Praise for Karen Armstrong's

THE GREAT TRANSFORMATION

"Armstrong's conviction, passion and intelligence radiate throughout the book, making us feel the urgency of the ideas it seeks to convey. . . . Above all, this is a book that aims to still the noise of our own troubled times."
—*The Baltimore Sun*

"Exhaustive. . . . *The Great Transformation* masterfully synthesizes mountains of information . . . and attends with care to how political and economic changes affected philosophy and religion."
—*The Boston Globe*

"Can the ideals of a few inspired lives 2,500 years ago be effectively applied to quell today's intolerance and warfare? Armstrong says those ideals can apply and urges that humanity abide by the ancient call to abandon selfishness and embrace compassion."
—*Los Angeles Times*

"Timely and necessary."
—*Herald* (London)

"An utterly enthralling reading experience. . . . It ranks with *A History of God* as one of her finest achievements."
—*Booklist*

"In her typical magisterial fashion, she chronicles these tales in dazzling prose with remarkable depth and judicious breadth. . . . A magnificent accomplishment."
—*Publishers Weekly*

KAREN ARMSTRONG

THE GREAT TRANSFORMATION

Karen Armstrong is the author of numerous other books on religious affairs, including *A History of God*, *The Battle for God*, *Holy War*, *Islam*, and *Buddha*. Her work has been translated into forty languages, and she is the author of three television documentaries. Since September 11, 2001, she has been a frequent contributor to conferences, panels, newspapers, periodicals, and other media on both sides of the Atlantic on the subject of Islam. She lives in London.

THE GREAT
TRANSFORMATION

To Mary, Fiona and Maeve

THE GREAT TRANSFORMATION

*The Beginning of
Our Religious Traditions*

With best wishes

KAREN ARMSTRONG

Karen Armstrong

ANCHOR BOOKS
A Division of Random House, Inc.
New York

FIRST ANCHOR BOOKS EDITION, APRIL 2007

Copyright © 2006 by Karen Armstrong

All rights reserved. Published in the United States by
Anchor Books, a division of Random House, Inc., New York.
Originally published in hardcover in the United States by
Alfred A. Knopf, a division of Random House, Inc., New York,
in 2006.

Anchor Books and colophon are registered trademarks
of Random House, Inc.

Owing to limitations of space, all acknowledgments
for permission to reprint previously published material
may be found at the end of the volume.

The Library of Congress has cataloged the Knopf edition
as follows:
Armstrong, Karen, [date]
The great transformation : the beginning of our religious
traditions / Karen Armstrong—1st ed.
p. cm.
Includes bibliographical references and index.
1. Religion—History. 2. Philosophy, Ancient.
3. History, Ancient. I. Title.
BL430.A76 2006
200.9'014—dc22
2005047536

Anchor ISBN: 978-0-385-72124-0

Maps by David Lindroth
Book design by Anthea Lingeman

www.anchorbooks.com

Printed in the United States of America
10 9 8 7 6 5 4 3

Contents

Maps and Plans

Maps and Plans

Acknowledgments

My thanks, as always, to my literary agents Felicity Bryan, Peter Ginsberg, and Andrew Nurnberg; and to my editors Jane Garrett, Robbert Ammerlaan, and Toby Mundy, who had the idea for this book. Their continued support and friendship has been a source of immense blessing and joy. I must also thank Michele Topham, Carole Robinson, and Jackie Head in Felicity Bryan's office for their constancy, patience, and kindness in helping me through the daily vicissitudes of a writer's life, and Emily Molanphy and Alice Hunt, assistants to Jane and Toby, who are such thoughtful intermediaries. As ever, I owe a great debt of gratitude to the production team at Knopf, whose passion for accuracy and elegance is quite indispensable: Chuck Antony (copyeditor), Patrice Silverstein and Chuck Thompson (proofreaders), Claire Bradley Ong (production), Anthea Lingeman (designer), David Lindroth (mapmaker), and Ellen Feldman (production editor). And even though their input is still to come at this writing, I cannot forget my friends in the publicity department, Sheila Kaye, Francien Schuursma, and Sheila O'Shea, who I know will promote the book with their usual dedication and generosity. Finally, I could not have completed this book without the love and practical support of my cousin, Jenny Wayman.

But this book is dedicated to Mitchell and Geraldine Bray, who understand the meaning of compassion, with my sincere and heartfelt gratitude.

Introduction

Perhaps every generation believes that it has reached a turning point of history, but our problems seem particularly intractable and our future increasingly uncertain. Many of our difficulties mask a deeper spiritual crisis. During the twentieth century, we saw the eruption of violence on an unprecedented scale. Sadly, our ability to harm and mutilate one another has kept pace with our extraordinary economic and scientific progress. We seem to lack the wisdom to hold our aggression in check and keep it within safe and appropriate bounds. The explosion of the first atomic bombs over Hiroshima and Nagasaki laid bare the nihilistic self-destruction at the heart of the brilliant achievements of our modern culture. We risk environmental catastrophe because we no longer see the earth as holy but regard it simply as a "resource." Unless there is some kind of spiritual revolution that can keep abreast of our technological genius, it is unlikely that we will save our planet. A purely rational education will not suffice. We have found to our cost that a great university can exist in the same vicinity as a concentration camp. Auschwitz, Rwanda, Bosnia, and the destruction of the World Trade Center were all dark epiphanies that revealed what can happen when the sense of the sacred inviolability of every single human being has been lost.

Religion, which is supposed to help us to cultivate this attitude, often seems to reflect the violence and desperation of our times. Almost every day we see examples of religiously motivated terrorism, hatred, and intolerance. An increasing number of people find traditional religious doctrines and practices irrelevant and incredible, and turn to art, music, literature, dance, sport, or drugs to give them the transcendent experience that humans seem to require. We all look for moments of ecstasy and rapture, when we inhabit our humanity more fully than usual and feel deeply touched within and lifted momentarily beyond ourselves. We are meaning-seeking creatures and, unlike other animals, fall very easily into despair if we cannot find significance and value in our lives. Some are looking for new ways of being religious. Since the late 1970s there has been a spiritual revival in many parts of the world, and the militant piety that we often call "fundamentalism" is only one manifestation of our postmodern search for enlightenment.

In our current predicament, I believe that we can find inspiration in the period that the German philosopher Karl Jaspers called the Axial Age because it was pivotal to the spiritual development of humanity.[1] From about 900 to 200 BCE,* in four distinct regions, the great world traditions that have continued to nourish humanity came into being: Confucianism and Daoism in China; Hinduism and Buddhism in India; monotheism in Israel; and philosophical rationalism in Greece. This was the period of the Buddha, Socrates, Confucius, and Jeremiah, the mystics of the Upanishads, Mencius, and Euripides. During this period of intense creativity, spiritual and philosophical geniuses pioneered an entirely new kind of human experience. Many of them worked anonymously, but others became luminaries who can still fill us with emotion because they show us what a human being should be. The Axial Age was one of the most seminal periods of intellectual, psychological, philosophical, and religious change in recorded history; there would be nothing comparable until the Great Western Transformation, which created our own scientific and technological modernity.

But how can the sages of the Axial Age, who lived in such different circumstances, speak to our current condition? Why should we look to Confucius or the Buddha for help? Surely a study of this distant period can only be an exercise in spiritual archaeology,

---

*Unless otherwise specified, all dates are BCE.

when what we need is to create a more innovative faith that reflects the realities of our own world. Yet, in fact, we have never surpassed the insights of the Axial Age. In times of spiritual and social crisis, men and women have constantly turned back to this period for guidance. They may have interpreted the Axial discoveries differently, but they have never succeeded in going beyond them. Rabbinic Judaism, Christianity, and Islam, for example, were all latter-day flowerings of the original Axial Age. As we shall see in the last chapter of this book, these three traditions all rediscovered the Axial vision and translated it marvelously into an idiom that spoke directly to the circumstances of their time.

The prophets, mystics, philosophers, and poets of the Axial Age were so advanced and their vision was so radical that later generations tended to dilute it. In the process, they often produced exactly the kind of religiosity that the Axial reformers wanted to get rid of. That, I believe, is what has happened in the modern world. The Axial sages have an important message for our time, but their insights will be surprising—even shocking—to many who consider themselves religious today. It is frequently assumed, for example, that faith is a matter of believing certain creedal propositions. Indeed, it is common to call religious people "believers," as though assenting to the articles of faith were their chief activity. But most of the Axial philosophers had no interest whatever in doctrine or metaphysics. A person's theological beliefs were a matter of total indifference to somebody like the Buddha. Some sages steadfastly refused even to discuss theology, claiming that it was distracting and damaging. Others argued that it was immature, unrealistic, and perverse to look for the kind of absolute certainty that many people expect religion to provide.

All the traditions that were developed during the Axial Age pushed forward the frontiers of human consciousness and discovered a transcendent dimension in the core of their being, but they did not necessarily regard this as supernatural, and most of them refused to discuss it. Precisely because the experience was ineffable, the only correct attitude was reverent silence. The sages certainly did not seek to impose their own view of this ultimate reality on other people. Quite the contrary: nobody, they believed, should ever take any religious teaching on faith or at second hand. It was essential to question everything and to test any teaching empirically, against your personal experience. In fact, as we shall see, if a prophet or philosopher did start to insist on obligatory doctrines, it was usually a sign that the Axial Age had lost its momentum. If the Buddha or Confucius had been asked whether he believed in God, he would probably have winced slightly and explained—with great courtesy—that this was not an appropriate question. If anybody had asked Amos or Ezekiel if he was a "monotheist," who believed in only one God, he would have been equally perplexed. Monotheism was not the issue. We find very few unequivocal assertions of monotheism in the Bible, but—interestingly—the stridency of some of these doctrinal statements actually departs from the essential spirit of the Axial Age.

What mattered was not what you believed but how you behaved. Religion was about doing things that changed you at a profound level. Before the Axial Age, ritual and animal sacrifice had been central to the religious quest. You experienced the divine in sacred dramas that, like a great theatrical experience today, introduced you to another level of existence. The Axial sages changed this; they still valued ritual, but gave it a new ethical significance and put morality at the heart of the spiritual life. The only way you could encounter what they called "God," "Nirvana," "Brahman," or the "Way" was to live a compassionate life. Indeed, religion *was* compassion. Today we often assume that before undertaking a religious lifestyle, we must prove to our own satisfaction that "God" or the "Absolute" exists. This is good scientific practice: first you establish a principle; only then can you apply it. But the Axial sages would say that this was to put the cart before the horse. First you must commit yourself to the ethical life; then disciplined and habitual benevolence, not metaphysical conviction, would give you intimations of the transcendence you sought.

This meant that you had to be ready to change. The Axial sages were not interested in providing their disciples with a little edifying uplift, after which they could return with renewed vigor to their ordinary self-centered lives. Their objective was to create an entirely different kind of human being. All the sages preached a spirituality of empathy and compassion; they insisted that people must abandon their egotism and greed, their violence and unkindness. Not only was it wrong to kill another human being; you must not even speak a hostile word or make an irritable gesture. Further, nearly all the Axial sages realized that you could not confine your benevolence to your own people: your concern must somehow extend to the entire world. In fact, when people started to limit their horizons and sympathies, it was another sign that the Axial Age was coming to a close. Each tradition developed its own formulation of the Golden Rule: do not do to others what you would not have done to you. As far as the Axial sages were concerned, respect for the sacred rights of all beings—not orthodox belief—was religion. If people behaved with kindness and generosity to their fellows, they could save the world.

We need to rediscover this Axial ethos. In our global village, we can no longer afford a parochial or exclusive vision. We must learn to live and behave as though people in countries remote from our own are as important as ourselves. The sages of the Axial Age did not create their compassionate ethic in idyllic circumstances. Each tradition developed in societies like our own that were torn apart by violence and warfare as never before; indeed, the first catalyst of religious change was usually a principled rejection of the aggression that the sages witnessed all around them. When they started to look for the causes of violence in the psyche, the Axial philosophers penetrated their interior world and began to explore a hitherto undiscovered realm of human experience.

The consensus of the Axial Age is an eloquent testimony to the unanimity of the spiritual quest of the human race. The Axial peoples all found that the compassionate ethic worked. All the great traditions that were created at this time are in agreement about the supreme importance of charity and benevolence, and this tells us something important about our humanity. To find that our own faith is so deeply in accord with others is an affirming experience. Without departing from our own tradition, therefore, we can learn from others how to enhance our particular pursuit of the empathic life.

We cannot appreciate the achievements of the Axial Age unless we are familiar with what went before, so we need to understand the pre-Axial religion of early antiquity. This had certain common features that would all be important to the Axial Age. Most societies, for example, had an early belief in a High God, who was often called the Sky God, since he was associated with the heavens.[2] Because he was rather inaccessible, he tended to fade from the religious consciousness. Some said that he "disappeared," others that he had been violently displaced by a younger generation of more dynamic deities. People usually experienced the sacred as an immanent presence in the world around them and within themselves. Some believed that gods, men, women, animals, plants, insects, and rocks all shared the same divine life. All were subject to an overarching cosmic order that kept everything in being. Even the gods had to obey this order, and they cooperated with human beings in the preservation of the divine energies of the cosmos. If these were not renewed, the world could lapse into a primal void.

Animal sacrifice was a universal religious practice in the ancient world. This was a way of recycling the depleted forces that kept the world in being. There was a strong conviction that life and death, creativity and destruction were inextricably entwined. People realized that they survived only because other creatures laid down their lives for their sake, so the animal victim was honored for its self-sacrifice.[3] Because there could be no life without such death, some imagined that the world had come into being as a result of a sacrifice at the beginning of time. Others told stories of a creator god slaying a dragon—a common symbol of the formless and undifferentiated—to bring order out of chaos. When they reenacted these mythical events in their ceremonial liturgy, worshipers felt that they had been projected into sacred time. They would often begin a new project by performing a ritual that represented the original cosmogony, to give their fragile mortal activity an infusion of divine strength. Nothing could endure if it were not "animated," or endowed with a "soul," in this way.[4]

Ancient religion depended upon what has been called the perennial philosophy, because it was present, in some form, in most premodern cultures. Every single person, object, or experience on earth was a replica—a pale shadow—of a reality in the divine world.[5] The sacred world was, therefore, the prototype of human existence, and because it was richer, stronger, and more enduring than anything on earth, men and women wanted desperately to participate in it. The perennial philosophy is still a key factor today in the lives of some indigenous tribes. The Australian aborigines, for example, experience the sacred realm of Dreamtime as far more real than the material world. They have brief glimpses of Dreamtime in sleep or in moments of vision; it is timeless and "everywhen." It forms a stable backdrop to ordinary life, which is constantly enervated by death, flux, and ceaseless change. When an Australian goes hunting, he models his behavior so closely on that of the First Hunter that he feels totally united with him, caught up in his more potent reality. Afterward, when he falls away from that primal richness, he fears that the domain of time will absorb him, and reduce him and everything that he does to nothingness.[6] This was also the experience of the people of antiquity. It was only when they imitated the gods in ritual and gave up the lonely, frail individuality of their secular lives that they truly existed. They fulfilled their humanity when they ceased to be simply themselves and repeated the gestures of others.[7]

Human beings are profoundly artificial.[8] We constantly strive to improve on nature and approximate to an ideal. Even at the present time, when we have abandoned the perennial philosophy, people slavishly follow the dictates of fashion and even do violence to their faces and figures in order to reproduce the current standard of beauty. The cult of celebrity shows that we still revere models who epitomize "superhumanity." People sometimes go to great lengths to see their idols, and feel an ecstatic enhancement of being in their presence. They imitate their dress and behavior. It seems that human beings naturally tend toward the archetypal and paradigmatic. The Axial sages developed a more authentic version of this spirituality and taught people to seek the ideal, archetypal self within.

The Axial Age was not perfect. A major failing was its indifference to women. These spiritualities nearly all developed in an urban environment, dominated by military power and aggressive commercial activity, where women tended to lose the status they had enjoyed in a more rural economy. There are no female Axial sages, and even when women were allowed to take an active role in the new faith, they were usually sidelined. It was not that the Axial sages hated women; most of the time, they simply did not notice them. When they spoke about the "great" or "enlightened" man, they did not mean "men and women"—though most, if challenged, would probably have admitted that women were capable of this liberation too.

Precisely because the question of women was so peripheral to the Axial Age, I found that any sustained discussion of this topic was distracting. Whenever I tried to address the issue, it seemed intrusive. I suspect that it deserves a study of its own. It is not as though the Axial sages were out-and-out misogynists, like some of the fathers of the church, for example. They were men of their time, and so preoccupied with the aggressive behavior of their own sex that they rarely gave women a second thought. We cannot follow the Axial reformers slavishly; indeed, to do so would fundamentally violate the spirit of the Axial Age, which insisted that this kind of conformity trapped people in an inferior and immature version of themselves. What we can do is extend the Axial ideal of universal concern to everybody, including the female sex. When we try to re-create the Axial vision, we must bring the best insights of modernity to the table.

The Axial peoples did not evolve in a uniform way. Each developed at its own pace. Sometimes they achieved an insight that was truly worthy of the Axial Age, but then retreated from it. The people of India were always in the vanguard of Axial progress. In Israel, prophets, priests, and historians approached the ideal sporadically, by fits and starts, until they were exiled to Babylon in the sixth century and experienced a short, intense period of extraordinary creativity. In China there was slow, incremental progress, until Confucius developed the first full Axial spirituality in the late sixth century. From the very start, the Greeks went in an entirely different direction from the other peoples.

Jaspers believed that the Axial Age was more contemporaneous than it actually was. He implied that the Buddha, Laozi, Confucius, Mozi, and Zoroaster, for example, all lived more or less at the same time. Modern scholarship has revised this dating. It is now certain that Zoroaster did not live during the sixth century, but was a much earlier figure. It is very difficult to date some of these movements precisely, especially in India, where there was very little interest in history and no attempt to keep accurate chronological records. Most Indologists now agree, for example, that the Buddha lived a whole century later than was previously thought. And Laozi, the Daoist sage, did not live during the sixth century, as Jaspers assumed. Instead of being the contemporary of Confucius and Mozi, he almost certainly lived in the third century. I have tried to keep abreast of the most recent scholarly debates, but at present many of these dates can only be speculative, and will probably never be known for certain.

But despite these difficulties, the general development of the Axial Age does give us some insight into the spiritual evolution of this important ideal. We will follow this process chronologically, charting the progress of the four Axial peoples side by side, watching the new vision gradually taking root, rising to a crescendo, and finally fading away at the close of the third century. That was not the end of the story, however. The pioneers of the Axial Age had laid the foundations upon which others could build. Each generation would try to adapt these original insights to their own peculiar circumstances, and that must be our task today.

THE GREAT
TRANSFORMATION

1

THE AXIAL PEOPLES

(c. 1600 to 900 BCE)

The first people to attempt an Axial Age spirituality were pastoralists living on the steppes of southern Russia, who called themselves the Aryans. The Aryans were not a distinct ethnic group, so this was not a racial term but an assertion of pride and meant something like "noble" or "honorable." The Aryans were a loose-knit network of tribes who shared a common culture. Because they spoke a language that would form the basis of several Asiatic and European tongues, they are also called Indo-Europeans. They had lived on the Caucasian steppes since about 4500, but by the middle of the third millennium some tribes began to roam farther and farther afield, until they reached what is now Greece, Italy, Scandinavia, and Germany. At the same time, those Aryans who had remained behind on the steppes gradually drifted apart and became two separate peoples, speaking different forms of the original Indo-European. One used the Avestan dialect, the other an early form of Sanskrit. They were able to maintain contact, however, because at this stage their languages were still very similar, and until about 1500 they continued to live peacefully together, sharing the same cultural and religious traditions.[1]

It was a quiet, sedentary existence. The Aryans could not travel far, because the horse had not yet been domesticated, so their horizons were bounded by the steppes. They farmed their land, herded their sheep, goats, and pigs, and valued stability and continuity. They were not a warlike people, since, apart from a few skirmishes with one another or with rival groups, they had no enemies and no ambition to conquer new territory. Their religion was simple and peaceful. Like other ancient peoples, the Aryans experienced an invisible force within themselves and in everything that they saw, heard, and touched. Storms, winds, trees, and rivers were not impersonal, mindless phenomena. The Aryans felt an affinity with them, and revered them as divine. Humans, deities, animals, plants, and the forces of nature were all manifestations of the same divine "spirit," which the Avestans called *mainyu* and the Sanskrit-speakers *manya*. It animated, sustained, and bound them all together.

Over time the Aryans developed a more formal pantheon. At a very early stage, they had worshiped a Sky God called Dyaus Pitr, creator of the world.[2] But like other High Gods, Dyaus was so remote that he was eventually replaced by more accessible gods, who were wholly identified with natural and cosmic forces. Varuna preserved the order of the universe; Mithra was the god of storm, thunder, and life-giving rain; Mazda, lord of justice and wisdom, was linked with the sun and stars; and Indra, a divine warrior, had fought a three-headed dragon called Vritra and brought order out of chaos. Fire, which was crucial to civilized society, was also a god, and the Aryans called him Agni. Agni was not simply the divine patron of fire; he *was* the fire that burned in every single hearth. Even the hallucinogenic plant that inspired the Aryan poets was a god, called Haoma in Avestan and Soma in Sanskrit: he was a divine priest who protected the people from famine and looked after their cattle.

The Avestan Aryans called their gods *daevas* ("the shining ones") and *amesha* ("the immortals"). In Sanskrit these terms became *devas* and *amrita*.[3] None of these divine beings, however, were what we usually call "gods" today. They were not omnipotent and had no ultimate control over the cosmos. Like human beings and all the natural forces, they had to submit to the sacred order that held the universe together. Thanks to this order, the seasons succeeded one another in due course, the rain fell at the right times, and the crops grew each year in the appointed month. The

Avestan Aryans called this order *asha,* while the Sanskrit-speakers called it *rita.* It made life possible, keeping everything in its proper place and defining what was true and correct.

Human society also depended upon this sacred order. People had to make firm, binding agreements about grazing rights, the herding of cattle, marriage, and the exchange of goods. Translated into social terms, *asha/rita* meant loyalty, truth, and respect, the ideals embodied by Varuna, the guardian of order, and Mithra, his assistant. These gods supervised all covenant agreements that were sealed by a solemn oath. The Aryans took the spoken word very seriously. Like all other phenomena, speech was a god, a *deva.* Aryan religion was not very visual. As far as we know, the Aryans did not make effigies of their gods. Instead, they found that the act of listening brought them close to the sacred. Quite apart from its meaning, the very sound of a chant was holy; even a single syllable could encapsulate the divine. Similarly, a vow, once uttered, was eternally binding, and a lie was absolutely evil because it perverted the holy power inherent in the spoken word.[4] The Aryans would never lose this passion for absolute truthfulness.

Every day, the Aryans offered sacrifices to their gods to replenish the energies they expended in maintaining world order. Some of these rites were very simple. The sacrificer would throw a handful of grain, curds, or fuel into the fire to nourish Agni, or pound the stalks of soma, offer the pulp to the water goddesses, and make a sacred drink. The Aryans also sacrificed cattle. They did not grow enough crops for their needs, so killing was a tragic necessity, but the Aryans ate only meat that had been ritually and humanely slaughtered. When a beast was ceremonially given to the gods, its spirit was not extinguished but returned to Geush Urvan ("Soul of the Bull"), the archetypical domestic animal. The Aryans felt very close to their cattle. It was sinful to eat the flesh of a beast that had not been consecrated in this way, because profane slaughter destroyed it forever, and thus violated the sacred life that made all creatures kin.[5] Again, the Aryans would never entirely lose this profound respect for the "spirit" that they shared with others, and this would become a crucial principle of their Axial Age.

To take the life of any being was a fearful act, not to be undertaken lightly, and the sacrificial ritual compelled the Aryans to confront this harsh law of existence. The sacrifice became and would remain the organizing symbol of their culture, by which they explained the world and their society. The Aryans believed that the universe itself had originated in a sacrificial offering. In the beginning, it was said, the gods, working in obedience to the divine order, had brought forth the world in seven stages. First they created the *Sky*, which was made of stone like a huge round shell; then the *Earth*, which rested like a flat dish upon the *Water* that had collected in the base of the shell. In the center of the Earth, the gods placed three living creatures: a *Plant*, a *Bull*, and a *Man*. Finally they produced Agni, the *Fire*. But at first everything was static and lifeless. It was not until the gods performed a triple sacrifice—crushing the Plant, and killing the Bull and the Man— that the world became animated. The sun began to move across the sky, seasonal change was established, and the three sacrificial victims brought forth their own kind. Flowers, crops, and trees sprouted from the pulped Plant; animals sprang from the corpse of the Bull; and the carcass of the first Man gave birth to the human race. The Aryans would always see sacrifice as creative. By reflecting on this ritual, they realized that their lives depended upon the death of other creatures. The three archetypal creatures had laid down their lives so that others might live. There could be no progress, materially or spiritually, without self-sacrifice.[6] This too would become one of the principles of the Axial Age.

The Aryans had no elaborate shrines and temples. Sacrifice was offered in the open air on a small, level piece of land, marked off from the rest of the settlement by a furrow. The seven original creations were all symbolically represented in this arena: Earth in the soil, Water in the vessels, Fire in the hearth; the stone Sky was present in the flint knife, the Plant in the crushed soma stalks, the Bull in the victim, and the first Man in the priest. And the gods, it was thought, were also present. The *hotr* priest, expert in the liturgical chant, would sing a hymn to summon *devas* to the feast. When they had entered the sacred arena, the gods sat down on the freshly mown grass strewn around the altar to listen to these hymns of praise. Since the sound of these inspired syllables was itself a god, as the song filled the air and entered their consciousness, the congregation felt surrounded by and infused with divinity. Finally the primordial sacrifice was repeated. The cattle were slain, the soma pressed, and the priest laid the choicest portions of the victims onto the fire, so that Agni could convey them to the land of the gods. The ceremony ended with a holy communion, as priest and participants shared a festal meal with the deities, eating the consecrated meat and drinking the intoxicating soma, which seemed to lift them to another dimension of being.[7]

The sacrifice brought practical benefits too. It was commissioned by a member of the community, who hoped that those *devas* who had responded to his invitation and attended the sacrifice would help him in the future. Like any act of hospitality, the ritual placed an obligation on the divinities to respond in kind, and the *hotr* often reminded them to protect the patron's family, crops, and herd. The sacrifice also enhanced the patron's standing in the community. Like the gods, his human guests were now in his debt, and by providing the cattle for the feast and giving the officiating priests a handsome gift, he had demonstrated that he was a man of substance.[8] The benefits of religion were purely material and this-worldly. People wanted the gods to provide them with cattle, wealth, and security. At first the Aryans had entertained no hope of an afterlife, but by the end of the second millennium, some were beginning to believe that wealthy people who had commissioned a lot of sacrifices would be able to join the gods in paradise after their death.[9]

This slow, uneventful life came to an end when the Aryans discovered modern technology. In about 1500, they had begun to trade with the more advanced societies south of the Caucasus in Mesopotamia and Armenia. They learned about bronze weaponry from the Armenians and also encountered new methods of transport: first they acquired wooden carts pulled by oxen, and then the war chariot. Once they had learned how to tame the wild horses of the steppes and harness them to their chariots, they experienced the joys of mobility. Life would never be the same again. The Aryans had become warriors. They could now travel long distances at high speed. With their superior weapons, they could conduct lightning raids on neighboring settlements and steal cattle and crops. This was far more thrilling and lucrative than stock breeding. Some of the younger men served as mercenaries in the armies of the southern kingdoms, and became expert in chariot warfare. When they returned to the steppes, they put their new skills to use and started to rustle their neighbors' cattle. They killed, plundered, and pillaged, terrorizing the more conservative Aryans, who were bewildered, frightened, and entirely disoriented, feeling that their lives had been turned upside down.

Violence escalated on the steppes as never before. Even the more traditional tribes, who simply wanted to be left alone, had to learn the new military techniques in order to defend themselves. A heroic age had begun. Might was right; chieftains sought gain and glory; and bards celebrated aggression, reckless courage, and military prowess. The old Aryan religion had preached reciprocity, self-sacrifice, and kindness to animals. This was no longer appealing to the cattle rustlers, whose hero was the dynamic Indra, the dragon slayer, who rode in a chariot upon the clouds of heaven.[10] Indra was now the divine model to whom the raiders aspired. "Heroes with noble horses, fain for battle, selected warriors call on me in combat," he cried. "I, bountiful Indra, excite the conflict, I stir the dust, Lord of surpassing vigour!"[11] When they fought, killed, and robbed, the Aryan cowboys felt themselves one with Indra and the aggressive *devas* who had established the world order by force of arms.

But the more traditional, Avestan-speaking Aryans were appalled by Indra's naked aggression, and began to have doubts about the *daevas*. Were they all violent and immoral? Events on earth always reflected cosmic events in heaven, so, they reasoned, these terrifying raids must have a divine prototype. The cattle rustlers, who fought under the banner of Indra, must be his earthly counterparts. But who were the *daevas* attacking in heaven? The most important gods—such as Varuna, Mazda, and Mithra, the guardians of order—were given the honorific title "Lord" (*ahura*). Perhaps the peaceful *ahuras*, who stood for justice, truth, and respect for life and property, were themselves under attack by Indra and the more aggressive *daevas*? This, at any rate, was the view of a visionary priest, who in about 1200 claimed that Ahura Mazda had commissioned him to restore order to the steppes.[12] His name was Zoroaster.

When he received his divine vocation, the new prophet was about thirty years old and strongly rooted in the Aryan faith. He had probably studied for the priesthood since he was seven years old, and was so steeped in tradition that he could improvise sacred chants to the gods during the sacrifice. But Zoroaster was deeply disturbed by the cattle raids, and after completing his education, he had spent some time in consultation with other priests, and had meditated on the rituals to find a solution to the problem. One morning, while he was celebrating the spring festival, Zoroaster had risen at dawn and walked down to the river to collect water for the daily sacrifice. Wading in, he immersed himself in the pure element, and when he emerged, saw a shining being standing on the riverbank, who told Zoroaster that his name was Vohu Manah ("Good Purpose"). Once he had been assured of Zoroaster's own good intentions, he led him into the presence of the greatest of the *ahuras:* Mazda, lord of wisdom and justice, who was surrounded by his retinue of seven radiant gods. He told Zoroaster to mobilize his people in a holy war against terror and violence.[13] The story is bright with the promise of a new beginning. A fresh era had dawned: everybody had to make a decision, gods and humans alike. Were they on the side of order or evil?

Zoroaster's vision convinced him that Lord Mazda was not simply one of the great *ahuras,* but that he was the Supreme God. For Zoroaster and his followers, Mazda was no longer immanent in the natural world, but had become transcendent, different in kind from any other divinity.[14] This was not quite monotheism, the belief in a single, unique deity. The seven luminous beings in Mazda's retinue—the Holy Immortals—were also divine: each expressed one of Mazda's attributes and was linked, in the traditional way, with one of the seven original creations. There was, however, a monotheistic tendency in Zoroaster's vision. Lord Mazda had created the Holy Immortals; they were "of one mind, one voice, one act" with him.[15] Mazda was not the only deity, but he was the first to exist. Zoroaster had probably reached this position by meditating on the creation story, which claimed that in the beginning there had been one plant, one animal, and one human being. It was only logical to assume that originally there had been one god.[16]

But Zoroaster was not interested in theological speculation for its own sake. He was wholly preoccupied by the violence that had destroyed the peaceful world of the steppes, and was desperately seeking for a way to bring it to an end. The Gathas, the seventeen inspired hymns attributed to Zoroaster, are pervaded by a distraught vulnerability, impotence, and fear. "I know why I am powerless, Mazda," cried the prophet, "I possess few cattle and few men." His community was terrorized by raiders "yoked with evil acts to destroy life." Cruel warriors, fighting under the orders of the evil Indra, had swept down on the peace-loving, law-abiding communities. They had vandalized and looted one settlement after another, killed the villagers, and carried off their bulls and cows.[17] The raiders believed that they were heroes, fighting alongside Indra, but the Gathas show us how their victims saw the heroic age. Even the cow complained to Lord Mazda: "For whom did you shape me? Who fashioned me? Fury and raiding, cruelty and might hold me captive." When Lord Mazda replied that Zoroaster, the only one of the Aryans who listened to his teachings, would be her protector, the cow was not impressed. What use was Zoroaster? She wanted a more effective helper. The Gathas cried aloud for justice. Where were the Holy Immortals, the guardians of *asha*? When would Lord Mazda bring relief?[18]

The suffering and helplessness of his people had shocked Zoroaster into a torn, conflicted vision. The world seemed polarized, split into two irreconcilable camps. Because Indra and the cattle raiders had nothing in common with Lord Mazda, they must have given their allegiance to a different *ahura*. If there was a single divine source for everything that was benign and good, Zoroaster concluded that there must also be a wicked deity who had inspired the cruelty of the raiders. This Hostile Spirit (*Angra Mainyu*), he believed, was equal in power to Lord Mazda, but was his opposite. In the beginning, there had been "two primal Spirits, twins destined to be in conflict" with each other. Each had made a choice. The Hostile Spirit had thrown in his lot with *druj*, the lie, and was the epitome of evil. He was the eternal enemy of *asha*, of everything that was right and true. But Lord Mazda had opted for goodness and had created the Holy Immortals and human beings as his allies. Now every single man, woman, and child had to make the same choice between *asha* and *druj*.[19]

For generations, the Aryans had worshiped Indra and the other *daevas*, but now Zoroaster concluded that the *daevas* must have decided to fight alongside the Hostile Spirit.[20] The cattle raiders were their earthly counterparts. The unprecedented violence in the steppes had caused Zoroaster to divide the ancient Aryan pantheon into two warring groups. Good men and women must no longer offer sacrifice to Indra and the *daevas;* they must not invite them into the sacred precinct. Instead, they must commit themselves entirely to Lord Mazda, his Holy Immortals, and the other *ahuras*, who alone could bring peace, justice, and security. The *daevas* and the cattle raiders, their evil henchmen, must all be defeated and destroyed.[21]

The whole of life had now become a battlefield in which everybody had a role. Even women and servants could make a valuable contribution. The old purity laws, which had regulated the conduct of the ritual, were now given a new significance. Lord Mazda had created a completely clean and perfect world for his followers, but the Hostile Spirit had invaded the earth and filled it with sin, violence, falsehood, dust, dirt, disease, death, and decay. Good men and women must, therefore, keep their immediate environment free from dirt and pollution. By separating the pure from the impure, good from evil, they would liberate the world for Lord Mazda.[22] They must pray five times a day. Winter was the season when the *daevas* were in the ascendant, so during this time all virtuous people must counter their influence by meditating on the menace of *druj*. They must rise up during the night, when wicked spirits prowled the earth, and throw incense into the fire to strengthen Agni in the war against evil.[23]

But no battle could last forever. In the old, peaceful world, life had seemed cyclical: the seasons had followed one another, day succeeded night, and harvest followed the planting. But Zoroaster could no longer believe in these natural rhythms. The world was rushing forward toward a cataclysm. He and his followers were living in the "bounded time" of raging cosmic conflict, but soon they would witness the final triumph of good and the annihilation of the forces of darkness. After a terrible battle, Lord Mazda and the Immortals would descend to the world of men and women and offer sacrifice. There would be a great judgment. The wicked would be wiped off the face of the earth, and a blazing river would flow into hell and incinerate the Hostile Spirit. Then the cosmos would be restored to its original perfection. Mountains and valleys would be leveled into a great plain, where gods and humans could live side by side, worshiping Lord Mazda forever. There would be no more death. Human beings would be like deities, free from sickness, old age, and mortality.[24]

We are now familiar with this kind of apocalyptic vision, but before Zoroaster there had been nothing like it in the ancient world. It sprang from his outrage at the suffering of his people and his yearning for justice. He wanted the wicked to be punished for the pain they had inflicted on good, innocent people. But as time passed, he began to realize that he would not be alive to see the Last Days. Another would come after him, a superhuman being, "who is better than a good man."[25] The Gathas call him the Saoshyant ("One Who Will Bring Benefit"). He, not Zoroaster, would lead Lord Mazda's troops into the final battle.

When—centuries later—the Axial Age began, philosophers, prophets, and mystics all tried to counter the cruelty and aggression of their time by promoting a spirituality based on nonviolence. But Zoroaster's traumatized vision, with its imagery of burning, terror, and extermination, was vengeful. His career reminds us that political turbulence, atrocity, and suffering do not infallibly produce an Axial-style faith, but can inspire a militant piety that polarizes complex reality into oversimplified categories of good and evil. Zoroaster's vision was deeply agonistic. We shall see that the agon ("contest") was a common feature of ancient religion. In making a cosmic agon between good and evil central to his message, Zoroaster belonged to the old spiritual world. He had projected the violence of his time onto the divine and made it absolute.

But in his passionately ethical vision, Zoroaster did look forward to the Axial Age. He tried to introduce some morality into the new warrior ethos. True heroes did not terrorize their fellow creatures but tried to counter aggression. The holy warrior was dedicated to peace; those who opted to fight for Lord Mazda were patient, disciplined, courageous, and swift to defend all good creatures from the assaults of the wicked.[26] *Ashavans,* the champions of order (*asha*), must imitate the Holy Immortals in their care for the environment. "Good Purpose," for instance, who had appeared to Zoroaster on the riverbank, was the guardian of the cow, and *ashavans* must follow his example, not that of the raiders, who drove the cattle from their pastures, harnessed them to carts, killed, and ate them without the proper ritual.[27] "Good Dominion," the personification of divine justice, was the protector of the stone Sky, so *ashavans* must use their stone weapons only to defend the poor and the weak.[28] When Zoroastrians protected vulnerable people, looked after their cattle tenderly, and purified their natural environment, they became one with the Immortals and joined their struggle against the Hostile Spirit.

Even though his vision was grounded in ancient Aryan tradition, Zoroaster's message inspired great hostility. People found it too demanding; some were shocked by his preaching to women and peasants, and by his belief that everybody—not just the elite—could reach paradise. Many would have been troubled by his rejection of the *daevas:* Might not Indra take revenge?[29] After years of preaching to his own tribe, Zoroaster gained only one convert, so he left his village and found a patron in Vishtaspa, the chief of another tribe, who established the Zoroastrian faith in his territory. Zoroaster lived in Vishtaspa's court for many years, fighting a heroic battle against evil to the bitter, violent end. According to one tradition he was killed by rival priests who were enraged by his rejection of the old religion. We know nothing about the history of Zoroastrianism after his death. By the end of the second millennium the Avestan Aryans had migrated south and settled in eastern Iran, where Zoroastrianism became the national faith. It has remained a predominantly Iranian religion. Strangely enough, it was the Aryan cattle rustlers, whom Zoroaster had condemned, who would eventually create the first sustained religion of the Axial Age, based upon the principle of *ahimsa,* nonviolence.

While some of the Sanskrit-speaking Aryans were creating havoc on the steppes, others had begun to migrate south, traveling in small bands through Afghanistan and settling finally in the fertile lands of the Punjab, among the tributaries of the river Indus. They called their new home Sapta-Sindhu, "Land of the Seven Rivers." There has been much debate about the Aryan settlement of India.[30] Some scholars even deny that it took place, arguing that it was the indigenous people of India who created the civilization that developed in the Punjab at this time. The Aryans have left no archaeological record of this early period in India. Theirs was an itinerant society, and people lived out in the open or in temporary encampments. Our only sources of information are the ritual texts, composed in Sanskrit, known collectively as the Vedas ("Knowledge"). The language of the Vedas is so similar to Avestan and its cultural assumptions so close to the Gathas that it is almost certainly an Aryan scripture. Today most historians accept that during the second millennium, Aryan tribes from the steppes did indeed colonize the Indus Valley. But it was neither a mass movement nor a military invasion. There is no evidence of fighting, resistance, or widespread destruction. Instead there was probably continuous infiltration of the region by different Aryan groups over a very long period.

When the first Aryans arrived, they would have seen the remains of a previous civilization in the Indus Valley.[31] At the height of its power and success (c. 2300–2000), this ancient Indian empire had been larger than either Egypt or Mesopotamia. It had two impressive capital cities: at Mohenjo-Daro, in modern Sind, and Harappa, some 250 miles to the east. But hundreds of other, smaller towns have also been excavated, extending 800 miles

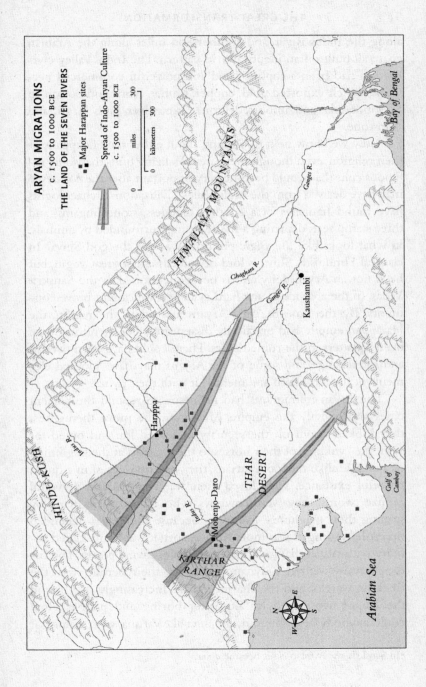

ARYAN MIGRATIONS
c. 1500 to 1000 BCE
THE LAND OF THE SEVEN RIVERS

■ Major Harappan sites

Spread of Indo-Aryan Culture
c. 1500 to 1000 BCE

miles   0   300

kilometers 0   300

HINDU KUSH

HIMALAYA MOUNTAINS

Harappa

Indus R.

Mohenjo-Daro

KIRTHAR
RANGE

THAR
DESERT

Ghaghara R.

Ganges R.

Ganges R.

Kaushambi

Bay of Bengal

Gulf of
Cambay

Arabian Sea

N
W   E
S

along the Indus River, and another 800 miles along the Arabian coast, all built on an identical grid pattern. The Indus Valley civilization had been a sophisticated and powerful commercial network, which exported gold, copper, timber, ivory, and cotton to Mesopotamia, and imported bronze, tin, silver, lapis lazuli, and soapstone.

Sadly, we know next to nothing about either the Harappans or their religion, even though there are tantalizing hints that some religious cults that would become very important after the Axial Age may have derived from the Indus Valley civilization. Archaeologists have found figurines of a Mother Goddess, stone lingams, and three stamp seals depicting a figure sitting, surrounded by animals, in what looks like the yogic position. Was this the god Shiva? In classical Hinduism, Shiva is lord of animals and a great yogin, but he is not an Aryan deity and is never mentioned in the Sanskrit Vedas. In the absence of any hard evidence, we cannot prove continuity. By the time the first Aryans arrived in the region, the Harappan empire had practically disappeared, but there may have been squatters in the ruined cities. There could have been overlap and interchange, and some of the Aryans may have adopted elements of the local faith and merged it with their own.

The Aryan immigrants had no desire to rebuild the ancient cities and revivify the empire. Always on the move themselves, they looked down on the security of settled life and opted for *yoga,* the "yoking" of their horses to the chariots at the beginning of a raid. Unlike the Zoroastrians, they had no interest in a quiet, peaceful existence. They loved their war chariots and powerful bronze swords; they were cowboys, who earned their living by stealing their neighbors' livestock. Because their lives depended on cattle rustling, it was more than a sport; it was also a sacred activity with rituals that gave it an infusion of divine power. The Indian Aryans wanted a dynamic religion; their heroes were the trekking warrior and the chariot fighter. Increasingly, they found the *asuras** worshiped by Zoroaster boring and passive. How could anybody be inspired by an *asura* like Varuna, who simply sat

---

*In Sanskrit, the Avestan *ahura* became *asura.*

around in his celestial palace, ordering the world from a safe distance? They much preferred the adventurous *devas,* "who drove on wheels, while the *asuras* sat at home in their halls."[32]

By the time they had established themselves in the Punjab, the cult of Varuna, the chief *asura,* was already in decline and Indra was becoming the Supreme God in his place.[33] With his wild, flowing beard, his belly full of soma, and his passion for battle, Indra was the archetypal Aryan to whom all warriors aspired. At the beginning of time, he had hurled his glittering, deadly thunderbolt at Vritra, the three-headed dragon who had blocked the flow of the life-giving waters, so that the earth was parched with drought. Indra had thus made the world habitable by fighting terrifying battles against overwhelming odds, not by feebly sitting at home like Varuna. In the Vedic texts, all the attributes of Varuna—the administration of law, the guardianship of the truth, and the punishment of falsehood—pass to Indra. But the uncomfortable fact remained that for all his glamour, Indra was a killer, who had only managed to defeat Vritra by lying and cheating. This was the violent and troubled vision of a society constantly involved in desperate warfare. The Vedic hymns saw the entire cosmos convulsed by terrifying conflict and passionate rivalries. *Devas* and *asuras* fought each other in heaven, while the Aryans struggled for survival on earth.[34] This was an age of scarcity; the only way that the Aryans could establish themselves in the Indus Valley was by stealing the cattle of the indigenous settled communities—the earthly counterparts of the stay-at-home *asuras.*[35]

The Aryans were hard-living, hard-drinking people who loved music, gambling, and wine. But even at this very early stage they showed spiritual genius. Shortly after they arrived in the Punjab, a learned elite began to compile the earliest hymns of the Rig Veda ("Knowledge in Verse"), the most prestigious portion of the Vedic scriptures. When completed, it would consist of 1,028 hymns, divided into ten books. This was just one part of a vast corpus of literature, which included anthologies of songs, mantras (short prose formulae used in ritual), and instructions for their recitation. These texts and poems had all been inspired; they were *shruti,* "that which is heard." Revealed to the great seers (*rishis*) of antiquity, they were absolutely authoritative, unmarked by human redaction, divine, and eternal.

Some hymns of the Rig Veda could be very old indeed, because by the time the Aryan tribes arrived in India, its language was already archaic. The poems were the property of a small group of seven priestly families, each with its own "copyrighted" collection, which they chanted during the sacrificial rituals. Family members learned the hymns by heart and transmitted them orally to the next generation; the Rig Veda was not committed to writing until the second millennium of the common era. Since the advent of literacy, our powers of memory have declined, and we find it hard to believe that people were able to learn such lengthy texts. But the Vedic scriptures were transmitted with impeccable accuracy, even after the archaic Sanskrit had become almost incomprehensible, and still today, the exact tonal accents and inflections of the original, long-lost language have been preserved, together with the ritually prescribed gestures of the arms and fingers. Sound had always been sacred to the Aryans, and when they listened to these holy texts, people felt invaded by the divine. As they committed them to memory, their minds were filled by a sacred presence. Vedic "knowledge" was not the acquisition of factual information but was experienced as divine possession.

The poems of the Rig Veda did not tell coherent stories about the gods or give clear descriptions of the sacrificial rituals but alluded in a veiled, riddling fashion to myths and legends that were already familiar to the community. The truth that they were trying to express could not be conveyed in neat, logical discourse. The poet was a *rishi,* a seer. He had not invented these hymns. They had declared themselves to him in visions that seemed to come from another world.[36] The *rishi* could see truths and make connections that were not apparent to ordinary people, but he had the divinely bestowed talent to impart them to anybody who knew how to listen. The beauty of this inspired poetry shocked his audience into a state of such awe, wonder, fear, and delight that they felt directly touched by divine power. The sacred knowledge of the Veda did not simply come from the semantic meaning of the words but from their sound, which was itself a *deva.*

The visionary truth of the Rig Veda stole up on the audience, who listened carefully to the hidden significance of the paradoxes and the strange, riddling allusions of the hymns, which yoked together things that seemed to be entirely unrelated. As they listened, they felt in touch with the mysterious potency that held the world together. This power was *rita,* divine order translated into human speech.[37] As the *rishi* physically enunciated the sacred syllables, *rita* was made flesh and became an active, living reality in the torn, conflicted world of the Punjab. The listeners felt that they were in touch with the power that made the seasons follow one another regularly, the stars remain in their courses, the crops grow, and enabled the disparate elements of human society to cohere. Scripture, therefore, did not impart information that could be grasped notionally but gave people a more intuitive insight that was a bridge, linking the visible with the invisible dimension of life.

The *rishis* learned to hold themselves in a state of constant readiness to receive inspired words that seemed to come from outside but were also experienced as an inner voice. They may already have begun to develop techniques of concentration that enabled them to penetrate the subconscious. They discovered that if they got rid of their usual distracting preoccupations, "the doors of the mind may be opened,"[38] and that Agni, the inventor of brilliant speech, the light of the world, enabled them to see in the same way as a god. The *rishis* had laid the foundations for the Indian Axial Age. At this very early date, they had made a deliberate effort to go beyond empirical knowledge and intuit a deeper, more fundamental truth.

Yet the *rishis* represented only a tiny minority of the Aryan community. The warriors and raiders lived in an entirely different spiritual world. Their lives alternated between the village (*grama*) and the jungle (*aranya*). During the monsoon rains, they had to live an *asura*-like existence in temporary, makeshift encampments. But after the winter solstice they yoked their horses and oxen and set off into the wilderness on a new cycle of raids, to replenish the wealth of the community. The opposition of the village and the forest became a social and spiritual paradigm in India.[39] Each complemented the other. The inhabitants of the settled commu-

nity provided crops and bred the cattle that the warriors needed;
yet they constantly feared attack from the bands of cattle rustlers,
who roamed on the outskirts of society. The tropical forest was the
place where the warrior proved his valor and explored the unknown. Later, during the Axial Age, hermits would retire to the
forest to pioneer the spiritual realm. In the *aranya,* therefore, the
Aryans experienced violence as well as religious enlightenment;
and from this very early stage, the two were inextricably entwined. Instead of waiting patiently and emptying his mind and
heart, like a *rishi,* a warrior knew that he would have to fight his
way to vision and insight.

Ever since they had taken up raiding on the steppes, the
Aryans had altered the patterns of their rituals, to reflect the agonistic tenor of their daily existence. Zoroaster had been very disturbed by the new sacrificial rites of the cattle rustlers, though he
did not describe them in any detail. "We must do what the gods
did in the beginning," an Indian ritual text of a later period explained.[40] "Thus the gods did, thus men do," said another.[41] In
their raids and battles, the Aryan warriors reenacted the heavenly
wars between *devas* and *asuras.* When they fought, they became
more than themselves and felt united with Indra; these rituals gave
their warfare a "soul," and by linking their earthly battles with
their divine archetype, they made them holy.

Sacrifice was therefore at the spiritual heart of Aryan society
in India, but it was also central to the economy. The old peaceful
rites of the steppes had become far more aggressive and competitive, and reflected the dangerous lives of the cattle rustlers. Aryan
sacrifice was now similar to the potlatch celebrated by the Native
American tribes of the northwest, who proudly displayed the
booty they had won and slaughtered large numbers of beasts for
lavish sacrificial banquets. If a community accumulated more animals and crops than it needed, this surplus had to be "burned
up." It was impossible for a nomadic group that was perpetually
on the move to store these goods, and the potlatch was a rough-
and-ready way of redistributing the wealth of society. The ritual
also showed how successful the chief had been and enhanced his
prestige.

In India the *raja* ("chief") commissioned a sacrifice in a similar spirit.[42] He invited the elders of his own tribe and some of the neighboring chieftains to a special sacrificial arena, where he exhibited his surplus of booty—cattle, horses, soma, and crops. Some of these goods were sacrificed to the gods and eaten in a riotous, sumptuous banquet; anything left over was distributed to the other rajas as gifts. This placed an obligation on the patron's guests to return these favors, and rajas vied with one another in putting on ever more spectacular sacrifices. The *hotr* priest, who chanted hymns to the gods, also sang the praises of the patron, promising that his munificence would bring even greater riches his way. Thus while the patron sought to curry favor with the gods and identify with Indra, who was himself an extravagant host and sacrificer, he also wanted to win praise and respect. At a time when he was supposed to leave his mundane self behind and become one with his heavenly counterpart, he was also engaged in aggressive self-assertion. This paradox in the ancient ritual would be a matter of concern to many of the reformers of the Axial Age.

Sacrifice also increased the violence that was already endemic in the region. After it was over, the patron had no cattle left and would have to inaugurate a new series of raids to replenish his wealth. We have no contemporary descriptions of these sacrifices, but later texts contain fragmentary references that give us some idea of what went on. The sacrifice was a solemn occasion, but it was also a large, rowdy carnival. Vast amounts of wine and soma were consumed, so people were either drunk or pleasantly mellow. There was casual sex with slave girls laid on by the officiating raja, and lively, aggressive ritual contests: chariot races, shooting matches, and tugs of war. Teams of dancers, singers, and lute players competed against one another. There were dice games for high stakes. Groups of warriors conducted mock battles. It was enjoyable, but also dangerous. In this highly competitive atmosphere, mock battles between professional warriors, all hungry for fame and prestige, could easily segue into serious fighting. A raja might wager a cow in a game of dice, and lose his entire herd. Carried away by the excitement of the occasion, he could also decide to lead an attack against his "enemy," a neighboring raja who was on bad terms with him or who was holding a rival sacrifice of his own. The texts indicate that *devas* and *asuras* often interrupted each other's sacrifices and carried off plunder and hostages, which suggests that this kind of violent intrusion was also common on earth.[43] A raja who had not received an invitation to a ritual was insulted; he felt honor-bound to fight his way into the enemy camp and carry off booty. In these liturgically inspired raids, people could and did get killed.

The sacrifice reenacted, in a heightened, ceremonial setting, the glory and terror of the Aryan heroic code.[44] A warrior's entire life was an agon, a deadly, dangerous contest for food and wealth, which could end in his death. Ever since they had lived on the steppes, the Aryans had believed that the best and wealthiest among them would join the gods in heaven. Now they were convinced that a warrior who died nobly in battle went immediately to the world of the gods. In the heroic code, therefore, enlightenment was inseparable from violent death. An ancient story made this clear. A group of warriors had gathered to perform a long, elaborate sacrifice. But as so often happened, they were surrounded by a rival tribe, and there was a fierce battle. Tragically Sthura, their leader, was killed. When it was all over, his clansmen sat in a circle, mourning his loss, but one of them had a vision. He saw Sthura walking through the sacrificial ground to the sacred fire, and then beginning his ascent to heaven. "Do not lament," he cried to his companions, "for he whom you are mourning has gone upward from the hearth of the offering fire and entered heaven."[45] Sthura joined the gods simply because he had been slain in the course of a dangerous ritual. His companion had this glorious vision only because his leader had been prematurely and pointlessly slain.

Some of the warriors recognized the futility of their heroic ethos. A few of the later poems of the Rig Veda express a new weariness and pessimism. People felt worn out. "Indigence, nakedness and exhaustion press me sore," the *rishi* complained; "my mind is fluttering like a bird's. As rats eat weaver's threads, cares are consuming me."[46] This vulnerability marked the beginning of the late Vedic period, a time of disturbing social change.[47] During the tenth century, the old egalitarian tribal structures had begun to crumble, and an aristocracy of warrior families, known as the kshatriyas ("the empowered ones"), became dominant. Those of less noble lineage, the vaishyas, the clansmen, started to give up raiding and become farmers. When the kshatriyas yoked their horses to their chariots at the beginning of the new raiding season, the vaishyas stayed behind in the village. Like the shudras, the non-Aryan population, they now resembled the asuras, who stayed at home in their halls, and were fair game for plunder.[48]

A few chiefs began to create embryonic kingdoms. A king was never elected for life. Every year, he had to submit to the ordeal of the rajasuya, the ritual of consecration, in order to prove that he was worthy of office. Somebody was always ready to challenge him, and the old raja had to win power back by leading a successful raid in the course of the rite and beating his opponent at dice. If he lost, he would go into exile in the forest, but would usually return and challenge his rival to another rajasuya. The instability of the Indian kingdom was so ingrained that an early manual of statecraft actually made the king's enemy a constituent part of the state.[49]

During the late Vedic period, there was a new wave of migration. In the tenth century, some of the Aryans began to push steadily eastward, settling in the Doab, between the Yamuna and Ganges rivers. This region became the arya varta, the "Land of the Arya." Here too small kingdoms developed. The kings of Kuru-Panchala settled on the northwest fringe of the Ganges plain, with their capital at Hastinapura, while the Yadava clan settled in the area of Mathura, to the south. The terrain here was very different from the Punjab. The lush forests of exotic trees were a green paradise, but to build their little towns and encampments, the pioneers had to set fire to the trees in order to clear the land. Agni, god of fire, therefore became integral to this new phase of colonization. Settlement was slow and steplike. Each year, during the cool season, the Kuru-Panchala dispatched teams of warriors who penetrated deeper into the dense forest, subjugated the local population, and made a new outpost a little farther to the east than the previous year.[50] They raided the farms of the *shudras,* seized their crops and cattle, and returned home before the monsoon to cultivate their own fields.[51] Slowly the Aryan frontier crept forward—a disciplined, persevering process that foreshadowed the Aryans' systematic conquest of inner space during the Axial Age.

New rituals were devised that sanctified this gradual, incremental drive toward the east. Mobility was still a sacred value: the sacrificial ground was used once only, and was always abandoned after the completion of the rite. At the western end of the sacrificial area, a thatched hut represented the hall of the settled householder. During the rite, the warriors solemnly carried the fire from the hut to the eastern end of the enclosure, where a fresh hearth was built in the open air. The next day, a new sacrificial ground was established, a little farther to the east, and the rite was repeated. The ceremony reenacted Agni's victorious progress into the new territory, as a ritualist of a later period explained: "This Fire should create room for us; this Fire should go in front, conquering our enemies; impetuously this Fire should conquer the enemies; this Fire should win the prizes in the contest."[52]

Agni was the patron of the settlers. Their colony was a new beginning and, like the first creation, had wrested order from chaos. Fire symbolized the warriors' ability to control their environment. They identified deeply with their fire. If he could steal fire from the hearth of a *vaishya* farmer, a warrior could also lure his cattle away, because they would always follow the flames. "He should take brightly burning fire from the home of his rival," says one of the later texts; "he thereby takes his wealth, his property."[53] Fire symbolized a warrior's power and success; it was—an important point—his alter ego. He could create new fire, control and domesticate it. Fire was like his son; when he died and was cremated, he became a sacrificial victim and Agni would carry him to the land of the gods. The fire represented his best and deepest self (*atman*),[54] and because the fire was Agni, this self was sacred and divine.

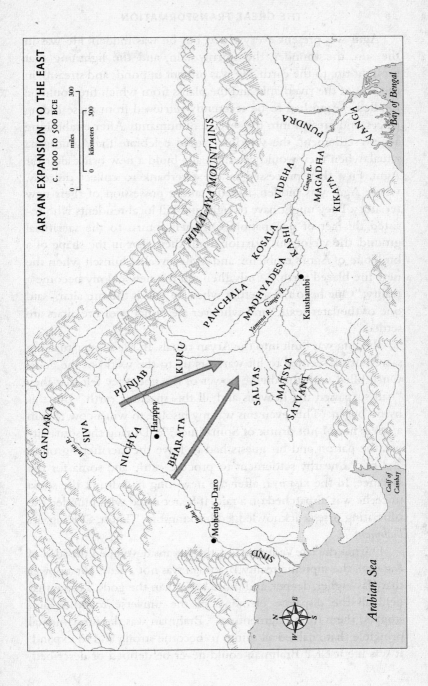

ARYAN EXPANSION TO THE EAST
c. 1000 to 500 BCE

300 miles

300 kilometers

Bay of Bengal

HIMALAYA MOUNTAINS

PUNDRA

VANGA

VIDEHA

MAGADHA

Ganges R.

KIKATA

KOSALA

KASHI

PANCHALA

MADHYADESA

Ganges R.

Kaushambi

Yamuna R.

KURU

SALVAS

MATSYA

PUNJAB

SATVANT

Indus R.

Harappa

GANDARA

SIVA

BHARATA

NICHYA

Indus R.

Mohenjo-Daro

Gulf of Cambay

SIND

Arabian Sea

N
E
W
S

Agni was present everywhere, but he was hidden. He was in the sun, the thunder, the stormy rain, and the lightning that brought fire to the earth. He was present in ponds and streams, in the clay of the riverbank, and the plants from which fire could be kindled.[55] Agni had to be reverently retrieved from these hiding places, and pressed into the service of humanity. After establishing a new settlement, the warriors would celebrate the Agnicayana ritual, when they would ceremonially build a new brick altar for Agni. First they processed to the riverbank to collect the clay, where Agni was hidden, ritually taking possession of their new territory. They might have to fight and kill local residents who resisted this act of occupation. On their return to the sacrificial ground, the victorious warriors built their altar in the shape of a bird, one of Agni's emblems, and Agni revealed himself when the new fire blazed forth.[56] Only then did the new colony become a reality: "One becomes a settler when he builds the fire altar," said one of the later texts, "and whoever are builders of fire altars are settled."[57]

Raiding was built into the Aryan rituals. In the soma ritual, the sacred drink seemed to lift warriors up to the world of the gods. Once filled with the divine power of the god, they felt that they "had surpassed the heavens and all this spacious earth." But this hymn began: "This, even this was my resolve, to win a cow, to win a steed: have I not drunk of Soma juice?"[58] During the soma ritual, the patron and his guests had to leave the sacrificial ground and raid a nearby settlement to procure cattle and soma for the sacrifice. In the *rajasuya*, after the new king had drunk the soma juice, he was dispatched on a raid. If he returned with plunder, the officiating priests acknowledged his kingship: "Thou, O King, art *brahman*!"[59]

During the late Vedic period, the Aryans developed the idea of *brahman*, the supreme reality. Brahman was not a *deva*, but a power that was higher, deeper, and more basic than the gods, a force that held all the disparate elements of the universe together, and stopped them from fragmenting.[60] Brahman was the fundamental principle that enabled all things to become strong and to expand. It was life itself.[61] Brahman could never be defined or described,

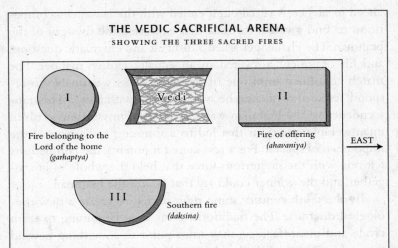

THE VEDIC SACRIFICIAL ARENA
SHOWING THE THREE SACRED FIRES

I

Vedi

II

Fire belonging to the
Lord of the home
(garhaptya)

Fire of offering
(ahavaniya)

EAST →

III

Southern fire
(daksina)

I) The "fire belonging to the Lord of the home" (garhaptya), used to prepare food for the sacrifice. It had a round altar, representing the earth.

II) The "fire of offering" (ahavaniya), where the prepared offerings were placed. A square altar, representing the four-directional sky. The offerings from earth (I) to heaven (II) by Agni.

III) The "southern fire" (daksina)—less used in major rituals— to ward off evil spirits and receive offerings to special ancestors. A semicircular altar representing the atmosphere between the earth and overarching heavens.

The Vedi was a grass-lined pit in which oblations and utensils were placed when not in use to preserve their powers.

The altars were usually made of sand, earth, pebbles, and pieces of wood.

because it was all-encompassing: human beings could not get out-side it and see it objectively. But it could be experienced in ritual. When the king arrived back safely from his raid, with the spoils of battle, he had become one with the brahman. He was now the axis, the hub of the wheel that would pull his kingdom together, and enable it to prosper and expand. Brahman was also experi-

enced in silence. A ritual often ended with the *brahmodya* competition to find a verbal formula that expressed the mystery of the
brahman. The challenger asked a difficult and enigmatic question,
and his opponent answered in an equally elusive manner. The
match continued until one of the contestants was unable to respond: reduced to silence, he was forced to withdraw.[62] The transcendence of the brahman was sensed in the mysterious clash of
unanswerable questions that led to a stunning realization of the
impotence of speech. For a few sacred moments, the competitors
felt one with the mysterious force that held the whole of life together, and the winner could say that he *was* the brahman.

By the tenth century some *rishis* started to create a new theological discourse. The traditional *devas* were beginning to seem
crude and unsatisfactory; they must point to something beyond
themselves. Some of the late hymns of the Rig Veda sought a god
who was more worthy of worship. "What god shall we adore
with our offering?" asked one of the *rishis* in Hymn 121 of the
tenth book of the Rig Veda. Who was the true lord of men and
cattle? Who owned the snowcapped mountains and the mighty
ocean? Which of the gods was capable of supporting the heavens? In this hymn, the poet found an answer that would become
one of the seminal myths of the Indian Axial Age. He had a vision of a creator god emerging from primal chaos, a personalized
version of the brahman. His name was Prajapati: "the All." Prajapati was identical with the universe; he was the life force that
sustained it, the seed of consciousness, and the light that emerged
from the waters of unconscious matter. But Prajapati was also a
spirit outside the universe, who could order the laws of nature.
Immanent and transcendent, he alone was "God of gods and
none beside him."

But this seemed far too explicit to another *rishi*.[63] In the beginning, he maintained, there was nothing. There was neither existence nor nonexistence, neither death nor immortality, but only
"indiscriminate chaos." How could this confusion become ordered and viable? The poet decided that there could be no answer
to this question:

Who verily knows and who can here declare it, whence it
was born and whence comes this creation?
The Gods are later than this world's production. Who
knows then whence it first came into being?
He, the first origin of this creation, whether he formed it
all or did not form it,
Whose eye controls this world in highest heaven, he
verily knows it—or perhaps he knows not.[64]

The poem was a *brahmodya*. The *rishi* asked one unfathomable question after another, until both he and his audience were reduced to the silence of unknowing.

Finally, in the famous Purusha Hymn, a *rishi* meditated on the ancient creation story of the Aryans, and laid the foundation for India's Axial Age.[65] He recalled that the sacrifice of the first man had brought the human race into being. Now he described this primordial Person (*Purusha*), walking of his own free will into the sacrificial ground, lying down on the freshly strewn grass, and allowing the gods to kill him. This act of self-surrender had set the cosmos in motion. The Purusha was himself the universe. Everything was generated from his corpse: birds, animals, horses, cattle, the classes of human society, heaven and earth, sun and moon. Even the great *devas* Agni and Indra had emerged from his body. But like Prajapati, he was also transcendent: 75 percent of his being was immortal and could not be affected by time and mortality. Unlike the agonistic rituals of the warriors, there was no fighting in this sacrifice. Purusha gave himself away without a struggle.

Purusha and Prajapati were shadowy, remote figures, with no developed mythology. There was very little to say about them. Indeed, it was said that Prajapati's real name was a question: "Who?" (*Ka?*) On the brink of its Axial Age, the visionaries of India were moving beyond concepts and words into a silent appreciation of the ineffable. But as the Purusha Hymn shows, they were still inspired by the ancient ritual. Even though the rites were so dangerous and violent, they would remain the inspiration of the great transformation in India. By the end of the tenth century, the *rishis* had established the complex of symbols that would create the first great Axial Age spirituality.

The Chinese kings of the Shang dynasty, who had ruled the Yellow River Valley since the sixteenth century, believed that they were the sons of God. It was said that Di, a supremely powerful deity who usually had no contact with human beings, had sent a dark bird down to the great plain of China. The bird had laid an egg, which was eaten by a lady. In the course of time, she had given birth to the first ancestor of the Shang monarchs.[66] Because of his unique relationship with Di, the king was the only person in the world who was allowed to approach the High God directly. He alone could win security for his people by offering sacrifices to Di. With the help of his diviners, he would consult Di about the advisability of undertaking a military expedition or founding a new settlement. He could ask Di whether or not the harvest would be successful. The king derived his legitimacy from his power as a seer and intermediary with the divine world, but on a more mundane level, he also relied on his superior bronze weaponry. The first Shang cities may have been founded by the masters of the guilds that had pioneered the manufacture of the bronze weapons, war chariots, and gleaming vessels that the Shang used in their sacrifices. The power of the new technology meant that the kings could mobilize thousands of peasants for forced labor or warfare.

The Shang knew that they were not the first kings of China. They claimed that they had wrested power from the last king of the Xia dynasty (c. 2200–1600). There is no archaeological or documentary evidence for the Xia, but there was probably some kind of kingdom in the great plain by the end of the third millennium.[67] Civilization had arrived slowly and painfully in China. The great plain was isolated from the surrounding regions by high mountains and swampy, uninhabitable land. The climate was harsh, with broiling summers and icy winters, when settlements were attacked by freezing, sand-laden winds. The Yellow River was difficult to navigate and prone to flooding. The early settlers had to cut canals to drain the marshland and build dikes to stop the floods from ruining the crops. The Chinese had no historical memory of the people who had created these ancient works, but they told stories of the feudal kings who had ruled the Chinese empire before the Xia, and made the countryside habitable. Huang-Di, the Yellow Emperor, had fought a monster and fixed the courses of the sun, moon, and stars. Shen Nong had invented agriculture, and in the twenty-third century, the wise emperors Yao and Shun had established a golden age of peace and prosperity. During Shun's reign, the land had been overwhelmed by terrible flooding, and Shun had commissioned Yu, his chief of public works, to solve the problem. For thirteen years Yu had built canals, tamed the marshes, and led the rivers to the sea, so that they flowed in as orderly a fashion as lords going to a great reception. Thanks to Yu's herculean efforts, the people were able to grow rice and millet. Emperor Shun was so impressed that he arranged for Yu to succeed him, and thus Yu became the founder of the Xia dynasty.[68] All these legendary sage kings would be an inspiration to the philosophers of the Chinese Axial Age.

The Shang aristocrats were certainly familiar with some of these stories. They knew that civilization was a precarious and hard-won achievement, and believed that the fate of the living was inextricably bound up with the spirits of those who had gone before them. The Shang may not have been as powerful as Yao, Shun, or Yu, but they controlled extensive territory in the great plain.[69] Their domain extended to the Huai Valley in the southeast, to Shantung in the east, and their influence could be felt as far away as the Wei Valley in the west. They did not rule a centralized state but had founded a network of small palace-cities, each governed by a representative of the royal house. The towns were tiny, consisting simply of a residential complex for the king and his vassals, surrounded by high walls of packed earth to guard against flooding or attack. At Yin, the last of the Shang capitals, the walls were a mere eight hundred yards in perimeter. Shang towns followed a uniform pattern; they were usually rectangular in shape, each wall oriented to one of the four compass directions, with all dwellings facing south. The royal palace had three courtyards and an audience chamber for ritual and political occasions; to the east of the palace was the temple of the ancestors. The market was north of the king's home, and the craftsmen, chariot builders, makers of bows and arrows, blacksmiths, and potters lived in the southern districts of the city with the royal scribes, diviners, and ritual experts.

This was not an egalitarian society. The Shang showed the passionate preoccupation with hierarchy and rank that would become one of the hallmarks of Chinese civilization. As the son of Di, the king was at the top of the feudal pyramid, in a class of his own. Next in rank were the princes of the royal house, rulers of the various Shang cities; below them came the heads of the great families, who held posts at court, and the barons, who lived on the revenues from rural territories outside the city walls. Finally, at the base of the feudal pyramid, were the ordinary gentlemen, the warrior class.

The city was a small aristocratic enclave, a world unto itself. The Shang nobility devoted their time exclusively to religion, warfare, and hunting. They took a surplus of agricultural produce from the local peasants in return for military protection. But very little of the region was given over to cultivation at this date. Most of the Yellow River valley was still covered by dense woods and marshes. In the Shang period, elephants, rhinoceroses, buffaloes, panthers, and leopards still roamed through the forests, together with deer, tigers, wild oxen, bears, monkeys, and game. The animals could become pests, so hunting was a duty as well as a pleasure. On the king's triumphant return to the city, the victims were sacrificed and eaten in huge, rowdy, drunken banquets.

There was little difference between war and hunting. Warfare was an activity that was limited to the aristocrats, who alone were allowed to own weapons and chariots. A typical military expedition was a modest affair, consisting of about a hundred chariots; the peasants who followed on foot did not take part in the fighting but acted as valets, servants, and carriers, and looked after the horses. The Shang had no great territorial ambitions; they made war simply to punish rebellious cities by carrying off valuable

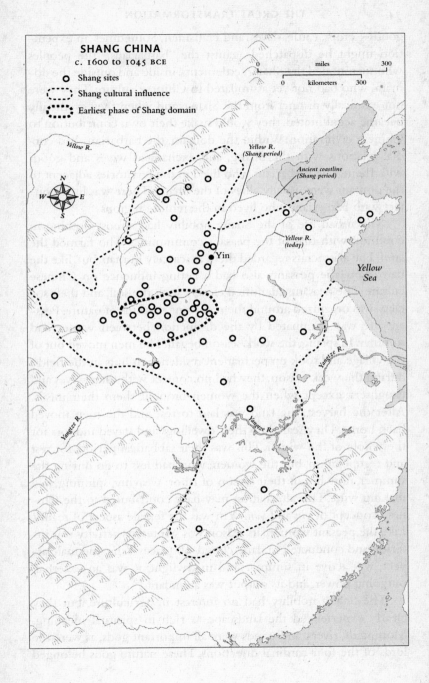

SHANG CHINA
c. 1600 to 1045 BCE

○ Shang sites

⬝⬝⬝ Shang cultural influence

●●● Earliest phase of Shang domain

Yellow R.

Yellow R.
(Shang period)

Ancient coastline
(Shang period)

N
W — E
S

Yellow R.
(today)

●Yin

Yellow
Sea

Yangtze R.

Yangtze R.

Yangtze R.

miles   0 — 300
kilometers 0 — 300

goods—crops, cattle, slaves, and craftsmen. Sometimes an expedition might be dispatched against the "barbarians," the peoples who surrounded the Shang settlements, inside and outside the domain, who had not yet assimilated to Chinese culture. They were not ethnically distinct from the Shang, and when they eventually became acculturated, they would make their own contribution to Chinese civilization. Within the domain, the barbarians had cordial relations with the Shang, and exchanged wives and goods with them. The barbarians who lived in the territories adjacent to the domain were usually allies of the Shang. There was little contact with barbarians who lived in the remote regions.

The urban life of the Shang nobility had almost nothing in common with that of the peasant communities who farmed the land. The aristocrats regarded them as scarcely human, but, like the barbarians, the peasants also had a lasting influence on Chinese culture. The peasants identified closely with the soil, and their society was organized around the recurrent rhythms of nature. Peasant life was dominated by the distinction between winter and summer. In spring, the work season began. The men moved out of the village and took up permanent residence in huts in the fields; during the work season, they had no contact with their wives and daughters, except when the women brought them their meals. After the harvest, the land was laid to rest and the men moved back home. They sealed up their dwellings and stayed indoors for the whole of the winter. This was their sabbatical period, for rest and recuperation, but the women, who had less to do during the summer, now began their season of labor: weaving, spinning, and making wine. This alternation may have contributed to the Chinese concept of *yin* and *yang*. Yin was the female aspect of reality. Like the peasant women, its season was winter; its activity was interior, and conducted in dark, closed-off places. Yang, the male aspect, was active in summer and in daylight; it was an external, outgoing power, and its output was abundant.[70]

The Shang nobility had no interest in agriculture, but they clearly experienced the landscape as rich in spiritual meaning. Mountains, rivers, and winds were all important gods, as were the lords of the four cardinal directions. These nature gods belonged to the Earth, which was the divine counterpart of Di, the Sky God. Because they could affect the harvest, they were placated and cajoled by sacrifice. Of even greater importance, however, were the ancestors of the royal house, whose cult was at the heart of Shang religion. Excavations at Yin (modern Anyang) have uncovered the tombs of nine kings; they lay in their coffins on a central platform, surrounded by the remains of soldiers who had been sacrificed at their funerals. After his death, a king achieved divine status; he lived in heaven with Di and could ask him to help his living relatives on earth.[71]

The Shang were convinced that the fate of the dynasty depended upon the goodwill of the deceased kings. While Di had no special cult of his own, and the nature gods no regular rites, the ancestors were worshiped in lavish ceremonies; each had his or her festival day in the ritual calendar. The kings held ceremonies, "hosting" (bin) their forefathers. Members of the royal family would dress up as their deceased relatives, feeling themselves to be possessed by the ancestor they impersonated, and when they entered the court, the king would bow down before them. The nature gods were summoned to share the feast in the palace courtyard, where quantities of animals were sacrificed and cooked. Then gods, ancestors, and human beings would feast together.

But behind this elaborate ritual lurked a deep anxiety.[72] Di was the guardian of towns and cities. He ruled the rains and the winds, and gave orders to the nature gods in the same way as the Shang king gave directions to his officials and soldiers. But Di was unpredictable. He often sent drought, flooding, and disaster. Even the ancestors were unreliable. The Shang believed that the spirits of the dead could be dangerous, so relatives buried the deceased in thick wooden coffins, treated their bodies with jade, and stuffed their orifices, lest the spirit escape and prey upon the living. Rituals were devised to turn a potentially troublesome ghost into a helpful, benevolent presence. The deceased was given a new name and assigned a special day for worship in the hope that he would now be kindly disposed toward the community. With the passing of time, an ancestor became more powerful, so rituals were designed to persuade the newly deceased to plead their cause with the more exalted ancestors, who might, in their turn, intercede with Di.

Most of our information about the Shang comes from the animal bones and turtle shells on which the royal diviners inscribed questions for Di, the nature gods, and the ancestors.[73] Archaeologists have unearthed 150,000 of these inscribed oracle bones. They show that the kings submitted all their activities to the scrutiny of these powers, asking their advice about a hunt, a harvest, or even a toothache. The procedure was simple. The king or his diviner addressed a charge to a specially prepared turtle shell or cattle bone, while applying a hot poker. "We will receive millet harvest," he might say, or, "To Father Jia [the seventeenth Shang king] we pray for good harvest."[74] He would then study the cracks that developed in the shell and announce whether or not the oracle was auspicious. Afterward the royal engravers carved the charge. Sometimes they also noted the prediction that came from the god or ancestor concerned and—very occasionally—included the result. It was obviously not a rational process, but the diviners were clearly trying to keep genuine records. Some of them, for example, noted that the king had foretold that his wife's childbearing would be "good" (that is, that she would bear a boy), even though she gave birth to a girl and the king had got the day wrong.[75]

The Shang kings' attempt to control the spiritual world often failed. The ancestors frequently sent bad harvests and ill luck. Di sometimes sent propitious rain, but, the oracle also observed, "It is Di who is harming our harvests."[76] Di was an unreliable military ally. He could "confer assistance" on the Shang, or inspire their enemies. "The Fang are harming and attacking us," mourned the oracle. "It is Di who orders [them] to make disaster for us."[77] Ineffective and undependable, Di met the usual fate of the Sky God and began to fade away. The Shang never developed a routine liturgy to ask for his help, and by the twelfth century they had stopped addressing him directly at all, and appealed only to the ancestors and nature spirits.[78]

Shang society was a strange mixture of refinement, sophistication, and barbarity. The Shang appreciated the beauty of their environment. Their art was sophisticated and inventive, and their bronze ritual vessels showed close observation of the wild animals and their cattle, oxen, and horses. They created wonderfully inventive urns in the shape of sheep, rhinoceroses, or owls. But they were not squeamish about slaughtering the beasts they observed so tenderly, sometimes slaying as many as a hundred victims in a single sacrifice. During the royal hunt, the Shang killed wild beasts with reckless abandon, and consumed hecatombs of domestic animals at a *bin* banquet or a funeral. The kings and nobles had acquired great wealth, which they measured in livestock, metal, crops, and game. Their environment teemed with wildlife, and the peasants provided an endless flow of grain and rice, so their resources seemed inexhaustible. There was no thought of saving for the morrow.[79]

Later Mozi, one of the Axial philosophers, recalled the lavish funerals of the Shang kings, the "sons of Heaven," clearly revolted by the prodigal, vulgar extravagance and the ritual murder of hapless servants and retainers:

> On the death of a prince, the store houses and treasures are emptied. Gold, jade and pearls are placed on the body. Rolls of silk and chariots with their horses are buried in the grave. But an abundance of hangings are also needed for a funerary chamber, as well as tripod vases, drums, tables, pots, ice-containers, war axes, swords, plumed standards, ivories and animal skins. No one is satisfied unless all these riches accompany the deceased. As for the men who are sacrificed in order to follow him, if he should be a Son of Heaven, they will be counted in hundreds or tens. If he is a great officer or a baron, they will be counted in tens or units.[80]

There was cruelty and violence in Shang religion, and in the end, it seemed to the Chinese that even Di, who had little sense of moral responsibility, had run out of patience with his ruling dynasty.

In 1045, King Wen of the Zhou, a people who ruled a principality in the Wei Valley, invaded the Shang domain while the king was away from the capital. Tragically, King Wen was killed in battle, but his son King Wu continued to advance into Shang territory, and defeated the Shang army at the battle of Mu-Ye, north of the Yellow River. The Shang king was beheaded, and the Zhou occupied Yin. King Wu then divided the spoils. He decided that he would remain in the old Zhou capital in the Wei Valley, so he put his son Cheng in charge of Yin, and entrusted the administration of the other Shang cities to Wu-Keng, the son of the last Shang king. King Wu then returned to the Wei Valley, where he died shortly afterward.

After his death, the Shang prince seized the opportunity to rebel against Zhou rule. But King Wen's brother Dan, usually known as the duke of Zhou, quashed the revolt, and the Shang lost control of the central plain. Prince Cheng became the new king, but because he was still a minor, the duke of Zhou acted as regent and devised a quasi-feudal system. The princes and allies of the Zhou were each given a city, as a personal fief, and the Zhou built a new capital to maintain a presence in the eastern territories of their domain. It was named Chengzhou in honor of the new king.

In many ways, the Zhou stepped straight into the shoes of the Shang. Like the Shang, they enjoyed hunting, archery, chariot driving, and extravagant parties. They organized their cities on the old Shang model, worshiped the nature gods and ancestors, and cast oracles. They also continued to worship Di but—in a way that was typical of ancient religion—they merged Di with their own Sky God, whom they called Tian ("Heaven"). But here they ran into a difficulty. The Shang had ruled for hundreds of years with the apparent blessing of Di. If they were to win over the Shang nobility who still lived on the great plain, continuity was essential. The Zhou wanted to worship the deceased Shang kings alongside their own ancestors. But how could they worship the Shang spirits when they had destroyed their dynasty?

The duke of Zhou found a solution. Di had sometimes used enemy tribes to punish the Shang. Now, it seemed, he had made the Zhou his instrument. On the occasion of the consecration of

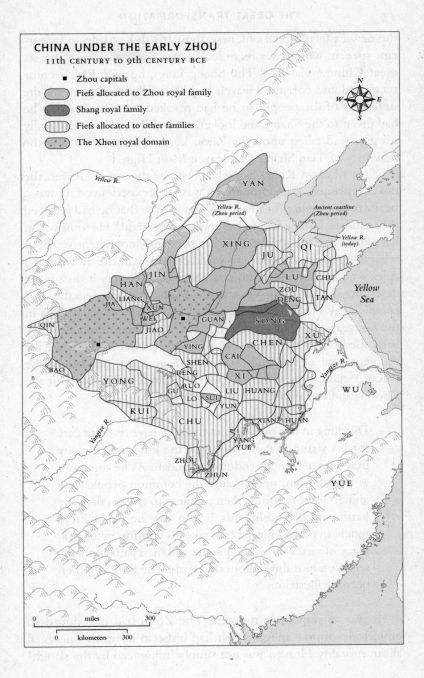

CHINA UNDER THE EARLY ZHOU
11th CENTURY to 9th CENTURY BCE

- ■ Zhou capitals
- Fiefs allocated to Zhou royal family
- Shang royal family
- Fiefs allocated to other families
- The Xhou royal domain

N
W E
S

Yellow R.

YAN

Yellow R.
(Zhou period)

Ancient coastline
(Zhou period)

Yellow R.
(today)

XING

JU

QI

JIN

HAN

LIANG

HA

XUN

WEI

JIAO

QIN

BAO

LU

CHU

ZOU

DENG

TAN

Yellow
Sea

GUAN

SONG

CHEN

XU

YING

CAI

SHEN

DENG

XI

GU

RUO

LO

SUI

YUN

LIU

HUANG

YONG

KUI

CHU

XIAN

HUAN

YANG
YUE

ZHOU

ZHUN

WU

YUE

0   miles   300

0   kilometers   300

the new eastern capital of Chengzhou, the duke made an important speech, which was recorded in the *Shujing,* one of the six great Chinese classics.[81] The Shang kings, he said, had become tyrannical and corrupt. Heaven had been filled with pity for the sufferings of the people, so he had revoked the mandate that he had given to the Shang, and looked around for new rulers. Finally his gaze had fallen upon the Zhou kings, who thus became the new sons of Tian Shang Di, Heaven Most High.

That was how King Cheng had become the son of Heaven, the duke explained, even though he was so inexperienced. It was a heavy responsibility for the young man. Now that he had received the mandate, Cheng had to be "reverently careful." He must be "in harmony with the little people . . . prudently apprehensive about what the people say." Heaven would take its mandate away from a ruler who oppressed his subjects, and would bestow it on a more deserving dynasty. This was why the Shang and Xia dynasties had failed. Many of the Shang kings had been virtuous rulers, but in the last years of the dynasty the people had been miserable. They had called out in anguish to Heaven, and Heaven "too grieved for the people of all the lands," decided to give the mandate to the Zhou because they were "deeply committed" to justice. But the Zhou could not afford to be complacent.

> Dwelling in this new city, let the king have reverent care for his virtue. If it is virtue that the king uses, he may pray Heaven for an enduring mandate. As he functions as king, let him not, because the common people stray and do what is wrong, then presume to govern them by harsh capital punishments. In this way, he will achieve much. In being king, let him take his position in the primacy of virtue. The little people will then pattern themselves on him throughout the world. The king will then become illustrious.[82]

It was an important moment. The Zhou had introduced an ethical ideal into a religion that had hitherto been unconcerned about morality. Heaven was not simply influenced by the slaughter of pigs and oxen, but by compassion and justice. The mandate of Heaven would become an important ideal during the Chinese Axial Age. If a ruler was selfish, cruel, and oppressive, Heaven would not support him, and he would fall. A state might appear to be weak and insignificant—like the Zhou before the conquest—but if its ruler was wise, humane, and truly concerned for the welfare of his subjects, people would flock to him from all over the world, and Heaven would raise him to the highest position.

At the beginning, however, there was some disagreement about the interpretation of the mandate.[83] The duke of Zhou and his brother Gong, duke of Shao, had a serious difference of opinion. The duke of Zhou believed that Heaven had given the mandate to *all* the Zhou people; the new king should, therefore, rely on the advice of his ministers. But Shao Gong argued that the king alone had received the mandate. He reverted to the old idea that because the king was the son of God, he was the only person who could approach Heaven directly. Certainly, the king would consult advisers, but he had received a unique, mystical potency that gave him the mandate to rule.

For obvious reasons, King Cheng found his uncle Gong's argument appealing. The two joined forces, and put pressure on the duke of Zhou to retire. He took up residence in the city of Lu, in the east of the central plain, which had been assigned to him as his personal fief. He became a hero to the people of Lu, who revered him as their most distinguished ancestor. The duke's conviction that virtue was more important than magical charisma was an insight worthy of the Axial Age. Instead of revering a man who had lived an immoral life simply because he was an ancestor, the cult should honor men of worth and merit.[84] But the Chinese were not yet ready for this moral vision and retreated into the paranormal rituals of the past.

We know almost nothing about the kings who ruled after King Cheng, but a hundred years after the Zhou conquest, it was clear that despite its mandate from Heaven, the Zhou dynasty had started to decline. The feudal system had an inbuilt weakness. Over the years, the blood ties that linked the rulers of the various cities to the royal house became attenuated, so that the princes of the cities were merely distant cousins of the king, twice or even thrice removed. The kings continued to rule from their western capital, and by the tenth century it was clear that the more easterly cities were becoming restive. The Zhou empire was beginning to disintegrate, but the dynasty retained a religious and symbolic aura long after the Zhou kings had ceased to be important politically. The Chinese would never forget the early years of the Zhou dynasty; their Axial Age would be inspired by the search for a just ruler, who would be worthy of Heaven's mandate.

In the twelfth century, the eastern Mediterranean was engulfed in a crisis that swept away the Greek, Hittite, and Egyptian kingdoms and plunged the whole region into a dark age. We do not know exactly what happened. Scholars used to blame the "sea peoples" mentioned in Egyptian records, anarchic hordes of rootless sailors and peasants from Crete and Anatolia who raged through the Levant and vandalized towns and villages. But it seems that the sea peoples may have been a symptom of the catastrophe rather than its cause. Climatic or environmental change may have led to extensive drought and famine that wrecked the local economies, which lacked the flexibility to respond creatively to the disruption. For centuries, the Hittites and Egyptians had divided the Near East between them. The Egyptians had controlled the whole of southern Syria, Phoenicia, and Canaan, while the Hittites had ruled Asia Minor and Anatolia. By 1130, Egypt had lost most of its foreign provinces; the Hittite capital was in ruins; the large Canaanite ports of Ugarit, Megiddo, and Hazor had been devastated; and in Greece, the Mycenaean kingdom had disintegrated. Desperate, dispossessed peoples roamed the region in search of employment and security.

The terrible finality of the crisis made an indelible impression on everybody who had experienced it. Two of the Axial peoples emerged during the ensuing dark age. A new Greek civilization rose from the rubble of Mycenae, and a confederation of tribes called Israel appeared in the highlands of Canaan. Because this re-

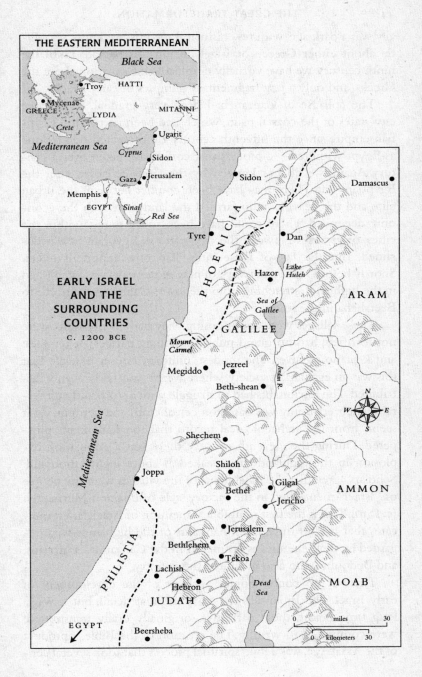

THE EASTERN MEDITERRANEAN

Black Sea

HATTI

Troy

Mycenae
GREECE

LYDIA

MITANNI

Mediterranean Sea

Crete

Cyprus

Ugarit

Sidon

Gaza

Jerusalem

Memphis

EGYPT

Sinai

Red Sea

EARLY ISRAEL
AND THE
SURROUNDING
COUNTRIES

C. 1200 BCE

Sidon

Damascus

PHOENICIA

Tyre

Dan

Hazor

Lake
Huleh

ARAM

Sea of
Galilee

GALILEE

Mount
Carmel

Megiddo

Jezreel

Beth-shean

Jordan R.

N
W E
S

Mediterranean Sea

Shechem

Shiloh

Bethel

Gilgal

Jericho

AMMON

Joppa

Jerusalem

Bethlehem

Tekoa

PHILISTIA

Lachish

Hebron

Dead
Sea

MOAB

JUDAH

EGYPT

Beersheba

0   miles   30

0   kilometers   30

ally was a dark age, with few historical records, we know very little about either Greece or Israel during this period. Until the ninth century, we have virtually no reliable information about the Greeks, and only a few, fragmentary glimpses of early Israel.

The collapse of Canaan had been very gradual.[85] The large city-states of the coastal plain, which had been part of the Egyptian empire since the fifteenth century, disintegrated one by one as Egypt withdrew—a process that could have taken over a century. Again, we do not know why the cities collapsed after the Egyptians left. There may have been conflict between the urban elite and the peasants who farmed the land on which the economy depended. There could have been social unrest within the cities, or rivalries between the city-states as Egyptian power declined. But the fall of these cities had one important effect. Shortly before 1200, a network of new settlements was established in the highlands, stretching from the lower Galilee in the north to Beersheba in the south.[86]

These villages were not imposing: they had no city walls; were not fortified; had no grand public buildings, palaces, or temples; and kept no archives. The modest, uniform houses indicate that this was an egalitarian society, where wealth was fairly evenly distributed. The inhabitants had to struggle with a stony, difficult terrain. Their economy was based on cereal crops and herding, yet it seems from the archaeological record that the settlements prospered. During the eleventh century, there was a population explosion in the highlands that peaked at about eighty thousand. Scholars agree that the inhabitants of the villages were the people of "Israel" mentioned in the victory stele of Pharaoh Mernepteh (c. 1210). This is the first nonbiblical mention of Israel, and it indicates that by this time, the inhabitants of the highlands were regarded by their enemies as distinct from the Canaanites, Hurrians, and Bedouins who also inhabited the country.[87]

There is no contemporary account of the development of early Israel. The Bible tells the story in great detail, but it was a long time before these narratives, originally orally transmitted, were committed to writing. The creation of the Bible, a product of the Axial Age, was a long spiritual process that took several centuries. The earliest biblical texts were written during the eighth century and the biblical canon was finalized sometime during the fifth or fourth century. During their Axial Age, Israelite historians, poets, annalists, prophets, priests, and lawyers meditated deeply on their history. The founding fathers of the nation—Abraham, Moses, Joshua, David—were as spiritually important to Israel as Yao, Shun, and the duke of Zhou were to the Chinese. Israelites reflected on the story of their beginnings as relentlessly as the sages of India would ponder the meaning of the sacrificial ritual. The story of Israel's origins would become the organizing symbol around which its Axial breakthrough revolved. As we shall see, the Israelites developed their saga, changed it, embroidered it, added to it, reinterpreted it, and made it speak to the particular circumstances of the time. Each poet, prophet, and visionary added a new layer to the evolving narrative, which broadened and deepened in significance.

The definitive narrative claims that the people of Israel were not native to Canaan. Their ancestor, Abraham, had come from Ur, in Mesopotamia, and settled in Canaan at the behest of his god in about 1750. The patriarchs had lived in different parts of the hill country: Abraham in Hebron; Isaac, his son, in Beersheba; and Jacob, Abraham's grandson (also called Israel), in the region of Shechem. Yahweh promised the patriarchs that he would make Israel a mighty nation and give them the land of Canaan as their own. But during a famine, Jacob/Israel and his twelve sons (founders of the Israelite tribes) had migrated to Egypt. At first they prospered there, but eventually the Egyptians enslaved them and the Israelites languished in captivity for four hundred years. Finally, in about 1250, their god, Yahweh, took pity on them and, with a mighty display of power, liberated them under the leadership of Moses. As the Israelites fled Egypt, Yahweh miraculously parted the waters of the Sea of Reeds, so that they crossed to safety dry-shod, but he then drowned Pharaoh and the Egyptian army, who had followed them into the sea in hot pursuit. In the desert region to the south of Canaan, Yahweh made a covenant with Israel on Mount Sinai, and gave them the Law that would make them a holy people. But the Israelites had to wander in the wilderness for forty years before Yahweh finally led them to the borders of Canaan. Moses died before entering the Promised Land, but in about 1200 Joshua led the armies of Israel to victory. Under Joshua, the Israelites destroyed all the Canaanite towns and cities, killed their inhabitants, and made the land their own.

The excavations of Israeli archaeologists since 1967, however, do not confirm this story. They have found no trace of the mass destruction described in the book of Joshua, no signs of foreign invasion, no Egyptian artifacts, and no indication of a change in population. The scholarly debate has been as fierce and often as antagonistic as the discussion about the origins of Vedic culture in India. The general scholarly consensus is that the story of the exodus from Egypt is not historical. The biblical narrative reflects the conditions of the seventh or sixth century, when most of these texts were written, rather than the thirteenth century. A number of scholars believe that many of the settlers who created the new colonies in the highlands were probably migrants from the failing city-states on the coast. Many of the first Israelites were, therefore, probably not foreigners but Canaanites. The earliest parts of the Bible suggest that Yahweh was originally a god of the southern mountains, and it seems likely that other tribes had migrated to the highlands from the south, bringing Yahweh with them. Some of the Israelites—notably, the tribe of Joseph—may even have come from Egypt. Israelites, who had lived under Egyptian rule in the coastal city-states, may have felt that they had indeed been liberated from Egypt—but in their own land. The biblical writers were not attempting to write a scientifically accurate account that would satisfy a modern historian. They were searching for the meaning of existence. These were epic stories, national sagas that helped the people to create a distinct identity.[88]

Why would the Israelites claim to be foreigners if they were in fact native to Canaan? Archaeologists have found evidence of considerable socioeconomic disruption in the highlands, major demographic shifts, and two centuries of life-and-death struggles between competing ethnic groups.[89] Even the biblical account suggests that Israel was not descended from a single ancestor, but consisted of a number of different ethnicities—Gibeonites, Jerahmeelites, Kenites, and Canaanites from the cities of Hepher and Tirzah—who all became part of "Israel."[90] These groups and clans seem to have bound themselves together by a covenant agreement.[91] All had made a brave, deliberate decision to turn their backs on the ancient urban culture of Canaan. In this sense, they were indeed outsiders, and the experience of living on the periphery may have inspired both their belief in Israel's foreign origins and the anti-Canaanite polemic in the Bible. Israel was a newcomer in the family of nations, born of trauma and upheaval, and constantly threatened with marginality. The Israelites developed a counteridentity and a counternarrative: they were different from the other nations in the region, because they enjoyed a unique relationship with their god, Yahweh.[92]

The tribal ethos demanded that its members avenge the death of their kinsfolk. Kindred were one flesh; tribesmen shared a single life.[93] Hence they had to love their fellow clansmen as themselves. The term *hesed,* often translated as "love," was originally a tribal term, denoting the loyalty of a kinship relationship that demanded generous and altruistic behavior toward one's family group.[94] People who were not blood relations could be incorporated into the tribe by marriage or a covenant treaty that gave them the status of brothers. The tribesmen had to love these new members as themselves, because they were now flesh of their flesh, bone of their bone. Many of the early covenants of the Middle East used these kinship terms, and it is likely that this ethos informed the covenant that bound together the different ethnic groups of the new Israel.[95] As social units became larger in the western Semitic world, kinship terminology was used even more frequently than before, in order to emphasize the sanctity of the bond that tied the larger confederation together. The institutions and laws of early Israel were thus dominated by the tribal ideal. Like other peoples in the region, Israelites felt related to their national god, calling themselves *am Yahweh,* the "kindred" or the "people" of Yahweh.[96]

The archaeological record shows that life was violent in the hill country. It was a chaotic time in the eastern Mediterranean, and the early settlers almost certainly had to fight for the land they were trying to colonize. The Bible preserves a memory of a great victory at the river Jordan: the tribes who migrated from the south, through the territory of Moab, may have had to contend with local groups who wanted to stop them from crossing the river. Once settlers were established in a village, they had to learn to coexist with their neighbors and unite against people who threatened the security of their fledgling society. Archaeologists believe that the sporadic warfare described in the books of Judges and 1 Samuel is probably a reasonably accurate description of conditions in the eleventh and tenth centuries. Israel had to compete with such groups as the Philistines, who had settled on the southern coast of Canaan in about 1200, at about the same time as the first villages were established in the highlands. A tribal leader (*sopet:* "judge") had to be able to muster support from neighboring settlements if his clan was attacked. Hence the institution of *herem* ("holy war") was crucial to Israelite society. If his tribe was attacked, the judge summoned other clans to the militia of Yahweh. The central cult object of Israel was a palladium called the Ark of the Covenant, symbol of the treaty that bound the *am Yahweh* together, which was carried into battle. When the troops set out, the judge called upon Yahweh to accompany the Ark:

> *Arise, Yahweh, may your enemies be scattered*
> *And those who hate you run*
> *For their lives before you.*[97]

Living constantly poised against attack, and ready for war, the beleaguered people developed an embattled cult.

Even though the people of Israel felt so separate from their neighbors, the biblical record suggests that until the sixth century Israel's religion was not in fact very different from that of the other local peoples. Abraham, Isaac, and Jacob had worshiped El, the High God of Canaan, and later generations merged El's cult with that of Yahweh.[98] Yahweh himself referred to this process when he explained to Moses that at the beginning of Israel's history the patriarchs had always called him El, and that only now was he revealing his real name, Yahweh.[99] But the Israelites never forgot El. For a long time, Yahweh's shrine was a tent, like the tabernacle in which Canaanite El presided over his divine assembly of gods.

In Canaan, El eventually met the fate of most High Gods, and by the fourteenth century his cult was in decline. He was replaced by the dynamic storm god Baal, a divine warrior, who rode on the clouds of heaven in his chariot, fought battles with other gods, and brought the life-giving rains. In the early days, Yahweh's cult was very similar to Baal's, and some of Baal's hymns were even adapted for use in Yahweh's temple in Jerusalem. Middle Eastern religion was strongly agonistic, dominated by stories of wars, hand-to-hand combat, and fearful battles among the gods. In Babylon, the warrior god Marduk had slaughtered Tiamat, the primal ocean, split her carcass in two like a giant shellfish, and created heaven and earth. Each year this battle was reenacted in the temple of Esagila during the new year ceremony to keep the world in existence for another year. In Syria, Baal fought Lotan, a seven-headed sea dragon, who is called Leviathan in the Bible. He also fought Yam, the primordial sea, symbol of chaos, and Mot, god of drought, death, and sterility. To celebrate his victory, Baal built himself a palace on Mount Sapan, his holy mountain. Until the sixth century, the Israelites also imagined Yahweh fighting sea dragons like Leviathan to create the world and save his people.[100]

The hymns of Ugarit show that the approach of Baal, the divine warrior, convulsed the entire cosmos: when he advanced on his enemies with his retinue of "holy ones," brandishing his thunderbolt,

> The heavens roll up like a scroll,
> And all their hosts languish
> As a vine leaf withers
> As the fig droops.[101]

Baal's holy voice shattered the earth, and the mountains quaked at his roar.[102] When he returned victoriously to Mount Sapan, his voice had thundered from his palace, and brought the rain.[103] His worshipers shared his struggle against drought and death by reenacting these battles in the liturgy of Ugarit. After his life-and-death battle with Mot, Baal had been joyously reunited with Anat, his sister-spouse. His worshipers celebrated this too in ritualized sex in order to activate the sacred energy of the soil and bring a good harvest. We know that, to the disgust of their prophets, the Israelites took part in these sacred orgies well into the eighth century and beyond.

In the very earliest texts of the Bible—isolated verses written in about the tenth century and inserted into the later narratives—Yahweh was presented as a divine warrior just like Baal. At this time, the tribes were living a violent, dangerous life and needed the support of their god. The poems usually depicted Yahweh marching from his home in the southern mountains and coming to the aid of his people in the highlands. Thus the Song of Deborah:

> *Yahweh, when you set out from Seir,*
> *As you trod the land of Edom,*
> *Earth shook, the heavens quaked,*
> *The clouds dissolved into water.*
> *The mountains melted before Yahweh,*
> *Before Yahweh, the God of Israel.*[104]

In another of these early poems, when Yahweh comes from Mount Paran, "he makes the earth tremble," and at his approach the ancient mountains are dislodged; the everlasting hills sink into the ground. His fury blazed against the primal sea and the nations that opposed Israel quaked with terror.[105]

In early Israel, there was no central sanctuary but a number of temples, at Shechem, Gilgal, Shiloh, Bethel, Sinai, and Hebron. As far as we can tell from isolated texts in the later biblical narrative, the Ark of the Covenant was carried from one shrine to another, and the Israelites gathered at their local temple to renew their covenant treaties in the presence of Yahweh. The temples were often associated with the great figures of Israel's past: Abraham was the local hero of the southern tribes around Hebron; Jacob had founded the shrine at Bethel; and Joseph, one of Jacob's favorite sons, was especially revered by the tribes of the northern hill country. Moses was also very popular in the north, especially at Shiloh.[106] During the covenant festivals, bards, priests, and judges told the stories of these great men. They would recall that Abraham had once entertained three strangers in his tent at Mamre, near Hebron, and that one of the strangers was Yahweh himself; that Jacob had a dream vision of Yahweh at Bethel, in which he saw a great ladder linking heaven and earth; and that after his conquest of the land, Joshua had bound the tribes together in a covenant at Shechem. Each shrine probably had its own saga, which was transmitted orally from one generation to another and recited on solemn occasions to remind the tribes of their kinship obligations.

The Israelites probably reenacted these great deeds at their ceremonies. Some scholars believe, for example, that the book of Joshua contains a record of the spring festival at Gilgal, which celebrated the tribes' victorious crossing of the river Jordan.[107] The biblical historian interrupts the ritual account by explaining that in the springtime, during the harvest season, "the Jordan overflows the whole length of its banks."[108] It appears that the water was specially dammed up for the festival, which commemorated a great miracle. When Joshua had led the people to the brink of the floodwater, he told them to stand still and watch what happened. As soon as the feet of the priests carrying the Ark touched the waters, they parted miraculously and the whole people crossed over safely, dry-shod, and entered the Promised Land at Gilgal. When the local people—"the kings of the Amorites on the west bank of the Jordan and all the kings of the Canaanites in the coastal region"—heard what had happened, "their hearts grew faint and their spirit failed them, as the Israelites drew near."[109] Every year, at the spring festival of the crossing (*pesach*), the tribes ritually enacted this great moment. They assembled on the east bank of the Jordan, purified themselves, crossed the dammed-up waters to the west bank, and entered the temple of Gilgal, where a ring of standing stones (*gilgal*), one for each of the twelve tribes, commemorated the event. There the Israelites pitched their camp, renewed the covenant, and celebrated the *pesach* by eating unleavened bread (*mazzoth*) and roasted corn, in memory of their forefathers, who had "tasted the produce of the country for the first time" after their triumphant entry into the land.[110]

Finally, perhaps, there was a reenactment of the vision that Joshua experienced after the Israelite army had set out from Gilgal.

> When Joshua was near Jericho, he raised his eyes and saw a man standing there before him, grasping a naked sword. Joshua walked towards him and said to him, "Are you with us or with our enemies?" He answered, "No, I am captain of the army of Yahweh." . . . Joshua fell on his face to the ground and worshipped him and said, "What are my Lord's commands to his servant?" The captain of the army of Yahweh answered Joshua, "Take your sandals off your feet, for the place you are standing on is holy." And Joshua obeyed.[111]

The festival of *pesach* had been a preparation for the holy war for the Promised Land that began with an assault on Jericho. The walls came miraculously tumbling down, and the Israelites stormed the city. "They enforced the *herem* on everything in the town: men and women, young and old, even the oxen and sheep and donkeys, massacring them all."[112]

Yahweh was a god of war. The festival of Gilgal took place at the time of the spring harvest, but there were no prayers for a good crop, but simply the commemoration of a military campaign. Israel's deity was called Yahweh Sabaoth, god "of armies"; he was accompanied by his heavenly host, and his captain led the Israelites into battle. War was a sanctified activity. The people purified themselves before the battle as for a religious rite, and the battleground, where Joshua had his vision, was a holy place. Many peoples in the Middle East reenacted cosmic battles, but Israel was beginning to do something different. Instead of commemorating a victory achieved in sacred time in the primordial world of myth, the Israelites celebrated a triumph that, they believed, had taken place in human time in the not-so-distant past.

This shift from myth to history is clear in one of the very earliest poems of the Bible. It was probably chanted during the Gilgal festival, and could be as old as the tenth century.[113] In the final biblical text, the Song of the Sea[114] was included in the story of the exodus, just after the crossing of the Sea of Reeds, and put on the lips of Miriam, the sister of Moses. But the Song of the Sea makes it clear that originally the enemies of Israel were not drowned in the Sea of Reeds but in the river Jordan. The people who witnessed the miracle were not the people of Egypt or Sinai, but the inhabitants of Canaan and the kingdoms on the east bank of the Jordan:

> *Pangs seize on the inhabitants of Philistia,*
> *Edom's chieftains are now dismayed,*
> *The princes of Moab fall to trembling,*
> *Canaan's inhabitants are all unmanned.*
> *On them fall terror and dread.*[115]

The song described Yahweh leading his people on a triumphant march through the Promised Land, not through the Sinai peninsula. It was adapted later to fit the story of the exodus, but it seems that originally the early ritual celebrating the crossing of the Jordan helped to shape the later biblical account of the crossing of the Sea of Reeds.[116]

It was easy to conflate the victory at the Sea of Reeds with the miracle at the Jordan. In Canaanite mythology, Baal made the cosmos habitable by fighting and killing Yam, the primal sea, which, in the Middle East, was always a symbol of the destructive forces of chaos. But Yam was also called Prince River. Sea and river were interchangeable. The Song of the Sea shows the strong influence of the cult and mythology of Baal.[117] Like Baal, Yahweh was extolled as a divine warrior.

> *Your right hand, Yahweh, shatters the enemy.*
> *So great your splendour, you crush your foes;*
> *You unleash your fury, and it devours them like stubble.*[118]

Like Baal, Yahweh forcefully controlled the sea/river: a single blast from his nostrils caused the waters to "stand upright like a dyke,"[119] and after his victory, Yahweh marched to his holy mountain, where he was established as king forever, just as Baal was enthroned on Mount Sapan after his victory over Yam. But there were striking differences. When Baal marched forth, mountains, forests, and deserts were convulsed; in the Song of the Sea it was the local people who were paralyzed with terror as Yahweh passed by. The ancient mythical undertones gave transcendent meaning to Israel's historical battles.

As we shall see in the next chapter, the Israelites would later become very hostile to Baal, but at this stage they found his cult inspiring. They were not yet monotheists. Yahweh was their special god, but they acknowledged the existence of other deities and worshiped them. Yahweh would not become the *only* god until the late sixth century. In the very early days, Yahweh was simply one of the "holy ones," or "sons of El," who sat in the divine assembly. At the beginning of time, it was said, El had assigned a "holy one" to be the patronal god of each nation, and Yahweh had been appointed the "holy one of Israel." Another early poem, included in the book of Deuteronomy, expressed this ancient theology:

> When the Most High gave the nations their inheritance,
> He fixed their bounds according to the number of the sons of God;
> But Yahweh's portion was his people,
> Jacob his share of inheritance.[120]

The Akkadian word for holiness was *ellu,* "cleanliness, brilliance, luminosity." It was related to the Hebrew *elohim,* which is often simply translated as "god" but originally summed up everything that the gods could mean to human beings. The "holy ones" of the Middle East were like *devas,* the "shining ones" of India. In the Middle East, holiness was a power that lay *beyond* the gods, like brahman. The word *ilam* ("divinity") in Mesopotamia referred to a radiant power that transcended any particular deity. It was a fundamental reality and could not be tied to a single, distinct form. The gods were not the source of *ilam,* but like human beings, mountains, trees, and stars, they participated in this holiness. Anything that came into contact with the *ilam* of the cult became sacred too: a king, a priest, a temple, and even the ritual utensils became holy by association. It would have seemed odd to the early Israelites to confine the sacred to a single divine being.[121]

By the beginning of the first millennium, Israelite society had developed and become more complex; the old tribal organization was no longer adequate. Even though many resisted this step, it was decided that Israel needed a monarchy. Originally, according to the Bible, Kings David (c. 1000–970) and Solomon (c. 970–930) ruled a united kingdom from their capital in Jerusalem. But by the tenth century, this had split into two separate states. The kingdom of Israel—in the north—was the larger and more prosperous, with 90 percent of the population. The land was fertile and productive, communication and transport relatively easy, and the Jezreel Valley had long been a major trade route between Egypt and Mesopotamia. The little kingdom of Judah in the south, ruled by the descendants of King David, was much smaller and more isolated; its rugged terrain was difficult to farm.[122]

We know more about the religion of Judah, however, because the biblical writers favored the southern kingdom. This was a typical Canaanite monarchy. The cult centered on the person of the Davidic king, the earthly counterpart of the divine warrior and a sacred figure because of his cultic relationship with Yahweh. At his coronation, he became one of the holy ones, a son of God. He was adopted by Yahweh, who declared: "You are my son; today I have become your Father."[123] As Yahweh's special servant, he sat on the divine assembly with the other sons of God. As Yahweh's regent, he would destroy his earthly rivals, just as Yahweh had defeated the cosmic powers of sea and river.

The covenant rituals were pushed to the background, and the covenant that allied Yahweh and the tribes was eclipsed in Judah by the covenant that Yahweh had made with King David, promising that his dynasty would last forever. The old covenant festivals had focused on Israelite history, but the royal cult returned to the ancient mythology. The temple psalms of the tenth century described Yahweh striding across the sea, like Baal, his thunder and lightning flickering over the world, as he hastened to the aid of Jerusalem.[124] At the new year festival, perhaps, a great procession reenacted Yahweh's triumphal march to Zion, his holy mountain, and carried the Ark into the temple built by King Solomon. Choirs chanted antiphonally: "Yahweh, the strong and valiant, Yahweh valiant in battle!" The other "sons of El," divine patrons of rival nations, must pay tribute to Yahweh, who shattered the cedars of Lebanon and sharpened the shafts of lightning, as he entered his sacred courts.[125] The voice of Yahweh shook the desert, and stripped the forest bare. "Yahweh sits enthroned upon the sea; Yahweh sits enthroned forever!"[126]

Yahweh was still a warrior god, but he was not the only deity worshiped in Israel. Other gods and goddesses were gentler; they symbolized harmony and concord, and made the land fertile. After he had defeated Mot and was reunited with Anat, even the fierce Baal had declared that his victory had inaugurated a profound concord between heaven and the very depths of the earth: "A word of tree and a whisper of stone, converse of heaven with earth, of Deeps to the Stars."[127] Israelites needed the support of their divine warrior, and were proud of Yahweh, but most wanted other forms of holiness too. This would eventually lead to conflict with a small minority who wanted to worship Yahweh alone.

The Axial Age had not yet begun. All these traditions were characterized by a high level of anxiety. Before life on the steppes had been transformed by the violence of the cattle rustlers, Aryan religion had been peaceful and kindly, but the shock of this unprecedented aggression had impelled Zoroaster to evolve a polarized, agonistic vision. In Israel and India too, insecurity and the difficulties of maintaining a society in new, hostile territory introduced violence and aggressive imagery into the cult. But people cannot live indefinitely with this degree of tension. Ritual taught them to look into the abyss, and realize that it was possible to face up to the impossible and survive. In the ninth century, the Greeks, the fourth of our Axial peoples, were starting to emerge from their dark age; their experience showed how the dramas of ritual helped the people of the ancient world to deal creatively with historical catastrophe and despair.

2

RITUAL

(c. 900 to 800 BCE)

The crisis in the eastern Mediterranean hit Greece in about 1200. It is possible that in a last burst of energy the Mycenaean Greeks destroyed the city of Troy in Asia Minor: archaeologists have unearthed evidence of devastation, which they believe took place in the second half of the thirteenth century. But like the kingdoms of the Near East, the Mycenaean kingdom also collapsed, and Greece entered a dark age that lasted for four hundred years. The Mycenaeans had controlled the region since the fourteenth century. They had established a commercial network of cities, which exported olive oil to Anatolia and Syria in return for tin and copper. Unlike the Minoan civilization (c. 2200 to 1375) that preceded it, Mycenaean society was aggressive and martial. The Minoans, who had ruled from Knossos in Crete, seem to have been gentle, peaceful people. Their palaces, beautifully decorated with lyrical, brilliantly colored frescoes, were not fortified, and war was a distant threat. But the Mycenaean Greeks dominated the masses by showy displays of the latest military technology. They had war chariots imported from the Hittite empire, powerful citadels, and impressive tombs. The king had developed an efficient administration. From their capital in Mycenae, the Mycenaeans had ruled Messenia, Pylos, Attica, Boetia, Thessaly, the Greek islands, and Cyprus. By the thirteenth century, according to Hittite sources, they had begun to raid the coastal cities of Asia Minor.

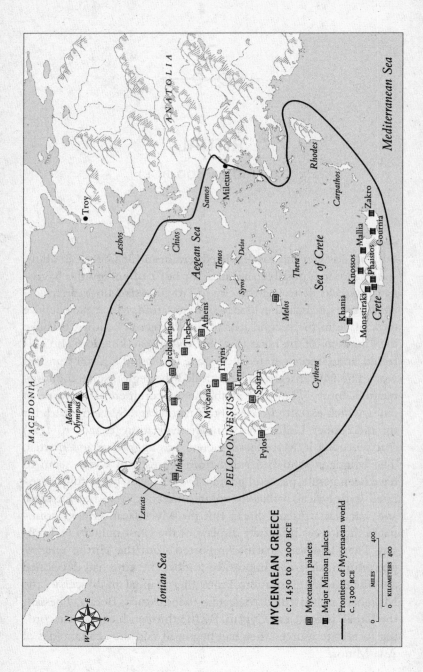

MYCENAEAN GREECE
c. 1450 to 1200 BCE

⊞ Mycenaean palaces
▦ Major Minoan palaces
── Frontiers of Mycenaean world
     c. 1300 BCE

0   MILES   400

0   KILOMETERS   400

Mediterranean Sea

Ionian Sea

Aegean Sea

Sea of Crete

A N A T O L I A

MACEDONIA

Mount
Olympus ▲

Troy ●

Lesbos

Chios

Samos

Miletus ●

Rhodes

Carpathos

Tenos

Delos

Syros

Melos

Thera

Khania

Monastiraki

Knossos

Mallia

Zakro

Phaistos

Gournia

Crete

Orchomenos

Thebes

Athens

Tiryns

Mycenae

Lerna

Sparta

Cythera

PELOPONNESUS

Pylos

Ithaca

Leucas

N
W · E
S

This powerful civilization virtually disappeared overnight. The cities of the Mycenaean heartland—Pylos, Tiryns, and Mycenae—were all destroyed, possibly by the sea peoples. Some of the population migrated to Arcadia and Cyprus, and Achaea in the northern Peloponnesus became an enclave for Mycenaeans, who would henceforth be known as the Achaeans.[1] But otherwise, they left scarcely a trace. The Mycenaeans had adapted the Minoan script to their own language, but the texts that have survived are simply lists of equipment, provisions, and purchases, so we know very little about their society. But it seems to have been run on Cretan and Near Eastern lines and bore little relationship to the Greek culture that would develop during the Axial Age.

The Greeks were an Indo-European people, who had begun to settle in the region in about 2000.[2] Like the Aryans of India, they had no memory of the steppes, and assumed that their ancestors had always lived in Greece. But they spoke an Indo-European dialect, and had some of the same cultural and religious customs as the Indo-Aryans. Fire was important in the Greek cult, and Greeks were also passionately competitive, making a contest out of anything they could. At first the Greek tribes had settled on the fringes of Minoan society, but by 1600 they had begun to establish a strong presence on the mainland, and were ready to take control and establish the Mycenaean kingdom when, after a series of natural disasters, Minoan civilization declined.

We know very little about either Minoan or Mycenaean religion. From the sculpture and votive offerings discovered by archaeologists, it appears that the Minoans loved dancing and processions; they had a cult of sacred trees, offered animal sacrifices to their gods on mountain peaks, and had ecstatic visions. Gold rings and statuettes show men and women, alert and erect, with eyes straining toward a goddess figure floating in the sky. Burial grounds were holy places. The king was the partner of the gods: seals show him in conversation with a goddess, who hands him a spear or staff. Some of these rituals would survive in later Greek religion, and the Mycenaean texts mentioned gods who would continue to be important in the later Greek pantheon: Zeus, Athena, Poseidon, and Dionysus.

But the disastrous collapse of the eastern Mediterranean severed the Greeks irrevocably from both these civilizations. Greece lapsed into illiteracy and relative barbarism; there was no central authority, and local chieftains ruled the various regions. Communities were isolated, and there were no more contacts with the Near Eastern countries, which were also in crisis. There was no more monumental building, no more figural art, and craftsmanship declined. Poets kept some of the old legends alive. They looked back on the Mycenaean period as a heroic age of magnificent warriors. They told stories about Achilles, the greatest of the Achaeans, who had been killed during the Trojan War. They recalled the tragic fate of Agamemnon, king of Mycenae, who had died in a divinely decreed vendetta. They kept alive the memory of Oedipus, king of Thebes, who, not realizing who they were, had killed his father and married his mother. The bards wandered around Greece and helped to give the scattered communities a shared identity and a common language.

One of the few cities to survive the crisis was Athens, in eastern Attica, which had been an important Mycenaean stronghold. The city declined and its population diminished, but the site was never entirely abandoned. By the middle of the eleventh century, however, Athenian craftsmen had begun to produce sophisticated pottery, decorated in what is now called the Proto-Geometric style, and at the same time, some Athenians migrated to Asia Minor, where they founded settlements along the Aegean coast that preserved the city's Ionian dialect. In the late tenth century, new villages began to appear in the countryside around Athens, and the population of Attica was divided into four tribes (*phylai*), which were administrative rather than ethnic units—like "houses" in a British public school. The tide was beginning to turn for Athens. Later this resurgence was attributed to Theseus, the mythical king of Athens.[3] Every year the Athenians would celebrate Theseus's unification of their region in a religious festival on the Acropolis, the sacred hill beside the city.

In the ninth century, Greek society was still predominantly rural. Our chief sources are the epics of Homer, which were not committed to writing until the eighth century, but which pre-

served some ancient oral traditions. The wealth of the local *basileis*
("lords") was measured in sheep, cattle, and pigs. They lived in a
world apart from the farmers and peasants, and still thought of
themselves as warriors. They boasted loudly about their exploits,
demanding acclaim and adulation, and were fiercely competitive
and individualist. Their first loyalty was to themselves, their families, and their clans, rather than to the city as a whole. But they felt
kinship with their fellow aristocrats throughout the Aegean, and
were prepared to cooperate generously with them and offer hospitality to travelers.

But toward the end of the dark age, trade revived in the
Aegean. The aristocrats needed iron for their weapons and armor,
and luxury goods to flaunt in their rivals' faces. Their first trading
partners were Canaanites from the northern coastal cities, whom
the Greeks called Phoenicians because they had the monopoly on
the only colorfast purple (*phoinix*) dye in antiquity. At first the
Greeks had resented the Phoenicians, whose culture was far more
sophisticated than their own. But by the ninth century, they had
begun to work creatively together. The Phoenicians established a
base in Cyprus, and Phoenician craftsmen came to work in
Athens, Rhodes, and Crete. Phoenician colonists began to open
up the western Mediterranean, and in 814 they established
Carthage on the north African coast. They showed the Greeks the
mercantile potential of the sea, and the Greeks began to make
new foreign contacts in Syria. In the late ninth century, Phoenicians, Cypriots, and Greeks founded the commercial center of Al-
Mina at the mouth of the river Orontes, which traded slaves and
silver in return for iron, metalwork, ivories, and fabric.[4]

Greece was coming back to life, but the people remained in a
spiritual limbo. A few elements of the old Minoan and Mycenaean
cults remained: there was, for example, a sacred olive tree on the
Acropolis.[5] But the thirteenth-century crisis had shattered the old
faith. The Greeks had watched their world collapse, and the
trauma had changed them. The Minoan frescoes had been confident and luminous; the men, women, and animals depicted had
been expectant and hopeful. There were apparitions of goddesses
in flowery meadows, dancing, and joy. But by the ninth century,

Greek religion was pessimistic and uncanny, its gods dangerous, cruel, and arbitrary.[6] In time, the Greeks would achieve a civilization of dazzling brilliance, but they never lost their sense of tragedy, and this would be one of their most important religious contributions to the Axial Age. Their rituals and myths would always hint at the unspeakable and the forbidden, at horrible events happening offstage, just out of sight, and usually at night. They experienced the sacred in catastrophe, when life was turned inexplicably upside down, in the breaking of taboos, and when the boundaries that kept society and individuals sane were suddenly torn asunder.

We can see this dark vision in the terrifying story of the birth of the Greek gods. In the Greek world, there was no benevolent creator god and no divine order at the beginning of time but only relentless hatred and conflict. At first, it was said, there had been two primal powers: Chaos and Gaia (Earth). They were too hostile to procreate, so they generated their offspring independently. Gaia produced Uranus (Heaven), the Sky God, and then gave birth to the seas, rivers, hills, and mountains of our world. Then Gaia and Uranus lay together, and Gaia gave birth to six sons and six daughters. These were the Titans, the first race of gods.

But Uranus hated his children, and forced all twelve of them back into Gaia's womb the minute they were born. Eventually, in agony, Gaia begged her children for help, but only Cronus, her youngest son, had the courage to do as she asked. Crouched in his mother's womb, he lay in wait for his father, armed with a sickle, and the next time Uranus penetrated Gaia, he cut off his genitals and threw them to the earth. High Gods were often overthrown by their more dynamic children, but few myths make the primordial struggle as perverse as this. Cronus was now the chief god, and he released his brothers and sisters from the depths of Earth. They mated with one another to produce a second generation of Titans, which included Atlas, who supported the earth on his shoulders, and Prometheus, who stole fire from heaven and gave it to human beings.

Instead of learning from the horror of the past, however, Cronus was as tyrannical as his father. He married his sister Rhea, who gave birth to five children—the second race of gods: Hester (guardian of the sacred hearth), Demeter (goddess of grain), Hera (patron of marriage), Hades (lord of the underworld), and Poseidon (god of the sea). But Cronus had been told that one of his children would supplant him, so he swallowed each infant immediately after its birth. Pregnant with her sixth child, Rhea turned to her mother, Gaia, in desperation, and when baby Zeus was born, Gaia hid him on the island of Crete, while Rhea presented Cronus with a stone, wrapped in swaddling clothes, which he duly swallowed, without noticing anything amiss. When Zeus grew up, he forced his father to disgorge his brothers and sisters, and the family took up residence on Mount Olympus. Cronus tried to fight back. For ten years he and some of the other Titans waged war on the Olympians, in a battle that shook the cosmos to its foundations, until Zeus achieved the final victory, and imprisoned his father and those Titans who had supported him in Tartarus, a dark and horrible region in the depths of the earth.

Meanwhile, Chaos, the second primal power, had generated his own terrifying offspring: Erebus (the "Dark Place," in the deepest recesses of the earth) and Night. Night then produced a brood of daughters, who included the Fates (Moirai), the Death Spirits (Keres), and the three Furies (Erinyes).[7] The Erinyes were particularly frightening; the Greeks imagined them as repellent hags, wreathed in snakes, crawling on all fours to scent their prey, whining and howling like dogs. One myth says that they were born from the drops of blood that fell upon the earth when Cronus hacked off Uranus's genitals. So they were older than the Olympians, and family violence was inscribed into their very being.

These chthonian powers, who lived in the depths of earth, dominated Greek religion during the dark age. In the ninth century, people believed that it was they, not the Olympians, who ruled the cosmos. As a later poet explained, these dark gods "tracked down the sins of men and gods, and never cease from awful rage until they give the sinner punishment,"[8] because a single atrocity against one's kin violated the entire social order. As Uranus, Cronus, and Zeus were all guilty of horrendous family crime, the chthonian gods represented, as it were, the shadow side of the Olympians. Once activated, their power worked automatically and could not be recalled. As soon as a victim cursed his assailant and cried aloud for vengeance, the Erinyes were released and hounded the transgressor like a pack of wild dogs, until he atoned for his sin by a violent, horrible death.

The Erinyes never entirely lost their hold on the Greek imagination. Long after the dark age, Greeks continued to be preoccupied by tales of men and women who murdered their parents and abused their children. These unnatural deeds, even if committed unwittingly, contained a contagious power (*miasma*) that had an independent life of its own. Until it had been purged by the sacrificial death of the wrongdoer, society would be chronically infected by plague and catastrophe. The myth of the house of Atreus, for example, tells of a hideous struggle between two brothers, Atreus and Thyestes, for the throne of Mycenae. On one occasion, Atreus invited his brother to a banquet and served Thyestes a delicious stew, containing the bodies of his own sons. This appalling deed released a contaminating *miasma* that was transmitted to the entire family of Atreus. All were caught up in a monstrous vendetta in which one violent and unnatural crime led to another. Atreus's son Agamemnon, king of Mycenae, was forced to sacrifice his daughter Iphigenia to secure a favorable wind to take the Greek fleet to Troy. His wife, Clytemnestra, retaliated by murdering him on his return from the Trojan War, and her son Orestes was then obliged to kill her in order to avenge his father. This perverse and convoluted story would become one of the most formative of the Greek myths. Like many other Greek tales, it presents human beings as utterly impotent. In the eighth century, Homer clearly believed that Clytemnestra and Orestes had no choice but to behave as they did; their actions were even lauded as virtuous, because they had rid the earth of the defiling *miasma*.[9]

However powerful they became, the Greeks never truly felt that they were in charge of their fate. As late as the fifth century, when Greek civilization was at its peak, they still believed that people were compelled by the Fates, or even by the Olympian gods, to act as they did, and once a crime had been committed, it inflicted untold woes upon innocent human beings who simply happened to live in the polluted environment. People could expect no help from the Olympians, who intervened in human life irresponsibly, supporting their favorites and destroying those who incurred their wrath, with no heed for the consequences. The only gods who showed any ethical sense were the Erinyes, who were outraged by these violent deeds but completely lacking in pity and compassion. Hence in some versions of the story, having been constrained to kill his mother, Orestes was pursued through the world by the Erinyes, until the *miasma* unleashed by his doomed family had been eliminated.

The Greeks were haunted by images of violence and disaster. The Olympians were not merely cruel to human beings; they could also persecute and maim one another. Hera, wife of Zeus, for example, was so disgusted by her crippled son, Hephaestus, when he was born that she flung him down to the earth. A savage, angry deity, she relentlessly hounded the children born of her husband's illicit amours. She plotted with the Titans to kill Dionysus, son of Zeus by the mortal woman Semele, and eventually made him insane. For years Dionysus ran frenziedly through the countries of the east, before he finally found healing. Hera also tried to kill Heracles, another son of Zeus, by putting snakes into his cradle, and drove him mad too, so that he killed his wife and children. The family was the foundation of society. In other cultures, as we shall see, it was regarded as a sacred institution, where people learned the values of respect and reverence for others. In Greece it was a lethal battleground, and Hera, goddess of marriage, showed that the most basic relationships could inspire murderous, cruel emotions. Her cult was pervaded by guilt, terror, and profound anxiety.

The first Greek temple to be built after the dark age was Hera's temple on the island of Samos, off the coast of Asia Minor. Her cult there showed that she was an uncanny, unreliable goddess who could disappear at a moment's notice and take all the good things of life with her. On the eve of her festival each year, her effigy—a shapeless plank—mysteriously vanished from the shrine. Its loss was discovered at daybreak, and all the people of Samos

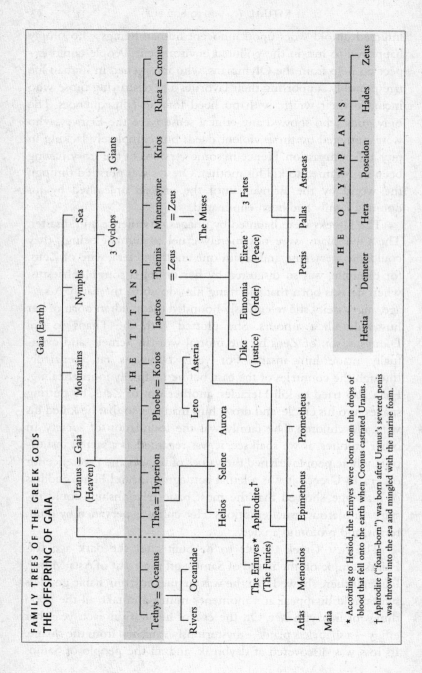

FAMILY TREES OF THE GREEK GODS
THE OFFSPRING OF GAIA

Gaia (Earth)

Uranus = Gaia
(Heaven)

Mountains   Nymphs   Sea

Tethys = Oceanus   Thea = Hyperion   Phoebe = Koios   Iapetos   Themis   Mnemosyne   Krios   Rhea = Cronus
                                                                        = Zeus   = Zeus

Rivers   Oceanidae   Leto   Asteria   3 Cyclops   3 Giants

         Helios   Selene   Aurora

The Erinyes*   Aphrodite†   The Muses
(The Furies)

Atlas   Menoitios   Prometheus   Epimetheus

Maia

Dike   Eunomia   Eirene   Persis   Pallas   Astraeas
(Justice) (Order) (Peace)

3 Fates

THE OLYMPIANS

Hestia   Demeter   Hera   Poseidon   Hades   Zeus

* According to Hesiod, the Erinyes were born from the drops of blood that fell onto the earth when Cronus castrated Uranus.

† Aphrodite ("foam-born") was born after Uranus's severed penis was thrown into the sea and mingled with the marine foam.

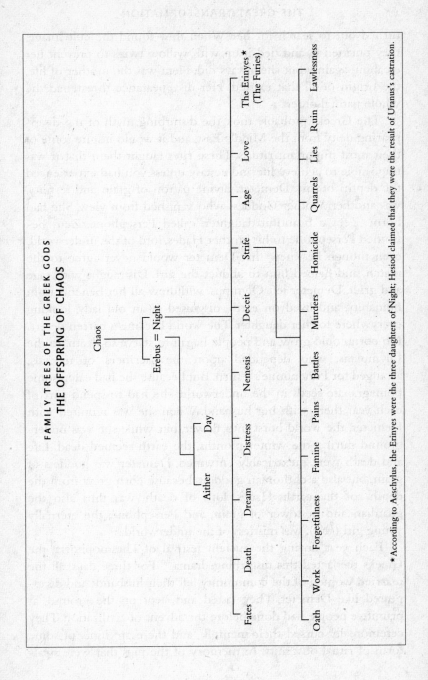

FAMILY TREES OF THE GREEK GODS
THE OFFSPRING OF CHAOS

Chaos

Erebus = Night

Aither — Day

Fates
Oath
Work
Death
Forgetfulness
Dream
Distress
Famine
Pains
Battles
Nemesis
Murders
Deceit
Homicide
Strife
Quarrels
Age
Lies
Love
Ruin
The Erinyes ★
(The Furies)
Lawlessness

★ According to Aeschylus, the Erinyes were the three daughters of Night; Hesiod claimed that they were the result of Uranus's castration.

turned out to search for her. When they found the cult image, they purified it, and tied it up with willow twigs to prevent her escaping again—but she always did. Hera was the mother of life, the origin of all that existed. Her disappearance threatened the whole natural order.

The Greeks probably took the disturbing myth of the disappearing deity from the Middle East, and it would inspire some of their most important rituals. These rites taught them that it was impossible to achieve life and ecstasy unless you had experienced the depths of loss. Demeter, divine patron of grain and fertility, was another Mother Goddess who vanished from view. She had borne Zeus a beautiful daughter, called Persephone. Zeus betrothed Persephone to his brother Hades, lord of the underworld, even though he knew that Demeter would never agree to the match, and helped him to abduct the girl. Distraught with rage and grief, Demeter left Olympus, withdrew all her benefits from humanity, and lived on earth, disguised as an old lady, looking everywhere for her daughter. The world became a barren desert. No corn could grow, and people began to starve to death, so the Olympians, who depended upon the sacrifices of mortals, arranged for Persephone's return. But because she had eaten some pomegranate seeds in the underworld, she had to spend part of each year there with her husband. When she was reunited with Demeter, the world burst into flower, but while she was underground during the winter months, the earth seemed dead. Life and death were inextricably entwined. Demeter was goddess of grain, but also a chthonian goddess, because corn grew from the depths of the earth. Hades, lord of death, was thus also the guardian and bestower of grain, and Persephone, the eternally young girl (*kore*), was mistress of the underworld.

Each year during the ancient festival of Thesmophoria, the Greeks reenacted this disturbing drama.[10] For three days, all the married women of the community left their husbands and disappeared like Demeter. They fasted and slept on the ground, as primitive people had done before the advent of civilization. They ceremonially cursed their menfolk, and there are hints of some form of ritual obscenity. In memory of the pigs that were swallowed up by the earth when Hades abducted Persephone, the women sacrificed piglets, threw their bodies into a pit, and left them to rot. There was no happy ending: the women did not celebrate the return of Persephone. The city had been turned upside down; family life, on which society depended, was disrupted; and the Greeks were forced to contemplate the prospect of the destruction of civilization, the profound antipathy of the sexes, and the cosmic catastrophe that had threatened the world when Demeter withdrew her favor.[11] At the end of the festival, the women went home, and life returned to normal. But the cult had made Greeks confront the unspeakable. They had watched their society collapse during the dark age, though they seem to have repressed the memory of this calamity. But some buried recollection of that time made them aware that whatever they achieved could vanish in a trice, and that death, dissolution, and hostility were perpetual, lurking menaces. The ritual compelled the Greeks to live through their fear, and to face it, and then showed them that it was possible to come through safely to the other side.

The religious traditions created during the Axial Age in all four regions were rooted in fear and pain. They would all insist that it was essential not to deny this suffering; indeed, to acknowledge it fully was an essential prerequisite for enlightenment. Even at this early stage, long before their Axial Age had begun, the Greeks already understood the importance of this. It was clear in the festival in honor of Dionysus, god of wine, which was held in the spring month of Anthesterion at the time of the new vintage.[12] Dionysus had learned the mystery of viticulture in the east, and—legend had it—revealed it to the people of Athens. The strange rites of the Anthesteria festival, which probably dates back to the dark age, reenacted this story and celebrated the divinely transforming power of wine, which lifted people to another dimension, so that, for a short time, they seemed to share in the beatitude of the Olympian gods.

The sampling of the new wine should have been a joyful occasion, but it was a festival of death. The mythical narrative associated with the ritual explained that Dionysus had presented the first vine to Ikarios, a farmer of Attica, and shown him how to harvest the grapes. But when his friends tasted the wine, the alcohol went straight to their heads and they fell to the ground in a stupor. Because they had never seen drunkenness before, the villagers assumed that Ikarios had killed them. They clubbed him to death and Ikarios's blood mingled with the liquor. As a tragic coda, when his daughter Erigone found his broken body, she hanged herself. Only the Greeks could have transformed a joyous spring festival into a memorial of such gratuitous horror.

The festival began at sunset in a small temple of Dionysus in the marshes outside the city. The whole population of Attica, including slaves, women, and children, marched out together to attend the opening ceremony, when a libation of wine was poured out as a gift to the god. But the next day, all the temples were closed and the doors of the houses were daubed with pitch. Everybody stayed at home, and each family member had to drink at least two liters of wine. It was a somber, deadly drinking competition. There was no merriment, no singing, and no conversation— a complete reversal of an ordinary social occasion in Athens. Each drinker sat alone, at his own table, drinking from a separate jug in sepulchral silence. Why? Local legend claimed that while he was fleeing from the Erinyes, Orestes had arrived in Athens. The king had feared the *miasma* he carried with him but had not wanted to turn him away. He invited Orestes to share the new wine but made him sit by himself, and nobody had spoken to him. Yet despite these precautions, the city had been polluted, and henceforth shared in the blood guilt of Orestes' crime. So, conscious of their impurity, the Athenians drank in grim silence. Suddenly the eerie quiet was interrupted by a grotesque masquerade. Masked mummers, representing the Keres, the chthonian Death Spirits, burst into the streets, riding on wagons that were crammed with pots of wine, aggressively demanding hospitality, laughing raucously, yelling insults, and making wild threats. But in the evening, order was restored. The whole population reeled drunkenly back to the little temple in the marshes, singing and laughing, and carrying their empty jugs. A priestess was presented to Dionysus as a bride, the god was placated, and the mummers, the envoys of death, were driven away.

The third day inaugurated another year and a fresh start. There was a lighter, more ebullient atmosphere. To mark the new era, everybody ate a cereal dish that—it was said—the first farmers had eaten in primordial times, before the invention of milling and baking. There were competitions, including a special swinging competition for little girls. But horror lurked even here, because the swinging girls recalled the hanging body of poor Erigone. You could never forget the inherent tragedy of life. All Greek ritual ended in *katharsis* ("purification"). The god was appeased, the *miasma* dispersed, and there was new life, new hope. Even the memory of Erigone's tragic death was combined with the spectacle of laughing, excited children at the beginning of their lives. The participants had experienced an *ekstasis,* a "stepping out." For three days, they had been able to stand aside from their normal existence, confront their buried fears, and pass through them to renewed life.

There was no introspection, and no attempt to analyze the hidden trauma that haunted the Greek psyche. This was touched upon only indirectly by the external rituals. By reenacting the ancient myth, the participants were not behaving as individuals. They laid aside their ordinary selves and did the opposite of what came naturally. Greeks loved banquets and jollity, but for a whole day they had denied their usual inclinations, and drunk their wine in sorrowful silence. By imitating the drama of the past, they had left their individual selves behind and felt touched and transformed by Dionysus, who was present in the intoxicating wine. The ritual had been an initiation, a rite of passage through sorrow, through the fear of death and pollution, to renewed life. When they came to die, some might remember the Anthesteria, and see death as just another initiation.

The eastern Mediterranean was coming to life again. By the end of the ninth century, the northern kingdom of Israel had become a major power in the region. When the Egyptian pharaoh Shishak had invaded Canaan in 926, he had not only sacked Jerusalem and

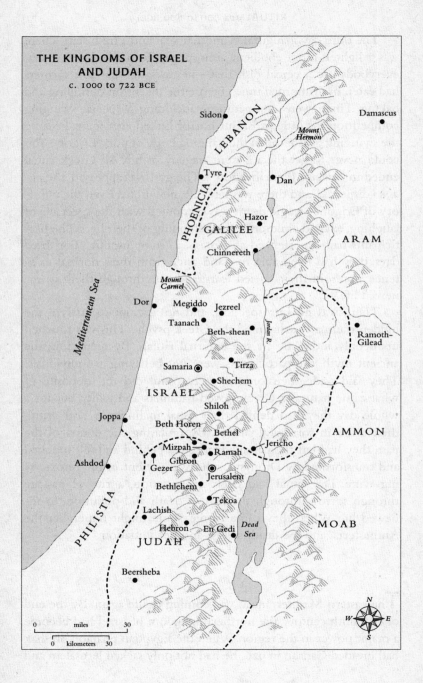

THE KINGDOMS OF ISRAEL
AND JUDAH
c. 1000 to 722 BCE

Mediterranean Sea

Sidon

LEBANON

Mount
Hermon

Damascus

Tyre

PHOENICIA

Dan

Hazor

GALILEE

ARAM

Chinnereth

Mount
Carmel

Dor

Megiddo

Jezreel

Taanach

Beth-shean

Jordan R.

Ramoth-
Gilead

Samaria

Tirza

Shechem

ISRAEL

Shiloh

Joppa

Beth Horen

Bethel

Mizpah

Ramah

Jericho

AMMON

Gibron

Ashdod

Gezer

Jerusalem

Bethlehem

PHILISTIA

Tekoa

Lachish

Dead
Sea

MOAB

Hebron

En Gedi

JUDAH

Beersheba

0   miles   30

0   kilometers   30

N
W   E
S

devastated 150 towns in Israel and Judah, but had also destroyed the ancient Canaanite strongholds of Megiddo, Rehob, Beth-shean, and Taanach. Canaanite culture never recovered. Israel expanded into the old Canaanite territories, absorbed the inhabitants of the ruined cities, and exploited their skills.[13] King Omri (885–874) built a marvelous new capital in Samaria, with a large, five-acre royal acropolis. His son Ahab (874–853) built a magnificent ivory palace there and established trade links with Phoenicia, Cyprus, and Greece. He also married Jezebel, a Phoenician princess, whose name has become a byword for wickedness.

The biblical historian who wrote a very negative account of Ahab in the first book of Kings was appalled by Jezebel, because she had imported the cult of Phoenician Baal into Israel. But he was writing in the seventh century, in a very different world. In the ninth century, Ahab's marriage would have been considered a political coup. It was important for the kingdom of Israel to integrate with the region, and hold its own against Damascus, Phoenicia, and Moab. Ahab was doing nothing new. Solomon had also made diplomatic marriages with foreign princesses, had included their gods in the royal cult, and built temples for them in the hills outside Jerusalem.[14] But Ahab had the misfortune to inspire the wrath of a small but passionately committed minority, who believed that the people of Israel should worship Yahweh alone.

Ahab was not an apostate. He regularly consulted the prophets of Yahweh and saw nothing amiss in his wife's devotion to Baal. For centuries, Yahweh's cult had been nourished by the hymns and rites of Baal. As archaeologists have discovered, most of the population worshiped other local gods besides Yahweh, and Baal worship flourished in Israel until the sixth century.[15] But by the ninth century, some Israelites were beginning to cut down on the number of gods they worshiped. In Syria and Mesopotamia, the experience of the divine was too complex and overwhelming to be confined to a single symbol. The imagery of the divine assembly, with its carefully graded ranks of consorts, divine children, and servants, showed that divinity was multifaceted and yet formed a coherent unity.[16] The symbolism of the divine assembly was very important to the people of Israel and Judah, but by the ninth century it was becoming more streamlined. Instead of presiding over a large divine household, like El and his consort, Asherah, Yahweh presided alone over a host of lesser celestial beings.[17] They were his "heavenly host," the warriors in his divine army.

As the national God, Yahweh had no peers, no rivals, and no superiors. He was surrounded by an "assembly of the holy ones" and "sons of God," who all applauded his fidelity to his people:

> Yahweh, the assembly of holy ones in heaven
> Applaud the marvel of your faithfulness.
> Who in the skies can compare with Yahweh?
> Which of the sons of God can rival him?
>
> God, dreaded in the great assembly of holy ones,
> Terrible to all around him,
> Yahweh, God of armies, who is like you?
> Mighty Yahweh, clothed in your faithfulness![18]

When people cried, "Who is like Yahweh among the other gods?" they were obviously not denying the existence of other deities, but declaring that their patronal god was more effective than the other "sons of El," the national gods of their neighbors. None could rival Yahweh's faithfulness.[19] But Yahweh was a warrior god. He had no expertise in agriculture or fertility, and so many Israelites, as a matter of course, performed the ancient rituals of Baal and Anat to ensure a good harvest, because Baal was the power that fertilized the land.

A small group of prophets, however, wanted to worship Yahweh alone, and were convinced that he could provide for all the wants of his people. Prophecy was an established spirituality of the ancient Middle East. From Canaan to Mari in the middle Euphrates, ecstatic prophets "spoke for" their gods.* In Israel and Judah, prophets were usually associated with the royal court. The

---

*A prophet is not a person who foretells the future. The word comes from the Greek prophetes, one who speaks on behalf of the deity.

biblical sources indicate that they often criticized the monarch, and were concerned to preserve the purity of Yahweh's cult. We know very little about early Israelite prophecy, however, because our main source is the seventh-century biblical historian who was writing long after the events he describes. But the legends about the ninth-century prophet Elijah and his disciple, Elisha, in the first and second books of Kings bear the marks of older, oral tradition. The material is not entirely historical, but these stories may reflect the very early stirrings of what scholars call the "Yahweh alone movement."

These tales describe the bitter clash between Elijah and Ahab. They present Jezebel as an evil woman who supported the priests of Baal but persecuted the prophets of Yahweh.[20] Elijah's name means "Yahweh is my God!" He is the first prophet on record to insist on the exclusive worship of Yahweh. In the old Middle Eastern theology, El had appointed a god to each of the nations. Yahweh was the holy one of Israel; Chemosh the holy one of Moab; and Milkom the holy one of Ammon. But some prophets were beginning to feel that Yahweh would be undermined if a king imported a foreign deity into the royal cult, and favored him over the holy one of Israel. Elijah did not doubt the existence of Baal, but because he was not the god of Israel, Elijah believed that he should stay in Phoenicia.

When, despite Baal's patronage, Israel was afflicted by a severe drought, Elijah saw his opportunity, and challenged 450 of Jezebel's priests to a contest on Mount Carmel.[21] First he harangued the people who had come to watch. It was time that they made a choice between Yahweh and Baal, once and for all. Next he called for two bulls—one for Yahweh and the other for Baal—to be placed on two altars. He and the Baal priests would call upon their respective gods and see which one sent down fire to consume the victim. For a whole morning, the Baal priests shouted Baal's name, yelling and gashing themselves with swords and spears and performing a hobbling dance around their altar. Nothing happened. But the second Elijah called on Yahweh, fire fell from heaven and devoured both bull and altar. The people fell on their faces: Yahweh was their god! Elijah ordered all the prophets of

Baal to be slaughtered in a nearby valley and then climbed up Mount Carmel and sat with his head between his knees, deep in prayer, begging Yahweh to end the drought. The rain fell in torrents, and Elijah tucked his hairy cloak into his leather loincloth and ran in ecstasy beside Ahab's chariot. Yahweh had successfully usurped the function of Baal, proving that he was as effective at maintaining the fertility of the land as at war.

In proposing that Israel worship only one god, Elijah had introduced a new tension into its traditional religion. Ignoring Baal required the people to relinquish an important and valuable divine resource. Thousands of them had found that the cult of Baal had enhanced their understanding of the world, had made their fields fertile, and given meaning to the backbreaking struggle against sterility and famine. When they performed the rites, they believed that they were tapping into the sacred energies that made the earth productive. Elijah was asking Israelites to give all that up and put their entire faith in Yahweh, who had no reputation in the field of fertility.[22]

After the storm, Elijah fell into depression and feared for his life, convinced that Jezebel would avenge the massacre of her prophets. He left Israel and took sanctuary in Yahweh's shrine on Mount Sinai, which the people of the northern kingdom called Mount Horeb. There Elijah hid in a cleft of the rock and waited for a revelation.[23] In the past, like Baal, the divine warrior Yahweh had often revealed himself in the convulsions of nature. The mountains had shaken, the trees had writhed, and the rivers had quailed at his approach. But this time it was different:

> Then Yahweh himself went by. There came a mighty wind, so strong it tore the mountains and shattered the rocks before Yahweh. But Yahweh was no longer in the wind. After the wind came an earthquake. But Yahweh was no longer in the earthquake. After the earthquake came a fire. But Yahweh was no longer in the fire. And after the fire there came the sound of a gentle breeze. And when Elijah heard this, he covered his face with his cloak.[24]

This was a hidden deity, no longer manifest in the violent forces of nature, but in a thin whisper of sound, the scarcely perceptible timbre of a tiny breeze, and in the paradox of a voiced silence.

It was a transcendent moment. Instead of revealing the divine as immanent in the natural world, Yahweh had become separate and other. Historians often speak of the "transcendental break-through" of the Axial Age. This was clearly such an event, but like the ancient religion of Israel, it was also deeply agonistic. It followed hard upon the heels of a massacre, and preceded a new round of hostilities. Standing outside the cave, covered in his cloak, Elijah heard Yahweh sentence Ahab's successors to death. They would all die, saving only those "who have not knelt before Baal."[25] When people concentrated on defining the god that they were transcending *to,* instead of focusing on the greed, hatred, and egotism that they were transcending *from,* there was a danger of stridency and aggressive chauvinism. Freedom was an essential value of the Axial Age, and Elijah's strong-arm tactics were what some later Axial sages would call "unskillful." It was counterproductive to force people into a spirituality for which they were not ready. It was unhelpful to be dogmatic about a transcendence that was essentially indefinable.

Elijah's contest with the prophets of Baal marked the beginning of a new conflict in Israel and Judah. From this time forward, the bitter contest with rival deities would inform the spirituality of the prophets. In some respects the cult became more peaceful. The ancient imagery of the divine warrior fell out of favor, because it was too reminiscent of Baal. Instead of seeing Yahweh in a dramatic storm, prophets henceforth had visions of Yahweh in the divine assembly.[26] But even this became competitive and agonistic. This Hebrew psalm shows Yahweh fighting for preeminence against the other sons of God in the council:

> *Yahweh stands up in the divine assembly,*
> *Among the gods he dispenses justice:*

> *"No more mockery of justice,*
> *No more favouring the wicked!*

> Let the weak and the orphan have justice,
> Be fair to the wretched and the destitute;
> Rescue the weak and needy,
> Save them from the clutches of the wicked!"
>
> Ignorant and senseless, they carry on blindly,
> Undermining the very basis of earthly society.
> I once said, "You too are gods,
> Sons of the Most High, all of you,"
> But all the same, you shall die like other men;
> As one man, gods, you shall fall.
>
> Rise, Yahweh, dispense justice throughout the world,
> Since no nation is excluded from your ownership.[27]

In the old days, the psalm implies, Yahweh had been prepared to accept the other "sons of God" as *elohim*, but now they are obsolete; they would wither away like mortal men. Yahweh, who had won the leadership of the divine council, had sentenced them all to death.

Yahweh accused the other deities of neglecting the primal duty of social justice. Elijah also insisted on compassion and consideration for the poor and oppressed. When Jezebel had Naboth, a landowner in the Jezreel Valley, stoned to death simply because he had refused to hand over a vineyard that adjoined Ahab's property, Yahweh sentenced the king to a horrible end: "In the place where the dogs licked the blood of Naboth, the dogs will lick your blood too."[28] When he heard this oracle, Ahab was overcome with remorse; he fasted, slept in sackcloth, and Yahweh relented. Concern for social justice was not a new development, nor was it peculiar to Israel and Judah. The protection of the weak had long been common policy throughout the ancient Near East.[29] As early as the third millennium, the kings of Mesopotamia had insisted that justice for the poor, the orphan, and the widow was a sacred duty, decreed by the sun god Shamash, who listened to their cries for help. The prologue of the Code of Hammurabi

(1728–1686) decreed that the sun would shine over the people only if the king and the mighty did not oppress their vulnerable subjects. The kings of Egypt were also commanded to take care of the destitute,[30] because Re, the sun god, was the "vizier of the poor."[31] In Ugarit, famine and drought could be held at bay only if justice and equity prevailed in the land; the protection of the weak preserved the divine order, achieved by Baal in his battle with Mot.[32] Throughout the Middle East, justice was an essential pillar of religion. It was also good pragmatic policy. There was no point in conquering foreign and cosmic foes if your iniquitous social policies created enemies at home.

Elijah and Elisha were both remembered for their acts of practical kindness as well as for their fiery words. These stories are given just as much prominence as Elijah's battles with Baal.[33] Like the other gods of the Middle East, Yahweh was moved by the plight of the needy and rewarded practical compassion as much as cultic purity. When a poor woman of Sidon shared her last handful of meal and oil with Elijah during a drought, Yahweh promised to keep her supplied with food for as long as the famine lasted.[34] But these tales do not indicate the beginning of a new Axial Age spirituality; social justice was already deeply rooted in the ancient traditions of the region.

To the east of Israel, an entirely different kind of empire was slowly coming into being. In 876, the Assyrian king had subdued the Phoenician towns on the Mediterranean coast, and when Shalmaneser III came to the throne in 859, a powerful confederation of local kings, led by Hadadezer of Damascus, tried to block Assyria's western advance. Ahab contributed a chariot squadron to the army that marched against Assyria in 853 and was defeated at the battle of Qarqar on the river Orontes. Assyria was not yet strong enough to annex territory in the west, however, and Damascus remained the strongest state in the area. Later that year, Ahab tried to challenge its power but died in a battle against his former ally. That was the end of the house of Omri; in a palace coup, Jehu, a candidate supported by Elisha, seized the throne and made an alliance with Assyria. In 841, Assyria defeated Damascus and became master of the region. As a favored vassal, the kingdom of Israel enjoyed a new period of peace and prosperity.

The story of the covenant ceremony at Shechem, recounted in the twenty-fourth chapter of the book of Joshua, probably dates from this period.[35] It is an older text, which the seventh-century historian included in his chronicle, and was probably based on the ancient covenant festival celebrated at this shrine. When the Israelites first arrived in Canaan, we are told, Joshua bound them solemnly to Yahweh in a formal treaty. If they wished to become Yahweh's people, they must put away the gods they had worshiped on the other side of the Jordan River, and serve Yahweh alone. They had to choose between Yahweh and the other gods of the region. Joshua warned them that this was a serious decision. Yahweh was a "jealous god, who will not forgive transgressions. . . . If you desert Yahweh to follow alien gods, he in turn will afflict and destroy you." But the people were adamant. Yahweh was their *elohim*. "Then cast away the alien gods among you," Joshua cried, "and give your hearts to Yahweh, the God of Israel."[36]

In the late ninth century, other gods were still alluring, but they had to stay on the opposite side of the Jordan. This was not a monotheistic text. If no other gods existed, it would be unnecessary for the people to make such a choice.[37] Monolatry (the worship of a single god) was a liturgical arrangement. The "Yahweh alone" movement urged Israelites to offer sacrifice only to Yahweh and to ignore the cult of other deities. But this position required courage, a narrowing of divine resources, and a loss of familiar and beloved sanctities. Israel was about to embark on a lonely, painful journey of severance from the mythical and cultic consensus of the Middle East.

No such painful rupture was required of the Chinese, whose Axial Age would not break with the past but would develop from a deeper understanding of the ancient rituals practiced by the

Zhou kings. The ninth century was a time of great weakness in China. The old feudal system was disintegrating and the Zhou domain was under constant attack from the barbarian peoples in the surrounding lands. We know very little about the historical events of this period, but there are sporadic references to palace intrigues, which, on at least two occasions, forced the king to flee his capital. The king could exert little control over the cities of the central plain, and the old monarchy had in effect been replaced by a confederation of lords united by their ideological loyalty to the Zhou, but in practice operating independently.[38] The only thing that held them all together was the cult. The rites reminded the king's vassals that the monarch was the Tianzi, the "son of Heaven." He had received a mandate from Tian Shang Di, Heaven Most High, to rule the Chinese people. He alone was permitted to sacrifice to the High God, and Zhouzhuang, his capital in the Wei Valley, was the religious center of the entire network of Zhou cities. No other city was allowed to hold the prestigious royal rites in honor of the deceased kings of China except Lu, whose prince was a direct descendant of the duke of Zhou.

In the rest of the great plain, each walled city (*kuo*) was ruled by a prince who held his domain as a fief from the king. Each city was modeled on the Zhou capital, with the prince's residence at the center of town, next to the temple of his own ancestors. The prince was served by the barons (*dai fu*) and the great officers (*qing*), who held key posts in the administration, presided over the big sacrificial banquets, took part in the prince's military campaigns, and provided the army with contingents of chariots and warriors. Beneath the barons and officers were the *shi,* the ordinary gentlemen, who were descendants of the junior branches of the great families and served in the chariot units. The cities had steadily increased their territories over the years, and were becoming substantial principalities. The most important were Song, whose prince claimed descent from the Shang kings and preserved Shang traditions, and Lu, which was passionately loyal to the Zhou rituals. By the end of the eighth century, there would be a dozen of these feudal principalities in the plain.

In all these cities, life was entirely dominated by religion.[39] The cult centered on the person of the king, the son of Heaven, who had inherited the mandate and had been born with a magical power, which he transmitted to the feudal lords of the principalities. Like most other religious systems at this time, that of the Chinese was preoccupied with preserving the natural order of the universe by rituals (*li*), which would ensure that human society conformed to the Way (*dao*) of Heaven. The ceremonial actions performed by the king, it was thought, could control the forces of nature and ensure that the seasons followed one another in due succession, rain was sent at the correct time, and the celestial bodies stayed on their prescribed courses. The king was, therefore, a divine figure, because he was the counterpart of the High God on earth. But there was no ontological separation between Heaven and Earth. The Chinese would never be interested in a god who transcended the natural order. Elijah's experience of a god who was entirely separate from the world would have puzzled them. Heaven and Earth were complementary: divine and equal partners.

Heaven, the High God, had humanlike characteristics, but never acquired a distinct personality or gender. He did not thunder commands from mountaintops, but ruled through his representatives. Heaven was experienced in the king, the son of Heaven, and the princes, each of whom was the son of Heaven in his own domain. Earth had no human counterpart, but every city had two Earth altars: one south of the palace near the ancestral temple, the other in the southern suburbs, beside the harvest altar. Location was everything in Chinese religion. The position of the Earth altar showed that the cultivation of the soil and the harvesting of crops put people directly into contact with the ancestors, who had tilled the ground before them, and thus established the Way of Heaven. Before and after the harvest, hymns of gratitude were sung around the Earth altar; the Way (*dao*) of Heaven was "delectable," linking past and present in sacred continuity:

> It is the glory of the region . . .
> It is the comfort of the old!

> *It is not just here that things are as they are here!*
> *It is not just today that things are as they are today!*
> *Among our most ancient forefathers it was so!*[40]

When people worked the land, they were not simply interested in their own individual achievements, "as they are today." Their efforts had united them to the ancestors, the archetypal human beings, and thus with the Way things ought to be.

Without the work of human beings, Heaven could not act.[41] Ordinary earthly actions were therefore sacramental, sacred activities, which enabled people to share in a divine process. When they had cleared the forests, pacified the countryside, and built roads, the Zhou kings had completed the creation that Heaven had begun. In the *Classic of Odes,* the poet used the same word to describe the divine work of Heaven and the earthly activity of human beings. Kings Tai and Wen had become Heaven's partners, and now their living descendants must continue this holy task:

> *Heaven made* [zuo] *the high mountain.*
> *King Tai enlarged it;*
> *He cleared* [zuo] *it.*
> *King Wen made it tranquil,*
> *He marched* [about]
> *And Qi had level roads.*
> *May their sons and grandsons preserve it!*[42]

Instead of seeing a gulf between Heaven and Earth, the Chinese saw only a continuum.[43] The most powerful ancestors were now with Tian Shang Di, the supreme ancestor, but they had once lived on earth. Heaven could communicate with earth through oracles, and human beings, the inhabitants of earth, could share a meal with the ancestors and gods in the *bin* ritual.

When the Chinese spoke of earth, the cosmos, or even the Chinese empire, these mundane categories included the sacred. They were less interested in finding something holy "out there" than in making this world fully divine, by ensuring that it conformed to Heaven's prototype. The Way of Heaven, revealed in the cosmic and natural processes, was more important than any clearly defined deity on high; they experienced the sacred in the daily, practical effort to make everything conform to Heaven's Way here on earth. Heaven was more sublime, but Earth was central to the political life of the city. All the great feudal assemblies were held at the Earth altar. The Zhou still saw warfare as a way of punishing rebels and miscreants, and thus restoring the order of the *dao*. A military expedition always started out from the Earth mound, and on their return, the troops sacrificed subversive prisoners there. When a lord was invested with a fief and became one of the sons of Heaven, the king gave him a clod of soil taken from the Earth altar. At an eclipse of the sun, the king and his vassals gathered around the Earth altar, each in his correct position, to restore cosmic order. Earth was thus the partner of Heaven, which could not implement its *dao* without the help of its counterparts here below.

When the king was invested with the royal mandate and became the chief son of Heaven, this "opened the Way" for Heaven on earth. He received a magical efficacy called *daode*, "the Potency of the Way," which enabled him to subdue his enemies, attract loyal followers, and impose his authority. If the king did not exercise *daode* correctly, it became malign.[44] Once he had this power, it was said, the mere presence of the king was efficacious; it exerted an influence that compelled men and natural phenomena to behave correctly. A king's passing thought was immediately translated into action:

> The thought of the King is boundless—
> He thinks of horses and they are strong.
> The thought of the King is wholly correct—
> He thinks of horses and they break into a gallop.[45]

When the king's power was strong, the earth broke into flower. If it was in decline, his subjects fell sick and died prematurely, the harvests failed, and the wells dried up. Again, the vision was holistic. The natural world and human society were inescapably bound up with each other.

The king's task was to ensure that the human and natural worlds really were in harmony. According to traditional lore, the sage kings had maintained the regular cycle of the seasons by traveling around their territories, following the path of the sun.[46] Thus Huang Di, the Yellow Emperor, had walked around the whole world, visiting the four points of the compass in due order. But Yao's potency was so strong that he did not need to make these perambulations personally; instead he sent delegates to the four poles to establish the seasons on his behalf. Shun went one better. He simply performed a ceremony at the four gates of his capital, each of which was oriented to one of the cardinal directions.[47] The Zhou kings, however, did not even need to leave their palace. They built a special hall and inaugurated the seasons by standing in each of its four corners, facing east, south, west, or north. As the year ran its course, the king had to change his clothes, accessories, and diet to bring his whole person into accord with the natural order. In the winter, he dressed in black, rode a black horse, traveled in a dark carriage, and carried a black standard. To establish this season he had to stand in the northwestern corner of the hall, and eat millet and pork, the food of winter. As spring approached, he dressed in green, carried a green flag, ate sour food, and stood in the northeast corner of the building. In the autumn, he wore white clothes and stood in the west; in summer he dressed in red and stood in a southerly position.

The king had supreme power, but he could not do as he chose. In every moment of his life he was obliged to conform to the celestial model; his personal likes and dislikes were wholly unimportant. His function was not to devise foreign or domestic policies of his own, but simply to follow the Way. This archaic ideal would later inspire many of the spiritualities of the Chinese Axial Age. If the king carried out his ritual duties correctly, it was said, his power (daode) made all things "calm and docile."[48] The earth, waters, plants, beasts, gods, men, women, princes, and peasants all flourished, without encroaching on one another's domains. This state of divine stability was called the Great Peace (tai-ping). But if for any reason the king failed and his power declined, there was chaos. The rain fell at the wrong time and ruined the crops, the sun and moon lost their way, and there was a solar eclipse or an earthquake. Then the king knew that he had to restore order. He would strike a great drum, put all his subjects on military alert, and summon the princes from their cities. When they arrived in the capital, dressed in clothes that corresponded to the compass direction of their fiefs—in black, green, red, or white—they would stand in their proper place in a square in the middle of the capital. If there was a drought, the king publicly confessed his faults, admitting that his bad government, mediocre officials, and the extravagance of his court were responsible, and offered a sacrifice at the Earth altar in the southern suburbs. This magical reordering of the human world would bring peace to the cosmos, and reestablish the Way of Heaven.

In the ninth century, the ritual became more public.[49] In the early Zhou period, these royal rites were probably private, family affairs, but now they were performed in front of a large audience. Ritual specialists (ru) presided, making sure that the ceremonies were carried out correctly. The new public liturgy meant that the people could observe and participate in the implementation of the Way. Thus all the inhabitants of the capital would turn out to watch the king and queen inaugurate the new year each spring. The king rode in a chariot, dressed in a robe embroidered with the sun and moon, to the Earth altar in the south of the city, and performed the first religious act of the new year, sacrificing a victim to Heaven. The king modeled his life on Heaven, and the people followed the lead of the king, who had to be the first to perform any seasonal activity. He was the living archetype; in imitating the son of Heaven, the people brought their own lives into harmony with the Way. Thus the king had to plow the first furrow after the winter rest; only then could the peasants begin their work of cultivation. In the spring, his wives ceremonially presented themselves to the king, so that he could open the matrimonial season. At the end of autumn, the king rode out to the northern suburbs, with his ministers and officers, to greet winter and bring back the cold. There he announced that the season of rest and darkness had begun, and ordered the peasants to return to their villages. As usual, he led the way, offering sacrifice and sealing his own palace gates. Then townsfolk and peasants followed his example, and retired to their homes.

Our information about the royal rites comes from the ancient Chinese classics. We do not know how historical these descriptions were; they could be largely utopian, but the ideals they expressed were deeply embedded in the Chinese imagination and would be crucial to the Axial Age. In the other cities, the princes, the local sons of Heaven, probably officiated at similar ceremonies. They served as retainers at the royal court and ate at the king's table; by sharing the food that he gave them, they absorbed some of his *daode*. In the capital, the king revered the deceased Shang and Zhou monarchs in elaborate, dramatic rites, while in the principalities the princes honored their own forebears, the founding fathers of the city, in the ancestral temple next to their residence.

Like the Shang, the Zhou held a special "hosting" (*bin*) sacrifice every five years and invited the nature gods and ancestors to a great banquet. For ten days, the court made elaborate preparations, fasting, cleaning the temple, and bringing the memorial tablets of the ancestors from their niches and setting them up in the palace courtyard. On the day of the feast, the king and queen processed separately to the courtyard; then the younger members of the royal family, each impersonating an ancestor, were led in by a priest, greeted reverently, and escorted to their places. Animals were slaughtered in their honor, and while the meat was cooking, priests ran through the streets calling any stray gods to the feast, crying, "Are you here? Are you here?" There was beautiful music, stately feasting, and everybody played their roles with the utmost decorum. After the banquet—a holy communion with the ancestors, who were mystically present in their young descendants—hymns celebrated the perfect performance of the rite: "Every custom and rite is observed," the participants sang; "every smile, every word is in place."[50] Every single facial gesture, every movement of their bodies, and every word that they uttered during the *bin* was prescribed. The participants left their individuality behind to conform to the ideal world of the ritual. "We have striven very hard," they continued, "that the rites may be without mistake."

> *All was orderly and swift.*
> *All was straight and sure.*[51]

The festival was an epiphany of a sacred society, living in close proximity with the divine; everybody had his or her unique and irreplaceable role, and by leaving their everyday selves behind, they felt caught up in something larger and more momentous. The ritual dramatically created a replica of the court of Heaven, where the High God, the First Ancestor (represented by the king), sat in state with the Shang and Zhou ancestors and the nature gods. The spirits conferred blessings, but they too submitted to the rituals of the sacred drama. The Shang had used the rites to gain the good offices of the ancestors and gods, but by the ninth century, it was becoming more important to perform the rituals precisely and beautifully. When they were perfectly executed, something magical occurred within the participants that gave them intimations of divine harmony.[52]

The ceremony concluded with an elaborate six-act ballet, which reenacted the campaign of Kings Wen and Wu against the last Shang king. Sixty-four dancers, clad in silk and carrying jade hatchets, represented the army, while the king himself played the part of his ancestor King Wen. Each act had its special music and symbolic dances, and hymns celebrated the establishment of the mandate:

> *The Mandate is not easy to keep,*
> *may it not end in your persons.*
> *Display and make bright your good fame,*
> *and consider what Yin had received from Heaven.*
> *The doings of high Heaven*
> *have no sound, no smell.*
> *Make King Wen your pattern*
> *and all the states will trust in you.*[53]

The ballet concluded with a peaceful dance (*da xia*), which was attributed to Yu, the founder of the Xia dynasty. It symbolized good government and universal peace, and—it was believed—would magically bring order and tranquillity to the Zhou domain.

The Chinese understood the importance of artifice; by acting out these intricate dramas, they felt that they became more fully humane. By the ninth century they had begun to appreciate that the transformative effect of ritual was far more important than the manipulation of the gods. By playing a role, we become other than ourselves. By taking on a different persona, we momentarily lose ourselves in another. The ritual gave the participants a vision of harmony, beauty, and sacredness that stayed with them when they returned to the confusion of their ordinary lives. During the rite, something new came alive in the dancers, actors, and courtiers. By submitting to the minute details of the liturgy, they gave themselves up to the larger pattern, and created—at least for a time—a holy community, where past and present, Heaven and Earth were one.

The Chinese were only at the beginning of their journey, however. They had not yet started to reflect upon the effects of these ceremonies. Thus far, they lacked the self-consciousness to analyze what they were doing. But later, during the third century, Xunzi, one of the most rationalistic philosophers of the Chinese Axial Age, reflected upon these ancient rites and was able to understand their spiritual importance. "The gentleman utilizes bells and drums to guide his will, and lutes and zithers to gladden his heart," he explained. In the war dance he brandished weapons; in the peace dance he waved feather ornaments, passing symbolically from belligerence to harmony. These external gestures had an effect on his inner self: "Through the performance of music the will is made pure, and through the practice of rites the conduct is brought to perfection, the eyes and ears become keen, the temper becomes harmonious and calm, and customs and manners are easily reformed."

Above all, these elaborate rituals helped the participants to transcend themselves. "The mature person," Xunzi continued, "takes joy in carrying out the Way; the petty man takes joy in gratifying his desires." During the Axial Age, people would realize that getting beyond the limitations of selfishness brought deeper satisfaction than mere self-indulgence: "He who curbs his desires in accordance with the Way will be joyful and free from disorder, but he who forgets the Way in the pursuit of desire will fall into delusion and joylessness."[54]

During the Chinese Axial Age, some of the philosophers would reject the artifice of ritual, but others would build a profound spirituality based upon these liturgical ceremonies. The establishment of the rites was one of the great achievements of the Zhou, and later generations recognized this. The *Record of Rites,* a text that was only completed after the Axial Age, remarked that the Shang had put the spirits in first place, and the rites second, but the Zhou put the rites first and the spirits second.[55] The Shang had wanted to use their rituals to control and exploit the gods, but the Zhou had intuitively realized that the rites themselves contained a much stronger transformative power.

By the end of the ninth century, it was clear that the Zhou dynasty was in dire straits. In 842, King Lih was deposed and forced into exile. The embarrassing failure of the kings made some people skeptical. If the sons of Heaven were so incompetent and shortsighted, what did that say about the High God himself? Poets began to write satirical odes: "Di on High is so contradictory, that the people below are all exhausted," one wrote. The kings and their royal rites no longer embodied the Way: "You utter talk that is not true . . . and there is no substance at the altar."[56] When King Lih died in exile in 828, his son was restored to power. But the Way was not reestablished; poets noted that in these days there was one natural disaster after another. Despite the meticulous performance of the rites, drought was burning up the country, and the ancestors did nothing at all to help:

> The great mandate is about to end.
> Nothing to look ahead to or back upon.
> The host of dukes and past rulers
> Does not help us.

> As for Mother and Father and the ancestors
> How can they treat us so?[57]

The rituals were still performed beautifully, and still had a profound effect on the participants, but a few tough-minded critics were beginning to lose faith in their magical efficacy. Yet the response to this growing crisis would be more ritual—not less.

By the ninth century, ritual experts in India had embarked on a liturgical reformation that inaugurated India's Axial Age. In the course of a systematic analysis of the sacrificial rituals, they discovered the inner self. We know little about these ritualists as individuals. We do not know their names, and they left no personal record of their journey toward this new vision. We know only that they belonged to the Brahmin priestly class, which had risen to new prominence during the late Vedic period.[58] Their work was preserved in the *Brahmanas,* technical ritual texts compiled between the ninth and seventh centuries. What does emerge from these somewhat dry treatises is that the reformers were motivated by the desire to eliminate violence from the sacrificial rites.

Aryan life was becoming more settled. The economy was beginning to depend more upon agricultural produce than raiding, and even though we have no documentary evidence, it seems that there was a growing consensus that the destructive cycle of raid and counterraid had to stop. The traditional rites not only legitimized this pattern but gave it sacred significance. The rituals themselves often degenerated into real fighting, and one aggressive sacrifice led inexorably to another.[59] The priestly experts decided to make a systematic appraisal of the sacrificial liturgy, taking out any practice that was likely to lead to violence. Not only were they able to persuade the *kshatriya* warriors to accept these expurgated rites, but their reform led to a spiritual awakening.[60]

At first sight, it seems that no texts could be further removed from the spirit of the Axial Age than the *Brahmanas,* which seem obsessed with liturgical minutiae. How could these stultifying discussions of the type of ladle that should be used for a particular oblation or how many steps a priest should take when he carried the firepot to the altar have inspired a religious revolution? Yet the *Brahmanas* were making a courageous attempt to find a new source of meaning and value in a changing world.[61] The ritualists wanted a liturgy that would not inflict harm or injury on any of its participants. The climax of the old sacrifices had been the dramatic decapitation of the animal victim, which reenacted Indra's slaying of Vritra. But Indra was no longer the towering figure that he had been when the Aryans first arrived in India. His importance had been steadily declining. Now, in the reformed ritual, the victim was suffocated as painlessly as possible in a shed *outside* the sacrificial arena. "You do not die, nor do you come to harm," the ritualists assured the beast; "to the gods you go, along good paths."[62] In these texts, the killing of the animal was frequently described as "cruel," an evil that had to be expiated. The victim should sometimes be spared, and given as a gift to the officiating priest. Already, at this very early date, the ritualists were moving toward the ideal of *ahimsa* ("harmlessness") that would become the indispensable virtue of the Indian Axial Age.[63]

The reformed ritual also banned any hint of aggression toward human beings. There were to be no more competitions, chariot races, mock battles, or raids. These were all systematically expunged from the rites and replaced by anodyne chants and symbolic gestures. To ensure that there could be no possibility of conflict, the patron or sacrificer, who commissioned the rite, would henceforth be the only warrior or *vaishya* present. The old noisy, crowded sacrificial arena was now empty, except for the single, lone sacrificer and his wife. No hostile enemies could interrupt the rite; there were no challengers, and the patron could invite no guests. Their place had been taken by the four priests and their assistants, who guided the patron through the ceremonies, taking care that every action and mantra conformed exactly to the regulations. All the fire, fury, and fun of sacrifice had been eradicated. The only danger that could occur in these innocuous rituals was a mistake in the procedure, which could easily be rectified by a special rite to "heal" the sacrifice.

We know what the ritualists removed, because the old agonistic practices left clear traces in the reformed rites. There are incongruous references to warfare in the most unlikely contexts. The *Brahmana* texts explained that the pressing of the soma plant reenacted Indra's slaughter of Vritra; they compared a stately antiphonal chant to Indra's deadly thunderbolt, which the priests were hurling back and forth "with strong voices."[64] A serene hymn, once chanted during a chariot race, was still called "The Chariot of the *Devas.*" The *Brahmanas* frequently mentioned the "enemy," whose absence had left an awkward gap. One of the three sacred fires in the arena still belonged to "the enemy"; mantras referred to a fight that never happened—"Indra and Agni have scattered my rivals!"[65] Any reference to warfare was rigorously excluded from the Agnicayana, which had originally sacralized the easterly migration of the warrior bands and the conquest of new territory. First the sacrificer was simply told to pick up the firepot, take three steps to the east, and set it down again. But this seemed a little too tame, so at a later stage, the firepot was pushed across the consecrated ground in a cart.[66]

The ritualists claimed that the reformed rites had been founded by Prajapati, the creator god mentioned in the late hymns of the Rig Veda, and told a story that became the charter myth of their movement.[67] One day, Prajapati and Death had performed a sacrifice together, competing in the usual chariot races, dice games, and musical competitions. But Death was soundly beaten by Prajapati, who refused to fight with traditional "weapons." Instead he used the new ritual techniques, and not only defeated Death but swallowed him up. Death had been eliminated from the sacrificial arena, and like the patron in the reformed rites, Prajapati found himself alone: "Now there is no ritual competition!" the ritualists concluded triumphantly. Prajapati had become the archetypal sacrificer. Henceforth anybody who imitated him in the new liturgy would not overcome Death by defeating his opponents in a contest, or by fighting and killing. A sacrificer could conquer death only by assimilating it and taking it into himself, so that "Death has become his self (*atman*)."[68] It was a striking image; by making Prajapati swallow Death, the ritualists were directing attention away from the external world and into the interior realm. By making Death a part of himself, Prajapati had internalized and therefore mastered it; he did not need to fear it anymore. Human sacrificers must do the same.

In the old rites, the patron had passed the burden of death on to others. By accepting his invitation to the sacrificial banquet, the guests had to take responsibility for the death of the animal victim. In the new rite, the sacrificer made himself accountable for the death of the beast. He took death into his own being instead of projecting it onto others, and thus became one with the sacrificial offering. Dying a symbolic death in the new rites, he would offer himself to the gods and—like the animal—he would experience immortality: "Becoming himself the sacrifice," one ritualist explained, "the sacrificer frees himself from death."[69]

The *Brahmanas* merged the figure of Prajapati, the creator god, with Purusha, the archetypal human "Person" in the late Vedic hymn, who had allowed the gods to immolate him so that the world could come into being. Prajapati/Purusha was thus both sacrificer and victim, and every time he went through the sacrificial procedure, the patron identified with this primordial ritual, and became one with Prajapati: "There is only one sacrifice," explained the ritualist; all sacrifices were identical to the original oblation at the beginning of time, and "Prajapati is the sacrifice."[70] Prajapati was now the model to be followed; instead of gaining immortality by becoming a killer like Indra, the patron became the victim, died a ritualized death, and—at least for the duration of the ceremony—entered the timeless world of the gods.

But the *Brahmanas* insisted that the sacrificer had to understand what he was doing. It was no use going mindlessly through the motions: he had to *know* that Prajapati was the sacrifice; he had to be familiar with the new ritual lore. In his contest with Death, Prajapati's "weapons" had been his knowledge of the *bandhus,* the "correspondences" between heavenly and earthly realities. Vedic religion had always seen physical objects as the replicas of divine beings. But the reformers made this early intuitive insight into a rigorous discipline. The ritualist learned to discover

likenesses and connections that linked every single action, implement, or mantra in the sacrificial ritual with a cosmic reality.[71]
It was a collective *yoga,* a "yoking" of different levels of reality
together.[72] Similarity and resemblance constituted an identity.
When the rites were performed in the full consciousness of this
connective network, everything appeared in a new guise: gods
were linked with humans, humans with animals, plants, and utensils, the transcendent with the immanent, and the visible with the
invisible.

Prajapati, for example, was the counterpart (*bandhu*) of the
year (the cycle of the seasons), because time had emanated from
his corpse on the day of creation; he *was* the animal victim, because he too had given himself up for immolation; the gods, who
had emerged from his corpse, were also *bandhus* of Prajapati.
While he was performing the rites of sacrifice, the patron *was* the
offering that he fed to the fire, because he was really offering
himself; he *was* the animal victim, for the same reason. And he
was, therefore, Prajapati, because he was the sacrificer, who had
commissioned the ritual, as well as its victim. Because he was re-
peating the primal sacrifice, he had become one with Prajapati,
had abandoned the profane world of mortality, and had entered
the divine realm. He could, therefore, declare: "I have attained
heaven, the gods; I am become immortal!" This archetypal thinking was, of course, typical of ancient thought. What distinguished
the Indian ritual reform, however, was that these links were actually forged in the course of the ritual by means of a mental effort. The ritualists tried to make the participants aware of these
bandhus, and thus become more self-conscious. Even the smallest
implement, such as a fire stick, had to be fused in their minds
with the fire stick that had been used in the primordial rite.
When the priest threw clarified butter into the fire, he uttered
exactly the same cry as Prajapati (*Svaha!*) when he had made this
offering. By means of the mental activity of the sacrificer and the
priests, these earthly objects were "perfected"; they left behind
the frail particularity of their profane existence to become one
with the divine.

Like all ancient peoples, the Vedic Indians believed that ritual could and must repair the constantly depleted energies of the natural world. The reformers told another story about Prajapati's creation. They explained that in the beginning Prajapati had awoken to the fact that he was alone in the universe; he longed for offspring, so he had practiced asceticism—fasting, holding his breath, and generating heat—and gradually the whole of reality had emanated from his person (*purusha*): *devas, asuras,* Vedas, humans, and the natural world. But Prajapati was not a very efficient progenitor and his creation was a mess. The creatures were not yet separate from Prajapati.[73] They were still a part of him, and when, exhausted by his labors, he fell into a stupor, they almost died.[74] They dropped away from him, disintegrated, and some actually fled, fearing that Prajapati would devour them. When he woke up, Prajapati was horrified: "How can I put these creatures back into myself?" he asked.[75] There was only one solution. Prajapati had to be put together again, so Agni reconstructed him, building him up piece by piece. The lost and scattered creatures regained their identity, and the world became viable.[76] Thus, by the ritual law of similarity, when the sacrificer built a new fire altar during the Agnicayana, he was really reconstructing Prajapati, and giving life to the whole of creation. Every ritual made the world stronger.[77] The reformers had replaced the old self-destructive rites with ceremonies that symbolized the building of a new world order. Gods and humans had to work together in a joint project of continuous renovation.

Fundamental to the ritual reform was the conviction that human beings were fragile creatures and, like Prajapati, could easily fall apart. They were born defective and unfinished, and could only build themselves up to full strength in the ritual. When he took part in the soma sacrifice, the patron experienced a second birth, and went through an initiation process that symbolically reproduced the various stages of gestation.[78] Before the rite began, he made a retreat, crouched in a hut (representing the womb), dressed in a white garment and black antelope skin (representing the caul and placenta), with his hands clenched into fists, like an embryo. He was fed on milk, and had to stammer when he spoke, like an infant.[79] Finally he sat beside the fire and sweated, as Prajapati had done, in order to effect a new creation. Once he had drunk the intoxicating soma, he experienced an ascent to the gods without having to die a violent death, as in the old ritual.[80] He could not stay long in heaven, but after his death, if he had accumulated sufficient liturgical credit, he would be reborn in the world of the gods.

In ritual, therefore, the sacrificer reconstructed his self (atman), just as Prajapati had done. In the workshop of sacrifice, he had put together the daiva atman (divine self), which would live on after his death. By performing the rituals correctly, with the knowledge of the bandhus firmly in his mind, the warrior could rebuild his own purusha (person). The Brahmin priests "make the person, consisting of the sacrifices, made of ritual actions," explained the ritualist.[81] The rites of passage also built up the human being. An Aryan boy had to undergo the upanayana that initiated him into the study of the Veda and the sacrificial procedure, or he would never be able to build a fully realized atman. Only married men could commission a ritual, and begin the process of self-building, so marriage was another rite of passage for both men and women (who could attend the sacrifice only in the company of their husbands). After a person's death, the corpse resembled the exhausted Prajapati and had to be reconstructed by means of the correct funeral rites.[82]

But the system did not work automatically. Unless a person was proficient in ritual science, he would be lost in the next world. He would not be able to recognize the "divine self" that he had created during his lifetime, nor would he know which of the heavenly realms he should go to. "Bewildered by the cremation fire, choked with smoke, he does not recognize his own world. But he who knows, he, indeed, having left this world, knows the atman, saying: 'This am I' and he recognizes his own world. And now the fire carries him to the heavenly world."[83] The phrase "he who knows" beats insistently through the Brahmana texts. The priests could not do all the work. The kshatriya and vaishya sacrificer also had to be proficient in liturgical lore, because knowledge alone could unlock the powers of the rites.

The liturgy created by the reformers must have been spiritually satisfying, or the Brahmins never could have persuaded the warriors to give up their war games. It is difficult for us to appreciate the aesthetic, transformative power of these rites, because we have only the flat statements of the *Brahmanas*. Before the rite, the sacrificer made a retreat that isolated him from the pressing concerns of his ordinary life; the fasting, meditation, and asceticism, the intoxication of the soma drink, and the beauty of the chant would all have given emotional resonance to the dry, abstract instructions of the ritualists. To read the *Brahmanas* without the experience of the liturgy is like reading the libretto of an opera without hearing the music. The "knowledge" of ritual science was not a notional acceptance of the metaphysical speculations of the Brahmins, but was like the insights derived from art, achieved by the compelling drama of the cult.

But the most important effect of the ritual reform was the discovery of the interior world. By placing such emphasis on the sacrificer's mental state, the ritualists had directed his attention within. In antiquity, religion was usually directed outward, to external reality. The old rites had focused on the gods, and their goal had been the achievement of material goods—cattle, wealth, and status. There was little or no self-conscious introspection. The ritual reformers were pioneers. They redirected sacrifice from its original orientation, and focused instead on the creation of the atman, the self. But what exactly was the atman? The priests who were immersed in the ritual science of the *Brahmanas* began to speculate on the nature of the self, and gradually the word "atman" came to refer to the essential and eternal core of the human person, which made him or her unique.

The atman was not what we in the West would call the soul, because it was not wholly spiritual. In the early stages of this speculation, some of the Brahmins believed that the self was physical: the trunk of the body, as opposed to the limbs. Others began to look deeper. Sound was such a powerfully sacred reality that perhaps a man's atman resided in his speech? Others thought that breath, without which life was impossible, must constitute the essential core of the human being, and a strong case could also be made for the heat (*tapas*) that welled up within the sacrificer while he sweated beside the sacred fire and that filled him with divine energy. From this point, it was logical to go a step further and suggest that the atman was the inner fire of the human being. For a long time now, fire had been regarded as the alter ego of the Aryan. Now some of the ritualists claimed that in the beginning Agni alone had possessed immortality. But by "continuously chanting and by ritual exertion," the other *devas* had discovered how to create an immortal atman for themselves. They had built a fire altar and constructed a new self in the workshop of the liturgy. In the same way, by meditating on the fire cult, by chanting mantras, and by the disciplined experience of *tapas,* human beings could achieve godlike immortality too.[84]

Finally, some of the later ritual texts made a revolutionary suggestion. A person who was expert in ritual lore need not take part in the external liturgy at all. Solitary meditation could be just as efficacious as the external rites. Somebody *who knew* ritual science could find his way to heaven without attending a ritual.[85] If the sacrificer *was* Prajapati, he must also have Prajapati's creative powers. At the beginning of time, before anything or anyone else existed, Prajapati had brought forth his own form, the gods, human beings, and the material world simply by his own mental exertions. Surely the lone ascetic could at the very least manage to create his own divine atman?

Ritualists argued that once the inner fire—the atman—had been created within the sacrificer, it became his permanent and inalienable possession. They developed a fresh ritual to make this explicit. When he ignited new fire during a rite by blowing on the sparks, the priest or patron should inhale and draw the sacred fire into his being.[86] This was what the *devas* had done, when they had acquired their eternal atman and achieved immortality. From that moment, therefore, the sacrificer was equal to the gods and did not need to worship them anymore. He *who knows thus* was no longer a *devayajnin* (a "sacrificer to *devas*") but an *atmayajnin*, a "self-sacrificer."[87] He no longer had to service his atman by continually participating in the external ceremonies of the liturgy, because his inner fire did not need fuel. He had achieved his atman once and for all. All that was necessary for the self-sacrificer was to speak the truth at all times, the special virtue of *devas* and warriors alike. By acting and speaking in accordance with truth and reality, he would be imbued with the power and energy of the brahman.[88]

The Axial Age of India had begun. In our modern world, ritual is often thought to encourage a slavish conformity, but the Brahmin ritualists had used their science to liberate themselves from the external rites and the gods, and had created a wholly novel sense of the independent, autonomous self. By meditating on the inner dynamic of the ritual, the priestly reformers had learned to look within. They would now begin to pioneer the exploration of the inner world as assiduously as the Aryan warriors had pressed forward into the unknown jungles of India. The stress on saving knowledge would also be important during the Axial Age; the ritualists were demanding that everybody reflect upon the rites and become aware of the implications of what they were doing: a new self-consciousness had been born. Henceforth, the spiritual quest of India would not focus on an external god, but on the eternal self. It would be a difficult quest, because this inner fire was difficult to isolate, but the ritual science of the *Brahmanas* had taught the Aryans that it was possible to build an immortal self. The reform, which had begun with the elimination of violence from the sacrificial rites, had led the Brahmins and their lay patrons in a wholly unexpected direction. Still lacking in India was a strong ethical commitment, which would save this proud self-sufficiency from becoming a monstrous egotism.

3

◦⊙ ⊙◦

KENOSIS

(c. 800 to 700 BCE)

The eighth century was a period of religious transition in the kingdoms of Israel and Judah, and at this time we see the first stirrings of the Axial spirituality that would come to fruition there some two hundred years later. Where the Vedic Indians had achieved fresh insight by meditating on the sacrificial rituals, the people of Israel and Judah analyzed the current events of the Middle East, and found that the unfolding history of their region challenged many of their notions of the divine. Some were also beginning to be critical of ritual and wanted a more ethically based religion. During the eighth century, the art of literacy spread through the western Semitic world and the eastern Mediterranean. Hitherto writing had been used chiefly for practical, administrative purposes, but now scribes began to develop a royal archive to preserve the ancient stories and customs. Toward the end of the century, the earliest part of the Pentateuch, the first five books of the Bible, was probably committed to writing. But more important, we find the seeds of the self-abandonment that would be crucial to all the religious traditions of the Axial Age. Here too the catalyst of change was the eruption of violence in the region.

During the first half of the eighth century, the northern kingdom of Israel was riding high. Assyria was growing from strength to strength, and would soon dominate the entire region, and as Assyria's loyal vassal, Israel enjoyed an economic boom under

King Jeroboam II (786–746). The kingdom was prosperous, exporting olive oil to Egypt and Assyria, and there was a marked rise in population. Jeroboam conquered new territory in Transjordan, and undertook major building works in Megiddo, Hazor, and Gezer. The kingdom now had a sophisticated bureaucracy and a professional army.[1] In Samaria, the nobility lived in luxurious houses with delicately carved ivory panels.

But as in any agrarian state, wealth was confined to the upper classes, and the gulf between rich and poor became distressingly obvious. In the rural districts, the peasants, whose labor funded the cultural and political projects of the king, were heavily taxed and subject to forced labor. In the towns, artisans fared little better.[2] This systemic injustice was a religious as well as an economic problem. In the Middle East, a king who abused his obligations to the needy violated the decrees of the gods and called his legitimacy into question, so it was not surprising that prophets rose up in the name of Yahweh to attack the government. Amos and Hosea were the first literary Hebrew prophets. Their disciples transmitted their teachings orally, and at the end of the eighth century, wrote them down and compiled anthologies of prophetic oracles. The final texts included the words of later prophets too, so it is difficult to be certain about the authenticity of individual oracles, but it is clear that both Amos and Hosea were disturbed by the social crisis of their time.

In about 780, a shepherd from Tekoa in the southern kingdom of Judah suddenly felt overwhelmed by the power of Yahweh. He was not prepared for this. "I was no prophet, neither did I belong to any of the prophetic guilds," Amos protested later. "I was a shepherd, and looked after sycamores. It was Yahweh who took me from herding the flock and Yahweh who said, 'Go prophesy to my people Israel.' "[3] He was not even allowed to remain in Judah, but was directed by Yahweh to Jeroboam's kingdom. Amos experienced the divine as a disruptive force that snatched him away from everything that was familiar to him. He felt that he had no choice. "The lion roars; who can help feeling afraid?" he said; "the Lord Yahweh speaks; who can refuse to prophesy?"[4] The Hebrew prophets were not mystics. They did not experience enlightenment within, at the end of a long, disciplined quest that they had initiated themselves. Amos's experience was quite different from the illumination that would, as we shall see, characterize the Axial Age in India or China. He felt possessed by a power that seemed to come from outside; it dislocated the normal patterns of his conscious life, so that he was no longer in command. Yahweh had taken the place of his controlling, purposeful ego and had hurled Amos into a completely different world.[5] The Hebrew prophets would experience the divine as a rupture, an uprooting, and a shattering blow; their religious experience was often accompanied by strain and distress.

At this time, the religion of Israel and Judah was highly visual. Psalmists were consumed with the desire to *see* Yahweh, "to gaze at you in the Temple and to see your power and glory."[6] When Amos arrived in the north, he had a vision of Yahweh in the temple of Bethel, one of the royal shrines of Israel. He had beheld Yahweh standing beside the altar, commanding the members of his divine council to destroy the temple and the people of Israel: "'Strike the capitals,' he commanded, 'and let the roof tumble down! I mean to break their heads, every one, and all who remain I will put to the sword; not one shall get away, not one escape!'"[7] Amos brought no message of consolation: Jeroboam, who had neglected his duties to the poor, would be killed, Israel destroyed, and its people "taken into exile, far distant from its own land."[8]

Amos did not necessarily need a divine inspiration to make this prediction. He could see that Assyria was building a powerful empire and reducing the smaller kingdoms of the region to vassal states. The subject king had to swear an oath of loyalty, and disobedience was punished by deportation of the elite. The prophets of Israel were like modern political commentators. Amos could see that by throwing his lot in with this great power, Jeroboam was playing a dangerous game. A single mistake could bring the wrath of Assyria to bear upon the kingdom of Israel. He brought a shocking new message. Yahweh was no longer reflexively on the side of Israel, as he had been at the time of the exodus. He would use the king of Assyria to punish Jeroboam for his neglect of the poor.

The king was informed of Amos's preaching, and the chief priest expelled him from Bethel. But undeterred, Amos continued to preach. He had, of course, no choice, because Yahweh compelled him to speak out. His teaching was shocking, because it overturned so many traditional certainties. Israel had always seen Yahweh as a divine warrior; from the earliest days, they had imagined their god marching from the southern mountains to come to their aid. Now Yahweh was back on the warpath. He would shatter the kingdoms of Damascus, Philistia, Tyre, Moab, and Ammon, but this time he would not be fighting on Israel's side. He was leading a holy war *against* Israel and Judah, using Assyria as his favored instrument.[9]

The spirituality of the Axial Age could often be iconoclastic. Religion was not about holding on to cherished practices and beliefs; it often demanded that people question their traditions and criticize their own behavior. Besides turning the ancient devotion to Yahweh, the divine warrior, upside down, Amos also poured scorn on Israel's beloved rituals. "I hate your feasts," Yahweh complained; "I take no pleasure in your solemn festivals." He was sick of listening to his people's noisy chanting and their devout strumming of harps. Instead, he wanted justice to "flow like water and integrity like an unfailing stream."[10] Finally, Amos undermined the Israelites' pride in their unique relationship with Yahweh. Other peoples had been liberated by Yahweh too; he had brought the Philistines from Caphtor and the Arameans from Kir and settled them in *their* promised lands.[11] Now he was preparing to wipe the kingdom of Israel off the map.

Amos had delivered a swingeing blow to Israel's self-esteem. He wanted to puncture the national ego. This was one of the earliest expressions in Israel of the spirituality of self-surrender, which was at the heart of the Axial ideal. Instead of using religion to shore up their sense of self-worth, the Israelites had to learn to transcend their self-interest and rule with justice and equity. The prophet was a walking example of what the Greeks would call *kenosis,* "emptying." Amos felt that his subjectivity had been taken over by God.[12] He was not speaking his own words, but Yahweh's; the prophet had left himself behind in passionate empathy with his

God, who had experienced the injustice committed by Israel as a personal humiliation.[13] This was an important moment. Axial Age religion would be conditioned by a sympathy that enabled people to *feel with* others. Amos did not experience anger on his own part; he felt the anger of Yahweh himself.

Hosea, who was active in the northern kingdom at about the same time as Amos, learned sympathy with Yahweh through a tragedy in his own life, when his wife, Gomer, became a sacred prostitute in the fertility cult of Baal.[14] This, Hosea realized, was what Yahweh, the holy one of Israel, must feel when his people went whoring after other gods. He saw his longing to win Gomer back as a sign that Yahweh also yearned after unfaithful Israel, and was prepared to give her another chance.[15] Here again, Hosea was assailing a cherished tradition—in this case, Baal worship. He would have to convince the people that Yahweh was not simply a god of war but could also bring them a good harvest. Like Elijah, he was trying to oust Baal and persuade Israelites to worship Yahweh alone. But where Elijah had concentrated on purifying the cult, Hosea's concern was ethical. Baal worship had led to moral decline—to "perjury and lies, slaughter, theft, adultery and violence, murder after murder."[16] There was sexual laxity, because everybody was frequenting the sacred prostitutes, and sprawling around drunkenly after sacrificial banquets. Instead of giving spiritual and moral guidance, priests consulted idols that were only blocks of wood.[17]

All this was caused by a lack of inwardness in Israelite religion.[18] The people followed other gods only because they did not truly *know* Yahweh. Their understanding of religion was superficial. Like the ritualists of India, Hosea was demanding greater awareness. Religious practices must no longer be taken for granted and performed by rote; people must become more conscious of what they were doing. Hosea was not talking about purely notional knowledge; the verb *yada* ("to know") implied an emotional attachment to Yahweh, and an interior appropriation of the divine. It was not enough merely to attend a sacrifice or a festival. "I desire loyalty [*hesed*]," Yahweh complained, "and not sacrifice; the knowledge of God, not holocausts."[19] Hosea constantly tried to make the Israelites aware of the inner life of God. The exodus, for example, had not simply been an exercise of power on Yahweh's part. When Yahweh had lived with the Israelites for forty years in the wilderness, he had felt like a parent teaching his children to walk, carrying them in his arms, and leading them like a toddler "with reins of kindness, with leading strings of love." Yahweh had been like one "who lifts an infant against his cheek"; he had "stooped down" when he gave the people their food.[20] Hosea was trying to make the people look beneath the surface of the ancient stories and appreciate the pathos of God.

Amos and Hosea had both introduced an important new dimension to Israelite religion. Without good ethical behavior, they insisted, ritual alone was worthless. Religion should not be used to inflate communal pride and self-esteem, but to encourage the abandonment of egotism. And Hosea, in particular, was urging the Israelites to examine their inner lives, analyze their feelings, and develop a deeper vision based on introspection. Some of these qualities also appeared in the early portions of the Pentateuch, which were being produced in Israel and Judah at about this time.

Scholars have long recognized that there are different layers in the Pentateuch. In the books of Genesis, Exodus, and Numbers, it seems that two early texts were first combined, and then, later, in about the sixth century, edited by a priestly writer ("P"), who added his own traditions. One of these early sources is called "J," because the author called his god "Yahweh," and the second "E," because this writer preferred the more formal divine title *elohim*. But J and E were not original compositions; they simply recorded and brought together into a coherent narrative the ancient stories that had been recited by bards at the covenant festivals of early Israel and had been transmitted orally from one generation to another. Even though the kingdoms of Israel and Judah both utilized writing for administrative purposes, they had not used it to record the history and ideology of the state. Until the eighth century, writing was regarded as a divine, uncanny skill that was potentially dangerous for human beings.[21] The wisdom of the community belonged to everybody, and should not become the possession of a literate minority. But by the end of the eighth century, literacy was becoming more widespread in the Near East, and new political circumstances prompted kings to record traditions that were favorable to their rule in a library of written texts.

Even though we cannot put an exact date to J and E, there is no sign of extensive literacy in either Israel or Judah until the eighth century. It seems likely that while they both contain older material, they represent two different strands of tradition—one southern, one northern—that were combined and written down in the late eighth century and included in the royal archive in Jerusalem.[22] They were an early attempt at historical writing, but they would not satisfy a modern historian, who is principally concerned to find out exactly what happened and when. The narratives of J and E are more than history. They had evolved over a long period of time, and were concerned not simply to describe the events of the past accurately but to discover what they meant, so they both included mythical material alongside their more historically based narratives. From the perspective of the early biblical writers, human life was not confined to the mundane but had a transcendent dimension, which threw light on the deeper significance of events and gave them paradigmatic significance. But nobody imagined that J and E were definitive texts. Theirs was not the last word. Later generations would feel at liberty to add to these scriptures and even to contradict them. J and E reflected the religious ideas of Israelites and Judahites at the end of the eighth century, but during the seventh, sixth, and fifth centuries, other authors added to the original stories, introduced new material, and rewrote the history of Israel in a way that spoke to the conditions of their own time.

The stories told in J and E had probably been used in the early cult of Israel. But by the eighth century, the covenant festivals had been replaced by the royal liturgies of Jerusalem and Samaria. This freed these narratives from their cultic setting, and enabled the bards and other tradents to develop a more sustained chronicle of the history of early Israel.[23] The basic outline is much the same in both J and E. The story began with Yahweh calling the patriarchs—Abraham, Isaac, and Jacob—into a close relationship. He promised that they would be the fathers of a great nation, and

would one day take possession of the land of Canaan. The saga
continued with the migration of the Israelites to Egypt, their victory over the Egyptians at the Sea of Reeds, the formation of a
covenantal league at Mount Sinai/Horeb, and the march to the
Promised Land. But within this basic framework, J and E had different emphases, which reflected local traditions.

Thus J almost certainly developed in the southern kingdom of
Judah. In J's narrative, the pivotal figure was Abraham rather than
Moses. E did not include the primeval history recounted in Genesis 1–11 (the creation of the world; the fall of Adam and Eve; the
murder of Abel by his brother, Cain; the flood; and the rebellion
at the Tower of Babel), but this was very important to J. He
wanted to show that before Abraham, history had been a succession of disasters; humanity seemed caught in a downward spiral of
rebellion, sin, and punishment, but Abraham had reversed this
grim trend. The covenant with Abraham had been the turning
point of history. Abraham was special to J because he was a man of
the south. He had settled in Hebron; his son Isaac lived in Beersheba; and Abraham had been blessed by Melchizedek, king of
Salem/Jerusalem. The career of Abraham also looked forward to
King David, who was born in the southern town of Bethlehem,
was crowned king of Israel and Judah in Hebron, and had made
Jerusalem his capital. For the people of Judah, the eternal covenant
that God had made with the house of David was far more significant than the covenant with Moses on Sinai.[24] J was much more
interested in God's promise that Abraham would be the father of
a great nation and a source of blessing to the whole of humanity
than in the Sinai covenant.

E's narrative of the patriarchs, however, never mentioned the
covenant with Abraham, and gave more prominence to Jacob, his
grandson, whom God renamed "Israel." But of even greater importance to E was the story of the exodus, in which the little-
known god Yahweh had defeated Egypt, the greatest power in the
region. It showed that it was possible for a marginal people to
overcome oppression and break out of obscurity, as the little kingdom of Israel had become a major power in the Near East during
the ninth century.[25] For E, Moses was the prophet par excellence.

It was he, not Abraham who turned history around. J was some-times quite critical of Moses,[26] while E was filled with sympathy for his hero during the long march through the wilderness to the Promised Land. When Yahweh's anger flared out against his peo-ple, E poignantly described Moses' anguish: "Why do you treat your servant so badly?" he demanded of his god. "I am not able to carry this nation by myself alone. The weight is too much for me. If this is how you want to deal with me, I would rather you killed me! If only I had found favour in your eyes, and not lived to see such misery as this!"[27] There is nothing similar to this in J's por-trait of Moses.

Neither J nor E presented Moses as a great lawgiver. When they described the covenant on Mount Sinai, they did not even mention the Ten Commandments. J has no legislation at all in his narrative, while E included only a collection of ninth-century laws—often called the Covenant Code—which stressed the im-portance of justice to the poor and weak.[28] Law had not yet be-come numinous in Israel and Judah. Sinai was significant to J and E because Moses and the elders had *seen* Yahweh there. They de-scribed them climbing to the summit to meet their god. "They saw the God of Israel beneath whose feet there was, it seemed, a sapphire pavement pure as the heavens themselves. . . . They gazed on God. They ate and drank."[29] This is the oldest account of the Sinai apparition, and may reflect an ancient liturgical reenactment of the theophany, which had included a communion banquet.[30]

J had no problem about this, and described God in strongly anthropomorphic terms. In his account, Yahweh strolled through the Garden of Eden like a potentate, enjoying the cool evening air; he closed the door of Noah's ark; he smelled the delicious aroma of Noah's sacrifice after the flood; and Abraham saw Yah-weh in the form of a stranger whom he entertained in his en-campment.[31] But in E, God was becoming more transcendent. He did not appear to human beings directly, but sent his "angel" as an intermediary. E believed that Moses' vision of God in a burning bush marked a new phase in the self-disclosure of Israel's *elohim*. "What is your name?" Moses had asked the god that summoned him from the burning bush. Abraham, Isaac, and Jacob had called him El, Yahweh replied, but now he was ready to reveal his real name to his people. It was *ehyeh asher ehyeh:* "I am what I am."[32] This enigmatic phrase was a Hebrew idiom of deliberate vagueness, which meant, in effect, "Never mind who I am!" or even "Mind your own business!" In the ancient world, to know somebody's name meant that you had power over him. God was not to be controlled and manipulated in this way.

In both J and E we see early signs of the spirituality of kenosis. It was clearly present in J's story of Abraham's vision of Yahweh at the oak of Mamre, near Hebron.[33] Abraham had looked up and seen three men standing near his tent. Instantly he ran to them "and bowed to the ground."[34] Strangers were potentially dangerous people, who were not bound by the laws of the local vendetta. They could kill and be killed with impunity. But instead of attacking them, in order to defend his family, Abraham prostrated himself as though they were gods. He then gave his visitors an elaborate meal to refresh them on their journey. The act of personal surrender, combined with practical compassion to three total strangers, led to a divine encounter: in the course of the ensuing conversation, it transpired quite naturally that one of these strangers was none other than Yahweh.

Even more striking was E's story of the binding of Isaac.[35] Abraham had been promised that he would become the father of a mighty nation, but he had only one remaining son. Then, E tells us, "It happened some time later that *elohim* put Abraham to the test." He called him by name, and Abraham cried, *Hinneni!* "Here I am!" Patriarchs and prophets often responded to God with this cry, which indicated their total readiness and presence. But God then issued the shocking command, "Take your son, your only child Isaac, whom you love, and go to the land of Moriah. There you shall offer him as a burnt offering, on a mountain I will point out to you."[36] This story marked a new conception of the divine. In the ancient world, a firstborn child was often regarded as the property of a god, and had to be returned to him in human sacrifice. The young blood restored the deity's depleted energies and ensured the circulation of power in the cosmos. But there was no such rationale here. *Elohim* was making a purely arbitrary demand, to which

Abraham could only respond in faith.[37] This god was entirely different from the other deities of the region; he did not share the human predicament, he did not require an input of energy from men and women, but could make whatever demands he chose.

Abraham did not falter. He immediately saddled his ass, and set out for the land of Moriah with Isaac and two servants, carrying in his own hands the knife that would kill his son and the wood for the holocaust. He bound Isaac, laid him on the altar, and seized the knife. It was an act of total obedience that threatened to drain his life of significance. The god he had served so long had shown that he was a breaker of promises and a heartless slayer of children. Only at the very last moment did *elohim* send his "angel" to stop the killing, commanding Abraham to sacrifice a ram instead. The story is supposed to mark an important cultic transition, when animal oblation was substituted for human sacrifice. But the pain of the story goes far beyond its liturgical relevance. Israel's *elohim* was not only a friendly, benevolent presence, but was sometimes terrifying and cruel, leading his devotees to the brink of meaninglessness. The story casts both Abraham and his god in a dubious light. It shows the destructive potential of an experience of the divine, before it was established that any violence—physical or psychological—was incompatible with the sacred.

A gap was beginning to open between the human world and the divine that had not been there before. In 740 a new prophet had a vision of Yahweh in the Jerusalem temple.[38] Like J, Isaiah, a member of the Judean royal family, was a southerner, and had no problem with seeing God in human form, but Yahweh was no longer a genial deity with whom it was possible to share a companionable meal. As the incense filled the cult hall, Isaiah saw the terrifying reality that lay behind the temple rituals. Yahweh sat on his heavenly throne, surrounded by his council of holy ones. On either side, two angels covered their faces: "Holy [*qaddosh*] is Yahweh, god of armies. His glory fills the whole earth." The foundations of the temple shook and the hall filled with smoke, engulfing Yahweh in an impenetrable cloud. He was no longer merely the holy one of Israel but the ruler of the world. And above all, he was *qaddosh,* totally "other" and "separate" from humanity. Isaiah was filled with terror. "What a wretched state I am in!" he cried. "I am lost!" A frail, unclean mortal, he had gazed upon the Lord of the heavenly host. One of the seraphs purified his lips with a burning coal and Yahweh asked: "Whom shall I send? Who will be our messenger?" and Isaiah immediately replied: "*Hinneni!* Send me!"

The divine message was bleak. The people would not listen to Yahweh until it was too late:

> *Until the towns have been laid waste and deserted,*
> *Houses left untenanted,*
> *Countryside made desolate,*
> *And Yahweh drives the people out.*
> *There will be a great emptiness in the country,*
> *And, though a tenth of the people remain,*
> *It will be stripped like a terebinth.*[39]

When Isaiah delivered the message, this fearful description of a desolate, depopulated land was becoming a daily reality in the Middle East. Tiglath-pileser III had become king of Assyria in 745, and had started to create an entirely new type of empire, gradually dismantling the old system of vassalage and incorporating all subject peoples directly into the massive Assyrian state. He had a superbly efficient professional army, equipped with the latest war chariots and a highly skilled cavalry, which terrorized the region. At the first sign of rebellion, a subject king was replaced by an Assyrian governor, the army invaded the country, and the entire ruling class was deported and replaced by people from other parts of the empire. Tiglath-pileser's first achievement was to subjugate Babylonia; then he turned his attention to the west. Seeing that the kingdom of Israel was in disarray after the death of Jeroboam II, the Assyrian army marched into the country in 738, and subdued its northern territories.

The Middle East had never seen military might on this scale before, and the region would never be the same again. The deportations caused widespread spiritual and physical dislocation, as whole populations were forcibly moved around the empire. When the Assyrian army attacked a country, it left a trail of devastation in its wake, and the countryside was deserted as the people fled to take refuge in the towns. Assyria was determined not only to dominate the Middle East militarily, but to create a unified culture. There was to be one empire, one economy, and one language. Tiglath-pileser adopted the Aramean language and script, which was easier to export than Assyrian cuneiform, to facilitate the administration of his growing empire. Writing became increasingly important in administrative and economic activities, and more people learned to read and write. This would facilitate the development of written rather than orally transmitted sacred texts.

The rise of Assyria posed a theological problem. Each of the subject peoples had a national god, a "holy one" like Yahweh, who was the custodian of its territory. The system worked well as long as each kingdom retained its independence, but when the god of one country encroached upon another, this could become a problem, as Elijah and Ahab had discovered. Once Assyria had begun to swallow up one nation after another, the balance of power between the gods had also changed. Like other kings in the region, the Assyrian king was the vicar of the national god Asshur, who had promised that the dynasty of Tiglath-pileser would endure forever. "You have given him his lordly destiny for power and said that his high-priestly seed should stand for ever."[40] If Asshur's vicar had conquered the kingdom of Israel, did it follow that Asshur was more powerful than Yahweh?

When Isaiah had his vision in 740, the little kingdom of Judah was still too insignificant to attract the attention of Assyria, but that changed in 734, when the kings of Israel and Damascus organized a coalition to oppose Assyria's westward advance. When King Ahaz of Judah refused to join them, they sent an army to besiege Jerusalem, depose Ahaz, and put a more amenable king on the throne of Judah. Ahaz had no option but to ask Tiglath-pileser for help and become a vassal of Assyria.[41] Judah's long period of peaceful obscurity was over; almost against its will, it had been dragged into the unfolding tragedy of the region. Tiglath-pileser lost no time in punishing his rebellious vassals. He swept down upon Damascus, executed King Rezin, and stormed down the Mediterranean coast, destroying any city that seemed about to defect. Finally it was the turn of Israel. In 732 the Assyrian army seized Galilee and the Jezreel Valley, and invaded Israel's territories on the east bank of the Jordan. Overnight the once-powerful kingdom of Israel had been reduced to a tiny rump state in the northern hills, with a puppet king on the throne. The people of Judah looked on aghast.

But Isaiah was not worried. He had seen Yahweh enthroned as king of the whole world, and knew that Jerusalem was safe. He belonged to a different religious world from Amos and Hosea, who had worked in the northern kingdom. He never referred to the exodus from Egypt or the long years of wandering in the desert. The royal court of Judah did not seek comfort in these northern traditions, but in the eternal covenant that Yahweh had made with King David and the traditions of the Jerusalem temple. Yahweh was king in Jerusalem, with the Davidic monarch as his earthly counterpart. As long as Yahweh reigned in Jerusalem—and Isaiah had seen with his own eyes that he did—the city could never be overcome:

> God is inside the city, she can never fall,
> At crack of dawn, God helps her;
> To the roaring of nations and tottering of kingdoms,
> When she shouts, the world disintegrates.[42]

The people of Judah must trust in Yahweh alone; the northern kingdom had fallen because it had taken pride in its weapons and diplomacy.[43] Jerusalem was a refuge for the "poor," so its people must rely only on Yahweh, instead of putting their trust in wealth and military power.[44]

Isaiah told the people that the divine warrior was once again on the march—fighting *for* his people. Judah had nothing to fear from Assyria, which was simply Yahweh's instrument, "the rod of my anger, the club brandished by me in my fury."[45] Isaiah evoked the ancient images of Yahweh coming to the aid of his people, while their enemies cowered in fear. At "the sight of the terror of

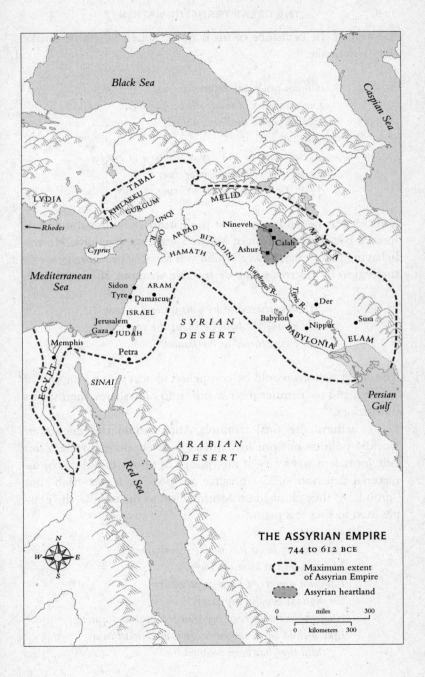

THE ASSYRIAN EMPIRE
744 to 612 BCE

⌐⌐⌐ Maximum extent
of Assyrian Empire

Assyrian heartland

0 ——— miles ——— 300
0 ——— kilometers ——— 300

Yahweh, at the brilliance of his majesty," when he rises to make the earth quake,

> *Human pride will lower its eyes,*
> *The arrogance of men will be humbled.*
> *Yahweh alone shall be exalted,*
> *On that day.*
> *Yes, that will be the day of Yahweh of armies*
> *Against all pride and arrogance,*
> *Against all that is great to bring it down.*[46]

Yahweh was becoming not just the national god but the god of history. But this exaltation of Yahweh was also aggressive. He was behaving like a great power, which was forcibly bringing peace to the region by destroying the destructive weapons of his enemies:

> *All over the world he puts an end to wars*
> *He breaks the bow, he snaps the spear,*
> *He gives shields to the flames.*[47]

The other nations would be compelled to accept the kingship of Yahweh and to hammer their swords into plowshares, their spears into sickles.[48]

To achieve the final triumph, Ahaz should not engage in worldly politics, but put his faith in Yahweh alone. In the Zion cult, Jerusalem was a city of the "poor." But poverty did not mean material deprivation. The obverse of "poor" was not "rich" but "proud." As they climbed up Mount Zion to the temple, the people used to sing this psalm:

> *Yahweh, my heart has no lofty ambitions,*
> *My eyes do not look too high.*
> *I am not concerned with great affairs*
> *Or marvels beyond my scope.*
> *Enough for me to keep my soul tranquil and quiet*
> *Like a child in its mother's arms, as content as a*
> *   child that has been weaned.*

Israel, rely on Yahweh,
Now and for always![49]

Now Isaiah told Ahaz that he should not depend on human strength, foreign alliances, or military superiority, but on Yahweh. It was idolatry to depend arrogantly upon mere human armies and fortifications. This reliance on Yahweh alone was a Judean version of the northern cultic movement to worship Yahweh exclusively, and Isaiah's insistence on humility and surrender seems at first sight similar to the Axial spirituality of kenosis. Yet it also inflated the national ego of Judah at a perilous juncture of history. Isaiah's revolutionary idea that Yahweh was not simply the patronal god of Israel, but could control the gods of other nations, was based upon a defiant patriotism. In many ways, Isaiah belonged to the old cultic world. He preached a violent, agonistic vision, which absorbed and endorsed the aggressive politics of the time. It was also an essentially magical theology, which encouraged people to believe that a divine potency made Jerusalem invincible. Reliance upon Yahweh alone would prove to be a very dangerous basis for foreign policy.

The northern kingdom did not wish to leave everything in Yahweh's hands. When Tiglath-pileser died, in 724, King Hoshea of Israel joined other vassals in a resistance movement, refused to pay tribute, and appealed to Egypt for support. Immediately, the new Assyrian king, Shalmaneser V, threw Hoshea into prison and besieged Samaria. The city capitulated in 722, the ruling class was deported to Assyria, and new settlers were drafted in to rebuild the region according to the Assyrian worldview. Now, instead of two official Yahweh traditions, there was only one. The little kingdom of Judah was one of a handful of nations to retain a degree of independence after the Assyrian campaigns. The archaeological record shows that Jerusalem expanded dramatically at the end of the eighth century.[50] New suburbs were built to house the Israelite refugees from the north, and within a few years Jerusalem was transformed from a modest highland town of ten to twelve acres to a city of 150 acres of densely packed houses and public buildings. The countryside surrounding the city was also developed extensively.

The refugees brought their own northern traditions to Judah, including, perhaps, the prophecies of Amos and Hosea, who had foretold the catastrophe of 722. The destruction of the kingdom of Israel was a painfully recent memory, and there was at this time a desire to preserve the northern traditions. Like other kings in the region, the kings of Judah began to assemble a royal library that probably included J and E, which may have been fused into a single text at this time. There was a longing to restore the united kingdom of David and Solomon, merging what remained of the kingdom of Israel with the resurgent kingdom of Judah.

This desire was reflected in the reform of King Hezekiah, who succeeded his father in 715.[51] We have no contemporary account, but the biblical tradition suggests that Hezekiah wanted to centralize the cult, permitting worship only in the Jerusalem temple and abolishing the rural shrines. The reform was short-lived, and archaeologists show that the general public continued to worship other gods, but because of his religious reform, the biblical historians remember Hezekiah as one of the greatest kings of Judah. His foreign policy, however, was disastrous. In 705, the remarkable Assyrian king Sargon II died, leaving his untested son Sennacherib to succeed. In the ensuing turmoil, when it appeared that Assyria might not be able to control the peripheral territories, Hezekiah foolishly entered an anti-Assyrian coalition and began to prepare Jerusalem for war. In 701, Sennacherib arrived in Judah at the head of a formidable army, and began systematically to devastate the countryside. Finally his soldiers surrounded Jerusalem itself. It seemed that the city could not survive, but at the last moment there was a reprieve. The biblical author tells us that the "angel of Yahweh slew 185,000 men in the Assyrian camp and the army was forced to withdraw."[52] We have no idea what happened. There may have been a sudden epidemic of plague in the Assyrian army, and the apparently miraculous deliverance seemed proof positive that Jerusalem was indeed inviolable. But it was impossible to ignore the damage that archaeologists have uncovered in the Judean countryside.[53] Lachish, the second city of Judah, was razed to the ground: fifteen hundred men, women, and children were buried in a mass grave. Hezekiah had inherited a thriving kingdom, but his imprudent foreign policy left him with only the tiny city-state of Jerusalem. Patriotic pride and chauvinistic theology had almost annihilated the nation.

The eighth century was an astonishing period in Greece. In a remarkably short space of time, the Greeks emerged from the dark age and laid the foundations of their unique culture. Their star was in the ascendant, as Judah's seemed in decline. Assyria had no interest in the Aegean, so the Greeks could develop their institutions without the threat of military invasion. They built peaceful contacts with the east and were eager to learn from foreign peoples. Their politics became radical and innovative, and they began to experiment with different forms of government, but this did not touch their religion. At a time when the Hebrew prophets were preaching monolatry, the worship of only one God, the Greeks became committed polytheists. Instead of moving away from the older forms of religion, the Greeks were becoming more systematically traditional.

The most important development of the eighth century was the creation of the polis, the small, independent city-state, where citizens learned the art of self-government. After the dark age, the old political institutions had been so thoroughly destroyed that the Greeks could start again with a clean slate.[54] The eighth century saw a rapid growth in population and an improvement in agricultural technique, which enabled farmers to produce a surplus of crops. They needed security and some form of social organization to guard their land and crops from rivals. The Greeks could now use their extra produce for trade, could fund civic projects, and from the start, the whole community may have been involved in the decision making.[55] By the end of the century, poleis had been established throughout the Hellenic world, all bearing a marked family resemblance. A polis had to have a city wall, a temple, an assembly, and a harbor.[56] There was no distinction between the countryside, on which the economy depended, and the urban center, the core of social identity. Peasants and city dwellers had

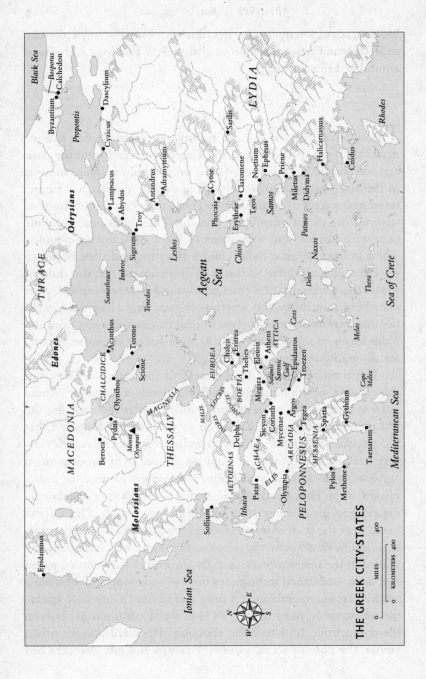

THE GREEK CITY-STATES

MILES 0 — 400

KILOMETERS 0 — 400

Black Sea

Bosporus
Calchedon
Byzantium

Propontis

Dascylium
Cyzicus

LYDIA

Sardis

Odrysians

Lampsacus
Abydos
Troy
Sigeum

Antandrus
Adramyttium
Cyme
Phocaia
Clazomene
Erythrae
Teos
Noetium
Ephesus
Priene
Miletus
Didyma
Patmos

Rhodes

Halicarnassus
Cnidus

THRACE

Samothrace
Imbros
Tenedos
Lesbos
Chios
Samos

Edones

MACEDONIA

Acanthus
CHALCIDICE
Olynthos
Torone
Scione

Beroea
Pydna
Mount Olympus

Aegean Sea

Delos
Naxos

Sea of Crete

Thera
Melos
Ceos

MAGNESIA

THESSALY

Molossians

Epidamnus

Ionian Sea

Sollium

Ithaca

AETOLINAS

MALIS
DORIS
LOCRIS
PHOCIS
Delphi

EUBOEA
Chalcis
Eritrea
Thebes
BOETIA
Eleusis
Megara
Athens
ATTICA
Salamis
Saronic
Gulf
Epidauros
Troezen

ACHAEA
ELIS
Patai
Olympia
Sicyon
Corinth
Mycenae
ARCADIA
Tegea
Argos

PELOPONNESUS
MESSENIA
Pylos
Methone
Sparta
Gythium
Taenarum
Cape Malea

Mediterranean Sea

N
E
W
S

the same rights and responsibilities, and sat in the same governing assemblies. All citizens were free to use the public buildings and the agora, an open space at the heart of each city, where they could do business and hold discussions. Each polis had its own patronal deity, and each developed distinctive sacrifices and festivals that helped to bind the citizens together.

The polis was an egalitarian society. From a very early date, farmers were highly critical of the old nobility and refused to accept a subservient role. Everybody could become a citizen—except slaves and women. The polis was an aggressively male state. During the dark age, women had enjoyed a better status, but in the new cities they were marginalized, segregated in secluded courtyards of the family home, and were rarely seen on the streets. There had also been an increase in the number of slaves. Most citizens owned their own land, and it was considered degrading to work for others or earn a salary. In other parts of the ancient world, kings had to limit the independence of their subjects in order to achieve a monarchical state, but Greek peasants refused to give up their traditional freedoms, and the aristocrats created autonomous city-states rather than large kingdoms that required local rulers to submit to an overlord. This ideal of independence was not a Greek invention. The Greeks probably preserved the old tribal assemblies and councils that other peoples abandoned when they developed large states and empires.[57]

As we see in the epics of Homer, for a Greek aristocrat of the eighth century, public speaking was as important as military prowess.[58] In the Mycenaean period, the king had been simply *primus inter pares*, and had to listen to the advice of the lords. Discussion of public policy continued in the polis, and because the farmers took part in government, they also had to develop debating skills. Everybody was forced, in however rudimentary a way, to think about abstract principles of justice and morality, as they argued about practical problems. The farmers were starting to become more like the nobility; an important characteristic of the polis was that the whole citizenry would gradually take over the old aristocratic ethos.[59]

Debate was an *agon*, a contest between the various speakers, in which the person who argued best was the victor. The Greeks retained the ancient Indo-European passion for competition that some of the Vedic Indians were beginning to discard. The agon was a law of life, and paradoxically, the nobility achieved a sense of solidarity by competing with one another.[60] Now that the entire polis was becoming an aristocratic, warrior society, farmers were beginning to acquire this agonistic spirit too. Homer shows that the Greek warlords were driven to excel, even at the expense of others. There was no esprit de corps, because each lord strove to fulfill his own personal destiny. Everybody was expected to be remarkable, and that meant everybody was a rival in the battle for singularity that informed every activity. Instead of self-surrender, therefore, there was fierce egotism in the polis. There was also an inherent aggression. The creation of the poleis had often been violent. The establishment of a community that could resist its neighbors and rivals had not always been peaceful. Village communities had often been forced to join a polis against their will. Synoeicism ("unification") had meant uprooting, resistance, and a good deal of misery—a birth agony reflected in many of the founding myths of the poleis.[61] The city had drawn people together, but had all too often achieved this violently. Each polis also had to compete constantly with the other poleis for power and wealth.

But the Greeks were also proud of their cultural unity, and celebrated this in Panhellenic festivals and institutions. One of the most famous was the athletics competition at Olympia, which was first recorded in 776 and was attended by aristocrats from all over Greece. Competing at the games was a political act: it put your polis on the map, and an Olympic victor achieved legendary fame when he returned home. But like all things Greek, the games had an uncanny, chthonian side. The earliest athletic competitions had been held during the funeral of a great warrior.[62] The extraordinary physical feats performed by the mourners had been a defiant assertion of life in the presence of death, and expressed the rage, frustration, and grief of the bereaved. Eventually the games became a religious rite, performed in a sanctuary in honor of a local

hero. The Olympic games were held in honor of Pelops, the legendary lover of Poseidon, who had also been a great athlete.

At Olympia, athletes were not simply competing for personal
fame, but were making a symbolic rite of passage from death to
life.[63] At the western end of the stadium was the tomb of Pelops,
a dark pit leading down to the depths of the earth. It faced the
altar of Zeus in the east, a huge pile of earth and ash, the residue
of innumerable sacrificial pyres. The god and the hero were like
night and day, death and life. On the night before the race, the
athletes sacrificed a ram in the precinct of Pelops, pouring its
blood into the chthonian depths. On the next morning, they
sprinted from Pelops's tomb to the summit of the Zeus altar, into
the rising sun, running away from death and bloody sacrifice toward the purifying fire. Like Pelops, the Olympian champion
would eventually die, but his victory in the agon gave the victor a
glory (*kleos*) that lived on in the memories of future generations.

The cult of the hero was a unique feature of Greek religion.[64]
The mortal hero was the chthonian counterpart of the immortal
gods. By the end of the eighth century, the grave of an outstanding warrior would occupy a place of honor in most of the poleis.
A constant reminder of the superior race of mortals who had lived
in the heroic age, the hero was revered as a demigod. Now that he
was dead, he lived a shadowy life in the depths of the earth, but his
spirit was still an active presence in the community; the qualities
that had made him so exceptional lived on. But his death had
filled the hero with rage, and an unpredictable, disturbing aura
emanated from his grave, which people passed in reverent silence. Unlike the gods, who lived on the heights of Mount
Olympus, the mortal hero was close at hand. The rites at his tomb
were designed to appease his anger and enlist his help. Worshipers
visited his shrine without garlands, unkempt, with hair unbound,
yet each polis was proud of its hero, who symbolized its special
qualities. His grave was often placed next to the temple of the patronal deity, as its dark, chthonian complement.

In Delphi, a sanctuary founded in the mid-eighth century, the
joyous cult of Apollo, god of music and poetry, was offset by the

tragic memory of Pyrrhus, son of Achilles, one of the warriors who had entered Troy in the wooden horse. After the war it was said that Pyrrhus had visited Delphi to claim redress from Apollo, whom he blamed for the death of his father, but he was hacked to pieces beside the sacred hearth by temple servants, who were quarreling over some sacrificial meat.[65] He was buried under the temple threshold. The sacrificial ritual of Delphi reflected the violence of his death. While the victim was killed, the local people stood around with their knives at the ready. As soon as the animal was dead, they would close in and savagely cut off as much of the meat as they could, often leaving the priest with nothing. The savagery of the sacrifice, which violated the civilized values of the polis, formed a sinister counterpoint to the luminous cult of Apollo, god of order and moderation.

Apollo had fought and killed a monstrous she-dragon at Delphi, a triumph that symbolized the victory of the Olympians over the chthonian powers. He called the dragon Python, because her carcass had rotted away (*pythein*) in the earth. Later he founded the Pythian games in her memory, and people came from all over the Greek world to consult Apollo's prophetess, the Pythia.[66] She sat on a tripod beside the sacred fire in the inner sanctum. When possessed by Apollo, she would shudder with anguish and sing or even scream the inspired words, but in fact her advice was often quite practical and sensible.

Unlike most of the other shrines, Delphi was not attached to a polis, but was isolated on a steep mountain, far from arable land. It was independent, therefore, a religious center based on insight rather than political power. Delphi had no agenda of its own, and became an agora, an "open space," where petitioners and pilgrims could meet and discuss the problems and ideals that, they discovered, were shared by most of the poleis. Delphi played an important role in the new wave of colonization that began in the middle of the eighth century.[67] Before leaving home, colonists would often consult the Pythia, who helped them to arrive at a reasoned decision. By the end of the century, new Greek settlements had been established all around the Aegean. Greece was coming to life again; there was a dawning excitement, a sense of discovery, fresh opportunities for trade, expanding horizons, and the stimulus of foreign culture.

Increase in trade led to new contacts with the east.[68] Greek merchants traveled to the Middle East, and refugees from the Assyrian invasions migrated to the Greek poleis, bringing new skills and crafts. The Greeks adapted the Phoenician script for their own use, and were thus able to participate in the new literary culture that now stretched from the Euphrates to Italy. The Greeks also imported eastern religious ideas. During the eighth century, they began to build large temples on the Near Eastern model, to house the effigy of a god. The cult of the Pythia may have been influenced by the ecstatic prophecy of the Middle East. The poets' descriptions of the underworld began to resemble the Mesopotamian world of the dead. Some of their most popular gods may have come from the East. Apollo, for example, who would become the most quintessentially Greek of all the gods, originally came from Asia Minor. The Greeks probably met the Middle Eastern goddess Ishtar on the island of Cyprus, and introduced her into their own pantheon as Aphrodite, goddess of love and fertility. The tragic figure of Adonis, the lover of Aphrodite, was almost certainly the vegetation god Tammuz, whose death was extravagantly mourned by women throughout the Middle East, who invoked him as *adon*—"Lord!"[69]

But nobody had such a formative influence on Greek religion as Homer, who committed orally transmitted epic traditions to writing in the late eighth century, at about the same time as the JE saga was being put together in Jerusalem. For centuries, bards had recited these ancient stories at games and festivals; by Homer's time, some of them could have been over a thousand years old.[70] His two poems—the *Iliad* and the *Odyssey*—preserved only a small portion of a much larger epic cycle; there may have been as many as eight poems about the Trojan War.[71] And there were other epic sagas: one traced the history of Oedipus, king of Thebes, and his blighted family; another recounted the adventures of Heracles; and a third told of Jason's quest for the golden fleece.

These ancient epics had changed and developed over the centuries, but once they had been written down, the *Iliad* and the

Odyssey were set for all time. Like all epics, they included some very ancient material, but they also reflected the conditions of Homer's own day. He was living in a time of transition. The new civilization that was emerging in Greece after the dark age was only a couple of generations old. Set in the late Mycenaean period at the time of the Trojan War (c. 1200), Homer's long narrative poems grafted the new culture onto the old. We will probably never know whether "Homer" was one poet or two—or even two different poetic schools—but it is impossible to exaggerate his influence. The *Iliad* and the *Odyssey* have been called the Greek Bible, because their ideals and values made an indelible impression on the new Hellenic culture.

The *Iliad* describes one small incident in the Trojan War—a quarrel, a bitter clash of egos, between Agamemnon, king of Mycenae and leader of the Greek army, and Achilles, captain of one of its squadrons. Once he felt that his honor had been impugned, Achilles endangered the entire Greek cause by withdrawing all his men from the fray. In the course of the ensuing conflict, Achilles' best friend, Patroclus, was tragically killed by Hector, son of King Priam of Troy. The *Odyssey* was set after the war and described the ten-year voyage of Odysseus, who had to journey through many strange lands until he was finally reunited with his wife in Ithaca. In both poems, Homer celebrated the excitement of battle, the joy of comradeship, and the glory of the *aristeia,* when a warrior lost himself in a "victorious rampage" and became an irresistible force, sweeping all before him. In war, Homer seemed to suggest, men lived more intensely. If his glorious deeds were remembered in epic song, the hero overcame the oblivion of death and achieved the only immortality that was possible for moribund human beings.

Fame was thus more important than life itself, and the poems show warriors desperately competing with one another in order to acquire it. In this quest for glory, every man was out for himself. The hero was an egotist, obsessed with questions of honor and status, loudly boasting about his exploits, and prepared to sacrifice the good of the whole to enhance his own prestige. There was no kenosis, no self-surrender; the only way a warrior could "step outside" the confines of self was in the *ekstasis* of killing. When possessed by Ares, god of war, he experienced a superabundance of life and became divine, losing himself in *aristeia* and slaughtering anything that stood in his way. War was, therefore, the only activity that could give meaning to life. Every warrior was expected to excel, but to be the "best" (*aristos*) meant simply to excel in battle.[72] No other quality or talent counted. In the heightened state of *aristeia,* the hero experienced a superabundance of life that flared up gloriously in contempt of death.

In India, priests and warriors alike were gradually moving toward the ideal of *ahimsa* (nonviolence). This would also characterize the other Axial spiritualities. But the Greeks never entirely abandoned the heroic ethos: their Axial Age would be political, scientific, and philosophical—but not religious. In presenting a warrior like Achilles as the model of excellence to which all men should aspire, Homer seems to have nothing in common with the spirit of the Axial Age. Yet standing on the threshold of a new era, Homer was able to look critically at the heroic ideal. He could see a terrible poignancy in the fate of the warrior, because in order to achieve the posthumous glory that was his raison d'être, the hero had to die. He was wedded to death, just as, in the cult, he was confined to the dark chthonian regions, tortured by his mortality. For Homer too, death was a catastrophe.

The *Iliad* was a poem about death, its characters dominated by the compulsion to kill or be killed. The story moved inexorably toward inevitable extinction: to the deaths of Patroclus, Hector, Achilles, and the beautiful city of Troy itself. In the *Odyssey* too, death was a black transcendence, ineffable and inconceivable.[73] When Odysseus visited the underworld, he was horrified by the sight of the swarming, gibbering crowds of the dead, whose humanity had obscenely disintegrated. Yet when he met the shade of Achilles, Odysseus begged him not to grieve: "No man has ever been more blest than you in days past, or will be in days to come. For before you died, we Achaeans honoured you like a god, and now in this place, you lord it among the dead." But Achilles would have none of this. "Don't gloss over death to me in order to console me," he replied, in words that entirely discounted the aristo-

cratic warrior ethos. "I would rather be above ground still and
labouring for some poor peasant man than be the lord over the
lifeless dead."[74] There was a fearful void at the heart of the heroic
ideal.

In the *Iliad,* the violence and death of the warrior is often presented as not only pointless, but utterly self-destructive. The third
person to be killed in the poem was the Trojan Simoeisios, a beautiful young man who should have known the tenderness of family life, but instead was beaten down in battle by the Greek hero
Ajax:

> He dropped then to the ground in the dust, like some black
> 　poplar
> Which in the land low-lying about a great marsh grows
> Smooth trimmed yet with branches growing at the uttermost
> 　tree-top:
> One whom a man, a maker of chariots, fells with the shining
> Iron, to bend it into a wheel for a fine-wrought chariot,
> And the tree lies hardening by the banks of a river.
> Such was Anthemion's son Simoeisios, whom illustrious
> 　Ajax killed.[75]

Homer dwelt on the pity of it all; the young man's life had been
brutally truncated, cruelly twisted from its natural bias, and transformed into an instrument of killing.

There was a similar hardening and distortion in the character of
Achilles, who was revered as the greatest of the Achaeans.[76] He is
presented as a man of great love (*philotes*) and tenderness; we see it
in his behavior to his mother, Patroclus, and his old tutor. But in the
course of his quarrel with Agamemnon, this love was quenched by
anger, a hard, self-righteous wrath that isolated him from the people he loved. "He has made savage the high-hearted spirit within his
body," his colleague Ajax explained.[77] He had become hard and
pitiless.[78] Achilles was trapped in a violent, damaging ethos, which
he questioned but could not abandon. After the death of Patroclus,
for which he was largely responsible, his *philotes* was turned to inhuman hatred. In his duel with Hector, to avenge the death of his

friend, he became demonic. When the dying Hector asked that his body be returned to his family for burial, Achilles replied that he would rather eat his own raw flesh,[79] and foully mutilated Hector's corpse, tying him to his horses and dragging the body round and round Patroclus's grave. The old, noble Achilles would never have behaved like this. In the course of his egotistic struggle, he had lost himself. As Apollo explained in the divine council, he had become an impersonal, destructive force, with neither pity nor justice, and had entirely relinquished the shame that holds humans back from the worst atrocities. And what had he achieved? "Nothing," said Apollo, "is gained for his good or his honour."[80]

But at the very end of the poem, Achilles recovered his loving heart in an extraordinary scene, when King Priam of Troy came to beg him to return the body of his son Hector. The old man had left Troy, walked unnoticed into the enemy camp, and to the astonishment of Achilles' companions, silently appeared in his tent, "caught the knees of Achilles in his arms, and kissed the hands that were dangerous and man-slaughtering and had killed so many of his sons."[81] The Greeks believed that weeping together created an important bond between men. The utter self-abasement of the old man stirred in Achilles "a passion of grieving for his own father." He took Priam's hand

> . . . . *and the two remembered, as Priam sat huddled*
> *At the feet of Achilles and wept close for*
>   *man-slaughtering Hector,*
> *And Achilles wept now for his own father, now again*
> *For Patroclus. The sound of their mourning moved in*
>   *the house. Then*
> *When great Achilles had taken full satisfaction in*
>   *sorrow*
> *And the passion for it had gone from his mind and*
>   *body, thereafter*
> *He rose from his chair and took the old man by the*
>   *hand, and set him*
> *On his feet again, in pity for the grey head and the*
>   *grey beard.*[82]

In an act of compassion for the father of the man who had killed his beloved friend, Achilles recovered his humanity and his *philotes*. He handed back Hector's corpse with great tact and tenderness, concerned that the heavy body would be too much for the old man. Then, while they shared a meal, the erstwhile enemies contemplated each other in silent awe.

> Priam, son of Dardanos, gazed upon Achilles,
>   wondering
> At his size and beauty, for he seemed like an
>   outright vision
> Of gods. Achilles in turn gazed on Dardanian Priam
> And wondered, as he saw his brave looks, and
>   listened to him talking.[83]

This experience of self-emptying sympathy enabled each to see the divine and godlike in the other.[84] In this scene, if not in the rest of the poem, Homer had perfectly expressed the spirit of the Axial Age.

Homer's gods, however, felt no compassion. Where some of the Hebrew prophets were beginning to explore the pathos of God, Homer depicted the Olympians as entirely indifferent to the suffering of humanity. If Zeus felt a passing pang for Hector, it was only a fleeting sensation and caused no lasting pain. The gods were mere spectators, who observed the antics of men and women like aristocrats watching a race at the games.[85] After the death of Patroclus, Achilles' divine horses wept for the fallen hero, their warm tears streaming to the ground. Zeus felt a momentary pity, breathed new vigor into them, and immediately they shook the dust from their manes and returned to the field, their transient pain in stark contrast to the wrenching, ugly grief of Achilles.

As a result, the gods seem less serious than the human characters in the poem. The gods risked nothing essential; they could not die, and nothing mattered to them very much. When Ares was wounded in battle by one of the Greek warriors, his wound quickly healed, and he was able to take his seat beside Zeus, after this momentary humiliation, exultant in "triumphant glory."[86]

When Zeus and Hera quarreled, little damage was done. And when fighting broke out between the gods who supported the Greeks and those who supported the Trojans, there were no serious consequences; the battle was almost comical in comparison to the lethal war being fought by human beings below.[87] The gods' easy lives threw the tragic, limited, and death-bound nature of human life into poignant relief.

Nevertheless, Homer's vivid portrait of the Olympian gods fixed their personalities for all time. He gave them clarity, and the pantheon a coherence that it had never had before. At a time when other Axial peoples were either beginning to find the old gods unsatisfactory or were changing their notion of divinity, the Greeks were becoming more committed to the older patterns of religion. Instead of seeing the divine as transcendent, they reaffirmed the traditional immanence of their gods. An encounter with the divine was not a devastating shock; instead a Greek god was felt to be quite compatible with humanity. A god or goddess was manifest in any kind of outstanding success or exceptional achievement.[88] When a warrior was carried away by the ecstasy of battle, he knew that Ares was present. When his world was transfigured by the overwhelming power of erotic love, he called this "Aphrodite." The divine craftsman Hephaestus was revealed in the inspiration of an artist, Athena in each and every cultural achievement.

A pantheon of gods symbolized the complexity of divinity. In the Canaanite divine assembly, none of the "sons of God" could exist by himself; he made sense only in his relation to his fellow deities. The Olympian family of gods was also an expression of a divine unity, which expressed the relationship and interdependence of the sacred powers that the Greeks experienced in the world around them. The only thing that distinguished the Greek pantheon was its high degree of coherence and organization. The Greeks of the classical period never departed from the old paganism. Instead they used their extraordinary talent for analysis to enhance the old vision, and give it system and rationale. The Olympian family had a pleasing symmetry and balance; it consisted of the parents (Zeus and Hera); the uncle and aunt (Poseidon and

Demeter); three sons (Apollo, Ares, and Hephaestus) and three daughters (Athena, Artemis, and Aphrodite). There were also outsiders: Hermes, messenger of the gods; Hecate, goddess of sorcery; and Dionysus, whose role was to challenge the Olympian order.

The gods could not be seen independently, as individual, isolated figures. Each was an indispensable component of the whole, and could only be understood vis-à-vis the other family members. The Greek pantheon has been compared to a language, where the semantic meaning of every word is conditioned by its similarity to and difference from the other words in the lexicon.[89] In fact, it was dangerous to worship only one god and neglect the cult of others. In the Greek world monolatry was taboo and could lead to a terrible punishment.[90] No god prohibited the worship of any other, and it was forbidden to pick and choose your favorites and neglect the cult of any single member of the pantheon. Gods might fight and quarrel, but each represented an authentic aspect of reality, without which the cosmos would be permanently disfigured. By revering the entire array of gods, it was possible to glimpse a unity that drew the contradictions together. Sacrifice would rarely be offered to only one god at a festival, and a sanctuary was generally dedicated to more than one deity. In Athens, for example, Poseidon was honored on the Acropolis alongside Athena, the patronal goddess.

Gods were frequently paired together in a way that brought out the tensions and paradox of life. The quarrels of Zeus and Hera, the archetypal married couple, reflected the inherent difficulty of the patriarchal order, which affirmed itself through a clash of opposites.[91] Ares and Athena were both warrior gods, but Ares represented the cruel, abhorrent aspect of warfare, while Athena embodied the splendor of victory.[92] Poseidon and Athena were often worshiped as a duo: Poseidon, lord of the sea, representing the primal, elemental forces, which Athena, goddess of civilization, was able to tame, control, and make accessible to human beings. Poseidon sired the horse, while Athena invented the bit and bridle; Poseidon stirred up the waves, and Athena built a ship. And yet because she was also a war goddess, Athena reflected the violence at the heart of any civilization and the struggle of any polis to survive.

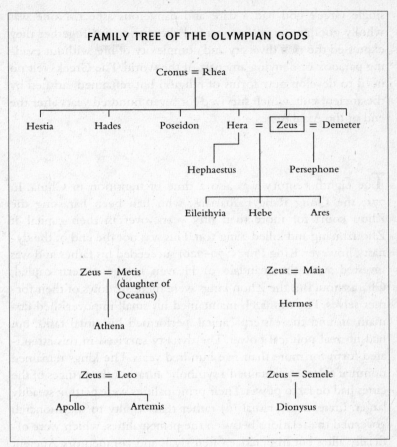

FAMILY TREE OF THE OLYMPIAN GODS

Cronus = Rhea

Hestia   Hades   Poseidon   Hera = Zeus = Demeter

Hephaestus   Persephone

Eileithyia   Hebe   Ares

Zeus = Metis   Zeus = Maia
(daughter of
Oceanus)   Hermes

Athena

Zeus = Leto   Zeus = Semele

Apollo   Artemis   Dionysus

Poseidon was also coupled with Apollo; together they represented old age and youth, which were polar opposites but also complementary. Hera and Dionysus were profoundly antagonistic to each other; but both were associated with madness, which could be a divine scourge or a liberating ecstasy. Apollo and Dionysus were brothers, who balanced and counterbalanced each other: Apollo standing for form, clarity, definition, and purity, while Dionysus embodied the forces of dissolution—at Delphi he was honored as Apollo's mysterious, chthonic counterpart. Every single Greek god had a dark and dangerous aspect. None was wholly good; none was concerned about morality. Together they expressed the rich diversity and complexity of life, without evading paradox or denying any part of the world. The Greeks felt no need to develop new forms of religion but remained satisfied by the ancient cult, which survived for seven hundred years after the end of the Axial Age.

The eighth century was also a time of transition in China. In 771, the Qong Rang barbarians, who had been harassing the Zhou court for more than fifty years, overran their capital at Zhouzhuang and killed King Yon. This was not the end of the dynasty, however. King Ping (770–720) succeeded his father and was invested with the mandate of Heaven in the eastern capital, Changzhou. But the Zhou kings were mere shadows of their former selves. The monarch maintained his small impoverished domain around the eastern capital, performed his ritual tasks, but had no real political power. The dynasty survived in this attenuated form for more than five hundred years. The kings remained nominal rulers and retained a symbolic aura, but the princes of the cities had de facto power. Their principalities were getting steadily larger. Increasingly, ritual (*li*) rather than loyalty to the monarch governed the relations between the principalities, which were officially allies but in practice often rivals and competitors. Ancient custom replaced the royal authority, acting as a kind of international law to control wars, vendettas, and treaties, and supervised the interchange of goods and services. This was the start of the era that historians call *Chunqiu* (Spring and Autumn), the name given to the laconic annals of the principality of Lu, which covered the era from 722 to 481. At the time, it seemed a chaotic period of conflict and fragmentation, but with hindsight we can see that China was making a complex transition from archaic monarchy to a unified empire. We know very little about the eighth century in China, but it seems that these years saw the emergence of a new sensibility.

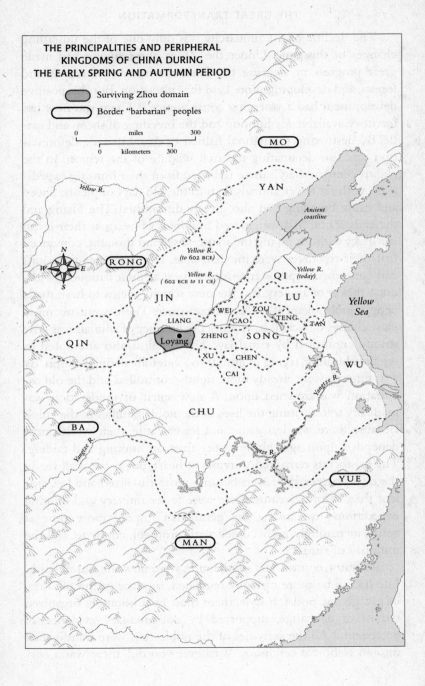

THE PRINCIPALITIES AND PERIPHERAL KINGDOMS OF CHINA DURING THE EARLY SPRING AND AUTUMN PERIOD

Surviving Zhou domain

Border "barbarian" peoples

miles 0 — 300

kilometers 0 — 300

MO

Yellow R.

YAN

Ancient coastline

Yellow R. (to 602 BCE)

Yellow R. (602 BCE to 11 CE)

RONG

QI

Yellow R. (today)

JIN

LU

Yellow Sea

WEI

ZOU

LIANG

CAO

TENG

QIN

ZHENG

SONG

TAN

Loyang

XU

CHEN

WU

CAI

CHU

Yangtze R.

BA

Yangtze R.

Yangtze R.

YUE

MAN

The decline of the monarchy was only one of the unsettling changes of this time. Under the Zhou, the Chinese had made great progress in clearing the land, cutting down woods and forests, and developing more land for cultivation. But this positive development had a worrying consequence.[93] There was now less territory available for hunting and the breeding of sheep and cattle. By destroying the natural habitat of many species, deforestation was also decimating the rich wildlife of the region. In the eighth century, the Chinese returned from their hunting expeditions with far fewer animals than in the old days of plenty. Sheep and cattle breeding had also greatly diminished. The Shang and the early Zhou had slaughtered hundreds of beasts at their lavish sacrifices without giving the matter a second thought, convinced that their resources were inexhaustible. They gave generous gifts and consumed copious amounts of meat at their banquets, without a flicker of anxiety. But the new scarcity seems to have made people look askance at this extravagance. There were no more mass killings of sacrificial victims; the number of animals was now strictly controlled by ritual law. The ritualists also attempted to regulate hunting, trying to limit it to a carefully defined season. By 771, funerals were already more tightly controlled, and the old ostentation was frowned upon. A new spirit of moderation was gradually transforming the lives of the noble families in the cities. Because there was less game and fewer cattle, their wealth now depended upon agriculture rather than on hunting and raiding. The aristocrats remained warriors at heart, but as we shall see in the next chapter, their wars became more ritualized and less violent than before. Because there were fewer military and hunting expeditions, the *junzi* ("the gentleman") spent more time at court, increasingly preoccupied with protocol, etiquette, and the minutiae of ritual.[94]

Restraint, control, and moderation were now the watchwords. Life had to be more carefully regulated. In place of the old orgy of gift giving, potlatch style, there must be a minutely organized system of exchange, supported by documentary evidence of precedent.[95] All the activities of the noble class were transformed into an elaborate ceremony. Whatever you did, there was a correct way of doing it. Over time, the nobility in the Zhou cities had evolved customs designed to promote social harmony and the welfare of the group. As in all societies, these traditions had developed more by trial and error than by conscious deliberation. These patterns of behavior had probably taken centuries to evolve, and were passed from one generation to another.[96] The *junzi* lived by an elaborate code of manners: there were some things that he did and other things that he did not do. Now, during the Spring and Autumn period, this customal law began to be written down and made into a coherent system. In this time of transition and uncertainty, people wanted clear directives. They had to rethink their religion. The king had been crucial to the old liturgy. How could his subjects venerate his potency when he had become a helpless puppet? How could you maintain the ancient sacrifices in a time of scarcity?

It seems that the new ritual science was developed in the principalities of the great plain by small groups of scribes, diviners, astronomers, and archivists. For some time, the *shi,* the minor nobility, had been assuming a more prominent role in the cities. The children of younger sons or second-class wives, they were beneath the ranks of the barons and great officers. They did the less prestigious jobs, serving as men-at-arms, guardians of the written traditions, and specialists in the various branches of knowledge. Some of the scribes had compiled the anthologies that would become the Chinese classics: the *Classic of Documents,* the *Classic of Odes,* the *Classic of Changes* (*Yijing*), the *Classic of Music* (which has not survived), and *Chunqiu,* the *Spring and Autumn Annals.* Now some of the *shi* literati started to codify the ceremonial and customal practices of the noble families. These ritualists (*ru*) made the principles of the noble life accessible and clear to everybody. A *junzi* must know exactly where he should place himself in a feudal gathering, how he should stand, greet people, and comport himself. He must know precisely when to speak, and when to remain silent. He must wear the correct clothes, use the appropriate gestures, and assume the right facial expressions for each occasion. Everything had a religious value. In the days of the early Zhou, the royal ceremonies had been designed to maintain the natural order. Now that the monarchy was in decline, the *ru* transformed the whole of life into an elaborate ritual performance in order to bring peace and order to the great plain.[97]

Every prince found that he needed a team of good ritual consultants, who could ensure that the official sacrifices, the "hosting" (*bin*) banquets for the ancestors, and the ritual ballets were carried out correctly. The *ru* helped the princes and ministers to use the rites politically, so that they were not worsted in the feudal assemblies, and would know how a *junzi* should prepare his case and voice his opposition. The chronicles show that knowledge of the *li* was vital in diplomacy. On one occasion, the prince of a small city called upon one of the more important princes, who died during his visit. The ministers tried to force the guest to dress the corpse—a calculated move, since this was the job of a vassal. If he obeyed, the guest would forfeit his political independence to the larger state, but how could he in courtesy refuse? His advisers solved the problem. The minor lord went along to dress the body, but took a sorcerer with him. According to the *li,* this was what a prince did in his own domain when making a condolence call on one of his retainers. This adroit manipulation of the *li* had completely reversed the situation, and discomfited the scheming ministers. The story shows that despite the apparent humility that they seemed to express, there was really no kenosis in the performance of these rites. The ritualized lifestyle of the nobility did teach aristocrats to behave with apparent reverence and modesty to one another, but the *li* were usually informed by self-interest. Everything was a matter of prestige. Aristocrats were jealous of their privileges and their honor, and exploited the *li* to enhance their status.[98]

The most able and authoritative school of ritual was based in the principality of Lu, which had always regarded itself as the custodian of sacred tradition. There ritualists and scribes gradually developed the *Lijing,* the ritual code that would become the sixth Chinese classic.[99] The Lu ritualists formulated two important principles: first, the efficacy of a ceremony depended upon the perfect performance of every single one of the actions that contributed to it; second, this perfection was possible only when each one of the participants was fully aware of the value and significance of the rite as a whole. In the late sixth century, one of the ritualists of Lu would initiate China's Axial Age, taking these two principles as his starting point, and would reveal the latent spiritual power of this apparently self-serving and potentially stultifying discipline.

Yet even at this early stage, some of the Lu ritualists understood the importance of self-surrender.[100] They greatly revered Yao and Shun, the sage kings of remote antiquity, and may have been responsible for the "Canon of Yao and Shun," one of the earliest chronicles in the *Classic of Documents*. Unlike the other culture heroes, Yao and Shun performed no magical feats; they did not fight a monster, like the Yellow Emperor, or control the floods, like Yu, the founder of the Xia dynasty. They governed their people by charisma alone. This was quite different from the ascendency achieved by a warrior, who ruled by military domination. Yao, the canon tells us, was a truly gentle man: "He was reverent, intelligent, accomplished, sincere, and mild. He was sincerely respectful and capable of modesty."[101] The power inherent in these qualities radiated out to the four corners of the earth, reached up to highest heaven and down to the depths of earth. It extended to all the families and clans of China, enabling them to live harmoniously together, and established the Great Peace (*dai ping*). The *daode*, the royal potency, was beginning to change. Instead of a purely magical efficacy, it was becoming an ethical power that brought spiritual benefit to the people.

Shun's origins were very humble indeed. Some said that he had been born into one of the eastern barbarian tribes; others claimed that he had been a peasant, a potter, or a fisherman. His father and older brother tried to kill him, but Shun managed to escape; he bore them no ill will, but, a model of filial piety, he continued to treat them gently and reverently. Despite his lowly status, Shun's self-control and moderation commended themselves to the emperor Yao, who was pondering the question of the succession. Yao's own son Zhu was deceitful and quarrelsome. How could he receive the mandate of Heaven? In his perplexity, Yao consulted the gods, and the Spirit of the Four Mountains told him about Shun: "He is the son of a blind man. His father is stupid, his mother deceitful, his half brother Xiang is arrogant. Yet he has been able to live in harmony with them and be splendidly filial. He has controlled himself and has not come to wickedness."[102]

After testing Shun, to make sure that he really was a good man, Yao bequeathed the empire to him, passing over his own son. Shun felt that he was unworthy, and after Yao's death, withdrew to the southern regions of China, leaving Yao's son in possession of the throne. But the feudal lords of the empire came to consult Shun, not Yao's son, and poets would sing only the praises of Shun. So finally Shun accepted the mandate of Heaven. Even as emperor, he continued to treat his father with respect, and when he retired, he followed the example of Yao, passing over his own son in favor of Yu, his minister of works, who founded the Xia dynasty.

Yao and Shun had become saints, men of kindness and humanity, who had established a golden age of peace. Their legend in the *Classic of Documents* was clearly a tacit criticism of rule based on force and coercion and inherited by dynastic succession. Instead of clinging to their own status and prestige, Yao and Shun had both put the good of the people before their natural preferences. They were the archetypal models, who exemplified the moderation, modesty, self-control, and reverence that the *li* were supposed to cultivate. The legend of Yao and Shun continued to be an inspiration when the political life of China became even more self-serving and ruthless. The Axial sages would argue that every single human being had the potential to become like these great men.

The new ritualized moderation gradually took root in the principalities of the central plain. Despite the tensions of the period, it did help to keep the peace in these ancient cities, which remained loyal to the Chinese ideal as expressed in the *li*. But they had new, aggressive rivals. During the eighth century, three of the kingdoms on the periphery of the plain were steadily acquiring large, rich territories by infiltrating barbarian lands: Jin, in the mountainous north; Qi, a rich maritime region in northwest Shantung; and Chu, a massive state in the middle Yangtze. These three states still preserved Chinese traditions, but they now had a large, indigenous population, which was not wedded to the *li*. Chu would be the first to throw off the old Zhou traditions. China was heading for a clash of civilizations.

Life was becoming more settled in the Ganges region of north India, and the family man had become the mainstay of society. As soon as he was married, a householder was allowed to have a sacred fire in his own home, and could perform the daily rites that were a scaled-down version of the reformed public liturgy. His home had become a private sacrificial arena, where he could build the self that would survive death and enter the world of the gods. But some men took the extraordinary step of leaving their families, turning their back on society, and retiring to the forest. Instead of making the household the focus of their lives, they were deliberately homeless. They lived rough, owned no property, and begged for their food. Some let their hair grow wild and matted, some wore yellow robes, and others went naked. These "renouncers" (*samnyasins*) put themselves beyond the pale, but they became central to India's spiritual quest. Henceforth the renouncer, not the householder, would become the agent of religious change.[103] It was he, not the Brahmin priest, who shaped the next stage of the Indian Axial Age.

It is difficult to date this development precisely, but it seems to have begun in the eighth century.[104] Renunciation may have been rooted in much older disciplines. Some scholars believe that it was practiced by the native inhabitants of India before the arrival of the Aryans,[105] while others argue that it was either a natural development of Vedic ritualism[106] or an entirely new ideology.[107] The Rig Veda mentions wanderers with "long, loose locks" and "garments of soiled yellow hue" who were able to fly through the air, "go where the gods had gone before," and see things from far away. They were devoted to Rudra, a frightening god with long braided hair, who lived in the mountains and jungles and preyed upon children and cattle.[108] In the Rig Veda there are very few references to Rudra, who may have been one of the gods of the in-

digenous population. The renouncers also resembled the Vratya
warriors, who roamed ceaselessly on the fringes of Vedic society.[109] They spoke an Indo-European dialect, and could have been
early Aryan immigrants who never accepted Vedic religion. When
Vratyas needed food, they stole it from the settled communities.
Their gowns were black (Rudra's color); they wore ram skins over
their shoulders, observed their own rituals, and practiced the
"three breaths," inhaling and exhaling in a controlled manner to
induce a change of consciousness. This early form of yoga, which
would become central to the spirituality of the renouncers, indicates that there may have been an ideological link between the
Vratyas and the new ascetics.

The ritualists had taken the violence out of the liturgy and had
begun to develop a more interior spirituality, and now ancient
warrior bands had become the unlikely model for nonviolent
communities of mendicant monks. The renouncers were returning to the old mobile lifestyle of the cattle raiders. Where their
forebears had opened up new territory, they would explore the
inner world and transform the old battles into an interior struggle
for enlightenment.[110] During the Indian Axial Age, the disciplines
of warfare would often be converted into a peaceful, spiritualized
practice. This was apparent in the young *brahmacarin,* who left his
family and went to live in his teacher's house to study the Veda,[111]
and whose life was also similar to the Vratyas'. Besides memoriz-
ing the sacred texts, he had to tend his teacher's fire, collect fuel
from the forest, and beg for his food. Like the Vratyas, the *brahmacarin* wore an animal skin and carried a staff. In other parts of
the world, Indo-European youths often had to spend some time
in the wild as part of their initiation into the warrior ethos—an
ordeal that taught them hunting, self-sufficiency, and other survival skills. The *brahmacarin* also had to spend time alone in the
forest as part of his initiation into adult life, but was expressly forbidden to hunt, to harm animals, or to ride in a war chariot.[112]

The *brahmacarya* ("holy life") was an initiation into Vedic life.
The student had to be chaste and commit no act of violence. He
could not eat meat, practiced the austerities of *tapas,* sitting by the
fire, sweating, and controlling his breathing. He memorized the

Rig Veda, and learned the correct sacrificial procedures, but far more crucial was the knowledge (*vidya*) he acquired that could not be put into words. In India, education was never simply a matter of acquiring factual information. A pupil learned by *doing* things—chanting mantras, performing tasks, rituals, or ascetical exercises—that were just as important as textual study, and that, over time, transformed him, so that he saw the world differently. Living in a limbo between the sacred and profane worlds, the *brahmacarin* was revered as a holy figure. His teacher was indispensable. By the eighth century, the Brahmin priest was considered a "visible deity."[113] Because he was one *who knew* Vedic science, he was filled with the power of the brahman that became manifest during the rituals. Constantly disciplining his senses, speaking the truth at all times, practicing nonviolence, and behaving with detached equanimity to all, the Brahmin teacher embodied the "holy life." By imitating his teacher in the smallest details of the daily round, the student became one with him, and learned the inner meaning of the Vedic knowledge. The teacher was thus a midwife, laboring, day by day, to bring to birth his pupil's new self (atman), which could move mountains.[114] His initiation complete, the fully fledged Brahmin could return to the world, take a wife, light his sacred fire, perform the duties of his class, and start a family.

But at some point during the eighth century, mature Brahmins whose apprenticeship was long behind them felt compelled to undertake a solitary *brahmacarya* without a teacher; this, they believed, would make their ritual practice more effective.[115] Once again, they retired to the forest to live the holy life. Some did this only for a limited period, but others became lifelong *brahmacarins*. During the Vedic rites, the sacrificer and priests had made a mystical ascent to heaven but could remain there only for a short time. The divine and profane worlds were incompatible. If the sacrificer descended immediately to earth after his sojourn in heaven, it was thought, he would die instantly. Special rites were designed to desacralize him, so that he could return safely to profane time. But the renouncer did not want to make this reentry; he wanted to remain in the realm of brahman all the time, and that meant that he could not live in the world anymore. The sacrificer turned his back on society simply for the duration of the ritual, but the renouncer rejected it forever.[116]

The early renouncers interpreted the holy life differently. Some lived in community and kept a sacred fire in their forest retreats, performing the rituals there. Others lived in solitude, returning to the village to take part in the sacrifices from time to time. Some renouncers, however, started to feel positively hostile to the external cult.[117] On the night before he left his home to take up permanent residence in the forest, one of these radical renouncers would gather together all his sacrificial utensils and churn a new fire. The next day, he bathed, shaved his head and beard, threw one last offering of butter or milk into the hearth, and then extinguished the flames. This rite was said to "internalize" the sacred fire that the renouncer would henceforth carry around within himself. It was the rite to end all rites, his last act before leaving the village forever. Then he donned his yellow robe, picked up his begging bowl and staff, and set off to find a guru to teach him the rudiments of his new life.[118]

The renouncer regarded his *brahmacarya* as a higher form of sacrifice. His sacred fire burned within, and was manifest in every life-giving breath that he drew. Every meal he ate was an offering to this invisible, internal fire. There was no need to throw fuel onto any physical flames. The ritual reformers had taught that a man's atman, his inner self, *was* Prajapati; it *was* the sacrifice, so why go through the external motions? The renouncer was not giving up sacrifice but making it an interior act. He was asking, in effect: What is a true sacrifice? Who is the true Brahmin—the priest who performs an external rite, or the renouncer who carries his sacred fire with him wherever he goes?[119] He had made the transition from a religion externally conceived to one that was enacted within the self. Renouncers were among the first to achieve the internalization of religion that was one of the hallmarks of the Axial Age. The ritualists had long claimed that the sacrificial rites created the divine, eternal self; that the sacrifice *was* the atman; and that the rituals contained the power of the brahman. The renouncers took this a step further. One's atman could give one access to the power that held the universe together. Renunciation, asceticism, and the disciplines of the holy life would unite the renouncer to the brahman that was mysteriously contained within his atman, the core of his being.

Life in the forest was hard and painful—an endless sacrifice. Gradually two kinds of ascetics emerged, side by side, competing with each other for new members. The hermit detached himself physically from the village and human society, dwelt in the forest subsisting on roots and fruit, and practiced *tapas*. Some lived with their wives and children and created a household in the jungle, centered around the sacred hearth. The hermit could not consume food grown in the settlement, but he could eat the flesh of an animal that had been killed by other predators. His whole demeanor partook of the wild. He was a man of the forest, the obverse of the settled householder. He wore his hair long and unkempt, his clothes were made of bark, and he was not even allowed to walk over the plowed fields, the symbol of human culture.

The renouncer was more radical, his withdrawal ideological rather than physical. He was permitted to beg his food in the villages, but could have no home—not even a hermitage in the forest—no family, no sex, no fire, no ritual, and no possessions. He was allowed to stay in one place during the monsoon, but otherwise he had to keep on the move, never spending more than two nights in any one location. He had to practice iron self-discipline, and control his speech and senses. Unlike the hermit, with his wild, matted hair, the renouncer shaved his head, practiced *ahimsa,* and refrained from "injuring seeds," while "treating all animals alike, whether they cause him harm or treat him with kindness."[120] Like the Brahmin, who reduced his opponents to silence in the *brahmodya* contest, the renouncer must be a "silent sage" (*muni*), striving to attain a reality that lay beyond words.

The rationale for this rigorous asceticism was given in the Aranyakas, the "Forest Texts," which developed an esoteric interpretation of the old rites. Fasting, celibacy, and *tapas* were no longer simply a preparation for ritual, as in the old Vedic religion; they *were* the ritual itself. Asceticism "heated up" the individual in the fires of *tapas,* like a sacrificial victim; the renouncer's deepest self *was* the sacrifice, which contained the supreme reality of the brahman. Because the gods existed within the brahman, they too dwelt in the core of the individual's being. By directing his spiritualized offering within, therefore, the silent sage was sacrificing to the internal and external *devas,* who were in fact one and the same.[121]

The new spirituality had grown organically and logically from the old. First, the ritualists had reformed the old tumultuous sacrificial contests, where the sacrificial arena was crowded with participants. In their new rites, the sacrificer became a lone figure, who was cut off from profane society during the ritual. Now the renouncer took this solitude a stage further. But even though the later literature would present the renouncer as the ideal Brahmin, and tried to incorporate him into Vedic orthodoxy, in fact he challenged the entire system.[122] People admired the renouncers and saw them as spiritual heroes, bravely pioneering a new spiritual path. The renouncer had declared his independence of the village, lived in a world of his own making, submitted to no rituals, performed none of the ordinary social duties, and embraced a radical freedom. At a time when social ideology decreed that a man's lifestyle was determined by the class that he was born into, the renouncer made his own decisions. While the householder was defined by the social network, his dependents, and children, the renouncer was an individual, existing for and by himself. The new hero of the Axial Age was not a heroic warrior, proudly vaunting his martial prowess, but a monk dedicated to *ahimsa,* who was determined to discover the absolute by becoming aware of the core of his being. The renouncers were seeking *yathabhuta,* an "enlightenment" that was also an "awakening" to their authentic selves.

4

⊸୭ ୭⊶

KNOWLEDGE

(c. 700 to 600 BCE)

Vedic religion came of age in the scriptures known as the
Upanishads, also called the Vedanta, "the end of the Vedas."
The ancient Vedic religion had been inspired by ceaseless migration and the appropriation of new territory. It had emerged from
a world of violent conflict. In the Upanishads, a group of mystics
embarked on the peaceful conquest of inner space. This marked a
major step forward in religious history. External ritual was replaced by rigorous introspection, and yet this was regarded not as
an innovation but as the fulfillment of ancient tradition. The thirteen classical Upanishads, produced between the seventh and second centuries, were accorded the same status as the Rig Veda.
They too were *shruti,* "revealed," regarded as scripture par excellence. They are not easy to interpret, but they have been more influential in shaping Hindu spirituality than any other part of the
Vedic corpus.

The two earliest Upanishads emerged seamlessly from the
world of the *Brahmanas.* Like the Aranyakas, or Forest Texts, they
were esoteric sections added onto the Brahmana commentaries of
the different priestly schools. The first of the Upanishads actually
called itself an Aranyaka. The Brhadaranyaka Upanishad is the
"Great Forest Text" of the White Yajur Veda School. It opened
with a discussion of the Vedic horse sacrifice, one of the most important of the royal ceremonies and the speciality of the White
Yajur Veda. The author of the Upanishad pointed out *bandhus*

("connections") in the traditional way, identifying various parts of the horse with the natural world. The stallion's head was the dawn, his eyes were the sun, and his breath was the wind. But in the Upanishad, the ritual could be performed and completed mentally. It had ceased to be linked with a physical, external sacrifice but took place entirely in the mind of the sage (*rishi*).

The Chandogya Upanishad was the Vedantic text of the Udgatr priests who were responsible for the chant, and it began appropriately with a meditation on the sacred syllable "Om," with which the Udgatr priest began each hymn. Sound had always been divine in India; it was the primal reality, because, it was said, everything else derived from it. Now, the Chandogya Upanishad made this single syllable stand for all sound and for the entire cosmos. Om was the essence of everything that existed—of the sun, moon, and stars. It was the brahman in form of sound, the vital power that held everything together: "As all leaves are held together by a stalk, so all speech is held together by *Om*. Verily, the whole world is nothing but *Om*."[1] But the chant was not merely a transcendent reality external to the priest who intoned it. It was also one with the human body, with the atman, with breath, speech, ear, eye, and mind. The Chandogya Upanishad directed the attention of the audience back to the inner self. When a priest intoned this sacred syllable with these "connections" firmly in his mind, he attained the goal of the spiritual quest. Because Om was the brahman, it was "the immortal and the fearless."[2] A person who chanted this immortal and fearless sound while contemplating these *bandhus* would himself become immortal and free from fear.

This brings us to the heart of the Upanishadic vision. The focus was no longer on the external performance of a rite, but on its interior significance. It was not sufficient simply to establish the connections (*bandhus*) between the ritual and the cosmos; you had to know what you were doing, and this knowledge would take you to the brahman, the ground of being. The worshiper no longer directed his attention to *devas* outside himself; he turned within, "for in reality each of these gods is his own creation, for he himself is all these gods."[3] The focus of the Upanishads was the atman, the self, which was identical with the brahman. If the sage could discover the inner heart of his own being, he would automatically enter into the ultimate reality and liberate himself from the terror of mortality.

To an outsider, this sounds frankly incredible—a series of abstract statements that are impossible to verify. And indeed, it is very difficult to follow the teachings of the Upanishads.[4] The sages did not give us rational demonstrations of their ideas. The texts have no system and the logic frequently seems bizarre. Instead of reasoned arguments, we have accounts of experiences and visions, aphorisms and riddles that are hard to penetrate. Certain phrases recur that clearly bear a weight of meaning that the Western reader cannot easily share. "This self is the brahman"—*Ayam atma brahman*—the sage tells us. "That is the teaching."[5] The Chandogya is even more elliptical: "That you are!" the sage tells his son. *Tat tvam asi.*[6] These are the "great sayings" (*maha-vakyas*), but it is hard to see why we should accept them. Instead of developing an argument systematically, the sages often presented their audience with a string of apparently unrelated insights. Sometimes they preferred to give negative information, telling us what was *not* the case. Thus Yajnavalkya, the most important *rishi* in the Brhadaranyaka Upanishad, refused to define what he meant by atman:

> About this self [atman], one can only say "not . . . not" [*neti . . . neti*]. He is ungraspable, for he cannot be grasped. He is undecaying, for he is not subject to decay. He has nothing sticking to him, for he does not stick to anything. He is not bound; yet he neither trembles in fear nor suffers injury.[7]

Often a debate ends in one of the contestants falling silent, unable to proceed, and this gives us a clue. The sages are conducting a *brahmodya,* the contest in which the competitors tried to formulate the mystery of the brahman. The competition had always ended in silence, indicating that the reality lay beyond the grasp of speech and concepts. The "great sayings" are not accessible to normal, secular modes of thought. They do not proceed from logic or sense perception, but can be apprehended only after a long period of training, meditation, and cultivating a habit of inwardness that transforms our way of looking at ourselves and the world. A reader who has not adopted the Upanishadic method will not be able to comprehend its conclusions.

The word "Upanishad" meant "to sit down near to." This was an esoteric knowledge imparted by mystically inclined sages to a few spiritually gifted pupils who sat at their feet. It was not for everybody. Most Aryans continued to worship and sacrifice in the traditional manner, since they lacked either the talent or the desire to undertake this long and arduous quest. The sages were exploring new ways of being religious. In penetrating the uncharted world of the psyche, they were pioneers, and only a talented few would be able to accompany them. But life was changing, and this meant that some people needed to find a spirituality to meet their altered circumstances. The first Upanishads were set in a society that was at the very beginning of the process of urbanization.[8] There is little agricultural imagery in these texts, but many references to weaving, pottery, and metallurgy. People were traveling long distances to consult these sages, which meant that transport was improving. Many of the debates took place in the court of a raja. Life was becoming more settled, and some had more leisure for contemplation. The Brhadaranyaka was almost certainly composed in the kingdom of Videha, a frontier state on the most easterly point of Aryan expansion in the seventh century.[9] Videha was scorned as an unsophisticated, newfangled place by the Brahmins in the "Land of the Arya" to the west, but there was a great admixture of peoples in these eastern territories, including Indo-Aryan settlers from earlier waves of migration, tribes from Iran (later known as the Malla, Vajji, and Sakya), as well as peoples who were indigenous to India. These new encounters were intellectually stimulating. The renouncers were also generating fresh ideas, as they experimented with their ascetic lifestyle.

Certainly the two earliest Upanishads both reflect this intense intellectual and spiritual excitement. Neither the Brhadaranyaka nor the Chandogya was written by a single author; they were anthologies of separate texts that were put together later by an editor. Authors and editors alike all drew upon a common stock of anecdotes and ideas circulating in the courts and villages. People thought nothing of traveling from Gandhara to Videha, which were a thousand miles apart, to consult one of the distinguished teachers of the day: Sandiliya, who speculated about the nature of the atman; Janaka, king of Videha; Pravahna Jaivali, king of Kuru-Panchala; Ajatashatru, king of Kashi; and Sanatkumara, who was famous for his lifelong celibacy.[10] The new ideas may originally have been developed by Brahmin priests, but *kshatriyas* and kings also took part in the debates and discussions, as did women—notably Gargi Vacaknavi and Maitreyi, Yajnavalkya's wife. Both women seem to have been accepted by the other contestants in the *brahmodya,* and their contributions were included by the editors as a matter of course. But the two most important *rishis* in the early Upanishads were Yajnavalkya of Videha and Uddalaka Aruni, a famous teacher of the Kuru-Panchala region, both of whom were active in the second half of the seventh century.[11]

Yajnavalkya was the personal philosopher of King Janaka of Videha, who was himself a leading exponent of the new spirituality. Like all the Upanishadic sages, Yajnavalkya was convinced that there was, as it were, an immortal spark at the core of the human person, which participated in—was of the same nature as—the immortal brahman that sustained and gave life to the entire cosmos. This was a discovery of immense importance and it would become a central insight in every major religious tradition. The ultimate reality was an immanent presence in every single human being. It could, therefore, be discovered in the depths of the self, the atman. The *Brahmanas* had already concluded that the core of the human being—variously identified as breath, water, or fire—was identical to the sacrifice, and that the power at the heart of the sacrifice was brahman, the essence of everything that existed. Yajnavalkya and the other Upanishadic sages developed this concept and freed it from external ritual. The atman was no longer simply the breath, which gave life to the human being, but that which inhaled and exhaled; it was the agent behind all the senses and was, therefore, beyond description. "You can't see the

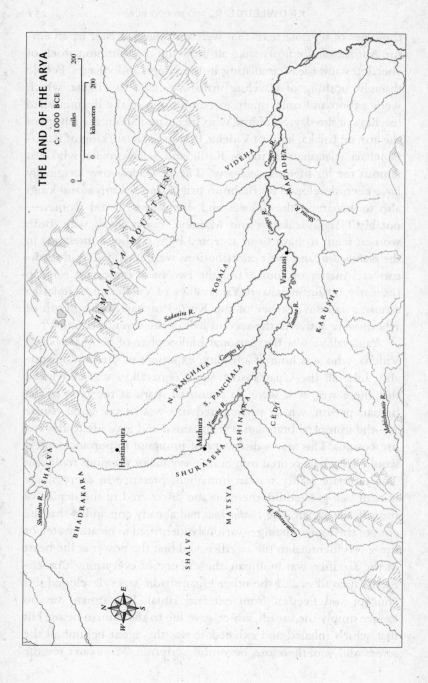

THE LAND OF THE ARYA

c. 1000 BCE

miles
0   200

kilometers
0   200

HIMALAYA MOUNTAINS

VIDEHA

MAGADHA

KOSALA

KARUSHA

Sadanira R.

Varanasi

Ganges R.

Sbona R.

Yamuna R.

N. PANCHALA

Ganges R.

S. PANCHALA

Hastinapura

Mathura

Yamuna R.

CEDI

Mahishmati R.

SHALVA

Shatadru R.

BHADRAKARA

SHURASENA

USHINARA

MATSYA

SHALVA

Chambatmati R.

N
W   E
S

Seer who does the seeing," Yajnavalkya explained. "You can't hear the Hearer who does the hearing; you can't think with the Thinker who does the thinking; and you can't perceive the Perceiver who does the perceiving. The Self within the All [brahman] is this *atman* of yours."[12] For the first time, human beings were systematically making themselves aware of the deeper layers of human consciousness. By disciplined introspection, the sages of the Axial Age were awakening to the vast reaches of selfhood that lay beneath the surface of their minds. They were becoming fully "self-conscious."

Because the self was identical with the immortal, unchangeable brahman, it was also "beyond hunger and thirst, sorrow and delusion, old age and death."[13] It was, Yajnavalkya explained to his wife, Maitreyi, "imperishable . . . indestructible." But like the brahman itself, it was transcendent, "ungraspable." It was only possible to define or comprehend something when there was duality. A person can see, taste, or smell something that is separate and apart from him- or herself. But when "the whole [brahman] has become a person's very self [atman], then who is there for him to see and by what means? Who is there for me to think of and by what means?"[14] It was impossible to perceive the perceiver within oneself. So you could only say *neti . . . neti* ("not this"). The sage affirmed the existence of the atman while at the same time denying that it bore any similarity to anything known by the senses.

Yet the goal of the new spirituality was knowledge of the unknowable atman. How could this be achieved? Yajnavalkya did not impart factual information, but used the traditional form of the *brahmodya* debate to show his interlocutor that when he considered brahman or atman, he had come to the end of what the ordinary thought processes could usefully do. It was a technique similar to the dialectic method developed later by Socrates. By eliminating his opponent's inadequate definitions of the atman, taking them apart one after the other, Yajnavalkya gradually led him or her from the consideration of external phenomena to an apprehension of the more elusive realities of the internal world. When, for example, King Janaka listed what other Brahmins had told him about the atman—that it was speech, breath, the eye, the wind, or the heart—Yajnavalkya insisted that these answers were only half true.[15] The reality they were looking for lay at the base of these phenomena, supporting them like the foundations of a house. They could not define but only participate in this more fundamental reality, live in it, as in a home. By systematically removing layer after layer of superficial knowledge, Yajnavalkya led his disciples to perceive everyday realities as manifestations of the absolute and to see that the core of the self was not the individual "I" that ruled our daily lives, hemmed in as it was with physical needs, desires, and fears, but an ultimate reality in its own right. They must undertake a long, slow quest for self-discovery. This was one of the clearest expressions of a fundamental principle of the Axial Age. Enlightened persons would discover within themselves the means of rising above the world; they would experience transcendence by plumbing the mysteries of their own nature—not simply by taking part in magical rituals.

Instead of discussing the external ceremonies of the cult, as the ritual reformers had done, Yajnavalkya had begun to explore the psychological makeup of the human being in an attempt to locate the true self, the inner person that controlled and animated the "I" of our mundane experience. We had to go beyond this "I" and discover modes of being that were different from our normal consciousness, which was dominated by sense perception, common sense, and rational thought. Yajnavalkya taught his disciples to consider their dreaming state, when they were no longer bound by space or time. In our dreams, we take the external world apart and create our own joys, pleasures, and delights. We become creators like Prajapati, bringing pools, wagons, roads, and teams of oxen into existence, and building up a whole new world by means of "the inner light that is in our heart."[16] In dreams, we become aware of a freer and higher self, since, for a short time, we are released from the constraints of the body. We also have nightmares, however, when we become acutely aware of our pain, fear, and desire. But in deep sleep, which is dreamless, the self is liberated from even these mental appearances of activity. In deep sleep, a person is "beyond fear." Deep sleep, Yajnavalkya believed, was not oblivion, but a state of unified consciousness. He compared it to the experience of sexual intercourse, when "a man embraced by a woman he loves is oblivious to everything within or without." He loses all sense of duality: "There isn't a second reality there that he could see as something distinct and separate from him."[17] Conscious only of oneness, the self experiences *ananda,* the "bliss" of brahman.

But the temporary release that we experience in sleep or orgasm is only a foretaste of the permanent liberation that is the goal of the spiritual quest, an experience of complete freedom and serenity. This enlightened state comes when the sage experiences the atman. At one with the inner core of his being, he "becomes calm, composed, cool, patient and collected," because he is in the world of the brahman. Suffused by the immortal, fearless brahman, he is "free from evil, free from stain, free from doubt." Because he knows the "immense and unborn self, unaging, undying, immortal and free from fear," he knows the brahman and is himself released from terror and anxiety.[18]

Thus knowledge of the self was an experience of pure bliss, an *ekstasis.* This knowledge lay beyond concepts and did not depend upon logical deduction. It was rather an awareness of an "inner light within the heart," a direct and immediate intuition, beyond any ordinary joy. This "knowledge" transformed the individual. It could be attained only after a long training in inwardness, which the aspirants could achieve by practicing Yajnavalkya's dialectical method: systematically dismantling normal habits of thought; cultivating an awareness of their interior world, their dreams, and subconscious states; and by constantly reminding themselves that the knowledge they sought was beyond words and of an entirely different order from their secular thoughts and experiences. Yajnavalkya could not impart this knowledge, as if it were ordinary, factual information. He could only teach the method that enabled his disciples to arrive at this state.

Yajnavalkya believed that a person who *knows thus*—who had realized his or her identity with brahman—would go to brahman at death, taking their "knowledge" with them. In the traditional Vedic ritual, a person constructed the self that would survive in the world of the gods by means of his liturgical action (*karma*).

But for Yajnavalkya, the creation of an immortal self was not achieved by external rites, but by this carefully acquired knowledge. The ritualists had believed that the self was built by accumulating a stock of perfectly executed sacrifices, but Yajnavalkya was convinced that the eternal self was conditioned by *all* our actions and experiences. "What a man turns out to be depends on how he acts and on how he conducts himself. If his actions are good, he will turn into something good. If his actions are bad, he turns into something bad." Yajnavalkya was not simply talking about our external deeds. Our mental activities, such as our impulses of desire and feelings of attachment, were also crucial. After his death, a man whose desires were fixed on the things of this world would return to earth, after a brief stay in heaven. His mind and character still clung to the mundane, and so he would be born again to endure a new life here below, "back to this world, back to action." But a man who sought only his immortal self, and was not attached to this world, belonged to the brahman: "A man who does not desire—who is without desires, who is freed from desires, whose desires are fulfilled, whose only desire is his self—his vital functions do not depart. *Brahman* he is, and to *brahman* he goes."[19] He would never again return to this life of pain and mortality.

This is the first time we hear of the doctrine of "action" (*karma*), which was about to become crucial to Indian spirituality. In Yajnavalkya's time, however, it was a new and controversial idea. When his Brahmin friend Artabhaga asked Yajnavalkya what happened to a person after death, he replied, "We cannot talk about this in public. Take my hand, Artabhaga, let's go and discuss this in private."[20] The new doctrine of karma seemed subversive. Sacrifice was supposed to ensure permanent residence in heaven, but some people were losing faith in the efficacy of ritual. Yajnavalkya and the other Upanishadic sages were beginning to believe that, however many perfectly executed sacrifices he performed, a person might have to return to this world of pain and death again and again. He would not only have to undergo a traumatic death once, but would have to endure sickness, old age, and mortality repeatedly, with no hope of final release. He would be liberated from this ceaseless cycle (*samsara*) of rebirth and redeath only by the ecstatic knowledge of the self, which would free him of the desire for ephemeral things here below.

But to become free of desire and attachment is extremely difficult. We instinctively cling to this life and to our personal survival. We think that our individuality is worth preserving, but, the sages insisted, this is an illusion. Once a person became aware that his or her self was identical with the brahman, which contained the whole universe, it became crystal clear that there was nothing to be gained by hanging on to this present, limited existence. Some of the sages were convinced that the best way to attain this liberating knowledge was to become a renouncer, giving up worldly gain, and eliminating desire by a life of austerity. This was not yet considered obligatory, but eventually Yajnavalkya embraced the life of a "striver" (*shramana*), leaving his wife, departing from the court, and going into "homelessness" in the forest.[21]

But Uddalaka Aruni, one of the most important sages of the Chandogya Upanishad, remained a Brahmin householder in the region of Kuru-Panchala all his life. This Upanishad ended by affirming the value of a devout existence in the world. Once a householder had completed his period of study as a *brahmacarin*, he must return home and put into practice everything that he had learned from his teacher. He must chant the sacred Vedas, bring up his children, meditate, and practice *ahimsa*, refraining from violence and acting with kindness to others. "Someone who lives in this way all his life," the text concludes, "attains the world of *brahman*, and he does not return [to this world] again."[22] A gentle, kindly man, Uddalaka agreed in essentials with Yajnavalkya. He saw brahman, the ultimate reality, as identical with the atman of a human being, taught the new doctrine of karma, and meditated on the experience of sleep as a foretaste of enlightenment. Like Yajnavalkya, he was convinced that liberation (*moksha*) from the painful cycle of death and rebirth was the goal of the spiritual life, and that it could not be achieved by external ritual practice, but only by the quest for interior knowledge.

In chapter six of the Chandogya, we see Uddalaka initiating his son Shvetaketu into the esoteric lore of the new spirituality, a precious glimpse of the way this teaching was transmitted. Shvetaketu would eventually become an important sage in his own right, but in this chapter he had only just finished his twelve-year stint as a *brahmacarin* and had returned home, "swell-headed and arrogant," thinking that he knew everything there was to know about Vedic life.[23] Uddalaka patiently undermined this misplaced confidence, teaching his son a different way of perceiving the world, himself, and the ultimate. He began by explaining that the identity of any object was inseparable from the material of which it was made—clay, copper, or iron. The same was true of the universe, which had originally consisted of being itself—absolute, undivided simplicity: "One only, without a second."[24] Like Prajapati, the One propagated itself by means of heat (*tapas*), which eventually brought forth, from itself, the entire range of creatures. In this way, the One became the origin, the essence, and therefore, the true self of every single creature: "The finest essence here— *That* constitutes the self of this whole world," Uddalaka explained, again and again. "*That* is the truth; *That* is the self [atman]. And you are *That*, Shvetaketu."[25] These sentences run like a refrain through the whole chapter, reinforcing the central teaching. Shvetaketu was brahman, the impersonal essence of the universe, which Uddalaka, like other sages, refers to as the neutral, elliptical "*that*."

But metaphysical instruction alone would not suffice. Shvetaketu had to appropriate this knowledge internally, make it his own, and fuse these external teachings with his personal mental landscape. He had, as later thinkers would put it, to "realize" them, make them a reality in his own life, and Uddalaka had to act as a midwife, slowly and carefully bringing this new insight to birth within his son. This was not a wholly academic, abstract education. Shvetaketu had not only to listen to his father's metaphysical explanations, but to perform tasks that made him look at the world in a different way. Uddalaka drew upon everyday examples, and made Shvetaketu take an active part in a series of experiments. In the most famous of these, he told his son to leave a chunk of salt in a beaker of water overnight. The next day, the lump had completely dissolved, but when his father made him take a sip from various parts of the cup, asking each time how it tasted, Shvetaketu had to reply: "Salty." The salt was still there, in every part of the beaker. "You, of course, did not see it there, son, yet it was always right there." So too was the invisible brahman, essence and self of the whole world. "And you are *that,* Shvetaketu."²⁶

Like the salt, the brahman could not be seen, but it could be experienced. It was manifest in every single living thing. It was the subtle essence in the banyan seed, from which a great tree grows, yet when Shvetaketu dissected the seed, he could not see anything. The brahman, Uddalaka explained, was the sap that was in every part of the tree and gave it life.²⁷ It was, therefore, the atman of the tree, as it was the atman of every single human being; all things shared the same essence. But most people did not understand this. They imagined that they were special and unique, different from every other being on the face of the earth. Instead of appreciating the deepest truth about themselves, they clung to those particularities that, they thought, made them so precious and interesting. But in reality, these distinguishing characteristics were no more durable or significant than rivers that flowed into the same sea. Once they had merged, they became "just the ocean" and did not stridently assert their individuality, crying, "I am that river," "I am this river." "In exactly the same way, son," Uddalaka persisted, "when all these creatures reach the existent, they are not aware that 'we are reaching the existent.' " They no longer cling to their individuality. Whether they were tigers, wolves, lions, or gnats, "they all merge into *that,*" because *that* is what they have always been, and they can only ever be *that.* To cling to the mundane self was, therefore, a delusion that would lead inescapably to pain and confusion. People could escape this only by acquiring the deep, liberating knowledge that the brahman was their atman, the truest thing about them.²⁸

But this knowledge was not easy to acquire. How could you find the unknowable atman? The atman was not what Western people call the "soul" or the psyche.[29] The Upanishads did not separate body from spirit, but saw human beings as a composite whole. Uddalaka made his son fast for fifteen days, allowing him to drink as much water as he liked. At the end of this, Shvetaketu was so weak and malnourished that he could no longer recite the Vedic texts that he had mastered so competently with his guru. He had learned that the mind was not pure intellect but was also "made up of food, of breath, of water, and speech, and heat."[30] The atman was physical and spiritual; it was immanent in the heart and in the body, the ultimate, immutable, inner core of *all* things, material and ephemeral. It could not be identified with or compared to any single phenomenon. It was "no thing," and yet it was the deepest truth of everything.[31] It could be discovered only within the human being, after a long, disciplined effort.

It took years to open up the depths of the self, through silence and a spiritual discipline that led the aspirant to realize the futility of desiring things that were only transient, and that it was stupid to prize individual qualities that were of no more importance than the grains of pollen that eventually made up a pot of honey.[32] The pupil must work patiently with a guru, who would help him to see what was really there, what was really important.

The early Upanishads were not rebelling against the old Vedic ritualism so much as moving beyond it. Unless a sage learned to look through the external rites to their inner meaning, he would never become aware of the absolute reality of brahman at their core. The Chandogya said that priests who chanted the syllable *Om* mindlessly and mechanically were like dogs baying for food.[33] The gods had faded into the background. In these early Upanishads, Prajapati, the personalized expression of brahman, was no longer the lofty creator god but had become an ordinary guru, who taught his pupils that they must not regard him—Prajapati—as the highest reality, but seek their own atman: "The self that is free from evils, free from old age and death, free from sorrow, free from hunger and thirst," he told them, "that is the self that you should try to discover."[34]

Devas and *asuras* also had to learn this important truth and had undergone exactly the same arduous training in inwardness as human beings. The Chandogya tells a story about the moment when *devas* and *asuras* first heard about the atman. "Come," they said to one another, "let us discover that self by discovering which one obtains all the worlds and all one's desires are fulfilled."[35] So Indra, representing his *devas,* and Virocana, one of the leading *asuras,* arrived on Prajapati's doorstep as humble Vedic students, carrying wood for their teacher's fire. They studied with Prajapati for thirty-two years but were still no closer to finding the atman. Prajapati told them to dress up in their best clothes and look at their reflections in a pan of water. What did they see? A replica of themselves, beautifully attired and spruced up, they replied. "That is the *atman;* that is the immortal," Prajapati told them, "that is the one free from fear; that is *brahman.*"[36] They left, delighted with themselves, and Virocana took this knowledge back to the *asuras.* The body was the atman, he told them; a person could win his heart's desire in this life and the next simply by taking care of his physical needs: there was no need for sacrifice or ritual.

But before Indra returned to heaven, he stopped in his tracks. Even an elegantly clothed body, he realized, would become old, sick, and eventually die. So he returned to Prajapati, carrying his firewood, and studied for another sixty-nine years, going deeper and deeper into himself. Prajapati told him that the atman was found in the dreaming state, when the self was free from physical constraints, and at first Indra was happy with this explanation. But then he reflected that in sleep a person could feel afraid, fear death, and even weep. So he returned to Prajapati again. This time Prajapati told Indra that he would find the atman in profound, dreamless sleep, when he was "totally collected and serene . . . that is the self; that is the immortal; that is the one free from fear; that is *brahman.*"[37] Again, Indra was attracted by this idea, but after a while found it disappointing; in such profound unconsciousness, a person might as well be dead. So he stayed with Prajapati for another five years, until he was ready to hear the truth.

Finally Prajapati told Indra that the enlightened person had to learn to look beyond his mind and his body before he could find the inner self that was independent of all his physical and mental functions. The atman was that which enabled a man to smell, to see, to think:

> The one who is aware: "Let me say this"—that is the self; the faculty of speech enables him to speak. The one who is aware: "Let me listen to this"—that is the self; the faculty of hearing enables him to hear. The one who is aware: "Let me think about this"—that is the self; the mind is his divine faculty of sight. This very self rejoices as it perceives with his mind, with that divine sight, these objects of desire found in the world of *brahman*.[38]

The story illustrates the long process of self-discovery. The teacher could not simply give his pupil the answers, but could only lead him through the stages of introspection. Just when it seemed that they had got to the root of the matter, the student discovered *for himself* that this was not the end of his quest, and that he had to go still deeper. Even the mighty Indra took 101 years to discover the atman that gave the gods immortality.[39]

The sages of the Upanishads were seeking the essence of the personality, and in the course of that process some experienced an ineffable joy and peace. Guru Prajapati called the person who had made this interior journey "the deeply serene one," who "emerges in his own true appearance."[40] He had somehow come to himself, not by receiving privileged information, but by living differently. The process was just as important as the achievement of the final goal. Somebody who merely reads the text of the Chandogya, however, cannot have this experience. There could be no enlightenment unless the student had actually made the meditation, and gone through the long and difficult journey of introspection. Most important, metaphysical contemplation was only a small part of the initiation. Like a *brahmacarin,* the Upanishadic student had to live in a humble, self-effacing way, and this was as crucial as the intellectual content of the quest. Indra, a god who never stopped boasting about his exploits, had to gather wood for his teacher, look after his fire, clean Prajapati's house, be chaste, give up warfare, and practice *ahimsa.* Human sages and gods were discovering a spiritual technology that would work only if people abandoned the aggressively self-assertive ego.

Meanwhile, the Greeks were taking an entirely different path. Where the Indian sages of the Axial Age were abandoning their heroic code and reducing Indra, the archetypal Aryan warrior, to a lowly Vedic student, the Greeks were militarizing the entire polis. The gods of India were beginning to merge into the mental processes of the renouncer, but the Greeks were giving their gods greater definition than ever before. In one sense, the Hellenic world prospered during the seventh century. At this point, Athens lagged behind the other poleis, but some cities were thriving, especially in the Peloponnesus.[41] This was the century of Corinth, which was superbly placed for Mediterranean trade, had a thriving crafts industry, and, under the influence of Egypt, was experimenting with monumental architecture. The most radical state, however, was Sparta, which had a unique political system that subjugated the interests of the individual wholly to the polis.[42] Citizens were known as *homoioi* (the "equal" or the "uniform" ones). In some ways this system was a parody of the Axial ideal of self-surrender, because the kenosis of Sparta was geared not to *ahimsa* but to military efficiency. Further, the equality of the Spartan citizens depended upon the ruthless subjection of others. At the end of the eighth century, Sparta had conquered Messenia to the southwest, appropriated its land, and divided it among the Spartan *homoioi*. The helots, the native people of Messenia, became their slaves. Such a system was bound to generate tension. In 670, Messenia broke away from Sparta, only to be reconquered after a brutal war.

But Sparta was not the only trouble spot. Despite its new economic prosperity, the Greek world was in crisis.[43] At first, colonization had been a solution to the internal problems of the poleis: troublemakers were simply sent away to found another settlement. But by the middle of the seventh century, contact with the more developed societies in the east led to widespread discontent with conditions at home. People wanted to enjoy the material luxuries they had seen abroad, but demand outstripped resources. Some families became rich, while others lived beyond their means and fell into debt. By 650, there were intense clan rivalries, bloody battles, and factional strife in many of the city-states. The details of the crisis remain obscure, but it seems that to solve their financial problems, some of the aristocrats tried to exploit the poorer farmers, reserving public land for their own use. Some tenants were obliged to give a sixth of their produce to the local nobility, and as the aristocrats controlled the courts, they had little hope of redress. A dangerous gap was developing between the nobility and the farmers, who were the mainstay of the economy.

The farmers had troubles of their own. Greeks had learned new methods of agricultural production from the east, and were beginning to invest in the future, planting vineyards and olive trees, which take ten years to bear fruit. They were also developing their livestock for long-term productivity. But in the meantime, many were finding it hard to make a living, and were either spending capital or selling land to fund their projects. There were bad cases of debt, which often ended in the enslavement of a debtor who failed to pay his creditors. All this unrest led to broader social problems. The old values seemed to be eroding. The poet Hesiod, writing in the early seventh century, noted that in some of the poleis, children were no longer obedient to their parents, generations were estranged from one another, and elders could no longer guide the young. His poetry was an attempt to fill this moral vacuum.

Hesiod was a different kind of poet from Homer, and perfectly placed to assess the crisis.[44] He was not a member of the warrior aristocracy, but a farmer in Boetia, and was inspired by many of the newer ideas coming from the east. His father had migrated from Asia Minor to the Greek mainland, and in some ways Hesiod seemed more at home with Near Eastern, Hurrian, or Hittite mythology than with the Greek heroic tradition. He certainly saw himself as a Greek bard and once even won a prize for his poetry, but he used the heroic formulae awkwardly and may have composed his poems in writing rather than orally.[45] He was the first

Greek poet to write in his own voice and put a name to his compositions. In some ways, Hesiod was more like a Hebrew prophet than a Homeric bard. Like Amos, he felt the first stirrings of divine inspiration "while he was shepherding his lambs." The Muses, the daughters of Zeus, commanded him to speak the truth, and then

> *Plucked and gave a staff to me,*
> *A shoot of blooming laurel, wonderful to see,*
> *And breathed a sacred voice into my mouth*
> *With which to celebrate the things to come*
> *And things which were before.*[46]

He experienced his poetry as a revelation; it could soothe men's hearts and build a bridge to the gods.

So did the practice of social justice. This preoccupation brought Hesiod even closer to Amos. In *Works and Days,* a long hymn to the sacred task of agricultural labor and wise husbandry, Hesiod explained that he was involved in a dispute with his brother Perses. Their inheritance had been divided between them, but Perses had tried to get more than his share, and had brought his case before the local *basileis.* Hesiod had little faith in the legal system, and warned Perses that the only people who would benefit from this litigation were the aristocrats themselves, who would charge a crippling fee. Hesiod's personal experience gave him a special insight into the agricultural crisis that was escalating into a major political dispute all over Greece. Like a prophet, Hesiod warned the *basileis:*

> *You lords, take notice of this punishment.*
> *The deathless gods are never far away. . . .*
> *The eye of Zeus sees all, and understands,*
> *And when he wishes, marks and does not miss*
> *How just a city is, inside.*[47]

Individual legal decisions (*dikai*) came from the goddess Dike (Justice), who was hurt when a judgment was perverted; she immediately informed her father, Zeus, when a *basileus* took bribes or committed perjury to feather his own nest, and Zeus, the protector of society, punished the guilty polis with plague, famine, and political disaster.[48] This was a naïve solution, requiring direct divine intervention, which, presumably, was not often forthcoming. But it marked a change. The old aristocratic code of honor had been essentially self-regarding. The development of the polis, which required the close cooperation of *basileis* and farmers, had brought the heroic ideal into conflict with the ordinary people's need for fair and equal opportunity. Hesiod believed that his generation faced a stark choice. Would justice (*dike*), or the prideful, selfish excess (*hubris*) of the heroic warrior, characterize Greek society?

To bring his point home, Hesiod created a new version of the old Indo-European myth of the Four Ages of Men.[49] Traditionally, there were four successive eras, each more degenerate than the last and each named after a metal: Gold, Silver, Bronze, and Iron. But Hesiod altered the story by adding the Heroic Age, which he inserted between the Bronze Age and the current Age of Iron, the worst era of all. In the Golden Age, at the very beginning of human history, there had been no gulf between men and gods; human beings had lived happy lives, and knew neither sickness nor old age. Death came to them as naturally and as peacefully as sleep. They did not have to work for their living, because "the fertile land gave up its fruits unasked." This race passed, so the Olympian gods fashioned a Silver race of human beings, who took a very long time to mature, but when they eventually reached their prime lived "brief, anguished lives," dominated by hubris. They "could not control themselves" and recklessly, heedlessly exploited and injured one another, neglecting the worship of the gods. Angrily, Zeus replaced them with the men of Bronze, who were even worse. They were "strange and full of power," addicted to "the groans and violence of war," "terrible men," their hearts "flinty hard," their limbs massive and invincible. This society was so self-indulgent and aggressive that the men of the Bronze Age eventually destroyed one another. So Zeus made the race of Heroes. These men were demigods, "just and good," who turned their backs on the hubris of their forebears, but even so, they fought the terrible Trojan War, which finally destroyed them. Now the heroes lived on in the Blessed Isles at the very edge of the world.

The Heroic Age was succeeded by the Age of Iron, the contemporary era. Ours was a world turned upside down, lurching toward inevitable destruction. Life was hard and hopeless. "By day, men work and grieve unceasingly," Hesiod reflected; "by night they waste away and die."[50] But the gods still granted human beings some blessings. In the Iron Age, good and evil, pain and pleasure were inseparable: people could eat and thrive only if they engaged ceaselessly in backbreaking toil. It was a time of ambiguity and ambivalence. Everything was mixed up together. But the men of Iron had a choice. They must either submit to the demands of justice or abandon themselves to the aristocratic sin of *hubris*. If they neglected *dike,* they would witness the triumph of evil, where might was right, where fathers felt nothing for their sons, where children despised their aged parents, and the old brotherly love of past ages would vanish. "Nothing will be any longer as it was in days past."[51]

The moral of the story was clear. Those races that practiced social justice were loved and honored by the gods. The violent warriors of the Bronze Age were killed; the heroes were transported to a happy, carefree life. Justice brought mortals closer to the gods, so they must behave decently to one another, and honor the Olympians in sacrifice. They must also know their place. The Age of Heroes was over. It was, therefore, Hesiod implied—though he did not explicitly say so—time to abandon the old, self-destructive warrior ethos. The men of Iron could not behave as if they were Achilles or Odysseus; they were mere farmers, tillers of the soil, involved in a humbler kind of strife (*eris*), the struggle with the land. Instead of trying to emulate their rivals' military prowess, they should be spurred on to healthy competition with a neighbor who had produced a good crop. This was the strife that made the farmer dear to the gods. This period of history was different from the Golden Age, when there had been no need to plow a field. In the Iron Age, Zeus had decreed that men could thrive only if they accomplished the hard, disciplined toil of husbandry, which was a form of sacrifice, a daily act of devotion to the gods.[52]

Hesiod explored these ideas more fully in his *Theogony,* which described the triumph of the Olympian gods over their rivals.[53] It became a textbook of Greek religion. Many were confused about some details of the mythology that had emerged from the obscurity of the dark age. How exactly were the various chthonic powers related to one another? Why had the Titans revolted against Zeus? What had caused the separation of men and gods? Hesiod tied up these loose ends, making use of Mesopotamian and other Near Eastern mythology. He told the traditional story in a way that made the horrible struggle of the theogony—the emergence of the gods from primal formlessness—represent a striving for greater clarity, order, and definition. This had begun when the bottomless abyss of Chaos was replaced by the more solid realities of Gaia and Uranus; it ended with the victory of the Olympians over those Titans who had opposed the rule of law. Hesiod wanted these frightening stories of divine fathers and sons murdering and mutilating one another to warn the Greeks of the dangers of the current internecine strife in the poleis. In his hands, the just and regulated regime established by Zeus was in pointed contrast to the unnatural chaos that had gone before. Hesiod's *Theogony* also raised questions that would later preoccupy the Greek philosophers: What were the origins of the cosmos? How did order come to prevail over chaos? How could the many derive from the one? How could the formless relate to what was defined?

Hesiod also fixed the place of human beings in the divine scheme, by telling the story of the Titan Prometheus.[54] During the Golden Age, gods and human beings had lived on equal terms and had regularly feasted together. But at the end of the Golden Age, the gods began to recede from the world of men; now the only way for humans to maintain contact with the Olympians was the ritual of animal sacrifice, when gods and men consumed their allotted portions of the victim. But Prometheus thought that the arrangement was unfair and wanted to help humans to improve their lot. After one of these sacrifices, he tried to trick Zeus into accepting the inedible bones of the victim, so that men could enjoy the meat. But Zeus saw through the ruse: gods did not need food; they could sustain themselves on the smoke that rose when the victim's bones were burned on the altar. Sacrifice, therefore, revealed the gods' superiority to mortals, who could survive only by eating the flesh of dead animals. Angered by Prometheus's crafty stratagem, Zeus decided to penalize humans by depriving them of the fire they needed to cook their food. Yet again, Prometheus defied him, stole the fire, and gave it back to humanity. Zeus took his revenge by chaining Prometheus to a pillar, and this time he punished humans by sending them a woman who had been put together by the divine craftsman Hephaestus. In the Golden Age, there had been no division between the sexes; humans had not been defined by gender. Pandora, the first woman, was a "beautiful evil." She carried a jar that she opened "and scattered pains and sufferings among men." Men were fatally paired with womankind, who brought sickness, old age, and suffering into their world.

This is one of the few overtly misogynous moments of the Axial Age. Hesiod intended it to illustrate the ambiguous nature of life in the Iron Age, representing humanity's fall from grace.[55] Henceforth good and evil were inextricably combined. Sacrifice brought men and gods together, but it also revealed the impassable distinction between them. Suffering was now an inescapable fact of life—a major theme of the Axial Age. In India, the sages were determined to create the spiritual technology that would enable human beings to transcend pain and mortality. Hesiod had no such ambition. Indeed, he was convinced that men should not seek to ascend to the divine world. The story of Prometheus put humans firmly in their place, midway between gods and animals and surrounded on all sides by the evils released by Pandora. Men of the Iron Age could not escape their suffering. They might want to rebel like Prometheus, but hubris was self-destructive: all that Prometheus's rebellion had achieved was pain for himself and ceaseless toil for humanity.

Other Greeks felt that resignation was not the answer. Increasingly, as the political crisis became more acute, farmers and peasants demanded economic relief, return of confiscated property, and security before the law, and gave their support to ambitious aristocrats who championed their cause, using this popular acclaim to achieve political power.[56] The first *tyrannos* gained control of Corinth in 655, and other poleis followed suit. These new rulers were not "tyrants" in our modern sense, but simply leaders who seized power unconstitutionally and ruled outside customal laws for the benefit of the people.[57] As the champion of justice, the tyrant was initially respected, but tyranny was not a sustainable political system. Inevitably the masses, who had been empowered by the tyrant, became more confident. By the time he died, his unconstitutional rule began to appear brutal and arbitrary, so the people usually rose up against his successors, and remembered the tyranny with hatred. But the experiment showed the people that, properly organized, they could put a brake on exploitation by the ruling class and take their destiny into their own hands.

Of still greater significance was a military innovation that coincided with the rise of tyranny. By the end of the eighth century, the manufacture of weapons had advanced considerably, and the poleis now had the military technology to equip large armies instead of relying on a small aristocratic squadron of charioteers.[58] Between 700 and 650, the city-states began to rely on heavily armed infantry, and the old-fashioned Homeric-style warriors, who had fought in single combat, were phased out. Manpower was crucial, and warfare could no longer be the privilege of the nobility. Henceforth anybody who could afford to equip himself with the requisite weapons (*hopla*)—be he lord or farmer—could join this prestigious troop, regardless of rank or birth. With the hoplite army, a new equality was born.

Hoplite fighting was distinguished by the phalanx, a tightly packed body of men, standing shoulder to shoulder, eight deep. Each soldier held his circular shield to protect his left side and gripped the right shoulder of the man next to him. The phalanx would push forward as one against the enemy, stabbing above and below the wall of shields. Eventually one side would break and run. The phalanx proved to be extraordinarily effective, but it inflicted particularly horrible wounds on the enemy. The hoplite army was a people's army, drawing on a larger proportion of the male population than ever before. And conversely, that meant that the people, the *demos,* were now essentially an army. In India, fighting had become the sole prerogative of the *kshatriya* class; warfare was now a specialized activity, from which the other three classes were barred. It was thus circumscribed and contained and, as the ideal of *ahimsa* took hold, was regarded increasingly as impure, tragic, and evil. But not so in Greece, which was going in the opposite direction. During the seventh century, the entire polis had become militarized. The citizenry had become an army, which could be mobilized at very short notice.

This was a radical break with the past. Hesiod had suggested that it was time to abandon the traditional heroic ideal; the hoplite army effected this severance. The individual warrior, yearning for personal glory, had become an anachronism: the new ideal was collective. The hoplite soldier was essentially one of a team. Hoplites fell or succeeded together, en masse; there could be no private glory. The hubris of an Achilles, which had put the whole army at risk, was now redundant. "Excellence" (*arete*) was redefined: it now consisted of patriotism and devotion to the common good. Writing in the late seventh century, the Spartan poet Tyrtaios described the new hero:

> *This is excellence, this the finest possession of men,*
> *The noblest prize that a young man can win:*
> *This is the common good for all the city and all the*
>   *people;*
> *When a man stands firm and remains unmoved in*
>   *the front rank*
> *And forgets all thought of disgraceful flight*
> *Steeling his spirit and heart to endure*
> *And with words encourages the man standing next to*
>   *him.*[59]

Instead of aggressively seeking his own fame and glory, the hoplite submerged his own needs for the good of the entire phalanx. Like the Axial ideal of kenosis, it promoted an ethic of selflessness and devotion to others. The difference was that this self-surrender was acted out on the battlefield in a savagely effective killing machine.

The hoplite reform transformed Greece and laid the foundations of democracy. A farmer who fought next to a nobleman in the phalanx would never see the aristocracy in the same way again. Old habits of deference could no longer be maintained. It would not be long before the lower classes demanded that *their* organization—the people's assembly—should take a central role in the government of the city. The hoplite reform altered the self-image of the polis. It was a peaceful revolution; instead of eliminating the upper classes, the farmers and peasants adopted the aristocratic ethos, so that the entire city became, in effect, a class of gentlemen warriors.

Free speech was originally the privilege of the noble hero. In Homer, the *basileis* of the Greek army were all at liberty to speak their minds forcefully to King Agamemnon. Now this right was extended to all members of the phalanx. The new army spoke a different language. *Logos* ("dialogue speech") was quite different from the allusive poetry of Homer and the Heroic Age.[60] Mythical discourse attempted to express the more elusive truths, and was not expected to conform too closely with objective realities in the external world. *Logos,* however, had to be practical, effective, and accurate. On the battlefield and in councils of war, soldiers confronted questions of life and death. Instead of asking, "What is the ultimate meaning of this event?" the men of *logos* asked, "What happened?" and "What shall we do?" *Logos* was driven by immediate, practical need, and it was vital that any soldier feel able to challenge the battle plan that would affect all alike, because the group needed all the expertise available. The *logos* of the hoplites would never replace the *mythos* of the poets. The two coexisted, each with its own sphere of competence. But as more citizens became hoplites, *logos* became the distinctive language and mode of thought of government.

In the seventh century, Sparta was the state that most perfectly enshrined the hoplite ethos.[61] By 650, all male citizens were hoplites, and the *demos,* the people, were sovereign. Ancient rituals were put to new, brutally pragmatic use. In the ancient fertility ritual of the Orthia, young boys had tried to steal cheeses from the altar of Artemis and were beaten away by other youths. In hoplite Sparta, the rite was used to teach young warriors fighting skills. It was no longer a mock battle, but was for real, and blood flowed freely. Instead of simply sending their young men into the wilderness, to learn courage and self-reliance during their initiation into civic life, the Spartans selected budding hoplites for special sodalities. By day, they were kept out of sight, but at night they were sent out into the countryside to kill as many of the helots as they could lay their hands on. In India, the emerging ethic of the Axial Age had extracted the violence from the ancient rites; in Greece, the old rites were being transformed by the demands of the military.

The Chinese, however, were attempting to moderate warfare by subordinating practical utility to the beauty of ritual. The seventh century was a turbulent time in the Yellow River region, but despite the constant wars between the principalities, violence was successfully kept within bounds. This was due, in no small measure, to the ritual reform initiated by the literati of Lu. By the seventh century, life in the principalities was minutely regulated by the *li,* so much so that social, political, and military life began to resemble the elaborate ritual ceremonies of the Zhou court. Even though, at first sight, this regularized conformity seems far from the spirit of the Axial Age, some of these rites had considerable spiritual potential. As yet, the Chinese did not realize this; they would not begin their Axial Age for another two hundred years, but the specialists of Lu were laying a strong foundation for the future, even though in the seventh century their primary aim was to create a society of gentlemen, who lived gracious lives of moderation and self-control.

The Zhou king had virtually retired to the royal domain, and was no longer at the forefront of political life. His place had been taken by the princes who ruled the ancient cities, which were collectively known as the *jung kuo,* "cities of the center." The prince had taken over many of the ritual attributes of the king.[62] He had become a holy figure. His vassals had to fast and purify themselves before they entered his presence, because, as Heaven's counterpart on earth, he had to be shielded from contamination and impurity. He too possessed the power that had radiated from the king, but—an important point—this *daode* depended upon and was nourished by his vassals' faithful performance of the courtly rites. Lu's ritual reform was based on a principle of far-reaching significance: the *li* not only transformed the person who practiced the rites; they also enhanced the sanctity of the one who received this ceremonial attention. This was an essentially magical notion, but it was based on a profound psychological insight. When people are consistently treated with the utmost respect, they learn to feel worthy of reverence; they realize that they have absolute value. So in China, the *li* sacralized relationships and conferred holiness on other people. When the vassals stood before their prince in the prescribed posture—with bodies bent, sashes hanging to the ground, their chins stretched out, like gargoyles on the eaves of a house, and their hands "clasped together, and as low as possible," their respectful attitude maintained and increased the prince's virtue.[63]

But the prince's own life was also minutely regulated. The potency of his office did not give him carte blanche to do as he pleased. In fact—another principle that would later inspire the philosophers of the Axial Age—his behavior should be characterized by *wu wei* ("doing nothing"). He was not like a modern head of state, who must formulate policies and objectives that express his vision for the country. The prince had to be entirely passive. He did not direct the administration; he gave no orders. His sole task was to concentrate the potency within himself and delegate it to the officers who acted on his behalf. To achieve this, he had to obey strict rules. If he made a mistake, it was the duty of his vassals to call him to order. An annalist noted down his every word and gesture. He was not allowed to play games or to joke; he could only listen to carefully selected music, and eat prescribed meals, prepared according to the ritual code.[64] His vassals must move energetically in his presence, showing that they were activated by the power that emanated from him. They must walk quickly "with their elbows spread out like the wings of a bird," whereas the prince had to walk with exactly measured steps or remain "immobile, inactive, and almost dumb."[65] In council, the prince made no eloquent speeches. If his ministers asked permission to undertake a certain course of action, he could reply only with a simple "Yes," but once that command had been given, the new policy had already come into effect: as the ancient song had expressed it, "when he thinks of horses, they break into a gallop." The ritualists of Lu claimed that Shun, the ancient sage king, had concentrated the potency so perfectly within himself that he did nothing at all, except stand in the correct position. His *daode* was so great that it sufficed by itself to guide and transform his subjects. He "ruled by inactivity [*wu wei*]. . . . For what action did he take? He merely placed himself gravely and reverently with his face due south; that was all."[66]

The rites were designed to enhance the status and prestige of the *junzi,* the "gentleman." But if performed in the right spirit, they also took the egotism out of government. There was a paradox here, which was also evident in the *li* of the battlefield. During the seventh century, the principalities began to wage a form of courtly warfare that was strictly regulated by the new spirit of moderation.[67] The rituals strictly limited the violence permitted in battle, and forbade warriors to take advantage of the enemy's weakness. Warfare became an elaborate pageant, governed by courtesy and restraint. In an aristocratic society where the noble families were obsessed with their honor, vendetta was a constant danger. The *li* attempted to restrain this tendency and ensure that warriors fought like gentlemen. Wars were usually quite short. They could not be waged for personal gain, but only to repel barbarian invasion or bring a rebellious city to heel, thus restoring the Way of Heaven. Warfare was regarded as a penal exercise; convicted criminals were pardoned on condition that they vowed, if necessary, to sacrifice themselves on the battlefield. Victory revealed the righteousness of the winning side, but only if the battle had been conducted according to the *li*.

The prince accompanied his troops, but, of course, the minis-

ter of war made all the decisions. To determine the manpower and
weaponry at his disposal, he began by taking a census, which was
itself an act of defiance and had immediately to be balanced by an
act of generosity. "When the great census had been taken," explained the author of the *Zuozhuan,* a commentary on the *Spring
and Autumn Annals,* "debtors were set free, alms were given to the
poor and widows, the guilty were pardoned."[68] Next the army assembled in the temple of the ancestors, and weapons were distributed. As they were thought to exude a malign influence, they were
usually kept under lock and key, and warriors had to fast before
they took them in their hands.[69] Finally the men gathered around
the Earth altar, while the prince performed a sacrifice.

The army set off, marching, as far as possible, with their faces
in a southerly direction. The infantry consisted of conscripted
peasants, who had been dragged away from their fields without
hope of return; reluctant soldiers, they lamented so loudly and
continuously that they were gagged during the march. Their role,
however, was strictly peripheral. They did not take part in the
fighting, but were simply carriers, valets, and servants, marching
separately from the main army and camping on the edges of the
forest.[70] The noblemen, in contrast, were calm and cheerful, riding
in their chariots to the accompaniment of lutes; each chariot team
consisted of an archer, a lancer, and a driver, their weapons
brightly painted and beribboned. The horses were draped in furs
and skins, and the bells on their harnesses were supposed to ring
in time with the music.[71]

When they pitched camp, facing the enemy, the layout of the
encampment exactly replicated that of the city. Warfare was a religious rite; it began with a spiritual retreat, and prayers and sacrifices were offered to the ancestors. At this time, the war minister
had to gauge the enemy's intentions: Did they really intend to
fight?[72] If the enemy was a barbarian tribe or a prince who had
lost the Way, it would be a battle to the death: in these very exceptional circumstances, the war minister marched toward the
enemy lines at the head of the pardoned criminals, a suicide
squad, who, with a bloodcurdling cry, cut their own throats in
unison at the first encounter, and battle was joined. Usually, how-

ever, warriors were required to fight politely, and the battle became a courtesy contest. On both sides, the *junzi* vied with one
another to perform ever more outrageous acts of generosity and
noblesse oblige.

The *li* demanded an external attitude of "yielding" (*rang*) to
the enemy, but they were generally performed in a spirit of pride
and bravado. In this chivalric game, the sport was to bully the
enemy with acts of kindness. Before battle was joined, warriors
boasted loudly of their prowess, and sent pots of wine over to the
enemy, removing their helmets whenever they caught sight of
their prince. If its driver paid a ransom on the spot, a true *junzi*
would always let an enemy chariot escape. During a battle between Chu and Jin, a Chu archer used his last arrow to shoot a
stag that was blocking the path of his chariot, and his lancer immediately presented it to the team in the Jin chariot bearing
down upon them. The Jin at once conceded defeat, crying in admiration: "Here is a worthy archer and well-spoken warrior!
These are gentlemen!"[73]

A nobleman lost status if he killed too many people. A prince
once rebuked a warrior who was boasting that he had slain six
enemy soldiers: "You will bring great dishonour on your country.
Tomorrow you will die—victim of your proficiency!"[74] After a
victory, it was essential that a *junzi* not get carried away. A truly
noble warrior was never supposed to kill more than three fugi-
tives and, ideally, was supposed to shoot with his eyes shut. Courtesy should always take precedence over efficiency. On one
occasion, when two chariots were locked in combat, one of them
turned aside and seemed about to retreat. The archer in the winning chariot shot, missed, and was about to take aim again, when
the enemy archer cried: "You must let me exchange my arrow for
yours, or it will be an evil deed!" So without more ado, the first
archer took the arrow from his bow and calmly waited for death.[75]
The battle was a clash of competing honors, and the clash of arms
was secondary.

In 638, the duke of the principality of Song was waiting for
the arrival of the Chu army, which greatly outnumbered his own.
When they heard that the Chu were crossing a nearby river, the

duke's vassals urged him to attack at once, but he refused. He also rejected the suggestion that he should attack the Chu while they were drawing up their battle lines. When finally the fighting began, Song was defeated and the duke badly wounded, but he was unrepentant. "A *junzi* worthy of the name does not seek to overcome the enemy in misfortune," he said. "He does not beat his drum before the ranks are formed."[76] A few years later, the large state of Jin was preparing for war with Qin, one of the peripheral states in the Wei Valley. The Qin sent a messenger to the Jin, telling them to be ready to fight at dawn, but the Jin commander noticed that the messenger looked very nervous. Some of his officers were jubilant: Qin was afraid! They should herd them toward the river immediately! But the commander quoted from the battle code: "It is inhuman not to gather up the dead or wounded. It is cowardly not to wait for the time arranged or to press the enemy in a dangerous passage!"[77]

There must be no unseemly gloating in victory. One victorious prince refused to build a monument to commemorate his triumph: "I was the cause that two countries exposed the bones of their warriors to the sun! It is cruel!" he cried. This was not like the battles that the first Zhou kings had fought against evildoers. "There are no guilty here," the prince concluded, "only vassals who have been faithful to the end."[78] A *junzi* was quick to pardon and show mercy, because it added to his prestige. Most ministers refused to make hard terms, for fear of future reprisals. Many liked a qualified victory better than an out-and-out success, and some even preferred temporary defeat with minimum casualties. Victory could be dangerous. A prince would have to give conquered territory to a vassal, who, with these extra resources, might then be tempted to rebel against his rule. The feudal system depended upon everybody keeping his place. If a vassal became too powerful, he could endanger the delicate equilibrium of the state.

In court life too, each *junzi* must keep to the role assigned to him and thus contribute to the beauty and elegance of the palace.[79] A gentleman should always be perfectly dressed; his manner must be "grave, majestic, imposing, and distinguished,"[80] and his expression "sweet and calm, the forms and dispositions conformable to the rules."[81] Instead of expressing his individuality, the vassal surrendered his entire being to the chivalric archetype. This "yielding" must be wholehearted. The first duty of a *junzi* was *cheng:* "sincerity." He could not conform to the *li* in a shallow, grudging, or hypocritical manner; his goal was to give himself up so thoroughly to the rules of etiquette that they became integral to his personality. By wholly identifying with the paradigmatic *junzi,* he would become a fully humane person. His personality would be perfected by this artifice, in the same way as a block of untreated jade was transformed by an artist into a beautiful ritual vessel. Court life was thus an education in true humanity. "The *li* teach us," the ritualists of Lu explained, "to give free rein to one's feelings, to let them follow their bent is the Way of barbarians. The Way of *li* is quite different. The ceremonial fixes degrees and limits."[82] If the rites became an authentic part of his being, the gentleman learned moderation, self-control, and generosity, because the *li* were designed to hold violence and hubris in check: "Rites obviate disorders, as dykes obviate floods."[83]

The archery contest revealed a *junzi*'s quality. This was not simply a test of skill and military efficiency, but a musical ceremony designed to promote peace and concord. Any barbarian could hit the target, but the *junzi* was aiming for nobility. He did not really want to win, because it was more honorable to lose. He had to *pretend* that he wanted to win, but that in itself was an act of humility, since naked ambition was vulgar, the sign of an inferior person. The presentation of the cup to the losing contestant was, therefore, really an act of homage. Before he picked up his bow, each competitor must have a sincere (*cheng*) attitude of mind, as well as an upright (*che*) bodily posture, or he would besmirch the power of his prince.[84] They both had to shoot their arrows at exactly the same moment, in time with the music. As it flew, whirring, from the bow, each arrow must sing out the correct note. Instead of hitting the target, the arrows were supposed to meet in midair: violence and confrontation had been deflected into concord and harmony. At the end of the contest, both archers wept: the winner out of pity for the defeated competitor, and the vanquished out of compassion for the victor, who, of course, was the real loser. The two warriors would kneel and promise to live henceforth as father and son.

The *li* were designed to check the aggressive chauvinism that could so easily inspire a vendetta. The spirit of "yielding" was also supposed to characterize political life.[85] Instead of vehemently expressing their own opinions and jockeying for position, counselors of the prince ceremonially deferred to him and to one another. Because they all derived whatever insight they had from the prince's power, serious conflict was a contradiction in terms. Even if he disagreed with a policy, once the prince had said yes, a vassal must carry it out to the best of his ability. Rejecting the decision would cut him off from the group, because it amounted to a denial of the power that animated the entire court. If he was convinced that the prince was departing from the Way of Heaven, the counselor had a duty to correct him. But he must not do this in a spirit of righteous indignation. Once he had registered his protest, the vassal must resign his office and leave the country—an act that involved the loss of his very self, because he broke with the *daode* of the court. For three months, he must remain in exile, putting pressure on the prince by this act of ritual suicide in the hope that he would return to the Way.

Family life was regulated by the same spirit. The relationship of father and son was based not on natural affection but on the bond between the prince and his vassal.[86] Chinese ritual always attempted to refine and improve upon the biological, and the *li* created the filial link between a father and his son, which did not exist at the son's birth. For the first thirty years of his life, a son scarcely saw his father. As a small child, he lived in the women's quarters and then went to study the *li* in the house of his maternal uncle. Only when his education was complete could he begin to perform the acts of service that affiliated him to his father and created the sacred link between them. Respect and reverence were far more important than affection or intimacy. Like a prince, a father was the representative of Heaven; the bond between the two was supposed to be remote and stern. It would be as inappropriate for him to be on familiar, friendly terms with his sons as for a prince to fool around with his vassals.

The son revered his father as a future ancestor. His meticulous performance of the rites of filial piety created within his parent the holiness that would make him a heavenly being after death. The rites nourished the *shen,* the divine, numinous quality that made each human being unique. If the *shen* was strong, this sacred individuality would survive the death of the body. By treating his father with absolute reverence, therefore, the eldest son empowered him to fulfill his humanity. Each morning, he rose at dawn, dressed carefully in full ceremonial costume, and waited upon his parents, together with his wife. He could not belch, sneeze, cough, or yawn in his father's presence. He never trod the same staircase as his father, never used his father's bowl, staff, or cup. He mended and washed his parents' clothes, prepared the eight ritually prescribed dishes, and waited on his parents while they ate, respectfully urging them to make a hearty meal. A son always addressed his father in a low, humble voice. If he believed that he was losing the Way, he should reprove him, but must express his views gently and pleasantly, with a modest expression. If his father persisted in wrongdoing, the son's behavior must be even more courteous, and he must never express anger or resentment. At seventy years old, the father retired from public life. In this last phase, the son's duty was to empathize with his every mood; he must be happy when his father was well, sad when he was ill, eat when his father had a good appetite, and fast when the old man was ailing.[87] He thus learned the empathic virtue of *shu* ("likening to oneself"), which would become central to the Chinese Axial Age.

When his father passed away, the son shared the experience of death insofar as he could. He withdrew from the family home, lived in a hut, slept on the ground with a clod of earth for a pillow, kept silence, fasted, and so weakened himself that he could rise only with the help of a staff. For three years, the son officiated at the rites of mourning that transformed the father's ghost into *shen,* while the deceased gradually made his way toward those forefathers who had also earned personal survival. At the end of the mourning period, his father's apotheosis was complete, and the son then presided over his cult. For ten days, he prepared for the *bin* ("hosting") ritual by making a spiritual retreat, during which he fasted and thought only about the way his father had behaved, smiled, and talked. At the *bin* ceremony, his own son played the part of the newly deceased and during the ritual felt that his grandfather's spirit was alive in him. When the bereaved son finally saw his "father" arriving at the banquet, he bowed low and escorted him to his place at the table, knowing that his task was done. He had, as the *Record of Rites* observed, communed with the "refulgent *shen* of his ancestor" and gained "a perfect enlightenment."[88]

Even after his father's death, the son did not own his life, but devoted all his talents to cultivating his father's honor, just as he promoted the power of his prince on the battlefield. He had a duty to take care of his health, because his body was the property of the family. He must not take unnecessary risks, but must "preserve his nature intact," keeping himself alive and well for as long as possible—an attitude that would also surface in a new form during the Chinese Axial Age. In many ways, the cult of filial piety is abhorrent to the modern sensibility, because it seems to reduce the son to a mere cipher. But in fact the Chinese family was organized to prevent paternal tyranny. The authority of the father was qualified by other figures. The rights of the eldest uncle were equal to and even could supersede those of a father. The son became a parent himself, and received homage from his children at the same time as he was serving his father. At the *bin* ceremony, when he greeted the *shen* of his "father," he was actually bowing before his *own* son. There was, therefore, an interchange of reverence. The chief duty of a younger son was not to serve his father but to revere and support his older brother. Many siblings would have older *and* younger brothers. The system was so designed that each family member received a measure of absolute respect. While the *li* required a son to submit to his father, the father was also obliged to behave fairly, kindly, and courteously to his children. We have no idea how thoroughly the Chinese followed these *li* in practice. The *Record of Rites* may have been a utopian rather than a historical reality. Nevertheless, by the seventh century the ideal does seem to have transformed Zhou China from a society addicted to rough extravagance into one that prized moderation and self-control.[89]

The ideal would set the Chinese Axial Age in motion, and give it unique direction.

At this point, even the less traditional states on the periphery of the great plain—Qi, Jin, Chu, and Qin—accepted the ritual imperative. But times were changing. During the second half of the seventh century, the barbarian tribes of the north began to invade the Chinese states more assiduously than ever before. The new southern state of Chu was also becoming a serious problem. Eager to expand, Chu increasingly ignored the rules of courtly warfare and threatened the principalities. The Zhou king was too weak to provide effective leadership against Chu, so in 679 Prince Huan of Qi called himself the "first noble" (*pa*) of China and founded a league of defense.[90]

At this point, Qi was the most powerful Chinese state and Prince Huan was an enlightened ruler, with Zhou connections. He organized conferences to discuss principles of cooperation between the states; the states and principalities that joined his league bound themselves by an oath, and this gave the political arrangement a religious character. An ox was sacrificed, delegates moistened their lips with the victim's blood, and everybody present repeated the words of the pact, calling upon the local gods, mountains, rivers, and ancestors:

> We all, who swear this treaty together, we will not gather up the harvests, we will not monopolise profits, we will not protect the guilty or harbour troublemakers; we will help those who are victims of calamity or disaster. We will have compassion on those in misfortune or trouble. We will have the same friends and the same enemies. We will help the royal house.[91]

The purpose was to create solidarity. These rites of alliance created family ties between the princes of the different states, who even promised to observe the funeral rites of their new "kin." Anyone who betrayed the league risked fearful penalties, which were endorsed by the gods and ancestors: "He shall lose his people, his appointment shall fail, his family perish, and his state and clan will be

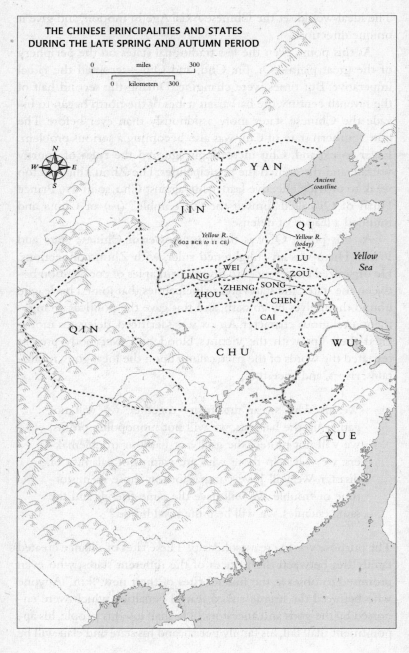

THE CHINESE PRINCIPALITIES AND STATES DURING THE LATE SPRING AND AUTUMN PERIOD

0   miles   300

0   kilometers   300

N W E S

YAN

JIN

Ancient coastline

QI

Yellow R. (602 BCE to 11 CE)

Yellow R. (today)

LU

WEI

ZOU

LIANG

SONG

ZHENG

CHEN

ZHOU

CAI

QIN

CHU

WU

Yellow Sea

YUE

utterly overthrown."[92] The first noble collected tribute from the member states and supervised common defense; even though he still recognized the sovereignty of the Zhou monarchy, he had in fact replaced the king. This league did not survive, however. After King Huan's death in 643, his sons fought for succession, and Qi never fully recovered from this civil war. Chu resumed its aggression and the prince of Jin organized a new confederation, but in 597 Chu defeated the league.

It seemed as though brute force had triumphed over moderation. But in the face of the growing menace of Chu, the old principalities clung even more closely to their rituals and customs. They could not compete with the military power of the new states, so they turned to diplomacy and persuasion. But the larger peripheral states were beginning to turn away from the ideals of concord and "yielding." People had noticed that even though the states had bound themselves to the league with the most ferocious oaths, the spirits failed to punish defectors; indeed, states that remained true to the covenant suffered most.[93] A growing skepticism was beginning to undermine old assumptions.

In Israel, the seventh century was a watershed that saw the beginnings of the religion of Judaism. Hezekiah had left a grim legacy. Determined not to repeat his father's mistakes, his son Manasseh (687–642) remained a loyal vassal of Assyria, and Judah prospered during his long reign.[94] The Assyrians did not expect their allies to worship Asshur, their national god, but inevitably, some of their religious symbols became highly visible. Manasseh was not interested in the worship of Yahweh alone. He rebuilt the rural shrines that Hezekiah had destroyed, set up altars to Baal, brought an effigy of Asherah into the Jerusalem temple, set up statues of the divine horses of the sun at the entrance of the temple, and instituted child sacrifice outside Jerusalem.[95] The biblical historian was appalled by these developments, but few of Manasseh's subjects would have found them very surprising, since, as archaeologists have discovered, many had similar icons in their own homes.[96]

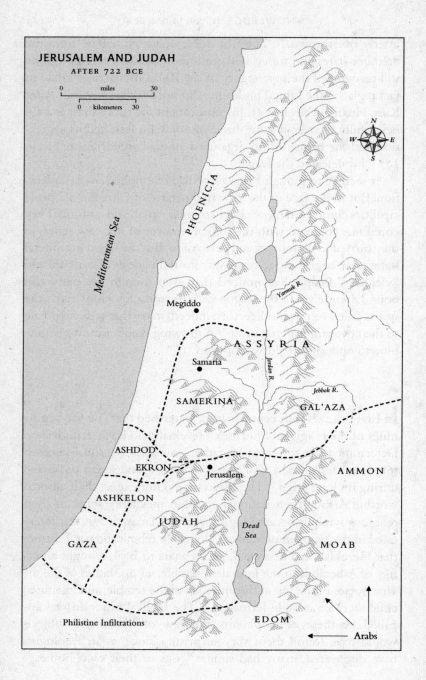

JERUSALEM AND JUDAH
AFTER 722 BCE

0 miles 30
0 kilometers 30

Mediterranean Sea

PHOENICIA

Megiddo

Yarmuk R.

ASSYRIA

Samaria

Jordan R.

SAMERINA

Jebbok R.

GAL'AZA

ASHDOD

EKRON

Jerusalem

AMMON

ASHKELON

JUDAH

Dead Sea

GAZA

MOAB

EDOM

Philistine Infiltrations

Arabs

Nevertheless, there was widespread unrest in the rural districts, which had been devastated during the Assyrian invasions.[97] Even though Hezekiah's nationalist policies had been so disastrous, some may have harbored dreams of a golden age when their fore-fathers had lived peacefully in their land, without the constant threat of enemy invasion and domination by foreign powers. This smoldering discontent erupted after the death of Manasseh. His son Amon reigned for only two years before he was assassinated in a palace uprising led by the rural aristocracy, whom the Bible calls *am ha-aretz* ("the people of the land").[98]

The leaders of the coup put Amon's eight-year-old son, Josiah, on the throne; because his mother came from Bozkath, a small vil-lage in the Judean foothills, he was one of their own.[99] Power had shifted away from the urban elites to the leaders of the country-side, and at first everything seemed to be going their way. By this time, Assyria was in decline and Egypt was in the ascendancy. In 656 Pharaoh Psammetichus I, founder of the Twenty-sixth Dy-nasty, forced the Assyrian troops to withdraw from the Levant. With astonishment and joy, the Judahites watched the Assyrians vacating the territories of the old northern kingdom of Israel. True, Josiah had now become the vassal of Egypt, but Pharaoh was too busy taking control of the lucrative trade routes in the Canaanite lowlands to bother about Judah, which—for the time being—was left to its own devices.

When Josiah was about sixteen years old, he had some kind of religious conversion, which probably meant that he wanted to worship Yahweh exclusively.[100] This principled devotion to the national god could also have been a declaration of political inde-pendence. In 622, some ten years later, Josiah began extensive building work on Solomon's temple, the great memorial of Judah's golden age. During the construction, the high priest Hilkiah made a momentous discovery, and hurried to Shaphan, the royal scribe, with this exciting news: "I have found the book of the law [*sefer torah*] in the temple of Yahweh."[101] This, he said, was the authentic Law, which Yahweh had given to Moses on Mount Sinai. At once Shaphan took the scroll to the king and read it aloud in his presence.

Most scholars believe that the scroll contained an early version of the book of Deuteronomy, which describes Moses gathering the people together on Mount Nebo in Transjordan shortly before his death, and delivering a "second law" (Greek: *deuteronomion*). But instead of being an ancient work, as Shaphan and Hilkiah claimed, it was almost certainly an entirely new scripture. Until the eighth century there had been very little reading or writing of religious texts in either Israel or Judah. There was no early tradition that Yahweh's teachings had been written down. In J and E, Moses had passed on Yahweh's commands by word of mouth, and the people had responded verbally: "All that Yahweh has *spoken* we will do."[102] J and E did not mention the Ten Commandments; originally the stone tablets—"written with the finger of God"[103]—probably contained the divinely revealed plans for the tabernacle where Yahweh had dwelt with his people during the years in the wilderness.[104] It was only later that the Deuteronomist writers added to the JE narrative, explaining that Moses "wrote down all the words of Yahweh" and "took the scroll of the covenant [*sefer torah*] and read it in the hearing of the people."[105] Now Shaphan claimed that this was the very scroll that Hilkiah had discovered in the temple. For centuries this precious document had been lost, and its teachings had never been implemented. Now that the *sefer torah* had been discovered, Yahweh's people could make a new start.

This was not a cynical forgery, however. At this time, it was customary for people who wished to impart a new religious teaching to attribute their words to a great figure in the past. The Deuteronomists believed that they were speaking for Moses at a time of grave national crisis. The world had changed drastically since the time of the exodus, and the religion of Yahweh was in danger. In 722, the northern kingdom of Israel had been destroyed, and thousands of its citizens had disappeared without trace. The kingdom of Judah had narrowly escaped extermination in the days of King Hezekiah. Only Yahweh—not the gods whose cult Manasseh had revived—could save his people. Many of the prophets had urged the people to worship Yahweh alone, and now at last Judah had a king who could revive the glories of the past.

This was what Moses would say to Josiah and his people, if he were delivering a "second law" today.

As soon as he had heard the words on the scroll, Josiah tore his garments in great distress. "Great indeed must be the anger of Yahweh blazing out against us," he cried, "because our ancestors did not obey what this book says by practising everything written within it."[106] The switch from the oral transmission of religion to a written text was a shock. Here—as elsewhere in the Bible—it evoked a sense of dismay, guilt, and inadequacy.[107] Religious truth sounded completely different when presented in this way. Everything was clear, cut-and-dried—very different from the more elusive "knowledge" imparted by oral transmission. In India, people did not believe that it was possible to convey a spiritual teaching in writing: you could not, for example, understand the full meaning of the Upanishads simply by perusing the texts. But the Deuteronomists made Yahwism a religion of the book. Henceforth in the West, the benchmark of religious orthodoxy would be a written scripture.

Josiah immediately consulted the prophetess Huldah, for whom the *sefer torah* meant one thing and one thing only. She received an oracle from Yahweh: "I am bringing disaster on this place and those who live in it, carrying out everything said in the book the king of Judah has read, because they have deserted me and sacrificed to other gods."[108] Reform was clearly essential, and Josiah summoned the whole people to listen to the clear directives of the scroll:

> In their hearing, he read out everything that was said in the book of the covenant found in the Temple of Yahweh. The king stood by the pillar and made a covenant before Yahweh, to follow Yahweh, keeping his commandments, his decrees and his statutes, with all his heart and soul, to perform the words of the covenant as written in that book. All the people gave their allegiance to the covenant.[109]

Josiah at once inaugurated a program that followed Yahweh's *torah* by the book.

First he eradicated the cultic traditions that his grandfather Manasseh had reintroduced, burning the effigies of Baal and Asherah, abolishing the rural shrines, pulling down the house of sacred male prostitutes in the temple, the furnace where Israelites had sacrificed their children to Moloch, and the effigies of the Assyrian horses of the sun. It reads like an orgy of destruction. When he turned to the old territories of the kingdom of Israel, however, Josiah was even more merciless. There he not only demolished the ancient temples of Yahweh in Bethel and Samaria, but slaughtered the priests of the rural shrines and contaminated their altars.[110]

The *sefer torah* revealed that for centuries the kings of Israel and Judah had condoned practices that Yahweh had expressly forbidden from the very beginning. It showed that Yahweh had sternly demanded exclusive allegiance: "Listen, Israel," Moses had told the people on Mount Nebo, "Yahweh is our *elohim,* Yahweh alone!" They must love him with all their heart and soul.[111] The love of Yahweh meant that Israelites must not "worship other gods, gods of the peoples around you."[112] Moses had insisted that when the people entered the Promised Land, they must have no dealings with the native inhabitants of Canaan. They must make no treaties with them, show them no pity, and wipe out their religion: "Deal with them like this: tear down their altars, smash their standing-stones, cut down their sacred poles, and set fire to their idols."[113] In his reform, Josiah had obeyed the clear instructions of Yahweh—to the letter.

The Deuteronomists claimed to be conservatives, who were returning to the original faith of Israel. In fact they were radically innovative. They outlawed symbols such as the sacred pole (*asherah*) and the "standing stones" (*masseboth*) that had always been perfectly acceptable.[114] In their law code, they introduced some startling new legislation.[115] First, the worship of Israel was stringently centralized: sacrifice could be offered only in one shrine, the place where "Yahweh had set his name."[116] Jerusalem was not mentioned explicitly, but by the seventh century it was the only temple capable of fulfilling this role. This meant that the other temples and the rural shrines, where the people had worshiped Yahweh for centuries, must be destroyed. Second, the

Deuteronomists condoned the secular slaughter of animals.[117] In the ancient world, it was generally permissible to eat only meat that had been sacrificed ceremonially in a sacred area. But now that the local temples had been abolished, people who lived too far away from Jerusalem were allowed to slaughter an animal in their hometown, provided that they did not eat its blood, which contained the life force, but poured it reverently on the ground.

The Deuteronomists had created a secular sphere, with its own rules and integrity, functioning alongside the cult.[118] The same principle applied to the Deuteronomists' judicial reform. Traditionally, justice had been administered by tribal elders in the local shrines, but now the Deuteronomists appointed state judges in every city, with a supreme court in Jerusalem for problematic cases.[119] Finally, the Deuteronomists stripped the king of his traditional powers.[120] He was no longer a sacred figure. In an astonishing departure from Near Eastern custom, the Deuteronomists drastically limited the sovereign's prerogatives. His only duty was to read the written *torah,* "diligently observing all the words of this law and these statutes, neither exalting himself above other members of the community nor turning aside from the commandments, either to the right or the left, so that he and his descendants may reign long over his kingdom in Israel."[121] The king was no longer the son of God, the special servant of Yahweh, or a member of the divine council. He had no special privileges but, like his people, was subject to the law. How could the Deuteronomists justify these changes, which overturned centuries of sacred tradition? We do not know exactly who the Deuteronomists were. The story of the discovery of the scroll suggests that they included priests, prophets, and scribes. Their movement could have originated in the northern kingdom and come south to Judah after the destruction of the kingdom of Israel in 722. They may also reflect the views of the disenfranchised *am ha-aretz,* who had put Josiah on the throne.

Josiah was crucial to the Deuteronomists. They revered him as a new Moses and believed that he was a greater king than David.[122] Besides reforming the law, the Deuteronomists also rewrote the history of Israel, which, they believed, had culminated in the reign of Josiah. First, they edited the earlier J and E narratives, adapting them to seventh-century conditions.[123] They made no additions to the stories about the patriarchs Abraham, Isaac, and Jacob, who did not interest them, but concentrated on Moses—who had liberated his people from slavery in Egypt—at a time when Josiah was hoping to become independent of the pharaoh. Next, they extended the chronicle of the exodus to include the book of Joshua and the story of his conquest of the northern highlands. The Deuteronomist historians saw the time of Joshua as a golden age, when the people were truly devoted to Yahweh,[124] and were convinced that Israel was about to embark on another glorious era. Like Moses, Josiah would shake off the yoke of Pharaoh; like Joshua, he would conquer the territories vacated by Assyria, and restore the true faith of Yahweh. Finally, in the books of Samuel and Kings, the Deuteronomists wrote a history of the kingdoms of Israel and Judah, which strongly condemned the northern kingdom and argued that the Davidic kings of Judah were the rightful rulers of the whole of Israel. The Deuteronomic corpus thus gave powerful endorsement to Josiah's religious and political programs.

But this was not cheap propaganda. The Deuteronomists were learned men and their achievement was remarkable. They drew on earlier materials—old royal archives, law codes, sagas, and liturgical texts—to create an entirely new vision, making the ancient traditions speak to the new circumstances of Israel under Josiah. In some ways, Deuteronomy reads like a modern document. Its vision of a secular sphere, an independent judiciary, a constitutional monarchy, and a centralized state look forward to our own day. The Deuteronomists also developed a much more rational theology, discounting much ancient myth.[125] God did not come down from heaven to speak to Moses on Mount Sinai; you could not actually see God, as some of the Israelites believed, nor could you manipulate him by offering sacrifice. God certainly did not live in the temple: the authors put a long prayer on the lips of Solomon after his dedication of the temple, which made it clear that the shrine was simply a house of prayer, not a link between heaven and earth. "Can God really live with man on earth?" Solomon asked incredulously. "Why the heavens and their own heaven cannot contain you—how much less this house that I have built!"[126] Israel did not own its land because Yahweh had chosen to dwell on Mount Zion, as the old mythology had claimed, but because the people observed Yahweh's statutes and worshiped him exclusively.

It was also essential that the Israelites behave with justice and kindness to one another. They would possess the land and succeed in their enterprises only if they gave a portion of their income to orphans and widows, or set aside for the poor some of their grapes, olives, or wheat in the fields after the harvest. They must remember that they had been oppressed in Egypt and imitate the generosity of Yahweh himself.[127] "You are not to toughen your hearts; you are not to shut your hand to your brother, the needy one," Moses told the people. "Rather you are to open—yes, open your hand to him."[128] Israelites must secure the inheritance of wives abandoned by their husbands, secure the rights of the resident alien (*ger*), and free their slaves after six years of service.[129] The Deuteronomists' passionate insistence upon the importance of justice, equity, and compassion went even further than the teaching of Amos and Hosea.

If their reform had been fully implemented, the Deuteronomists would have completely altered the political, social, religious, and judicial life of Israel. This is an important point. The Deuteronomist lawyers and historians had given a wholly new centrality to the written text. Today people often use scripture to oppose change and to conserve the past. But the Deuteronomists, who pioneered the idea of scriptural orthodoxy, used the texts they had inherited in order to introduce fundamental changes. They rewrote the old laws of the ninth-century Covenant Code, inserting phrases and altering words to make it endorse their novel legislation about secular slaughter, a central sanctuary, and the religious calendar.[130] Instead of allowing the old laws, oral sagas, or cultic customs to impede or confine their reform, they used these traditions creatively. The sacred lore of the past was not cast in stone; the Deuteronomists saw it as a resource that could shed light on their current situation.

The Deuteronomists made Judaism a religion of the book. But

it seems that there was considerable opposition to this development. Literacy changed the people's relationship with their her-
itage, and not always for the better. In India, for example, oral
transmission required a long apprenticeship, dynamic interchange
with a charismatic teacher, and a disciplined, self-effacing lifestyle.
But solitary reading encouraged a more individual and independent education. The pupil was no longer reliant on his guru, but
could peruse the texts by himself and draw his own conclusions,
and his knowledge might be shallower, because he might see no
need to look beneath the words on the page or experience the luminous silence that took him beyond its words and concepts.

The prophet Jeremiah began his ministry at about the same
time as Hilkiah discovered the scroll. He linked his own calling
with the finding of the *sefer torah,* and even though he was not
himself a scribe, his disciple Baruch committed his oracles to writing. Jeremiah greatly admired Josiah and probably had connections with Hilkiah and Shaphan. At several points, the book of
Jeremiah shared the style and vision of the book of Deuteronomy.[131] And yet he had reservations about the written *torah:* "How
dare you say: 'We are wise, and we possess the law of Yahweh'?" he
asked his opponents. "See how it has been falsified by the lying
pen of the scribes!" The written text could subvert orthodoxy by
a mere sleight of the pen, and distort tradition by imparting information rather than wisdom. The scribes, Jeremiah concluded,
would be dismayed and confounded. They had "rejected the word
[*davar*] of Yahweh, so what is their wisdom?"[132] In biblical Hebrew, *davar* was the spoken oracle of God, uttered by the prophets,
and "wisdom" (*mishpat*) referred to the oral tradition of the community. Already at this early stage, there was concern about the
spiritual value of a written scripture.

In a study of modern Jewish movements, the eminent scholar
Haym Soloveitchik argues that the shift from oral tradition to
written texts can lead to religious stridency, giving a student misplaced clarity and certainty about matters that are essentially elusive and ineffable.[133] The Deuteronomists were bold and creative
thinkers but their theology was often strident. "You must destroy
completely all the places where the nations you dispossess have

served their gods," Moses instructed the people. "You must tear
down their altars; smash their pillars, cut down their sacred poles,
set fire to the carved images of their gods, and wipe out their
name from that place."[134] Yahweh may have instructed Israelites to
be kind to one another, but they must have no mercy on foreigners. The Deuteronomist historian described, with apparent approval, Joshua's massacre of the inhabitants of Ai:

> When Israel had finished killing all the inhabitants of Ai
> in the open ground and where they followed them into
> the wilderness, and when all to a man had fallen by the
> edge of the sword, all Israel returned to Ai and slaugh-
> tered all its people. The number of those who fell that
> day, men and women together, was twelve thousand, all
> people of Ai.[135]

Too much certainty and clarity could lead to cruel intolerance.

The Deuteronomist probably ended his history with a description of the first Passover ever held in the Jerusalem temple.
After Joshua had destroyed the temples of Samaria and killed their
priests, he summoned the whole people to celebrate Pesach, "as
prescribed in this scroll of the covenant." This was another of the
Deuteronomists' innovations. Hitherto Passover had been a private, family festival, held in the home; now it became a national
convention.[136] At last, the historian suggests, the people were celebrating Pesach in the way that Yahweh intended.

> No Passover like this one had ever been celebrated since
> the days when the judges ruled Israel or throughout the
> entire period of the kings of Israel and the kings of
> Judah. The eighteenth year of King Josiah was the only
> time when such a Passover was celebrated in honour of
> Yahweh in Jerusalem.[137]

It was the beginning of a new political and religious era. The little
kingdom of Judah was about to pass over to a new golden age.

But Josiah's great experiment ended in tears. The map of the

Middle East was changing. The Assyrian empire was in the final stages of its decline and Babylon was in the ascendant. In 610 Pharaoh Psammetichus died, and was succeeded by Necho III, who the following year marched through Palestine to come to the aid of the beleaguered Assyrian king. Josiah intercepted the Egyptian army at Megiddo, and was killed at the first encounter.[138] None of the reforms survived his death. The dream of political independence had been shattered, and Judah was now a bit player in the struggle between Egypt and the new Babylonian empire, which threatened its very survival.

5

SUFFERING

(c. 600 to 530 BCE)

During the sixth century, Israel embarked fully upon its Axial Age, and yet again, the catalyst of change was the experience of unbridled, shocking violence. Shortly after Josiah's untimely death, Nebuchadnezzar, king of Babylon, became the undisputed master of the region, and for the next twenty years, the Neo-Babylonian empire contended with Egypt for the control of Canaan. The kings of Judah veered uneasily between the two powers, opting now for one, then relying on the protection of the other. But it proved dangerous to oppose Babylon. Each time Judah rebelled against Babylonian rule, Nebuchadnezzar descended on the little kingdom with his powerful army and subjugated the region, in three brutal military campaigns. In 597, the young King Jehoiachin of Judah submitted to Babylon and was deported with eight thousand exiles; they included members of the royal family, the aristocracy, the military, and the skilled artisans: "all of them men capable of bearing arms, [they] were led into exile in Babylon."[1] It was this first group of deportees who created the new Axial Age vision.

Nebuchadnezzar had torn the heart out of the Judean state, but it struggled on for another ten years, with Zedekiah, a Babylonian appointee, on the throne. When Zedekiah rebelled in 587, Nebuchadnezzar showed no mercy. His army fell upon Jerusalem, destroyed its temple, and razed the city to the ground. Zedekiah was forced to watch the slaughter of his sons before his eyes were torn out, and he too was carried off to Babylon, with five thousand more deportees, leaving only the poorer people and those who had defected to Babylon in the devastated land. Judah was incorporated into the administrative structure of the empire, and in 581, a third group was taken into exile.[2]

This was a period of intense suffering. Recently some scholars have argued that the Babylonian exile was not really very traumatic: about 75 percent of the population remained behind, and life continued as before. The deportees were well cared for in Babylonia. They settled down and made lives for themselves as rent collectors, business agents, and managers of canals. Some even owned fiefs of land.[3] But recent archaeological investigations have revealed the fury of the Babylonian attack on Jerusalem, Judah, and the entire Levant, which was far more destructive than the Assyrian onslaught. The country entered a dark age, one of the most miserable periods of its history.[4] Jerusalem and its temple remained a desolate ruin. The book of Lamentations described its empty squares, crumbling walls, and damaged gates; the crowded, prosperous city was now the abode of jackals. People clawed at garbage dumps for food, mothers killed and boiled their babies, and handsome young men roamed the ruined streets with blackened faces and skeletal bodies.[5] The people of Israel had looked into a terrifying void, but having lost everything, some were able to create a new vision out of the experience of grief, loss, and humiliation.

The prophet Jeremiah was not deported, because he had consistently supported the Babylonians, realizing that rebellion was utter folly. Some prophets thought that because Yahweh dwelt in his temple, Jerusalem could not be destroyed, but Jeremiah told them that this was dangerous nonsense. It was useless to chant "This is the temple of Yahweh!" like a magic spell. If the people did not mend their ways, Yahweh would destroy the city.[6] This was treason, and Jeremiah was almost executed, but after his acquittal he continued to wander through the streets, uttering his grim oracles. His name has become a byword for exaggerated pessimism, but Jeremiah was not being "negative." He was right. His unflinching and courageous stand expressed one of the essential

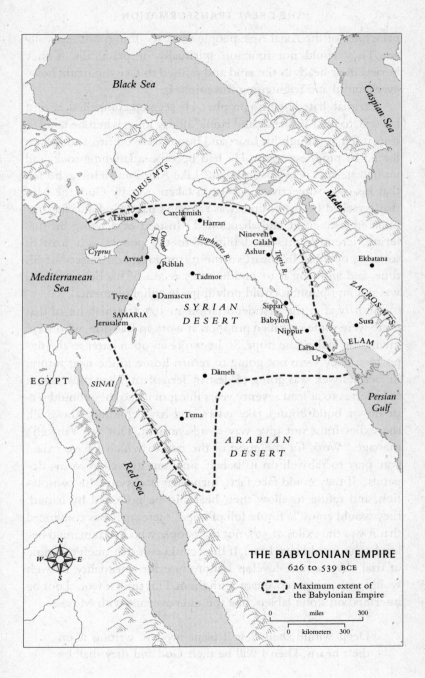

THE BABYLONIAN EMPIRE
626 to 539 BCE

- - - Maximum extent of
the Babylonian Empire

0   miles   300

0   kilometers   300

Black Sea

Caspian Sea

TAURUS MTS.

Medes

Tarsus

Carchemish

Harran

Nineveh

Calah

Ashur

Euphrates R.

Tigris R.

Ekbatana

Cyprus

Arvad

Riblah

Orontë R.

ZAGROS MTS.

Mediterranean
Sea

Tadmor

Tyre

Damascus

Sippar

Babylon

Susa

SYRIAN
DESERT

Nippur

SAMARIA

Jerusalem

Larsa

Ur

ELAM

EGYPT

SINAI

Dûmeh

Persian
Gulf

Tema

Red Sea

ARABIAN
DESERT

N
W   E
S

principles of the Axial Age: people must see things as they really are. They could not function spiritually or practically if they buried their heads in the sand and refused to face the truth, however painful and frightening this might be.

Jeremiah hated being a prophet. He seemed compelled, against his will, to cry "Violence and ruin!" all day long; when he tried to stop, it felt as though his heart and bones were on fire, and he was forced to prophesy again. He had become a laughingstock, and wished he had never been born.[7] Like Amos and Hosea, he felt that his own subjectivity had been taken over by God; the pain that wracked his every limb was Yahweh's pain: God also felt humiliated, ostracized, and abandoned.[8] Instead of denying his suffering, Jeremiah presented himself to the people as a man of sorrows, opening his heart to the terror, rage, and misery of his time, and allowing it to invade every recess of his being. Denial was not an option; it could only impede enlightenment.

Shortly after the first deportation, in 597, Jeremiah heard that there were some so-called prophets at work in Babylon, who were giving the exiles false hope. So he wrote an open letter to the deportees. They were not going to return home in the near future; in fact, Yahweh was going to destroy Jerusalem. They must resign themselves to at least seventy years in captivity, so they should settle down, build houses, take wives, and have children. Above all, the exiles must not give way to resentment. This was Yahweh's message. "Work for the good of the city to which I have exiled you; pray to Yahweh on its behalf, since on its welfare yours depends." If they could face facts, turn their backs on false consolation, and refuse to allow their hearts to be poisoned by hatred, they would enjoy "a future full of hope."[9] Jeremiah was convinced that it was the exiles of 597, not the people who had remained behind, who would save Israel. If they could come through this time of trial, they would develop a more interior spirituality. Yahweh would make a new covenant with them. This time it would not be inscribed on stone tablets, like the old covenant with Moses:

> Deep within them I will plant my law, writing it on
> their hearts. Then I will be their God and they shall be

my people. There will be no further need for neighbour
to try to teach neighbour, or brother to say to brother,
"Learn to know Yahweh!" No, they will all know me,
the least no less than the greatest.[10]

Having lost everything, some of the people of Israel were turning
within. Each individual must take responsibility for him- or herself; they were starting to discover the more interior and direct
knowledge of the Axial Age.

Far from seeking the welfare of the Babylonians, however,
some of the exiles wanted to smash their children's heads against a
rock.[11] Exile is not simply a change of address. It is also a spiritual
dislocation. Cut off from the roots of their culture and identity,
refugees often feel that they have been cast adrift, have lost their
orientation, that they are withering away and becoming insub-
stantial.[12] The Judean exiles were reasonably well treated in Babylon. They were not kept in a prison or a camp. King Jehoiachin,
who had freely surrendered to Nebuchadnezzar in 597, was under
house arrest, but was given a stipend and lived in comfort with his
entourage in the southern citadel of Babylon.[13] Some of the deportees lived in the capital, while others were housed in undeveloped areas, near newly dug canals.[14] They could, to an extent,
manage their own affairs.[15] But they were still displaced persons.
In Jerusalem, many had been men of authority and influence; in
Babylonia they had no political rights and were on the margins of
society, their position lower than that of the poorest of the local
people. Some were even forced into the corvée.[16] They had suffered a shocking loss of status. When they described the exile, they
frequently used words like "bonds" (*maserah*) and "fetters" (*zig-
gin*).[17] They may not technically have been slaves, but they felt as
though they were.

Some of the refugees could no longer worship Yahweh, who
had been so soundly worsted by Marduk, god of Babylon.[18] The
book of Job, based on an ancient folktale, may have been written
during the exile. One day, Yahweh made an interesting wager in
the divine assembly with Satan, who was not yet a figure of towering evil but simply one of the "sons of God," the legal "adver-

sary" of the council.[19] Satan pointed out that Job, Yahweh's favorite human being, had never been truly tested but was good
only because Yahweh had protected him and allowed him to prosper. If he lost all his possessions, he would soon curse Yahweh to
his face. "Very well," Yahweh replied, "all that he has is in your
power."[20] Satan promptly destroyed Job's oxen, sheep, camels, servants, and children, and Job was struck down by a series of foul
diseases. He did indeed turn against God, and Satan won his bet.

At this point, however, in a series of long poems and dis-
courses, the author tried to square the suffering of humanity with
the notion of a just, benevolent, and omnipotent god. Four of
Job's friends attempted to console him, using all the traditional arguments: Yahweh only ever punished the wicked; we could not
fathom his plans; he was utterly righteous, and Job must therefore
be guilty of some misdemeanor. These glib, facile platitudes simply enraged Job, who accused his comforters of behaving like God
and persecuting him cruelly. As for Yahweh, it was impossible to
have a sensible dialogue with a deity who was invisible, omnipotent, arbitrary, and unjust—at one and the same time prosecutor,
judge, and executioner.

When Yahweh finally deigned to respond to Job, he showed no
compassion for the man he had treated so cruelly, but simply uttered a long speech about his own splendid accomplishments.
Where had Job been while he laid the earth's foundations, and
pent up the sea behind closed doors? Could Job catch Leviathan
with a fishhook, make a horse leap like a grasshopper, or guide the
constellations on their course? The poetry was magnificent, but irrelevant. This long, boastful tirade did not even touch upon the
real issue: Why did innocent people suffer at the hands of a sup-
posedly loving God? And unlike Job, the reader knows that Job's
pain had nothing to do with the transcendent wisdom of Yahweh, but was simply the result of a frivolous bet. At the end of the
poem, when Job—utterly defeated by Yahweh's bombastic display
of power—retracted all his complaints and repented in dust and
ashes, God restored Job's health and fortune. But he did not bring
to life the children and servants who had been killed in the first
chapter. There was no justice or recompense for them.

If Job was indeed written by one of the exiles, it shows that some of the community may have lost all faith in Yahweh. But others responded creatively to the catastrophe and began to develop an entirely new religious vision. The royal scribes continued to edit earlier texts. The Deuteronomists added passages to their history to explain the disaster, while priests began to adapt their ancient lore to life in Babylonia, where the Judeans had no cult and no temple. Deprived of everything that had given meaning to their lives—their temple, their king, and their land—they had to learn to live as a homeless minority, and once again, they were not afraid to rewrite their history, revise their customs, and find a radically innovative interpretation of their traditional sacred symbols.

We can see the development of this Axial vision in the prophetic career of the young priest Ezekiel, who was deported to Babylon in 597 and settled in the village of Tel Aviv—Springtime Hill—near the Chebar Canal. He had a series of visions, which marked his painful passage from agonizing terror to a more peaceful, interior spirituality. In 593, just five years after he had been taken into exile, while Jerusalem and its temple were still standing, Ezekiel had a bewildering vision on the banks of the Chebar.[21] There was a strong wind; he saw flashes of lightning, thunder, and smoke; and in the midst of this stormy obscurity, Ezekiel could just make out four extraordinary creatures, each with four heads, pulling a war chariot. They beat their wings with a deafening sound, like "rushing water, like the voice of Shaddai, like a storm, like the noise of a camp." On the chariot was something "like" a throne, on which sat a "being that looked like a man," with fire shooting from its limbs, yet it also "looked like the glory of Yahweh." A hand reached out, clasping a scroll "inscribed with lamentations, wailings, moanings," and before he could bring the divine message to his people, Ezekiel was forced to eat it, painfully assimilating the violence and sorrow of his time.

God had become incomprehensible—as alien as Ezekiel felt in Tel Aviv. The trauma of exile had smashed the neat, rationalistic God of the Deuteronomists; it was no longer possible to see Yahweh as a friend who shared a meal with Abraham, or as a king presiding powerfully over his divine council. Ezekiel's vision made no sense; it was utterly transcendent, beyond human categories. The scroll that was handed to him contained no clear directives, like the Deuteronomists' *sefer torah;* it offered no certainty, but expressed only inchoate cries of grief and pain. It was a martial vision, filled with the confusion and terror of warfare. Instead of a celestial throne, Yahweh appeared on a war chariot—the equivalent of today's tank or fighter jet. The message that Ezekiel was to deliver was little more than a threat. He was simply to warn the "defiant and obstinate" exiles that "there is a prophet among them—whether they listen or not." There could be no tenderness or consolation. Yahweh was going to make Ezekiel as defiant and obstinate as the rest of the people, "his resolution as hard as a diamond and diamond is harder than flint." Finally Ezekiel was lifted up amidst tumultuous shouting. He felt the hand of Yahweh lying "heavy" upon him; his heart overflowed "with bitterness and anger," and he lay in Tel Aviv for a week, "like a man stunned."[22]

And yet there was consolation. When Ezekiel ate the scroll and accepted its overwhelming sorrow and fear, he found that "it tasted as sweet as honey."[23] And even though Yahweh had brought no comfort, the fact remained that he had come to his people in exile. The temple was still standing, yet Yahweh had left his shrine in Jerusalem and thrown in his lot with the exiles. In later visions, Ezekiel would see that Yahweh had been driven out of his city by the idolatry and immorality of the Judeans who had remained behind.[24] But the exiles must realize that they bore some responsibility for the catastrophe. Ezekiel's mission was to bring this home to the deportees of 597. There were to be no fantasies of restoration; their job was to repent and—somehow—to build a rightly ordered life in Babylon. But they could not do this unless they allowed themselves to experience the full weight of their sorrow.

Ezekiel's personal dislocation was, perhaps, revealed in his strange, distorted actions—the weird mimes he felt compelled to perform to bring the people's predicament home to them. When Ezekiel's wife died, Yahweh forbade him to mourn; another time, Yahweh commanded Ezekiel to lie on one side for 390 days and on the other for 40. Yahweh tied him up, shut him in his house, and stuck Ezekiel's tongue to the roof of his mouth, so that he could not speak. Once Yahweh forced him to pack his bags and walk around Tel Aviv like a refugee. He was afflicted with such acute anxiety that he could not stop trembling, could not sit still, and had to keep moving about restlessly. This—he seemed to be telling his fellow exiles—was what happened to displaced people: they no longer had normal responses, because their world had been turned upside down. They could not relax or feel at ease anywhere at all. Unless the exiles appreciated this to the full—saw things as they were—they would not be able to heal. It was no good looking on the bright side or telling themselves that they would soon be home, because this was simply not true. They must strip themselves of these delusions.

Ezekiel was a priest, and he interpreted the crisis in terms of the temple rituals, but used traditional liturgical categories to diagnose the moral failings of his people. Sometime before the destruction of Jerusalem in 586, Ezekiel had a vision that showed him why Yahweh had been driven out of Jerusalem. Taken on a guided tour of the temple, he saw to his horror that, poised as they were on the brink of catastrophe, the people of Judah were still worshiping gods other than Yahweh. The temple had become a nightmarish place, its walls painted with writhing snakes and repellent animals. The priests performing these "filthy" rites were presented in a sordid light, almost as if they were engaged in furtive, disreputable sex: "Son of man, have you seen what the elders of the throne of Israel do in the dark, each in his painted room?"[25] In another chamber, women sat weeping for Tammuz, the Anatolian vegetation god. Other Judeans worshiped the sun with their backs to the Holy of Holies, where Yahweh dwelt.

But the people were also rejecting Yahweh ethically as well as ritually. Ezekiel's divine guide told him that the guilt of Israel and Judah "is immense, boundless; the country is full of bloodshed, the city overflows with wickedness, for they say, 'Yahweh has abandoned the country, Yahweh cannot see.' The city is filled with the corpses of murdered men."[26] In this world of international aggression, it is significant that Ezekiel was preoccupied with the violence that Judeans were inflicting upon one another. Reform must begin with an objective, clearsighted examination of their own failings. Instead of blaming the Babylonians for their cruelty, projecting their pain onto the enemy, Ezekiel forced his fellow exiles to look nearer home. Blood was of crucial importance in the temple cult. Most priestly discussions of blood had hitherto centered on the ritual. But Ezekiel now made blood a symbol for murder, lawlessness, and social injustice.[27] Ritual was being interpreted by the new moral imperative of the Axial Age. These social crimes were just as serious as idolatry, and Israel had only itself to blame for the impending disaster. At the end of his vision, Ezekiel watched Yahweh's war chariot fly away over the Mount of Olives, taking the divine glory away from the holy city.

There was no hope for the Judeans who had stayed behind and whose sinfulness and political chicanery would result in the destruction of Jerusalem. Like Jeremiah, Ezekiel had no time for these people. But because Yahweh had decided to dwell among the deportees in exile, there was hope for the future. Despite his distress and apparent derangement, Ezekiel had a vision of new life. He saw a field full of human bones, which represented the exiled community; they kept saying: "Our bones are dried up, our hope has gone; we are as good as dead." But Ezekiel prophesied over the bones and "the breath entered them; they came to life again and stood up on their feet, a great and immense army."[28] One day when they had fully repented, Yahweh would bring the exiles home. But this would not be a simple restoration. Like Jeremiah, Ezekiel knew that the suffering of exile must lead to a deeper vision. Yahweh promised: "I will give them another heart, and I will put a new spirit in them. I will remove the heart of stone from their bodies, and give them a heart of flesh instead, so that they will keep my laws."[29] In his first vision, Yahweh had told Ezekiel that he was going to make his heart as hard as flint. But because Ezekiel—and, presumably, some of the exiles—had assimilated their pain, acknowledged their own responsibility, and allowed their hearts to break, they had become humane.

Finally, perhaps toward the end of his life, after the destruction of Jerusalem, Ezekiel had a vision of a city called Yahweh Sham ("Yahweh is there!"), situated on the summit of a very high mountain. These chapters may have been edited and expanded by some of Ezekiel's disciples, but the core idea probably came from the prophet himself.[30] Even though Jerusalem and its temple lay in ruins, they lived on in the prophet's mind, and Ezekiel saw their mystical significance. Solomon's temple had been designed as a replica of the Garden of Eden, and Ezekiel now found himself looking at an earthly paradise. There was a temple in the center of the city; and a river bubbled up from beneath the sanctuary and flowed down the sacred mountain, bringing life and healing to the surrounding countryside. Along the riverbanks, there grew trees "with leaves that never wither and fruit that never fails . . . good to eat, and with leaves medicinal."[31] The temple was the nucleus of the whole world; divine power radiated from it to the land and people of Israel in a series of concentric circles. In each zone, the farther it got from its source, this holiness was diluted.

The first circle surrounding the city was the home of the king and priests, the sacred personnel. The next zone, for the tribes of Israel, was a little less holy. But beyond the reach of holiness, outside the land, was the world of the *goyim,* the foreign nations. In the temple cult, Yahweh had been *qaddosh:* "separate" and "other." Now that the temple was gone, Israel could still participate in his holiness by living apart from the rest of the world. This vision of the restored community was not a detailed blueprint for the future or an architectural plan. It was what the people of India would call a mandala, an icon for meditation,[32] an image of the properly ordered life, centered on the divine. Yahweh was with his people, even in exile; they must live as though they were still living beside the temple, separately from the *goyim*. They must not fraternize or assimilate, but gather in spirit around Yahweh. Even though they were peripheral people in Babylonia, they were closer to the center than their idolatrous neighbors, who were scarcely on the map. But given the emphasis on the inner life at this time, it is also possible that the description enabled Ezekiel's disciples to internalize the temple and make it an interior reality. By contemplating the circles of holiness, they could discover their own "center," the orientation that enabled them to function fully. The exiles did not analyze the psyche as rigorously as the sages of the Upanishads, but it is possible that while meditating upon this mandala, some were discovering a divine presence at the core of their being.

In his meditation on Yahweh Sham, Ezekiel expended a great deal of time on detailed discussion of sacrifice, vestments, and the measurements and proportions of the temple. In times of social uncertainty, anthropologists tell us, ritual acquires a new importance.[33] Among displaced people, in particular, there is pressure to maintain the boundaries that separate the group from others, and a new concern about purity, pollution, and mixed marriage, which help the community to resist the majority culture. Certainly Ezekiel's vision showed a fortress mentality. No foreigners were allowed in his imaginary city; there were walls and gates everywhere, barricading the holiness of Israel from the threatening outside world.

Ezekiel was one of the last of the great prophets. Prophecy had always been linked with the monarchy in Israel and Judah, and it became less influential as the monarchy declined. But the priests, who had officiated in the temple, acquired a new importance, as the last link with a world that seemed irrevocably lost. They could have fallen into despair after their temple had been destroyed, but instead, a small circle of exiled priests began to construct a new spirituality on the rubble of the old. We know very little about them. Scholars call this priestly layer of the Bible "P," but we do not know whether P was a single editor or, more probably, a school of priestly writers and editors. Whoever they were, P had access to several old traditions, some written down and others orally transmitted.[34] Perhaps they worked in the royal archive housed in the court of the exiled King Jehoiachin. The documents available to P included the JE narrative, the genealogies of the patriarchs, and ancient ritual texts that listed the places where the Israelites were believed to have camped during their forty years in the wilderness. But P's most important sources were the Holiness Code[35] (miscellaneous laws collected during the seventh century) and the Tabernacle Document, the centerpiece of P's narrative, which described the tent shrine that the Israelites had built in the wilderness to house the divine presence.[36] It was called the tent of meeting because Moses consulted Yahweh there and received his instructions. Some of P's material was very old indeed, and his language was deliberately archaic, but his aim was not antiquarian. He wanted to build a new future for his people.

P made some important additions to the JE saga, and was also responsible for the books of Leviticus and Numbers. Most readers find this priestly lore impossibly difficult; they usually skip the interminable accounts of convoluted, bloody sacrifices and the incomprehensibly detailed dietary laws. Why bother to describe ceremonies that, now that the temple was in ruins, were obsolete? Why such concentration on purity when the exiles were living in an impure land? At first sight, P's apparent obsession with external rules and rituals seems far removed from the Axial Age. Yet he was preoccupied with many of the same issues as the reformers who had revised the Vedic sacrifices. P wanted the deportees to live in a different way, convinced that, if faithfully observed, these laws would not imprison them in soulless conformity, but would transform them at a profound level.

The first chapter of Genesis, which described how Israel's God had created heaven and earth in six days, is probably P's most famous work, and it is a good place to start. When his first audience listened to a creation story, they expected to hear tales of violent struggle. The exiles were living in Babylon, where Marduk's victory over Tiamat, the primal sea, was reenacted in a spectacular ritual at the new year, and there were many stories about Yahweh slaying a sea dragon when he created the world. So the audience would not have been surprised to hear the sea mentioned in P's opening words: "In the beginning God created the heavens and the earth. Now the earth was wild and waste, there was darkness over the face of Ocean, rushing-spirit of God hovering over the face of the waters." But then P surprised them. There was no fighting or killing. God simply spoke a word of command: "Let there be light!" And—without any struggle at all—the light shone forth. God ordered the world by issuing a further series of edicts: "Let the waters under the heavens be gathered in one place!" "Let the earth sprout forth with sprouting growth!" "Let there be lights in the dome of the heavens, to separate the day from the night!" And finally: "Let us make humankind [*adam*] in our image!" And each time, without a single battle, "it was so."[37] In the same way as the Indian ritualists had systematically taken the violence out of the traditional ritual, P methodically extracted aggression from the traditional cosmogony.

This was a remarkable spiritual achievement. The deportees had been the victims of a horrifying assault. The Babylonians had devastated their homeland, reduced their city to rubble, razed their temple to the ground, and forcibly driven them into exile. We know that some of them wanted to pay back the Babylonians in kind:

> *Destructive Daughter of Babel,*
> *A blessing on the man who treats you*
> *As you have treated us,*
> *A blessing on him who takes and dashes*
> *Your babies against the rock!*[38]

But this, P seemed to tell them, was not the way to go. His creation story can be seen as a polemic against the religion of their Babylonian conquerors. Yahweh was far more powerful than Marduk. He did not have to fight a battle against his fellow gods when he ordered the cosmos; the sea was not a terrifying goddess, but simply the raw material of the universe; and the sun, moon, and stars were mere creatures and functionaries. Marduk's creation had to be renewed annually, but Yahweh finished his work in a mere six days and was able to rest on the seventh. He had no divine competition but was incomparable, the only power in the universe and beyond opposition.[39]

Israelites could be extremely scathing about other people's faith, but P did not take that road. There were no cheap jibes against Babylonian religion. His narrative was serene and calm. Even though the exiles had experienced such violent uprooting, this was a world where everything had its place. On the last day of creation, God "saw *everything* that he had made, and here: it was exceedingly good."[40] He also blessed all that he had made—and that, presumably, included the Babylonians. Everybody should behave like Yahweh, resting calmly on the Sabbath, serving God's world, and blessing all his creatures.

P deliberately linked the building of the tabernacle with the creation of the world.[41] In his instructions to Moses about the construction of this shrine, Yahweh ordered that the work should take six days, "but the seventh is to be a holy day for you, a day of complete rest, consecrated to Yahweh."[42] When the tent of meeting was finished, "Moses examined the whole work, and he could see they had done it as Yahweh had directed him. And Moses blessed them."[43] The exodus from Egypt was crucial to P's vision, but he interpreted the story very differently than the Deuteronomists. P did not describe the covenant made on Mount Sinai, which had become a painful, problematic memory now that Israel had been exiled from the land that Yahweh had promised them there.[44] For P the climax of the story was not the giving of the *sefer torah* but the gift of the life-giving presence of God in the tent of meeting.

Yahweh told Moses that he had brought the people out of Egypt "in order to live [*skn*] myself in their midst."[45] In his mobile shrine, the divine presence accompanied the people of Israel wherever they were. The root word *shakan,* usually translated as "to live," originally meant "to lead the life of a nomadic tent dweller." P preferred this word to *yob* ("to dwell"), which suggested permanent habitation. God had promised to "tent" with his wandering people. He had no fixed abode, was not tied to any one shrine, but had promised to *shakan* with the Israelites wherever they went.[46] When he edited the JE narrative, P concluded the book of Exodus with the completion of the tent of meeting, when God fulfilled his promise, when the glory of Yahweh filled the tabernacle (*mishkan*) and the cloud of his presence covered it:

> *Whenever the cloud goes up from the* mishkan
> *the Children of Israel march on, upon all their marches. . . .*
> *For the cloud of YHWH is over the* mishkan *by day*
> *and fire is by night in it,*
> *before the eyes of all the House of Israel*
> *upon all their marches.*[47]

The present tense was of great importance. Yahweh was *still* with his people in their latest march to Babylonia. Like their God, Israel was a mobile people. Unlike the Deuteronomists, P did not end the saga with Joshua's conquest but left the Israelites on the border of the Promised Land.[48] Israel was not a people because it dwelt in a particular country, but because it lived in the presence of its God, who traveled with the people wherever in the world they happened to be.

P's description of Israel's encampment in the wilderness revealed the exile's passion for order.[49] When they pitched camp at night or marched during the day, each of the tribes had its divinely appointed position around the tent. In the book of Numbers, Israel's history, which had been so brutally disrupted, was presented as a stately procession from one place to another. Adding his own priestly lore to the JE narrative, P recast the history of his people, showing that the exile to Babylon was just the latest in a long series of tragic migrations: Adam and Eve had been forced to leave Eden; Cain had become a perpetual wanderer after killing his brother; human beings were scattered over the face of the earth after the rebellion at the Tower of Babel. Abraham had left Ur, the tribes had migrated to Egypt, and Yahweh had liberated them from captivity. But he had "tented" with his people in the Sinai desert for forty years, and—the implication was—he was still living in the midst of his people in this latest migration to Babylon.

The community of exiles probably went in for quite a lot of grumbling and complaining. In his narrative, P developed the stories about Israel's "murmuring" against God in the wilderness.[50] The exiles were also a "stiff-necked generation," but P showed them the way forward. Even in exile, they could create a community to which God's presence could return, provided that they all lived according to the ancient priestly laws. This was a startling innovation. P was not reviving old legislation that had fallen into disuse. The ceremonial laws, purity regulations, and dietary rules that had governed the lives of the priests who served in the temple had never been intended for the laity.[51] Now, P made an astonishing claim. Israel, whose national temple had been destroyed, was a nation of priests. All the people must live as though they were serving the divine presence in the temple, because God was still living in their midst. P's legislation ritualized the whole of life, but he used these ancient temple laws to initiate a new ethical revolution, based on the experience of displacement.

Even though the exiles were living in an impure land, P insisted that there was a profound link between exile and holiness. In the Holiness Code, God had told the Israelites: "You must be holy, because I, Yahweh your God, am holy."[52] To be "holy" was to be "separate." Yahweh was "other," radically different from ordinary, profane reality. The law proposed by P crafted a holy lifestyle based on the principle of separation. The people must live apart from their Babylonian neighbors and keep the natural world at a distance. By imitating the otherness of God in every detail of their lives, they would be holy as Yahweh was holy and would be in the place where God was. Because exile was essentially a life of alienation, Babylonia was the perfect place to put this program into practice. In Leviticus, Yahweh issued detailed regulations about sacrifice, diet, and social, sexual, and cultic life. If Israel observed these laws, Yahweh promised, he would always live in their midst. God and Israel traveled together. If they chose to disregard his commandments, Yahweh would "walk with them" as a punitive force.[53] He would devastate their land, destroy their shrines and temples, and scatter them among the nations. This— P implied—had come to pass. The people of Israel had not lived lives of holiness, and that was why they were now in exile. But if they repented, Yahweh would remember them, even in the land of their enemies. "I will place my 'Tabernacle' [*mishkan*] in your midst and I myself will not despise you. I will walk about among you."[54] Babylonia could be a new Eden, where God had walked with Adam in the cool of the evening.

For P, a man of the Axial Age, holiness had a strong ethical component and was no longer a merely cultic matter. It involved absolute respect for the sacred "otherness" of every creature. In the law of freedom,[55] Yahweh insisted that nothing could be enslaved or owned, not even the land. In the Jubilee Year, which must be proclaimed every fifty years, all slaves must be freed and all debts canceled. Even though they lived separate, holy lives, Israelites must not despise the stranger: "If a stranger lives with you in your land, do not molest him. You must treat him like one of your own people and love him as yourselves. For you were strangers in Egypt."[56] This was a law based on empathy. The experience of suffering must lead to the appreciation of other people's pain. Your own sorrow must teach you to feel with others. P was a realist, however. The commandment to "love" did not require the people to be constantly filled with warm affection. P was not writing about feelings. This was a law code, and P's language was as technical and reticent as any legal ruling, where emotion would be out of place. In Middle Eastern treaties, to "love" meant to be helpful, loyal, and to give practical support. The commandment to love was not excessively utopian, therefore, but was within everybody's grasp.

From start to finish, P's vision was inclusive. Yet at first reading, the dietary laws seem harsh and arbitrarily selective. How could a God who had blessed all the animals on the day of creation dismiss some of his creatures as "unclean" or even as "abominations"? We naturally endow words such as "impure" or "abomination" with ethical and emotional significance, but the Hebrew *tamei* ("impure") did not mean "sinful" or "dirty." It was a technical term in the cult, and had no emotive or moral overtones. As in Greece, certain actions or conditions activated an impersonal *miasma* that contaminated the temple and drove God out.[57] For P, death was the basic and prototypical impurity: the living God was incompatible with dead bodies. It was an insult to come into his presence after contact with the corpse of any one of his creatures. All major pollutants—improperly shed blood, leprosy, discharge— were impure because they were associated with death, and had encroached into an area where they did not belong.[58] In the temple, priests who served the divine presence had to avoid all contact with dead bodies and symbols of decay. Now all Israelites must do the same, because they too were living with their God.

But—a very important point—P did not teach that other human beings were unclean or contaminating.[59] The laws of holiness and impurity were not designed to keep outsiders beyond the pale; in P, the foreigner was not to be shunned but "loved." Contamination did not come from your enemies, but from yourself. The code did not command Israelites to avoid impure strangers, but to honor all life. In the dietary laws that forbade the consumption of "unclean" animals, P came very close to the Indian ideal of *ahimsa*. Like other ancient peoples, Israelites did not regard the ritualized sacrifice of animals as killing. It transformed the victim into a more airy, spiritual substance,[60] and it was forbidden to kill and eat an animal that had not been consecrated in this way. P forbade the "secular slaughter" that had been permitted by the Deuteronomists, and ruled that Israelites could sacrifice and eat only the domestic animals from their flocks of sheep and herds of cattle. These were the "clean" or "pure" animals that were part of the community and, therefore, shared in God's covenant with Israel; they were his possessions and nobody could harm them. The "clean" animals must be allowed to rest on the Sabbath, and they could be eaten only if they were given some kind of posthumous life.[61]

But the "unclean" animals, such as dogs, deer, and other creatures that lived in the wild, must not be killed at all. It was forbidden to trap, slaughter, exploit, or eat them, under any circumstances. They were not dirty or disgusting. Israelites were not forbidden to touch them while they were alive. They became unclean only after their death.[62] The law that forbade any contact with the corpse of an unclean animal protected it, because it meant that the carcass could not be skinned or dismembered. It was, therefore, not worthwhile to hunt or trap them. Similarly the animals classed as "abominations" (*sheqqets*) were not abhorrent during their lifetime. The Israelites must simply avoid them when they were dead, for the same reason. These "swarming creatures" of sea and air were vulnerable and should inspire compassion. Quails, for example, were tiny and easily blown off course. And because they were prolific and "teemed," they were blessed by God and belonged to him.[63] All God's animals were his beautiful creation.[64] P made it clear that God had blessed clean and unclean animals on the day he created them, and had saved pure and impure animals alike at the time of the flood. Harming any one of them was an affront to his holiness.

There was, however, an undercurrent of anxiety in P. The legislation surrounding leprosy, discharge, and menstruation, inspired by a fear of the body's walls being breached, revealed the displaced community's concern to establish clear boundaries. P's evocation of a world in which everything had its place sprang from the trauma of dislocation. The national integrity of the exiles had been violated by a ruthless display of imperial power. The great achievement of the exilic priests and prophets had been the avoidance of a religion based on resentment and revenge, and the creation of a spirituality that affirmed the holiness of all life.

At the beginning of the sixth century, the social crisis that had disrupted many of the poleis in the Greek world finally hit Athens. The farmers in the rural areas of Attica complained of exploitation and banded together against the aristocrats. Civil war seemed inevitable. The noblemen were vulnerable: they were not united, had no army or police force at their disposal, and many of the farmers were trained hoplites, and therefore armed and dangerous. The only way out of the impasse was to find an impartial mediator who could arbitrate fairly between the contending parties. Athens chose Solon, and in 594 appointed him city magistrate, with a mandate to reform the constitution.

Solon belonged to the circle of independent intellectuals who gave advice to various poleis during crises. At first they had been consulted on purely practical matters: the economy, unemployment, or bad harvests. But increasingly, the "wise men" had started to consider more abstract, political issues. Solon had traveled widely in Greece, and in his discussions with other members of the circle had considered the besetting problems of the polis. He told Athenians that they were living in *dysnomia* ("disorder") and heading for disaster. Their only hope was to create *eunomia* ("right order") by returning to the norms that had originally governed Greek society. Farmers were essential to the polis, both as hoplites and as producers of wealth. By attempting to suppress them, the aristocrats had created an unhealthy imbalance in society that could only be self-destructive.

Solon was not content simply to pass a few laws. He wanted to make farmers and aristocrats alike aware of the problems of government and the principles that lay at the heart of any well-ordered society. All citizens must accept a measure of responsibility for the state of *dysnomia*. It was not a divine punishment but the result of human selfishness, and only a concerted political effort could restore peace and security. The gods did not intervene in human affairs and would not reveal a divine law to rectify the situation. This was an Axial breakthrough. At a stroke, Solon had secularized politics. In the holistic vision of antiquity, justice was part of a cosmic order that ruled even the gods; a bad government, which flouted these sacred principles, could disrupt the course of nature. But Solon had no time for this. Nature was governed by its own laws, which could not be affected by the actions of men and women. The Greeks were beginning to think in a new, analytic way, separating the different components of the problem, giving each its integrity, and then proceeding to find a logical solution. The circle of wise men had begun to study the process of cause and effect that would enable them to predict the outcome of a crisis. They were learning to look beyond the particular problems of a polis and find abstract general principles that could be applied universally.[65]

Solon's principle of *eunomia* was not only decisive in Greek political thought, but would help to shape early Greek science and philosophy. It was based on the idea of balance. No one sector of society should dominate the others. The city must work in the same way as the hoplite phalanx, in which all the warriors acted in concert. The farmers must be freed of the burdens placed upon them, so that they could counter the powers of the aristocrats who oppressed them. So Solon canceled the farmers' debts; the Popular Assembly of all the citizens, which went back to the old tribal days, must balance the aristocratic Council of Elders. He also created the Council of Four Hundred, to supervise all the official assemblies of the polis. To further dilute the power of the aristocracy, Solon defined status by wealth rather than by birth: anybody who produced over two hundred bushels of grain, wine, or oil each year was now eligible for public office. Finally, Solon reformed the judiciary, and permitted any citizen to prosecute the city magistrates.[66] He had the new laws inscribed on two wooden tablets, so that any literate Athenian could consult them.

Solon probably imagined that once the imbalance in society had been rectified, the aristocrats would automatically rule more justly. But of course, they resented their loss of privilege, and when the new measures were not fully implemented, there was unrest and disappointment among the poorer classes. Many urged Solon to establish a tyranny in Athens, so that he could enforce his reforms, but he refused because tyranny was an unbalanced polity. In the short term, Solon failed: the people were not yet ready for his ideas. But the widespread interest in his reforms had put Athens, which had fallen behind the other poleis, in the vanguard of progress. By rejecting tyranny, Solon had also set a new standard of the ideal citizen, who served without hope of personal reward and did not seek to become superior to the ordinary people.[67]

But in 547 a tyrant did seize power in Athens. Peisistratos, from the nearby city of Brauron, whose family controlled the northern plains near Macedon, became the champion of many disaffected people in Athens. He and his sons would govern the city until 510. Generous, charming, and charismatic, Peisistratos was good for the city. He gave generous loans to the impoverished farmers, initiated important construction projects, and repaired the water-supply system and the roads around the city. Trade expanded, poets frequented his court, and the people enjoyed a spiritual renewal.

Peisistratos wanted to create a distinctive religious center in Athens. He and his sons transformed the Acropolis, making it a spectacular cult site with a stone temple and a convenient approach up the rocky hillside. Wealthy patrons commissioned statues of the gods, which stood around the sanctuary like an enchanted stone forest.[68] Peisistratos also gave new life to the grand festival of Panathenaea, which celebrated the birth of the city, was held every four years, and had its own athletic games.[69] It was the climax of the new year's celebrations, and followed some dark, perplexing rites that reenacted the early history of Athens. In one of these rites, an ox was sacrificed on the Acropolis in a way that induced a profound guilt. The priest who had inflicted the fatal blow had to flee; a court was convened; and the knife, convicted of murder, was thrown into the sea. Behind the burlesque of this "ox murder" (*bouphonia*) lurked a horror of the violence that lay at the heart of every civic sacrifice and of civilization itself—a horror that was all too often blunted by routine—for which somebody or something would always have to pay.

The triumph of the Panathenaea dispelled the uncanny aura of these unsettling rituals.[70] The centerpiece of the festival was a procession through the city, which finished on the Acropolis at the eastern end of Athena's new temple. There the city presented the goddess with a fresh saffron robe for her cult statue, embroidered with scenes of her battle with the Cyclops, which symbolized the triumph of civilization over chaos. All citizens were represented in the procession: the young ephebes (the adolescent boys who were becoming full citizens), hoplites, girls in yellow chitons, old men, craftsmen, resident aliens, delegates from other poleis, and the sacrificial victims. Athens was on display, to itself and to the rest of the Greek world, in a dazzlingly proud assertion of identity.

But Greeks were beginning to long for a more personal religious experience. One of the new buildings constructed by Peisistratos was a cult hall at the city of Eleusis, some twenty miles west of Athens, where, it was said, the goddess Demeter had stayed while searching for Persephone. The Eleusinian mystery cult now became an integral part of the religious life of Athenians.[71] It was an initiation, in which participants experienced a transformed state of mind. Because the rites were shrouded in secrecy, we have only an incomplete idea of what went on, but it seems that the initiates (*mystai*) followed in the footsteps of Demeter; they shared her suffering—her grief, desperation, fear, and rage—at the loss of her daughter. By participating in her pain and, finally, the joy of her reunion with Persephone, some of them found that, having looked into the heart of darkness, they did not fear death in the same way again.

Preparations began in Athens. The *mystai* fasted for two days;

they stood in the sea and sacrificed a piglet in honor of Perse-phone; and then in a huge throng they set off on foot for Eleusis. By this time they were weakened by their fast and apprehensive, because they had no idea what was going to happen to them. The *epoptai,* who had been initiated the previous year, made the jour-ney with them; their behavior was threatening and aggressive. The crowds called rhythmically and hypnotically upon Dionysus, god of transformation, driving themselves into a frenzy of excitement, so that when the *mystai* finally arrived in Eleusis, they were ex-hausted, frightened, and elated. By this time, the sun was setting; torches were lit, and in the unearthly, flickering light, the *mystai* were herded to and fro through the streets, until they lost their bearings and were thoroughly disoriented. Then they plunged into the pitch-darkness of the initiation hall. After this the picture becomes very confused. Animals were sacrificed; there was a ter-rifying, "unspeakable" event, which may have involved the sacri-fice of a child who was reprieved only at the eleventh hour. There was a "revelation"; something was lifted out of a sacred basket. But finally the reunion of Kore and Demeter was reenacted and the mystery concluded with rhapsodic scenes and sacred tableaux that filled the initiates with joy and relief. At Eleusis, they had achieved an *ekstasis,* "stepping outside" their normal, workaday selves, and experienced new insight.

No secret doctrine was imparted. As Aristotle would explain later, the *mystai* did not go to Eleusis to learn anything, but to have an experience, which, they felt, transformed them.[72] "I came out of the mystery hall," one of the *mystai* recalled, "feeling a stranger to myself."[73] The Greek historian Plutarch (c. 46–120 CE) thought that dying might be like the Eleusinian experience:

> Wandering astray in the beginning, tiresome walking in circles, some frightening paths in darkness that lead nowhere; then, immediately before the end, all the ter-rible things—panic and shivering, sweat and amaze-ment. And then some wonderful light comes to meet you, pure regions and meadows are there to greet you,

with sounds and dances and solemn, sacred words and
holy views.[74]

The final rapture, orchestrated by the intense psychodrama, gave
people intimations of the beatific bliss enjoyed by the gods.

The Greeks were learning to think with logical, analytical
rigor, and yet periodically they felt the need to surrender themselves to the irrational. The Athenian philosopher Proclus (c. 412–
485 CE) believed that the initiation of Eleusis created a *sympatheia*,
a profound affinity with the ritual, so that they lost themselves and
became wholly absorbed in the rite "in a way that is unintelligible
to us and divine." Not all the *mystai* achieved this; some were simply "stricken with panic," and remained imprisoned in their fear,
but others managed to "assimilate themselves to the holy symbols,
leave their own identity, become one with the gods, and experience divine possession."[75] In India, people were beginning to
achieve similar bliss in the techniques of introspection. There
was no such interior journey at Eleusis; this was quite different
from the solitary *ekstasis* achieved by some of the mystics of the
Axial Age. The illumination of Eleusis did not happen in a remote
forest hermitage, but in the presence of thousands of people.
Eleusis belonged to the old, pre-Axial world. By imitating Demeter and Persephone, reenacting their passage from death to life,
the *mystai* left their individual selves behind and became one with
their divine models.

The same was true of the mysteries of Dionysus.[76] Here too
the participants united themselves to a suffering god, following
Dionysus's frenzied wanderings when, driven mad by his step-
mother, Hera, he had journeyed through the forests of Greece and
through the eastern lands of Egypt, Syria, and Phrygia in search of
healing. The mythical stories about Dionysus spoke of destructive
insanity and terrifying extremity, but his city cult was orderly,
though there was a carnival atmosphere, with just a hint of trans-
gression.[77] Men wore women's clothes, like the young Dionysus
while he was hiding from Hera. Everybody drank wine, and there
was music and dancing. The Maenads, Dionysus's female devotees,

ran through the streets wearing crowns of ivy leaves and carrying magical willow wands. But sometimes, the whole group fell into a trance, a heightened state of consciousness, which spread from one celebrant to another. When this happened, worshipers knew that Dionysus was present among them. They called this experience of divine possession *entheos:* "within is a god."

There had always been an element of the burlesque in the cult of Dionysus. In his civic processions all the inhabitants of the polis would mingle together, slaves marching side by side with aristocrats. It was the exact opposite of the Panathenaea, where every sector of the populace had a clearly defined place in the procession.[78] Dionysian religion contained a hint of rebellion, which appealed to the craftsmen, artisans, and peasants from whom the tyrants drew their support, and so they often encouraged the cult of Dionysus. In 534, Peisistratos established the City Dionysia in Athens, and built a small temple to Dionysus on the southern slope of the Acropolis. Beside it was a theater, which had been cut out of the rocky hillside. On the morning of the festival, the god's effigy was ceremonially carried into the city and placed on the stage. For the next three days, the citizens gathered in the theater to listen to the choral recitations of the ancient myths, which would slowly develop into a full-scale drama. In the dramatic rituals of the City Dionysia, the Greeks would come closest to the religious experience of the Axial Age.

A few Greeks, in two marginal movements of the sixth century, also moved toward the vision of the Axial Age emerging in other parts of the world. The first was the Orphic sect, which rejected the aggressive ethos of the polis and embraced the ideal of nonviolence.[79] Orphics would not even sacrifice an animal ceremonially, adopted a strict vegetarian diet, and because the sacrifice was essential to the political life of the city, they withdrew from the mainstream. Their model was Orpheus, a mythical hero of Thrace, which was a wild, peripheral, and "uncivilized" region of Greece. A man of sorrows, Orpheus mourned the loss of his wife, Eurydice, for his entire life and died a violent, horrible death: he had so enraged the women of Thrace by refusing to marry again that they tore him to pieces with their bare hands. Yet Orpheus was a man of peace, whose inspired poetry tamed wild beasts, calmed the waves, and made men forget their quarrels.[80] The second of these movements was initiated by Pythagoras, a mathematician from Samos, who migrated to Italy in 530, traveled in the east, and taught a version of the Indian doctrine of karma. We know very little about him personally, except that he established an esoteric sect whose members purified the body by abstaining from meat, refused to take part in the sacrificial rituals, and sought enlightenment through the study of science and mathematics. By concentrating on pure abstractions, Pythagoreans hoped to wean themselves away from the contaminations of the physical world and glimpse a vision of divine order.

Most Greeks, however, continued to worship the gods in the traditional, time-honored way, though in the sixth century there were stirrings of an entirely new rationalism. A few philosophers had begun to study science, not, like the Pythagoreans, as a means of gaining spiritual enlightenment, but for its own sake.[81] These first scientists lived in Miletus, an Ionian polis on the coast of Asia Minor, a prosperous port with extensive links to the Black Sea and the Near East. The first to gain notoriety was Thales, who became an overnight sensation by predicting a solar eclipse in 593. This had simply been a lucky guess, but his real achievement was to see the eclipse as a natural rather than a divine event. Thales was not against religion. The only sentence of his to have survived was "Everything is water and the world is full of gods." The primal sea had long been regarded as the divine raw material of the cosmos, but Thales' approach to this mythical intuition was strictly logical. In the fragments of his work that have been preserved in the writings of other philosophers, it appears that he argued that all other creatures had derived from the element of water, and that life was impossible without it. Because water could change its form and become ice or steam, it was capable of evolving into something different. Following the same line of thought, Anaximenos (560–496), another Milesian philosopher, believed that air was the primal stuff: air was also essential to life and could mutate— becoming wind, cloud, and water.

In the absence of empirical proof, these speculations were little more than fantasies; they were significant, however, because they showed that some Greeks were beginning to feel it necessary to follow the promptings of *logos* through to the bitter end, even if this overturned conventional wisdom. In attempting an analysis of the material world to discover a single, simple cause, Thales and Anaximenos were both starting to think like scientists. Anaximander (610–546), the most innovative of the three, went a step further: in order to find the primal substance, a philosopher had to go beyond what could be perceived by the senses in search of a more fundamental, intangible substance. He argued that the basic stuff of the universe was wholly "indefinite" (*apeiron*). Because it lay beyond our experience, it had no qualities that we could discern, yet everything had existed within it *in potentia*. The *apeiron* was divine, but went beyond the gods; it was the immeasurable and inexhaustible source of all life. By a process that Anaximander never explained, individual phenomena had "separated out" from the *apeiron,* and all the elements of the cosmos were now at war, constantly encroaching and preying upon one another. Time had imposed a form of *eunomia* on the universe, decreeing that each element was confined in its proper place, and that no one component of the universe could dominate the others. But eventually all things would be reabsorbed into the *apeiron.*

The *apeiron* had the potential to become what theologians have called a "god beyond the gods," except that it had no relevance to the daily lives of human beings. In the past, cosmology had not attempted to describe the origins of life in a literal manner. Creation myths had been designed to reveal fundamental insights about the perplexities of life on earth. The stories of gods fighting monsters to bring order out of chaos had laid bare the fundamentally agonistic struggle at the heart of life, which always depended on the death or destruction of other beings. Stories of a primal sacrifice had shown that true creativity required that you give yourself away. In his creation account, P had insisted that everything in the world was good, at a time when the exiles could have given way to despair. But it would be impossible to use any of the Milesian cosmologies therapeutically. That was not what they were for; they had nothing to do with spiritual insight. The Milesians developed their speculations for their own sake, and the seeds of future Western rationalism had been sown. At about the same time, however, philosophers in India had developed a creation myth that moved the religious Axial Age another step forward.

A new philosophy had emerged in India that was quite different from the Upanishads and paid scant attention to the Vedic scriptures. It was called Samkhya ("discrimination"), though originally the word may simply have meant "reflection" or "discussion." Samkhya would become extremely influential in India. Almost every single school of philosophy and spirituality would adopt at least some of its ideas—even those which disapproved of Samkhya. Yet, despite its importance, we know very little about the origins of this seminal movement. A sixth-century sage called Kapila was credited with the invention of Samkhya, but we know nothing about him, and cannot even be sure that he actually existed.

Like the Milesians, Samkhya analyzed the cosmos into separate component parts, looked back to the very beginning, and described a process of evolution that brought our world into being. But there the resemblance ended. Where the Greek philosophers were oriented to the external world, Samkhya delved within. Where the Milesians still claimed that "the world is full of gods," Samkhya was an atheistic philosophy. There was no brahman, no *apeiron,* and no world soul into which everything would merge. The supreme reality of the Samkhya system was *purusha* (the "person" or "self"). But the *purusha* of Samkhya was nothing like the Purusha figure in the Rig Veda, and was quite different from the self (*atman*) sought by the sages of the Upanishads. Unlike any of the other twenty-four categories of the Samkhya world, the *purusha* was absolute and not subject to change. But *purusha* was not a single, unique reality. In fact, the *purusha* was bewilderingly multiple. Every single human being had his or her own individual and eternal *purusha,* which was not caught up in samsara, the ceaseless round of death and rebirth, and which existed beyond space and time. Like the atman, *purusha* was impossible to define because it had no qualities that we could recognize. It was the essence of the human being, but was not the "soul," because it had nothing to do with our mental or psychological states. *Purusha* had no intelligence, as we know it, and no desires. It was so far from our normal experience that our ordinary waking selves were not even aware that we had an eternal *purusha*.

At the very beginning, *purusha* had somehow become entangled with *prakrti,* "nature." This word is also difficult to translate. It did not simply refer to the material, visible world, because *prakrti* included the mind, the intellect, and the psychomental experience that unenlightened human beings regard as the most spiritual part of themselves. As long as we were confined within the realm of *prakrti,* we remained in ignorance of the eternal dimension of our humanity. But *purusha* and *prakrti* were not enemies. "Nature," depicted as female, was in love with *purusha*. Her job was to extricate each person's *purusha* from her embrace, even if this required humans to turn against what, in their ignorance, they regarded as their true selves.[82] Nature yearned to liberate us, to free the *purusha* from the toils of illusion and suffering that characterize human life. Indeed, the whole of nature—did we but know it—existed in order to serve the eternal self (*purusha*) of each one of us. "From *brahman* down to the blade of grass, the whole of creation is for the benefit of the *purusha,* until supreme knowledge is attained."[83]

How did *purusha* fall into the toils of nature? Was there some kind of original sin? Samkhya does not answer these questions. Its metaphysical scheme was not intended to offer a literal, scientific, or historical account of reality. In India, truth was measured not by its objective but by its therapeutic value. The followers of Samkhya were supposed to meditate upon this description of nature's relationship with the *purusha* in order to discover what a human being had to do to find his way back to his true self. The ideas of Samkhya were almost certainly born in the circles of renouncers who were not satisfied by the spirituality of the Upanishads. Instead of losing themselves in the impersonal brahman, they wanted to retain their individuality. It was quite clear to them that life was unsatisfactory. Something had gone wrong, but it was pointless to speculate on how this unhappy state of affairs had come to pass. In their meditations they had glimpsed some kind of inner light, which indicated to them that they had another, more absolute self, if only they could separate it from the mess of illusion and desire that impeded their spiritual growth. The word *samkhya* may have once referred to the "dissociation" of the self from the "natural" realm of mind and matter. The renouncer had already withdrawn from society; now he had to take the next step, and find the true center of his being: the true spirit, his real self, his immortal *purusha*.

Samkhya attempted an analysis of reality that was simply designed to help the renouncer to achieve this liberation. In his forest retreat he could meditate upon it in order to understand the different components of his human nature. Only by becoming acquainted with the complexities of the human predicament could he hope to transcend it. Samkhya taught that nature had three different "strands" (*gunas*), which could be discerned in the cosmos as a whole and in each individual person.

- *Satta,* "intelligence," which is closest to the *purusha*
- *Rajas,* "passion," physical or mental energy
- *Tamas,* "inertia," the lowest of the *gunas*

At the beginning of time, before individual creatures had come into existence, the three *gunas* coexisted harmoniously in primal matter, but the presence of *purusha* disturbed this equilibrium and set off a process of emanation. The first of the new categories to emerge from the original undifferentiated unity was the intellect (*buddhi*), known as the "Great One." This was the highest part of our natural selves, and if we could isolate and develop it, it could bring us to the brink of enlightenment. The intellect was very close to the *purusha,* and could reflect the self in the same way as a mirror reflects a flower, but in the unenlightened human being it was clouded by the grosser elements of the world.

The next category to emerge was the ego principle (*ahamkara*). All other creatures emanated from the *ahamkara:* gods, hu-

mans, animals, plants, and the insensate world. The ego principle
was the source of our problem, because it transmitted nature to all
the different beings, with the three *gunas* in different proportions.
Satta (intelligence) was dominant in *devas* and holy men; *rajas*
characterized ordinary people, whose passionate energy was often
misdirected; and the lives of animals were obscured by the mental
darkness of *tamas*. But whatever our status, the root of our unhappiness was our sense of ego, which trapped us in a false self
that had nothing to do with our eternal *purusha*. We experienced
thoughts, feelings, and desires. We said, "I think," "I want," or "I
fear," imagining that "I" represented our entire being, so we expended far too much energy preserving and propping up this "I"
and hoped for its eternal survival in heaven. But this was an illusion. The ego on which we lavished so much attention was
ephemeral, because it was subject to time. It would become sick,
weak, diminish in old age, and finally flicker out and die, only to
start the whole miserable process again in another body. And in
the meantime, our true self, our *purusha,* which was eternal, autonomous, and free, was yearning to be liberated. Nature itself was
longing to achieve this. If we wanted to get beyond the pain and
frustrations of our lives, we must learn to recognize that the ego
was not our real self. Once we had attained this saving knowledge, in an intense act of cognition, we would achieve *moksha*
("liberation").

Ignorance held us back. We were so imprisoned in the delusions of nature that we confused the *purusha* with our ordinary
psychomental life, imagining that our thoughts, desires, and emotions were the highest and most essential part of our humanity.
This meant that our lives were based on a mistake. We assumed
that the self was simply an enhanced version of the ego that governed our daily existence. The renouncer had to rectify this ignorance in a course of meditation and study. The aspirant must
become aware of the forms of nature and the laws that govern its
evolution. He would thus acquire a knowledge that was not simply an intellectual mastery of the Samkhya system but an awakening to his true condition. In the course of his meditation, he
learned to concentrate on the *buddhi* to the exclusion of all else in

the hope of catching a glimpse of the *purusha*. Once he had seen the *purusha* reflected in his intellect, he achieved a profound realization that this was his true self. He cried, "I am recognized,"[84] and immediately nature, which had been longing for this moment, withdrew, "like a dancer, who departs after satisfying the master's desire."[85]

After that moment, there was no going back. Once he had woken up to his true nature, the enlightened renouncer was no longer prey to the sufferings of life. He went on living in the natural world; he would still get sick, grow old, and die, but now that he was one with the *purusha* the pain could no longer touch him. Indeed, he would find himself saying, "It suffers," rather than, "I suffer," because sorrow had become a remote experience, distant from what he now understood to be his true identity. When he finally died, nature ceased to be active, and the *purusha* attained perfect freedom and could never enter another mortal, time-bound body.

In one sense, Samkhya seemed to have detached itself entirely from Vedic religion. From the Samkhyan perspective, sacrifice was useless. The gods were also imprisoned by nature, so it was pointless to ask for their help. It was also counterproductive to try, by means of ritual, to build an atman that would survive in heaven, because the ego-self had to die. Only the special knowledge that was an awakening to our truest reality could bring permanent liberation. But even though it conflicted with Vedic orthodoxy, Samkhya was really a development of the traditional, archetypal vision of the perennial philosophy. People had always yearned to lose themselves in a celestial model, but Samkhya told them that this was not an external reality but existed within. They would not find the absolute by imitating a god, but by awakening to their most authentic self. The archetype did not exist in a remote, mythical realm but was inherent in the individual. Instead of merging with an external paradigmatic figure, they must identify with the internalized *purusha*.

Samkhya marked a new stage in self-consciousness. People in India were becoming aware of a self that was obscured by the confusions of daily life, hidden in our bodies, fettered by our instincts, and only dimly aware of itself. The metaphysical drama of Samkhya revealed that which was specifically human yearning for liberation. People could reach beyond themselves by cultivating a greater self-awareness. But this did not mean self-indulgence, because it was the ego that held the self in thrall. The people of India were becoming aware of the grasping, selfish orientation of our mundane existence. The ego made us unable to look at anything without asking: "Do I want this?" "How can I benefit from it?" "Does this threaten me?" "Why have I not got this?" As a result, we never saw anything as it truly was because we were imprisoned in the toils of selfishness. Samkhya could envisage liberation from this clinging, frightened egotism into a state of being that, in our normal ego-obsessed existence, we could not conceive. Such a state was not divine; it was not supernatural; it was the fulfillment of our human nature, and anybody who was ready to work for this freedom could acquire it.

Samkhya made two important contributions to Indian spirituality. First was the perception that all life was *dukkha,* a word that is often translated as "suffering" but that has a wider meaning: "unsatisfactory, awry." For reasons that nobody could ever know, our birth into this desacralized world was fraught and painful. Our experience was conditioned by ignorance and sorrow. Everything in the cosmos was disintegrating, mortal, and ephemeral. Even when the false "I" felt happy or satisfied, there was something amiss. If "I" achieved success, my rivals were disconsolate. Often "I" yearned for a goal or material object, only to find that it was ultimately disappointing and unsatisfactory. Moments of happiness were nearly always followed by periods of grief. Nothing lasted very long. Our chaotic inner world could shift from one state to another in a matter of seconds. Our friends died; people became ill, old, and lost their beauty and vitality. To deny this universal *dukkha*—as many preferred to do—was a delusion, because it was a law of life. But, Samkhya argued, this imperfect nature was also our friend, because the more "I" suffered and identified with this ephemeral world, the more "I" yearned for the absolute, unconditioned reality of *purusha.* Constantly, as we looked around us and into our turbulent inner selves, we found ourselves longing for something else: like the Upanishadic sages, we had to cry, *Neti, neti,* "Not this!" Samkhya might sound pessimistic, but it was actually optimistic and ambitious. It insisted that nature was not the final reality. People could and did experience liberation; they did find their *purusha,* their true self. All creatures suffered—gods, humans, animals, and insects—but only human beings were capable of *moksha* and liberation from pain.

But many renouncers found that in practice liberation was extremely difficult. Some people did achieve *moksha* by means of study and meditation, but others felt that something more was needed. Nature held human beings in such a powerful grip that tougher measures were necessary. This led some renouncers to develop the discipline that is now practiced throughout the world in meditation halls and gyms. Yoga is one of India's greatest achievements and, in its most evolved form, almost certainly was first designed in Samkhya circles to release the *purusha* from the entanglement of nature. This classical yoga was very different from the version of yoga that is often taught in the West today.[86] It was not an aerobic exercise, and it did not help people to relax, to suppress excessive anxiety, or feel better about their lives—quite the contrary. Yoga was a systematic assault on the ego, an exacting regimen that over a long period of time taught the aspirant to abolish his normal consciousness with its errors and delusions, and replace it with the ecstatic discovery of his *purusha.*

Again, we do not know the names of the renouncers who developed yoga. It was associated with Patanjali, who wrote the Yoga Sutras in the first centuries of the common era. But Patanjali did not invent these practices, which were very old indeed. Some scholars believe that a form of yoga may have been evolved by the indigenous inhabitants of India, before the arrival of the Aryan tribes. Some of the yogic techniques, particularly the breathing exercises, were mentioned in the early Upanishads and were practiced during the Vedic rituals. But however it began, yoga had become an established part of the spiritual landscape of India by the sixth century. It was practiced by Brahmins, orthodox Vedic renouncers, and the so-called heretical sects. Different groups developed different versions of yoga, but the basic disciplines, as described in the Yoga Sutras, were fundamental.

The term *yoga* is itself significant. It means "yoking." It was the word once used by the Vedic Aryans to describe the tethering of the draught animals to their war chariots before a raid. Warriors were men of yoga. They were like *devas,* perpetually on the move and constantly engaged in militant activity, while the sluggish *asuras* stayed at home. By the sixth century, however, the new men of yoga were engaged in the conquest of inner space; instead of waging war, they were dedicated to nonviolence. Yoga amounted to a raid on the unconscious mind, which was the root cause of so much of our pain. Patanjali listed five *vrittis* ("impulses") that held us in thrall: ignorance, our sense of ego, passion, disgust, and the lure of this transient life. These instincts surfaced one after the other, with inexhaustible and uncontrollable energy. They were basic to our humanity and, the yogins believed, were too deeply entrenched to be eliminated by the simple act of knowledge envisaged by the Samkhya teachers. We were deeply conditioned by what the yogins called *vasanas,* subconscious sensations that produced everything that was specific to the individual personality. They were the result of heredity and the karma of past and present lives. Long before Freud and Jung developed the modern, scientific search for the soul, the yogins of India had already begun to explore and analyze the unconscious realm with unprecedented vigor. These *vrittis* and *vasanas* had to be annihilated, "burned up." Only then could the self detach itself from the chaos of its psychic life, throw off the toils of nature, and experience the bliss of *moksha.* And this herculean feat could be achieved only by sheer mental force.

First, however, the yogin had to undergo a long period of preparation. He was not allowed to perform a single yogic exercise until he had completed an extensive moral training. The aspirant began by observing the *yamas* ("prohibitions"). At the top of the list was *ahimsa,* "harmlessness." The yogin must not kill or injure other creatures; he could not even swat a mosquito or speak unkindly to others. Second, he was forbidden to steal, which also

meant that he could not grab whatever he wanted, whenever he
wanted it; he must simply accept the food and clothing that he
was given without demur, cultivating an indifference to material
possessions. Third, he must not lie, but must speak the truth at all
times, not distorting it by making an incident more entertaining
or more flattering to himself, for example. Finally, he must abstain
from sex and from intoxicating substances, which could cloud his
mind and enervate the mental and physical energies that he
would need in this spiritual expedition. The preparatory program
also demanded the mastery of certain bodily and psychic disciplines (*niyama*). The aspirant must keep himself scrupulously
clean; he must study the teaching (*dharma*) of his guru; and he
must cultivate a habitual serenity, behaving kindly and courteously
to everybody, no matter how he was feeling inside.

This preparatory program showed the spiritual ambition of
the yogins. They were not interested in simply having a transient,
inspiring experience. Yoga was an initiation into a different way of
being human, and that meant a radically moral transformation.
The prohibitions and disciplines were a new, Axial Age version of
the traditional imitation of the archetypal model. Yogins had to
leave their unenlightened selves behind, abandon the ego principle, and behave as though the *purusha* had already been liberated.
When people in the past had ritually imitated a god, they had experienced a "stepping out" of their normal lives and an enhancement of being. The same was true of the *yama* and *niyama*. By dint
of practice, these ethical disciplines would become second nature,
and when this happened, Patanjali explained, the aspirant would
experience "indescribable joy."[87] As he left the "ego principle" behind, he had intimations of the final liberation.

Once his teacher was satisfied that the aspirant had mastered
the *yama* and *niyama,* he was ready to learn the first properly yogic
discipline: *asana,* "sitting." He had to sit with crossed legs, straight
back, and in a completely motionless position for hours at a time.
This was uncomfortable at first, and sometimes unbearably
painful. Motion is what characterizes living creatures. Everything
that moves is alive. Even when we imagine that we are sitting still,
we are in constant motion: we blink, scratch, shift from one but-

tock to another, and turn our heads in response to stimulus. Even in sleep, we toss and turn. But in *asana,* the yogin was learning to sever the link between his mind and his senses. He was so still that he seemed more like a statue or a plant than a human being. In the old days, the Aryans had despised the *asuras,* who had sat at home all day. Now the new men of yoga sat for hours in one place, without a sign of life.

Next the yogin learned to control his breathing, an even greater assault on his instinctual life. Respiration is the most fundamental and automatic of our physical functions, and is absolutely essential to life. In *pranayama,* however, the yogin learned to breathe more and more slowly. His aim was to pause for as long as possible between exhalation and inhalation, so that it seemed as though respiration had entirely ceased. His heart rate slowed down; he might even appear to be dead, and yet, once he had become adept at *pranayama,* he experienced a new kind of life. This controlled respiration, which is entirely different from the arrhythmic breathing of ordinary life, has been shown to have physical and neurological effects. It produces a sensation of calm, harmony, and equanimity, said to be comparable to the effect of music. There was a feeling of grandeur, expansiveness, and nobility—a sense of presence.

Once he had mastered these physical exercises, the trainee yogin was ready for the mental discipline of *ekagrata,* concentration "on one point." Here he refused to think, learning to focus uninterruptedly on a single object or idea. It could be a flower, the tip of his nose, or one of the teachings of his guru. The important thing was to exclude rigorously any other emotion or association, and to push away each one of the distractions that inevitably rushed into his mind. There were various forms of *ekagrata.* The aspirant learned *pratyahara* (withdrawal of the senses), contemplating the object with the intellect alone. In *dharana* (concentration), he was taught to visualize the *purusha* in the depths of his being, and imagine it gradually emerging like a lotus rising from a pond. Each *dharana* was supposed to last for twelve *pranayamas,* and by means of these combined physical and mental techniques, the adept yogin had sunk so deeply into his inner world and away from his ordinary, secular consciousness that he entered a state of trance.

The trainee found that he had achieved an astonishing invulnerability. As he became more expert, he found that he was no longer aware of the broiling heat of summer or the freezing cold of the winter rains. Now that he was able to control his psychic life, he had become impervious to his environment. He also found that he saw the object that he was contemplating in a new way. Because he had suppressed the flood of memories and personal associations that it evoked, he was no longer distracted by his own concerns. He did not subjectivize or privatize it; instead of viewing it through the distorting lens of his own needs and desires, he could see it as it really was. The "I" was beginning to disappear from his thinking, and as a result, even the most humdrum objects revealed wholly unexpected qualities. When the yogin meditated in this way on the ideas of his particular school, such as the Samkhya creation myth, he experienced them so vividly that a rationalistic formulation of these truths paled in comparison. His knowledge was no longer simply notional; he knew these truths directly. They had become a part of his inner world.

Yogins did not believe that they were touched by a god; there was nothing supernatural about these experiences. Samkhya, after all, was an atheistic creed and had no interest in *devas*. Yogins were convinced that they were simply developing the natural capacity of the human person. Anybody who trained hard enough could achieve these mental feats. They had discovered a new dimension of their humanity. This transcendence was not an encounter with an external deity "out there," but a descent into the depths of their own being. By systematically separating himself from his normal, ego-bound existence, the yogin was attempting to isolate his real self from the toils of nature. Again, these men of the Axial Age were achieving an ecstatic "stepping out" of the norm by becoming more fully aware of their own nature.

Once he had entered the state of trance, the yogin progressed through a series of increasingly deep mental states, which bore no relation to their usual experience. There was *samadhi,* a state of pure consciousness, where the sense of "I" and "mine" had completely disappeared; the yogin felt wholly at one with the objects of his meditation, and was aware of nothing else. He was certainly not conscious of himself contemplating them. There were other, more extreme states that were achieved by a very few, especially talented yoga practitioners, who could describe them only paradoxically: there was a sense of absence that was also a presence; an emptiness that was plenitude; an eternal present; a life in death. Yogins called such experience "nothingness" because there were no words to describe it; they compared it to the sensation of walking into a room and finding simply emptiness, space, and freedom.

The yogins interpreted their meditative discoveries differently. Those who subscribed to the teachings of the Upanishads believed that they had finally become one with the brahman; those who followed the Samkhya philosophy claimed that they had liberated the *purusha*. But the basic experience remained the same. Whatever they thought they had done, the yogins had opened up new possibilities. An acute appreciation of the suffering that was endemic to the human condition had led these extraordinarily ambitious men to find a radical way out. They had evolved a spiritual technology that would free them of *dukkha*. Yoga was not for everybody, however. It was a full-time job that could not be combined with the demands of everyday life. But other sages would later find a way to develop a yoga that would give the laity intimations of enlightenment.

Meanwhile, China was in crisis. When Chu had defeated the armies of the league of Chinese states in 597, the region became engulfed in an entirely new kind of aggression. The gloves were off. Chu had no time for the old ritualized warfare, and the other large states also began to cast aside the constraints of tradition, determined to expand and conquer more territory, even if this meant the destruction of the enemy. Warfare became very different from the stately campaigns of the past. In 593, for example, during a lengthy siege, the people of Song were reduced to eating their own children. The old principalities faced political annihilation. They knew that they could not compete with the bigger states but were drawn into the fray against their will, as their territories became a battleground of competing armies. Qi, for example, so frequently encroached on the tiny principality of Lu that Lu was forced to appeal to Chu for aid—but all to no avail. By the end of the sixth century, Chu had been defeated and Qi had become so dominant that the duke of Lu only managed to retain a modicum of independence with the help of the western state of Qin.

The states were also weakened by internal problems. During the sixth century, Qi, Jin, and Chu were all fatally debilitated by chronic civil wars. In Lu, three competing baronial families had reduced the legitimate duke to a mere puppet. This in itself was a sign of the times. The descendant of the great duke of Zhou had been stripped of all power except his ritual duties, and was financially dependent upon the usurpers. Old political and social structures were disintegrating, and China seemed to be rushing headlong into anarchy. Yet these struggles signaled a deeper change. The noblemen who rebelled against their princes were certainly motivated by greed and ambition, but they were also trying to free themselves from the domination of the older families. The Chinese were painfully moving toward a more egalitarian polity that would undermine the hitherto unchallenged rule of the hereditary princes.[88] In Cheng and Lu, there were fiscal and agricultural reforms that improved the lot of the peasants. In the second half of the sixth century, Zichan, prime minister of the principality of Cheng, inscribed and displayed the penal laws on large bronze cauldrons. There was now a definite law code, which anybody could consult to challenge arbitrary rule.

As archaeologists have discovered, there was a growing contempt for ritual observance: people were placing profane objects in the tombs of their relatives instead of the prescribed ritual vessels. The old spirit of moderation was in decline: many of the Chinese had developed a new taste for luxury, which put an unbearable strain on the economy, as demand outstripped resources. Some of the ordinary gentlemen (*shi*) at the bottom of the feudal hierarchy had begun to ape the lifestyle of the great families. As a result, there were now too many aristocrats, so a worrying number of the *shi* were fatally impoverished. There were now so many nouveaux riches that some members of the nobility could no longer own a fief, because there was not enough land to go around. Many gentlemen, including some who were close relatives of the princes, lost their lands and titles and were reduced to the rank of commoners. Some of the demoted *shi* were scribes, ritualists, or captains in the army, who were now forced to leave the city and take their skills into the countryside, where they lived with the common people.

This was not simply a social and political crisis. Heaven and earth were so interdependent that many people feared that the current scorn for the Way of Heaven endangered the entire cosmos. The ritualists of Lu saw the new greed, aggression, and materialism as a blasphemous assault on the sacred rites. Others were more skeptical. In 534, many of the Chinese states were devastated by a typhoon, which was followed by deadly forest fires. In Cheng, the master diviner approached Zichan, the prime minister, and asked him to offer a special sacrifice to appease Heaven. Zichan shook his head. "The Way of Heaven is far removed; it is the Way of man that is near us," he replied. "We cannot reach the former; what means have we of knowing it?"[89] Since Heaven was beyond our ken, it was better to concentrate on what lay within our grasp.

At about this time, a young man called Kong Qiu (551–479) had almost completed his studies and was about to take a minor post in the administration of Lu. His family were newcomers to the principality, since his ancestors had been members of the ducal house of Song, but like so many other aristocrats, the family was forced to emigrate. Kong Qiu was thus brought up in genteel poverty, and had to earn his living. He was drawn to the ritualists and was passionately devoted to the Zhou dynasty, especially the great duke of Zhou, who sometimes visited him in his dreams. Kong Qiu was an avid student. By the age of thirty, he had mastered his study of the *li,* and by the time he was forty, he says, he had become a learned man. Many of the *shi* who had been reduced to penury were bitter and resentful, but Kong Qiu understood the deeper meaning of the rites and was convinced that, properly interpreted, they could bring the people of China back to the Way of Heaven. Later Kong Qiu's disciples would proudly call him Kongfuzi, "our Master Kong." In the West, we call him Confucius. China's Axial Age was about to begin.

6

EMPATHY

(c. 530 to 450 BCE)

Toward the end of the sixth century, Lu was on the verge of total anarchy, as the three baronial families who had usurped the power of the legitimate duke battled against one another for supremacy. This was especially distressing to the ritualists. People from all over China came to Lu to attend the ceremonial liturgy and listen to the music that dated back to the early Zhou kings. One visitor from Jin exclaimed: "The ceremony [li] of Zhou is all in all here! Only now do I understand the potency of the Duke of Zhou and why Zhou reigned."[1] But by 518, the rightful ruler of Lu, the descendant of the duke of Zhou, was so poor that he could no longer pay musicians and dancers to perform these rites in the ancestral temple. Yet that year one of the usurpers had eight teams of dancers performing the rites of the royal house—quite illegally—in his *own* ancestral shrine. There was creeping dismay. The li no longer curbed the greed and ostentation of the noble families, and Heaven seemed indifferent.

When Confucius heard about this illicit performance of the royal rites, he was incensed. "The Way makes no progress," he lamented.[2] If the rulers could not implement the sacred values that kept society on the right path, then he must do so himself. As a commoner, he could not establish the *dao;* only a king could do that. But he could educate a band of holy, informed men who would instruct the rulers of China in the Way and recall them to their duty. Confucius had hoped for a political career, but was constantly disappointed. He was too blunt and honest to succeed in politics, and never managed to achieve anything more than a menial appointment in the departments of finance and accountancy. Yet this was the best thing that could have happened. His political failure gave him time to think, and he became an inspired teacher, determined that if he could not succeed himself, he would train others for high office. Like other marginalized *shi* at this time, he became a wandering scholar, traveling tirelessly from one state to another with his small, faithful band of disciples, hoping that at least one of the princes would finally take him seriously.

Confucius was no solitary ascetic, but a man of the world, who enjoyed a good dinner, fine wine, a song, a joke, and stimulating conversation. He did not lock himself away in an ivory tower, did not practice introspection or meditation, but always developed his insights in conversation with other people. In the Analects, our main source, we see him constantly engaged in discussion with friends and pupils. His kindness and brilliance—an unusual combination—drew students toward him like a magnet, and he never turned anyone away. Some of his students were aristocrats, others were of humble birth. His favorite was probably the poor but mystically gifted Yan Hui, but he loved all the members of his little company: calm, strong Mingzi; energetic Zilu; and Zigong, who was always so brave and honest. When a potential student presented himself, Confucius looked for one quality above all others. "Only one who bursts with eagerness do I instruct," he said. "Only one who bubbles with excitement do I enlighten."[3] He scolded his pupils, drove them on ruthlessly, but never bullied them. After marveling at the somewhat daunting attainments of the yogins, it is a relief to turn to Confucius, whose Way, properly understood, was accessible to anybody. Affable, calm, and friendly, Confucius never pontificated; there were no long lectures or sermons, and even if he disagreed with his students, he was usually ready to concede their point of view. Why should he not? He was no divinely inspired sage like Yao or Shun. He had no revelations or visions. His only merit was an "unwearying effort to learn and unflagging patience in teaching others."[4]

The Analects were put together by his disciples long after Confucius's death, so we cannot be sure that all the maxims attributed to him are authentic, but scholars believe that the text can be regarded as a reasonably reliable source.[5] It consists of hundreds of short, unconnected remarks, with no attempt to produce a clearly defined vision. The style is suggestive in the same way as a Chinese landscape: readers are supposed to search for what is *not* said, to look between the lines for the full meaning, and to connect one idea with another. In fact, despite first impressions, there is coherence in the Analects. Indeed, Confucius's vision is so densely interconnected that it is sometimes difficult to disentangle its various themes.

Like other philosophers of the Axial Age, Confucius felt profoundly alienated from his time. He was convinced that the root cause of the current disorder in China was neglect of the traditional rites that had governed the conduct of the principalities for so long. In the days of Yao and Shun and, later, under the early Zhou, he believed, the Way of Heaven had been practiced perfectly and human beings had lived together harmoniously. The *li* had encouraged a spirit of moderation and generosity. But these days, most princes never gave the *dao* a second thought. They were too busy chasing after luxury and pursuing their own selfish ambitions. The old world was crumbling, without anything of equal value emerging to take its place. In Confucius's view, the best solution was to return to the traditions that had worked so well in the past.

Confucius was horrified by the constant warfare that threatened to obliterate the small principalities. Yet, to his dismay, they did not seem fully alert to the danger. Lu could not compete militarily with a large state like Qi, but instead of marshaling all its resources to meet this external threat, the baronial families—all motivated by greed and vainglory—were fighting a self-destructive civil war. If the "three families" had observed the *li* correctly, this state of affairs could never have come to pass. In the past, the rites had helped to curb the danger of violence and vendetta, and had mitigated the horror of battle. They must do so again. As a ritualist, Confucius had spent far more time on the study of ceremony and the classics than on the princely arts of archery and chariot driving.[6] He now redefined the role of the *junzi:* the true gentleman should be a scholar, not a warrior. Instead of fighting for power, the *junzi* must study the rules of correct behavior, as prescribed by the traditional *li* of family, political, military, and social life. Confucius never claimed to be an original thinker. "I have transmitted what was taught to me without making up anything of my own," he once said. "I have been faithful to and loved the ancients."[7] Only a sage, who had been blessed with divine insight, could break with tradition. "I am simply one who loves the past, and who is diligent in investigating it."[8] And yet, despite these disclaimers, Confucius *was* an innovator. He was bent on "reanimating the Old to gain knowledge of the New."[9] The world had changed, but there could be no fruitful development unless there was also a measure of continuity.

Some of the ways in which Confucius interpreted tradition were radically different in emphasis. The old religion had focused on Heaven: people had often performed the sacrifices simply to gain the favor of the gods and spirits, but Confucius concentrated on this world. Like his contemporary Zichan, prime minister of Cheng, he believed that it was better to focus on what we knew. Indeed, he preferred not to speak of Heaven at all. His pupil Zigong noted: "We are allowed to hear our Master's views on culture and the outward insignia of goodness, but about the ways of Heaven, he will not tell us anything at all."[10] Confucius was not interested in metaphysics and discouraged theological chatter. When Zilu asked him how a *junzi* should minister to the gods, he replied: "Till you have learned to serve men, how can you serve spirits?" And when Zilu persisted, and asked what the life of the ancestors was actually like, Confucius replied again: "Till you know about the living, how are you to know about the dead?"[11] Confucius was no skeptic. He practiced the traditional ancestral rites punctiliously, and was filled with numinous awe when he thought of Heaven. Like the Indian sages, he understood the value of silence. "I would much rather not have to talk," he once complained. Zigong was distressed. "If our Master did not talk," he objected, "how can we little ones teach others about him?" "Heaven does not speak," Confucius replied, "yet the four seasons run their course by the command of Heaven, the hundred creatures, each after its own kind, are born thereby. Heaven does no speaking!"[12] Heaven might not talk, but it was supremely effective. Instead of wasting time on pointless theological speculation, people should imitate the reticence of Heaven and keep a reverent silence. Then, perhaps, they too would be a potent force in the world. Confucius brought the religion of China down to earth. Instead of concerning themselves about the afterlife, people must learn to be good here below. His disciples did not study with him in order to acquire esoteric information about the gods and spirits. Their ultimate concern was not Heaven but the Way. The task of the *junzi* was to tread the path carefully, realizing that this in itself had absolute value. It would lead them not to a place or a person but to a condition of transcendent goodness. The rituals were the road map that would put them on course.

Everybody had the potential to become a *junzi,* who—for Confucius—was a fully developed human being. In the old days, only an aristocrat had been a *junzi,* but Confucius insisted that anybody who studied the Way enthusiastically could become a "gentleman," a mature or profound person. Zigong once suggested that the company adopt as their motto: "Poor without cadging, rich without swagger." "Not bad," Confucius said. "But better still, Poor, yet delighting in the Way; rich, yet a student of ritual." Zigong immediately capped this by quoting a verse from the *Classic of Odes:*

> As thing cut, as thing filed,
> As thing chiselled, as thing polished.[13]

Confucius was delighted: at last Zigong was beginning to understand the *Odes!* These lines perfectly described the way a *junzi* used the rites to burnish and refine his humanity. A *junzi* was not born but crafted. He had to work on himself in the same way as a sculptor shaped a rough stone and made it a thing of beauty. A true *junzi* was always trying to go beyond what he was and become what he was supposed to be. "How can I achieve this?" asked Yan Hui. It was simple, Confucius answered: "Curb your ego and surrender to *li*."[14] A *junzi* must submit every detail of his life to the rituals of consideration and respect for others. The aim was "to look at nothing in defiance of ritual, to listen to nothing in defiance of ritual, to speak of nothing in defiance of ritual, never to stir hand or foot in defiance of ritual." If the princes of China did this, they would save the world. "If a ruler could curb his ego and submit to *li* for a single day, everyone under Heaven would respond to his goodness!"[15]

Like the Indian sages, Confucius saw the "ego principle" as the source of human pettiness and cruelty. If people could lose their selfishness and submit to the altruistic demands of the *li* at every moment of their lives, they would be transformed by the beauty of holiness. They would conform to the archetypal ideal of the *junzi,* the superior human being. The rites lifted ordinary biological actions onto a different plane; they ensured that we did not treat other people carelessly or relate to them perfunctorily; that we were not simply driven by utility and self-interest. The rules of filial piety, for example, instructed sons to serve their parents' food graciously, but these days many sons simply threw it on the table. "Even dogs and horses are cared for to that extent!" Confucius exclaimed in exasperation; but if the meal was eaten in an atmosphere of respect and appreciation, it became humane.[16] A man of the Axial Age, Confucius wanted people to become fully conscious of what they were doing. Performance of the *li* was not simply a matter of going through the motions; it required psychological acuity, sensitivity, and an intelligent appraisal of each circumstance.[17] "Filial piety does not consist merely in young people undertaking the hard work, when anything has to be done or serving their elders first with wine and food," Confucius explained; "it is something much more than that."[18] What was this elusive "something"? It was the "demeanor," Confucius decided.[19] The spirit in which you performed a rite would show in every single one of your gestures and facial expressions. A rite could become an insult if it was carried out with contempt or impatience.

In the past, however, the *li* had often had an aggressive edge.

They had been used for political advantage or simply to enhance a nobleman's personal prestige. Confucius systematically took this egotism out of the *li*. His prolonged study of the rites had taught him that they made sense only if sincerely performed in a spirit of "yielding" (*rang*). Sons had to yield to fathers, warriors to their enemies, and kings to their retainers. The rites taught them to give up their personal preferences, dethroning themselves from the center of their world and putting another person there. In political life, the rites had made it difficult for statesmen to promote purely self-interested policies. They had taught a disciplined habit of empathy. If performed in the right spirit, therefore, the rites were a spiritual education that helped people to get beyond the limitations of egotism. A reformed ritualism, which cut out the old obsession with status and preeminence, could make the whole of China a humane place, by restoring dignity and grace to human intercourse.

Li taught people to deal with others as equals. They became partners in the same ceremony: in the liturgical ballets, a person who performed even a minor role perfectly was indispensable and contributed to the beauty of the whole. The rites made people conscious of the holiness of life and also conferred sanctity. Traditionally, the *li* of reverence had nourished the divine power of the prince; the *li* of filial piety had created the divine *shen* that enabled a mortal man to become an ancestor. By treating others with absolute respect, the rituals introduced the person who performed the rite and the person who received his attention to the sacred dimension of existence.

In India, the yogins had embarked on a solitary quest for the absolute. Confucius would not have understood this. In his view, you needed other people to elicit your full humanity; self-cultivation was a reciprocal process. Instead of seeing family life as an impediment to enlightenment, like the renouncers of India, Confucius saw it as the theater of the religious quest, because it taught every family member to live for others.[20] This altruism was essential to the self-cultivation of a *junzi:* "In order to establish oneself, one should try to establish others," Confucius explained. "In order to enlarge oneself, one should try to enlarge others."[21]

Later Confucius would be criticized for concentrating too exclusively upon the family—because people should have concern for everybody—but Confucius saw each person as the center of a constantly growing series of concentric circles, to which he or she must relate.[22] Each of us began life in the family, so the family *li* began our education in self-transcendence, but it could not end there. A *junzi*'s horizons would gradually expand. The lessons he had learned by caring for his parents, spouse, and siblings made his heart larger, so that he felt empathy with more and more people: first with his immediate community, then with the state in which he lived, and finally with the entire world.

Confucius was one of the first people to make it crystal clear that holiness was inseparable from altruism. He used to say: "My Way has one thread that runs right through it." There were no abstruse metaphysics or complicated liturgical speculations; everything always came back to the importance of treating other people with absolute sacred respect. "Our Master's Way," said one of his disciples, "is nothing but this: doing-your-best-for-others [*zhong*] and consideration [*shu*]."[23] The Way was nothing but a dedicated, ceaseless effort to nourish the holiness of others, who in return would bring out the sanctity inherent in you. "Is there any single saying that one can act upon all day and every day?" Zigong asked his master. "Perhaps the saying about consideration [*shu*]," said Confucius. "Never do to others what you would not like them to do to you."[24] *Shu* should really be translated as "likening to oneself." Others have called it the Golden Rule; it was the essential religious practice and was far more difficult than it appeared. Zigong once claimed that he had mastered this virtue: "What I do not want others to do to me, I have no desire to do to others," he announced proudly. One can almost see Confucius's wry but affectionate smile, as he shook his head. "Oh! You have not quite got to that point yet."[25]

Shu required that "all day and every day" we looked into our own hearts, discovered what caused us pain, and then refrained, under all circumstances, from inflicting that distress upon other people. It demanded that people no longer put themselves into a special, separate category but constantly related their own experience to that of others. Confucius was the first to promulgate the Golden Rule. For Confucius it had transcendent value. A perfect mastery of the *li* helped people to acquire what he called *ren*. This word had originally meant "noble" or "worthy," but by Confucius's time, it simply meant a human being. Confucius gave the word an entirely new significance, but he refused to define it. Later some philosophers would equate *ren* with "benevolence," but this was too narrow for Confucius.[26] In Chinese script, *ren* had two components: first, a simple ideogram of a human being—the self; and second, two horizontal strokes, indicating human relations. So *ren* could be translated as "cohumanity"; some scholars also argue that its root meaning was "softness" or "pliability."[27] *Ren* was, therefore, inseparable from the "yielding" of ritual. But for Confucius, *ren* was inexpressible, because it could not be contained within any of the familiar categories of his time.[28] Only somebody who practiced *ren* perfectly could understand it. *Ren* resembled what Socrates and Plato would call "the Good." A person who had *ren* had become a perfectly mature human being, on a level with Yao, Shun, or the duke of Zhou. *Ren,* Confucius believed, was the "power of the Way" (*daode*) that had enabled the sage kings to rule without force. It should no longer be regarded as magical but as a moral efficacy that would change the world far more effectively than violence and warfare.

What is *ren,* asked one of Confucius's disciples, and how could it be applied to political life? The master replied:

> Behave away from home as though you were in the presence of an important guest. Deal with the common people as though you were officiating at an important sacrifice. Do not do to others what you would not like yourself. Then there will be no feelings of opposition to you, whether it is the affairs of a State you are handling or the affairs of a Family.[29]

If the prince behaved toward other rulers and states in this way, there could be no brutal wars. The Golden Rule would make it impossible to invade or devastate somebody else's territory, because no prince would like this to happen to his own state. Rulers could not exploit the common people, because they would see them as copractitioners in a beautiful ceremony and, therefore, "like themselves." Opposition and hatred would melt away. Confucius could not explain what *ren* was, but he could tell people how to acquire it. *Shu* taught you to use your own feelings as a guide to your treatment of others. It was quite simple, Confucius explained to Zigong:

> As for *ren,* you yourself desire rank and standing; then help others to get rank and standing. You want to turn your merits to account; then help others to turn theirs to account—in fact, the ability to take one's own feelings as a guide—that is the sort of thing that lies in the direction of *ren*.[30]

Any ruler who constantly behaved in this way, conferring benefits on the ordinary folk and seeking the good of the entire state rather than his own personal advantage, would be a sage on the same level as Yao and Shun.[31]

Confucius was not a timid conservative, therefore, clinging to traditional mores and preoccupied with liturgical minutiae. His vision was revolutionary. He gave a new interpretation to the customary *li*. They were not designed to enhance a nobleman's prestige, but to transform him by making the practice of self-forgetfulness habitual. By taking the egotism out of the ritual, Confucius brought out its profound spiritual and moral potential. He was not encouraging servile conformity. The *li* demanded the imagination and intelligence to see that each circumstance was unique and must be judged independently. Confucius also introduced a new egalitarianism. Previously only the aristocracy had performed the *li*. Now, Confucius insisted, anybody could practice the rites, and even somebody of humble origins, such as Yan Hui, could become a *junzi*.

Other Chinese philosophers of the Axial Age would propose a more realistic solution to the problems of China, but they were not always as ambitious as Confucius, who aimed at more than law and order. He wanted human dignity, nobility, and holiness, and knew that this could be achieved only by a daily struggle to achieve the virtue of *shu*. It was an audacious plan. Confucius was asking people to trust in the power of an enhanced humanity instead of coercion. Very few people really wanted to give up their egotism. But those who did try to put Confucius's Way into practice found that it transformed their lives. *Ren* was difficult because it required the eradication of vanity, resentment, and the desire to dominate others.[32] And yet, paradoxically, *ren* was easy. "Is *ren* indeed so far away?" Confucius asked. "If we really wanted *ren,* we should find that it was at our very side."[33] It came "after what is difficult is done"—after, that is, a person had mastered the education provided by the *li.*[34] It required perseverance, rather than superhuman strength, and was, perhaps, like learning to ride a bicycle: once you had acquired the skill, it became effortless. You had to keep at it, however. Either you constantly behaved toward other people—whoever they were—as though they had the same fundamental importance as yourself, or you did not. But if you did so, you achieved a moral power that was almost tangible.

The pursuit of *ren* was a lifelong struggle; it would end only at death.[35] Confucius did not encourage his students to speculate about what lay at the end of the Way. Walking along this path was itself a transcendent and dynamic experience. Yan Hui, Confucius's favorite disciple, expressed it beautifully when he said of *ren,* "with a deep sigh":

> The more I strain my gaze towards it the higher it soars.
> The deeper I bore down into it, the harder it becomes.
> I see it in front, but suddenly it is behind. Step by step,
> the Master skilfully lures one on. He has broadened me
> with culture, restrained me with ritual. Even if I wanted
> to stop, I could not. Just when I feel that I have ex-
> hausted every resource, something seems to rise up,
> standing over me sharp and clear. Yet though I long to
> pursue it, I can find no way of getting to it at all.[36]

Ren was not something you "got" but something you gave. *Ren* was an exacting yet exhilarating way of life. It was *itself* the transcendence you sought. Living a compassionate, empathic life took you beyond yourself, and introduced you into another dimension. The constant discipline of ritual and *ren* gave Yan Hui momentary glimpses of a sacred reality that was both immanent and transcendent, looming up from within yet also a companionable presence, "standing over me sharp and clear."

When Yan Hui died, in 483, Confucius wept bitterly, without his customary restraint. "Alas, Heaven has bereft me, Heaven has bereft me!"[37] If any man's death could justify such excessive grief, he said, it was Yan Hui's. He had always said that Yan Hui was further along the Way than himself.[38] Confucius's son died that same year, and three years later, his oldest disciple, Zilu, died. Confucius was desolate. "The phoenix does not come," he lamented, "the river gives forth no chart. It is all over with me."[39] Even his hero the duke of Zhou no longer came to him in sleep.[40] In 479 he died at the age of seventy-four. In his self-effacing way, he thought that he was a failure, and yet he had made an indelible impression on Chinese spirituality. Even the Axial philosophers who vehemently rejected his teaching would find it impossible to escape his influence.

A new power had appeared in the Middle East. In 559, Cyrus succeeded to the throne of Persia, in what is now southern Iran. Ten years later, he conquered Media; in 547 he defeated Lydia and the Greek poleis on the Ionian coast of Asia Minor; and finally, in 539, he invaded Babylonia and was greeted by the conquered peoples as a liberating hero. Cyrus had become the ruler of the largest empire the world had ever seen. He was probably a practicing Zoroastrian, but he did not impose his faith on his subjects. In Egypt, Cyrus was called the servant of Amun Re; in Babylon, he was the son of Marduk; and a Judean prophet called him the *messiach,* the "anointed king" of Yahweh.[41] We do not know this prophet's name. He was active in Babylonia during the second half of the sixth century, and because his oracles were preserved in the same scroll as those of Isaiah, he is usually called Second Isaiah. He

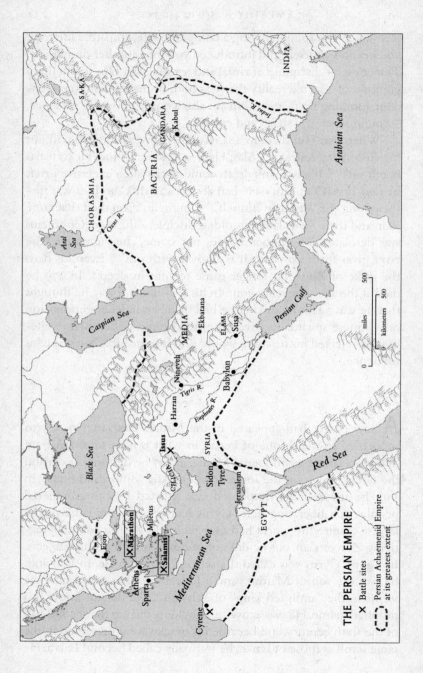

THE PERSIAN EMPIRE

X Battle sites

⌐ ⌐ Persian Achaemenid Empire
at its greatest extent

had watched Cyrus's progress with mounting excitement, convinced that the suffering of the exiled community was coming to an end. Yahweh had called Cyrus to be his servant, and his imperial mission would change the history of the world.[42] He had promised to repatriate all deportees, so Jerusalem would be rebuilt and the land restored. There would be a new exodus: once again, Jewish exiles would journey through the wilderness to their Promised Land.

Instead of the anguished, wrenching visions of Ezekiel, Second Isaiah could see a glorious future, which he described in lyrical, psalmlike poetry. He spoke of magical events and a transformed creation. Unlike the Deuteronomists, who had scorned the old mythology, Second Isaiah relied upon a mythical tradition that had little connection with the Pentateuch. Instead of P's orderly creation story, he revived the ancient tales of Yahweh, the divine warrior, slaying the sea dragon to bring order out of primordial chaos,[43] reinstating the violence that P had so carefully excluded from his cosmology. Yahweh, he announced joyfully, was about to repeat his cosmic victory over the sea by defeating the historical enemies of Israel.

But these exuberant prophecies were punctuated by four extraordinary poems about a man of sorrows, who called himself Yahweh's servant.[44] We have no idea who the servant was. Was he, perhaps, the exiled king of Judah? Or did he symbolize the whole community of deportees? Many scholars believe that these poems were not the work of Second Isaiah, and some have even suggested that the servant was the prophet himself, whose inflammatory oracles may have offended the Babylonian authorities. Others regard the servant as the archetypal exilic hero, who expressed a religious ideal that was deeply in tune with the ethos of the Axial Age. For some of the exiles, the suffering servant was their model—not the divine warrior.

In the first poem, the servant announced that he had been chosen by Yahweh for a special mission. Filled with God's own spirit, he was entrusted with the gigantic task of establishing justice throughout the world. But he would not achieve this by force of arms. There would be no battles and no aggressive self-assertion. The servant would conduct a nonviolent, compassionate campaign:

> He does not cry out or shout aloud
> or make his voice heard in the streets.
> He does not break the crushed reed,
> nor quench the wavering flame.[45]

The servant had sometimes felt hopeless, but Lord Yahweh always came to his aid, so he could stand firm, set his face like flint, and remain untouched by insult and humiliation. He had never retaliated violently, but resolutely turned the other cheek.

> For my part I made no resistance, neither did I turn away.
> I offered my back to those who struck me,
> my cheeks to those who tore at my beard;
> I did not cover my face
> against insult and spittle.[46]

God would judge and punish the servant's enemies, who would simply melt away, disintegrating like a moth-ridden garment.

The fourth song looked ahead to this final triumph. At present, the servant inspired only revulsion; he was "despised and rejected by men," so disfigured that he seemed scarcely human. People turned their faces away in horror and disgust. But, Yahweh promised, he would eventually be "lifted up, exalted, rise to great heights." The people who had watched his degradation would be speechless with astonishment, but they would eventually realize that he had suffered for them: "Ours were the sufferings he bore, ours the sorrows he carried. . . . He was punished for our faults, crushed for our sins." By his courageous, serene acceptance of pain, he had brought them peace and healing.[47] It was a remarkable vision of suffering. In their hour of triumph, the servant reminded Israel that pain was an ever-present reality, but his kenosis led to exaltation and ekstasis. His benevolence was universal, reaching out from his immediate circle to include the entire world—to the distant islands and the remotest peoples. It was not enough "to restore the tribes of Jacob," Yahweh told him; he was to be "the light of the nations, so that my salvation may reach to the ends of the earth."[48]

By contrast, the oracles of Second Isaiah had a harsh message for the nations who opposed Israel in any way. They would be "destroyed and brought to nothing," scattered like chaff on the wind. Even those foreign rulers who helped Israel would have to fall prostrate on the ground before the Israelites, licking the dust at their feet.[49] In these passages, Israel's role was not to be a humble servant of humanity, but to demonstrate the mighty power of Yahweh, the warrior god. There seem to be two contending visions in this text, and perhaps there were two schools of thought in the exiled community at this point. The servant triumphed by nonviolence and self-effacement; he saw the sufferings of Israel as redemptive. But other exiles anticipated a new order based on the subjection of others. One ethos was profoundly in tune with the Axial Age; the other straining to break free from it. This tension would continue within Israel.

Second Isaiah believed that the historic reversals of his time would enable both Israel and the foreign nations "to know that I am Yahweh."[50] These words recur again and again. This new exercise of divine power would show everybody who Yahweh was and what he could do. Motivated entirely by the desire to help his people, he had inspired the career of Cyrus, caused an international, worldwide political revolution, and cast down the mighty empire of Babylon. When Israel returned home, Yahweh would transform the wilderness into a lake, and plant cedars, acacias, myrtles, and olives to delight his people on their homeward journey. Could any other deity match this? No, Yahweh declared scornfully to the gods of the *goyim,* "you are nothing, and your works are nothingness." Nobody in their right mind would worship them.[51] Yahweh had annihilated the other deities and become in effect the *only* God, his vitality in sharp contrast with the lifeless, inanimate effigies of the Babylonian deities.[52] "I am Yahweh, unrivalled," he announced proudly. "There is no other god besides me."[53]

This is the first unequivocal biblical assertion of monotheism, the belief that only one God exists. The doctrine is often seen as the great triumph of the Jewish Axial Age, but in the way that it is phrased, it seems to retreat from some fundamental Axial principles. Instead of looking forward to a period of universal peace and compassion, Second Isaiah's aggressive deity looks back to the pre-Axial divine warrior:

> Yahweh advances like a hero,
> His fury is stirred like a warrior's.
> He gives the war shout, raises hue and cry,
> Marches valiantly against his foes.[54]

Unlike the self-emptying servant, this God cannot stop asserting himself: "I, I am Yahweh!" Where the servant refused to "break the crushed reed,"[55] this aggressive deity could not wait to see the *goyim* marching behind the Israelites in chains. Instead of recoiling from the violence, like so many of the other Axial sages, Second Isaiah gave it sacred endorsement.

The prophet's focus on the earthly city of Jerusalem also seemed to turn the clock back to an older, less developed theological vision. In India and China, the cult was being steadily internalized, and in Israel too Ezekiel's mandala of a holy city had represented an interior, spiritual ascent to the divine. But the pivot of Second Isaiah's hopes was the earthly Zion. Yahweh would work a miracle there, transforming its desolate ruins into an earthly paradise. The "glory" of Yahweh, which Ezekiel had seen leaving the city, would return to Mount Zion, and—most important—"all mankind shall see it."[56] Second Isaiah was expecting something dramatic. Before the exile, the "glory" had been evoked and reenacted in the temple rituals, but in the restored Jerusalem (whose walls and battlements would be studded with precious jewels), the divine presence would be more tangible. The returned exiles would experience the glory directly, and because Yahweh would be with his people in such a public, incontrovertible way, they would be safe forever. No nation would dare to attack them again:

> Remote from oppression, you will have nothing to fear;
> Remote from terror, it will not approach you. . . .
> Not a weapon forged against you will succeed.[57]

Second Isaiah's promises were disconcertingly close to those of the "false prophets" who had predicted that Jerusalem could never fall to the Babylonians. What would happen if these very precise prophecies were not fulfilled?

At first everything went wondrously according to plan. Shortly after Cyrus conquered Babylon, in the autumn of 539, he issued an edict ordering that the gods of the subject peoples, whose effigies Nebuchadnezzar had carried off to Babylonia, should be returned to their own lands, that their temples should be rebuilt, and their cultic furniture and utensils restored. Because gods needed worshipers, the deportees could also return home. Cyrus's policy was tolerant but also pragmatic. It was cheaper and more efficient than the massive resettlement programs that had characterized Assyrian and Babylonian imperialism. Cyrus would not only earn the gratitude of his subjects, but would also win the favor of their gods.

A few months after Cyrus's coronation, a party of Jewish exiles set out for Jerusalem, with the gold and silver vessels that Nebuchadnezzar had confiscated from the temple. The Bible tells us that 42,360 Judeans made the journey home, together with their servants and two hundred temple singers,[58] but in fact the first batch of returnees was probably quite small, since most of the exiles chose to stay in Babylon.[59] The leader of the returning party was Sheshbazzar, the *nasi* ("vassal king") of Judah. We know nothing about him. He may have been a member of the Davidic royal house, and if so, he would have kissed Cyrus's hands as a sign of fealty and was the official representative of the Persian government. Judah had become part of the fifth province (satrapy) of the Persian empire, which comprised all territories west of the Euphrates.

We know almost nothing about these early years in Judah, since the biblical account is confused and incomplete. Sheshbazzar disappeared from the record, and we have no idea what happened to him. We hear nothing more about the Golah, the community of returned exiles, until 520, the second year of the reign of Darius (521–486), the third Persian emperor. The leader of the Judean community in Jerusalem was now Zerubbabel, the grandson of King Jehoiachin, who shared power with Joshua, the high priest. He too disappeared mysteriously after his term of office, and for fifty years we have no information about events in Judah.

If the Golah had arrived in Judah with the prophecies of Second Isaiah ringing in their ears, they must have come down to earth very quickly when they saw their new home. Most of them had been born in exile, and Judah would have seemed bleak, alien, and desolate after the sophistication of Babylonia. Used to the Babylonian way of life, they must have felt like foreigners in their own land. The country was full of strangers, who, like themselves, had lost their national status after the Babylonian wars, and while they had been away, Philistines, Moabites, Ammonites, Edomites, Arabs, and Phoenicians had settled in the coastal plain, the Jezreel Valley, and the highlands. The returnees called them all the *am ha-aretz,* "the people of the land." The new arrivals were also reunited with their fellow Israelites after an absence of seventy years. Judah was administered from Samerina, as the capital of the old northern kingdom was now known, and the returning exiles had to present their letters to the Israelite governors there when they arrived.[60] In exile, the deportees had changed their religion quite radically. How would they relate to the Yahwists who had never left Judah, who worshiped other gods beside Yahweh, and adhered to practices that now seemed barbaric and alien?

The building project stalled, and twenty years after the return of the Golah, Yahweh still had no temple. The restoration was not proving to be as easy as Second Isaiah had predicted. The former exiles had no building experience, and had nowhere to live, so most of them agreed that the temple would have to wait until they had new homes. But in 520, a few months after the arrival of Zerubbabel, Haggai, a new prophet, told the returnees that their priorities were wrong. The reason that the harvests were so bad and the economy in recession was that they had built houses for themselves and left Yahweh's dwelling place in ruins.[61] Duly chastened, the Golah went back to work.

The foundations were completed by the autumn of 520, and on the date of the traditional autumn festival, the Golah assembled

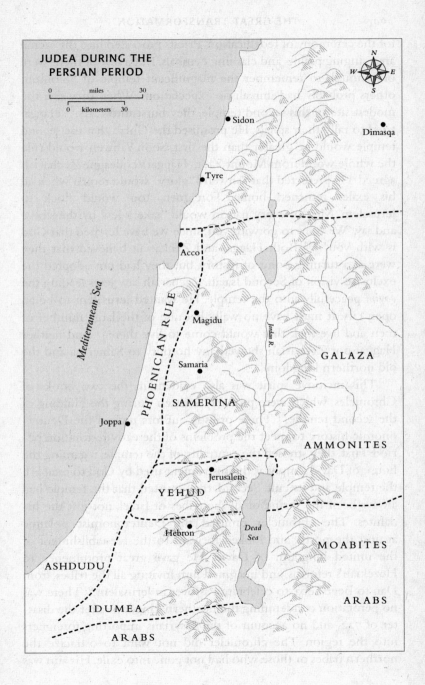

JUDEA DURING THE PERSIAN PERIOD

0   miles   30

0   kilometers   30

N
W   E
S

• Sidon

• Dimasqa

Mediterranean Sea

• Tyre

• Acco

PHOENICIAN RULE

• Magidu

Jordan R.

• Samaria

GALAZA

SAMERINA

• Joppa

AMMONITES

• Jerusalem

YEHUD

• Hebron

Dead Sea

MOABITES

ASHDUDU

IDUMEA

ARABS

ARABS

for the ceremony of rededication. Priests processed into the sacred area, singing psalms and clashing cymbals. But a few of them were old enough to remember the magnificent temple of Solomon; others probably had unrealistic expectations. When they saw the modest site of this second temple, they burst into tears.[62] Haggai tried to rally their spirits. He promised the Golah that the second temple would be greater than the first. Soon Yahweh would rule the whole world from Mount Zion. Haggai's colleague Zechariah agreed. He predicted that Yahweh's "glory" would return when all his exiles returned home. Foreigners too would flock to Jerusalem. Men of every nation would "take a Jew by the sleeve and say, 'We want to go with you, since we have learned that God is with you.' "[63] Both Haggai and Zechariah believed that they were at a turning point of history, but they had not adopted the exclusive vision of Second Isaiah. Zechariah saw Jews leading the *goyim* peacefully into the temple. He wanted Jerusalem to be an open city. It must have no walls, because of the large number of men and livestock that would come to live there.[64] And neither Haggai nor Zechariah showed any hostility to Samerina and the old northern kingdom.[65]

This inclusive spirit was also evident in the two books of Chronicles, which were probably written during the building of the second temple.[66] These priestly authors revised the Deuteronomic history to meet the problems of the early restoration period. First, they stressed the centrality of the temple, regarding the house of David simply as the instrument used by God to establish the temple and its cult. Second, they insisted that the temple had always been the shrine of all the tribes of Israel, not just the Judahites. The chronicler omitted the Deuteronomist polemic against the north, and looked forward to the reestablishment of the united kingdom of David. He gave great prominence to Hezekiah's reforms, and imagined him inviting all the tribes, from Dan to Beersheba, to celebrate Passover in Jerusalem.[67] There was no peroration condemning the northern kingdom after the disaster of 722, and no account of the Assyrians importing foreigners into the region. The chronicler did not want to ostracize the northern tribes or those who had not gone into exile. His aim was

to unite the people of Yahweh around their sanctuary. The first
version of Chronicles probably concluded with the consecration
of the second temple's foundations in 520. It was true, the chronicler admitted, that some of the old priests wept aloud, remember-
ing the glories of the old temple. But others raised their voices in
delight, "and nobody could distinguish the shouts of joy from the
sound of the people's weeping; for the people shouted so loudly
that the noise could be heard far away."[68] Pain and joy were inextricably combined at this complex moment. Yes, there was sorrow
for the tragedies of the past, but there was also happiness and an-
ticipation. A new beginning had been made, and the people of Israel, reunited in Jerusalem, seemed, like the servant, to be calling
out to the whole world.

Shortly after the Jews had completed their temple, Athens embarked on another important political change. The tyranny of the
Peisistrids had run its usual course, and Athenians were now eager
for a greater share in government. In 510, however, Sparta invaded
Athens, hoping to replace the Peisistrid tyrant with a pro-Spartan
puppet, but the Athenians rebelled, and with the help of Cleisthenes, son of the tyrant of Sicyon, they expelled the Spartans,
abolished the tyranny, and installed Cleisthenes as city magistrate.
During his year in office (508–507), Cleisthenes introduced
some startling reforms.[69] He completely reorganized the ancient
tribal system, in a way that weakened the authority of the aristocratic leaders. He also redesigned and enlarged Solon's Council of
Four Hundred: it now had five hundred members, who were chosen from each of the new tribes. Members were elected annually
from the middle classes, and could hold office only twice in their
lifetime, which meant that most farmers, artisans, and merchants
would serve on the council at some point, and thus became citizens in an entirely new and meaningful way. Athens was still ruled
by nine magistrates, elected from the upper classes, who were responsible for the festivals, the army, and the administration of justice; they were answerable to the aristocratic Council of Elders,

which met on the rocky hillock of the Areopagus, near the agora. Even though the nobility still governed the city, the Council of Five Hundred and the People's Assembly could challenge any abuse of power.

This was the most egalitarian polity yet devised, and it had an electrifying effect on the Greek world. Other poleis tried similar experiments, and there was a surge of fresh energy in the region. Cleisthenes was asking a great deal of his citizens. Since the Council of Five Hundred met three times a month, ordinary farmers and merchants were expected to dedicate about a tenth of their time to politics during their year in office. They did not lose their enthusiasm, however, and they learned a great deal from the experience. By the fifth century, the middle classes were able to participate in council debates and follow the thinking of the most intelligent people in Athens. The experiment showed that if citizens were properly educated and motivated, a government did not have to rely on brute force, and that it was possible to reform ancient institutions in a rational manner. The Athenians called their new system *isonomia* ("equal order").[70] The polis was now more evenly balanced, with farmers and traders on a more equal footing with the aristocrats.

Truth was no longer a secret, esoteric revelation for a select few. It was now *en mesoi* ("in the center") of the political domain,[71] but the Greeks still regarded their political life as sacred and the polis as the extension of divinity into human affairs. Athens remained a devoutly religious city, even though it was increasingly a city of *logos*. As more people participated in government, they began to apply the debating skills they had acquired on the council floor to other spheres of knowledge. Political speeches and laws were now subjected to stringent criticism, and *logos,* the speech of the hoplites, continued to be aggressive. Debate was characterized by conflict, antithesis, and the desire to exclude an opposing point of view.

The philosophy of the period reflected the agonistic quality of political life, as well as the Greek yearning for poise and harmony. This was especially evident in the work of Heraclitus (540–480), a member of the royal family of Ephesus, who was known as the "riddler" because he presented his ideas in lapidary, baffling maxims. "Nature," he once said, "loves to hide"; things were the opposite of what they seemed.[72] The first relativist, Heraclitus argued that everything depended upon context: seawater was good for fish, but potentially fatal for men; a blow was salutary if delivered as a punishment, but evil if inflicted by a murderer.[73] A restless, unsettling man, Heraclitus believed that even though the cosmos seemed stable, it was in fact in constant flux and a battlefield of warring elements. "Cold things grow hot, the hot cools, the wet dries, the parched moistens."[74] He was especially fascinated by fire: a flame was never still; fire transformed wood into ash, and water into steam. Fire was also a divine force that preserved order by preventing any one of the competing elements from dominating the rest—in rather the same way as the clash of opinions in the council maintained the equilibrium of the polis. Yet beneath this cosmic turbulence, there was unity. Flux and stability, which seemed antithetical, were one and the same; night and day were two sides of a single coin; the way up was also the way down, and an exit could serve as an entrance.[75] You could not rely on the evidence of your senses, but must look deeper to find the *logos,* the ruling principle of nature. And that also applied to human beings. Heraclitus had discovered introspection, a new activity for the Greeks. "I went in search of myself," he said.[76] You could learn a little about human nature by studying dreams, emotions, and people's individual qualities, but it would always remain an enigma: "You will not find out the limits of the soul by travelling, even if you travel over every pole."[77]

In their political reform, the Greeks had found that it was possible to jettison traditional institutions without calling down the wrath of the gods, and some began to question other time-honored assumptions. Xenophanes (560–480), another philosopher from the Ionian coast, rejected the Olympian gods as hopelessly anthropomorphic. People thought that gods "are born, and have clothes and speech and shape like our own." They were guilty of theft, adultery, and deception. It was clear that people had simply projected their own human form onto the divine. Horses and cows would probably do the same.[78] But, he believed, there was only "one god, greatest among gods and men," who transcended all human qualities.[79] Beyond time and change, he governed everything with his mind (*nous*); no sooner did he think of something than it was done.[80]

Xenophanes emigrated from Asia Minor to Elea in southern Italy, which now became an important center for the new philosophy. Parmenides, a native of Elea, who was slightly younger than Heraclitus, experienced his bleak philosophy as a divine revelation. He had traveled to heaven in a fiery chariot, he said, far beyond the Milky Way, where he met a goddess who took him by the hand and gave him this reassurance: "No ill fate has sent you to travel this road—far indeed does it lie from the steps of men—but right and justice. It is proper that you should learn all things."[81] Parmenides believed that by freeing humanity from delusion, he was performing a valuable spiritual service. Because nothing was as it appeared, human reason must rise above common sense, prejudice, and unverified opinion; only then could it grasp true reality.[82] But many of his contemporaries felt that he made it impossible to think constructively about anything at all.[83]

Parmenides argued that the world could not have developed in the way the Milesians had described, because all change was an illusion. Reality consisted of one, simple, complete, and eternal Being. He insisted that we could say nothing sensible about phenomena that did not exist. Thus, because Being was eternal and not subject to alteration, there was no such thing as change. We could, therefore, never say that something was born, because that implied that previously it had *not* existed, nor, for the same reason, could we say that it died or ceased to be. It *appeared* that creatures came into being and passed away, but this was an illusion, because reality was beyond time and change. Again, nothing could "move," in the sense that at a given moment an object shifted from one place to another. We could never say that something had "developed," that it had been one way once but become something different. So the universe was not in flux, as Heraclitus claimed; nor did it evolve, as the Milesians had argued. The universe was the same at all times and in all places. It was unchanging, uncreated, and immortal.

The Milesians had based their philosophy on their observation of such phenomena as water and air. But Parmenides did not trust the evidence of the senses, and relied, with remarkable, ruthless consistency, on a purely reasoned argument. He cultivated the habit of "second-order thinking," reflection upon the thought processes themselves. Like many of the Axial sages, he had arrived at a new, critical awareness of the limitations of human knowledge. Parmenides had also embarked on the philosophical quest for pure existence. Instead of contemplating individual creatures, he was trying to put his finger on quintessential being. But in the process, he created a world in which it was impossible to live. Why would anybody undertake any course of action, if change and movement were illusory? His disciple Melissus was a naval commander: How was he supposed to guide his moving ship? How should we evaluate the physical changes that we note within ourselves? Were human beings really phantoms? By divesting the cosmos of qualities, Parmenides had also deprived it of heart. Human beings do not respond to the world with *logos* alone; we are also emotional creatures, with a complex subconscious life. By ignoring this and cultivating his rational powers exclusively, Parmenides had discovered a void: there was nothing to think about. Increasingly, as philosophers of the Axial Age practiced sustained logical reflection, the world became unfamiliar and human beings appeared strange to themselves.

Yet pure, unflinching *logos* could work brilliantly in the world of affairs. At the beginning of the fifth century it inspired a naval victory that epitomized the new Greek spirit. In 499 Athens and Eritrea had unwisely sent help to Miletus, which had rebelled against Persian rule. Darius quashed the rebellion, sacked Miletus, and then turned his attention to its allies on the mainland. The Athenians had little conception of the power of the Persian empire, and probably did not realize what they had taken on. But they had no option now but to prepare for war. In 493, Themistocles, a general from one of the less prominent Athenian families, was elected magistrate, and persuaded the Areopagus Council to build a fleet.

This was a surprising decision. Athenians had no expertise in naval warfare; their strength lay in the hoplite army that was their pride and joy. They had no experience of shipbuilding. But the council agreed, navigational experts were brought in, and the Athenians began to build two hundred triremes and train a navy of forty thousand men.[84] This involved a radical break with tradition. Previously only men who could afford to equip themselves had been allowed to join the hoplite army, but now all Athenian males, including noncitizens, were drafted into the fleet. Aristocrats, farmers, and *thetes,* men of the lower classes, sat on the same rowing bench and had to pull together. In the hoplite phalanx, Athenians fought face-to-face; they found it dishonorable to sit in the trireme with their backs to the enemy. Many must have resented Themistocles' plan, especially when their first great triumph against the Persian army was on land. In 490, the Persian fleet sailed across the Aegean, conquered Naxos, sacked Eritrea, and landed on the plain of Marathon, some twenty-five miles north of Athens. Under the leadership of Militiades, the hoplite army of Athens set out to meet them, and against all the odds, inflicted a stunning defeat upon Persia.[85] Marathon became the new Troy; its hoplites were revered as a modern race of heroes. Why depart from tradition, when the old ways had been so spectacularly successful?

In 480, Xerxes, the new Persian king, sailed toward Athens with twelve hundred triremes and about one hundred thousand men.[86] Even with the help of Sparta and the other Peloponnesian cities, the Athenian navy was greatly outnumbered. Some of the magistrates wanted to jettison the fleet, but Cimon, the son of Militiades, the hero of Marathon, ceremonially left his riding tackle on the Acropolis and set out for the port of Piraeus: Marathon was in the past. Before the Persians' arrival, Themistocles evacuated the entire population of Athens, including women, children, and slaves, and sent them to the island of Salamis, across the Saronic Gulf.[87] When the Persians arrived, they found an eerily empty city; they rushed through the streets, looting and pillaging, and burned the magnificent new temples on the Acropolis, while the Athenians sat miserably on Salamis, scarcely able to bear this humiliation. But Themistocles had set a deadly trap. After they had finished their rampage, the Persian navy sailed over to

Salamis but could not fit all their ships into the narrow gulf. The triremes became gridlocked, jammed hopelessly together, and were unable to move. The Athenians could pick them off one by one. By evening the surviving Persian ships had fled, and Xerxes left Attica to put down an uprising at home.

Salamis changed the course of Greek history and marked the birth of something fundamentally new. The Greeks had overcome a massive empire by the disciplined exercise of reason. Themistocles could never have persuaded the citizens to adopt his plan had they not learned over the years to think logically, abstracting their emotions from their rational powers. His strategy displayed many of the values of the Axial Age. The Greeks had to turn their backs on the past, and embark on an experimental course. The plan demanded self-sacrifice. The hoplite phalanx was crucial to the Greeks' identity, but at Salamis they had to leave this "self" behind and—in defiance of their heroic tradition—allow the Persians to destroy their city and its holy places. Salamis was an Axial moment, and yet, as so often in Greece, it was a martial triumph and led to more warfare.

In 478, over a hundred poleis formed a military confederation under the leadership of Athens. Its objective was to counter a future Persian invasion, to liberate the Ionian cities from Persian rule, and to promote friendship among the Greeks. Members pledged ships and equipment, and agreed to meet every year on the island of Delos, the birthplace of Apollo, patron of the league. In 477, Athens went on the offensive, conquering the city of Eion, the most important Persian stronghold on the northern coast of the Aegean. But despite this triumph, there was buried fear and anxiety. At the Great Dionysia in 476, the playwright Phrynichus presented a trilogy about the Persian wars. *The Fall of Miletus* has not survived, but the historian Herodotus (485–425) remembered the effect it had on the audience. "The whole theater broke into weeping and they fined Phrynichus a thousand drachmas for bringing national calamities to mind that touched them so nearly and forbade forever the acting of that play."[88] The tragedies performed at the Great Dionysia did not usually depict current affairs. Phrynichus had not achieved the detachment necessary for the *katharsis,* or "cleansing," that Athenians expected from tragedy.

Tragic drama was now a treasured institution in Athens. Every year at the City Dionysia, the polis put itself on stage. The playwrights often chose subjects that reflected recent events, but usually presented them in a mythical setting that distanced them from the contemporary scene and enabled the audience to analyze and reflect upon the issues. The festival was a communal meditation, during which the audience worked through their problems and predicament. All male citizens were obliged to attend; even prisoners were released for the duration of the festival. As in the Panathenaea, Athens was on show; the City Dionysia was a mighty demonstration of civic pride. Member cities of the league sent delegates and tribute; garlands were presented to outstanding citizens; children of soldiers who had died in the service of Athens marched in procession, armed for war.[89]

But there was no facile chauvinism. The citizens assembled in the theater to weep. When the Greeks dramatized the myths that had always helped them to define their distinctive identity, they interrogated the certainties of the past and subjected traditional absolutes to stringent criticism. The tragedies also marked the internalization and deepening of ritual that characterized the spirituality of the Axial Age. The new genre may have originated in the secret mystery rites of Dionysus, when a chorus had recited the story of Dionysus's sufferings in formal poetic language, while the leader stepped forward to explain its esoteric meaning, in a more colloquial style, to newcomers who had not yet been initiated.[90] But in the City Dionysia, the once-private rites were performed in public; they had been democratized, placed *en mesoi*.

Over the years, new characters were introduced, who conversed with the leader of the chorus, giving a more dramatic immediacy to the proceedings. By the fifth century, the plays performed during the City Dionysia reflected the introspection of the Axial Age. They showed the well-known characters of myth—Agamemnon, Oedipus, Ajax, or Heracles—making an interior journey, struggling with complex choices, and facing up to the consequences. They displayed the new self-consciousness of the Axial Age, as the audience watched the mind of the protagonist turning in upon itself, meditating upon alternatives, and coming, tortuously, to a conclusion. And like the philosophers, the tragedians questioned everything: the nature of the gods, the value of Greek civilization, and the meaning of life. In the old days, nobody had subjected these stories to such radical scrutiny. Now the playwrights added to the original tales, embellished and changed them in order to explore the unprecedented perplexities that were emerging in the Hellenic world.

In tragedy there was neither a simple answer nor a single viewpoint.[91] The main protagonists were the mythical heroes of the past, while the chorus usually represented marginal people: women, old men, and foreigners, who often looked aghast at the principal characters, finding their world alien, incomprehensible, and dangerous. The chorus did not speak for the polis. Even though they were peripheral and often ill-educated people, they spoke in a stylized, lyrical Attic dialect, while the aristocratic protagonists used the colloquial idiom of the polis. There was thus a marked clash of perspectives, and neither the hero nor the chorus expressed the "correct" view. The audience had to weigh one insight against another, just as they did in the council. They could only make sense of the play by analyzing the arguments of the chorus—people who usually had no voice in the polis—or heroes of the mythical past, who lived in a far-off time and in distant places. Tragedy taught the Athenians to project themselves toward the "other," and to include within their sympathies those whose assumptions differed markedly from their own.

Above all, tragedy put suffering on stage. It did not allow the audience to forget that life was *dukkha,* painful, unsatisfactory, and awry. By placing a tortured individual in front of the polis, analyzing that person's pain, and helping the audience to empathize with him or her, the fifth-century tragedians—Aeschylus (c. 525– 456), Sophocles (c. 496–405), and Euripides (c. 484–406)—had arrived at the heart of Axial Age spirituality. The Greeks firmly believed that the sharing of grief and tears created a valuable bond between people.[92] Enemies discovered their common humanity thus, as Achilles and Priam had done at the end of the *Iliad:* their tears had been a *katharsis* that cleansed their grief of poisonous hatred. At the City Dionysia, Athenians wept loudly and unashamedly. This not only strengthened the bond of citizenship, but reminded individuals that they were not alone in their more personal sorrows. They realized in an entirely new way that all mortal beings suffered. Catharsis was achieved by the experience of sympathy and compassion, because the ability to *feel with* the other was crucial to the tragic experience. This was especially clear in Aeschylus's *The Persians,* which was presented at the City Dionysia in 472.

By choosing a contemporary subject, just four years after the debacle of Phrynichus's *The Fall of Miletus,* Aeschylus was taking a risk. But his play achieved the necessary distance by making the Athenians see the battle of Salamis from the Persians' point of view. The fact that there was no riot this time was a tribute not only to Aeschylus but to the Athenian audience. Only a few years earlier, the Persians had smashed their city to pieces and desecrated their holy places, yet now they were able to weep for the Persian dead. Xerxes, his wife Atossa, and the ghost of Darius all spoke movingly of the piercing grief of bereavement that ripped away the veneer of security and revealed the terror of life. There was no triumphant righteousness; no gloating. Aeschylus did not depict the Persians as enemies, but as a people in mourning. There was praise for Persian courage; Greece and Persia were described as "sisters of one race . . . flawless in beauty and grace."[93] The play ended with a ritual lament as the defeated Xerxes was led, gently and respectfully, into his palace. *The Persians* was an outstanding example of a sympathy that reached out to the erstwhile enemy at a time when memories of desperate conflict were still raw.

The play reflected on the lessons of the war. Xerxes had been guilty of hubris; he had overstepped the mark and refused to accept the divinely appointed boundaries of his empire. The ghost of Darius issued a solemn warning:

> . . . *Let no man,*
> *Scorning the fortune that he has, in greed for more*
> *Pour out his wealth in utter waste. Zeus throned on high*
> *Sternly chastises arrogant, boastful men.*[94]

But the Persians were not the only people guilty of this over-
weening pride. At this time, some Athenians were beginning to
worry about their own hubris in invading other poleis, and using
the spoils of war to fund their expensive building projects. Xerxes'
warning probably struck home.[95]

In 470, when the wealthy island of Naxos tried to secede from
the Delian League, Athens promptly attacked the city, razed its
walls, and forced it back into line. The league had been designed
to encourage friendship among the poleis, but it was becoming
clear that its real purpose was to serve Athenian interests. The following year, the cities of the league defeated the Persian fleet at
Pamphylia, in a battle that marked the end of the Persian wars.
Many must have wondered whether the league served any further
purpose, now that the Persian threat had been contained. There
was also tension at home. Since Salamis, the *thetes,* the lower
classes that formed the backbone of the navy, had become more
prominent in the city. They were not so constrained by traditional
ideas, and were likely to support any radical policy that gave them
a higher profile in the assembly. There was new friction between
the classes, and Athens was becoming a divided city.

All these anxieties surfaced in Aeschylus's *Seven Against Thebes,*
which was presented in 467 and told the story of the apparently futile war between Oedipus's two sons, Polynices and Eteocles. This
grim story of fraternal rivalry may have recalled the recent tragedy
of Naxos, when Greek had attacked Greek. Polynices, who had
invaded his native polis, was guilty of hubris, while Eteocles seemed
to embody the restraint and self-control that should characterize a
true citizen: he loathes the ancient, irrational religion of the chorus
of frightened women, who rush periodically onto the stage in ones
and twos, asking disconnected questions and uttering witless and
incomprehensible ritual cries. Yet Eteocles himself, the man of *logos,*
falls prey to the pollution that his father, Oedipus, had unleashed,
and that had contaminated the whole family.[96] At the end of the
play, this *miasma* finally drove the two brothers to kill each other
outside the walls of Thebes.

Aeschylus had depicted a torn society, painfully caught between two irreconcilable worlds. Like Eteocles and the philoso-

phers, some citizens looked down on the old religion, but could not entirely shake it off. It still held sway in the deeper, less rational regions of their minds. At the end of the play, the Erinyes, the ancient chthonian Furies, triumphed over the modern forces of *logos*. Athenians might regard themselves as rational men of the polis, in charge of their own destiny, but they still *felt* that they could be overtaken by a divinely inspired pollution that had a life of its own. Would Athenian hubris in Naxos produce fresh *miasma* and bring their city to ruin? The Greek mind was straining in two directions, and Aeschylus did not propose an easy solution. In their final lament, the chorus was split, half siding with Polynices, the others attending the funeral of Eteocles.

In 461 a group of young Athenians led by Ephialtes and his friend Pericles mounted a concerted attack on the elders in the Assembly, which then deprived the Areopagus Council of all its powers. Their slogan was *demokratia* ("government by the people"). The coup completely overturned the political order. The Areopagus was replaced by the Council of Five Hundred and decisions were henceforth made by all citizens in the Popular Assembly. But the new democracy was not entirely benign. Debates were often rude and aggressive. The courts were made up of citizens, who were both judge and jury. There was no rule of law, and a trial was essentially a battle between the accused and his accusers.

The *Oresteia*, a trilogy written by Aeschylus shortly afterward, shows how deeply Athens had been shaken by this revolution. Again, Aeschylus depicted a clash between old and new—between the Erinyes and the more modern, "political" gods of Olympus. The trilogy traced the emergence of the polis from tribal chaos and vendetta to the relative order of Athens, where citizens could take control of their lives; it marked the painful passage from an ethos of blind force to nonviolent debate. Yet Aeschylus made it clear that the ideal differed from the reality, that there were no easy answers, and that the final vision of law and order could only be an aspiration rather than an achieved fact.

The *Oresteia* confronted the problem of violence, a central preoccupation of the Axial Age. It told the story of the house of

Atreus, a family contaminated by unnatural murder and caught up in an unstoppable cycle of revenge killing. It began with the slaying of Agamemnon by his wife, Clytemnestra; continued with her murder by her son, Orestes, who was avenging the death of his father; and it ended with Orestes' headlong flight from the Erinyes, whose terrifying appearance onstage caused some women in the audience to miscarry. The protagonists could not stop the violence because each killing unleashed a fresh *miasma,* and the Olympians, who, as patrons of the poleis, were supposed to be on the side of law and order, seemed to take perverse delight in giving mortals impossible commands that involved them in no-win situations. Human life was, therefore, full of inescapable grief. "He who acts must suffer," observed the chorus; "that is the law."[97] But in his "Prayer to Zeus," Aeschylus offered a frail thread of hope. As long as Zeus—"whoever Zeus may be"—presided over heaven and earth, suffering would remain part of the human condition, and yet Zeus had "taught man to think," and set humanity on the path to wisdom:

> He issued the law: Learn through suffering.
> Sorrow enters even sleep, dripping into the heart,
> Sorrow which cannot forget suffering.
> And even those who are unwilling learn to be wise.

All life was indeed *dukkha,* but pain educated human beings, so that they learned to transcend their apparently hopeless plight.

In *Eumenides,* the last play of the trilogy, Orestes, still pursued by the Erinyes, arrived in Athens, and flung himself at the feet of Athena, who convened the Areopagus Council to judge his case. The brutal justice of the vendetta must yield to the peaceful process of law. The Erinyes argued that by slaying his mother Orestes had violated the sacred law of blood and must suffer the correct punishment. The jury was split, but Athena, who had the casting vote, acquitted Orestes, placating the Erinyes by offering them a shrine on the Acropolis. Henceforth they would be called the Eumenides, "the well-disposed ones." The virtues of the polis—moderation and the balance of opposing forces—had prevailed, but the dark deeds of the past were still alive. Men and women, gods and Furies must learn from suffering, assimilating and absorbing the memory of the dark deeds of the past. At the very end of the play, the Eumenides were escorted in solemn procession to their new shrine.[98] This ritual *pompe* symbolized the inclusion of tragedy within the polis. The bloodshed, hatred, and polluting nightmare of violence—symbolized by the Erinyes—could not be denied. The city must incorporate this weight of sorrow, take it into itself, accept it, honor it in the sacred heart of the polis, and make it a force for good.

But Athens was not learning the lessons of history. For all its fine talk of freedom, the city was resented throughout the Greek world as an oppressive power. The Delian League of free city-states had become in fact the Athenian empire; any polis that tried to break away was brutally subjugated and forced to pay tribute. In 438, the Parthenon, the magnificent temple of Athena on the Acropolis, had been completed, but it had been built by humiliating and exploiting fellow Greeks. The new shrine, which dominated the city landscape, was an assertion of communal pride and supremacy, yet Pericles warned the citizens that they had embarked on a dangerous course. It would be impossible for Athens to quash a widespread revolt. Its empire had become a trap. It had probably been wrong to establish it, but it would be dangerous to let it go, because Athens was now hated by the people whose lives it controlled.

Athens was beginning to realize that it had limits. Sophocles' *Antigone,* presented in the mid-440s, depicted an irreconcilable clash between family loyalty and the law of the polis, which neither of the chief protagonists—Creon, king of Thebes, and Antigone, daughter of Oedipus—was able to resolve. In fact, no resolution was possible. The play showed that firm beliefs and clear principles would not infallibly lead to a good outcome. All the characters had good intentions, none of them wanted the tragedy to occur, but despite their sincere and best efforts, the result was catastrophic and devastating loss.[99] Despite its proud claim to honor freedom and independence, the polis could not accommodate an Antigone, who disobeyed its laws for the most pious of motives, stood up for her convictions, and was able to argue for them with passionate, convincing *logos*. In their hymn to progress, the chorus of old men claimed that there was nothing beyond man's power. He had created the technology to overcome every obstacle, and had developed his reasoning powers to establish a stable society. He was lord of all he surveyed and seemed wholly invincible—except for the grim fact of death, which brought home his real helplessness. If he forgot this, he would fall prey to hubris, and walk "in solitary pride to his life's end."[100]

The Axial peoples were all becoming acutely aware of the limitations of the human condition, but in other parts of the world, this did not stop them from reaching for the highest goals or developing a spiritual technology that would enable them to transcend the suffering of life. Indeed, it was the agonizing experience of their inherent vulnerability that impelled many of them to find the absolute within their own fragile selves. But the Greeks, it seemed, could see only the abyss. Once Antigone realized that there was nothing more she could do, she accepted her destiny as the daughter of Oedipus, acknowledging that she too was helpless before the *miasma* that had infected the entire family. Instead of wavering, like her sister Ismene, Antigone proudly took possession of her suffering and—literally—"walked in solitary pride" into her tomb.

The dream of enlightenment, Sophocles seemed to be telling his polis, was an illusion. Despite their extraordinary cultural and intellectual achievements, human beings still faced overwhelming pain. Their skills, their principles, their piety, and their reasoning powers could not save them from *dukkha,* which they experienced not as the result of their own karma, but from a divine source outside themselves. Mortal men and women were not in charge of their destiny. They must do everything in their power to avoid tragedy—as Antigone did. But when they had come to the end of endeavor, they could only accept their fate unflinchingly and with courage. This, Sophocles suggested, was what constituted human greatness. But in India, the dream of enlightenment was

not dead. Indeed, it was becoming a tangible reality to more people than ever before.

A spiritual vacuum had also opened up in India, and new sages
worked energetically, even desperately, to find a fresh solution. By
the late fifth century, the doctrine of karma, which had been controversial at the time of Yajnavalkya, was now universally accepted.[101] Men and women believed that they were all caught up
in the endless cycle of death and rebirth; their desires impelled
them to act, and the quality of their actions would determine
their state in the next life. Bad karma would mean that they could
be reborn as slaves, animals, or plants. Good karma would ensure
their rebirth as kings or gods. But this was not a happy ending:
even gods would exhaust this beneficial karma, would die and be
reborn in a less exalted state on earth. As this new concept took
hold, the mood of India changed and many became depressed.
They felt doomed to one transient life after another. Not even
good karma could save them. When they looked around their
community, they could see only pain and suffering. Even wealth
and material pleasure was overshadowed by the grim reality of
impending old age and mortality. In fact, they believed, worldly
goods "sap . . . the energy of all the senses," and hastened their
decline.[102] As this gloom intensified, people struggled to find a
way out.

More and more people became disenchanted with the old
Vedic rituals, which could not provide a solution to this problem.
The best they could offer was rebirth in the world of the gods, but
in the light of the new philosophy, this could only be a temporary
release from the relentless recurrence of suffering and death. Further, people were beginning to notice that the rites did not even
produce the material benefits they promised. Some rejected the
ritual science of the *Brahmanas*. The Upanishads promised final
liberation, but this spirituality was not for everybody. It was based
on a close familiarity with the minutiae of Vedic thought that
most people simply did not have, and many were doubtful about

the identity of the brahman and atman, on which the whole system depended. Yoga offered *moksha,* but how did the yogin interpret the tranced states that he experienced? Could they be reconciled with Vedic orthodoxy? The Upanishads that were composed at about this time asserted that they could. The Katha Upanishad claimed that the atman (the true self) controlled the body in the same way as a rider managed his chariot. The yogin learned to keep his mind and senses under control like the good horses of a chariot driver. In this way, a person who "has understanding is mindful and always pure," and would achieve release from the endless cycle of rebirth.[103] But others were convinced that yoga was not enough. Something more was needed.

Yoga was a full-time job. It demanded hours of effort each day, and was clearly incompatible with the duties of a householder. By the sixth century, most people thought that the householder had no chance of achieving *moksha,* because he was a slave to karma, compelled by the duties of his class to perform one action after another, each fueled by the desire that was the root of the problem. A householder could not beget children without desire. He could not wage war, grow his crops, or engage in business without wanting to succeed. Each action led to a new round of duties that bound him to the inexorable cycle of samsara. The only way to find release was to "go forth" into the forest and become a hermit or a mendicant, who had none of these tasks. People in India did not regard the renouncers as feeble dropouts, but revered them as intrepid pioneers, who, at considerable cost to themselves, were trying to find a spiritual solution for humanity. Because of the prevailing despair in the region, many were longing for a Jina, a spiritual conqueror, or a Buddha, an Enlightened One, who had "woken up" to a different dimension of existence.

The spiritual malaise was exacerbated by a social crisis. Like the Greeks, the peoples of north India were undergoing major political and economic change. The Vedic system had been the spirituality of a highly mobile society, engaged in constant migration. But by the sixth and fifth centuries, people were settling down in ever larger permanent communities and were seriously engaged in agriculture. The introduction of iron technology, including the heavy plow, made it possible to reclaim more fields, to irrigate them, and to clear the dense forests. The villages were now surrounded by carefully supervised plots of land with a network of ditches. New crops were produced: fruit, rice, cereal, sesame, millet, wheat, grains, and barley. Farmers were becoming richer.[104] There was also political development. By the end of the sixth century, the small chiefdoms had been absorbed into larger units. The largest of these new kingdoms were Magadha in the southeast and Kosala in the southwest. They were ruled by kings who had, very gradually, imposed their rule by force and had slowly changed the old patterns of allegiance from clan loyalty to an incipient patriotism that focused on territory rather than kinship. As a result, the *kshatriya* warrior class, which was responsible for defense and administration, had become even more prominent. The new kings were no longer as deferential to the Brahmins as their forebears had been, though they might still pay lip service to the older ideals.

Monarchy was not the only form of government. To the east of the new kingdoms, a number of differently run states had also emerged, ruled by an assembly (*sangha*) of the elders of the old clans (*ganas*). This government by discussion had an obvious resemblance to the Greek polis, though in truth we know little about these Indian *sanghas*. It was not clear how many people were admitted to the tribal assembly, which classes were involved, or whether council members were elected. There were probably as many systems as there were states, but however they were organized, these "republics"—Malla, Koliya, Videha, Naya, Vajji, Shakya, Kalama, and Licchavi—were becoming more powerful, even though they felt threatened by the kingdoms of Kosala and Magadha, which wanted to expand their territory. The possibility of confrontation loomed, and people were aware that wars between these larger states would be far more destructive than the old raids, especially since weaponry had become more deadly since the manufacture of iron.

The new states stimulated trade in the Ganges basin. They built roads and secured trade routes. Coins replaced cattle as the symbol of wealth, and a merchant class developed, which traded in metals,

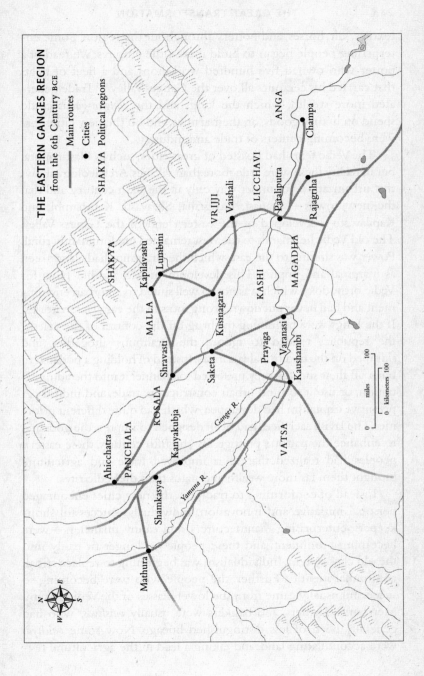

THE EASTERN GANGES REGION
from the 6th Century BCE

Main routes
● Cities
SHAKYA Political regions

ANGA
Champa
Pataliputra
Rajagriha
LICCHAVI
VRIJJI
Vaishali
MAGADHA
SHAKYA
Kapilavastu
Lumbini
MALLA
KASHI
Kusinagara
Shravasti
Saketa
Prayaga
Varanasi
Kaushambi
KOSALA
Kanyakubja
Ganges R.
VATSA
PANCHALA
Ahicchatra
Shamkasya
Yamuna R.
Mathura

100
miles
100
kilometers
0

N
W   E
S

textiles, salt, horses, and pottery throughout the region. Some enterprising people began to build mercantile empires. We read of a potter who owned five hundred workshops and a fleet of boats that carried his ceramics all over the Ganges Valley.[105] Trade generated more wealth, which the kings and the *sangha-ganas* could spend on luxury goods, on their armies, and on the new cities that were becoming centers of trade and industry.

The Vedic texts had boasted of great cities, such as Hastinapura, but in reality these were little more than villages. Archaeology shows that urbanization got under way only in the sixth century, and that the new towns—Varanasi, Rajagriha, Shravasti, Kaushambi, and Kapilavastu—developed in the eastern end of the Ganges Valley. The old Vedic heartlands to the west remained predominantly rural. Power was shifting to the east, which the Brahmins had always seen as marginal and impure. This development was another blow for Vedic orthodoxy, which was not so well suited to an urban environment and had never put down strong roots in the eastern territories. If the kings were beginning to shrug off the control of the priests, the republics tended to ignore the Brahmins altogether, and skimped on the traditional sacrifices. Instead of holding a potlatch to burn off their surplus, they preferred to channel it into the administration, or use it to fund urban construction, trade, and industry. A primitive capitalism had developed, which had quite different priorities. The lavish sacrifices had been designed to impress the gods and to enhance the patron's prestige. By the fifth century, these eastern peoples had realized that their improved trade and agriculture brought them far more wealth and status than the Vedic rites.

Instead of conforming to tradition, the new cities encouraged personal initiative and innovation. Individuals—successful shopkeepers, enterprising manufacturers, and canny financiers—were becoming prominent, and these people no longer fit easily into the old class system. Individualism was beginning to replace tribal, communal identity. Further, the people who were becoming so successful usually came from the lower classes of the Vedic system. Merchants, farmers, and bankers were usually *vaishyas,* who had generally been of less distinguished lineage. Now some *vaishyas* were accumulating land, and taking a lead in the agricultural revolution; others were going in for trade and industry, and becoming richer than the *kshatriyas*. Artisans usually came from the indigenous *shudra* class, who were not allowed to take part in the Vedic rituals and did not belong to the Aryan community. In the old days, their function had been to provide labor. But in the new towns, some *shudras,* such as the potter with the huge ceramic empire, were acquiring wealth and status that would once have been inconceivable.

These developments were positive but also unsettling. Urbanization involved massive social change that left many people feeling obscurely disoriented and lost. Some families had become rich and powerful, others had started to decline. Towns and trade encouraged greater personal mobility, and while it was stimulating to make new contacts with people in other regions, this also undermined the smaller, more parochial communities. There were new class divisions. Brahmins and *kshatriyas* tended to band together against *vaishyas* and *shudras*. The old rural elites felt alienated from the emerging urban classes, which had strong *vaishya* and *shudra* elements. The rich *vaishyas,* who had become merchants and bankers, were increasingly estranged from the agricultural *vaishyas* in the countryside. The rules that had governed relations between the four classes now seemed incongruous, and people had to learn fresh ways of living together. The loss of tribal identity left some feeling bereft and cast into a void.

These social tensions were particularly acute in the east, where urbanization was more advanced, and it was in this region that the next phase of the Indian Axial Age began. Here the Aryan settlers were in a minority, and indigenous traditions were still very much alive. People felt free to explore novel solutions. The rapid material developments in the towns made city dwellers more conscious of the pace of change than in the countryside, where people did the same thing at the same time, year after year. Life probably seemed even more ephemeral and transient, and this confirmed the now-ingrained belief that life was *dukkha,* as did the prevalence of disease and anomie in the crowded, disturbing cities. Traditional values had crumbled, and the new ways seemed frightening and alien. The cities were exciting; their streets were crowded with brilliantly painted carriages; huge elephants carried merchandise to and from distant lands; and merchants from all parts of India mingled in the marketplace. The urban class was powerful, thrusting, and ambitious. But the gambling, theater, dancing, prostitution, and rowdy tavern life of the towns seemed shocking to people who leaned toward the older values.

Life was becoming even more aggressive than before. In the republics, there was infighting and civil strife. The monarchies were efficient and centralized only because they could coerce their subjects. Armies professed allegiance to the king alone, instead of to the tribe as a whole, so he could impose order with his personal fighting machine, and use it to conquer neighboring territory. This new royal power gave greater stability to the region, but many were disturbed that the kings could force their will upon the people in this way. The economy was fueled by greed, and bankers and merchants, locked in ceaseless competition, preyed on one another. How did this ruthless society measure up to the ideal of *ahimsa*, which had become so crucial in north India? Life seemed even more violent and terrifying than when cattle rustling had been the backbone of the economy. Vedic religion appeared increasingly out of touch with contemporary reality. Merchants were constantly on the road, and could not keep the sacred fires burning or observe the traditional household rites. Animal sacrifice may have made sense when stock breeding had been the main occupation, but now that agriculture and trade had taken its place, cattle were becoming scarce and sacrifice seemed wasteful and cruel—too reminiscent of the violence of public life. People needed a different religious solution.

Naturally they looked to the renouncers, who, like the merchants, were the men of the hour. They too had stepped outside the confines of the Vedic system and struck out on their own. These days the renouncers were everywhere. Some communities of hermits remained in the forests, observing Vedic rituals, but others were very much in evidence in eastern society. By the sixth century, countless schools had sprung up. Groups of disciples clustered around a teacher who had advocated a special way of life, promising that his *dharma* ("teaching") would lead to liberation from death and rebirth. His pupils probably called him the Buddha or the Jina, because they believed that he had discovered the secret of enlightenment. We know very little about these schools. India was still an oral society and most of these gurus left no written scriptures; often we rely on the polemic of their rivals, who probably distorted their teaching. These teachers had imbibed the competitive spirit of the age and vied fiercely with one another for disciples, taking to the roads to preach their dharma. Crowds of renouncers in their yellow robes marched along the trade routes beside the merchants' caravans, and their arrival was anticipated as eagerly as the traders' wares. When a new teacher came to town, people turned up en masse to listen to him. There were passionate discussions involving all classes of society in the marketplace, the city hall, and the luxuriant tropical parks in the suburbs. Householders, who had no intention of leaving home but felt in need of new spiritual answers, often attached themselves to a school as lay supporters. The renouncers, the "silent sages," walked quietly through the towns, begging for their food by holding out their bowls, and householders and their wives were happy to fill them with leftovers. This was a good deed, and might ensure that in their next life they too could become monks, with a chance of achieving *moksha*.

The latest teachings had a number of common elements: life was *dukkha;* to become free, you must rid yourself of the desire that led to activity, by means of asceticism and meditation. There were no elaborate texts and commentaries. These dharmas were strictly practical. The guru taught a method that was accessible to anybody who wanted to learn it; you did not have to be a scholar or a ritual expert. The program was usually based on a teacher's own experience. If it worked and brought his disciple intimations of liberation and enlightenment, the dharma was valid. If it did nothing for him, he felt no compunction about abandoning his teacher to find another one. In fact it was customary for monks to hail each other on the road: "Who is your teacher? And what dharma are you following these days?"

Some of these schools taught extreme methods, which revealed the growing desperation.[106] The Hansas were entirely homeless, could stay only one night in a village, and lived on cow dung. The Adumbaras lived on fruit, wild plants, and roots. The Paramahansas slept under trees, in graveyards, and in deserted houses. Some followed the teachings of Samkhya and practiced yoga, intent on acquiring liberating knowledge. Others were more skeptical. A teacher called Sanjaya rejected the possibility of any final answer. All one could do was cultivate friendship and peace of mind; because truth was relative, discussion inevitably led to acrimony and should be avoided. Ajita, another teacher, was a materialist, who denied the doctrine of rebirth: since all humans were wholly physical creatures, they would simply return to the elements after their death. The way you behaved was therefore of no importance, because everybody had the same fate, but it was probably better to foster goodwill and happiness by doing as you pleased and performing only karma that fostered these ends.[107]

These teachings all showed a determination to find a way out of the samsaric impasse of rebirth and redeath: some believed that they could achieve this by performing formidable austerities, others by avoiding hostility and unpleasantness. The goal was not to find a metaphysical truth but to obtain peace of mind. Unlike Sophocles, these sages did not think that they had to accept their pain with dignity. They were convinced that it *was* possible to find a way out. One of the most important of these teachers was Makkhali Gosala (d. c. 385). A taciturn man and a severe ascetic, he preached religious fatalism: "Human effort is ineffective." People were not responsible for their behavior. "All animals, creatures, beings and souls lack power and energy. They are bent this way and that by fate, by the necessary condition of their class, and by their individual nature."[108] He founded a school called Ajivaka ("Way of Life"). Gosala believed that all human beings without exception were destined to live through a fixed number of lives before they attained *moksha,* so their actions could not affect their fate one way or the other. And yet, paradoxically, the Ajivakas adopted a harsh regime. They wore no clothes, begged for their food, and observed such strict dietary rules that some of them starved to death. They also inflicted intense pain on their bodies. When he was initiated into the sect, for example, the new member was buried up to his

neck and had his hairs pulled out one by one. They did not perform these penances because they believed that they would help
them, but simply because they had reached that stage in their personal cycle when it was their lot to practice austerity.

It is a sign of the intense anxiety of this period that this bleak
dharma was very popular. Gosala's rivals attacked him more vehemently than any other guru, because they feared his success. Inscriptions show that kings sent him gifts and donated property to
Ajivaka ascetics, and the sect survived in India until the tenth century CE. We may not have the full picture. Gosala probably taught
an especially effective form of meditation that was kept secret
from outsiders. The extremity of his *tapas* may have been designed
to shock initiates into a state beyond pain or pleasure, and his determinism could simply have been a method of achieving serenity and calm: if everything was predestined, there was no point in
worrying about the future.

Gosala was said to have been a disciple of Vardhamana Jnatr-
putra (c. 497–425), who became one of the most important teachers of this period. His disciples called him Mahavira, "Great Hero."
The second son of a *kshatriya* chieftain of Magadha, he had a spectacular physique, strength, and beauty but decided, at the age of
thirty, to abandon the world and become a renouncer. He was determined to achieve enlightenment by himself, without the help
of a guru, so he refused to join one of the established schools. We
are told that the gods performed his rite of initiation into homelessness, and for twelve and a half years he lived as a mendicant,
roaming through the Ganges Valley, practicing the usual austerities: he wore no clothes, exposing his body to the torrid heat of
summer and the cold of winter; he fasted, and deprived himself of
sleep and shelter. It was during this initial period that he accepted
Gosala as a disciple, and traveled with him for six years until Gosala announced that he had achieved *moksha* and could call himself
a Jina, a spiritual conqueror. This account, however, is a later in-
terpolation into an older text.[109] It is hostile to Gosala, suggesting
that he was merely jealous of Mahavira's spiritual superiority and
broke away prematurely. Eventually the two men were reconciled:
Gosala died acknowledging that Mahavira was a true teacher, and

Mahavira predicted that one day Gosala would achieve enlightenment. It is likely that there was some historical connection between the two schools, and that Mahavira was influenced by the
Ajivakas at an early stage, but went on to develop an independent
teaching.

Mahavira's harsh lifestyle had a special purpose. Like all ascetics, he wanted to release his true self from the constraints of the
body, and thus achieve inner control and peace of mind. But he
did not achieve *moksha* until he had developed an entirely new
way of looking at the world that was informed through and
through by *ahimsa:* "harmlessness."[110] Each human being had a
soul (*jiva*), a living entity within, which was luminous, blissful, and
intelligent. But animals, plants, water, fire, air, and even rocks and
stones each had *jivas* too; they had been brought to their present
existence by the karma of their former lives. All beings shared the
same nature, therefore, and must be treated with the same courtesy and respect that we would wish to receive ourselves.[111] Even
plants had some form of awareness; in future lives, they could become sacred trees, and then progress to human form and finally
achieve enlightenment. If they gave up all violence, animals could
be reborn in heaven. The same rule applied to human beings, who
could achieve *moksha* only if they did not harm their fellow creatures. Until an ascetic had acquired this empathic view of the
world, he could not attain *moksha.*

For Mahavira, liberation *was* nonviolence. When he achieved
this insight at the age of forty-two, he immediately experienced
enlightenment. At that time, according to the earliest texts, he was
living in a field beside a river.[112] He had fasted for two and a half
days, drunk no water, exposed himself to the full glare of the sun,
and achieved *kevala,* a unique knowledge that gave him an entirely different perspective. He could now perceive all levels of reality simultaneously, in every dimension of time and space, as
though he were a god. Indeed, for Mahavira, a *deva* was simply a
creature who had attained *kevala* by perceiving and respecting the
divine soul that existed in every single creature.

Naturally this state of mind could not be described, because it
entirely transcended ordinary consciousness. It was a state of ab-

solute friendliness with all beings, however lowly. In this enlightened state of being, "words return in vain, no statements of mundane logic can be made, and the mind cannot fathom it." You
could speak of it only by saying, "*Neti . . . neti*" ("Not this . . . not
this"). When an enlightened person had attained this perspective,
he or she would find that there was "nothing with which it can be
compared. Its being is without form. . . . It is not sound, nor form,
nor soul, nor heaven, nor touch or anything like that."[113] But, Mahavira was convinced, anybody who followed his regimen would
automatically attain this ineffable state, and become a Jina. Hence
his followers were known as the Jains, and his dharma was "the
Way of the Conquerors."

Mahavira was a *kshatriya*. He believed that he was simply the
latest in a long line of Jinas who had crossed the river of *dukkha* to
gain liberation. After his death, the Jains would develop an elaborate prehistory, claiming that, in previous eras, there had been
twenty-four of these "ford-makers," who had discovered the
bridge to *moksha*. Each one had been a *kshatriya,* had been physically strong and beautiful, and as brave as a lion. Mahavira, the
"Great Hero," was thus offering an alternative ethos to the warrior class; the new heroism utterly rejected fighting, but required
courage of its own. Later the Jain order would be sponsored by
kings and warriors who were not able to abandon their military
duties, but who hoped to do so in a future life. Despite its dedication to nonviolence, the dharma frequently used martial imagery.
The Jain ascetic was a warrior who was battling his own belligerent instincts and warding off the bad effects of the aggression that
characterized all unenlightened people. The ascetic would win as
much glory for himself, his family, and his order by his life of
ahimsa as a soldier on the battlefield. The Jain community was
called a *gana:* "a troop." To become a Jina required the valor, determination, and ruthlessness toward oneself that was the mark of
a true hero.

Few people ever pursued the ideal of *ahimsa* with such relentless consistency as Mahavira. Later Jains would develop an elaborate eschatology and cosmology; they would evolve a metaphysics
that saw karma as a form of fine matter, like dust, produced by the

different qualities of various actions, which settled on the soul, weighing it down and preventing it from soaring to the top of the universe. As far as we can tell, Mahavira and his early followers were not concerned with these matters. Nonviolence was their *only* religious duty. All other ethical practice was useless without *ahimsa,* and this could not be achieved until the Jain had acquired an empathy with every single creature: "All breathing, existing, living, sentient creatures should not be slain, nor treated with violence, nor abused, nor tormented, nor driven away. This is the pure, unchangeable, eternal law, which the enlightened ones who know have proclaimed."[114]

This understanding was not, of course, a notional assent. The Jains had to become aware at a profound level that even apparently inert entities, such as stones, had a *jiva* and were capable of pain, and that no living creature wished to suffer—any more than they themselves did.

Jains achieved this insight by a program of asceticism that made them conscious of this extraordinary truth. By learning to behave differently, they found that their outlook changed, and they began to see the world anew. They had to move with consummate caution lest they inadvertently squash an insect or trample on a blade of grass. They were required to lay down objects with care, and were forbidden to move around in the darkness, when it would be easy to damage another precious creature. They could not even pluck fruit from a tree, but had to wait until it had fallen to the ground of its own accord. Jains needed to eat, of course, and in the early days they were allowed to accept meat in their begging bowls, provided that they had not had the animals killed themselves. The ideal, however, was to abstain from any activity at all, because the tiniest movement or physical impulse was likely to cause injury.

But the *ahimsa* of the Jains was not entirely negative, preoccupied with *not* doing harm. Jains had to cultivate an attitude of positive benevolence toward all beings. All living creatures should help one another. They must approach every single human being, animal, plant, insect, or pebble with friendship, goodwill, patience, and gentleness. Like the yogins, Jains followed five "prohibitions" (*yama*) and vowed to forgo violence, lying, sex, stealing, and the ownership of property, but Mahavira's interpretation of these *yama* was informed by his vision of the life force in all things. Naturally the early Jains concentrated on the first vow, of *ahimsa* ("harm-lessness"), which they practiced in the smallest details of their lives, but the other vows were also informed by the spirit of non-violence. Not only must Jains refrain from lying, but their speech must be deliberate and controlled, in order to eliminate any hint of unkindness or impatience. Words could lead to blows, so they should talk as little as possible. It was even better *not* to speak the truth if it would hurt another creature. The Jain vows were de-signed to create an attitude of watchfulness and care. It was not enough for Jains to forgo stealing; they could not possess anything at all, because each being had its own sacred *jiva,* which was sov-ereign and free.[115]

At all times, Jains must make themselves aware of the life force in everything around them. If people did not see this, they could not relate properly to their fellow creatures, but this involved Jains in a truly heroic restraint that seemed to curtail their lives at every turn. They could not light fires, dig, or plow. They could drink only filtered water, must inspect their surroundings every time they took a single step, and avoid any thoughtless movement. If the vows were lived in this way, the Jains would find that they had achieved an extraordinary self-control and a compassion that would bring them to enlightenment. Empathy was crucial. First, Mahavira taught, the Jain must acquire "knowledge of the world," so that he understood that everything had a sacred life force. Once he had acquired this knowledge of the world, he must then culti-vate "compassion for it."[116]

Mahavira had arrived at his own version of the Golden Rule. Jains had to treat all others as they would wish to be treated them-selves. The *dukkha* that pervaded the entire world was caused by the actions of ignorant people, who did not realize what they were doing when they injured others. To deny the *jiva* of your fel-low creatures was tantamount to denying your own inner self.[117] Jains wanted friendship with all things and all people—with no exceptions whatsoever. Once they had achieved this attitude, they would immediately attain enlightenment. *Moksha* was not a reward bestowed on the deserving by an overseeing god. Jains were not interested in this kind of theology. But they found that this practice, rigorously followed, brought them transcendent peace.

After his enlightenment, Mahavira preached his first sermon at the shrine of a tree spirit on the outskirts of the city of Champa.[118] The first detailed account of this event is found in a relatively late text, of the first century, but it became central to the Jain tradition. The king and queen of Champa attended, together with a huge crowd of gods, ascetics, lay folk, and animals, who all listened intently to Mahavira's gospel of nonviolence. It was a symbolic moment. In Vedic sacrifice, the gods had gathered to watch human beings slaughtering animals, but at Champa, gods, humans, and beasts assembled to listen to the preaching of *ahimsa* and formed a single, loving community. This vision of unity and universal empathy was supposed to inform every action of life.

Jains were not interested in yoga but practiced their own type of meditation. Standing motionless, their arms hanging by their sides but not touching the body, monks rigorously suppressed every hostile thought or impulse, while, at the same time, they made a conscious effort to fill their minds with love and kindness toward all creatures.[119] An experienced Jain would achieve a quasi-meditative state called *samayika* ("equanimity"), in which he *knew*, in every fiber of his person, that all creatures on the face of the earth were equal; at this time he felt exactly the same goodwill to all things, had no favorites, no pet hates, and did not distinguish a single being, however lowly, unpleasant, or insignificant, from himself. Twice a day, Jains stood before their guru and repented of any distress that they might inadvertently have inflicted "by treading on seeds, green plants, dew, beetles, mold, moist earth, and on cobwebs." They concluded with these words: "I ask pardon from all living creatures. May all creatures pardon me. May I have friendship for all creatures and enmity toward none."[120] The new ideal was no longer merely to refrain from violence, but to cultivate a tenderness and sympathy that had no bounds.

7

CONCERN FOR EVERYBODY

(c. 450 to 398 BCE)

In Israel, the Axial Age was drawing to a close. By the second half of the fifth century, Jerusalem was a small, damaged city in an undistinguished corner of the Persian empire. The Great Transformation usually occurred in regions that were in the vanguard of change and development. Israel and Judah had suffered greatly from the imperial powers, but these empires had brought intimations of broader horizons and a wider world. Israel's Axial Age had reached its crescendo in Babylon, the regional capital. In Jerusalem, the returning exiles were no longer in the forefront of world events, but lived in obscurity; the struggle for survival had taken precedence over the search for fresh religious vision. A few chapters in the book of Isaiah may express the preoccupations of the community after the completion of the second temple.[1] The old dream of Second Isaiah had not died. People still hoped that Yahweh would create "a new heaven and a new earth" in Jerusalem, where there would be no weeping and the pain of the past would be forgotten.[2] Others looked forward to the time when the city of God should open its gates to everybody—to outcasts, foreigners, and eunuchs—for Yahweh had proclaimed, "My house will be a house of prayer for all the peoples." One day he would bring these outsiders into the city, and allow them to sacrifice to him on Mount Zion.[3] But in fact a more rigidly exclusive attitude heralded the end of the Axial Age.

In about 445, a new governor was appointed as the Persian

representative in Jerusalem. Nehemiah, a member of the Jewish community in Susa, the Persian capital, had held the post of cup-bearer to King Artaxerxes I. He had been shocked to hear that the walls of Jerusalem were still in ruins and begged the king to allow him to go to Judah and rebuild the city of his ancestors. He arrived incognito, and went out secretly one night for a ride around the old, desolate fortifications, "with their gaps and burnt-out gates." At one point, he could not even find a path for his horse. When Nehemiah made himself known to the elders the next day, the citizens, mounting a massive cooperative effort, managed to build new walls for the city in a mere fifty-two days. But relations between the Golah, the community of returned exiles, and their neighbors had deteriorated so badly that it was a dangerous task. Throughout his mission, Nehemiah had to contend with the determined opposition of some of the local dynasts: Sanballat, governor of Samerina, in the territories of the old northern kingdom; Tobiah, one of his officials; and Gershon, governor of Edom. The new walls were built in fear and tension: "Each did his work with one hand while gripping his weapon with the other. And as each builder worked, he wore his sword on his side."[4]

It is very difficult to date this period. Our chief sources are the books of Ezra and Nehemiah, which consist of a number of unrelated documents that an editor later attempted to string together. He assumed that Ezra and Nehemiah were contemporaries, and made Ezra arrive in Jerusalem first. But in fact there are good reasons for dating Ezra's mission much later, during the reign of Artaxerxes II.[5] Nehemiah did a great deal to revive the fortunes of the city. He managed to increase the population to about ten thousand citizens, and tried to prevent the suppression of the poor by the nobility. But it is significant that his first act in Jerusalem was to build a wall. In his second term of office, which began in about 432, Nehemiah made new legislation to prevent members of the Golah from marrying into the families of the local population, even those Israelites who had not been taken into exile. He expelled the chief priest, Eliashib, because he was married to Sanballat's daughter. In exile, some of the priests had warned against assimilation with foreigners. Now the Golah was forbidden to marry people who had once been members of the Israelite family, but were now regarded as strangers and enemies.

During the exile, the laity had been encouraged to adopt the purity laws of the priests, and this meant that ordinary Jews had to be instructed in the intricacies of the ritual law by experts. One of these was Ezra, who had "devoted himself to the study of the law of Yahweh, to practising it, and to teaching Israel its laws and customs."[6] He may also have been the minister for Jewish affairs at the Persian court. At this time, the Persians were reviewing the laws of the subject peoples, to make sure that they were compatible with the security of the empire. As a legal expert in Babylonia, Ezra could have worked out a satisfactory modus vivendi between the Torah and the Persian legal system. His mission was to promulgate the Torah in Jerusalem and make it the official law of the land.[7] The biblical writer saw Ezra's mission as a turning point in the history of his people: he described his journey to Judah as a new exodus and presented Ezra as a new Moses. When he arrived in Jerusalem, Ezra was appalled at what he found. Priests were still colluding with the *am ha-aretz,* and the people continued to take foreign wives. For a whole day, the inhabitants of Jerusalem had to watch in dismay as the king's emissary tore his hair and sat down in the street in the posture of deep mourning. Then he summoned all the members of the Golah to a meeting: anybody who refused to attend would be cast out of the community and have his property confiscated.

On New Year's Day, Ezra brought the Torah to the square in front of the Water Gate; standing on a wooden dais and surrounded by the leading citizens, he read the Torah to the crowd, expounding on it as he went along.[8] We have no idea which text he actually read to them, but it was certainly a shock to the people. Religious truth always sounded different when written down and read aloud, and the people burst into tears, shocked by the demands of Yahweh's religion. Ezra had to remind them that this was a festival, an occasion for rejoicing, and recited the text that commanded the Israelites to live in special booths during the month of Sukkoth, in memory of their ancestors' forty years in the wilderness. The people rushed into the hills to pick branches of olive, myrtle, pine, and palm, and soon leafy shelters appeared all over the city. There was a carnival atmosphere: each evening, the people assembled to listen to Ezra's reading of the law.

The next assembly was a more somber occasion.[9] It was held in the square in front of the temple, and the people stood shivering as the torrential winter rains deluged the city. Ezra commanded them to send away their foreign wives, and women and children were, therefore, expelled from the Golah to join the *am ha-aretz*. Membership in Israel was now confined to the descendants of those who had been exiled to Babylon and to those who were prepared to submit to the Torah, the official law code of Jerusalem. The lament of the outcasts may have been preserved in the book of Isaiah:

> For Abraham does not own us
> And Israel does not acknowledge us;
> Yet you, Yahweh, yourself are our father. . . .
> We have long been like people who do not rule,
> People who do not bear your name.[10]

Suffering and domination had led to a defensive exclusion that was alien to the unfolding spirit of the Axial Age in the other regions.

But that cold, rainy scene was not the end of the story. The books of Ezra and Nehemiah comprised only a small part of the Hebrew Bible. Their perspective was shared by many of the people but it was not the only viewpoint. During the fifth and fourth centuries, the Bible was compiled by editors and the more inclusive traditions of Israel and Judah were also represented. The traditions of P, who had insisted that no human beings were unclean, dominated the first three books of the Pentateuch and qualified the more exclusive vision of the Deuteronomists. Other books reminded Jews that King David himself was descended from Ruth, a woman of Moab. And the book of Jonah showed a Hebrew prophet being compelled by Yahweh to save the city of Nineveh, capital of the Assyrian empire, which had destroyed the kingdom of Israel in 722. When Jonah had remonstrated with

God, Yahweh had answered in words that could have been endorsed by many other sages of the Axial Age—especially, perhaps, the Jains: "Am I not to feel sorry for Nineveh, the great city, in which there are more than a hundred and twenty thousand people who cannot tell their right hand from their left, to say nothing of all the animals?"[11]

The first phase of the Axial Age of Israel was over, but, as we shall see in the final chapter, it would enjoy a second flowering: Rabbinic Judaism, Christianity, and Islam would all build on Israel's Axial insights, and create a faith based upon the Golden Rule and the spirituality of "yielding," empathy, and concern for everybody.

As they entered the second half of the fifth century, despite the apparent success of their city, some of the older Athenians felt uncertain about the future. Pericles had led the polis to the zenith of its power. The new buildings on the Acropolis were a triumph; sculptors were creating astonishing work, and the great tragedians continued to present their masterpieces at the City Dionysia. In 446, Athens and Sparta had negotiated a truce for thirty years, dividing the Hellenic world between them: Athens would control the Aegean, while Sparta, a land power, held the Peloponnesus. Athens could look forward to a period of peace and prosperity, and yet Pericles built long defensive walls, enclosing the city and the port of Piraeus. Many Athenians still felt vulnerable, grimly aware that the subject poleis resented their imperial rule. In 446 they had sustained heavy losses in Boetia; cities had tried to defect from the Delian League, and there was war on Samos, in which the Persians threatened to intervene. Athens was not a major world power but only a small, overextended city-state. How could forty thousand fighting men rule the whole of Greece? But the younger generation did not appreciate this. Born after the battle of Marathon, they had known only easy success. They were becoming impatient with Pericles, who was now sixty years old, and were ready to listen to the new ideas that had the city buzzing during the 430s.

There was a major intellectual shift during these years. People had started to feel frustrated and even baffled by the philosophers, whose work was becoming increasingly abstruse. Zeno (b. 490), the disciple of Parmenides, had tried to demonstrate the validity of his master's controversial ideas by formulating a series of mischievous paradoxes. Parmenides had claimed that despite the evidence of our senses, everything was immobile. Zeno illustrated this by stating that an arrow in flight was actually motionless. At each second it occupied a space that was exactly equal to itself and was therefore always at rest, wherever it was. "What is moving is moving neither in the place in which it is, nor in the place in which it is not."[12] Again Zeno argued that it was impossible for Achilles, who ran faster than anyone else, even to begin the race of the Panathenaea: before he could complete the course, he had to travel halfway; before he reached that point, he had to get a quarter of the way there. But this line of reasoning could continue ad infinitum: before Achilles covered *any* distance he had to cover half of it.[13] It was, therefore, impossible to talk sensibly about motion, so it was better, as Parmenides advised, to say nothing about it at all.

Zeno wanted to demonstrate the logical absurdity of common sense and had discovered that motion was really a succession of immobilities in a way that would fascinate later philosophers. Chinese logicians, as we shall see, would evolve similar conundrums. But many of Zeno's contemporaries felt that reason was undermining itself. If it was impossible to formulate any truth, what was the point of these discussions? The Sicilian philosopher Empedocles (495–435) tried to reinstate the normal world, while holding on to some of Parmenides' insights. He argued that the four elements were indeed unchanging, but that they moved about and combined to form the phenomena we see. Anaxagoras of Smyrna (508–428) believed that every substance contained parts of every other substance, even though their presence could not be discerned by the naked eye. It followed that because it contained the seeds of all that exists, anything could develop into absolutely anything else. Like the Milesians, he tried to find the source from which everything developed. He called it *nous* ("mind"). This cosmic intelligence was divine, but not supernatural; it was merely another form of matter. Once *nous* had set everything in motion, there was nothing more it could do. Impersonal, natural forces took over, and the process continued without guidance. Democritus (466–370) imagined innumerable tiny particles careering around in empty space. He called them "atoms," the word deriving from *atomos* ("uncuttable"). The atoms were solid, indivisible, and indestructible, but when they collided with one another, they stuck together, and created the familiar objects that we see around us. When the atoms dispersed, things fell apart and apparently died, but the atoms went on to create new forms of being.[14]

These philosophers were not lonely thinkers, shut away from the world in ivory towers. They were celebrities. Empedocles, for example, claimed that he was divine, wore a purple robe, a golden girdle, and bronze shoes. Crowds flocked to hear him speak. With hindsight, we can see that some of the intuitions of these philosophers were remarkable. Democritus's atoms would be developed by modern physicists; and Empedocles imagined a cosmic struggle between Love and Strife, which was not unlike electromagnetism and Big Bang theory.[15] But they had no way of proving their theories, so however insightful, they remained fantasies. Philosophy was becoming too remote for ordinary people. These fanciful cosmologies answered no human need and ran counter to basic experience. If you could not trust the evidence of your senses, how could you reach any conclusions at all? Why should anybody believe the extraordinary ideas of Parmenides or Democritus, when they could produce no sound evidence to support them? As common sense was relentlessly dismantled by these logicians, many began to feel disoriented. Science has continued to disturb the public in this way. The hypotheses of Copernicus, Galileo, and Charles Darwin all caused disquiet when they were first proposed. Increasingly, these natural scientists (*physikoi*) began to have a similar effect on their Greek contemporaries.

In about 460 Anaxagoras arrived in Athens, and he immediately became a controversial figure. This was the first time that Athens, a very religious polis, had been directly exposed to the new ideas. Many were intrigued, but others were dismayed. Anaxagoras became interested in astronomy, and was said to have predicted the fall of a meteorite in Thrace in 467. He could not have achieved this feat, but may well have been excited by stories of large, blazing rocks falling from the sky. At all events, he concluded that the sun was a stone and the moon a mass of earth. The heavenly bodies were not gods, but red-hot rocks; instead of worshiping them, people should keep out of their way.[16] This kind of remark may have been commonplace in Ionia, but it was not acceptable in Athens.

A new circle of intellectuals tried to bring philosophy down to earth and make it more relevant. They had a profound effect on Athenian thinkers, but many found them just as distressing as the scientists.[17] They were called Sophists ("wise men"). Later Socrates, Plato, and Aristotle would criticize them quite savagely, and as a result, the word "sophist" is used today to describe somebody who uses specious, fallacious arguments. But this is not fair to the original Sophists, who were seriously seeking truth in their own way, and believed that they had an important mission. They argued that philosophy had taken a wrong turn. Gorgias, a Sophist from Leontinum in Sicily, parodied the convoluted logic of the Milesian and Eleatic *physikoi* thus:

- Nothing whatever exists.
- If it did exist, it would be impossible to explain what it was.
- If this were possible, it would be impossible to communicate it to anyone else.[18]

What was the point of denying common sense and the utility of language? Instead of creating incredible fantasies, it was time to develop a philosophy that would actually help people.

The Sophists set themselves up as educators. Democracy had made it possible for any gifted man to make his mark in the assembly, if he could speak eloquently and persuasively. But the ordinary curriculum did not help young men to acquire these skills. Greek boys learned reading, writing, sport, and a great deal

about Homer, but their education finished when they were fourteen years old. The Sophists stepped in to fill the gap, offering a
higher education to anybody who could pay the required fee.
One of the most notable Sophists was Hippias of Elis, a regular
polymath, who gave courses in arithmetic, mnemonics, survey-
ing, history, music, poetry, and mathematics. Like Empedocles, he
was a celebrity. He recited his poems at the Olympic games and
lectured to huge crowds. He was also a craftsman, and made all
his own clothes and shoes. This self-sufficiency underlined his
philosophy. People must rely on their own insights. Instead of
undermining common sense, Hippias and his colleagues tried to
give their pupils confidence in the workings of their minds. They
could never know absolute truth, but once they realized that all
thought was subjective, they would at least be free of delusion.
Their ideas were as good as anybody else's, so they should regard
their own thoughts as sovereign and autonomous.

The Sophists touched on many themes of the Axial Age: the
desire for liberation, autonomy, individualism, and the ability to
reach out to ordinary people, instead of confining knowledge to a
small elite. But there was a fundamental difference. So far the
Greeks had shown no desire for radical transformation, such as
that sought by the yogins. They had a strong sense of their potential as human beings, but little interest in where this might take
them. They concentrated on what they were rather than on what
they might become.[19] Focused on the present, they were chiefly
interested in *techne,* a technology that would make them more effective here and now. The Sophists did not want a *techne* that
would take them out of this world; they had no ambition to create a different kind of person, but simply wanted to enhance their
pupils' mundane skills. Instead of renouncing possessions, the
Sophists were keen to make money. Other philosophers despised
this, but the Sophists were not sordid mercenaries. They sincerely
believed that they were performing a valuable service in helping
ordinary citizens to take advantage of their new opportunities, regardless of birth and status.

Some of them gave lessons on rhetoric and the art of persuasion. Gorgias, for example, wrote several handbooks on public

speaking, and taught his pupils that it was possible to argue any case. He once wrote a famous defense of the indefensible Helen of Troy, and was himself an electrifying lecturer. When he arrived in Athens as an ambassador for Leontinum in 427, Gorgias became an overnight sensation, and young Athenians crowded into his classes. One of his students was Alcibiades, the nephew of Pericles, who once soundly defeated his uncle in an argument about democracy, using Sophistic methods. Alcibiades became a brilliant speaker in the assembly, and as we shall see, this had terrible consequences for Athens. Some of the Sophists' pupils certainly abused the skills that they had learned, but this was not the Sophists' fault. Gorgias believed that effective oratory kept freedom alive. Somebody who truly understood how to marshal an argument could defend the innocent and advance his polis. In a democracy, the Attic orator Antiphon once observed, "Victory goes to him who speaks best."[20] This was not necessarily a cynical observation, but a statement of fact about the way democracy worked. If victory did indeed go to the person who argued most convincingly in the assembly, the Sophists' skills could indeed ensure that the right prevailed.

Not all Sophists concentrated on public speaking. The most prominent Sophist was Protagoras of Abdera, who had little interest in rhetoric. His specialty was law and government, but he also wrote about language and grammar, and produced a philosophical treatise on the nature of truth. He arrived in Athens during the 430s, and became a friend of Pericles, who commissioned him to write the constitution for the new settlement at Thurii in Italy. Protagoras taught his students to question everything. They must accept nothing on hearsay or at second hand, but test all truth against their own judgment and experience. There must be no more self-indulgent speculation about the cosmos, unsupported by hard evidence. Naïve reliance on traditional mythology was also unacceptable, if it contradicted the laws of common sense.

The Sophists taught systematic doubt at a time of deepening anxiety. They had traveled widely. They knew that other cultures had different customs that worked perfectly well and concluded that there were no absolute verities. Where Parmenides and

Democritus had castigated subjective conviction, Protagoras embraced it. One person's truth would be different from his neighbor's, but that did not mean that it should be dismissed as false. Every man's perception was valid for him. Instead of seeing truth as a remote reality that was inaccessible to ordinary mortals, Protagoras claimed that everybody had a share. He simply needed to look into his own mind. "The measure of all things is man," he wrote in his epistemological treatise, "for things that are, that they are; for things that are not, that they are not."[21] An individual must rely on his own human judgments; there was no transcendent authority, and no Supreme God who could impose his view upon humanity.

Some Athenians found this liberating and would discover that this habit of questioning basic assumptions opened new doors and gave them fresh insights about religion. One of these was the playwright Euripides (c. 480–406), and it was at his home that Protagoras read his notorious treatise on the gods. "Concerning the gods," he began, "I have no means of knowing whether they exist or not, nor of what form they are; for there are many obstacles to such knowledge, including the obscurity of the subject and the shortness of human life."[22] Without adequate information, he could make no statement about the divine. He had simply applied Parmenides' rule to theology. The reality of the gods was not demonstrable, and could not, therefore, be a proper object of either knowledge or conversation.

The treatise caused an uproar. In 432, the city passed a law that made it illegal to teach such impiety, and Protagoras and Anaxagoras were both expelled from Athens. But the new skepticism remained, eloquently expressed in the tragedies of Euripides, who constantly asked difficult questions about the gods: Did they exist? Were they good? If not, how could life have any meaning? He was strongly influenced by the Sophists. "Do you think there are gods in the heavens?" he wrote at about this time. "No, there is no such thing, unless someone is determined foolishly to stick with the old fairy tales. . . . Think for yourselves: don't just take my word for it."[23] His personal experience cried out against the old theology. Tyrants killed and plundered, but they fared better than people who lived decent lives. His hero Heracles, son of Zeus, was driven mad by the goddess Hera, and in this divinely inspired frenzy murdered his wife and children. How could anybody accept such a deity? "Who could pray to such a god?" Heracles asked Theseus, king of Athens, at the end of the play. "These tales are simply the wretched myths of poets."[24] But Euripides did not completely reject the divine. By ruthlessly questioning the ancient stories, he was beginning to evolve a new theology. "The *nous* [mind] in each one of us is a god," he maintained.[25] In *Trojan Women,* he made the bereaved and defeated Hecuba, wife of Priam, pray to an unknown god: "O you who give the earth support and are by it supported, whoever you are, power beyond our knowledge, Zeus, be you stern law of nature or intelligence in man, to you I make my prayers; for you direct in the way of justice all mortal affairs, moving with noiseless tread."[26]

In 431, Euripides' *Medea* was presented at the City Dionysia. It told the story of the woman of Colchis who married Jason, helped him to find the golden fleece, but was then cruelly rejected by her husband. In revenge, she killed Jason's new wife, his father, and—finally—the sons she had borne to Jason. But unlike former heroes, Medea was not acting under the orders of a god; she was driven by her own stringent *logos.* Arguing against her powerful maternal instincts, raising objections to her abominable plan only to demolish them, she realized that she could not truly punish Jason unless she murdered their boys. Reason was becoming a frightening tool. It could lead people to a spiritual and moral void, and, if skillfully used, it could find cogent reasons for cruel and perverse actions. Medea was too intelligent not to find the most effective revenge and too strong not to carry it out.[27] She could have been a pupil of Gorgias.

The exercise of logic was an essential part of the catharsis of tragedy. Aristotle would later claim that the "ability to reason well" was a sine qua non for the purifying emotion of pity.[28] Without analytical rigor, you could not see the other's point of view. For the Greeks, logic was not coolly analytical, but fraught with feeling. The arguments in the courts and assemblies were as passionate and dramatic as those in the theater, and here too citizens learned the *ekstasis* of "stepping out" of themselves and moving toward a different perspective.[29] Reason could compel an audience to feel compassion for people who might seem to have no claim on their sympathy. Euripides continued the tragic tradition of reaching out empathically to the "other," even toward Medea and Heracles, who had committed such unspeakable acts. At the end of *Heracles,* Theseus offered the polluted, broken man his sympathy. When he led Heracles offstage, the two heroes had their arms around each other in a "yoke of friendship," and the chorus lamented "with mourning and with many tears. . . . For we today have lost our noblest friend."[30] These words instructed the audience to weep too. This was Dionysian *ekstasis,* a "stepping out" of our ingrained prejudice and preconceptions to an act of compassion that, before the play, might have seemed impossible.

When Euripides presented *Medea,* he told the story of a woman who had argued herself into a terrible crime. His audience might have seen a reference to the prolonged debate in the Athenian assembly, which, after some highly dubious political maneuvering, had thrust the Greek world into the Peloponnesian War. In 431, while the audience watched the play, preparations for this offensive were in progress. Pericles' plan was to save the empire at the expense of Attica. He ordered all the country folk to move into the city, and a hundred thousand people from the rural districts crowded within Athens's long walls. There they stayed, while the Spartans burned and looted the Attic countryside and the Athenian fleet ravaged the Peloponnesus. In 430, an outbreak of plague made the overcrowded city a living hell. Some twenty thousand people—25 percent of the population—died. In their fear and grief, as they watched the devout suffering alongside unbelievers, many Athenians lost all faith in the gods. They also lost confidence in Pericles, who was stripped of office. Although he was reappointed a few months later, he would die in the autumn of 429. Meanwhile, as the plague raged in Athens, the war had reached a stalemate. Athenians and Spartans pillaged each other's territories, but rarely met in pitched battle, so neither side could claim decisive victory.

A few months after Pericles' death, Sophocles presented *Oedi-*

pus the Tyrant at the City Dionysia. The play opened in Thebes, which had been stricken by plague because the murder of King Laius, Oedipus's father, had not been avenged. Oedipus launched an inquiry and, of course, discovered that not only was he himself the unwitting slayer of his father but, without realizing who she was, he had married his own mother. The Sophists had claimed that man was free and independent, and could take control of his own life. But was an individual entirely responsible for his actions, as the law of Athens claimed? Even when a person carefully considered a plan, did not the full meaning and origin of his deeds elude him? Did they not remain opaque? All his life, Oedipus had tried to act rightly and had constantly taken the best advice available. Through no fault of his own, he had become a monstrous figure, the polluter of his city, hopelessly defiled by actions whose significance he had failed to grasp at the time. He was guilty and innocent, agent and victim.

Oedipus had a reputation for wisdom. He had once saved Thebes by guessing the riddle of the Sphinx. It has been suggested that his name may have derived from *oida:* "I know." But it turned out that he was the opposite of what he had believed himself to be. He had been lethally ignorant. The truth was insupportable, and—in a horrifying gesture that Sophocles added to the original story—when he learned what he had done, he gouged out his eyes.[31] Despite his famed vision (*oidos*), he had in fact been blind to the truth. His self-mutilation took Oedipus to the limits of knowledge, beyond speech and perception—almost in a parody of mystical insight. He began the play as a king revered by his subjects as divine; he ended as a contaminated criminal, who had brought the *miasma* of death and sickness to his city.

But his journey was not over. Oedipus's blindness brought him a wholly new emotional vulnerability.[32] His speech now larded with wordless exclamations ("*Ion . . . ion! Aiai . . . aiai!*"), Oedipus learned pathos. When he reached out to Ismene and Antigone, his distraught daughters, Oedipus forgot himself in sympathy for their plight. The chorus too was filled with terror, their dread so great that at first they could not look the mutilated man in the face. But gradually this spectacle of unspeakable suffering taught them compassion, their fear dissolving as they struggled to understand the depth of Oedipus's pain. They begin to speak tenderly to him, calling him "my friend" and "dear one."[33] As usual in the tragic genre, their sympathy issued a directive to the audience, instructing them to feel compassion for a man who was guilty of crimes that would normally fill them with disgust. The audience too would experience transcendence, as they left their former assumptions behind in the *ekstasis* of empathy.

When Oedipus finally retired from the stage and disappeared into his palace, he had learned the lesson of suffering that the tragedians wanted to teach. But it is difficult to define this new knowledge. What the characters and the audience learned was a sympathy that brought a purifying catharsis. Oedipus had to abandon his certainty, his clarity, and supposed insight in order to become aware of the dark ambiguity of the human condition. The sagacity that had brought him such prestige had to be dismantled. With great courage, he accepted his punishment, even though he had not deserved it. He was now irrevocably cut off from other human beings. In the ancient logic of Greek religion, he had become taboo, a figure separate, apart, and therefore holy. In *Oedipus at Colonus,* a play that Sophocles wrote at the very end of his life, Oedipus would be exalted—almost deified—at death and his grave would be a source of blessing to Athens, which had given him asylum.[34]

During the 420s, while the Peloponnesian War dragged on and one atrocity succeeded another, a new philosopher became a well-known personality in Athens. Unlike the smart Sophists, he cut a rather shabby figure. He had no interest in making money, and would have been appalled at the idea of charging his students a fee. An ugly man, with protruding lips, a flat, upturned nose, and a paunch, Socrates was the son of a stonecutter. He had, however, been able to afford the weapons that admitted him to the hoplite army and was a veteran of the Peloponnesian War. Despite his humble origins, Socrates attracted a small crowd of disciples from the best families in Athens, who were fascinated by him and revered him as a philosophical hero. Socrates would talk to anybody. Indeed, he needed conversation, yet he was also capable of

profound abstraction. During a military campaign, he once aston-
ished his fellow hoplites by standing motionless all night long,
wrestling with an intellectual problem. On another occasion, on
his way to a dinner party, he fell into deep study, lagged behind his
companions, and finally spent the evening lost in thought, on a
neighbor's porch. "It's quite a habit of his, you know," one of his
friends explained; "off he goes and there he stands, no matter
where he is."[35] But his thought was deeply practical: Socrates was
convinced that he had a mission to bring his fellow Athenians to
a better understanding of themselves.

Conversation with Socrates was a disturbing experience. Anyone with whom he felt an intellectual affinity "is liable to be
drawn into an argument with him; and whatever subject he starts,
he will be continually carried round and round by him," said his
friend Niceas, "until at last he finds that he has to give an account
of his past and present life; and when he is once entangled, Socrates
will not let him go until he has completely and thoroughly sifted
him."[36] Socrates' purpose was not to impart information, but to
deconstruct people's preconceptions and make them realize that in
fact they knew nothing at all. The experience was a milder version
of the kenosis endured by Oedipus. You did not receive true
knowledge at second hand. It was something that you found only
after an agonizing struggle that involved your whole self. It was a
heroic achievement, a discipline that was not simply a matter of assenting to a few facts or ideas, but that required the student to examine his past and present life to find the truth within.

Socrates described himself as a midwife: he was bringing the
truth to birth within his interlocutors. They usually began a conversation with clear, fixed ideas about the topic under discussion.
Laches, an army general, for example, was convinced that courage
was a noble quality. And yet, Socrates pointed out, relentlessly pil-
ing up one example after another, a courageous act was often
foolhardy and stupid—qualities that they both knew were "base
and hurtful to us." Niceas, another general, entered the conversation and suggested that courage required the intelligence to appreciate terror, so that animals and children, who were too
inexperienced to understand the danger of a situation, were not

truly brave. Socrates replied that in fact all the terrible things we feared lay in the future, and were, therefore, unknown to us; it was impossible to separate the knowledge of future good or evil from our experience of good and evil in the present and the past. We say that courage was only one of the virtues, but anyone who was truly valiant must also have acquired the qualities of temperance, justice, wisdom, and goodness that were essential to valor. If you wanted to cultivate one virtue, you also needed to master the others. So at base, a single virtue, such as courage, must be identical with all the rest. By the end of the conversation, the three hoplites had to admit that, even though they had all endured the trauma of the battlefield and should be experts on the subject, they were quite unable to define courage. They had not discovered what it was, could not decide what distinguished it from the other virtues, and felt deeply perplexed. They were ignorant and, like children, needed to go back to school.[37]

Socrates had invented dialectic, a rigorous dialogue designed to expose false beliefs and elicit truth. By asking questions and analyzing the implications of the answers, Socrates and his colleagues discovered the inherent flaws and inconsistencies of every single point of view. One definition after another would be rejected, and often the dialogue ended with the participants feeling as dizzy and stunned as Laches and Niceas. Socrates' aim was not to come up with a clever or intellectually satisfying solution. The struggle usually led to the admission that there *was* no answer, and the discovery of this confusion was far more important than a neat conclusion, because once you had realized that you knew nothing, your philosophical quest could begin.

Socrates' dialectic was a Greek, rational version of the Indian *brahmodya,* the competition that attempted to formulate absolute truth but always ended in silence. For the Indian sages, the moment of insight came when they realized the inadequacy of their words, and thus intuited the ineffable. In that final moment of silence, they had sensed the brahman, even though they could not define it coherently. Socrates was also trying to elicit a moment of truth, when his interlocutors appreciated the creative profundity of human ignorance.

The knowledge thus acquired was inseparable from virtue. Unlike the Sophists, Socrates did not believe that courage, justice, piety, and friendship were empty fictions, even though he could not define them. He was convinced that they pointed to something genuine and real that lay mysteriously just out of reach. As his dialogues demonstrated, you could never pin the truth down, but if you worked hard enough, you could make it a reality in your life. In his discussion with Laches and Niceas, he was interested in courage as a virtue, not as a concept. Knowledge *was* morality. If you understood the essence of goodness, you were bound to act properly. If you were confused or your understanding of goodness was self-serving or superficial, your actions would fail to meet the highest standards. For Socrates, the purpose of philosophy was not to propound abstruse theories about the cosmos; philosophy was about learning how to live. Why was there so much evil in the world? It was because people had inadequate ideas about life and morality. If they recognized the depth of their ignorance, they would be better placed to know how to behave.

It is difficult to know exactly what Socrates said or thought, because he wrote nothing down. Indeed, he disapproved of writing, which, he thought, encouraged a slick, notional conception of truth. Our main sources are the dialogues written by his pupil Plato years after Socrates' death. Plato attributed many of his own insights and attitudes to Socrates, especially in the middle and later works, but the early dialogues, such as *Laches: On Courage,* probably give us an accurate idea of the way Socrates operated. We see that his main preoccupation was goodness, which he believed to be indivisible. Socrates' conception of the Good was, therefore, not unlike Confucius's *ren;* he seemed to have been reaching toward a transcendent notion of absolute virtue that could never be adequately conceived or expressed. As we shall see in the next chapter, Plato would make the Good the supreme, ineffable ideal.

Socrates may have hoped to advance further than the perplexity and confusion that marked the end of each of his recorded discussions, but this seemed to be as far as he got. By rigorous use of *logos,* he had discovered a transcendence that he deemed essential to human life. However closely he and his companions reasoned, something always eluded them. Socrates took pride in the ignorance that he had discovered at the heart of each firmly held opinion, no matter how dogmatically maintained. He understood just how little he knew, and was not ashamed to encounter the limitations of his thought again and again. If he did feel that he had an edge over others, it was only because he realized that he would never find answers to the questions he raised. Where the Sophists had taken refuge from this ignorance in practical action, Socrates experienced it as an *ekstasis* that revealed the deep mystery of life. People *must* interrogate their most fundamental assumptions. Only thus could they think and act correctly, see things as they truly were, get beyond false opinion, and arrive at intimations of that perfect intuition that would make them behave well at all times. Those who did not do this could only live expediently and superficially. As he explained in one of the most memorable utterances attributed to him: "The life that is unexamined is not worth living."[38]

To fail to think deeply about meaning was a betrayal of the "soul" (*psyche*). The discovery of the psyche was one of the most important achievements of Socrates and Plato. Unlike the atman, the psyche was separate from the body; it had existed before the birth of the individual and would survive his or her death. It enabled human beings to reason and inspired them to seek goodness. The cultivation of the soul was the most important human task, far more crucial than the achievement of worldly success. The soul was damaged by wrong action but benefited from right and just deeds. "We ought not to retaliate or render evil for evil to anyone, whatever evil we may have suffered from him,"[39] Socrates said at the end of his life. It was tempting to respond in kind but retaliation was always unjust; it was, therefore, essential to turn the other cheek. This was a dramatic departure from Greek custom, which saw vengeance as a sacred imperative, but Socrates insisted that this was the only path to happiness, because forbearing behavior to everybody—friend and foe alike—was beneficial to the soul.[40]

These ideas were not presented as dogmas. When Plato came to record his master's teaching, he had to invent the literary form of the dialogue. Like Confucius, Socrates taught by discussion, and never proposed a definitive thesis. Each person had to work out what was just and good for himself in conversation with another. In the course of this agon, they would experience an illumination in which they woke up to themselves. The people who came to Socrates usually thought that they knew what they were talking about, but by systematically making them aware of their ignorance, Socrates led them to discover an authentic knowledge within, which had been there all along. When this finally came to light, it felt like the recollection of an insight that had been forgotten. This illuminating, almost visionary discovery, Socrates believed, would inspire right action.

Like any kind of oral transmission, the Socratic dialectic was not a purely cerebral exercise. It was an initiation. Plato's account of these Socratic dialogues was pervaded by profound emotion that informed the ideas at every stage of the argument. Participants became aware of an aspiration that brought them to the heart of their being. There was a sense of constant striving without fanaticism or dogmatic certitude. Instead, there was a receptive, eager openness to the absolute. In the Platonic dialogue, we sense the effect that Socrates had on others. Alcibiades, the nephew of Pericles, seemed to have fallen in love with Socrates, whom he saw as a mysterious figure, appearing just when one least expected to find him. He was like the little effigies of the satyr Silenus, which, when unscrewed, had a tiny statue of a god inside. He was like the satyr Marsyas, whose music propelled the audience into a trance and made them yearn for union with the gods. But Socrates did not need a musical instrument. His words alone stirred people to the depths. "Whenever I listen to him, my heart beats faster than if I were in a religious frenzy and tears run down my face," Alcibiades confessed. He never had this experience when listening to his uncle Pericles. When Socrates spoke, he made Alcibiades realize "that I am still a mass of imperfections." He was the only person in the world who could fill him with shame. Socrates seemed to be a buffoon, fooling around, joking, falling in love with young men, and drinking all night long. But, Alcibiades said,

I doubt whether anyone has ever seen the treasures that
are revealed when he grows serious and exposes what
he keeps inside. However I once saw them, and found
them so divine and beautiful and marvellous that, to put
the matter briefly, I had no choice but to do what
Socrates bade me.

The *logoi* of Socrates filled his audience with the same kind of
"frenzy" as a Dionysian initiation; the listener felt "unhinged" (*ek-plexis*), as though he were on the brink of illumination.[41]

Not everybody was enraptured by Socrates, however. At this
time of anxiety and war, people did not want to be confused,
stirred to the depths, and made hyperconscious of their imperfections. They wanted certainty. In 423, Aristophanes produced a
satirical portrait of Socrates in his comedy *Clouds*. The play
showed a profound unease with the relativism of the Sophists,
who could make a convincing case for the most impossible
propositions. Socrates was no Sophist, but Athenians who had not
experienced his method would probably have been unable to distinguish between his relentless undermining of received opinion
and the Sophists' denial of absolute truth. Aristophanes presented
Socrates in his "logic shop," where, arguing that wrong was right,
he instructed people to worship the clouds instead of Zeus. Eventually the protagonist, a loyal Athenian citizen, was so outraged
that he burnt the school down. The comedy turned out to be
prophetic in a way that Aristophanes could never have imagined.

By this time, Athens faced defeat in the Peloponnesian War.
Many saw this imminent catastrophe as a divine punishment for
the irreligion of the philosophers. They regarded Socrates' teaching as blasphemous, even though he was traditionally devout and
attended the public rituals as scrupulously as he performed his
military service. But anxiety was about to turn into hysteria. In
416, Alcibiades made an emotional speech in the assembly, arguing that Athens should go to the aid of its ally Segesta, in Sicily,
which was being attacked by the nearby city of Selinus. The general Niceas (Socrates' sparring partner) was against the expedition,
but Alcibiades and the younger generation carried the day. It was

a disastrous decision, since most of the citizens who voted for the war had no idea of the size and power of Sicily. Just before the fleet disembarked, somebody vandalized the Herms, the phallic statues of the god Hermes that were placed throughout the city to protect streets and houses. Nobody knew who was responsible, but the incident shook Athens to the core. People were convinced that this blatant sacrilege would call down divine vengeance. There were witch hunts, suspects were executed, and eventually Alcibiades himself was recalled from Sicily to answer charges of blasphemy.

There ensued a series of disasters. The Athenian navy was blockaded in the harbor at Syracuse, and the troops were incarcerated in nearby stone quarries. At a stroke, Athens lost about forty thousand men and half its fleet. In 411, a pro-Spartan cabal overturned the democratic government in Athens. The coup was short-lived, and democracy was restored the following year, but it was a sign of Athens's new vulnerability. The war with Sparta continued until 405, when the Spartan general Lysander forced Athens to surrender. Yet again, an oligarchy was established under a government of thirty pro-Spartan aristocrats, who killed so many citizens in the ensuing reign of terror that it was overthrown, and democracy reestablished after only a year. Athens had regained its independence, its democracy, and its fleet, but its power was broken, the empire dismantled, and Pericles' great defensive wall demolished.

Against this terrifying backcloth, two great tragedies were enacted in Athens. Just before Athens conceded defeat in 406, Euripides died, and his final dark, bitter plays, lurid with a sense of looming catastrophe, were performed posthumously. The last was *The Bacchae,* presented in 402.[42] As the play opened, the god Dionysus arrived incognito in Thebes, the city that had rejected his mother, Semele, when she had fallen pregnant, and had consistently prohibited his cult. But now most Thebans were enchanted by the fascinating stranger who had suddenly turned up in their midst. The women of the city, who had not been properly initiated into the Dionysian mystery, abandoned themselves to unbridled frenzy, roaming through the woods, clad in animal pelts. The young king Pentheus tried to restore order, but to no avail. Eventually he allowed himself to be dressed in women's clothes so that he could spy on these revels unobserved. But in their hysteria, the women tore him to pieces with their bare hands, thinking that they had killed a lion. Agaue, Pentheus's mother, triumphantly carried her son's head into Thebes at the head of a demented procession.

The tragic dramas had often depicted the slaying of kinsfolk, but by making Dionysus, the patron of tragedy, responsible for this unnatural murder, Euripides seemed to be calling the entire genre into question. There was no glimmer of hope at the end of the play. The royal house had been shattered, the women reduced to animals, enlightened reason defeated by savage *mania,* and Thebes—like Athens at this juncture—seemed doomed. What had been the value of the annual release of emotion in honor of a god who killed, tortured, and humiliated human beings without giving any plausible explanation?

Athens was beginning to grow beyond tragedy, and in so doing, was also parting company with the Axial Age. The play warned the polis that it was dangerous to refuse admittance to the outsider. In *Oedipus at Colonus* (406), Sophocles had shown Athens receiving with honor the polluted, sacred figure of the dying Oedipus, an act of compassion that would be a blessing for the city. But in *The Bacchae,* Pentheus rejected the stranger and was destroyed. Not only was it politically disastrous, but individuals also had to recognize and accept the stranger that they encountered within themselves during the mystery celebrations. By giving Dionysus his due in the annual festival, Athens had given the alterity that he represented an honored place in the heart of the city; but over the years it had failed to respect the inviolable separateness of the other poleis, had exploited and attacked them, and in the process had fallen prey to hubris.

In this last play, Euripides approached the heart of the Axial vision. The chorus of Maenads, the regular worshipers of Dionysus, had been correctly initiated into his cult; they experienced a vision of peace, rapture, and integration. But the women of Thebes, who were unschooled in the disciplines of transformation, were simply out of control, driven mad by the darker regions of their psyche that were unknown to them. As she entered the city, holding aloft the ghastly trophy of her son's head, Agaue did not achieve *ekstasis,* but was enchanted only by her own achievements:

> Great in the eyes of the world,
> Great are the deeds I have done
> And the hunt I've hunted there.[43]

The apotheosis of this barren selfishness was an act of unspeakable, unnatural violence.

In this play, Euripides also presented one of the most moving and truly transcendent Greek experiences of the divine. Dionysus might seem amoral, cruel, and alien, yet he was incontrovertibly present onstage, and could neither be willed nor driven away. In his human disguise as the stranger, he seemed uncanny. Dionysus had always been the masked god—the mask a constant reminder that he was other than he appeared. His supreme epiphany was not an anthropomorphic apparition but a sudden disappearance when, hiding himself from all who believed only in what they could see, he vanished abruptly from the stage. A great silence immediately descended upon earth, in which his presence was felt more strongly than ever before.[44] The older Olympian vision was reaching beyond itself to the ineffable reality behind the symbols.

The second great tragedy of this period was the death of Socrates in 399. At his trial, he was accused of failing to recognize the gods of the state, of introducing new gods, and of corrupting the young. The young Plato was at the trial, and it made a profound impression upon him. From a legal point of view, Socrates' defense was inept. He could not have corrupted the young, he said. He did not know enough to teach anybody anything. He had worked for the good of Athens, but the polis had failed to appreciate this. Yet he could not abandon his mission. The very best thing a man could do was "to let no day pass without discussing goodness and all the other subjects about which you hear me talking."[45] He failed to convince his judges and was condemned to death.

Socrates had long been the object of suspicion and fear. Some of his associates, such as Alcibiades, had been involved in Athens's military disasters, and Socrates became a scapegoat. He had said the right things at the wrong time. Devoted to Athens, he obeyed its laws to the end, refusing to escape from prison, even though the sentence was unjust, and turning down the option of exile: he was almost seventy years old, he said simply, and did not wish to live anywhere else. He was a champion of truth, and would die a witness (*martys*) to the untruth that was currently in the ascendant. Yet he died without anger or blame. There was nothing tragic about death, he told his pupils. Nobody knew what it was; it might even be a great good. Throughout his life, he believed that he had been accompanied by a *daimon,* a divine presence, which had spoken to him at crucial moments. It had never told him what to do, but had only warned him *against* a particular action. He found it encouraging that his inner voice had not spoken to him during his trial. He must be on the right track and going to the Good.

His friends gathered around his bed while he drank the prescribed poison. Before he took the hemlock, Plato says, he washed his body, to save the women the trouble after his death. He thanked his jailor courteously for his kindness, and even made some mild jokes about his predicament. He was able to look death calmly in the face, forbade his friends to mourn, and quietly and lovingly accepted their companionship. Instead of destructive, consuming sorrow, there was a quiet, receptive peace. Throughout the Axial Age, sages had been preoccupied with death. Socrates showed that it was possible for a human being to enjoy a serenity that transcended his circumstances, in the midst of pain and suffering.

Shortly after the death of Confucius, China entered a disturbing and frightening era, which historians call the period of the Warring States. It marked a decisive transition in Chinese history. In 453, three families rebelled against the prince of Jin, and created

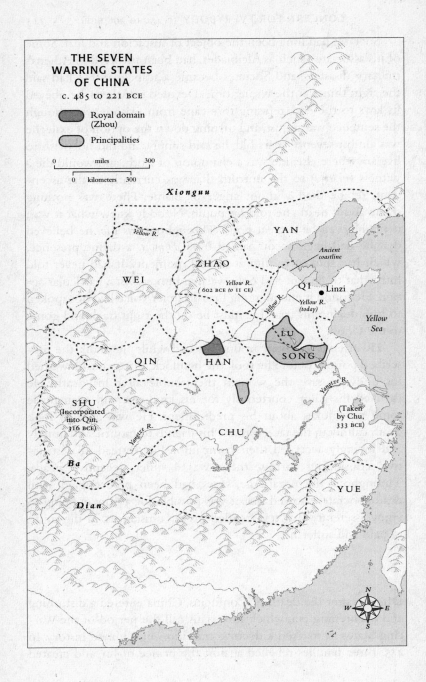

THE SEVEN
WARRING STATES
OF CHINA
c. 485 to 221 BCE

Royal domain
(Zhou)

Principalities

miles
0   300

0   kilometers   300

Xiongnu

YAN

Yellow R.

ZHAO

*Ancient
coastline*

WEI

*Yellow R.
(602 BCE to 11 CE)*

QI   ● Linzi

Yellow R.

*Yellow R.
(today)*

*Yellow
Sea*

LU

QIN   HAN   SONG

Yangtze R.

SHU
(Incorporated
into Qin,
316 BCE)

CHU

(Taken
by Chu,
333 BCE)

Yangtze R.

Ba

Dian

YUE

N
W   E
S

three separate states in Jin territory: Han, Wei, and Zhao. This was the real end of the long-declining Zhou dynasty: hitherto all the rulers of China had been enfeoffed by the Zhou king; these new states, however, were established simply by military force, and the Zhou king could do nothing about it. From this moment the larger and more powerful states were engaged in a desperate struggle for the sole domination of China. The chief contenders were the state of Chu in the south, which was only half Chinese; Qin, a rough, warlike state in western Shensi; the rich, maritime kingdom of Qi; the "three Jin"—the new states of Han, Wei, and Zhao; and Yan, near the northern steppes. At first the little principalities in the central plain tried to preserve themselves by diplomacy, but in the course of the next two hundred years, they were eliminated, one by one, and absorbed into the larger, more competitive kingdoms.

The Warring States era was one of those rare periods of history when a succession of changes, each reinforcing the other, accelerates the process of development, and leads to a fundamental alteration of society.[46] When these struggles finally came to an end in 221, the political, religious, social, economic, and intellectual life of China was entirely different. But in the early years of the Warring States, most people would only have been aware that life on the central plain had suddenly become more violent than ever before. The horror of this experience intensified the quest for a new religious vision.

Warfare itself had been transformed.[47] There were no more ritualized confrontations between courtly charioteers, each vying to outdo the others in generosity and courtesy. The militarized states fought to gain new territory, subjugate the population, and wipe out the enemy. Campaigns lasted longer and went farther afield. The fighting was characterized by deadly efficiency, which demanded unity of command, strategy, trained troops, and abundant resources. Warfare was now masterminded by military experts, and order, discipline, and effectiveness were far more important than honor and prestige. In the old days, nobody would have dreamed of killing women, children, the wounded, or the infirm. But now "all who have or keep any strength are our enemies even if they are old men," said one of the modern generals. "Why should we refrain from wounding a second time those whose wounds are not mortal?"[48]

Already in the late sixth century, the states had started to develop a new military technology. Specialists constructed mobile towers and wheeled ladders to attack city walls; they dug mines and underground passages, and devised bellows to drive smoke into the tunnels of the enemy. The landscape itself was mobilized for warfare: Chu and Qi built the first defensive walls in Honan and Shantung; Qin fortified the dikes of the Yellow River. Fortresses were built along frontiers and manned by professional garrisons. More land was drained, and the first canals were dug in order to increase agricultural production to fund these expensive campaigns.

More and more of the population was mobilized. In the old days of courtly feudal warfare, the peasants had been peripheral players, taking no real part in the action. Now hundreds of thousands of peasants were drafted into the infantry, which had become the most important part of the army. The defunct state of Jin had been the first to use infantry troops, in the late sixth century, when fighting in mountainous regions that were unsuitable for chariot warfare. Yue and Wu, whose swampy territory had too many lakes and waterways for chariots, followed suit. Gradually the warrior-peasant became a major factor in social and political life. The aristocratic chariot teams were phased out, and soldiering became a lower-class activity. The military specialists learned from the nomads of the steppes. In the fourth century they would introduce cavalry, which were more mobile than the cumbersome chariot armies, and could sweep down on a community in a surprise attack with devastating results. The new warriors also used the nomads' weapons: the sword and the crossbow, which was more accurate than the old retroflex bow and could kill at a distance of half a mile.

The kings of the large, aggressively expanding states had thrown aside the ideals of moderation and restraint. Funerals once again became cruel, lavish displays. One king buried vast riches with his daughter, and sacrificed troops of dancers and boys and girls of common stock.[49] Modern rulers now had colorful, extravagant households, filled with women, musicians, dancers, jugglers, clowns, and gladiators. Sophists, who had originally advised princes and vassals about the ritualized court palavers, now developed clever debating skills and gave advice on public relations and diplomacy. Impoverished wandering *shi* also clustered around the courts, showing off their talents in the hope of a job. Some of them were scholars. Duke Wen (446–395) of the new state of Wei became a patron of learning, supporting a circle of literati to advise him on matters of protocol and ethics. These kings no longer trusted the aristocrats, who had become their competitors, and turned increasingly for advice to these "men of worth." One of Duke Wen's protégés was Confucius's disciple Zixia.

But in these pragmatic times, the rulers tended to find Confucians too idealistic, and they turned increasingly to the *xie,* the bands of peripatetic military experts who, like other members of the *shi* class, had lost their foothold in the cities and roamed the countryside in search of employment. By the Warring States period, however, many of the *xie* were recruited from the lower classes. They were mercenaries, prepared to fight in any army, as long as they were rewarded adequately. Unlike the more aristocratic Confucians, they were aggressive men of action. According to a historian of a later period, "Their words were always sincere and trustworthy, their actions quick and decisive. They were always true to what they promised and without regard to their own persons they would rush into danger, threatening others."[50]

But toward the end of the fifth century, one of the *xie* turned his back on this militancy and preached a message of nonviolence. His was called Mozi, "Master Mo" (c. 480–390). We know very little about him, because the dialogues recorded in the book that bears his name are far more impersonal than the Analects, and Mozi the man disappears behind his ideas.[51] He headed a strictly disciplined brotherhood of 180 men.[52] Unlike Confucius's loosely organized band of disciples, Mozi's school resembled a sect. It had strict rules, followed a rigorously egalitarian ethic, and its members dressed like peasants or craftsmen. Instead of fighting as mercenaries, Mohists intervened to stop wars and defend cities in the smaller and more vulnerable states.[53] Nine chapters of the Mozi deal with the techniques of defensive warfare and the construction of equipment to protect city walls. But Mozi was also a philosopher. He did not stop at disciplined action, but traveled from court to court, preaching his highly original ideas to the rulers.

From the evidence of the Mozi, it seems that Master Mo could originally have been an artisan or craftsman. He used the imagery of a working man, comparing Heaven's organization of the world to the compasses and L-square of the wheelwright and the carpenter, who employed these instruments "to measure the round and the square throughout the world."[54] Unlike the graceful style of the Analects, Mozi's prose was somewhat humorless and ponderous, suggesting that he may have been a self-educated man who took up the pen with difficulty.[55] Despite his impressive grasp of tradition, a residual awkwardness of style indicates that Mozi was not wholly at ease with the high culture of the nobility. Mo and his followers were arrivistes, impatient with the aristocracy's preoccupation with prestige and status. He wanted a uniform control of expenditure, a curbing of extravagance, and a society that reflected the more frugal ethos of his own class.

Mozi was, for example, highly critical of the Zhou dynasty and had little time for Confucius's hero the duke of Zhou. He had very little interest in the Zhou ritual, music, and literature, which was so inspiring to Confucius. The poorer folk had never taken part in these elaborate court ceremonies, and the li seemed a complete waste of time and money to the Mohists. Mozi was deeply religious and believed that it was important to sacrifice to Heaven and the nature spirits, but he was disgusted by the extravagance of the elaborate ceremonial rites in the ancestral temples. He was especially incensed by the expensive funerals and the long, three-year mourning period. This was all very well for the idle rich, but what would happen if everybody observed these rites? It would ruin the workingman, bring down the economy, and weaken the state.[56] Mozi took a strictly pragmatic view of ritual. Rulers spent an inappropriate amount of money on these ceremonies, when the ordinary people did not have the wherewithal for food and clothes. The *li* did not elevate the soul; the ritualists had simply retreated from the problems of their time, taking refuge in the discussion of arcane ceremonies and abandoning all hope of redeeming the world.

The situation had already changed dramatically in the short time that had elapsed since Confucius's death. In the fourth and third centuries, as we shall see, Confucians would agonize about the plight of the poor and work indefatigably for the reform of society. But in Mozi's day, some of the ritualists might have been so shocked by the rapid changes in the great plain that they withdrew from public life in the way that Mo described. Mozi, however, was extremely distressed by the predicament of the peasants, who were dragged off to fight in wars, conscripted into the corvée, and impoverished by heavy taxation. It was essential to supply their basic need for shelter, clothing, and security. Mozi was not a revolutionary. He did not want to topple the ruling class, but he was convinced that Chinese values needed radical revision. Mozi believed that the sage kings had been content with the bare necessities of life. There must be a return to the ideals of Yao, Shun, and Yu, who had not lived lives of sophistication, luxury, and showy display at the expense of ordinary folk. They had built their houses just high enough to keep out the damp; their walls were just thick enough to keep out sleet and rain, and their inner partitions just high enough to segregate the sexes.[57] Mozi's favorite was Yu, who, despite his lofty status and great wealth, had spent his life developing a technology to control water distribution and prevent flooding, working practically for the good of the people.

Mozi's message was utilitarian and pragmatic, yet he nurtured utopian dreams. He believed that it was possible to persuade human beings to love instead of hate. As with Confucius, the single thread that held his philosophy together was *ren,* but he believed that Confucius had distorted this compassionate ethic by limiting it to the family. In his view, the clan spirit of the aristocracy was at the root of many of the current problems: family chauvinism, competitions for prestige, vendettas, and sumptuary expenses. He wanted to replace the egotism of kinship with a generalized altruism.[58] Everybody must feel toward all others exactly what he felt for his own people. "Others must be regarded like the self," he said; this love must be "all-embracing and exclude nobody."[59] Reform must come from the rulers: the only way to stop the Chinese from killing one another in these appalling wars was to persuade them to practice *jian ai*.

Jian ai is often translated as "universal love," but this is too emotive for Mozi's utilitarian ethos.[60] Mozi did not expect the Chinese to develop a warm affection and tenderness for everybody. He was more interested in justice than feelings. *Ai* was a deliberately cultivated attitude of benevolence, so that you wished everybody well, even—and perhaps especially—those who did not belong to your immediate community. *Jian ai* was based on a strong sense of equity, fairness, and an impartial concern for all human beings without exception. This, Mo was convinced, was indispensable for peace and security. At present, rulers only loved their own state and felt no qualms about attacking their rivals. But if they were taught to have as much concern for others as for themselves, this would be impossible. "Regard another's state as you regard you own, another's family as you regard your own, and another's person as you regard your own," Mo urged. "If the lords of the states are concerned for each other they will not go to war." If brothers had no respect for each other, they would quarrel; if the lords had no *jian ai,* they would summon their armies. "In all cases, the reason why the world's calamities, dispossessions, resentments and hatreds arise is lack of *jian ai.*"[61]

Mozi's version of the Golden Rule may have been less elegantly expressed than that of Confucius, but it was immediately regarded as more radical. Instead of seeing the family as the place where you learned to love other people, Mozi argued that, on the contrary, *jian ai,* "concern for everybody," made it possible to love your family or state appropriately. If people did not cultivate benevolence toward the whole human race, family love and patriotism would degenerate into collective egotism. In his view, the Confucian family was simply a special-interest group. Even criminals loved their families and robbed other people in order to enrich their kinsfolk. If people did not reach out beyond their family or nation, they became guilty of the potentially lethal selfishness that was the cause of the world's ills.

Jian ai led directly to nonviolence. In the chapter of his book entitled "Rejection of Aggression," Mozi carefully weighed the cost of war against its benefits. War ruined harvests, killed multitudes of civilians, wasted weapons and horses, and left the ancestors with no descendants to sacrifice on their behalf. Rulers argued that conquest benefited the state, but the capture of a small town could result in thousands of casualties at a time when men were desperately needed to farm the land. How could that be good for their kingdom? The larger states thought that they would gain by conquering the territory of their smaller neighbors, but their wars benefited only about five people out of ten thousand. Some chapters of the Mozi, probably written by later generations of Mohists, permitted warfare in self-defense; they included instructions for the defense of a city during a siege. But Mozi himself was probably a strict pacifist, who opposed all violence and traveled from one state to another to persuade rulers to break the cycle of warfare that was beginning to engulf all the states of the great plain.[62]

Many of the Chinese, for whom family values were sacrosanct, were shocked by Mo's ideas, so he developed a method of arguing rationally in support of his beliefs. This is why the Mozi contains the first Chinese essays in logic and dialectic; some of the later chapters, dating from the third century, show a sophisticated grasp of the principles of systematic argumentation, definition, and precise grammar. The approach was entirely different from the impressionistic style of the Analects. Confucius assumed that the *junzi* would acquire his insights and understanding intuitively after a long period of study and reflection. But Mozi's "men of worth" (*xian*) were men of action and argued their way to truth logically.[63] They excelled "in their virtuous behavior, and their skill in argument."[64] Their remarks must be precise in order to convince their opponents of the importance of *jian ai* at this desperate moment in history. The Mohist was more interested in *doing* good than *being* good. For Confucius, *ren* was primarily an interior virtue, but the "men of worth" were outwardly directed to the external world. Mohists were not interested in the slow process of self-cultivation, but wanted to put their practical skills, logic, and willpower at the service of society.

Mozi summed up his vision in ten theses, each of which was presented as a proposition. Should people have "concern for everybody"? Should they "reject aggression"? What did Mohists think about extravagant funerals, liturgical music, and the will of Heaven? Were people's actions determined by fate? How should Mohists approach their superiors? Each proposal was weighed against three criteria. Did it conform to the practice of the sage kings? Was it supported by common sense? And—most important—would it benefit the human race? If it failed any of these tests, it must be rejected. Lavish funerals and music did not benefit society, so they had to go. Nobody had ever seen "Fate," so the determinism that made the Confucians believe that they could not change the world was not a proper attitude for true men of worth.

Mozi's ethical vision was strictly utilitarian. An act was virtuous if it enriched the poor, prevented unnecessary death, increased the population, and contributed to public order. People had to be argued out of their selfishness; human beings were natural egotists, so they had to be convinced by irrefutable arguments that their well-being was entirely dependent upon the welfare of the whole of humanity and that a fair and just "concern for everybody" was essential for prosperity, peace, and security.[65] Mohists must convince rulers that aggression was not in their best interests. Warfare made their own subjects suffer; it ruined the economy; and victory stirred up hatred and jealousy. They would get the wealth, happiness, and success that they desired only if everybody behaved toward one another with equity and transcended self-interest. Rulers had to "learn not to be concerned for themselves alone."[66]

If they were selfish and violent, they would incur the wrath of Heaven. Unlike Confucius, who preferred not to speak about Heaven, Mozi backed up nearly every one of his arguments with a reference to the High God. Heaven loved all human beings without distinction and was the exemplary model of *jian ai.* "Heaven is all embracing and not selfish," Mozi insisted.

Heaven is generous and ungrudging; Heaven's understanding is eternal and never declines. . . . Heaven displays its love of all men by giving them all life and
sustaining them. If one flouts Heaven, Heaven will inflict calamities. Because the sages made Heaven their
standard, all their actions were effective.[67]

The aristocracy had long been moving toward an impersonal
conception of the divine, but Mozi probably expressed the beliefs
of the ordinary people, who still saw Heaven as a personalized
deity. Yet despite his strong, literal-minded beliefs in God and the
Spirits, Mozi had very little religious feeling. Unlike Confucius,
Mozi felt no awe or wonder in the presence of Heaven. His theology was as grimly practical as his ethics. Heaven was useful.
Heaven could pressure people into the belief that they *must* cultivate a concern for everybody, or suffer the consequences.

If everybody could be persuaded to respect others as they did
themselves, there would be peace and harmony throughout the
world. Nobody could raze a city to the ground or massacre the
population of a village if he practiced *jian ai*. Mozi was at his most
eloquent when he described this utopia:

Now if we seek to benefit the world by taking *jian ai* as
our standard, those with sharp ears and clear eyes will
see and hear for others, those with sturdy limbs will
work for others, and those with a knowledge of the Way
will endeavor to teach others. Those who are old and
without wives and children will find means of support
and be able to live out their days; the young and or-
phaned who have no parents will find someone to care
for them and look after their needs.[68]

Mozi did not believe that this was an impossible dream. Throughout this chapter, he repeatedly exclaimed: "When all these benefits
may be secured merely by taking *jian ai* as our standard, I cannot
understand how the men of the world can hear about this doctrine
and still criticize it!"[69] The sage kings had founded an empire based

on universal altruism; the ideal had worked in the past, and could do so again. It *was* possible to change the world, he argued, and men of worth must rise to the challenge.

During the Warring States period, Mozi was more widely revered than Confucius, because he spoke directly to the terror and violence of his time. As he watched the whole of China mobilizing for war, it seemed that human beings were about to erase themselves from the face of the earth. If they could not curb their selfishness and greed, they would destroy one another. The only way they could survive was by cultivating a boundless sympathy that did not depend upon emotional identification but on the reasoned, practical understanding that even their enemies had the same needs, desires, and fears as themselves.

Toward the end of the fifth century, a *kshatriya* from the republic of Sakka, in the foothills of the Himalayas, shaved his head and beard, put on the saffron robe of the renouncer, and set out on the road to Magadha. His name was Siddhatta Gotama, and he was twenty-nine years old. Later he recalled that his parents wept bitterly when he left home. We are also told that before leaving he stole into his wife's bedroom while she was asleep to take one last look at her and their newborn son, as though he did not trust his resolve should she beg him to stay.[70] He had begun to find his father's elegant house constricting: a miasma of petty duties weighed him down. When he looked at human life, Gotama could see only the grim cycle of suffering, which began with the trauma of birth and proceeded inexorably to "aging, illness, death, sorrow and corruption," only to start again with the next life cycle. But like the other renouncers, Gotama was convinced that these painful states must have their positive counterparts. "Suppose," he said, "I start looking for the *un*born, unaging, deathless, sorrowless, incorrupt and supreme freedom from all this bondage?"[71] He called this blissful liberation *nibbana** ("blowing

---

*In Sanskrit, the Pali *nibbana* becomes *nirvana*.

out"), because the passions and desires that tied him down would be extinguished like a flame. He had a long, arduous quest ahead, but he never lost hope in a form of existence—attainable in this life—that was not contingent, flawed, and transient. "There *is* something that has not come to birth in the usual way, which has neither been created and which remains undamaged," he insisted. "If it did not exist, it would be impossible to find a way out."[72]

He believed that he did find it, as did the monks who followed his teachings and transmitted them orally, until they reached their present form about a hundred years after Gotama's death. They called him the Buddha, the "enlightened" or "awakened" one. These Buddhist scriptures were composed in Pali, one of the Sanskrit dialects of northeast India, and are our main source of information about the Buddha's life. As in most of the new schools that were springing up in the eastern Ganges plain, Buddhist teachings and practices (*dhamma*)★ were based on the life experience of the founder, and the Pali texts therefore emphasize those aspects of his biography that would help others to achieve *nibbana*. If people wanted to become enlightened, they too had to leave home and family, as well as all their preconceptions, far behind, just as the Buddha had done.

Later Buddhists told a mythical story that brought out the deeper significance of Gotama's departure. When he was born, his father invited some Brahmins to examine the baby and tell his fortune. One of them predicted that Gotama would see four disturbing sights that would convince him to become a renouncer and discover a new spiritual truth. Gotama's father had more worldly ambitions for his son, so to shield him from these painful spectacles he posted guards around the palace to keep all distressing reality at bay. Thus, even though he lived in carefree luxury, the boy was a virtual prisoner. Gotama's pleasure palace is a striking image of a mind in denial. As long as we persist in closing our hearts to the sorrow that surrounds us on all sides, we remain incapable of growth and insight. But when Gotama was twenty-nine years old, the gods, who needed the Buddha's *dhamma* as much as human be-

★In Pali, the Sanskrit *dharma* becomes *dhamma*.

ings, decided to intervene. They sent four of their number past the guards, disguised as an old man, a sick man, a corpse, and a renouncer. Gotama was so shocked by these images of pain that he put on his yellow robe and left home that very night. Once the suffering that is an inescapable part of the human condition has broken through the cautionary barricades that we have erected against it, we can never see the world in the same way again. Gotama had allowed the knowledge of *dukkha* to invade his life, and his quest could begin.

As he walked down the road to Magadha, Gotama probably hailed other renouncers in the usual way, asking who their master was and what *dhamma* they followed, because he was looking for a teacher to instruct him in the rudiments of "homelessness." First he studied in Vaishali with two of the greatest yogins of the day, Alara Kalama and Uddalaka Ramaputta. He was an excellent pupil, and to the delight of his teachers soon achieved the very highest states of trance, but he could not accept their interpretations of these experiences. They followed the teachings of Samkhya, and believed that once they had entered these peak planes of the psyche, they had liberated the *purusha* from the bonds of nature. But Gotama, all his life, had been skeptical of metaphysical doctrines: How could this trance be the unconditioned and uncreated *purusha* when he knew perfectly well that he had manufactured it for himself, by his yogic expertise? Further, when he returned to himself, he found that there had been no real transformation. He was still his unregenerate, greedy, yearning self. His trance was not *nibbana,* because *nibbana* could not be temporary. Gotama had no problem with yoga, but he would not accept interpretations that did not coincide with his own experience.[73]

Gotama left his teachers and joined a group of ascetics. With them he practiced severe extremities that gravely damaged his health. He lay on a mattress of spikes, ate his own urine and feces, and fasted so rigorously that his bones stuck out "like a row of spindles . . . or the beams of an old shed." At one point, he became so weak that he was left for dead beside the road.[74] But all to no avail. However severe his penances—perhaps even because of them—his body still clamored for attention, and he continued to be plagued by the lust and cravings that bound him to the grim cycle of rebirth. There was no hint of the peace and liberation he sought.

Nevertheless, Gotama did not give up. Henceforth he would rely only on his own insights. This would become one of the central tenets of his spiritual method. He constantly told his disciples that they must not accept anybody's teachings, no matter how august, if those teachings did not tally with their own experience. They must never take any doctrine on faith or at second hand. Even his own teachings must be jettisoned if they failed to bring followers to enlightenment. If people relied on an authority figure, they would remain trapped in an inauthentic version of themselves and would never attain the freedom of *nibbana*. So in a moment of mingled despair and defiance, his health broken down by excessive penance, and at a spiritual dead end, Gotama resolved to strike out on his own. "Surely," he cried, "there must be another way to achieve enlightenment!" And as if to prove that his declaration of independence was indeed the way forward, the beginnings of a new solution declared itself to him.[75]

He suddenly recalled an incident from his early childhood. His nurse had left him under the shade of a rose apple tree while she watched the ceremonial plowing of the fields before the spring planting. The little boy sat up and saw that young shoots of grass had been torn up by the plow, and insects had been killed. Gazing at the carnage, Gotama had felt a strange pang of grief, as though his own relatives had died.[76] The surge of selfless empathy brought him a moment of spiritual release. It was a beautiful day, and the child had felt a pure joy welling up within him. Instinctively, he had composed himself in the yogic position, and entered a tranced state, even though he had never had a yoga lesson in his life.

As he looked back on this childhood event, Gotama realized that the joy he had felt that day had been entirely free of craving and greed. "Could this," he asked himself, "possibly be the way to enlightenment?" If an untrained child could achieve yogic ecstasy and have intimations of *nibbana,* perhaps the liberation of *moksha* was built into the structure of our humanity. Instead of starving his body into submission, and making yoga an assault on his psyche, maybe he should cultivate these innate tendencies that led to *cetovimutti,* the "release of the mind" that was *nibbana.* He should foster helpful (*kusala*) states of mind, such as the disinterested impulse of compassion that had surfaced so naturally, and at the same time avoid any mental or physical states that would impede this liberation.[77]

Like the Jains, Gotama realized that the traditional five "prohibitions" of the "unhelpful" (*akusala*) states of violence, stealing, lying, intoxication, and sex must be balanced by their positive counterparts. Instead of merely avoiding aggression, he must behave gently and kindly to everything and everybody, and cultivate thoughts of loving-kindness. It was important not to lie, but also crucial to ensure that whatever he said was "reasoned, accurate, clear, and beneficial."[78] Besides refraining from stealing, he must rejoice in possessing only the bare minimum. From now on, he was going to work *with* his human nature and not fight against it. For the first time in months, he took solid food and started to nurse himself back to health. He also began to develop a special type of yoga. First came the practice of "mindfulness" (*sati*), in which, as a prelude to meditation, he scrutinized his behavior at every moment of the day, noting the ebb and flow of feelings and sensations, together with the fluctuations of his consciousness, and making himself aware of the constant stream of desires, irritations, and ideas that coursed through his mind in the space of a single hour. This introspection was not designed to induce a neurotic, self-regarding guilt. Gotama was simply becoming acquainted with the workings of his mind and body in order to exploit their capacities and use them to best advantage, in the same way as an equestrian seeks an intimate knowledge of the horse he is training.

Like many other renouncers, Gotama was convinced that life was *dukkha,* and that desire was responsible for our suffering. The practice of mindfulness made him even more acutely aware of the impermanence and transitory nature of human existence and of its countless frustrations and disappointments. It was not simply the big traumas of old age, sickness, and death that made life so unsatisfactory. "Pain, grief and despair are *dukkha,*" he explained later. "Being forced into proximity with what we hate is suffering; being separated from what we love is suffering; not getting what we want is suffering."[79] He also observed the way one craving after another took possession of his mind and heart, noticing how he was ceaselessly yearning to become something else, go somewhere else, and get something that he did not have. In this endless stream of desire, it seemed as though human beings were continually seeking a new kind of existence—a new life, or rebirth. He could see it in his physical restlessness, the way he constantly shifted his position or set off for another part of the forest. "The world, whose very nature is to change, is constantly determined to become something else," he concluded. "It is at the mercy of change, it is only happy when caught up in the process of change, but this love of change contains a measure of fear, and this fear is itself *dukkha*."[80]

These were not simply logical reflections. Gotama was a very skilled yogin, and practiced this mindfulness with the disciplined concentration that enabled him to see these truths more "directly," without the filter of self-protecting egotism that distorts them. But he did not stop at contemplating these negative truths; he also fostered the more "skillful" (*kusala*) states while performing his yogic exercises, sitting cross-legged, and practicing the breathing rituals of *pranayama*. He was not only eliminating hatred from his mind, but making sure that it was also "full of compassion, desiring the welfare of all living beings." He was not only freeing himself of laziness and inertia, but cultivating "a mind that is lucid, conscious of itself, and completely alert." By systematically banishing one anxious thought after another, he found that his mind became "calm and still . . . had outgrown debilitating doubt," and was no longer plagued by "unprofitable [*akusala*] mental states."[81] If performed at sufficient depth, in the yogic manner, these mental exertions could, he believed, transform the restless and destructive tendencies of the unconscious and conscious mind.

In later years, Gotama claimed that this yogic mindfulness brought to birth a different kind of human being, one that was not dominated by craving, greed, and selfishness. He had almost killed himself by undergoing excessive mortification, and was convinced that disciplined, systematically acquired compassion could take the place of the old punitive asceticism, and give the aspirant access to hitherto unknown dimensions of his humanity. Every day, while practicing yoga, he entered into an alternative state of consciousness, fusing each successive trance with a feeling of positive benevolence toward the entire world.

He called these meditations "the immeasurables" (*appamana*). At each stage of his yogic journey into the depths of his mind, he deliberately evoked the emotion of love—"that huge, expansive and immeasurable feeling that knows no hatred"—and directed it to the four corners of the world, not omitting a single plant, animal, friend, or foe from this radius of sympathy. It was a fourfold program. First, he cultivated a disposition of friendship for everything and everybody. Next he learned to suffer with other people and things, empathizing with their pain, as he had felt compassion for the grass shoots and insects under the rose apple tree. In the third phase of his meditation, he summoned up a "sympathetic joy" that delighted in the happiness of others, without envy or sense of personal impairment. Finally, when he entered the deepest trance of all, so immersed in the object of his contemplation that he was beyond pain or pleasure, Gotama aspired to an attitude of total equanimity toward others, feeling neither attraction nor antipathy. This was extremely difficult, because Gotama had to divest himself completely of the egotism that constantly looks to see how other things and people might benefit or detract from the self. Where traditional yoga had built up in the yogin a state of impervious autonomy, Gotama was learning systematically to open his whole being to others, and thus transcending the ego in compassion and loving-kindness to all other creatures.[82] When these positive, skillful states were cultivated with yogic intensity, they could more easily take root in the unconscious and become habitual. The "immeasurables" were designed to pull down the barricades that we erect between ourselves and others in order to protect our fragile egos. As the mind broke free of its ordinary, self-oriented constriction, it felt "expansive, without limits, enhanced, without hatred or petty malevolence."[83] If taken to the very highest level, this yoga of compassion brought the aspirant the "release of the mind," or *nibbana*.[84]

We have no idea how long it took Gotama to recover his health and attain the supreme enlightenment after he had devised this regimen. The Pali texts give the impression that it was a speedy process, but Gotama himself explained that it could take as long as seven years to achieve this incremental transformation. Gradually, the aspirant would learn to live without the selfish cravings that poison our lives and relationships, and would become less affected by these unruly yearnings. As he became aware of the ephemeral nature of these invasive thoughts, it became difficult to identify with them, and he became increasingly adept at monitoring the distractions that deprive us of peace.[85] The texts depict Gotama attaining enlightenment in a single night, because they wanted to show the general contours of the process and were not interested in the historical details of the journey. But Gotama's enlightenment was, almost certainly, no instant "born again" experience. He later warned his disciples that "in this method, training, discipline and practice take effect by slow degrees, with no sudden perception of the ultimate truth."[86]

The traditional story has Gotama sitting down under a bodhi tree in a pleasant grove near the city of Uruvela, beside the Neranjara River. The Pali scriptures tell us that in the course of a single meditation, he gained an insight that changed him forever and was convinced that he had liberated himself from the cycle of rebirth.[87] But there seems little that is new in this insight, usually formulated as the Four Noble Truths. Most renouncers would have agreed with the first three: that existence was *dukkha,* that desire was the cause of our suffering, and that there was a way out of this predicament. The fourth truth may have constituted the breakthrough: Gotama claimed that he had discovered the path that leads from suffering and pain to its cessation in *nibbana.* This path, traditionally called the Noble Eightfold Path, was a plan of action, consisting of morality (the cultivation of the "skillful" states), meditation, and the wisdom (*panna*) that enabled the aspirant to understand Gotama's teaching "directly" through the practice of yoga and integrate it with his daily life. Gotama never claimed that the Noble

Truths were unique, but that he was the first person in this historical era to have "realized" them and made them a reality in his own life. He found that he *had* extinguished the craving, hatred, and ignorance that hold humanity in thrall. He *had* reached *nibbana,* and even though he was still subject to physical ailments and other vicissitudes, nothing could touch this inner peace or cause him serious mental pain. His method had worked. "The holy life has been lived out to its conclusion!" he cried triumphantly at the end of his meditation under the bodhi tree. "What had to be done has been accomplished; there is nothing else to do!"[88]

What was *nibbana*? The word, as we have seen, implies that Gotama, on achieving enlightenment, had been "snuffed out." After his enlightenment, he was often called the Tathagata ("gone"), implying that "he" was no longer there. But this did not mean personal extinction. What had been extinguished was not Gotama the man but the fires of greed, hatred, and delusion. By tamping out the "unhelpful" states of mind, the Buddha (as we must now call Gotama) had achieved the peace of complete selflessness. This was a state that those of us who are still enmeshed in the toils of egotism cannot begin to imagine. That is why the Buddha always refused to define *nibbana*: it would be "inappropriate" to do so, because there were no words to describe this state to an unenlightened person.[89] The Buddha would still suffer; he would grow old and sick like everybody else, but by assiduous meditation and ethical effort, he had found an inner haven, which enabled a man or woman who put this regimen into practice to live with pain, take possession of it, affirm it, and experience a profound serenity in the midst of suffering. Perhaps Socrates had discovered something similar through his lifelong discipline of passionate honesty, which made him capable of equanimity while undergoing an unjust execution. *Nibbana* was thus found within each person's inner being, and was an entirely natural state. It was a still center that gave meaning to life. People who lost touch with this quiet place within could fall apart, but once they had learned to access this oasis of calm, they were no longer driven hither and yon by conflicting fears and desires, and discovered a strength that came from being correctly centered, beyond the reach of selfishness.

The Buddha was convinced that though *nibbana* was not a supernatural reality, it was a transcendent state because it lay beyond the capacities of those who had not achieved this inner awakening. There were no words to describe it, because our language is derived from the sense data of our unhappy existence, in which we cannot conceive of a life entirely devoid of ego. In purely mundane terms, *nibbana* was "nothing," because it corresponded to no reality that we could recognize. But those who had managed to find this sacred peace discovered that they lived an immeasurably richer life.⁹⁰ Later monotheists would speak about God in very similar terms, claiming that God was "nothing" because "he" was not another being; and that it was more accurate to say that he did not exist, because our notions of existence were too limited to apply to the divine.⁹¹ They would also claim that a selfless, compassionate life would bring people into God's presence. But like other Indian sages and mystics, the Buddha found the idea of a personalized deity too limiting. The Buddha always denied the existence of a supreme being, because an authoritative, overseeing deity could become another prop or fetter that would impede enlightenment. The Pali texts never mention brahman. The Buddha came from the republic of Sakka, far from the Brahminical heartlands, and may have been unfamiliar with the concept. But his rejection of God or gods was calm and measured. He simply put them peacefully out of his mind. To inveigh vehemently against these beliefs would have been an unskillful assertion of ego. The old gods sometimes played a part in his life. Mara, god of death, for example, sometimes appeared in the Pali texts as the tempter of the Buddha, advising him to take an easier path, almost as though he were an aspect of the Buddha's own mind.

Yet when the Buddha tried to give his disciples a hint of what *nibbana* was like, he often mixed negative with positive terms. *Nibbana* was the "extinction of greed, hatred and delusion"; it was "taintless," "unweakening," "undisintegrating," "inviolable," "nondistress," and "unhostility." It canceled out everything that we find unbearable. One of the most frequent epithets used to describe *nibbana* was "deathless." But positive things could be said of *nibbana* too: it was "the Truth," "the Subtle," "the Other Shore,"

"Peace," "the Everlasting," "the Supreme Goal," "Purity, Freedom, Independence, the Island, the Shelter, the Harbour, the Refuge, the Beyond."[92] It was *the* supreme goal of humans and gods alike, an incomprehensible serenity, and an utterly safe refuge. Many of these images are reminiscent of words later used by monotheists to describe their experience of the ineffable God.

In finding *nibbana,* the Buddha had achieved his goal, but this was not the end of his life and mission. At first he had simply wanted to luxuriate in this transcendent peace. It occurred to him that he should, perhaps, spread the good news, but he rejected the idea as too exhausting and depressing. His *dhamma* was too difficult to explain. Far from wishing to give themselves up, most people positively relished their attachments and would not want to hear this message of self-abandonment.[93] But then the god Brahma (a popular manifestation of the brahman in the eastern Ganges) decided to intervene. In the Pali text, he seemed, like Mara, to represent an aspect of the Buddha's own personality: at some buried level, Gotama realized that he simply could not neglect his fellow creatures. In a complete reversal of their usual roles, the god left his heaven, descended to earth, and knelt before the enlightened man. "Lord," he prayed, "please teach the *dhamma.* Look down at the human race, which is drowning in pain, and travel far and wide to save the world." The Buddha listened carefully, and the Pali text tells us that "out of compassion, he gazed upon the world with the eye of a Buddha."[94] This is an important remark. A Buddha was not one who simply achieved his own salvation, but one who could still sympathize with the pain of others. Compassion and loving-kindness directed to the four corners of the earth had brought him to enlightenment. Selfish withdrawal would violate the essential dynamic of his *dhamma,* which demanded that he return to the marketplace and become involved in the sorrowing world. A crucial part of the insight he had gained under the bodhi tree was that to live morally was to live for others. For the next forty-five years of his life, the Buddha tramped tirelessly through the cities and towns of the Ganges plain, bringing his teaching to gods, animals, men, and women.

The Buddha's first disciples were already renouncers, and one of them was said to have achieved enlightenment during the Buddha's first sermon. The texts always described the process in the same way. As Kondanna listened to the Buddha expounding the Noble Truths, he began to experience the teaching "directly"; it "rose up" in him, as if from the depths of his own being, as though he recognized it, had always known it.[95] It was not long before young men from the *kshatriya* and Brahmin classes began to join the Buddha. *Vaishya* merchants were also attracted to his insistence upon self-reliance, and those who did not become monks often became lay followers and patrons. The Buddha's order (*sangha*) soon became a sizable sect. The monks spent hours each day practicing the Buddha's compassionate, mindful yoga, but they also had to teach the method to others. This was not a religion for the privileged elite, like the old Vedic rituals. It was "for the many." The monks often lived in parks in the suburbs of the cities, which made it easy for the townsfolk to consult them, and crowds of merchants, noblemen, and courtesans turned out to listen to the Buddha when he arrived in their region. But most of the time, the monks were on the road, traveling "for the welfare and happiness of the people, out of compassion for the world."[96]

One of the most popular ways of attaining *nibbana* was meditation on the distinctively Buddhist doctrine of *anatta* ("no self"). The Buddha did not believe that the eternal self (atman; *purusha*) was the supreme reality. The practice of mindfulness had made him aware that human beings were in constant flux; their bodies and feelings changed from one moment to the next. After systematically examining his shifting convictions, emotions, and perceptions an honest person had to conclude that none of these could be the self sought by so many of the renouncers, because they were so flawed and transitory: "This is not mine; this is not what I really am; this is not my Self."[97] But the Buddha went even further and denied the reality of a stable, "lowercase" self too. The terms "self" and "myself" were, he believed, mere conventions, since every sentient being was simply a succession of temporary, mutable states of existence. In our own day, some postmodernist philosophers and literary critics have come to a similar conclusion.

The Buddha liked to use metaphors such as a blazing fire or a rushing stream to describe the human personality. It had some kind of identity, but was never the same from one moment to the next. Unlike the postmodernist idea, however, *anatta* was not an abstract, metaphysical doctrine but, like all his teachings, a program for action. *Anatta* required Buddhists to *behave* day by day, hour by hour, as though the self did not exist. Not only did the concept of "self" lead to unskillful thoughts about "me" and "mine," but prioritizing the self led to envy, hatred of rivals, conceit, pride, cruelty, and—when the self felt threatened—violence. The Buddha tried to make his disciples realize that they did not have a "self" that needed to be defended, inflated, cajoled, or enhanced at the expense of others. As a monk became expert in the practice of mindfulness, he would no longer interject his ego into passing mental states, but would regard his fears and desires as transient, remote phenomena that had little to do with him. Once a monk had achieved this level of dispassion, the Buddha explained to his monks, he was ripe for enlightenment. "His greed fades away, and once his cravings disappear, he experiences the release of the mind."[98]

The texts tell us that when the Buddha's first disciples heard his explanation of *anatta,* their hearts were filled with joy and they immediately experienced *nibbana.* Why should they have been so happy to hear that the self that we all cherish did not exist? The Buddha knew that *anatta* could sound frightening. An outsider might panic, thinking, "I am going to be annihilated and destroyed; I will no longer exist!"[99] But the Pali texts show people accepting *anatta* with relief and delight. Once they lived as though the self did not exist, they found that they were happier and experienced the same kind of enlargement of being as they did when practicing the immeasurables. To live beyond the reach of hatred, greed, and anxieties about our status and survival proved to be liberating.

But there was no way of proving this rationally. The only way of assessing the Buddha's method was to put it into practice. He had no time for abstract doctrinal formulae divorced from action. A person's theology was a matter of total indifference to the Buddha.

Indeed, to accept a dogma on somebody else's authority was un-skillful; it could not lead to enlightenment because it amounted to an abdication of personal responsibility. Faith meant trust that *nib-bana* existed and a determination to realize it. He always insisted that his disciples test everything he taught them. A religious idea could all too easily become a mental idol, one more thing to cling to, while the purpose of the *dhamma* was to help people to let go. Even his own teachings must be jettisoned, once they had done their job. He liked to tell the story of a traveler who came to a great expanse of water and desperately needed to get across. But there was no bridge or ferry, so he cobbled together a raft and paddled over. But then, the Buddha would ask his audience, what should the traveler do with the raft? Should he decide that because it had been so helpful to him, he must load it onto his back and lug it around with him wherever he went? Or should he simply moor it and continue his journey? The answer was obvious. "In just the same way, monks, my teachings are like a raft, to be used to cross the river and not to be held on to," the Buddha concluded.[100] His task was not to issue infallible statements or satisfy intellectual curiosity, but to enable people to cross the river of pain and arrive at the "fur-ther shore." Anything that did not serve that end was irrelevant.

The Buddha had, therefore, no theories about the creation of the world or the existence of God. These topics were, of course, extremely fascinating, but he refused to discuss them. Why? "Be-cause, my disciples, they will not help you, they are not useful in the quest for holiness; they do not lead to peace and to the direct knowledge of *nibbana*."[101] He told one monk who kept pestering him about cosmology to the detriment of his yoga and ethical practice that he was like a wounded man who refused medical treatment until he learned the name of the person who had shot the arrow, and what village he came from. He would die before he got this useless information. What difference did it make to learn that a God had created the world? Grief, suffering, and pain would still exist. "I am preaching a cure for these unhappy conditions here and now," the Buddha explained to his metaphysically in-clined monk, "so always remember what I have not explained to you and the reason I have refused to explain it."[102]

The Buddha liked to keep explanations to a minimum. Like Socrates, he wanted the disciple to discover the truth within himself. This also applied to the laity. On one occasion, the Kalamans, a tribal people who lived on the northern bank of the Ganges, sent a delegation to the Buddha. One renouncer after another had descended upon them, they explained, but each one belittled the others' doctrines. How could they tell who was right? The Buddha replied that he could see why the Kalamans were so confused. He did not add to their perplexity by reeling off the Four Noble Truths, but held an impromptu tutorial. The Kalamans were expecting other people to tell them the answers, he explained, but if they looked into their own hearts they would find that they already knew the right way to live. Was greed, for example, good or bad? Had the Kalamans noticed that if somebody was consumed by desire, he was likely to steal, lie, or even to kill? Did not this type of behavior make the selfish person unpopular and, therefore, unhappy? And did not hatred and delusion also lead to pain and suffering? By the end of their discussion, the Kalamans found that they had indeed known the Buddha's *dhamma* all along. "That is why I told you not to rely on any teacher," the Buddha concluded. "When you know in yourselves that some things are helpful and others unhelpful, you should practise this ethic and stick to it, no matter what anybody else tells you."[103] He adapted a form of the meditation on the immeasurables to the laity to help them to acquire the skillful attitude described in an early Buddhist poem:

> *Let all beings be happy! Weak or strong, of high,*
> *   middle or low estate,*
> *Small or great, visible or invisible, near or far away,*
> *Alive or still to be born—may they all be perfectly*
> *   happy!*
> *Let nobody lie to anybody or despise any single*
> *   being anywhere.*
> *May nobody wish harm to any single creature, out of*
> *   anger or hatred!*
> *Let us cherish all creatures, as a mother her only*
> *   child!*

May our loving thoughts fill the whole world, above,
    below, across,—
Without limit; a boundless goodwill toward the
    whole world,
Unrestricted, free of hatred and enmity![104]

If they behaved in this way and there was a future life, the Buddha concluded, the Kalamans might accumulate some good karma and be reborn as gods. But if there was no afterlife, their considerate, genial lifestyle might encourage others to respond to them in the same way. At the very least, the Kalamans would know that they had behaved well, which was always a comfort.[105]

The Buddha always entered into the position of the people that he was addressing, even if he did not agree with it. As always, compassion was the key. One of his lay followers was King Pasenadi of Kosala, who remarked one day that he and his wife had recently admitted to each other that nothing was dearer to them than their own selves. Obviously this was not a view that the Buddha could share, but he did not scold the king or launch into a discussion of *anatta*. Instead he asked Pasenadi to consider this: If he found that there was nothing dearer to him than himself, others must feel the same. Therefore, the Buddha concluded, "a person who loves the self should not harm the self of others."[106] This was his version of the Golden Rule. Laypeople could not extinguish their egotism as thoroughly as a monk, who was devoted to the task full-time, but they could use their experience of selfishness to empathize with other people's vulnerability. This would take them beyond the excesses of ego and introduce them to the essential value of compassion.

Toward the end of his life, King Pasenadi's wife died and he fell into a chronic depression. He took to driving around the countryside aimlessly, and one day discovered a park full of wonderful old trees. Alighting from his carriage, he walked among their enormous roots and noticed the way that they "inspired trust and confidence." "They were quiet; no discordant voices disturbed their peace; they gave out a sense of being apart from the ordinary world and offered a retreat from the cruelty of life." Looking at these marvelous trees, the king immediately thought of the Buddha, jumped into his carriage, and drove for miles until he had reached the house where the Buddha—now an old man of eighty—was staying.[107] For many of his contemporaries, the Buddha was a haven of peace in a violent, sorrowful world. The search for a place apart, separate from the world, and yet wondrously within it, that is impartial, utterly fair, calm, and that fills us with a confidence that, against all odds, there is value in our lives, was what many people in the Axial Age sought when they looked for God, brahman, or *nibbana*. The Buddha seemed to encapsulate this in his own person. People were not repelled by his dispassion, not daunted by his lack of preference for one thing or person over another. He does not seem to have become humorless, grim, or inhuman, but inspired extraordinary emotion in all who met him. His constant, relentless gentleness, serenity, and fairness seemed to touch a chord and resonate with some of their deepest longings. Like Socrates and Confucius, he had become what Karl Jaspers called a paradigmatic personality—somebody who exemplified what a human being could or should be.[108] These luminaries of the Axial Age had become archetypal models; imitating them would help other people to achieve the enhanced humanity that they embodied.

One day a Brahmin found the Buddha sitting under a tree and the sight of his serenity, stillness, and self-discipline filled the priest with awe. The Buddha reminded him of a tusker elephant: there was the same sense of enormous strength and massive potential brought under control and channeled into an extraordinary peace. The Brahmin had never seen a man like that before. "Are you a god, sir?" he asked. "An angel . . . or a spirit?" No, the Buddha replied. He had simply revealed a new potential in human nature. It was possible to live in this world of pain at peace, in control, and in harmony with one's fellow creatures. Once people had cut the roots of their egotism, they lived at the peak of their capacity and would activate parts of their beings that were normally dormant. How should the Brahmin describe him? "Remember me," the Buddha told him, "as one who is awake."[109]

8

ALL IS ONE

(c. 400 to 300 BCE)

By the fourth century, the economic and political transformation of China was progressing at astonishing speed. The wars continued and the princes needed to fund their expensive campaigns, so they encouraged the development of the new mercantile economy.[1] In the late fifth century, the Chinese had discovered how to cast iron, and with their strong iron tools were able to clear an immense amount of forest land. By the end of the fourth century, the Wei Valley, the Chengdu basin, and the central plain were under continuous cultivation. Farmers learned to use manure, to distinguish different kinds of soil, and the best times to plow, sow, or drain the land. Harvests improved, and despite the destructive warfare, there was a rapid growth in population. A new class of merchants arose, who worked closely with the princes, building foundries and developing mines. The most enterprising merchants established large trading empires and took their goods north to Korea, the steppes, and even as far as India, trading in textiles, cereals, salt, metals, hides, and leather, and employing an ever-growing number of artisans, agents, and fleets of carts and boats.

The cities were no longer simply political and religious capitals, but had become centers of trade and industry, accommodating thousands of citizens. In the feudal period, the walls of the little palace towns had measured a mere five hundred yards; now some city walls were over two miles long. In the fourth century, Linzi, the capital of Qi, was the largest city in China, with three hundred thousand inhabitants. An urban class of craftsmen and artisans, no longer tied to the royal palace, had emerged there, and the wealthy enjoyed the new luxuries and the thriving entertainment industry. The princes of Qi became patrons of the leading scholars of China, and in 357 founded the Jixia Academy beside the western gate of Linzi, where *shi* literati lived in well-appointed apartments on generous stipends.[2]

Many enjoyed these changes, but others were becoming uneasily aware that their lives were very different from the ritualized existence of their forefathers. The princes of the big, successful states were no longer hedged around with ceremonial restrictions. Instead of "doing nothing," as the royal *li* required, the rulers enthusiastically pursued their own ambitious policies and were intent on monopolizing power. In the early fourth century, the king of Wei replaced the hereditary barons and ministers with a civil service of salaried officials. The old administrative offices had been tied to the great families, but now the king could choose his own functionaries, and if they were disobedient, he could simply get rid of them. Unsatisfactory politicians were summarily exiled or executed. As other states followed the example of Wei, politics became an extremely dangerous game. The princes occasionally consulted the *shi* moralists, but paid far more attention to the merchants. Increasingly their policies reflected the shrewd pragmatism and calculation of the new commercial ethos.

The economic boom accentuated inequalities and caused massive social disruption. Peasants were regularly drafted into the army and torn away from their homes and fields; some became successful farmers, but others fell into debt and were turned off their land. The rulers purloined many of the marshes and forests where peasants had fished, hunted game, or gathered wood. Village communities were fatally damaged, and many peasants were forced to become laborers in the factories and foundries. Some aristocratic families were ruined, and the small, old-fashioned principalities were in constant danger of annihilation. A great void had opened in the lives of many people. "What is lawful, what is unlawful?" asked Ku Yuan, prince and poet of Chu. "This country is a slough of despond! Nothing is pure any longer! Informers are exalted! And wise men of gentle birth are without renown!"[3] He had begged his prince to consult a holy man and return to the Way, but was dismissed, banished, and in 299 committed suicide.

Others wanted nothing whatever to do with this brave new world and retired to the forests. Hermits had been opting out of city life for some time; Confucius had met some of these anchorites, who had ridiculed his attempts to reform society.[4] These solitaries were nothing like the renouncers of India. They simply wanted a quiet life. Some took the high moral ground, however, speaking in a "critical and disparaging" way about the current state of affairs.[5] Their hero was Shen Nong, the legendary sage king who had invented agriculture.[6] Unlike the ambitious rulers of their own day, Shen Nong had not tried to centralize his empire but had allowed each fiefdom to remain autonomous; he had not terrorized his ministers and, apart from a regular inspection of the crops, had ruled by "doing nothing" (*wu wei*). Other hermits were content simply to live an idyllic life, hunting and fishing in the forests and marshlands,[7] but by the middle of the fourth century, they too had developed a philosophy, which they attributed to one Master Yang.[8]

Yangzi left no book, but his ideas were preserved in other texts. He issued a direct and disturbing challenge to the Confucians and Mohists. The family *li* had insisted that a person's life was not his own. Heaven had allotted humans a fixed life span, so if you put your life in danger, you violated Heaven's will. Now that life at court had become so dangerous, it was clearly wrong to seek political office.[9] Yangists, therefore, made a principled retreat from public life. They argued that Yao and Shun had not retired from government out of humility, as the Confucians believed, but because they refused to put their own or other people's lives at risk. Yangists liked to quote the example of Tan Fu, an ancestor of the Zhou kings, who had renounced the throne rather than fight an invading army: "To send to their deaths the sons and younger brothers of those with whom I dwell is more than I could bear," he explained in his abdication speech.[10]

Yangists had no time for either *ren* or "concern for everybody." Their philosophy was "Every man for himself."[11] This seemed monstrously selfish to the Confucians, who complained that if Yangzi "could benefit the empire by pulling out one hair, he would not do so."[12] But Yangists insisted that it was irresponsible to get involved with other people or institutions; your prime duty was to preserve your own life and do only what came naturally.[13] Yangists must not meddle with their human nature, but should follow the Way that had been established by Heaven. It was wrong to refuse pleasure or submit to the artificial rituals of court life, which distorted human relationships. You could not make real contact with people if you followed the *li* instead of your feelings. Life should be spontaneous and sincere.

Many people in China were attracted by the Yangist ideal, but others found it disturbing.[14] They had always believed that the rituals established the Way of Heaven on earth. Were these *li* really damaging? If Yangzi was right, virtuous kings who had denied themselves pleasure for the sake of their subjects had been foolish and wrongheaded, while immoral tyrants who simply enjoyed themselves were far closer to Heaven. Were human beings basically selfish? If so, what could be done to make the world a better place? What was the basis for morality? Was the Confucian ideal of self-cultivation perverse? And what exactly was the "human nature" that the Yangists prized so highly? These questions were discussed by the scholars of the Jixia Academy, one of whom wrote a Confucian riposte to Yangism in a mystical essay called *Inward Training* (*Xinshu Shang*) for the guidance of a ruler.

The author argued that *ren* was not a distortion of human nature but its fulfillment; indeed, the very word *ren* was synonymous with humanity. If a prince wanted to become truly "human hearted," he must discover the core of his own being. Instead of fleeing to the forest to find peace and security, he must cultivate an interior quiet by means of meditation. By learning to check his passions, still his desires, and empty his mind of distracting thoughts, the enlightened prince would find his true and authentic self. He would clarify his mental powers, his physical health would improve, and he would discover that without making any further effort, he had "naturally" become a man of *ren*. The Chinese had discovered introspection and by the fourth century had developed their own version of yoga. We know very little about these early forms of meditation, but they seem to have involved exercises of concentration and controlled breathing. In the old days, the kings had established the Way by adopting the correct physical orientation. Now, according to *Inward Training,* a prince could put the world to rights by finding his true center within.

Chinese meditation was based on the management of *qi,* a word that is difficult to translate. *Qi* was the raw material of life, its basic energy, and its primal spirit. It animated all beings and gave everything its distinctive shape and form. The dynamic, ceaselessly active substructure of reality, *qi* was not unlike the atoms of Democritus, except that it was more mystical. Under the guidance of the Way, the ultimate controlling force, it periodically accumulated in various combinations to form a rock, a plant, or a human being. But none of these creations was permanent. Eventually the *qi* would disperse: the person or plant would die, and the rock would disintegrate. But the *qi* was still alive; it would continue to roil in the cauldron of ceaseless change, and would eventually regroup and take on a different shape. Everything in the universe, therefore, shared the same life, albeit in different degrees of intensity.

The purest and most concentrated form of *qi* was being itself, the "quintessence" (*jing*) of reality. In meditation, the contemplative learned to liberate his *qi*. By systematically removing all the desire, hatred, and restless mental activity that blocked its natural course, the contemplative enabled his *qi* to flow unimpeded through his heart, mind, and body in the way Heaven intended. When he achieved this total alignment with the Way, he fell into a trance, and a sacred peace rose up from within; this was the *shen,* his deepest and most divine self, which was one with the quintessence (*jing*) of existence. In meditation, therefore, the enlightened prince discovered his true nature. Not only was his "heart" (*xin*), the organ of thought, perfected, but his hearing, sight, and limbs were healthier too.[15] He would thus be able to fulfill his allotted span of life. Because he was one with the *jing,* the "quintessence" of everything that existed, he experienced a sense of union with the whole of reality, and could exclaim: "All things are at my disposal, within myself."[16]

At a time when China was torn apart by terrifying wars, Chinese mystics were discovering a tranquillity within themselves that drew everything together. This desire for unification also informed the new vogue for dialectic and debate. The intense discussions between Mohists, Confucians, and Yangists had led to a fascination with the mechanics of argument. Like the Greek Sophists, the *bianzhe* ("debaters") delighted in their ability to prove both sides of an argument and undermine received ideas. Many people found them trivial and irresponsible, but the debaters saw their work as a cohesive force, which brought apparently disparate objects together and revealed an underlying unity. One of them exclaimed: "I brought together similarity and difference, discerned hardness and whiteness; what was certain and what was not, what was possible and what was not."[17]

The most famous of these early dialecticians was a remarkable man: Huizi (370–319) was prime minister of Wei, one of the most advanced of the warring states.[18] Very little of his writing has survived, but he seems to have felt a strong affinity with Mohism. The only work that has come down to us is a set of ten paradoxes that revealed the instability that he discerned at the heart of existence.[19] Huizi wanted to demonstrate that words were misleading because they gave things an illusory permanence and solidity. "*Today I left for Yueh,*" he said, "*and arrived yesterday.*" Time was entirely relative: the "yesterday" of today was the "today" of yesterday, and today's "today" would be tomorrow's "yesterday." In another paradox, he demonstrated the relativity of our spatial concepts: "*I know where the center is of the whole world: north of Yen and south of Yueh.*" Because Yan was in the north of China, and Yue was in the south, the "center" should logically lie between these two extremes. But when you stepped outside a strictly Chinese perspective, it was clear that any spot could become the center of the world, just as any point on a line could be the starting point of a circle.

The theses were really points for contemplation, designed to show that the distinctions we imagine we see were delusions. Even life and death were aspects of each other: "*When the sun is in the centre, it is in the decline,*" said Huizi. "*That which is born is dying.*"

Everything was in flux, so from the very first moment of its existence, the life of any creature had already started to decay. People used words such as "high" and "low" in an absolute sense, without realizing that an object is only "high" in comparison with something else, so *"Heaven is on the same level as Earth and the mountains are equal with the marshes."* It was a mistake to put things into hard-and-fast categories, because everything was unique, even objects that were superficially similar: *"That which is joined is separate."* All things were, therefore, one: Heaven and earth, life and death, superior and lowly. A politician, an activist, and a Mohist, Huizi may have wanted to suggest that all human beings had equal value, and that social fortune was also mutable.[20]

In the first of his theses, Huizi pointed to a reality that lay beyond anything we experienced in ordinary life. *"The greatest thing has nothing outside it and we call this the great One; the smallest thing has nothing inside it, and we call this the smallest One."* We called an object "big" only because it was larger than something else; but actually everything was "great" because there was nothing in our world that was not bigger than something else. Yet the categories "greatest" and "smallest" existed in our minds, which showed that we had the power to imagine the absolute. Language laid bare a transcendence that was built into the structure of our thought. Huizi's paradoxes had a spiritual and social resonance that Zeno's did not, and his ten propositions were framed by the notions of transcendence and compassion. In the first thesis, Huizi directed our attention to the great One that had nothing beyond itself. The tenth and last thesis was Mohist: *"Love embraces all forms of life and Heaven and Earth are of One."* Because the distinctions on which we based our likes and dislikes were delusions, we should feel equal concern for all beings. The last thesis looked back to the first, because the "great One" comprised the whole of reality: Heaven and Earth were not distinct and antithetical but one.[21] Everything, therefore, deserved our love and ultimate concern.

This spiritual vision helps to explain Huizi's unlikely friendship with Zhuangzi (c. 370–311), one of the most important figures of the Chinese Axial Age.[22] A Yangist and a hermit, Zhuangzi seems at first sight to have little in common with the dignified prime minister of Wei. He remained an outsider all his life. He once visited the king of Wei dressed in a worn, patched gown, his shoes tied together with string, and for some years he lived in a slum, earning his living by weaving sandals. But Zhuangzi had an ebullient, original, and brilliant mind, and never felt at a loss before the rich and powerful. He loved sparring with Huizi, and after his death complained that he no longer had anybody to talk to, but ultimately Zhuangzi felt that dialectic was too narrow. Huizi, for example, was a Mohist, but could not the Confucians also be right? If everything was relative, as Huizi suggested, why should only one philosophy be correct? In his view, the bickering and point scoring of the philosophers were pure egotism: the Way was beyond limited human notions of right and wrong, truth and falsehood.

The book attributed to Zhuangzi is actually an anthology of texts that date from the fourth to the end of the third century. Traditionally, only the first seven chapters are thought to contain Zhuangzi's own teachings, but modern analysis has revealed that these "Inner Chapters" include later material, and that some of the other sections are closer in style to the historical Zhuangzi. The book began as a defense of private life. Zhuangzi was irritated by the Mohists and Confucians, who, he thought, were positively bursting with self-importance, pompously convinced that they had a mission to save the world. Politics could not change human nature: when kings and politicians interfered with the lives of their subjects, they invariably made matters worse. Zhuangzi believed in nongovernment. It was unnatural and perverse to force people to obey man-made laws; it was like shortening the legs of a crane, putting a halter around a horse's neck or a string through an ox's nose.[23]

When Zhuangzi first retired from public life in search of peace and security, he had been a Yangist. But one day, he realized that it was impossible for any creature to live a wholly safe and protected life.[24] He had trespassed into a game reserve to poach some fowl, had spotted a large magpie, and taken careful aim, fully expecting the bird to fly off in alarm. But the magpie did not even notice Zhuangzi, because it had its eye on a delicious cicada that was basking in a lovely shady spot, heedless of its personal safety. A preying mantis was flexed ready to spring on the cicada, so intent upon the chase that it too ignored the magpie, which swept down on its prey in high excitement and gobbled them both up—still oblivious of Zhuangzi and his crossbow. Zhuangzi sighed with compassion. "Ah, so it is that one thing brings disaster upon another, and then upon itself." None of these creatures was aware of impending danger, because they were all programmed to hunt one another. Whether they willed it or not, they were involved in a chain of mutual destruction. No one could live a wholly isolated life—not even a hermit: Zhuangzi himself had been so busy taking aim at the magpie that he had not noticed the appearance on the scene of a gamekeeper, who angrily chased him out of the park. The incident made a great impression on Zhuangzi, and for three months he was depressed. He could now see that the Yangist creed was based on an illusion: it was impossible to protect yourself in the way Yangzi taught. We were conditioned to destroy and be destroyed, to eat and be eaten. We could not escape our destiny. Until we became reconciled to the endless process of destruction and dissolution, we would have no peace.

After the incident in the park, Zhuangzi found that he looked at the world quite differently. He began to realize that everything was in flux and constantly in the process of becoming something else—yet we were always trying to freeze our thoughts and experiences and make them absolute. This was not how the Way of Heaven operated. Anything that tried to close itself off from the endless transformation of life in an attempt to become autonomous and self-contained was going against the natural rhythm of the cosmos. Once he had fully appreciated this, Zhuangzi felt an exhilarating freedom. He found that he was no longer afraid of death, because it was futile to try to preserve your life indefinitely. Death and life, joy and sorrow succeeded each other, like day and night. When he died and ceased to be "Zhuangzi," nothing would change. He would remain what essentially he had always been: a tiny part of the endlessly mutating pageant of the universe.

Zhuangzi sometimes used shock tactics to bring this truth home to friends and disciples. When Zhuangzi's wife died, Huizi came to pay a condolence call, and was horrified to find him sitting cross-legged, singing rowdily, and bashing a battered old tub—flagrantly violating the dignified ceremonies of the mourning period. "She was your wife! She bore your children!" protested Huizi. "The least you can do is shed a tear for her!" Zhuangzi smiled. When she first died, he had mourned his wife like everybody else. But then he cast his mind back to the time before she was born, when she had simply been part of the endlessly churning *qi,* the raw material of the universe. One day there had been a wonderful change: the *qi* had mingled together in a new way, and suddenly, there was his dear wife! Now she was dead and had simply gone through another alteration. "She is like the four seasons in the way that spring, summer, autumn and winter follow each other," Zhuangzi reflected. She was now at peace, lying in the bosom of the *dao,* the greatest of mansions. If he wept and complained, he would be completely at odds with the Way things really were.[25]

Zhuangzi and his friends showed a bemused, detached delight in the change, death, and dissolution that filled so many of the other sages of the Axial Age with dismay. One day, Master Li, one of Zhuangzi's disciples, had visited a dying friend, and to his disgust found his wife and children sobbing at the bedside. "Out of the way! Shoo!" he cried. "Don't pester change in the making!" Then, leaning against the door of his sick friend's bedroom, he remarked whimsically: "It's amazing—that Maker-of-Things! What will it make of you next? Where will it send you? Will it make you into a rat's liver? Will it make you into a bug's arm?" "Our parents are part of us," the dying man replied.

> East and west, north and south—wherever we go, we follow their wishes. And we obey *yin* and *yang* even more completely. They've brought me here to the brink of death and to resist their wishes would be such insolence.
>
> We call our life a blessing, so our death must be a blessing too. Suppose a mighty metal-smith cast a piece of metal, which jumped up and said, "*No, no—I must be*

one of those legendary Moyeh swords!" Wouldn't the metal-
smith consider it ominous metal? And suppose, having
chanced upon human form, I insist, *"Human, human, and
nothing but human!"* Wouldn't the Maker-of-Change
consider me an ominous person? I see Heaven and
Earth as a mighty foundry and the Maker-of-Change as
a mighty metal-smith—so wherever they send me, how
could I ever complain? I'll sleep soundly—and then,
suddenly, I'll wake.[26]

Once they had given up thinking of themselves as unique and
precious individuals whose lives must be preserved at all costs,
Zhuangzi and his friends found that they could observe their
predicament with cheerful interest and detachment, and remain
calm and content.[27] Once you were entirely reconciled with the
Way of Heaven, you were at peace because you were attuned to
reality.

What exactly was the Way? Time and again, Zhuangzi insisted that the Way was unthinkable, inexpressible, and impossible to
define. It had no qualities, no form; it could be experienced but
never seen. It was not a god; it had existed before Heaven and Earth,
and was beyond divinity; it was more ancient than antiquity—yet
it was not old. It was both being and nonbeing.[28] It represented all
the myriad patterns, forms, and potential that made nature the way
it was.[29] The Way mysteriously ordered the shifting transformations
of the *qi,* but it existed at a point where all the distinctions that
characterize our normal modes of thought cease. Any attempt to
pontificate about these ineffable matters simply led to unseemly,
egotistic squabbling. We had to realize that we knew nothing. If we
selected one theory and rejected another, we were distorting reality, trying to force the creative flow of life into a channel of our
own making. The only valid assertion was a question that plunged
us into doubt and a luminous sense of unknowing. We should not
be dismayed to find that there was no such thing as certainty, because this confusion could lead us to the Way.

Egotism was the greatest obstacle to enlightenment. It was an inflated sense of self that made us identify with one opinion rather than another; ego made us quarrelsome and officious, because we wanted to change other people to suit ourselves. Zhuangzi often mischievously used the figure of Confucius to express some of his own ideas. One day, he said, Yan Hui told Confucius that he was off to reform the king of Wei, a violent, reckless, and irresponsible young man. Marvelous, Confucius remarked wryly, but Yan Hui did not fully understand himself. How could he possibly change anybody else? All he could do was lay down the law and explain a few Confucian principles. How would these external directives affect the obscure subconscious impulses that were the source of the king's cruelty? There was only one thing that Yan Hui could do. He must empty his mind, get rid of all this bustling self-importance, and find his inner core.

> "Centre your attention," Confucius began. "Stop listening with your ears and listen with your mind. Then stop listening with your mind and listen with your primal spirit [qi]. Hearing is limited to the ear. Mind is limited to tallying things up. But the primal spirit's empty: it's simply that which awaits things. Tao is emptiness merged and emptiness is the mind's fast."[30]

Instead of using every opportunity to feed the ego, we had to starve it. Even our best intentions could be grist to the mill of our selfishness. But qi had no agenda; it simply allowed itself to be shaped and transformed by the Way, and so everything turned out well. If Yan Hui stopped blocking the qi, deflecting it from its natural course, the Way could act through him. Only then could he become a force for good in the world. By the end of the conversation, however, Yan Hui seemed to have lost all interest in the project.

Once people stopped arguing about doctrines and theories, they could acquire what Zhuangzi called the Great Knowledge. Instead of claiming that *this* could not mean *that,* they began to see that all apparent contradictions formed a mysterious, numinous unity. This *coincidentia oppositorum* brought them to the hub of the wheel, the axis of the Way, "the pivot at the centre of the circle, for it can react equally to that which is and to that which is not."[31] The unenlightened state was like the vision of a frog who lived in a well and could see only a little patch of sky that he mistook for the whole. After he had seen the entire reality, his perspective was changed forever.[32] The Great Knowledge could never be defined; Zhuangzi would describe only its effects. It gave the sage a sensitive and intelligent responsiveness to each circumstance as it arose. He did not plan how he would act ahead of time; he did not agonize over alternative courses of action or stick to a rigid set of rules. Once he had ceased to obstruct the Way, he would acquire a spontaneity that resembled the knack of a talented craftsman.

Zhuangzi told another story about Confucius, who was traveling with his disciples through a forest and met a hunchback who was trapping cicadas with a sticky pole. To Confucius's astonishment, the hunchback never missed a single one. How did he manage it? He had clearly so perfected his powers of concentration that he had lost himself in his task, and achieved an *ekstasis,* a self-forgetfulness that brought him into perfect harmony with the Way. "Do you have the Way?" Confucius asked. "Indeed I have!" replied the hunchback. He had no idea how he did it! But he had practiced for months and could now bring himself into a state in which he was wholly focused on catching cicadas: "never tiring, never leaning, never being aware of any of the vast number of living beings, except cicadas. Following this method, how could I fail?" He had left his conscious self behind and let the *qi* take over, Confucius explained to his disciples: "He keeps his will undivided and his spirit energized," so that his hands seemed to move by themselves. Conscious deliberate planning would be distracting and counterproductive. The hunchback reminded Zhuangzi of the carpenter Bian, who explained: "When I work on a wheel, if I hit it too softly, pleasant as this is, it doesn't make for a good wheel. If I hit furiously, I get tired, and the thing doesn't work! So, not too soft, not too vigorous. I grasp it in my hand and hold it in my heart. I cannot express this by word of mouth, I just know it.

I cannot teach this to my son, nor can my son learn it from me."[33] In the same way, a sage who had learned not to analyze, make distinctions, and weigh alternatives had left the "ego principle" behind, did what came naturally, and became one with the deepest and most divine rhythm of the universe.

What did this feel like? Zhuangzi told his disciples about Ziqi, the contemplative, whose friends had come upon him one day "gazing into the sky, breath shallow and face blank, as if he were lost to himself." This had never happened before. Ziqi looked like an entirely different person. What had happened? "Do you understand such things?" asked Ziqi. "Just then I'd lost myself completely." He had "gone" in the same way as a craftsman disappeared into his work. When we tried to hold on to ourselves, we were alienated from the "great transformation" of the Way. Because he had lost himself, Ziqi was liberated from the constraints of selfishness. He could now see more clearly than ever before. "Perhaps you've heard the music of humans," he told his friends, "but you haven't heard the music of earth. Or if you've heard the music of earth, you haven't heard the music of Heaven." When you achieved this larger vision, you heard everything singing together, and yet you could distinguish each thing separately. This was the Great Knowledge; it was "broad and unhurried," while "small understanding is cramped and busy."[34]

You could not achieve this illumination unless you abandoned all previous habits of thought. The true sage did not amass knowledge, but learned to forget one thing after another, until finally he forgot about himself and could merge joyously into the Way. Zhuangzi told yet another story about Confucius and Yan Hui.

"I'm gaining ground!" Yan Hui had announced one day.

"What do you mean?" asked Confucius.

"I've forgotten Humanity [ren] and Duty [yi] completely," Yan Hui replied.

"Not bad!" admitted Confucius. "But that's still not it."

A few days later, Yan Hui exclaimed: "I've forgotten ritual and music completely."

"That's still not it," said Confucius.

But finally Yan Hui surprised his master. "I'm gaining ground!" he beamed. "I sit quietly and forget."

Confucius shifted uneasily. "What do you mean?" he asked.

"I let the body fall away and the intellect fade," said Yan Hui. "I throw out form, abandon understanding—and then move freely, blending away into the great transformation. That's what I mean by *sit quietly and forget*."

Confucius went pale; his disciple had surpassed him.

> "If you blend away like that, you're free of likes and dis-
> likes," he said. "If you're all transformation, you're free of
> permanence. So in the end, the true sage here is you! So
> you won't mind if I follow you from now on, will you?"[35]

To "know" a thing is to distinguish it from everything else. To forget these distinctions is to become aware of undifferentiated unity, and to lose all sense of being a separate individual.

Zhuangzi's enlightenment was different from the Buddha's; it did not seem to have happened once and for all time. He could not walk around in a perpetual trance; there were times when he had to analyze things and make distinctions in order to function in normal life.[36] Sometimes he was "with Heaven," and at other times he was "one with humanity."[37] But at the heart of his life, he felt at peace with the Way, the "root" or "seed" from which all things grow and the axis around which they revolved.

Zhuangzi was not entirely happy about the Mohist ideal of "love" or "concern," because it required people to fix their attention on individual beings that were too ephemeral for this degree of attention. But he did preach a spirituality of empathy. The sage, he believed, was essentially unselfish. "The perfect man has no self," he explained.[38] He regards other people as "I." "People cry, so he cries—he considers everything as his own being," because he had lost all sense of himself as separate and particular.[39] His heart had become "empty" and simply reflected other beings in their integrity, like a mirror, without the distorting lens of ego.[40] A true sage did not need rules about *ren*. He spontaneously sought the good of others, without ponderously thinking of himself as concerned for other people.[41] Once he had the Great Knowledge, he had acquired the knack of unselfconscious benevolence.

Zhuangzi probably considered his contemporary Meng Ke (371–288), who is known in the West as Mencius, an egotistic busybody, because he was so desperately eager to take an active role in public life.[42] A devout Confucian, Mencius became a scholar at the Jixia Academy, but his real ambition was to serve in the government. Like Confucius, however, he had no success. He failed to win the confidence of either King Xuan of Qi or King Hui of Liang, both of whom found his ideas ludicrously impractical. But Mencius did not give up easily, and for years traveled from one state to another, trying to persuade the princes to return to the Way. He could not turn his back on the world, like Zhuangzi, but believed that he had been appointed by Heaven to save it.

Mencius saw a pattern in history. A sage king appeared every five hundred years or so, and in the intervening period people were governed by ordinary "men of renown." Since it was over seven hundred years since the rule of the early Zhou kings, the new sage ruler was sadly overdue. Mencius was acutely aware that China had changed—in his view, for the worse. "The people have never suffered more under tyrannical government than today," he lamented. "It must be that Heaven does not desire to bring peace to the world." But if Heaven *did* want to save the world, who else but he could do it?[43] As a mere commoner, he could not be a sage king, but he did believe that he been appointed Heaven's messenger to the princes. The people were crying out for good leadership. They would flock to any ruler who treated them kindly, with benevolence and justice.

When it was clear that the princes would never take him seriously, Mencius retired and wrote a book that recorded his discussions with the rulers he had tried to serve. He believed that it was impossible to govern by force. The people submitted to coercive rule because they had no choice, but if a peace-loving king came to power, they would flock to him "with admiration in their hearts" because goodness had a "transformative power."[44] Instead of relying on military might, he told King Hui, he should "reduce punishment and taxation, and get the people to plough deeply and weed promptly." In their spare time, able-bodied young men must learn to live by the family *li,* and become good brothers and sons. Once they had received this moral grounding, they would, as a matter of course, be loyal subjects and a source of great strength. They would "inflict defeat on the strong armour and sharp weapons" of the larger states, even if they were "armed with nothing but staves."[45] Why? Because all the best ministers would want to serve in the administration of a just and compassionate king; farmers would want to cultivate his lands; merchants to trade in his cities. "Anyone with a grievance against their own rulers would come and complain to your Majesty," Mencius told King Hui. "If that happens, who could stop it?"[46]

Confucius had believed that ritual alone could transform society, but Mencius had witnessed the economic and agricultural revolutions of the Warring States period. Instead of admiring their ritual proficiency, Mencius revered Yao and Shun as engineers, practical men of action. At the time of Yao, China had been overwhelmed by a terrible flood, and Yao—alone of all the people—"was filled with anxiety."[47] He cut channels for the water, so that it could flow into the sea, and the people were able to level the ground and make it habitable. Shun appointed Yu his minister of works, and for eight long years Yu had dredged the rivers, deepened their beds, and built new dikes. In all that time, he never slept a single night in his own house. He had no time to spare for agriculture, so Shun appointed Hou Chi to show the people how to cultivate grain. But once the people had full bellies, moral standards declined, and this gave Shun much disquiet. He therefore appointed Fang Xun as his education minister, to instruct the people in the *li* of human relationships.[48]

Mencius stressed the loving concern that the sage kings had felt for the people. In his account, the first sign of emergent sagehood in both Yao and Shun was that they worried about their people, were made anxious by their plight, and filled with concern and distress. A sage could not bear to see other people suffering. Each had "a heart sensitive to the pain of others . . . and this manifested itself in compassionate government," Mencius argued. The sage kings were not content simply to feel sorry for their subjects; they energetically and creatively translated their concern into effective action. Their good, practical government sprang from compassion (*ren*), the ability to look beyond self-interest, "the extension of one's scope of activity to include others."[49]

The princes of the Warring States period might not have Yao and Shun's exceptional talents, but they could and must imitate their altruism. Confucius had refused to define *ren;* Mencius gave it a clear, narrow meaning: "benevolence," the essential virtue that made it impossible for him to turn his back upon the world. He distrusted Mozi's "concern for everybody," fearing that this generalized goodwill would undermine the family bonds that were essential to society,[50] even though he agreed that concern could not stop at the family. He told King Xuan to begin by treating the elderly members of his own family reverently. Once he had mastered this habit of respect, he would naturally extend it to old people in other families. Finally, he would be able to treat all his subjects with benevolence, and they would then submit gladly to his rule.[51]

Mencius did not agree that the rules of *ren* were artificial but believed that it was natural for people to respond compassionately to suffering. He reminded King Xuan that he had recently spared the life of an ox that was being led to sacrifice. When he had seen the poor beast crossing his hall and heard its pitiful cry, he had called out to the attendant: "Spare it! I cannot bear to see it shrinking in fear, like an innocent man going to the place of execution."[52] That had been a good impulse, but it was only the beginning. Next the king should apply this instinctive sympathy to his subjects and treat them more kindly, and finally he should extend his concern to other states. Mencius believed that human nature was basically good—that it inclined to *ren* spontaneously. Mohists believed that people could be moved only by self-interest and that goodness had to be drilled into them from outside, but Mencius argued that it was as natural for us to behave morally as it was for our bodies to develop into a mature human form. We could stunt both our physical and moral growth by bad habits, but the instinctive tendency toward goodness remained.

Every single person had four fundamental "impulses" (*tuan*) that, if properly cultivated, would grow into the four cardinal virtues: benevolence, justice, courtesy, and the wisdom to distinguish right from wrong. They were like the first shoots that would one day grow into a plant.[53] These "shoots" were as natural to us as our arms and legs. Nobody was wholly without sympathy for others. If a man saw a child teetering on the brink of a well, about to fall in, he would immediately lunge forward to save it—not in order to ingratiate himself with the parents, win the admiration of his friends, or because he was irritated by the child's cries. He would be moved by an instinctive impulse of compassion. There would be something fundamentally wrong with a person who could watch the child fall to its death without a flicker of disquiet. In the same way, somebody who had absolutely no sense of shame or who lacked any rudimentary sense of right or wrong would be a defective human being. You could stamp on these "shoots"—just as you could cripple or deform yourself—but if they were cultivated properly, they acquired a vibrant, dynamic power of their own. Once they were active, they would transform not only the person who practiced them but everyone with whom he came in contact—like the potency of the king. Somebody who had successfully cultivated all four "shoots" could save the world.[54]

Mencius was living in the troubled period of the Warring States. He knew that the embryonic seeds of goodness were easily destroyed. Everywhere he looked, he could see examples of greed and selfishness, which, he believed, obstructed the flow of *qi* and perverted the natural tendency to goodness. The "shoots" resided naturally in the "heart," the thinking, affective organ, but many people simply threw their hearts away. The common people had been corrupted by cruelty, hunger, and exploitation. The upper classes were so avid for luxury, pleasure, power, and fame that they had neglected the "shoots" and allowed them to shrivel and die.

Only the *junzi,* the mature person, had kept his heart alive.[55] Most people's hearts resembled Ox Mountain, which had once been covered in luxuriant, leafy groves, but had been stripped bare by reckless, brutal deforestation. It was hard to believe that there had ever been any trees on Ox Mountain, just as it was difficult to imagine that a bestial, selfish person had ever had any good qualities. But the potential had been there. "Given the right nourishment, there is nothing that will not grow, and deprived of it, there is nothing that will not wither away."[56]

Mencius was an optimist. Even if you had lost your heart, it was always possible to find it again. *Wu wei* ("doing nothing") was not the answer; the world needed *yu wei* ("self-effort"), which brought human beings into harmony with Heaven. The purpose of the Confucian education was to search for the compassionate heart that had gone astray. How strange it was that people were unconcerned about this diminution of their humanity! They spent a great deal of time and energy looking for missing chickens or dogs, but did nothing to recover their own hearts.[57] Everybody—without exception—had the capacity to cultivate the four essential virtues and become a sage like Yao or Shun. As soon as it was found and repaired, the sympathetic heart was so constructed that it would blaze forth like a forest fire or burst into the air like a spring that had forced its way up from the depths of the earth. A sage was simply a person who had fully realized his humanity and become one with Heaven.[58] Most of us found compassion difficult at first; we had to nourish our innate virtue by constantly repeated acts of benevolence, reverence, justice, and equity. Each time we acted well, we strengthened the "shoots," until the cardinal virtues became habitual. A vigorous campaign of *yu wei* would result in the creation of the "unmoved" or "steadfast" heart, which could keep unruly passions in check.

The person who persevered in this struggle for goodness would arrive at what Mencius called "floodlike *qi*" (*hao jan chi qi*)—a phrase that he coined himself and found difficult to explain. It was a special sort of *qi,* which lifted human beings to the divine:

This is a *ch'i*★ which is, in the highest degree, vast and unyielding (*hao jan*). Nourish it with integrity and place no obstacle in its path and it will fill the space between Heaven and Earth. It is a *ch'i* which unites rightness and the Way. Deprive it of these and it will collapse. It is born of accumulated rightness, and cannot be appropriated by anybody through a sporadic show of rightness.[59]

The practice of *ren* would bring ordinary, frail human beings into harmony with the Way. Zhuangzi had experienced something similar, but had claimed that self-consciousness could only impede the flow of the *qi*. Not so, Mencius replied; unity with the Way could be attained by disciplined, sustained moral effort.

The Golden Rule was crucial. This was the virtue that made the *junzi* truly humane, and brought the individual into a mystical relationship with the entire universe. "All the ten thousand things are there in me," Mencius said in one of his most important instructions. "There is no greater joy for me than to find, on self-examination, that I am true to myself. Try your best to treat others as you would wish to be treated yourself, and you will find that this is the shortest way to benevolence [*ren*]."[60] By behaving as though other people were as important as yourself, you could experience an ecstatic unity with all things. A *junzi* no longer felt that there was any distinction between him and other creatures. Such a person became a divine force for good in a troubled world.

When he looked back to the feudal period, a time when the king's egotism had been constrained by the *li*, Mencius believed that his subjects had been content. Those distant days seemed like a golden age compared with the violence and terror of the Warring States period. The king had radiated the potency of the Way and had exerted a profound moral influence on his people, who had been "happy," "expansive and content." They had "moved daily to-

---

★In his text, Lau uses the old Wade-Giles system of transliteration of Chinese characters rather than the Pinyin system used in this book. Hence *qi* is rendered *ch'i*.

ward goodness without realizing who brought this about." There were no kings of that caliber today, but anybody could become a *junzi,* a fully mature person, and have the same effect on his environment. "A *junzi* transforms where he passes, and works wonders where he abides. He is in the same stream as Heaven above and Earth below. Can he be said to bring but small benefit?"[61]

In China, the Axial Age had started late but was now in full flower. In the other regions, it was either running down or in the process of becoming something different. We see this clearly in the *Mahabharata,* the great epic of India.[62] The story is set in the Kuru-Panchala region during the period of the *Brahmanas,* before the rise of the state systems, but the oral transmission of the epic started in about 500; it was not committed to writing until the first centuries of the common era, when it achieved its final form. The *Mahabharata* is, therefore, a complex, multilayered text, an anthology of many strands of tradition. The general outline of the story, however, had probably been established by the end of the fourth century. Unlike the defining texts of the Axial Age, which were composed in priestly and renouncer circles, the epic reflects the ethos of the *kshatriya* warrior class. The religious revolution of the Axial Age left them with a perplexing dilemma. How could a king or warrior who admired the ideal of *ahimsa* become reconciled with his vocation, which demanded that he fight and kill in order to defend his community?

The duties of each class were sacred. Each had its own inviolable dharma, a divinely ordained way of life. A Brahmin's duty was to become expert in Vedic lore; the *kshatriya* was responsible for law, order, and defense; and the *vaishya* had to devote his energies to the production of wealth. The renouncers depended on the support of the warriors and merchants, who gave them the alms, food, and security that enabled them to dedicate themselves full-time to the religious quest. Yet in order to carry out their duties successfully, kings, warriors, and merchants were compelled to behave in ways that were—in Buddhist parlance—"unskillful" or even downright sinful. To perform successfully in the marketplace, *vaishyas* had to be ambitious, to want worldly goods, and to compete aggressively with their rivals, and this "desire" bound them inexorably to the cycle of death and rebirth. But the *kshatriya's* vocation was especially problematic. During a military campaign, he was sometimes forced to be economical with the truth or even to tell lies. He might have to betray former friends and allies, and to kill innocent people. None of these activities was compatible with the yogic ethos, which demanded nonviolence and a strict adherence to truth at all times. The *kshatriya* could only hope to become a monk in his next life, but given the nature of his daily karma, it seemed unlikely that he could achieve even this limited goal. Was there no hope? The *Mahabharata* agonized over these questions, but could find no satisfactory solution.

It is very difficult to date any single passage of the *Mahabharata* accurately or even to isolate the original story. In the long process of transmission, old and new material became inextricably combined, and in the first centuries of the common era, the epic was reinterpreted by priestly scholars. Yet the general movement of the narrative does yield some insight into the preoccupations of the *kshatriyas* as the Axial Age drew to a close. The *Mahabharata* tells the story of a catastrophic war between two sets of cousins, the Kauravas and the Pandavas, who were competing for control of the Kuru-Panchala region. Not only was the family torn apart; the war almost resulted in the annihilation of the entire human race. It brought the heroic age to an end, and ushered in the Kali Yuga, our own deeply flawed era.

This was an apocalyptic war, and yet it is not presented in the *Mahabharata* as a struggle between good and evil. The Pandavas were destined to win, but they managed to defeat the Kauravas only by resorting to some highly dubious maneuvers that were suggested by their friend and ally Krishna, the chieftain of the Yadava clan. Even though they had no choice but to act as they did, the Pandavas felt deeply impaired by their dishonorable conduct, and when they surveyed the devastated, depopulated world at the end of the war, their victory seemed hollow. In contrast, many of the Kauravas seemed noble, exemplary warriors. When their

leader Duryodhana was killed in battle, his spirit ascended immediately to heaven and a shower of heavenly petals covered his
corpse.

In some respects, the religious world of the *Mahabharata* seems
untouched by the Axial Age. The epic reminds us that only an
elite group was involved in the Great Transformation. Most people retained the older religious practices and—superficially, at
least—appeared to have been unaffected by the new developments. Indra, for example, was still the most important god in the
Mahabharata—he clearly remained popular among the *kshatriyas*
long after he had faded from the sophisticated priestly speculations. In the epic, the cosmic events of the ancient Vedic myths
were transposed into a historical setting: the war of the Pandavas
and Kauravas replicated the wars between *devas* and *asuras,* and
each of the Pandava brothers was the son and earthly counterpart
of a Vedic god. The epic was based on the theology of the early
Vedic period. A warrior who died in battle went straight to the
world of the gods; there was no hint that he would have to return
and suffer another death. There were no modern renouncers in
the poem, but only old-fashioned hermits tending their sacrificial
fires in the forest. There were a few yogins in the *Mahabharata,* but
they were usually more interested in exploiting the magical potential of their enhanced mental powers than in suppressing their
egos. The Axial Age had insisted on the personal responsibility of
the individual, but in the epic the main characters had no choice
at all, and were often compelled by the gods to act against their
better judgment. The archaic spirit of the *Mahabharata* is particularly evident in its preoccupation with the ancient sacrificial lore.
The five Pandava brothers, for example, were all married to their
sister, Draupadi. This was clearly highly unconventional, but the
marriage recalled the ancient ritual of the Asmavedya, the horse
sacrifice, which bestowed sovereignty on the king: during the rite,
the queen had some form of simulated sex with the sacrificial stallion, and was thus able to transmit the dominion it represented to
her husband. In the epic, Draupadi represented royal authority,
which she passed on to her brothers.

But the *Mahabharata* also reflects the terror inspired by the sacrificial contests, before they had been reformed by the ritualists. At the beginning of the story, Yudishthira, the oldest Pandava brother, having won the kingdom by force of arms, summoned the chieftains to his royal consecration (*rajasuya*). He had to prove that he possessed the brahman by submitting to the challenge and ordeal of the ritual. He was duly consecrated and anointed king, but the *rajasuya* had a disastrous outcome. Overcome with envy, Duryodhana challenged Yudishthira to the dice game that was mandatory during the rites, but the gods loaded the dice against Yudishthira, who lost his wife, his property, and his kingdom. The Pandavas were forced into exile for twelve years, and the war that would almost result in the destruction of the world became inevitable. The story's catastrophic view of the sacrificial contest gives us some insight into the anxiety that inspired the ritual reform of the *Brahmanas*.

The plight of Yudishthira shows that the *Mahabharata* was not, after all, untouched by the Axial Age. He seems to have been profoundly affected by the new ideals. He was—to the frequent exasperation of his brothers—gentle, tolerant, and singularly lacking in the warrior ethos. He not only had no desire to assert himself and trumpet his ego in the conventional way, but appeared to find it well-nigh impossible to do so and regarded war as evil, savage, and cruel.[63] Yudishthira was a man of the Axial Age, and this proved to be an almost intolerable handicap. He could not go off to the forest and practice *ahimsa*. He was the son of the god Dharma, a manifestation of Varuna, who upheld the order that made life possible. As his earthly representative, it was Yudishthira's inescapable duty to achieve the sovereignty that alone could bring order to the world. As the son of Dharma, he was also obliged to practice the traditional virtues of absolute truthfulness and fidelity to his sworn word, without which the social order could not be maintained. Yet during the war, Yudishthira was forced—quite disgracefully—to lie.

In the course of the eighteen-day battle, the Pandavas had to kill two of the generals fighting on the Kaurava side. As the epic was set in the heroic age, none of these men were ordinary mortals; they were demigods, with supernormal powers. When the

Pandavas rode into battle, for example, their chariots did not touch the earth. Warriors were not subject to the same constraints as the human beings of our own debased Kali Yuga; and Bhishma and Drona, who led the Kaurava troops, could not be killed by regular means. They had inflicted so many casualties on the Pandavas' army that the brothers despaired of victory. The future of the world hung in the balance, because if Yudishthira failed to achieve sovereignty, the divine order would be hopelessly violated. At this terrible moment, Krishna stepped in with advice that filled the brothers with dismay.

The Pandavas knew and respected the generals, who were men of outstanding courage and honor. When they were boys, Bhishma had initiated the Pandavas into the *kshatriya* code and the martial arts. He was a perfect warrior, famous for his scrupulous truthfulness. Drona had taught the Pandavas archery and chariot driving and, as a Brahmin, was a devoutly religious man. Neither would dream of lying or breaking an oath, and they would find it impossible to believe that Yudishthira, son of Dharma, would lie or try to exploit them. And yet this was what Krishna, in two successive councils of war, advised him to do. Yudishthira, he argued, must trap Bhishma into revealing, with his habitual scrupulous veracity, the only way that it was possible to kill him. And he must tell Drona a foul lie, informing him that his son Aswatthaman had been killed, so that, in the midst of the battle, Drona would lay down his weapons and make himself vulnerable to attack.

When Krishna outlined these stratagems in all their shabby detail, the Pandava brothers were horrified. Burning with grief and shame, Arjuna, the greatest warrior of them all, refused at first to take any part in Krishna's scheme. Krishna had told him that he would have to steal up on Bhishma, hiding behind another warrior, who, to add insult to injury, had been a woman in a past life! Arjuna was the son of Indra: How could he possibly behave in such a way? But Krishna pointed out that Arjuna had made a solemn vow to kill Bhishma, and this was the only way he could keep his word. How could the son of Indra break a sacred oath?[64]

When Bhishma was killed according to Krishna's plan, everybody behaved as nobly as they possibly could. Arjuna brought water from the depths of the earth with one of his arrows, so that his old teacher could slake his thirst and bathe his wounds, and the dying Bhishma's body did not touch the ground: he remained in a state of heroic and moral elevation. But Drona's death irreparably damaged the Pandavas. Krishna told Arjuna that they had to "cast virtue aside," in order to save the world, and Yudishthira reluctantly and "with difficulty" promised to tell Drona his cruel lie.[65] "Untruth may be better than truth," Krishna argued. "By telling a lie to save life, untruth does not touch us."[66]

But despite Krishna's reassurance, Yudishthira *was* tarnished. His chariot had always floated the width of four fingers from the ground, but as soon as he told Drona that his son had been killed, it came sharply down to earth. Drona, however, died the holiest of deaths and was taken directly up to heaven. When Yudishthira told him that his son Aswatthaman was dead, Drona had at first continued to fight, but was persuaded to lay down his weapons by a group of *rishis* who appeared to him in a vision and warned him that he was about to die; as a Brahmin, he should not spend his last moments fighting. Immediately Drona laid down his arms, sat in his chariot in the yogic position, fell into a trance, and peacefully ascended to the world of the gods. The life had already left his body when he was beheaded by an ally of the Pandavas. The contrast of Yudishthira's fall from grace and Drona's ecstatic ascension was devastating in its implications. Arjuna bitterly berated Yudishthira: his vile lie would taint them all.[67]

What are we to make of Krishna's dubious role? He was not a Satan, tempting the Pandavas to sin. Like the brothers, he was also the son of one of the Vedic gods. His father was Vishnu, the guardian of sacrifice.[68] In the *Brahmanas,* Vishnu's task was to "repair" a sacrifice that had been spoiled by a mistake in the ritual, so that it could still perform its function and renew the cosmic order. In the *Mahabharata,* Krishna was Vishnu's earthly counterpart. As the heroic age drew to its violent close, order had to be restored by a massive sacrificial ritual. The battle was this sacrifice; its victims—the warriors who died during the fighting—would put history back on track, by returning the sovereignty to Yudishthira. But the war could not be won by ordinary means: Drona and

Bhishma, Krishna pointed out, were supermen who "could not have been slain in a fair fight."[69] His desperate stratagems were like the special ritual procedures employed by a priest to put the sacrifice back on course.

In terms of the old Vedic ethos, Krishna's argument was impeccable; he was even able to cite the precedent of Indra, who had resorted to a similar lie when he slew the monster Vritra and brought order out of chaos. But Yudishthira was a man of the Axial Age, and was not convinced by this archaic ritual lore. He was inconsolable. Throughout the poem, he persisted in his despairing cry: "Nothing is more evil than the kshatriya's *dharma*."[70] Warfare was not a blood sacrifice acceptable to the gods; it was an atrocity. The epic story showed that violence bred more violence; and that one dishonorable betrayal led to another.

Crazed with sorrow, Drona's son Aswatthaman vowed to avenge his father's death, and offered himself to Shiva, the ancient god of the indigenous people of India, as "self-sacrifice" (*atma-yajna*). His martyrdom was a horrible parody of the nonviolent renunciation of self practiced by the renouncers. Shiva handed Aswatthaman a glittering sword, and took possession of his body, which now shone with unearthly radiance. In a divine frenzy, Aswatthaman entered the Pandavas' camp while everybody was asleep, and began to slaughter his enemies in a raid that was as dishonorable as Yudishthira's betrayal of his father. Aswatthaman was a Brahmin; he experienced the massacre as a holy ritual, but in fact it was a sacrifice that was out of control. In Vedic ritual, the animal was supposed to be killed swiftly and painlessly. But when Aswatthaman seized his first victim—the man who had decapitated his father—he kicked him to death, refusing to finish him quickly, and "made him die the death of an animal . . . grinding off his head."[71]

The Pandava brothers escaped the raid, because Krishna had advised them to sleep outside the camp that night, but most of their family—including the children—were slaughtered. When the Pandavas finally caught up with Aswatthaman, they found him sitting serenely beside the Ganges in a ritual garment, in classic

Brahminical pose, with a group of renouncers. As soon as he saw the Pandavas, Aswatthaman plucked a blade of grass and transformed it into a *brahmasiris,* a weapon of mass destruction, which he released with the cry "*Apandavaga!*"—"For the annihilation of the Pandavas!" There was an immediate fiery conflagration that threatened to engulf the world. In order to neutralize the effect of Aswatthaman's missile, Arjuna immediately fired off a *brahmasiris* of his own, and it too blazed up like the fire at the end of a yuga.[72]

There was a deadly impasse, and yet again, the fate of the world was in the balance. But two of the renouncers with Aswatthaman positioned themselves between the contending weapons. In the Axial spirit—"desiring the welfare of all creatures and of all the worlds"—they asked both warriors to recall their missiles. Arjuna had observed the "holy life" of a warrior: he practiced a form of yoga, and carefully observed the sacred *kshatriya* virtues of truth and fidelity.[73] He could control his anger, and because he had not fired his weapon in wrath, he was able to recall it. Aswatthaman, however, had hurled his *brahmasiris* in rage. He could not restrain it but could only alter its course: the weapon would now go into the wombs of the Pandavas' wives; they would bear no more children, and the Pandava line would become extinct. Krishna cursed him: for three thousand years Aswatthaman must wander the earth alone, a renouncer manqué, living in the forests and uninhabited tracts of land.

Yudishthira ruled for fifteen years, but the light had gone from his life. He could never reconcile the *kshatriya's* violent vocation with the dharma of *ahimsa* and compassion that he found in his heart. There are innumerable passages in the *Mahabharata* that defend the warrior's vocation and that exult in fighting and killing, but fundamental doubts remain. The epic shows the unsettling effect of the Axial spirituality on some of the laypeople in India, who felt thrust into a limbo. Trapped in a worldly dharma, they could not join the renouncers and yogins, but found that the old Vedic faith could no longer sustain them. Indeed, it sometimes seemed demonic: Aswatthaman's ecstatic "self-sacrifice" had almost destroyed the world. The story of his night raid—with its evocation of massacre, martyrdom, escalating retaliation, and the reckless firing of weapons—has almost prophetic resonance for us today. A destructive cycle of violence, betrayal, and economy with the truth could lead to tragic nihilism:

> The goddess Earth trembled and the mountains shook. The wind did not blow, nor did the fire, though kindled, blaze forth. And even the constellations in the sky, agitated, wandered about. The sun did not shine; the lunar disc lost its splendour. All confounded, space became covered with darkness. Then, overcome, the gods did not know their domains, the sacrifice did not shine forth, and the Vedas abandoned them.[74]

The only thing that had saved the world from destruction was the Axial spirit of the two sages, who desired "the welfare of all creatures and of all the worlds." Somehow this spirit had to become more accessible to the ordinary warrior and householder, some of whom were in danger of falling into despair.

When Socrates was put to death by the democracy of Athens in 399, his pupil Plato was thirty years old. The tragedy made an indelible impression on the young man and profoundly affected his philosophy.[75] Plato had hoped for a political career. Unlike his hero Socrates, he came from a rich, aristocratic family: his father was a descendant of the last king of Athens; his stepfather had been a close friend of Pericles; and two of his uncles had been active in the government of the thirty tyrants after Athens's defeat in the Peloponnesian War. They had invited Plato to join them. It seemed a great opportunity, but Plato could see the flaws of this disastrous administration. He was delighted when the democracy was restored, and believed that his time had come, but the trial and death of Socrates so shattered his hopes that he became disillusioned and withdrew from public life in disgust. Wherever he looked, in any polis, the system of government was bad:

Hence I was forced to say . . . that the human race will
not see better days until either the stock of those who
rightly and genuinely follow philosophy acquire political authority, or else the class who have political control
be led by some dispensation of providence to become
real philosophers.[76]

How could the insights of the Axial Age be integrated into the
violent and dishonest world of politics? Plato's philosophy often
seems to be otherworldly and to involve a flight from the mundane to the cold purity of abstraction. Yet Plato did not want his
philosophers to retire from the world. Like the Confucians, he believed that a sage should be a man of action and influence public
policy. Ideally, a philosopher should rule the people himself. Like
the Buddha, Plato insisted that after achieving enlightenment, the
sage must return to the agora and work there for the betterment
of humanity.

After the death of Socrates, Plato traveled in the eastern
Mediterranean, hoping for inspiration. He stayed for some time in
Megara with Euclides, one of the Eleatic philosophers who had
been a disciple of Socrates; he shared Plato's fascination with Parmenides. Plato was also attracted by the Pythagorean communities, with whom he forged lifelong friendships. He was especially
inspired by their passion for mathematics, which trained their
minds away from the confusing morass of the particular to a world
of pure numbers and geometric forms. He traveled in Egypt and
Libya, and in the court of the tyrant Dionysius I of Syracuse, he
met Dion, who became very enthusiastic about Plato's ideas. Plato
may have hoped that Dion would become a philosophical activist
in Sicily, but his first visit to Syracuse ended badly. It was said that
Dionysius had Plato sold into slavery, and that he was rescued only
at the last minute by his friends. Bruised by this experience, he returned home to Athens in 387.

There was little to cheer him there. Athens had tried to recover from the Peloponnesian War by making an alliance with
Thebes against Sparta. But there was no lasting peace. The events
of the next thirty years demonstrated the chronic instability of in-

tercity politics on the Greek mainland. The poleis continued to fight, no city was able to implement a coherent foreign policy, and all were debilitated by the ceaseless conflict; trade declined; and there was renewed conflict between rich and poor. These internal disputes sometimes exploded in atrocity. In 370, democrats in Argos brutally clubbed twelve hundred aristocrats to death, and in Tegea the leaders of the oligarchy were slaughtered by a violent mob.

Plato's response to this mayhem was to found a school of mathematics and philosophy. It was called the Academy, because the scholars met in a sacred grove on the outskirts of Athens dedicated to the hero Academius. Teaching was conducted by discussion in the Socratic manner rather than by lectures. Plato did not seek at this early stage to impose his own views on his pupils, but encouraged independent thinking. At the same time, he developed his personal ideas in writing and became the first philosopher whose oeuvre has survived in its entirety. He did not record his insights dogmatically, but used the dialogue form, in which different viewpoints were expressed. As Socrates was the hero of these dialogues, they arrived at no firm conclusions. Plato's dialogues were not definitive arguments but invitations to further thought that drew his readers into a deeper appreciation of the complexities of the issues discussed. Plato was not like a modern academic. Instead of expounding his ideas solemnly and logically, he often presented them playfully, indirectly, and allusively, speaking in parables and referring to fundamental truths elliptically and obscurely. He believed that the process of arriving at truth was hard, and required long, rigorous training in dialectic, but in his writing he also preserved the ancient methods of oral transmission, which recognized that truth could not be imparted by a simple recitation of facts, but demanded intuition, aesthetic insight, and imagination as well as empirical observation and disciplined logic.

Plato's philosophy is dominated by what is usually called the "doctrine of the forms," even though this never really became a consistent theory. Modern scholars have traced a development in his thought, and some believe that at the end of his life he abandoned the forms altogether, but it is a mistake to seek a clear intellectual evolution in Plato's work.[77] He probably started a new dialogue before finishing one that was already in progress, working on several at once. Sometimes he would try one approach, sometimes another; occasionally he described the forms mystically as divine figures; at other times he defined them more cerebrally. In each dialogue, he stole up on this difficult concept from a different starting point, so that what is preserved is a series of overlapping arguments that present a general idea of a form as an abstract object of thought by asking a number of different philosophical questions—but always trying to find out how this apparently abstruse notion had practical relevance in the unsettled and disturbing world of the fourth century.

Socrates had attempted to discover the true nature of goodness, but he does not seem to have formulated this in a way that satisfied anybody—perhaps not even himself. In the early dialogues, Plato probably stuck closely to his master's procedures. As we have seen, he made Socrates ask his interlocutors to consider different instances of a virtue such as courage, in the hope of finding a common denominator. If this type of behavior *was* brave and that was *not,* what did this tell us about the nature of courage per se? How could you behave virtuously if you did not know what virtue was? In the political turbulence of his time, in which the supporters of the competing polities—democracy, oligarchy, tyranny, aristocracy, monarchy—stridently argued their case, Plato believed that the only hope of achieving a solution was to find the underlying principles of good government. Like Socrates, Plato was disturbed by the relativism of the Sophists. He wanted to find a dimension of reality that was constant and unchanging but that could be grasped by a sustained effort of rational thought.

Yet Plato departed from Socrates by putting forward an extraordinary suggestion. Virtue, he argued, was not a concept that could be constructed by accumulating examples of behavior in daily life. It was an independent entity, an objective reality that existed on a higher plane than the material world. The ideas of goodness, justice, or beauty could not be experienced by the senses; we could not see, hear, or touch them, but they could be comprehended by the power of reasoning that resided in the soul (*psyche*) of each human being. Everything in our material world had an eternal, unchanging form: courage, justice, largeness—even a table. If we stood on a riverbank, we recognized that the body of water in front of us was a river rather than a pond or an ocean because we had the form of a river in our minds. But this universal concept was not something that we had created for our own convenience. It existed in its own right. In this world, for example, no two things were truly equal, yet we had an idea of absolute equality, even though we had no experience of it in our everyday lives. "Things have some fixed being or essence of their own," Plato made Socrates say. "They are not in relation to us and are not made to fluctuate by how they appear to us. They are by themselves, in relation to their own being or essence, which is theirs by nature."[78]

The Greek word *idea* did not mean "idea" in the modern English sense. An *idea* or *eidos* was not a private, subjective mental construct, but a "form," "pattern," or "essence." A form or *idea* was an archetype, the original pattern that gave each particular entity its distinctive shape and condition. Plato's philosophical notion can be seen as a rationalized and internalized expression of the ancient perennial philosophy in which every earthly object or experience has its counterpart in the divine sphere.[79] This perception had been crucial to pre-Axial religion, so Plato's idea of a world of absolutes that were imperfectly represented in the mundane sphere would have seemed less strange to his contemporaries than to a modern reader. The forms manifested themselves in the world of time, but they were superior, numinous, and timeless. They gave shape to our lives but transcended them. Everything here below was constantly changing and decaying. Plato pointed out that even though a beautiful person lost her looks and died, beauty itself continued to exist. She had not possessed absolute beauty—no earthly entity does—but she was informed by beauty and participated in this eternal quality. Her beauty was very different from the beauty of her sister, or from the beauty of a poem, a mountain, or a building, but people recognized it because each of us had innate knowledge of the eternal forms. When we fell in love with a beautiful person, we surrendered to the beauty that was revealed in her. The enlightened person will have trained him- or herself (Plato believed that women could enjoy this knowledge too) to see through the imperfect earthly manifestation of beauty to the eternal form that lay beneath it.

The realm of the forms was thus primary, and our material world was secondary and derivative, just as, in the perennial philosophy, the celestial sphere was superior and more enduring than the mundane. The forms had an intensity of reality that transitory phenomena could not possess. When we glimpsed the form that was imperfectly revealed in a person, an action, or an object, we saw its hidden essence and encountered a level of being that was more authentic than its earthly manifestation. Like Zhuangzi and the Buddha, Plato realized that everything that we saw here below was constantly becoming something else. The forms, however, were not involved in the flux of becoming. They were static, changeless, and immortal. The philosopher sought to encounter a deeper level of meaning by cultivating a knowledge that was based on the exercise of pure reason rather than sense data, which was always inherently unsatisfactory—or *dukkha,* as the Buddha would have said.

Plato may have harked back to an ancient mythical perception, but he was also inspired by the mathematics of his day. Inscribed over the door of the Academy was the motto "Let no one unacquainted with geometry enter here." Training in mathematics was essential. Like the Pythagoreans, Plato believed that the cosmos was ordered on the fundamental ideas of number and geometry. We never saw a perfect circle or triangle in natural objects, but these forms underlay all empirically observed objects. They were not, Plato believed, imposed by the ordering mind on the untidy world about us, but existed independently, transcending the intellect that perceived them. They were, therefore, *found,* and discovered not by ordinary modes of thought but by the trained intelligence. Mathematics exemplified the absolutely certain knowledge that Plato sought but that could not be derived from our ordinary experience.[80] Even today, mathematicians speak of their discipline in a Platonic way. "When one 'sees' a mathematical truth," Roger Penrose has explained, "one's consciousness breaks through into this world of ideas and makes contact with it."[81]

But even though this knowledge could only be acquired painfully and laboriously, it was—Plato was convinced—an entirely natural human capacity. We were born with it. It simply had to be awakened. Truth was not introduced into the mind from outside but had to be "re-collected" from a prenatal existence when each man or woman had enjoyed direct knowledge of the forms. Each soul (psyche) had been born many times, Plato's Socrates explained, "and has seen all things here and in the underworld. There is nothing which it has not learned, so it is in no way surprising that it can recollect the things it knew before, both about virtue and other things . . . because searching and learning are, as a whole, recollection."[82] He illustrated his theory by summoning a slave boy to his side and helping him to find the solution to a difficult geometrical problem, claiming that he had simply reminded the child of something that he had known in a previous existence but had forgotten.[83]

Plato shared the conviction of many Axial philosophers that there was a dimension of reality that transcended our normal experience but that was accessible to us and natural to our humanity. Yet where others believed that this insight could not be achieved by ratiocination, Plato believed that it could. But his insistence that knowledge was essentially recollection shows that this rigorous dialectic was not coldly analytic but intuitive; the recovery of this innate knowledge seemed to take the mind itself by surprise. It is true that in some of the dialogues Plato simply made use of the forms to investigate a concept or get to the root of a problem.[84] But it is also true that Plato's rational quest was passionate and romantic. In ancient Greece, reason was not "cold" but "hot," a spiritual quest for meaning and value.[85] It helped the psyche to identify its goals and harness its desires in order to attain them. Hitherto, as far as we can tell from the fragmentary texts that have survived, Greek philosophers had often confined themselves to a notional, cerebral interpretation of experience. In the Academy, Greek education became more spiritual.

Frequently Plato used the imagery and vocabulary of the Eleusinian and Dionysian mysteries to describe the process of illumination and recollection. Instead of achieving insight through rituals and dramatic representations, however, his disciples reached their vision of the forms through the exercise of a dialectic that was so rigorous and exacting that it seems to have pushed them into an alternative state of consciousness. The process was described as a mystical ascent to a higher state of being, an initiation that was not wholly unlike that experienced by the *mystai* at Eleusis, which had introduced the aspirant to a blessed state. In the *Symposium,* Plato made Socrates describe the quest as a love affair that grasped the seeker's entire being, until he achieved an *ekstasis* that took him beyond normal perception. Socrates explained that he had received this information from a priestess called Diotima, who showed her *mystai* how their love of a beautiful body could be purified and transformed into an ecstatic contemplation (*theoria*) of ideal beauty. At first the philosophical initiate was simply enraptured by the physical perfection of his beloved; then he began to see that this person was just one manifestation of a beauty that existed in other beings too. In the next stage of his initiation, he realized that beauty of body was of a lesser order than the more elusive beauty of soul that could exist even in a physically ugly person. Finally, Diotima explained, "As he approaches the end of the initiation, there bursts upon him that wondrous vision, which is the very soul of the beauty he has toiled so long to find." This beauty was eternal; it could no longer be confined to a particular object, but was "absolute, existing alone with itself, unique, eternal." All other things participated in it, "yet in such a manner that, while they come into being and pass away, it neither undergoes any increase or diminution nor suffers any change." The *psyche* had been "initiated into the mysteries of love," had left the material world behind, and attained an ecstatic knowledge of absolute beauty itself.[86]

We moderns experience thinking as something that we *do.* But Plato envisaged it as something that happened to the mind: the objects of thought were living realities in the *psyche* of the person who learned to see them. This vision of beauty was not merely an aesthetic experience. Once people had experienced it, they found that they had undergone a profound moral change and could no longer live in a shabby, unethical way. A person who had achieved this knowledge could "bring forth not mere reflected images of goodness, but true goodness, because he will be in contact not with a reflection but with the truth." He had undergone a fundamental transformation: "having brought forth and nurtured true goodness, he will have the privilege of being beloved of God, and becoming, if ever men can, immortal himself."[87] Plato's description of beauty was clearly similar to what others called God or the Way:

> This Beauty will not appear to the imagination like the beauty of a face or hands or anything else corporeal, or like the beauty of a thought or science, or like beauty that has its seat in something other than itself, be it in a living thing or the earth or the sky or anything else whatsoever.

Like God, brahman, or *nibbana,* it was utterly transcendent: "absolute, existing alone within itself, unique, eternal."[88]

But the vision of beauty was not the end of the quest. It pointed inexorably toward the Good, the essence of everything that human beings desired. All the other forms were subsumed within the Good, and were nourished by it. In the Good, all things became one. The Good was indescribable and Plato's Socrates could speak of it only in parables, most memorably in the allegory of the cave in *The Republic.*[89] Here Socrates imagined a group of men who had been chained up all their lives like prisoners in a cave. They were turned away from the sunlight and could see only shadows reflected from the outside world onto the rocky wall. This was an image of the unenlightened human condition in which it was impossible to see the forms directly. We were so conditioned by our deprived circumstances that we took these ephemeral shadows for true reality. If we were liberated from this captivity we would be dazzled and bewildered by the brilliant sunlight and vibrant existence of the world outside the

cave. It would probably be too much for us, and we would want
to go back to our familiar twilight existence.

So, Socrates explained, the ascent to the light must take place
gradually. The sunlight symbolized the Good. Just as physical light
enabled us to see clearly, so the Good was the source of true
knowledge. When, like the liberated prisoners, we saw the Good,
we perceived what was really there. The sun enabled things to
grow and flourish; like the Good, it was the cause of being and
thus lay beyond anything that we experienced in ordinary life. At
the end of its long initiation, the illuminated soul would be able
to see the Good as clearly as ordinary people see the sun. But even
this was not the end of the journey. The liberated men probably
wanted to stay outside and bask in the sunlight—just as the Buddha wanted to luxuriate in the peace of *nibbana*—but they had a
duty to go back to the darkness of the cave to help their com-
rades. "Therefore each of you in turn must go down to live in the
common dwelling place of the others," Socrates insisted. "You'll
see vastly better than the people there. And because you've seen
the truth about fine, just, and good things, you'll know each image
for what it is."[90] They would probably get a hostile reception.
They would now be bewildered by the darkness; their former
companions might laugh at them and tell them that they were de-
luded. How could an enlightened man "compete again with the
perpetual prisoners in recognizing the shadows"?[91] The captives
might even turn on their liberators and kill them, just as, Plato implied, the Athenians had executed the historical Socrates.

The parable of the cave was an integral part of Plato's political
description of the ideal republic. He always came back to the
practical application of his ideals, and the shadows on the wall, besides depicting the impoverished vision of the unenlightened, also
expressed the ephemeral illusions of contemporary politics, which
relied on coercion and self-serving fantasies. In *The Republic,* Plato
wanted to show that justice was rational, and that people could
live in the way that they should only if they were brought up in a
decent society, where the rulers were governed by reason. There is
much in this text that is distasteful and elitist. There would, for example, be genetic engineering in Plato's utopian city: less able cit-

izens would be discouraged from procreation; defective infants would be discreetly disposed of, and the more promising taken from their parents and brought up in state nurseries in a segregated sector of the polis. The most gifted would be subjected to a long, arduous education, which would culminate in their ascent from the cave. At the end of their initiation into enlightened civic life, they would see the Good for themselves and thereby attain an inner stability that would bring peace and justice to the republic.

> Thus, for you and for us, the city will be governed, not like the majority of cities nowadays, by people who fight over shadows and struggle against one another in order to rule—as if that were a great good—but by people who are awake rather than dreaming, for the truth is surely this: A city whose prospective rulers are least eager to rule must of necessity be most free from civil war.[92]

Plato almost certainly did not regard his imaginary republic as a blueprint for an actual state and probably used it simply to stimulate discussion, but the inherent cruelty of his utopia departed from the compassionate ethos of the Axial Age.

The Republic was authoritarian. It imposed its vision on others—an expedient that the Buddha, for example, would have found "unskillful." Plato had no time for the humanities. He looked askance at traditional Greek education, with its emphasis on poetry and music, because he believed that the arts aroused irrational emotion. Plato's republic would not encourage personal relationships: sex was simply a means to the end of breeding genetically acceptable citizens. And Plato wanted to ban tragedy from his ideal polis. In the fourth century, new tragedies continued to attract large audiences from all over Attica,[93] but Athenians looked back with nostalgia to the great days of Aeschylus, Sophocles, and Euripides and still hankered after their tragic insight.[94] But Plato turned his back on tragedy. He distrusted its pessimism, its negative appraisal of human potential, and believed that its skeptical view of the gods could induce a fatal nihilism. To sympathize with the tragic heroes was implicitly to condone their bleak valuation of life, and thus to encourage inconsolable grief and ungovernable rage. Tragedy had the power to "maim" even the souls of the virtuous citizens and make the lives of those exposed to it "worse and more wretched." Above all, tragedy tapped a natural tendency to sorrow and could inspire an "emotional surrender."[95] Grief for oneself and pity for others must be controlled and held in check. Indeed, to sympathize with others and share their suffering, as the chorus directed the audience to do, dangerously undermined the moderation and self-control of the good man. Society must take active measures to repress this natural sympathy, since it was incompatible with virtue.[96]

Instead of cultivating the "shoots" of compassion, like Mencius, Plato wanted to eliminate it. In his later work, we see a harshness that could have been accentuated by his second Sicilian adventure. After the death of the tyrant Dionysius I of Syracuse, Plato unwisely became involved in the political conspiracy that led to the assassination of his old protégé Dion in 354. At one point, Plato was put under house arrest and narrowly escaped execution. Not only had his philosophical ideas proved wholly ineffective, but he himself was personally scarred, and from this time forward he took a harder line.

Plato's vision of the forms had introduced a new dynamic into Greek religion. Since Homer, Greeks had been encouraged to accept reality as it was, and had no ambition to transcend it or radically change their condition. Poets, scientists, and tragedians had insisted that existence was transitory, moribund, and often cruelly destructive. Human life was *dukkha;* not even the gods could change this unsatisfactory state of affairs. This was the true reality, and a mature human must face up to it, either with heroic defiance or with tragic or philosophical insight. Plato reversed this. Our earthly, corporeal life was indeed miserable and awry, but it was *not* the true reality. It was *un*real, compared with the immutable, eternal world of the forms, and this perfect world was accessible to human beings. People did not have to put up with suffering and death. If they were prepared to devote themselves to a long, exacting philosophical initiation, their souls could ascend to the divine world without any help from the gods and achieve an immortality that had once been the prerogative of the Olympians. After Plato there was a yearning for an ineffable reality that existed beyond the gods.

In his later years, however, Plato turned back to the world and his theology became more concrete. In *Timaeus,* Plato suggested that the world had been created by a divine craftsman (*demiourgos*), who was eternal and wholly good but not omnipotent; he was not free to fashion the cosmos as he chose but had to model his creation upon the forms. The craftsman was not a figure that could inspire a religious quest, because he had no interest in humanity. He was not the Supreme God: a higher god existed, but he was also irrelevant to the human predicament. "To find the maker and father of this universe is hard enough," Plato remarked, "and even if I succeeded, to declare him to everyone is impossible."[97] Plato's aim was not religious. He simply wanted to devise a rational cosmology. Created according to the forms, imbued with reason, his universe had an intelligible pattern that could be investigated empirically. There would be no more arbitrary Olympian interventions. The cosmos was ruled by a comprehensive plan, which men could understand if they applied themselves to it logically.

Indeed, the cosmos thus created was itself a living being, with a rational mind (*nous*) and soul (*psyche*), which could be discerned in the mathematical proportions of the universe and the regular revolutions of the heavenly bodies. The stars themselves participated in the divinity of the creator; they were "visible and generated gods," and Gaia, the Earth, was "the foremost, the one with greatest seniority"; she too had been created according to the perfect model.[98] In the same way, the *nous* of each human being was divine; each had a *daimon,* a divine spark, within him- or herself, whose purpose was to "raise us up away from the earth and toward what is akin to us in heaven."[99] Human beings therefore lived in a perfectly rational world, the exploration of which was both a scientific and a spiritual enterprise. Plato had devised a new cosmic religion, which superseded the old Olympian vision and became the faith of the enlightened philosopher. It was accepted—though interpreted differently—by all Plato's pupils, and would, once merged with the monotheistic vision, remain the basic cosmological vision of Western Europe until the twelfth century CE.

Plato's sacred universe was an inspiration to philosophers; it encouraged them to investigate the cosmos empirically and to believe that it was possible to solve the mysteries of nature. It assured them that their minds, which contained a trace of the sacred, were equipped for the task. It also brought the divine into a human frame and made it perceptible. It was possible to actually see the gods—the sun, moon, and stars—every day, shining in the sky. When they investigated the earth, scientifically, they were delving into the mystery of the divine. But Plato's cosmic religion meant nothing to ordinary people who had no philosophical training. A deity who was uninterested in the human race could not give meaning to their lives. Plato tried to remedy this. The Olympian gods and heroes were now regarded as *daimones,* lesser deities who acted as tutelary spirits and carried messages to and from the ineffable celestial world. Nobody could ever have any intercourse with the supremely incomprehensible God, but they could revere Zeus, the guardian of city boundaries who took care of strangers; Hera, the patron of marriage; and Athena and Ares, who looked after hoplites during a campaign.[100] The Olympians had been reduced to guardian angels,* similar to the nature spirits who were being phased out of the Axial religions.

The Olympians may have lost status, but Plato insisted that their cult was essential to the polis. In *The Laws,* his last work, Plato described another utopian polis in which the old worship remained important. He denied that there was any conflict between reason and traditional Greek piety. There were no compelling proofs for the existence of the Olympian *daimones,* but it was irrational and unintelligent to deny the ancient myths, because like fairy tales, they contained a modicum of truth. Plato

---

*The Greek *aggelos* and Latin *angelus* meant "messenger," ministering spirit, a spiritual being superior to humans, who were the attendants of the deity.

wanted to reform the cult. He insisted that the Olympians could not be influenced by sacrifice or prayer, but that people should express their gratitude to these intermediaries with the ineffable, divine world.[101] Hester, Zeus, and Athena must have their shrines on the acropolis of his ideal city. Its agora would be surrounded by temples, and the festivals, processions, sacrifices, and prayers must all be carried out punctiliously. The most important deities of his imaginary city were Apollo and Helios, who had long been identified with the sun, and could easily be integrated with Plato's cosmic theology. Plato tried to merge old and new. During the festivals of his polis, gods and *daimones* would dance unseen beside the human celebrants. Indeed, the purpose of these rituals was precisely "to share [the gods'] holidays."[102] The festival involved *orgiazein,* a word used to describe the ecstatic mystery celebrations.[103] The sacrifices could not propitiate the Olympians, but they could still lift the spirit and give humans intimations of transcendence. Nevertheless, despite Plato's approval of the old religion, he considered it inferior to philosophy. It could not bring true enlightenment: the forms could only be apprehended through the reasoning powers of the mind, not in the insights of myth or the sacred drama of ritual. Traditional religion had been downgraded; *mythos* had become subservient to Plato's mystical *logos.*

There was a sinister directive in *The Laws* that took Plato even further away from the Axial Age.[104] His imaginary city was a theocracy. The first duty of the polis was to inculcate "the right thoughts about the gods, and then to live accordingly: well or not well."[105] Correct belief came first; ethical behavior only second. Orthodox theology was the essential prerequisite for morality. "No one who believes in gods as the law directs ever voluntarily commits an unholy act or lets any lawless word pass his lips."[106] None of the Axial thinkers had placed any great emphasis on metaphysics. Some even regarded this type of speculation as misguided. Ethical action came first; compassionate action, not orthodoxy, enabled human beings to apprehend the sacred. But for Plato, correct belief was mandatory, so important that a "nocturnal council" must supervise the citizens' theological opinions.

There were three obligatory articles of faith: that the gods existed; that they cared for human beings; and that they could not be influenced by sacrifice and prayer. Atheism and a superstitious belief in the practical efficacy of ritual would be capital crimes in Plato's ideal polis, because these ideas could damage the state. Citizens would not be permitted either to doubt the existence of the Olympian gods or to ask searching questions about them. Poets could use their fables to instruct the masses, but their stories must not be too fanciful. They must focus on the importance of justice, the transmigration of souls, and the punishments that would be inflicted on wrongdoers in the afterlife. These doctrines could thus guarantee the good behavior of the uneducated. Plato was aware that some atheists lived exemplary lives, so he allowed a convicted unbeliever five years to find his way back to the fold. During this time, he would be detained in a sequestered place for reflection. If he still refused to submit to the true faith, he would be executed.[107]

At the beginning of his philosophical quest, Plato had been horrified by the execution of Socrates, who had been put to death for teaching false religious ideas. At the end of his life, he advocated the death penalty for those who did not share his views. Plato's vision had soured. It had become coercive, intolerant, and punitive. He sought to impose virtue from without, distrusted the compassionate impulse, and made his philosophical religion wholly intellectual. The Axial Age in Greece would make marvelous contributions to mathematics, dialectics, medicine, and science, but it was moving away from spirituality.

Plato's most brilliant pupil made this divide even more absolute. Aristotle (c. 384–322) was not a native Athenian. He came from a Greek colony on the peninsula of Chalcidice. His father was the friend and physician of King Amyntas II of Macedon, and Aristotle grew up with Amyntas's son Philip. At the age of eighteen, however, Aristotle arrived in Athens, and for twenty years he studied under Plato at the Academy. During this period of his life, he was a loyal disciple of Plato and accepted his theory of the forms. But over time, he became convinced that the forms had no independent, objective existence. Qualities such as beauty, courage, roundness, or whiteness existed only in the material object in which they inhered. Aristotle became extremely critical of the notion that the ideal world was more real than the material universe. Some substances were indeed eternal, divine, and superior to perishable objects, but it was very difficult to gain any accurate knowledge about them, because they existed beyond the reach of our senses. It was better to concentrate on what lay within our grasp, such as the structure of plants and animals.

When Plato died in 347, Aristotle left Athens. He may have been disappointed not to have been appointed head of the Academy, but he may also have become persona non grata in Athens because of his Macedonian connections. His friend Philip had succeeded his father in 360. A soldier and politician of genius, he had made the failing, backward, and isolated state of Macedonia a major power in the region, so that it now threatened Athenian interests. After a series of military defeats, Athens was forced to sign a treaty with Macedonia in 346, but remained hostile to and resentful of this dynamic new state, which was steadily expanding its territory and encroaching onto the mainland.

In 342, Philip invited Aristotle to take up residence in Macedonia and educate his son Alexander. Aristotle remained Alexander's tutor for at least three years, by which time Philip had become master of Greece, and after inflicting a decisive defeat on Athens in 338, he brought a new stability to the region. All the poleis benefited from the more peaceful conditions, and Athens in particular enjoyed a new period of prosperity. Philip had planned to invade Persia, but was assassinated in 336 and succeeded by his son Alexander. The following year, Aristotle returned to Athens and established his own school, known as the Lyceum because it was close to the temple of Apollo Lyceus.

By this time he had become a biologist. He had spent some years in Asia Minor dissecting animals and plants and writing detailed descriptions of his investigations. Aristotle brought philosophy down to earth. He had become especially interested in the process of development and decay: he once broke an egg every day to chart the growth of the chick embryo. Where Plato and

other Axial sages had been disturbed by flux and mutability, Aristotle was simply intrigued by the whole process of "becoming."
Change was not *dukkha;* it was natural to all living beings. Instead
of seeking meaning in the immaterial world, Aristotle found it in
the physical forms of transformation. For him, a "form" was not
an eternal reality beyond the realm of the senses. It was an immanent structure within each substance that controlled its evolution until it attained maturity. Each person or thing had a *dynamis*
that impelled it to grow into its form, as the acorn contained
within itself the "potential" to become an oak tree. Change was
not to be feared but celebrated; it represented a universal striving
for fulfillment.

But this was a purely earthly achievement. Aristotle had no
ambition to leave Plato's cave. There was much beauty to be found
in the phenomenal world, if a philosopher knew how to use his
reason. After his return to Athens, Aristotle began to turn his attention to metaphysical and ethical subjects, but his focus remained fixed steadfastly upon the faculty and exercise of reason.
Aristotle was a man of *logos.* What distinguished the human being
from other animals was the ability to think rationally. Every creature strained to achieve the form within it. *Theoria,* the pursuit of
truth for its own sake, was the final "form" or goal of man (Aristotle had little opinion of the female, which he saw as a defective
form of humanity). The *eudaimonia* ("well-being") of man, therefore, lay in his intelligence. His "good" consisted of thinking
clearly and effectively, planning, calculating, studying, and working things out. A man's moral well-being also depended upon
logos, because such qualities as courage or generosity had to be
regulated by reason. "The life according to reason is best and
pleasantest," he wrote in one of his later treatises, "since reason,
more than anything else, *is* man."[108] A man's intelligence (*nous*)
was divine and immortal; it linked him with the gods, and gave
him the ability to grasp ultimate truth. Unlike sensual delight, the
pleasures of *theoria* did not ebb and flow, but were a continuous
joy, giving the thinker that self-sufficiency that characterized the
highest life of all. We "must, in so far as we can, strain every nerve

to live in accordance with the best thing in us," Aristotle insisted. We could not, like the gods, completely immerse ourselves in intellectual contemplation, but when we did, we activated a divine principle within. A man could only reach toward this divine attribute "in so far as something divine is present in him."[109]

In some respects, *theoria* was similar to the tranced states achieved by some of the other Axial sages, who were also seeking to fulfill their human potential, looking for a joy that did not wax or wane, and for absolute self-sufficiency. But they had tried to go beyond reason and *logos*. We do not know what Aristotle's *theoria* involved.[110] Did he include his scientific studies? Or was he engaged in a more meditative, transcendental activity? Certainly *noeton* ("thought") was for Aristotle the highest form of being. *Noesis noeseos* ("thinking about thinking") was being itself; it was the origin of all things and characterized the hidden life of God.

Like Plato, Aristotle believed that *theologia,* the study of God, was the "first philosophy" because it was concerned with the highest cause of being. He fully accepted Plato's cosmic religion, seeing the universe as divine, the stars as living gods, and imagining a supreme being that existed beyond the divine craftsman and his creation. Aristotle's God was not the first cause, because the universe was divine and eternal. Instead, he saw God as the Unmoved Mover. He noticed that everything that moved had been activated by something else. What had set the stars and the other heavenly bodies on their unchanging revolutions around the earth? Whatever had started them off must itself be immobile, or we would have to postulate a still higher being to initiate this action too. Reason demanded that the chain of cause and effect must have a single starting point. Aristotle's God was, therefore, the logical consequence of his cosmology rather than a mystically intuited reality. In the animal kingdom, he argued, desire could inspire movement. A hungry lion stalked a lamb because of his longing to eat. It followed that the stars might also have been set in motion by desire. They were themselves so perfect that they could yearn only toward a greater perfection, compelled by an intellectual love for a being engaged in the supreme activity. Aristotle's God was *noesis noeseos,* lost in contemplation of itself.

Hence Aristotle's Unmoved Mover was eternal; it was the supreme form, because it was the only form to exist apart from matter. As the highest divinity, it was pure *nous,* self-absorbed and self-sufficient, because it could take no heed of anything inferior to itself. God was pure *theoria.* Again, as in Plato's theology, there was nothing here for the ordinary person.[111] Not only was the Unmoved Mover unconcerned with the human race, but Aristotle also cast doubt on the idea that the lesser Olympians had any interest in humanity. For Plato, the Olympians' involvement in human affairs was an article of faith; for Aristotle, it was merely a hypothesis.[112] Yet, like Plato, Aristotle did not want to abolish the traditional cult. People always yearned toward superior beings. It was natural for them to honor the gods, and this type of worship should be accepted as a matter of fact. The old myths were highly suspect, but they probably contained a few fossils of ancient wisdom, such as ascribing divinity to the heavenly bodies. Religion could also be useful in giving a divine sanction to the laws and rulings of the polis.[113]

Philosophy had produced a new God, but it had nothing in common with Yahweh. Aristotle would have found the idea of a supreme deity who suddenly decided to create the world and involved himself in human history completely ludicrous. Even though monotheists would later use Aristotle's dubious "proofs" for the Unmoved Mover to demonstrate the existence of their God, the God of the philosophers was eventually regarded by the more discerning as *deus otiosus,* and useless to the spiritual quest.[114] Aristotle would have agreed. There was nothing sacred about his metaphysics. The term itself was coined by editors and librarians who put together his fragmentary writings and lecture notes. They simply combined fourteen essays on unrelated topics into a single volume, which they labeled *meta ta physika:* "After *The Physics.*"

In some respects, Aristotle seems to have had a better understanding of traditional spirituality than Plato. He was not preoccupied with orthodoxy, pointing out that the initiates who took part in the mysteries did not do so to learn facts and doctrines but to "experience certain emotions and to be put in a certain disposition."[115] This type of religion was about feeling (*pathein*), not thinking. Aristotle seemed more comfortable with emotion than Plato. It was, for example, sometimes good to be angry, as long as you did not allow your wrath to become extreme. Where Plato would have banned tragedy from his ideal republic, Aristotle believed that it still had a function. It was right to feel pity and fear on some occasions, and tragedy helped to educate the emotions and teach people to experience them appropriately.[116] When observing the sufferings of Oedipus, for example, a pusillanimous man would realize that his troubles were not so bad after all, and an arrogant person would learn to feel compassion for those weaker than he. By imitating serious and terrible events, tragedy accomplished the purification of such feelings.[117] The emotions were drained of their dangerous potential and became beneficial to the individual and the community. Indeed, these feelings were essential to the peculiar pleasure of tragedy. Aristotle understood rationally what ritualists had always intuited: a symbolic, mythical, or ritual reenactment of events that would be unendurable in daily life could transform our deepest fears into something pure, transcendent, and even pleasurable. And yet Aristotle saw the tragedies as literary texts for private perusal. In his discussion of tragedy, he stressed its effect on the individual rather than its civic, political function. He did not discuss its ritual dimension and showed scant interest in the gods. His literary criticism was anthropocentric and, like his philosophy, was wholly oriented to the mundane world. What had been a profound religious experience was being subtly altered by Aristotle's rational intelligence into something more pragmatic.

Aristotle was a pioneer of great genius. Almost single-handedly he had laid the foundations of Western science, logic, and philosophy. Unfortunately, he also made an indelible impression on Western Christianity. Ever since Europeans discovered his writings in the twelfth century CE, many became enamored of his rational proofs for the Unmoved Mover—actually one of his less inspired achievements. Aristotle's God, which was not meant to be a religious value, was foreign to the main thrust of the Axial Age,

which had insisted that the ultimate reality was ineffable, indescribable, and incomprehensible—and yet something that human
beings *could* experience, though not by reason. But Aristotle had
set the West on its scientific course, which would, nearly two
thousand years after the first Axial Age, introduce a second Great
Transformation.

9

EMPIRE

(c. 300 to 220 BCE)

At the beginning of the third century, the Axial Age, which was coming to an end in the other regions, was still flourishing in China, but even here some of the original ideals were hardening. For generations, Wei and Qin had been the most powerful kingdoms in the region. In a desperate struggle for survival, the smaller states had veered in their support from one to the other, but people were becoming weary of the endless strife. Many longed for a ruler who was powerful enough to create a united Chinese empire, as in the days of Yao and Shun. There was an almost palpable longing for peace. The Chinese were not interested in the scientific, metaphysical, and logical questions that fascinated the Greeks. The political situation was so grave that such issues seemed trivial. Their priority was to bring back law and order, and to that end Chinese philosophers, moralists, and mystics concentrated on solving the problems of government. By this time, it was clear that a new approach was necessary. Change was accelerating at such a rate that people could see major differences occurring between one generation and the next. There was a growing conviction that if a new empire did emerge from the chaos of the Warring States period, it could not be run like the archaic empire of Yao and Shun—or even the early Zhou. In the larger, constantly expanding kingdoms, the princes no longer relied on the magical potency (*daode*) of their office. They were realists, and could see that the economy was the key to success.

Victory would go to the ruler who had the largest territory, the greatest manpower, the most extensive resources, and the best grain reserves.

By the end of the fourth century, the rulers had abandoned even the pretense of listening to Confucian and Mohist advisers. Instead they turned to men from the new merchant class, who shared their hard-nosed realism. The merchants depended upon calculation and the laws of finance; instead of contemplating the Way, they speculated on the desire for gain and luxury and thought in terms of money and written contracts. But another philosophical school was also coming to the fore. In one state after another, rulers were turning to the political scientists, the "men of method." The Chinese historians referred to them collectively as the Fajia, often translated as "School of Law."[1] But this can be misleading. The men of method were certainly interested in law, but they were not preoccupied by jurisprudence. *Fa* meant "standard, model." It was used to describe a tool, such as a plumb line or a carpenter's square, that reshaped raw materials so that they conformed to a fixed pattern.[2] The Legalists wanted to make people adapt to their ideal, so they extended the word to include prescriptive methods of controlling social behavior. *Fa* was, therefore, often paired with *xing* ("punishment"). The state, they argued, must impose severe penalties to reform men and women, in the same way that an L-square forced irregular material into line. Mohists and Confucians believed that only a sage king who was imbued with benevolence and morality could reform society. The Legalists were not interested in a prince's morality; they believed that, if properly formulated, their method would work automatically, provided that it was backed up by draconian punishments and a rigorous penal code.

The men of method had probably always been active in government circles. Even in the idealized feudal days, there must always have been a measure of coercion in politics. But times had changed. During the last century, there had been a huge population explosion in the great plain; and because of the ceaseless wars of expansion, states were becoming much bigger than the little feudal principalities had ever been. A prince needed more than *ren* and ritual to govern these enormous kingdoms. The Legalists wanted to create a polity that would actually work. They did not see history as a lamentable decline from a golden age. This could only lead to nostalgia for the past, whereas salvation must lie in a rational appraisal of the present. Successful states, such as Wei and Qin, which were constantly expanding and having, therefore, to impose their rule on resentful, vanquished people, needed an efficient method of administration that did not rely on the ruler's charisma but would apply to all subjects alike, rich and poor, Chinese or barbarian.

The Legalists liked to compare the mechanism of the law to a pair of scales, which provided a standard measurement. Merchants and shopkeepers might want to extort more money from their customers, but the scales told them exactly how much they could charge. "Men don't try to change the scales because they know it would be useless," wrote a fourth century author.

> So when there is a clear-sighted ruler on the throne, officials have no opportunity to bend the law, magistrates have no opportunity to practise partiality. The people know that it would be useless to try to influence the magistrates; the scales stand level and correct, waiting for the load. So traitors and tricksters have no opportunity to get decisions partial to themselves.[3]

Once it had been set up, their political theory would work just as automatically and impartially. The Legalists had made the important intellectual transition from the person-to-person government of feudalism to an objective legal system, which was not unlike the concept of law in the modern West, except that in ancient China the law was not designed to protect the individual but to achieve control from above. The intellectual or moral status of the ruler was irrelevant, because the system could function without his personal intervention. He could—and should—sit back and "do nothing" (*wu wei*).

Strangely enough, Legalists felt an affinity with the Daoists, people like Zhuangzi, who had also taught the importance of "doing nothing" and insisted that the Way of Heaven operated independently of human intentions. The early Legalists agreed. Thus Shen Dao, who was a contemporary of Mencius at the Jixia Academy, had compared the impersonal institutions of authority in the well-ordered state to the activity of the Way of Heaven, which could not be affected by the desires and dispositions of individual human beings. Just as the sage refrained from purposeful activity (*yu wei*) because it blocked the workings of the Way, so the king must refrain from any personal interventions that impeded the mechanical working of the system. Shen Dao wanted to find an ideological context for his wholly pragmatic vision of government, and the Legalist ideal of the passive, inactive king had deep roots in China. The ritual law of the feudal period had also ruled that the prince must "do nothing" but must simply allow the magical power of the Way to work through him.

Legalism first developed in the kingdoms of Wei, Han, and Zhao, which had broken away from the old state of Jin in the early fifth century. These were rogue states, and their rulers were, therefore, less wedded to tradition and more open to radical theories of government. In about 370, an ambitious young man called Shang Yang (c. 390–338) had settled in Wei and joined the discussions of the local political scientists, who had no grand spiritual program but simply wanted to reform the military, increase agricultural production, bolster the power of the ruler by weakening the local nobility, and develop a clear and effective legal code. Shang failed to gain the favor of the king of Wei, but in 361 managed to become chief adviser to the prince of Qin. This was a great opportunity. Qin had a large barbarian population, which knew next to nothing about Zhou traditions, and the nobility was too weak and impoverished to put up any effective opposition to Shang's revolutionary program. His reform, which flouted many of the major principles of the Axial Age, made the backward, isolated kingdom of Qin the most powerful and advanced state in China. At the end of the third century, as a result of Shang's far-reaching measures, Qin would conquer all the other states, and in 221 its ruler would become the first historical emperor of China.

Lord Shang felt no loyalty to past tradition. "When the guiding principles of the people become unsuited to their circum-stances," he argued, "their standard [*fa*] of value must change. As conditions in the world change, different principles are prac-tised."[4] It was no use dreaming of a golden age of compassionate sage kings. If people were more generous in the past, this was not because they had practiced *ren,* but because the population was smaller and there was enough food to go round. Similarly, the cor-ruption and conflict of the Warring States period was not the re-sult of dishonesty, but occurred simply because resources were scarce.[5] Instead of promoting nonviolence, Lord Shang wanted the people of Qin to be as eager for war and bloodshed as a hun-gry wolf. He had only one objective: "the enrichment of the state and the strengthening of its military capacity."[6] To meet its targets, governments had to exploit the fear and greed of the population. Very few people wanted to expose themselves to the perils of modern warfare, but Shang devised such dire punishments for de-serters that death on the battlefield seemed preferable. He also re-warded the outstanding military service of peasants and noblemen alike with a grant of agricultural land.

Lord Shang's methodical, rational reform completely trans-formed daily life in Qin, which under his tutelage became a deadly efficient fighting machine. Conscription in the army and the corvée was compulsory, and the harsh discipline of army life was imposed on the whole country. Lord Shang's most important innovation was to link agricultural production with the military. Successful peasant-soldiers became landowners and were given ti-tles and pensions, while the old nobility was dismantled. Aristo-crats who did not perform well on the battlefield were demoted and became commoners; those who did not participate efficiently in Shang's ambitious land-clearance schemes were sold into slav-ery. Everybody was subject to the same laws: even the crown prince was executed when found guilty of a minor offense.

Not only was Lord Shang unconcerned about the morality of the prince; he believed that a virtuous sage would make a disas-trous king. "A state that uses good people to govern the wicked will be plagued by disorder and destroyed," he declared. "A state that uses the wicked to govern the good always enjoys order and becomes strong."[7] The Confucians, who preached peace, were dangerous. If everybody practiced the *li,* they would become so moderate and restrained that a prince would never persuade anybody to fight. Lord Shang was openly contemptuous of the Golden Rule. A truly effective prince would inflict upon the enemy exactly what he would *not* wish to have done to his own troops. "If in war you perform what the enemy would not venture to perform, you will be strong," he told his officials. "If in enterprises you undertake what the enemy would be ashamed to do, you have the advantage."[8]

His draconian reforms were a great success. In 340, Qin inflicted a massive defeat on Wei, its major rival, and became a major contender for imperial power. Lord Shang had expected to receive a generous gift of land as a reward for his services, but instead he became a victim of the new ruthlessness. In 338, after the death of his royal patron, his rivals got the ear of the new prince, and Shang was ripped to pieces by the war chariots he had procured for Qin. But a new generation of Legalists would continue along the lines that he had mapped out, and other states began to follow Qin's example.

One of the finest Legalist scholars was Han Fei (280–233), who became a minister of King Huang-Di of Qin. He was far less cynical than Lord Shang and believed that he had a noble mission to help humanity. In his essay "Solitary Indignation," he saw himself as quite different from the other wandering *shi* who peddled what in his view were useless, impractical ideas. He and the other Legalists should be men of unimpeachable morality, and must dedicate themselves unswervingly to the highest interests of the prince.[9] Han Fei knew that it was highly unlikely that a king would be a paragon of virtue, but he wanted to help an ordinary human being to become an effective ruler by setting up an efficient system. The ruler must find the right officials to work for him, and should be inspired by the desire to help his people. "He simply looks ahead for what will benefit the people. Therefore, when he imposes punishments on them, it is not out of hatred of the people, but he does so simply out of concern for them."[10] He should be impartial and unselfish, punishing friends and family if

necessary and rewarding his enemies. A poem attributed to Han
Fei gave the ruler's *wu wei* almost mystical significance:

> *By doing without knowledge, he possesses clear-sightedness,*
> *By doing without worthiness, he gets results,*
> *By doing without courage, he achieves strength.* [11]

The law was not supposed to be a method of punishment and
suppression. It was an education that would accustom king and
subjects to behave in a different way. Once this reformation was
complete, there would be no further need for punishments;
everybody would act in accordance with the best interests of the
state. Yet for all his good intentions, Han Fei also suffered a violent
end; he was slandered and imprisoned, and in 233, rather than
submit to execution, accepted the option of committing suicide.

Before he had become a Legalist, Han Fei had studied under
the most distinguished Confucian philosopher of his time and
probably acquired much of his idealism from his teacher. Xunzi
(c. 340–245), a passionate, poetic, yet rigorously rational thinker,
managed to absorb insights of other philosophers into his own
Confucian perspective and created a powerful synthesis. [12] He did
not think that Mohists, Yangists, and Legalists were wrong; they
simply stressed only one side of a complex argument, and it was
possible to learn something from them all. Xunzi was also profoundly influenced by Daoist ideas. His book was more cogently
argued and organized than any other text of Axial Age China, yet
at times his prose modulated easily into poetry and his logic into
mystical insight.

Xunzi was appalled by the new pragmatism, which he believed had led to a decline in moral standards. Everywhere he
went he saw "scheming and plotting," and the selfish pursuit of
wealth, power, and luxury. [13] Because princes refused to allow
themselves to be restrained by the *li,* they pursued their own ambitions ruthlessly, and violence and warfare became endemic.
Xunzi did not accept the realism of the Legalists; he still believed
that a compassionate king was the only person who could restore
peace and order, but he was prepared to consider any system that

might bring relief, even if it departed from traditional Confucian principles. Xunzi was an activist; he longed for a government post, but was no more successful than Confucius and Mencius. He was three times appointed master of the Jixia Academy, but had to leave Qi when its tyrannical King Min expelled the scholars from his kingdom. In 255, he moved to Chu, where the prime minister made him a magistrate, but he lost his post in 238 when his patron was assassinated. Sadly, Xunzi retired from public life, and edited his collected essays.

One of these described his visit to Qin. Even though the Legalist ideal could not have been further from his own, Xunzi was impressed with what he saw. The officials worked with efficiency and integrity; there was no corruption, no infighting in the administration, and the ordinary people were simple and unspoiled. They may have feared the government, but they obeyed it, and appreciated the stability and impartiality of the new laws.[14] Qin was not perfect, however. Xunzi realized that the reforms had only been possible because the people had no experience of high civilization. He believed that the harsh penal code was probably necessary, but he also noted that Qin was a troubled place; people seemed constantly afraid that "the world will unite to crush it."[15] Qin would never rule the whole of China, he believed, because its draconian style of government would alienate the subjects of other states; it would survive only if it accepted the guidance of a *junzi,* a mature and humane ruler. Xunzi was both right and wrong. Qin did manage to defeat the other states and establish an empire, but its ruthless methods of government resulted in the collapse of the dynasty, which fell after a mere fourteen years.

Nevertheless, Qin was a challenge to a Confucian. During an audience with King Zhao, Xunzi told him that he was sorry that there were no ritualists in the Qin administration. The king replied bluntly: "The Confucians [*ru*] are no use in running a state."[16] Given their dismal track record, it was difficult for Xunzi to argue with him. Nor could he find an effective answer to his ambitious young pupil Li Si. Xunzi had suggested that if a *junzi* came to power, there would be peace, because his morality (*yi*) and benevolence (*ren*) would be an irresistible force for good. It was a beautiful Confucian vision. The prince's compassion would radiate from him, like the potency of the sage kings, Xunzi explained; wherever he went, he would effortlessly transform his environment. Such a prince would never attack another state simply to further his own ambition.

> He takes up arms in order to put an end to violence, and to do away with harm, not in order to compete with others for spoil. Therefore when the soldiers of the benevolent man encamp they command a godlike respect; and where they pass, they transform the people. They are like the seasonable rain in whose falling all men rejoice.

"Dream on!" Li Si exclaimed. How did Xunzi explain the success of Qin, which had been consistently victorious for four generations? "Its armies are the strongest in the world and its authority sways the other feudal lords. It did not do this by *ren* and *yi* but by taking advantage of its opportunities—that's all."[17] Not long afterward, Li Si abandoned Xunzi, converted to Legalism, emigrated to Qin, became its prime minister, and presided over the lightning campaign that resulted in Qin's final victory in 221.

In 260, a few years after Xunzi's visit, the army of Qin conquered Xunzi's native state of Zhao. Even though the prince surrendered, the Qin troops massacred four hundred thousand Zhao soldiers. How could a *junzi,* who could not even keep a minor post in the administration, exert any restraining influence over such a ruthless regime? But as the political situation darkened, and more states adopted the Legalist system, Xunzi never lost faith. Against all odds, he continued to believe that the "yielding" spirit of the rituals and the compassionate ethic of *ren* could bring peace and order to China, even though he admitted that, in these hard times, they would probably have to be backed up by punishments and rewards. Sagehood was not an impossible ideal. If he made a passionate and committed effort to transform himself, any man in the street could become like Yao and save the world.

Throughout the *Xunzi,* we find an insistent plea for *yu wei,* disciplined, conscious effort. Xunzi had learned from his visit to Qin that if they tried hard enough, human beings could turn their society around. But they must take responsibility for themselves. Heaven was not a god who intervened in the affairs of the world. It was no use relying on Heaven for help, or trying to bend Heaven's will by consulting oracles. Xunzi hated these old manipulative superstitions. Heaven was nature itself; the Way of Heaven could be seen in the order and regularity of the heavenly bodies and the succession of the seasons. Heaven's Way was entirely separate from human beings. It could give them no guidance or help, but it had made available the resources they needed to find their own path. This was the mission of the *junzi*. It was pointless to contemplate the Way of Heaven and neglect human affairs, as Zhuangzi had done. It was wrong to withdraw from society. Civilization was a magnificent achievement; it had given human beings divine status, and made them equal partners with Heaven and Earth. "Is it better to obey Heaven and sing hymns to it," Xunzi asked, "or to grasp the mandate of Heaven and make use of it?" Was it better to yearn for Heaven, like the Daoists, or to make use of the resources that Heaven had provided and "bring them to completion"?[18] If we concentrated on Heaven and neglected what man could do, Xunzi insisted again and again, "we fail to understand the nature of things."[19]

But this involved hard, dedicated effort. Xunzi had learned from the Legalists that people needed to be reformed. Unlike Mencius, he believed that human nature was not good but evil. Everybody, he said, "is born with feelings of envy and hate, and if he indulges these, they will lead him into violence and crime, and all sense of loyalty and good faith will disappear."[20] He used the same imagery as the Legalists: "A warped piece of wood must wait until it has been laid against the straightening board, steamed and forced into shape, before it can become straight."[21] But if he worked hard enough, anybody could become a sage. He could not achieve this alone; first he must find a teacher and submit himself to the rites (*li*): only then would he be able to observe the dictates of courtesy and humility, obey the rules of society and achieve order.[22] It was no good doing what came naturally, like

Yangists and Daoists. Goodness was the result of conscious endeavor. The *junzi* used artifice to redirect his passions into constructive channels. This would not warp human nature, but bring out its full potential.

Xunzi was convinced that if they used their intelligence and reasoning powers, people would realize that the only way to restore peace and good order was to create a moral society. Education was crucial. He took a leaf out of the Legalists' book by admitting that the less intelligent would not understand this, and would have to be compelled, by a judicious system of law and punishments, to submit to a program of moral education. But wiser people would voluntarily choose to transform themselves by studying the wisdom of the past. When Yao, Shun, and Yu had contemplated the world, they realized that they could end the intolerable misery they saw all around them only by a massive intellectual effort that began with the transformation of their own selves. So they created the rituals of reverence, courtesy, and "yielding" (*rang*). These moderated their unruly passions, so that they achieved inner peace. By looking into their own hearts, critically observing their behavior, and observing their own reactions to life's pain and joy, the sages discovered how to order social relations.[23] The *li* were thus based on the principle of *shu,* "likening to oneself." Only when a ruler had mastered himself could he bring peace and order to society as a whole.

The sages had not imposed a set of alien rules on their subjects, therefore; the *li* had been inspired by their analysis of humanity. The rites humanized the emotions, shaping them as an artist brought form and beauty out of unpromising materials: they "trim what is too long, and stretch out what is too short, eliminate surplus and repair deficiency, extend the forms of love and reverence, and step by step, bring to fulfillment the beauties of proper conduct."[24] The *li* were a kind of natural law. The universe itself had to obey rules that brought order out of potential chaos. Even the heavenly bodies and the four seasons had to "yield" instead of encroaching aggressively upon one another. "Heaven and Earth are harmonised by the *li,* the sun and moon are illuminated by it; the four seasons derive their order from it; the stars and planets move by it," Xunzi pointed out.

If they did not, there would be chaos. The same *li*, which demanded that all things observe their due place in the order of the cosmos, would purify human emotions.[25] So far from being unnatural, the *li* would take people to the heart of reality. "The meaning of ritual is deep indeed," Xunzi repeated emphatically. "He who tries to enter it with the uncouth and inane theories of the system-makers will perish there."[26]

Even though Xunzi concentrated on earth rather than Heaven, he was not a secular humanist. Like all Chinese, he revered nature as "godlike" (*shen*). His religious rationalism was based on mystical silence. He deplored what he called "obsession," the egotistic insistence on a single doctrinal position. Before anybody attempted to reform society, he must understand the Way, and he could not do that by insisting that his opinions were right and everybody else's wrong. The Way could be comprehended only by a mind that was "empty, unified and still." Here Xunzi was entirely in agreement with Zhuangzi. The mind was "empty" if it remained open to new impressions, instead of clinging to its *own* opinion; it was "unified" if it did not force the complexity of life into a coherent, self-serving system; it was "still" if it did not indulge in "dreams and noisy fantasies," and nurture ambitious "plots and schemes" that hindered true understanding.[27] "Emptiness, unity and stillness," Xunzi explained, "these are the qualities of a great and pure enlightenment."

Divested of egotistic obsession, an ordinary human being could achieve the panoptic vision of a sage. Instead of being imprisoned in a parochially selfish point of view, he acquired an intuitive grasp of the deeper principles of government.

> He who has such enlightenment may sit in his room and view the entire area within the four seas, may dwell in the present and yet discourse on distant ages. He has a penetrating insight into all beings and understands their true nature, studies the ages of order and disorder and comprehends the principle behind them. He surveys all Heaven and Earth, governs all beings, and masters the great principle and all that is in the universe.[28]

His intelligence had become "godlike" (*shen*). The Legalists had not been ambitious enough. A reformed person was not simply a cog in the economic or military machine, but a divine being. "Broad and vast—who knows the limits of such a man?" Xunzi asked. "Brilliant and comprehensive—who knows his virtue? Shadowy and ever changing—who knows his form? His brightness matches the sun and moon; his greatness fills the eight directions. Such is the Great Man."[29] A man who had fulfilled the potential of his humanity in this way could save the world.

Nobody took Xunzi's political ideas very seriously, but by the middle of the third century, everybody was talking about another mystical manual of statecraft that immediately attracted widespread attention.[30] The Legalists in particular warmed to this new text. The *Daodejing* (*Classic of the Way and Its Potency*) has become a popular devotional classic in the West, even though it was not originally written for a private individual but for the ruler of a small state. We know very little indeed about its author, who wrote under the pseudonym Laozi, "Old Master." Various stories circulated about him, none of which have much historical validity, and the author, whose theme is anonymity and selflessness, has eluded us, as he probably would have wished.

The *Daodejing* consists of eighty-one small chapters, written in enigmatic verse. Even though Laozi was far more spiritual than the Legalists, there was an affinity between them, which the Legalists spotted immediately. Both despised the Confucians; both had a paradoxical view of the world, in which goals could be achieved only by pursuing their opposites; and both believed that the ruler should "do nothing" and intervene as little as possible in the life of the state. Unlike the Legalists, Laozi wanted his king to be virtuous, but not like a Confucian sage, who was endlessly trying to *do* things for his people. Instead, a prince who practiced the self-effacement and total impartiality of *wu wei* would bring the violence of the Warring States period to an end. The ancient kings, it was said, had ruled by the magical potency that established the Way of Heaven on earth by performing a series of external ceremonies. Laozi internalized these old rites, and advised the princes to acquire an interior, spiritualized conformity with the Way.

These were terrifying times for the small principalities, which were about to be obliterated by Qin. The fear of imminent annihilation runs like a leitmotif through the *Daodejing,* which offers the vulnerable prince a stratagem for survival. Instead of posturing aggressively, he must retreat and make himself small. Instead of plotting and scheming, he must abandon thought, calm his mind, relax his body, and free himself of conventional ways of looking at the world. He must allow his problems to solve themselves by the discipline of *wu wei.*[31] But this could be achieved only if he reformed his own heart, which must be rooted in stillness and emptiness. That is why Laozi devoted thirty chapters of his book to the mystical discipline that would transform the interior life of the prince and give him the power to replenish and restore the world, as the ancient kings had done.

The very first chapter introduces us to Laozi's method. The sage ruler had to learn to think in an entirely different way. Ordinary rational thought would be useless: doctrines, theories, and systems could only impede his progress, because he had to enter a dimension that existed beyond language and concepts. Hence Laozi began:

> *The way that can be spoken of is not the constant way;*
> *The name that can be named is not the constant name.*
> *The nameless was the beginning of heaven and earth.*

Everything in the world has a name, but Laozi was speaking of what was beyond the mundane and more fundamental than anything we could conceive: it was, therefore, nameless and unseen. But most people were unaware of this hidden dimension. It could be known only by the person who had rid himself forever of desire. Somebody who had never eliminated desire from his mind and heart could see only the manifestation of this nameless reality— the visible, phenomenal world. The unseen and the manifest, however, were both rooted in a still deeper level of being, the secret essence of all things, the "Mystery upon mystery." What should we call this? Perhaps, Laozi concluded, we should call it the Dark, to remind ourselves of its profound obscurity: "the gateway of the manifold secrets!"[32]

Laozi revealed ever deeper tiers of reality, as though he were peeling the layers of an onion. Before he could begin his quest, the sage ruler had to understand the inadequacy of language; just as he thought that he had glimpsed the unseen, he was made aware of a still deeper mystery. Next, he was warned that this knowledge was not a matter of acquiring privileged information; it demanded the kenosis upon which all the great Axial sages insisted. He had to give up the "desire" that constantly clamors "I want!" Even when he had realized this, he was still only at the "gateway" of the final mystery. In placing the Way at the center of his vision, Laozi emphasized the fluidity of the spiritual life; the goal was hidden and inaccessible, and the path always had a fresh twist or turn, constantly urged us further, at the same time as it receded into the distance:

> There is a thing confusedly formed,
> Born before heaven and earth,
> Silent and void
> It stands alone and does not change,
> Goes round and does not weary.
> It is capable of being the mother of the world.
> I know not its name
> So I style it "the way."
> I give it the makeshift name of "the great."
> Being great, it is further described as receding.[33]

There was insouciance in Laozi's attempt to name this elusive, recessive "thing" to which he would give only a "makeshift" name. We could not talk about this "thing," but if we modeled ourselves upon it, it became—somehow—known to us.

Laozi's elliptical poems made no logical sense. He deliberately confused his readers by pelting them with paradox. He told them that the sublime was nameless, and yet a few lines later he said that the "named" and the "nameless" came from the same source. The sage ruler was supposed to hold these contradictions in his heart and become aware of the inadequacy of his ordinary thought processes. Laozi's chapters were not speculations, but points for meditation. He wrote down only the conclusions, and did not trace the steps that led to these insights, because the sage ruler had to journey down the Way by himself, going from the manifest to the unseen, and finally to the darkest of the dark. He could not achieve these insights at second hand, relying on other people's reports of the Way. The Chinese had their own form of yoga (*zuo-wang*), which taught them to shut out the outside world and close down their ordinary modes of perception. Zhuangzi had called this "forgetting," the discarding of knowledge. Laozi occasionally referred to these yogic disciplines,[34] but did not describe them in any detail; they were, however, essential to the mystical process he outlined. The only way the reader could evaluate his conclusions was to make the journey.

Laozi often called the unseen reality "the Void," because it could not be defined, a name that suggested an emptiness that the busy *yu wei* mind feared. Our nature abhors a vacuum, and we fill our minds with ideas, words, and thoughts that seem to be full of life but take us nowhere. In the *Daodejing,* however, the Void is also called the Womb of all being, because it brings forth new life.[35] Laozi's images of the Void, the Valley, and the Hollow all speak of something that is not there. Besides pointing to the indescribable mystery of being, they also point to the kenosis of the *wu wei* mind, once the ego has been lost. There must be a void in the being of the sage ruler. In the trance of meditation, he could experience the "emptiness" that, according to Laozi, was a return to the authentic humanity that people had enjoyed before they were infected by civilization, which had introduced a false artifice into human life. By interfering with nature, human beings had lost their Way.

While other creatures kept to the Way designed for them, humans had separated themselves from their *dao* by constant, busy *yu wei* reflection: they made distinctions that did not exist, and formulated solemn principles of action that were simply egotistical projections. Laozi agreed with Zhuangzi about this. When the sage trained himself to lay aside these mental habits, he could return to his original nature, and get back on the right path.

> *I do my utmost to attain emptiness;*
> *I hold firmly to stillness.*
> *The myriad creatures all rise together*
> *And I watch their return.*
> *The teeming creatures*
> *All return to their separate roots.*
> *Returning to one's roots is known as stillness.*[36]

Everything else returned to its origins, in the same way as the leaves fell to the roots of the tree, became compost, and reentered the cycle of life. The leaves had emerged from the unseen world, had become manifest for a while, and then returned to the dark. The enlightened sage ruler stood aloof from this flux. Once he had aligned himself with the unseen, he attained perfect wisdom and impartiality. He can identify himself with the Way, the poem concluded; "he can endure, and to the end of his days will meet with no danger."[37]

Emptiness brought a release from the fear that pervaded the *Daodejing*. The ruler who dreaded annihilation was afraid of a chimera. We should not fear nothingness, because it was at the heart of reality. "The thirty spokes of the wheel share one hub," Laozi pointed out, "but it is where there is nothing [the hole for the axle] that the efficacy of the cart lies."[38] So too, when making a pot, we kneaded the clay into an attractive shape, but the raison d'être of the vessel was the place where there was nothing. Laozi concludes:

> *Thus we think we benefit from perceptible things*
> *But it is where we perceive nothing that true efficacy lies.*[39]

It was the same with public policy. Once he had discovered the fertile Void within himself, the prince was ready to rule. He had attained a "kingliness" modeled on Heaven and the *dao*.[40] The sage ruler must behave like Heaven, which pursued its own inscrutable course without interfering with the Ways of other creatures. This is the Way things ought to be, and this—not ceaseless, purposeful activism—would bring peace to the world.

Everywhere rulers, politicians, and administrative officials were plotting and scheming. Many of the philosophers had done more harm than good. Mohists stressed the importance of analysis, strategy, and action. Confucians glorified the culture that, Laozi believed, had interrupted the flow of the *dao*. The Confucian heroes Yao, Shun, and Yu had constantly meddled with nature—by directing the flow of rivers, and setting fire to forests and mountains to create arable land. By imposing their rituals on society, Confucians had encouraged people to concentrate on a purely external spirituality. There was far too much goal-directed, *yu wei* activity; it was incompatible with the gentle, unassertive and spontaneous course of the Way, which let creatures alone:

> *The way never acts, yet nothing is left undone.*
> *Should lords and princes be able to hold on to it,*
> *The myriad creatures will be transformed of their own accord.*

And, the Daoist ruler concluded: "If I cease to desire and remain still, the empire will be at peace of its own accord."[41]

The secret of survival was to act counterintuitively.[42] In political life, people always preferred frenzied activity to doing nothing, knowledge to ignorance, and strength to weakness, but—to the astonishment of his contemporaries, who were intrigued with this novel idea[43]—Laozi insisted that they should do the exact opposite.

> *In the world there is nothing more submissive and*
>   *weak than water*
> *Yet for attacking that which is hard and strong nothing*
>   *can surpass it.*
> *This is because there is nothing that can take its place.*
>   *That the weak overcomes the strong,*
>   *And the submissive overcomes the hard,*
> *Everyone in the world knows, yet no one can put this*
>   *knowledge into practice.*[44]

All human effort was directed against passivity, so to do the opposite of what was expected by the aggressively scheming politicians was to return to the spontaneity of the Way.[45] It was a law of nature that everything that went up must come down, so in strengthening your enemy by submission, you actually hastened his decline. The reason why Heaven and Earth endured forever was precisely because they did not struggle to prolong their existence:

> Therefore the sage puts his person last and comes
> first. . . .
> Is it not because he is without thought of self that he
> is able to accomplish his private ends?[46]

Such self-emptying required a long mystical training, but once the sage ruler had achieved this interior void, he would become as vital, fluid, and fecund as the so-called weaker things of life.

Force and coercion were inherently self-destructive. Here Laozi returned to the spirit of the ancient rituals of warfare, which had urged the warriors to "yield" to the enemy. "Arms are ill-omened instruments, and are not the instruments of the sage," Laozi maintained. "He uses them only when he cannot do otherwise."[47] Sometimes war was a regrettable necessity, but if he was forced to fight, the sage must always take up his weapons with regret. There must be no egotistic triumphalism, no cruel chauvinism, and no facile patriotism. The sage must not intimidate the world with a show of arms, because this belligerence would almost certainly recoil on him. The sage must always try to bring a military expedition to an end. "Bring it to a conclusion, but do not boast; bring it to a conclusion, but do not brag; bring it to a conclusion, but do not be arrogant; bring it to a conclusion, but only where there is no choice; bring it to a conclusion, but do not intimidate."[48]

Wu wei, therefore, did not mean total abstinence from action, but an unaggressive, unassertive attitude that prevented the escalation of hatred.

> *The good leader in war is not warlike*
> *The good fighter is not impetuous;*
> *The best conqueror of the enemy is he who never*
>   *takes the offensive.*
> *The man who gets the most out of men is the one*
>   *who treats them with humility.*[49]

This, Laozi concluded, "is what I call the virtue [*de*] of non-violence," and by acting in this way, Laozi concluded, the sage warrior "matched the sublimity of Heaven."[50]

It was our attitude, not our action, that determined the outcome of what we did. People were always able to sense the feeling and motivation that lay behind our words and deeds. The sage must learn to absorb hostility; if he retaliated to an atrocity there would certainly be a fresh attack. Challenges must be ignored. "To yield is to be preserved whole. . . . Because [the sage] does not contend, no one in the world is in a position to contend with him."[51] Tyrants were digging their own grave, because when a prince tried to act upon other human beings, they automatically resisted him, and the result was usually the opposite of what was intended. *Wu wei* must be combined with humility. The sage did not trumpet his principles from the rooftops; indeed, he had no fixed opinions. The sage did not try to make the people become what *he* wanted them to be, but "takes as his own the mind of the people."[52] Laozi was convinced that human nature was originally kind and good. It had become violent only when people had felt coerced by elaborate laws and moral codes.[53] Whenever he encountered the aggression of a bigger state, the sage ruler must ask whether hatred was breeding more hatred, or whether it was weakening in response to compassion, a virtue that Laozi rarely mentioned explicitly but that was implicit in his striving to put himself in the place of the other:

> *The reason there is great affliction is that I have a self.*
> *If I had no self, what affliction would I have?*
> *Therefore to one who honours the world as his self*

The world may be entrusted,
And to one who loves the world as one's self
The world may be consigned.[54]

Laozi was the last great Chinese sage of the Axial Age. His was an essentially utopian ideal. It is difficult to see how a sage who had reached this level of "emptiness" would ever come to power, since he would be incapable of the calculation that was necessary to win office.[55] Like Mencius, Laozi may have nurtured some kind of messianic hope that the horrors of his time would impel the people to gravitate spontaneously toward a mystically inclined ruler. But, of course, it was not a Daoist sage but the Legalist state of Qin that ended the violence of the Warring States and unified the empire. This spectacular success seemed to prove that universal kingship could not be achieved without recourse to military power. It brought a peace of sorts, but spelt the death knell to the Axial hopes for morality, benevolence, and nonviolence. Under the empire, the Axial spiritualities would effect a synthesis and transmute into something quite different.

The Chinese were isolated from the other Axial peoples, so they knew nothing about the extraordinary career of Alexander the Great, Aristotle's old pupil, who conquered the Persian empire in 333 when he routed the army of Darius III at the river Issus in Cilicia. He then led his army on a rampage through Asia, creating an empire that included most of the known world. His progress had been violent and ruthless. He brooked no opposition, but mercilessly destroyed any cities that had the temerity to stand in his way and massacred their populations. His empire was based on fear, and yet Alexander had a vision of political and cultural unity. But the empire did not survive his early death in Babylonia in 323. Almost immediately fighting broke out among his leading generals, and for the next two decades the lands conquered by Alexander were devastated by the battles of these six *diadochoi* ("successors"). The "peace" of the empire had given way to destructive warfare. Finally, at the very end of the century, two of the *diadochoi* eliminated the others and divided Alexander's territories between them. Ptolemy, one of the most shrewd of Alexander's generals, took Egypt, the African coast, Palestine, and southern Syria, while Seleucus, who had been appointed satrap of Babylonia by Alexander, controlled large parts of the old Persian empire, including Iran. Seleucus settled the far eastern boundary by relinquishing the Indian territories, which proved impossible to maintain.

Alexander made little impression on the people of India. He conquered only a few minor tribes, and his invasion was not even mentioned by some of the early Indian historians. His achievement was not the conquest of India, but the feat of actually getting there, and his two years in India were more of a geographical expedition than a military campaign. Alexander seemed the embodiment of the Greek ethos. He had been brought up on the Homeric myths, inspired by the ideals of Athens, and tutored by Aristotle. Greece had not participated as fully in the religious vision of the Axial Age as the other regions. Some of its most startling "axial" achievements had been military. Alexander's two-year adventure in India was another such moment: a Greek army had reached what they regarded as the end of the earth. They had pitted themselves against the ultimate as bravely as the yogins had struggled to break through the limits of the human psyche. Where mystics had conquered interior space, Alexander explored the farthest reaches of the physical world. Like many of the Axial sages, he was constantly "straining after more."[56] He wanted to go farther into India than the Persian kings, and reach the ocean that, he believed, circled the earth. It was the kind of "enlightenment" that would always appeal to Western explorers[57] but very different from the *nibbana* or *moksha,* characterized by self-effacement, *ahimsa,* and compassion, sought by the Indian mystics.

The Greek soldiers were enthralled and terrified by the magnificence of India, with its fearsome monsoons, its astonishing war elephants, blazing summers, and intractable mountain passes. They were especially intrigued by the "naked philosophers" they encountered, who may have been Jains. But even though the Indians had no enduring interest in the Greeks, Alexander and his successors decisively changed the fortunes of some of the other peoples we have met in this book. The Zoroastrians of Iran remembered Alexander as the worst sinner in history, because he killed so many priests and scholars and stamped out so many of their sacred fires. He was the "accursed" (*guzustag*), a title that he alone shares with the Hostile Spirit. The slaughter of the priests was an irreparable loss: Zoroastrian texts were still transmitted orally; many existed only in the minds of the murdered priests, and could never be recovered.

The Jews were more affected by the *diadochoi* than by Alexander himself. Since the time of Ezra and Nehemiah, Jerusalem had remained a backwater. It was not on any of the main trade routes: the caravans that stopped at Petra or Gaza had no reason to go to Jerusalem, which lacked the raw materials to develop its own industry. But during the wars of the *diadochoi,* Judea was continually invaded by one army after another, from Asia Minor, Syria, and Egypt, with their baggage, equipment, families, and slaves. Jerusalem itself changed hands no less than six times between 320 and 301. The Jews of Jerusalem experienced the Greeks as destructive, violent, and militaristic. In 301, Judea, Samerina, Phoenicia, and the entire coastal plain were captured by the armies of Ptolemy I Soter, and for the next hundred years, Jerusalem remained under the control of the Ptolemies, who did not, however, interfere much in local affairs.

But the region was changing. Alexander and his successors founded new cities in the Near East, which became centers of Hellenistic learning and culture: Alexandria in Egypt, Antioch in Syria, and Pergamum in Asia Minor. These were Greek poleis, which usually excluded the native inhabitants and were built on a scale never seen before in the Hellenic world. This was the cosmopolis, the "world city." It was a great age of migration. Greeks no longer felt wedded to the small city-state of their birth. Alexander's heroic expedition had expanded their horizons, and many now felt that they were cosmopolitans, citizens of the world. Greeks became world travelers, as merchants, mercenaries, and ambassadors, and many began to find the polis petty and

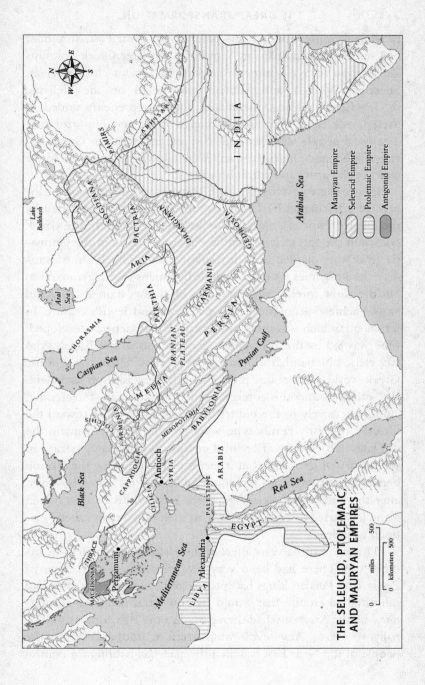

THE SELEUCID, PTOLEMAIC,
AND MAURYAN EMPIRES

Mauryan Empire

Seleucid Empire

Ptolemaic Empire

Antigonid Empire

provincial. Some founded new poleis in the Near East. Alexander had settled Macedonians in Samerina, and later Greek colonists also arrived in Syria and converted such ancient cities as Gaza, Shechem, Marissa, and Amman into poleis on the Hellenic model. Greek soldiers, merchants, and entrepreneurs settled in these Greek enclaves to take advantage of the new opportunities. The local people who learned to speak and write in Greek became "Hellenes" themselves, and were allowed to enter the lower ranks of the army and administration.

Hence there developed a clash of civilizations. Some of the locals were fascinated by Greek culture. Others were horrified by the secular tenor of polis life, the immoral activities of the Greek gods, and the spectacle of youths exercising naked in the gymnasia. Jews were divided in their response to the Greeks. In Alexandria, the Ptolemies refused to admit Egyptians to the gymnasium, but did allow foreigners to enter, so local Jews trained there and would achieve a unique fusion of Greek and Jewish culture. In Jerusalem, which was more conservative, two factions developed. One was led by the Tobiad clan, descendants of the Tobiah who had caused Nehemiah so much trouble. They felt at home in the Greek world, and became pioneers of the new ideas in Jerusalem. But others found this foreign influence extremely threatening, clung defensively to the old traditions, and gravitated toward the Oniads, a priestly family who were determined to maintain the old laws and customs. The third century is a shadowy period in the history of Jerusalem, but it seems that at this time the tension between the two camps remained under control. Later, however, after the end of the Axial Age, there was serious conflict, when some Jews tried to convert Jerusalem itself into a polis called "Antioch in Judea."

These turbulent years affected the history of Jerusalem in another way. There had been very few rebellions against imperial Persia. The Persian kings had propagated the myth that they had inherited an empire that would last forever: it had been inaugurated by the Assyrians, had then passed to the Babylonians, and finally, to Cyrus. Any revolt was, therefore, doomed. But as the people of the Near East watched the *diadochoi* battling for control of the region, one succeeding another, their mood changed. The world had been turned upside down, and some Jews began to entertain hopes of independence under their own *messiach*. When in 201 the Ptolemies were ousted from Judea by the Seleucids, these hopes flared again. The behavior of the Seleucid king Antiochus IV in the second century resulted in a surge of Jewish apocalyptic passion, which drew on the ancient theology of the Davidic monarchy. But this messianic piety had no roots in the Axial Age, and took Judaism in a different, post–Axial direction.

Alexander had won his empire at the peak of Greek intellectual achievement and his career marked the beginning of a new era. After his death, some poleis on the Greek mainland, including Athens, revolted against Macedonian rule, and Antipater, one of the six original *diadochoi,* took savage reprisals. This finished Athenian democracy. As Greek migrants and colonists settled in the new territories, Greek civilization began to merge with the cultures of the east. Scholars of the nineteenth century called this fusion "Hellenism." The challenge of this encounter was enriching, but in the process the intensity of the Greek experiment became diluted. Spread thinly over such a huge, foreign area, it fragmented and became Greek*ish* rather than truly Greek. Any period of major social change is troubled. The collapse of the old order and the inevitable political disruption were disturbing.[58] There was widespread bewilderment and malaise. Personal and political autonomy had always been crucial to the Greeks' sense of identity, but now their world had expanded so dramatically that people felt that their destiny was controlled by vast impersonal forces.

During the third century, three new philosophies, rooted in the pain of the period, tried to assuage this sense of alienation.[59] Epicurus (341–270), for example, experienced very little security for the first thirty-five years of his life. His family was expelled from Samos by the Macedonians, and he wandered from one polis to another before arriving in Athens in 306. There he bought a house with a garden near the Academy, and founded a community of close friends. Pleasure, he taught, was the chief goal of human existence, but this did not mean, as his detractors assumed, that he flung himself into a hectic round of hedonistic delights. In fact, the community adopted a quiet, simple regime in "the Garden." Pleasure did not consist in sensuality and self-indulgence, but in *ataraxia* ("freedom from pain"). Epicureans shunned all mental disturbances. Life in the polis was so tense and unpredictable that those who had the means should withdraw from public affairs and enjoy a peaceful existence with congenial people. They must avoid anything that caused them distress, including the superstitious belief in fickle deities who inflicted such great suffering on hapless men and women. Above all, Epicureans should not allow their mortality to poison their minds. They must realize that death was simply the extinction of consciousness, "seeing that when we exist, death is not present, and when death is present we do not exist," Epicurus pointed out. It was pointless to worry about it. "A correct understanding that death is nothing to us makes the mortality of life enjoyable, not by adding infinite time, but by ridding us of the desire for immortality."[60]

At the same time that Epicurus and his friends were enjoying retirement in the Garden, Zeno (342–270), a Hellenized Phoenician from Cyprus, was teaching in the Painted Stoa, a porch in the Athenian agora. Hence he and his followers were known as Stoics. Zeno had been greatly inspired by the extraordinary moment when Alexander had seemed to unite the world under his rule. The cosmos, he believed, was a unity. There was no split between body and spirit; the whole of reality was physical, animated, and organized by a sort of fiery, vaporous breath, which he called the Logos ("Reason"), the Pneuma ("Spirit"), or God. This intelligent, divine force pervaded everything. It was wholly immanent. Human beings could achieve happiness only by living in accordance with the rational Logos, which was revealed in the natural order. Freedom consisted in surrender to the will of God; since God had predetermined everything, it was useless to rebel against fate. The correct attitude was one of resigned acquiescence. Stoics should travel lightly through life, indifferent to their external circumstances. They must cultivate an inner peace, avoid all occasions of disquiet, do their duty conscientiously, conduct themselves with sobriety, and avoid all extremes. The objective was to live in harmony with the inexorable processes of the divine Logos, not to work against them.

Ataraxia was also the goal of Pyrrho of Elis (c. 365–275), founder of the Skeptics. We know very little about him. He wrote nothing and indeed no Skeptical texts were produced until about five hundred years after his death. Pyrrho seems to have insisted that it was impossible to be certain about anything, so the best way to live at peace was to suspend judgment. People who were dogmatic and self-assertive were doomed to unhappiness. "Nothing is honourable or base or just or unjust," he is reported to have said. "Convention and habit are the basis of everything that men do, for each thing is no more this than that."[61] This was inconsistent, of course. If it was true that we knew nothing, how could Pyrrho know that even this was true—or evolve a philosophy at all? But Pyrrho apparently saw Skepticism as a therapy, not as an epistemological theory. People became too agitated by their strong opinions; they were too anxious to discover the truth. So a Skeptic would kindly undermine their certainty, flushing all this intellectual turmoil out of their systems. Sextus Empiricus, the first Skeptical writer, who lived in the third century CE, explained that Pyrrho and his disciples began by trying to find truth in order to gain peace of mind. But when they were unable to achieve this to their satisfaction, they gave up and immediately felt much better. "When they suspended judgement, tranquillity followed as it were fortuitously, as a shadow follows a body."[62] So they became known as *skeptikoi* ("inquirers") because they were still looking, had not closed their minds, but had learned that an uncluttered attitude, open to all possibilities, was the secret of happiness.

The Axial Age was well and truly over for these Hellenistic philosophers, and yet in their work we find ghostly relics of the great pioneering spiritualities that sages and prophets had been exploring for more than five hundred years. The heroic striving of Confucius, the Buddha, Ezekiel, and Socrates had been replaced by a more modest, attainable, and, as it were, "budget" version. In Zeno's ideal of a life attuned to nature, there was a hint of Daoism, but instead of yearning to change the world by aligning himself with the natural process, the Stoic simply resigned himself to the status quo. There is a fatalism in all these third-century Greek philosophies that was anathema to the Axial Age. The Buddha had warned his disciples not to become attached to metaphysical opinions; the mystics of the Upanishads had reduced their interlocutors to silence by pointing out the fallacy of rational thought, but they had not simply "suspended judgement" like the Skeptics. They had used the experience of dismantling ordinary habits of thought to give people intimations of a mystery that lay beyond words and conceptual ideas. The renouncers of India had left the world behind, but not to live in the suburban Epicurean Garden, and the Buddha had insisted that his monks must return to the agora and practice compassion for all living beings.

Herein lay the difference. These Hellenistic philosophers made no heroic ethical demands. They all claimed to lay aside the abstruse metaphysics of Plato and Aristotle and go back to Socrates, who had tried to teach men how to live. They wanted the peace of mind that Socrates had possessed when he had faced his unjust death with equanimity. They were also popularizers like Socrates, who had talked to everybody, learned and uneducated alike. But Socrates had never claimed that a human being's sole aim should be to eliminate disturbance. Zeno, Epicurus, and Pyrrho all wanted a quiet life and were determined to avoid the extremity and striving of the great Axial philosophers. They simply wanted *ataraxia,* to be trouble-free. The Axial sages all pointed out that existence was inherently unsatisfactory and painful, and wanted to transcend this suffering. But they were not content merely to avoid distress and stop caring about anything or anybody; they had insisted that salvation lay in facing up to suffering, not retreating into denial. In Epicurus's sequestered Garden, there is more than a hint of the Buddha's pleasure park. The similarity becomes more pointed when we reflect that most Epicureans had private means to finance their retreat, which would not have been available to the hoi polloi.

Instead of seeking *ataraxia,* the Axial thinkers had forced their contemporaries to accept the reality of pain. Jeremiah had denounced those who retreated into denial as "false prophets." The

tragedians of Athens had put suffering onstage and commanded
the audience to weep. You could achieve liberation only by going
through sorrow, not by going to elaborate lengths to make sure that
it never impinged on your protected existence. The experience of
dukkha was a prerequisite for enlightenment, because it enabled
the aspirant to empathize with the grief of others. But the Hellenistic philosophies were entirely focused on the self. True, the
Stoics were urged to take part in public life and work generously
for the good of others. But they were not allowed to empathize
with the people they served, because that would disturb their
equilibrium. This cold self-sufficiency was alien to the Axial Age.
Friendship and kindness were crucial to Epicurus's commune, but
they were not extended outside the Garden. And however kindly
intentioned, there was more than a hint of aggression in the Skeptics' therapy, as they went around picking arguments with other
people in order to undermine their convictions. The approach
was markedly different from that of the Buddha and Socrates, who
always started from where their interlocutors actually were, not
where they thought they ought to be.

Many Axial thinkers were mistrustful of pure *logos* and reason,
but the Hellenistic philosophies were based on science rather than
intuition. Epicurus, for example, developed the atomism of Democritus to show that it was a waste of the precious lives we had to
fear death, which would inevitably occur when the atoms fell
apart. It was pointless to ask the gods for help, because they too
were composed of and ruled by the atoms. The Stoics taught that
it was possible to align yourself with the divine process of nature
only if you understood scientifically that it was programmed by
the Logos and could not be altered. The third century was the
great age of Greek science. The new Hellenistic kingdoms of
Ptolemy and Seleucus were far richer than the old poleis, and
kings vied with one another to attract scholars to their capitals,
bribing them with grants and salaries. Euclid and Archimedes
both lived and worked in Alexandria. The Milesian and Eleatic
philosophers had concentrated on those aspects of natural science
that related to human beings, rather like popular scientists today,
whereas the new scientists of the third century were at the cutting

edge of mathematics, physics, astronomy, and engineering. Science had now lost its early religious orientation and become a wholly secular pursuit.

The Hellenistic philosophies did not affect the old pagan religion: sacrifices, festivals, and rituals continued without interruption. The mysteries became even more popular, and were often combined with congenial eastern cults. In 399, Socrates had been executed for turning people away from the traditional gods. After the fourth century, no philosopher was persecuted for his religious views, even though Epicurus, Zeno, and Pyrrho attempted to discredit the old beliefs. There was a new tolerance that was never officially endorsed by the establishment, but that gained ground among the elite.[63] Most people continued to practice the ancient rites, which remained largely untouched by the Axial Age and would remain in place until Christianity was forcibly imposed as the state religion in the fifth century CE.

The Hellenistic philosophers may not have been as revolutionary as their predecessors, but they had lasting influence, and in many ways they epitomized the emerging Western spirit. In the West, people gravitated toward science and *logos,* and were less spiritually ambitious than the sages of India and China. Instead of making the heroic effort to discover a realm of transcendent peace within, the Hellenistic philosophers were prepared to settle for a quiet life. Instead of training the intuitive powers of the mind, they turned to scientific *logos.* Instead of achieving mystical enlightenment, the West was excited by a more mundane illumination. The Western genius for science eventually transformed the world, and in the sixteenth century its scientific revolution introduced a new Axial Age. This would greatly benefit humanity, but it was inspired by a different species of genius. Instead of the Buddha, Socrates, and Confucius, the heroes of the second Axial Age would be Newton, Freud, and Einstein.

A new empire had also been established in India, but it was very different from Alexander's. Magadha had dominated the Ganges

Valley since the fourth century, and had greatly expanded its territory under the powerful Nanda dynasty. But in 321, Chandragupta Maurya, a *vaishya* who may have come from one of the tribal republics, seized the throne, having already established a power base in the Punjab, where the Greeks' departure had left a power vacuum. We know very little about either his reign or his military campaign, but the Mauryan empire eventually extended from Bengal to Afghanistan, and Chandragupta then began to penetrate central and southern India. Coming from the more peripheral tribal states, the Mauryan emperors had no strong links with Vedic religion, and were more interested in the nonorthodox sects. Chandragupta himself favored the Jains, who accompanied his army and established themselves in the south. His son Bindusara Maurya promoted the Ajivakas, while the third emperor, Ashoka, who succeeded to the throne in 268, patronized the Buddhists, and his brother Vitashoka actually became a Buddhist monk. Pali sources claim that before his conversion, Ashoka had been a cruel, self-indulgent ruler, who managed to win the throne only by killing his other brothers. On his accession, he assumed the title Devanampiya, "the Beloved of the Gods," and continued to conquer new territory until he suffered a severe shock.

In 260 the Mauryan army conquered Kalinga in the region of modern Orissa. Ashoka recorded his victory in an edict, which he had inscribed on a massive rock face. He said nothing about his military strategy, and instead of celebrating his victory, he dwelt on the tragic number of casualties. One hundred thousand Kalingan soldiers had been killed during the battle; "many times that number" perished afterward from wounds and hunger, and 150,000 Kalingans had been deported. Ashoka was devastated by the spectacle of such suffering. The "Beloved of the Gods," he said, felt remorse,

> for when an independent country is conquered, the
> slaughter, death and deportation is extremely grievous
> to *Devanampiya* and weighs heavily on his mind. . . .
> Even those who were fortunate enough to have es-

caped, and whose love is undiminished, suffer from the misfortunes of their friends, acquaintances, colleagues and relatives. . . . Today if a hundredth or a thousandth part of those people who were killed or died or were deported when Kalinga was annexed were to suffer similarly, it would weigh heavily on the mind of *Devanampiya*.[64]

The purpose of the edict was to warn other kings against undertaking further wars of conquest. If they did lead a campaign, it must be fought humanely, and victory should be implemented "with patience and light punishment." The only true conquest was *dhamma,* by which Ashoka meant a moral effort that would benefit people in this life and the next.[65]

This was a significant moment. The *Arthashastra,* a manual of statecraft composed by the Brahmin Kautilya, the mentor of Chandragupta Maurya, made it clear that the conquest of neighboring territories was one of the king's sacred duties. Ashoka, however, proposed to replace military might with *ahimsa*. There is some doubt about the details of this incident. Ashoka probably exaggerated the casualty figures: the Mauryan army was only sixty thousand strong, so it is hard to see how it could have killed a hundred thousand Kalingans. It was well disciplined and did not usually harass noncombatants. If Ashoka was so distressed by the plight of the deportees, why did he not simply repatriate them? He may have wanted to deter rebellion by emphasizing the magnitude and ruthlessness of his victory, and he certainly did not abjure all warfare from that day forward. In other edicts, Ashoka admitted that war was sometimes necessary, and never disbanded his army.[66]

But perhaps this is to expect too much. It is clear that Ashoka was truly shaken by the violence and suffering in Kalinga, and that he tried to introduce a policy based on *dhamma*. He now ruled an Indian kingdom of unprecedented size. Throughout the length and breadth of his territory he inscribed edicts outlining his innovative policy on cliff faces and pillars. They were prominently sited and probably read aloud to the populace on state occasions.

Written in Pali, inscribed with animal figures and such motifs as the Buddhists' wheel, each one begins, "Thus speaks the Beloved of the Gods," and preaches a humane ethic of nonviolence and moral reform. The extent of these edicts is amazing; it is comparable to finding identical runes in the Grampians, Italy, Germany, and Gibraltar.[67]

The fact that Ashoka felt that such a policy was feasible suggests that the Axial virtues of compassion and *ahimsa* had taken firm root, even if they could never be fully implemented by a politician. Ashoka may sincerely have believed that violence simply bred more violence, and that slaughter and conquest could only backfire. His *dhamma* was not specifically Buddhist but could appeal to any of the main schools. Ashoka probably hoped to promote a policy based on consensus, which could bind the subjects of his far-flung empire together. The *dhamma* did not mention the uniquely Buddhist doctrine of *anatta* ("no self") or the practice of yoga, but concentrated on the virtues of kindness and benevolence.[68] "There is no gift comparable to the gift of *dhamma* . . . the sharing of *dhamma*," Ashoka wrote in the Eleventh Major Rock Edict. This consisted of

> good behaviour towards slaves and servants, obedience
> to mother and father, generosity towards friends, ac-
> quaintances and relatives, and towards renouncers and
> brahmins, and abstention from killing living beings. Fa-
> ther, son, brother, master, friend, acquaintance, relative
> and neighbour should say "this is good, this we shall do."
> By doing so, there is gain in this world and in the next
> there is infinite merit through the gift of *dhamma*.[69]

Far from imposing Buddhism on his subjects, the edicts insisted that there must be no religious chauvinism. Brahmins were to be honored as well as those renouncers who rejected the Vedic system. The king "honours all sects and both ascetics and laymen with gifts and recognition," reads the Twelfth Major Rock Edict. "The advancement of the essential doctrines of all the rest" was of the greatest importance. Nobody must disparage anybody else's teaching. In this way, all the different schools could flourish. "Concord is to be commended, so that men may hear one another's principles."[70]

Ashoka was a realist. He did not outlaw violence; there were occasions when it might be unavoidable—if, for example, the forest dwellers stirred up trouble. Capital punishment remained an option. But Ashoka did cut down on the consumption of meat in his household and listed birds, animals, and fish that could not be hunted. It was a brave experiment, but it failed. During the last ten years of his reign, Ashoka made no new inscriptions, and his vast empire may already have been falling apart. After his death in 231, the *dhamma* lapsed. Social tensions and sectarian conflicts set in, and the empire began to disintegrate. It has been suggested that Ashoka's preoccupation with nonviolence emasculated the army and made the state vulnerable to invasion, but Ashoka was never doctrinaire about *ahimsa*. It is more likely that the empire simply outgrew its resources. Ashoka was never forgotten. In Buddhist tradition, he is a *chakkavatti*, a universal king whose reign turned the wheel of law. Later leaders, such as Guru Nanek, founder of Sikhism, and Mahatma Gandhi, would revive the ideal of concord and unity across sectarian and social divides.

After Ashoka's death, India entered a dark age. Even though a number of documents survived, we have little reliable information about the kingdoms and dynasties that rose and fell during these centuries of political instability, which lasted until the accession of the Gupta dynasty in 320 CE. But we do know that India experienced major spiritual change. During this time, Indian religion became theistic, and the people discovered God. The stark, aniconic religion of the Vedas and the renouncers, which had so drastically reduced the role of the gods, had given way to the Hindu extravaganza of brilliantly painted temples, colorful processions, popular pilgrimages, and devotion to the images of a multitude of exotic deities.

The first sign of this development can be seen in the Shvetashvatara Upanishad, the teachings of "the Sage with the white mule," which was probably composed in the late fourth century. Traditional Vedic religion had never been very visual. Even in their heyday, nobody had been particularly interested in what Indra or Vishnu had looked like. People had experienced the divine in chants and mantras, not in statues and icons. The Shvetashvatara Upanishad is strongly influenced by the teachings of Samkhya yoga, an originally atheistic school, but here brahman, the absolute reality, was identified with the personalized god Rudra/Shiva, and it was he who would liberate the yogin from the painful cycle of samsara. When he achieved this *moksha,* the enlightened yogin would *see* the deity within himself.

This was probably not a complete innovation. Vedic religion had been practiced and promoted by the upper classes, but it is possible that ordinary worshipers had always made images of the gods in perishable materials that did not survive.[71] By the end of the Axial Age, this popular faith, which may have existed continuously ever since the days of the Indus Valley civilization, had begun to fuse with the sophisticated practices of the sages. In the Rig Veda, Rudra was a very marginal god. Now, merged with the indigenous god Shiva, he had come to the foreground as the personalized embodiment of brahman and the Lord of the universe, who made himself known to his devotees in the practice of yoga. The yogin could break the bonds of samsara only by becoming one with the Lord, the ruler of nature and the self (atman): "When he comes to know God, he is freed from all fetters. . . . By meditating on him, by striving toward him, and further in the end by becoming the same reality as him, all illusion disappears."[72] All impediments fell away, and at the moment of death the self was indissolubly united to Lord Rudra.

The Lord was not simply a transcendent being but lived within the self, in rather the same way as the form (*murti*) of fire was potentially present in wood: we could not see it until the friction of the fire drill caused the flame to blaze forth. The Lord resided within us like oil in sesame seeds or butter in curds. Meditation brought the yogin into direct contact with "the true nature of the *brahman,*" which was no longer an impersonal reality, but the "unborn, unchanging" Rudra, the mountain dweller.[73] He was even "higher than *brahman,* the immense one hidden in all beings, in each according to its kind, and who alone encompasses the whole universe."[74] Yet Rudra was also "the size of a thumb," hiding within the self.[75] Meditation had enabled the yogin to see the god's physical form (*murti*) in the deeper regions of his personality.

To create a coherent theistic vision, the Shvetashvatara Upanishad drew upon a number of diverse spiritualities: on the Upanishadic notion of the identity of brahman and atman, on the concepts of rebirth and *moksha,* on Samkhya, yoga, and the chanting of the sacred syllable Om. It joined all these a-theistic disciplines with the image of the creator god. In later, classical Hinduism, this synthesis would create a new theology, which could be applied to any deity, not merely to Rudra/Shiva. The specific identity of the Lord in question was less important than the fact that he had become accessible in meditation. The yogin knew that this god existed, not because of a set of metaphysical proofs, but because he had seen him.

In the very last verse of the Shvetashvatara, we find an important new word. The Upanishad explained that the liberation it described would shine forth "only in a man who has the deepest love [*bhakti*] for God and who shows the same love towards his teacher."[76] A religious revolution was afoot. People who felt excluded from the abstruse mysticism of the Upanishads and the world-renouncing ascetics were beginning to create a spirituality that suited their way of life. They wanted to participate in the insights of the Axial Age, but needed a less abstract and more emotive religion. So they developed the notion of *bhakti* ("devotion") to a deity who loved and cared for his worshipers.[77] The central act of *bhakti* was self-surrender: devotees stopped resisting the Lord and, conscious of their helplessness, were confident that their god would help them.

The word *bhakti* is complex. Some scholars believe that it comes from *bharij,* "separation": people became aware of a gulf between them and the divine, and yet, at the same time, the god of their choice slowly detached himself from the cosmos he created and confronted them, person to person. Other scholars believe that the word relates to *bhaj*—to share, participate in—as the yogin in the Shvetashvatara becomes one with Lord Rudra. At this stage *bhakti* was still in its infancy. A crucial text was the *Bhagavad-Gita,* which—some scholars believe—was written during the late third century. It developed the theology of the Shvetashvatara Upanishad, taking it in a new direction that had a profound effect on the Hindu spirituality that emerged during the dark age.

The *Bhagavad-Gita* ("The Song of the Lord") may originally have been a separate text, but at some point it was inserted into the sixth book of the *Mahabharata.* It takes the form of a dialogue between Arjuna, the greatest warrior of the Pandava brothers, and his friend Krishna. The terrible war that Yudishthira, Arjuna's eldest brother, had hoped to avoid was about to begin. Standing in his war chariot, with Krishna as his driver, Arjuna gazed in horror at the battlefield. Until this point in the story, Arjuna had been less disturbed than Yudishthira about the prospect of war, but now he was struck by the enormity of what was about to happen. The family was tragically divided against itself; the Pandavas were about to attack their kinsfolk. According to ancient teaching, a warrior who killed his relatives consigned the entire family to hell. He would rather give up the kingdom than slaughter his brave cousins and his beloved teachers Bhishma and Drona. There would be anarchy; the social order would be destroyed. If he was responsible for the death of his cousins, he would never know happiness again, and evil would haunt the Pandavas for the rest of their lives. "What use to us is kingship, delights, or life itself," he asked Krishna.[78] It would be far more glorious to be killed in battle, unarmed, and offering no resistance.

> *Saying this in the time of war*
> *Arjuna slumped into his chariot*
> *And laid down his bow and arrows*
> *His mind tormented with grief.*[79]

The *Bhagavad-Gita* was one of the last great texts of the Axial Age, and it marks a moment of religious transition. As so often in our story, a new religious insight was inspired by revulsion from violence. Krishna tried to put some heart into Arjuna by citing all the traditional arguments for war. The warriors who fell in the coming battle would not really die, he said, because the atman was eternal; and since a warrior who died in battle would go straight to heaven, Arjuna would be doing his cousins a favor. If he refused to fight, Arjuna could be accused of cowardice and, more seriously, would violate the dharma of the *kshatriya* class. As a warrior, it was his sacred duty to fight. It was required of him by the gods, by the divine order of the universe, and by society. Like his brother Yudishthira, Arjuna was facing the tragic dilemma of the *kshatriya* dharma. The emperor Ashoka had been committed to nonviolence but he could not decommission his army. Brahmin priests could abjure warfare; renouncers could turn their backs on the whole sorry mess and take refuge in the forest. But somebody had to defend the community, and to preserve law and order. That, most unfortunately, would mean fighting, if only in self-defense. How could a warrior do his sacred duty to society without incurring the bad effects of the violent karma that he was forced to commit?

Arjuna was not impressed by Krishna's first set of arguments. "I will not fight!" he insisted.[80] Warfare on this scale must be wrong. It could not be right to shed blood for worldly gain. Perhaps he should become a renouncer? But he respected Krishna, and turned back to him in desperation, begging for his help. In agreeing to be Arjuna's guru, Krishna had the difficult job of countering the arguments of the Jains, the Buddhists, and those ascetics who believed that all worldly action was incompatible with liberation. But this meant that the vast majority had no hope of salvation. Arjuna had put his finger on a major flaw of the Indian Axial Age. Krishna wanted him to consider the problem from a different perspective, but instead of proposing a wholly new teaching that canceled out the other schools, he attempted a new synthesis of the old spiritual disciplines with the new concept of *bhakti*.

Krishna proposed that Arjuna practice an alternative kind of yoga: karma-yoga. He made a shocking suggestion: even a warrior who was fighting a deadly battle could achieve *moksha*. To achieve this, he had to dissociate himself from the effect of his action—in this case the battle, and the death of his kinsfolk. Like any yogin, the man of action (karma) must give up desire. He could not permit himself to lust after the fame, wealth, or power that would result from the military campaign. It was not the actions themselves that bound human beings to the endless round of rebirth, but attachment to the fruits of these deeds. The warrior must perform his duty without hope of personal gain, showing the same detachment as a yogin:

> Be intent on action
> Not on the fruits of action;
> Avoid attraction to the fruits
> And attachment to inaction!
>
> Perform actions, firm in discipline,
> Relinquishing attachment;
> Be impartial to failure and success—
> This equanimity is called discipline.[81]

But greed and ambition were deeply rooted in human consciousness, so the warrior could achieve this state of dispassion only by the exercise of yoga, which would dismantle his ego. The warrior must take the "me" and "mine" out of his deeds, so that he acted quite impersonally. Once he had achieved this, he would in fact be "inactive," because "he" would not be taking part in the war: "always content, independent, he does nothing at all even when he engages in action."[82] A *kshatriya* had responsibilities; he could not simply retire to the forest. But by practicing karma-yoga he would in fact be detached from the world, even while he was living and active in it. Krishna instructed Arjuna in the usual yogic disciplines, but the meditation he proposed was tailor-made for the *kshatriya,* who could not spend hours every day in contemplation. There was a more exacting form of meditation for a professional ascetic, but karma-yoga could be performed by a man or woman who had worldly duties. The traditional yoga had never centered on a god, but karma-yoga did. The Shvetashvatara Upanishad had instructed the yogin to focus on Rudra/Shiva, but Krishna told Arjuna that he must meditate on Vishnu.

Krishna had a surprise for Arjuna. He explained that he, Krishna, was not only the son of Vishnu, but he actually *was* the god in human form. Even though he was "unborn, undying, the Lord of creatures," Vishnu had descended into a human body many times.[83] Vishnu was the creator of the world and kept it in being, but whenever there was a serious crisis—"whenever sacred duty decays and chaos prevails"—he created an earthly form for himself and came into the world:

> To protect men of virtue
> And destroy men who do evil
> To set the standard of sacred duty,
> I appear in age after age.[84]

Now that he had imparted this astonishing news, Krishna could speak more openly to Arjuna about the devotion of *bhakti*. Arjuna could learn how to detach himself from his egocentric desires by imitating Krishna himself. As Lord and Ruler of the world, Krisha/Vishnu was continually active, but his deeds (*karman*) did not damage him:

> These actions do not bind me,
> Since I remain detached
> In all my actions, Arjuna,
> As if I stood apart from them.[85]

But if he wanted to imitate Krishna, Arjuna had to understand the nature of divinity; he had to *see* Krishna/Vishnu as he truly was.

Right there on the battlefield, Krishna revealed his divine nature to Arjuna, who was aghast and filled with terror when he saw his friend's eternal form as the god Vishnu, creator and destroyer, to whom all beings must return. He saw Krishna transfigured by the divine radiance, which contained the entire cosmos. "I see the gods in your body!" he cried.

> *I see your boundless form*
> *Everywhere,*
> *The countless arms,*
> *Bellies, mouths, and eyes;*
> *Lord of all,*
> *I see no end,*
> *Or middle or beginning*
> *To your totality.*[86]

Everything—human or divine—was somehow present in the body of Krishna, who filled space and included within himself all possible forms of deity: "howling storm gods, sun gods, bright gods, and gods of ritual." But Krishna/Vishnu was also "man's tireless spirit," the essence of humanity.[87] All things rushed toward him, as rivers roiled toward the sea and moths were drawn inexorably into a blazing flame. And there too Arjuna saw the Pandava and Kaurava warriors, all hurtling into the god's blazing mouths.

Arjuna had thought that he had known Krishna through and through, but now, "Who are you?" he cried in bewilderment. "I am Time grown old," Krishna replied—time, which set the world in motion and also annihilated it. Krishna/Vishnu was eternal; he transcended the historical process. As destroyer, Krishna/Vishnu had *already* annihilated the armies that were apparently drawing up their battle lines, even though, from Arjuna's human perspective, the fighting had not even begun. The outcome was fixed and immutable. In order to keep the cosmos in being, one age must succeed another. The war between the Pandavas and the Kauravas would bring the heroic era to an end, and inaugurate a new historical epoch. "Even without you," Krishna told Arjuna, "all these warriors arrayed in hostile ranks will cease to exist."

> *They are already*
> *Killed by me.*
> *Be just my instrument,*
> *The archer at my side.*[88]

Arjuna, therefore, must go into the battle, and play the role allotted to him in restoring dharma to the world.

It was a perplexing vision. Krishna's teaching seemed to absolve human beings of any responsibility for the carnage they committed. Too many politicians and warriors have insisted that they were simply the instruments of destiny, and used this to justify horrendous acts. But few have emptied themselves of the desire for personal gain that, Krishna insisted, was essential. Only the disciplined action of the warrior-yogin could bring order to a destructive world. Krishna seemed pitiless, and yet, he told Arjuna, he was a savior god, who could rescue those who loved him from the ill effects of their karma. Only people of *bhakti* could see Krishna's true nature, and this devotion required complete self-surrender:

> Acting only for me, intent on me,
> Free from attachment,
> Hostile to no creature, Arjuna,
> A man of devotion can come to me.[89]

Detachment and indifference were the first steps toward the union with God, which could save human beings from all the suffering of life.[90]

The *Bhagavad-Gita* has probably been more influential than any other Indian scripture. Its great merit was its accessibility. Where other spiritualities confined salvation to a few gifted, heroic ascetics, this was a religion for everybody. Very few people had the time or talent to dedicate their lives to yoga. Not many could renounce their family and take themselves off to the forest. But "if they rely on me, Arjuna," Krishna promised, "women, vaishyas, shudras, even men born in the womb of evil, reach the highest way."[91] Anybody could love and imitate the Lord, and learn to transcend selfishness in the ordinary duties of daily life. Even a warrior, whose dharma obliged him to kill, could practice karma-yoga. After the great epiphany, Krishna explained that the whole material world was a battlefield in which mortal beings struggle for enlightenment with the weapons of detachment, humility, nonviolence, honesty, and self-restraint.[92] The *Bhagavad-Gita* did not negate the spirituality of the Axial Age but instead had made it possible for everybody to practice it.

10

THE WAY FORWARD

The spiritual revolution of the Axial Age had occurred against a backcloth of turmoil, migration, and conquest. It had often occurred between two imperial-style ventures. In China, the Axial Age finally got under way after the collapse of the Zhou dynasty and came to an end when Qin unified the warring states. The Indian Axial Age occurred after the disintegration of the Harappan civilization and ended with the Mauryan empire; the Greek transformation occurred between the Mycenaean kingdom and the Macedonian empire. The Axial sages had lived in societies that had been cut loose from their moorings. Karl Jaspers suggested, "The Axial Age can be called an interregnum between two ages of great empire, a pause for liberty, a deep breath bringing the most lucid consciousness."[1] Even the Jews, who had suffered so horribly from the imperial adventures in the Middle East, had been propelled into their Axial Age by the terrifying freedom that had followed the destruction of their homeland and the trauma of deportation that severed their link with the past and forced them to start again. But by the end of the second century, the world had stabilized. In the empires that were established after the Axial Age, the challenge was to find a spirituality that affirmed the new political unification.

The Chinese had yearned for peace and integration for a very long time. When Qin conquered the seven remaining states and established a centralized empire in 221, many must have been relieved, but they had a shocking introduction to imperial rule. The

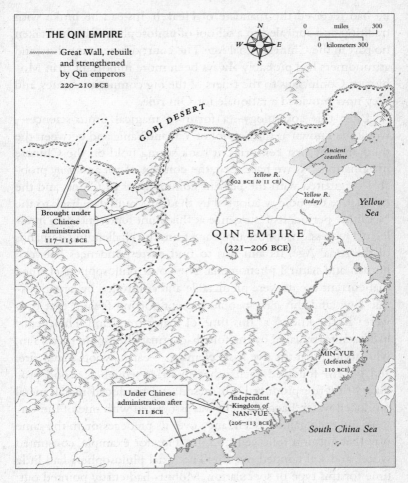

THE QIN EMPIRE

~~~~~~~~ Great Wall, rebuilt
and strengthened
by Qin emperors
220–210 BCE

GOBI DESERT

Ancient coastline

Yellow R.
(602 BCE to 11 CE)

Yellow R.
(today)

*Yellow
Sea*

Brought under
Chinese
administration
117–115 BCE

QIN EMPIRE
(221–206 BCE)

MIN-YUE
(defeated
110 BCE)

Under Chinese
administration after
111 BCE

Independent
Kingdom of
NAN-YUE
(206–113 BCE)

South China Sea

triumph of Qin had been a great victory for the Legalists. Even the legendary sage kings, who had been feudal suzerains, had not achieved an empire of this kind. Qin knew that it had no precedent in China, and the king styled himself "the first emperor." The court historian exulted: "Now within the four seas everywhere, there are commanderies and counties, decrees issue from a single centre, something that has never been from the remotest past."[2] Because this was a new era, the emperor did not claim that he had received the mandate of Heaven. Instead he broke with tradition and appealed to a school of philosophers who had taken no part in the Chinese Axial Age. The court diviners, annalists, and astronomers had probably always been more important than Mohists or Confucians to the rulers of the big competitive states, and they now provided a rationale for Qin rule.

Later this cosmology—a form of magical proto-science—would be known as the School of Yin and Yang, and between the third and the first centuries, it took strong hold on the Chinese imagination.[3] As we have seen, the concept of *yin* and *yang* probably originated with the peasant communities of China, and the correlative cosmology adopted by the Qin could date back to the Neolithic period. Its resurgence at this point represented an intellectual regression, almost an escape from the challenging demands of the Axial Age. Its aim was to find correspondences between human and natural phenomena. The court philosophers claimed that current events were predictable and controlled by larger, cosmic laws, and this gave people the comforting feeling that they were "in the know" at this time of major transition. The theory had been formulated by the fourth-century philosopher Zou Yan, who argued that the five basic elements—earth, wood, metal, fire, and water—followed each other in strict sequence: wood produced fire; fire produced ash or soil; soil produced metal; metal produced water. Each element was associated with one of the seasons, and each gained ascendancy over its predecessor, in the same way that autumn followed summer. Fire, for example, consumed wood, and soil tamped out fire. The Axial philosophers had little time for this type of speculation. Mohists had curtly pointed out: "The five elements do not always win ascendancy over one another."[4] Zou Yan, however, believed that he could also apply this scheme to the historical succession of the great dynasties. The Yellow Emperor was linked with the ocher-colored earth of China, the Xia with wood, the Shang with their bronze metal, and the Zhou with fire. The new Qin dynasty must, therefore, be dominated by water, which was associated with the season of winter.

The first emperor seized upon this idea as an endorsement of his rule. He dressed in black, the color of winter, which seemed appropriate to the dark, cold policies of Legalism, with its "resolute harshness, deciding all things by law, incising and deleting without benevolence, generosity, mildness or righteousness."[5] At the same time, he supported the latest experiments to find the elixir of life. Some of Zou Yan's disciples in the Qin court were trying to concoct herbal and mineral recipes for immortality—a debased form of magic that would later be associated with philosophical Daoism.[6] Some of these early scientists experimented with medicines; others cultivated longevity by breathing and gymnastic exercises; geographical expeditions were even dispatched to find the Isles of the Blest off the northeast coast of China, where, it was thought, privileged human beings could live forever. All this represented a desire to achieve control, to predict the future and keep death at bay by physical rather than spiritual means, but it was also a retreat from the vision of the Axial sages, who had believed that the quest for this type of permanence and security was immature and unrealistic.

The first emperor had to decide how to organize the vast territories he had conquered. Should he give his sons feudal domains, like the Zhou? His prime minister, Li Si, Xunzi's old pupil, advised him to grant his sons stipends instead of land, and to maintain absolute control of his empire. When in 213 a court historian criticized this breach with tradition, Li Si presented the emperor with a fateful memorandum. In the old days, he argued, people had consulted independent scholars and followed different schools of thought, but this could not be allowed to continue:

> Your Majesty has united the world. Yet some with their
> private teachings mutually abet each other, and discredit
> our laws and customs. If such conditions are not pro-
> hibited, the imperial power will decline above and par-
> tisanships will rise from below.[7]

Li Si therefore counseled that "all historical records, save those of Qin, all the writings of the hundred schools, and all other literature, save that kept in the custody of the official scholars, and some works on agriculture, medicine, pharmacy, divination, and arbori-culture should be delivered to the government and burned."[8] Not only was there a massive book burning, but 460 teachers were ex-ecuted. The Axial philosophers of China had arrived at a spiritual apprehension of the unity of all things. For Li Si, unification meant the violent destruction of the opposition. There was one world, one government, one history, and one ideology.

Fortunately, the emperor allowed the seventy official philoso-phers of the regime to keep copies of the Chinese classics, or everything might have been lost. But these savage policies were counterproductive. After the death of the first emperor in 209, the people of the empire rose up in rebellion. After three years of chaos, Liu Bang, a commoner who had started life as a local ad-ministrator, led his forces to victory and founded the Han dynasty. He wanted to preserve the centralized political system of the Qin, and even though he could see that Li Si's policy had been mis-guided, he knew that the empire needed the realism of the Legal-ists as well as a more edifying ideology. He found a compromise in the philosophy known as Huang Lo, a synthesis of Legalism and Daoism.[9] The two schools had always felt an affinity, and they probably chose Huang Di, the legendary Yellow Emperor, as their patron because he had never been important to the Confucians or the Mohists. People were weary of arbitrary imperial rule, and, it was said, Huang Di had ruled by "doing nothing." The emperor must delegate power to his ministers and refrain from personally intervening in public policy; there would be a rational penal law, but no draconian punishments.

The last Chinese sages of the Axial Age had been wary of dog-matic adherence to a single orthodox position, and were moving toward syncretism. But many people felt confused and found it hard to choose between the different schools. The author of the essay "Under the Empire," which was probably written in the early years of the Han, felt that the spiritual world of China was disintegrating. The teaching of the sage kings had been crystal clear. But now:

Everywhere under Heaven is in great disarray, the worthy ones and the sages have no light to shed, the Tao and
Virtue [*de*] are no longer united, and the whole world
tends to see only one aspect and think that they have
grasped the whole of it.[10]

The Chinese had absorbed an important lesson of the Axial Age.
They knew that no school could possibly have the monopoly on
truth, because the *dao* was transcendent and indescribable. At this
time, Daoism was in the ascendancy. For the author of "Under the
Empire," nearly all the sages had important insights, but Zhuangzi
was the most reliable. He had "taught what he believed, yet was
never partisan, nor did he view things from just one perspective."
Because he was so open-minded and unfettered by human orthodoxy, he was "in accord with the Dao and went to the highest
heights."[11]

But gradually the merits of Confucianism became apparent.[12]
The Han emperors had always appreciated the importance of ceremony and ritual. The first Han emperor had commissioned the
local ritualists to draw up a court liturgy and when it was performed for the first time, he had cried: "Now I realize the nobility of being a son of Heaven!"[13] Once people had recovered from
the trauma of the Qin inquisition, Daoism began to seem impractical. It had always had more than a hint of anarchy and lawlessness, and it was felt that the people needed some kind of moral
guidance. Whatever the merits of *wu wei,* the emperors could not
rule entirely by "emptiness." The popularity of Huang Lo peaked
during the reign of the Han emperor Wen (179–157), and after
that the regime was ready for change.

In 136, the court scholar Dong Zhongshu presented a memorial to Emperor Wu (140–87), arguing that there were too many
competing schools and recommending that the six classics, taught
by the Confucians, should become the official teaching of the
state. The emperor agreed, but instead of abolishing all the
schools, as the Qin had done, he permitted the other schools to
continue. Confucian philosophy endorsed the meritocratic sys-

tem of the Han, which now selected its civil servants by means of a public examination. The Confucians had always believed that a man of virtue and learning should take a high position in government, regardless of his birth. They supported the family, the basic unit of society, and above all, they were scholars as well as thinkers, intimately familiar with the cultural history that was essential to the Chinese national identity.

By the first century, therefore, Confucianism was very highly regarded, but the Chinese still appreciated the insights of the other philosophies of the Axial Age. In his account of the main schools of China, the historian Liu Xin (c. 46 BCE–23 CE) argued that the Way of the ritualists was "the loftiest of all." They "take pleasure in the elegance of the Six Classics, lodge their thoughts within the bounds of Benevolence and the Right, pass on the tradition of Yao and Shun, and have kings Wen and Wu as their authorities and Confucius as their founder." But Confucianism did not have the whole truth: "There are gaps in its knowledge, which can be filled by the other schools." Each philosophy had its strengths and weaknesses. The Daoists knew how to get to the center of the spiritual life, "grasp the crucial, cling to the basic, maintain oneself by clarity and emptiness, uphold oneself by humility and yielding," but they underestimated the role of ritual and the rules of morality. The cosmologists could instruct the people in natural science, but this school could degenerate into superstition. The Legalists knew that government depended upon laws and deterrents; their failing was to jettison benevolence and morality. The Mohists' condemnation of extravagance and fatalism and their "concern for everybody" were valuable, but Liu Xin was not happy with their rejection of ritual and their tendency to ignore "the distinction between kin and stranger."[14]

The Chinese understood that nobody had the last word on truth; no orthodoxy, however august, could claim anybody's entire allegiance. Respect for others' opinions was more important than achieving a single, infallible vision. China's inclusive spirit is unique.[15] Later the Chinese would be able to absorb Buddhism alongside their homegrown spiritualities. In India and the West, religions are often aggressively competitive, but in China it is

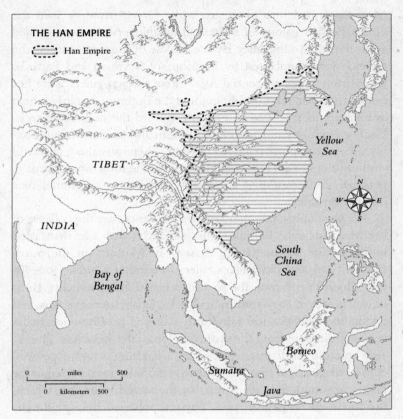

THE HAN EMPIRE
- - - Han Empire

TIBET

INDIA

Yellow Sea

South China Sea

Bay of Bengal

Borneo

Sumatra

Java

0   miles   500

0   kilometers   500

often said that a person can be a Confucian by day and a Daoist at night. Not even Legalism was discarded. The Chinese needed its insights as their empire expanded, so much so that orthodox Confucians often accused their rulers of being "Confucians in appearance but Legalists in practice."[16] It is generally acknowledged that each faith has its proper sphere—an Axial attitude that is sorely needed in our own time.

In India, the Mauryan empire rapidly disintegrated after the death of Ashoka in 232. Regional kingdoms developed in the south,

Magadha lapsed into obscurity, while Greek invaders from the Greco-Persian colony of Bactria in northern Afghanistan gained control of the Indus Valley. By the middle of the first century, the Greeks were supplanted by invasions of Scythian and Parthian tribes from Iran and central Asia. These foreign rulers were not hostile to Indian religion, but because the Brahmins regarded them as unclean, they tended to gravitate toward the non-Vedic sects. Between 200 BCE and 200 CE, Buddhism and Jainism were probably the most popular religions in India. There was also a powerful explosion of *bhakti* faith, reflecting a yearning for a more intimate, personal, and emotional spirituality that almost amounted to a popular revolution.

We have only a fragmentary idea of events after the collapse of the Mauryan state, because India entered a dark age that lasted until the rise of the Gupta dynasty in Mathura in the north (319–415 CE) and the Pallava rulers in southern India (300–888 CE), which swept away the so-called heretical movements. Buddhism, however, took root in Sri Lanka, Japan, southeast Asia, and China. In India, classical Hinduism achieved preeminence, but it was very different from the Vedic religion of the Axial Age. The severe aniconic faith was replaced by a dazzling array of colorful deities, effigies, and temples. Indians, who used to experience the divine in sound, now wanted to *see* the sacred in images, which, they believed, housed the gods' physical presence. Because the divine was infinite, it could not be confined to a single expression; each deity enshrined a particular aspect of the impersonal brahman. But the most popular gods were Shiva and Vishnu, the gods of *bhakti*. In some respects, it seemed that the elite religion of the Vedas had been submerged by the less developed faith of the masses.

It is, however, unwise to talk in too schematic a way about the development of Indian religion. Some of these apparently "new" devotions could date back to the Indus Valley civilization or to the non-Aryan Dravidian culture of southern India,[17] and despite appearances, Vedic religion was far from dead. Indeed, Brahminical religion made important developments after the collapse of the

Mauryan empire.[18] New ritual texts reinterpreted the domestic sacrifices of the householder along Axial lines. They were no longer seen as a pale shadow of the public rites but as their quintessence. Provided that the householder knew what he was doing, a simple action, such as throwing a cup of milk into the sacred fire, could epitomize the entire complex ceremonial of the sacrificial cult and discharge all his sacrificial obligations. Very few people could afford to commission an expensive Vedic ceremony, but anybody could throw a fuel stick into the fire as a symbol of his own "self-sacrifice." "He must recite a portion of the Veda, even if it is only the syllable *Om*. That fulfils the sacrifice to *brahman*."[19] By these minimal actions, the householder not only paid his "debts" to the gods, but made reparation for the inescapable violence of his daily life. The Axial ideal of *ahimsa* was now deeply rooted in the Indian religious consciousness. People were acutely aware of the harm that could be inflicted upon apparently inanimate objects. These new texts noted that the householder had five "slaughterhouses" in his home—the hearth, the grinding stone, the broom, the mortar and pestle, and the water jar—that "bind" him every day with the sin of "killing." The conscious performance of these scaled-down domestic rites constituted an act of "redemption."[20]

These texts also record a development that diverged sharply from the Axial ideal.[21] There had probably long been an "untouchable" caste in India; it has been suggested that the Brahmin and the "untouchable" classes had been established at about the same time, as opposite poles of the hierarchy.[22] But the *Law of Manu* did not reject this archaic idea, and affirmed the degradation of the three lowest ranks. The carpenters, carvers, and fierce "untouchables" (*candelas*) were the result of mixed marriages between *vaishyas, kshatriyas,* and Brahmins, respectively. They must be totally excluded from Vedic society, live on the outskirts of the villages, and perform such menial and polluting tasks as leatherwork and sweeping dung from the village.[23]

The *bhakti* revolution tried to adapt the austere religion of the *Brahmanas* and renouncers to the ordinary people. The popularity of these devotional cults revealed the new hunger for theism. Not everybody wanted to merge with the impersonal brahman; they preferred a more human encounter with a god to whom they could relate. *Bhakti* was defined as "the passionate longing for the Lord from one's whole heart"; the love of the Lord would take people beyond their selfishness, making them "perfect, satisfied, free from hatred, pride and self-interest."[24] *Bhakti* was, therefore, another way of emptying the heart of egotism and aggression. People who could not model their lives on an interior, intellectualized paradigm of humanity could imitate a god whose love and selflessness were easily apparent. Thus Krishna had instructed Arjuna in the *Bhagavad-Gita*:

> *Focus your mind on me,*
> *Let your understanding enter me;*
> *Then you will dwell*
> *In me without doubt.*
>
> *If you cannot concentrate*
> *Your thoughts firmly upon me*
> *Then seek to reach me, Arjuna,*
> *By discipline in practice.*[25]

The *bhakti* religions recognized that not everybody had the same powers of concentration; some might find the disciplined imitation of Krishna in their daily lives easier than long hours of meditation.

This was not a daunting faith; it could be cultivated over time by simple acts of devotion. Devotees could begin by listening to talks about Vishnu/Krishna; then they could start to recite his names, while thinking about his great feats of love for humanity. They could make a simple offering before his shrine and learn to consider him as a friend, until eventually they were able, without any excessive straining, to surrender to him entirely.[26] Self-surrender was the central act of *bhakti;* it was an act of kenosis that transformed the person into a *bhakta*. At this point, the worshiper stopped resisting the Lord and learned to behave as lovingly toward others as he did. The *Bhagavad-Gita* gave the highest praise to the *bhakta* who had learned to practice what the Confucians called *shu,* "likening to oneself."

> When he sees identity in everything
> Whether joy or suffering,
> Through analogy with the self,
> He is deemed a man of pure discipline.[27]

Bhakti encouraged the worshiper to acknowledge his helplessness and need, and this experience of his own vulnerability made it possible to empathize with others. The new spirituality was, therefore, deeply in tune with the Axial Age.

The Lord himself was the exemplar of love. Central to the cult of Vishnu was the *avatara,* a "manifestation" or "descent" of the god into an earthly or human form. At times of historical crisis, Vishnu gave up the bliss of heaven to save the world.[28] It was said that he had made ten such appearances: Krishna was the most important of these avatars, but Vishnu had also become manifest as a fish, a bear, a dwarf, and a tortoise—creatures that may have been the symbols of indigenous deities, which were thus grafted onto the Vedic system. The development of the *avatara* idea is complex: it probably derived from the amalgamation of many different cults, some of which could have been extremely ancient. But in *bhakti,* they acquired Axial significance. By making the loving "descent" into his *avatara,* Vishnu revealed himself to be the savior god par excellence, who laid aside the outward trappings of divinity to help suffering humanity.

Vishnu had always had this potential. He had been mentioned only infrequently in the Rig Veda, but his name probably derived from *vish:* "to enter."[29] Not only did he participate in and pervade the world, but he was the *axis mundi* that tirelessly supported the earth upon his shoulders. He was also a creator god, but unlike Indra, he had not brought order out of chaos by violence and deception. Instead he had conquered the world for gods and humans by taking three giant strides that encompassed the entire cosmos, "widely pacing, with three steppings forth over the realms of earth for freedom and for life."[30] A benevolent god, he was the friend of human beings and the protector of the unborn child.[31] The *Brahmanas* identified him with the healing power of sacrifice; in Vedic lore he was associated with the Purusha, the primordial Person who had voluntarily laid down his life to enable the world to come into being, and thus enshrined the principle of self-emptying love.

Shiva, the other god of *bhakti,* was very different.[32] Linked with the terrifying Rudra, the uncanny mountain god whom people implored to stay away from their settlements and cattle, he was frightening as well as gracious. There was violence in his *mythos,* but he was also the source of great happiness. Shiva was implacable if you did not worship him, but would always save his *bhakta.* Yet he was a jealous god. In one of the earliest tales, he killed Daksha, a devotee of Vishnu, who had refused to invite Shiva to his sacrifice; there was fierce rivalry between the two sects. However, as the lover of Parvati, Shiva became the enchanting Lord of the Dance and an icon of salvation: the dwarf under Shiva's foot was an image of the evil that Shiva had subdued; his outstretched hand a sign of grace; his raised foot an emblem of freedom; and the snake around his neck a symbol of immortality. Shiva was creator and destroyer, a householder as well as a great yogin. In his person, he synthesized the apparent contradictions of the spiritual life and gave his worshipers intimations of transcendence and unity that went beyond earthly categories.

The effigy was very important in *bhakti:* the image (*murti*) of Shiva, Vishnu, or Krishna was their "embodiment," thought to contain a real and physically manifest divine presence.[33] The god had descended into his statue at the moment of its consecration, so that it became the abode of the divine. In some of the old temples, it was said to have been "found," sent by a god, or its whereabouts revealed in a dream. The statue was, therefore, itself an *avatara,* manifesting the self-sacrificing love of the god. Some texts even spoke of the god's suffering when he compressed himself into the man-made image out of compassion for humanity. When it became the focus of contemplation, the statue was thus an icon of al-

truism. Buddhists and Jains were also influenced by this new
Hindu devotion. In the first century CE, as never before, they
began to create statues of the Buddha and of the twenty-four spiritual leaders called *tirthankaras* ("ford-makers"), who had preceded
Mahavira in charting the path to enlightenment. These images first
appeared in Gandhara in northwest India and Mathura on the Yamuna River.

The Buddha had always discouraged the cult of personality
and had tirelessly deflected the attention of his disciples from
himself to the message and method that he taught. Devotion to a
human being could be a "fetter" that encouraged unenlightened
habits of dependence and attachment. In the centuries that followed his death, Buddhists would have felt it unseemly to honor
a statue of the Buddha, because he had "gone" into the bliss of *nibbana*. But the icons of the Buddha would become very important.
When they looked at the serenity and fulfillment of his face, people became aware of what a human being could become. He was
an image of enlightened humanity, so suffused with the ineffable
nibbana that he was identical with it. In an important sense, therefore, he was *nibbana,* and expressed the transcendent reality in a
human form.

By this time, Buddhism had split into two separate schools,
both regarded as authentic versions of the faith. Historically there
has been little animosity or rivalry between the two. The more
austere and monastically inclined Theravada retired from the
world, and sought enlightenment in solitude. The Mahayana was
more democratic and emphasized the virtue of compassion. They
pointed out that the Buddha had returned to the marketplace
after his enlightenment and worked for forty years to show people how to deal with the ubiquitous pain of life. In the first century CE, this gave rise to a new Buddhist hero: the bodhisattva, a
person who was on the brink of achieving enlightenment. Instead
of disappearing into the bliss of *nibbana,* however, the bodhisattvas
sacrificed their own happiness for the sake of the people and returned to the world of samsara to teach other people to find liberation. They were not unlike the savior gods of *bhakti,* who
descended from heaven to help suffering humanity. As this first-

century text explained, the bodhisattvas were not interested in achieving a privatized *nibbana*.

> On the contrary, they have surveyed the highly painful world of being, and yet desirous of winning supreme enlightenment, they do not tremble at birth-and-death. They have set out for the benefit of the world, for the ease of the world, out of pity for the world. They have resolved: "We will become a shelter for the world, the world's place of rest, the final relief of the world, islands of the world, lights of the world, and the guides of the world's means of salvation."[34]

The bodhisattva was a new model of compassion, one that translated the old ideal of the Axial Age into a new form.

The Jewish Axial Age had been cut short, stifled, perhaps prematurely, by the difficulties of dispersion and resettlement, but it was brought to fulfillment by marvelous secondary and tertiary flowerings. During the first century CE, when the Holy Land had been occupied by the Roman empire, the country was in turmoil. A group of political Jewish zealots fiercely opposed Roman rule and in 66 CE orchestrated a rebellion that, incredibly, held the Roman armies at bay for four years. Fearing that it would spread to the Jews of the diaspora, the Roman authorities crushed the insurgency mercilessly. In 70 CE, the emperor Vespasian conquered Jerusalem and burned the temple to the ground. This second destruction was a bitter blow, but, with hindsight, it seems that the Jews of Palestine, who tended to be more conservative than the diaspora Jews, had already prepared themselves for the disaster. The Essenes and the Qumran sect had already withdrawn from mainstream society, believing that the Jerusalem temple was corrupt; their purified community would be a new temple of the spirit. They had imbibed the apocalyptic piety that had developed after the Axial Age and, like the Zoroastrians, looked forward to a great battle at the end of time between the children of light and the children of darkness, internalizing the violence of their time and giving it sacred endorsement.

But the most progressive Jews in Palestine were the Pharisees, who developed some of the most inclusive and advanced spiritualities of the Jewish Axial Age. They believed that the whole of Israel was called to be a holy nation of priests and that God could be experienced in the humblest home as well as in the temple. He was present in the smallest details of daily life, and Jews could approach him without elaborate ritual. They could atone for their sins by acts of loving-kindness rather than animal sacrifice. Charity was the most important commandment of the law. Perhaps the greatest of the Pharisees was Rabbi Hillel (c. 80 BCE–30 CE), who migrated to Palestine from Babylonia. In his view, the essence of the Torah was not the letter of the law but its spirit, which he summed up in the Golden Rule. In a famous Talmudic story, it was said that one day a pagan approached Hillel and promised to convert to Judaism if the rabbi could teach him the entire Torah while he stood on one leg. Hillel replied simply: "What is hateful to yourself, do not to your fellow man. That is the whole of the Torah and the remainder is but commentary. Go learn it."[35]

The Pharisees wanted no part in the violence that was erupting destructively around them. At the time of the rebellion against Rome, their leader was Rabbi Johanan ben Zakkai, Hillel's greatest student. He realized that the Jews could not possibly defeat the Roman empire, and argued against the war, because the preservation of religion was more important than national independence. When his advice was rejected, he had himself smuggled out of Jerusalem hidden in a coffin in order to get past the Jewish Zealots who were guarding the city gates. He then made his way to the Roman camp and asked Vespasian for permission to live with his scholars in Javne, on the coast of southern Palestine. After the destruction of the temple, Javne became the new capital of Jewish religion. In Rabbinic Judaism, the Jewish Axial Age came of age.

The Golden Rule, compassion, and loving-kindness were central to this new Judaism; by the time the temple had been destroyed, some of the Pharisees already understood that they did not need a temple to worship God, as this Talmudic story makes clear:

> It happened that R. Johanan ben Zakkai went out from Jerusalem, and R. Joshua followed him and saw the burnt ruins of the Temple and he said: "Woe is it that the place, where the sins of Israel find atonement, is laid waste." Then said R. Johanan, "Grieve not, we have an atonement equal to the Temple, the doing of loving deeds, as it is said, 'I desire love and not sacrifice.' "[36]

Kindness was the key to the future; Jews must turn away from the violence and divisiveness of the war years and create a united community with "one body and one soul."[37] When the community was integrated in love and mutual respect, God was with them, but when they quarreled with one another, he returned to heaven, where the angels chanted with "one voice and one melody."[38] When two or three Jews sat and studied harmoniously together, the divine presence sat in their midst.[39]

Rabbi Akiba, who was killed by the Romans in 132 CE, taught that the commandment "Thou shalt love thy neighbor as thyself" was "the great principle of the Torah."[40] To show disrespect to any human being who had been created in God's image was seen by the rabbis as a denial of God himself and tantamount to atheism. Murder was a sacrilege: "Scripture instructs us that whatsoever sheds human blood is regarded as if he had diminished the divine image."[41] God had created only one man at the beginning of time to teach us that destroying only one human life was equivalent to annihilating the entire world, while to save a life redeemed the whole of humanity.[42] To humiliate anybody—even a slave or a non-Jew—was equivalent to murder, a sacrilegious defacing of God's image.[43] To spread a scandalous, lying story about another person was to deny the existence of God.[44] Religion was inseparable from the practice of habitual respect to all other human be-

ings. You could not worship God unless you practiced the Golden
Rule and honored your fellow humans, whoever they were.

In Rabbinic Judaism, study was as important as meditation in
other traditions. It was a spiritual quest: the word for study, *darash,*
meant "to search," "to go in pursuit of." It led not to an intellectual grasp of somebody else's ideas, but to new insight. So rabbinic
midrash ("exegesis") could go further than the original text, discover what it did *not* say, and find an entirely fresh interpretation;
as one rabbinic text explained: "Matters that had not been disclosed to Moses were disclosed to Rabbi Akiba and his generation."[45] Study was also inseparable from action. When Rabbi Hillel
had expounded the Golden Rule to the skeptical pagan, he told
him, "Go and study it." The truth of the Golden Rule would be
revealed only if you put it into practice in your daily life.

Study was a dynamic encounter with God. One day, somebody
came to Rabbi Akiba and told him that Ben Azzai was sitting expounding the scripture with fire flashing around him. Rabbi Akiba
went to investigate. Was Ben Azzai, perhaps, discussing Ezekiel's vision of the chariot, which inspired the mystically inclined to make
their own ascent to heaven? No, Ben Azzai replied.

> I was only linking up the words of the Torah with one
> another, and then with the words of the prophets, and
> the prophets with the writings, and the words rejoiced,
> as when they were delivered from Sinai, and they were
> sweet as at their original utterance.[46]

Scripture was not a closed book, and revelation was not a historical event that had happened in a distant time. It was renewed
every time a Jew confronted the text, opened himself to it, and applied it to his own situation. This dynamic vision could set the
world afire.

There were, therefore, no "orthodox" beliefs. Nobody—not
even the voice of God himself—could tell a Jew what to think. In
one seminal story, Rabbi Eliezer ben Hyrcanus was engaged in an
intractable argument with his colleagues about a point of Jewish
law. He could not convert them to his point of view, so he asked

God to back him up by performing some spectacular miracles. A carob tree moved four hundred cubits of its own accord; water in a conduit flowed backward; the walls of the house of studies shook so dramatically that the building seemed about to collapse. But Rabbi Eliezer's companions were not impressed. Finally, in desperation, he asked for a "voice from heaven" (*bat qol*) to come to his aid. Obligingly the divine voice declared: "What is your quarrel with Rabbi Eliezer? The legal decision is always according to his view." But Rabbi Joshua rose to his feet and quoted the book of Deuteronomy: "It is not in heaven." The teaching of God was no longer confined to the divine sphere. It had been promulgated on Mount Sinai, and was therefore the inalienable possession of every single Jew. It did not belong to God anymore, "so we pay no attention to a *bat qol.*"[47]

The rabbis fully accepted the Axial principle that the ultimate reality was transcendent and ineffable. Nobody could have the last word on the subject of God. Jews were forbidden to pronounce God's name, as a powerful reminder that any attempt to express the divine was so inadequate that it was potentially blasphemous. The rabbis even warned Israelites not to praise God too frequently in their prayers, because their words could only be defective. When they spoke of God's presence on earth, they were careful to distinguish those traits of God that he allowed us to see from the divine mystery that would always be inaccessible to us. They liked to use such phrases as the "glory" (*kavod*) of God; the "Shekhinah," the divine presence; and the "Holy Spirit" rather than "God" *tout court,* as a constant reminder that the reality they experienced did not correspond to the essence of the Godhead. No theology could be definitive. The rabbis frequently suggested that on Mount Sinai, each of the Israelites had experienced God differently. God had, as it were, adapted himself to each person "according to the comprehension of each."[48] What we call "God" was not the same for everybody. Each of the prophets had experienced a different "God," because his personality had influenced his conception of the divine. This profound reticence would continue to characterize Jewish theology and mysticism.

Christianity began as another of the first-century movements that tried to find a new way of being Jewish. It centered on the life and death of a Galilean faith healer who was crucified by the Romans in about 30 CE; his followers claimed that he had risen from the dead. They believed that Jesus of Nazareth was the long-awaited Jewish messiah, who would shortly return in glory to inaugurate the kingdom of God on earth. He was the "son of God," a term they used in the Jewish sense of somebody who had been assigned a special task by God and enjoyed a privileged intimacy with him. The ancient royal theology had seen the king of Israel as the son and servant of Yahweh; the suffering servant in Second Isaiah, who was associated with Jesus, had also suffered humiliation for his fellow humans and had been raised by God to an exceptionally high status.[49] Jesus had no intention of founding a new religion and was deeply Jewish. Many of his sayings, recorded in the gospel, were similar to the teachings of the Pharisees. Like Hillel, Jesus taught a version of the Golden Rule.[50] Like the rabbis, he believed that the commandments to love God with your whole heart and soul and your neighbor as yourself were the greatest *mitzvoth* of the Torah.[51]

The person who made Christianity a gentile religion was Paul, the first Christian writer, who believed that Jesus had also been the messiah, the anointed one (in Greek, *christos*). Paul was a diaspora Jew from Tarsus in Cilicia; a former Pharisee, he wrote in koine Greek. Bridging both worlds, he was convinced that he had a mission to the *goyim,* the foreign nations: Jesus had been a messiah for the gentiles as well as the Jews. Paul had the universal—"immeasurable"—vision of the Axial Age. God felt "concern for everybody." He was convinced that Jesus' death and resurrection had created a new Israel, open to the whole of humanity.

Writing to his converts in Philippi in Macedonia during the mid-fifties, about twenty-five years after Jesus' death, Paul quoted an early Christian hymn that shows that from the very beginning, Christians had experienced Jesus' mission as a kenosis.[52] The hymn began by pointing out that Jesus, like all human beings, had been in the image of God, yet he did not cling to this high status,

> But emptied himself [heauton ekenosen]
> To assume the condition of a slave. . . .
> And was humbler yet, even to accepting death, death
>   on a cross.

But because of this humiliating "descent," God had raised him high and given him the supreme title *kyrios* ("Lord"), to the glory of God the Father. This vision was not dissimilar to the ideal of the bodhisattva, who voluntarily laid aside the bliss of *nibbana* for the sake of suffering humanity. Christians would come to see Jesus as an *avatara* of God, who had made a painful "descent" out of love in order to save the human race. But Paul did not quote the hymn to expound the doctrine of the incarnation. As a former Pharisee, he knew that religious truth had to be translated into action. He therefore introduced the hymn with this instruction to the Christians of Philippi: "In your minds, you must be the same as Christ Jesus." They must also empty their hearts of egotism, selfishness, and pride. They must be united in love, "with a common purpose and a common mind."[53]

> There must be no competition among you, no conceit;
> but everybody is to be self-effacing. Always consider the
> other person to be better than yourself, so that nobody
> thinks of his own interests first, but everybody thinks of
> other people's interests instead.[54]

If they revered others in this selfless way, they would understand the *mythos* of Jesus' kenosis.

Jesus was the paradigmatic model of the Christians. By imitating him, they would enjoy an enhanced life, as "sons of God." In the rituals of the new church, they made a symbolic descent with Christ into the tomb when they were baptized, identified with his death, and now lived a different kind of life.[55] They would leave their profane selves behind and share in the enhanced humanity of the *kyrios*.[56] Paul himself claimed that he had transcended his limited, individual self: "I now live not with my own life but with the life of Christ who lives in me."[57] It was the old archetypal religion in a new Axial configuration, dominated by the virtue of love. Later Christians would set great store by orthodoxy, the acceptance of the "correct teaching." They would eventually equate faith with belief. But Paul would have found this difficult to understand. For Paul, religion was about kenosis and love. In Paul's eyes, the two were inseparable. You could have faith that moved mountains, but it was worthless without love, which required the constant transcendence of egotism:

> Love is always patient and kind; it is never jealous; love
> is never boastful or conceited; it is never rude or selfish;
> it does not take offence, and is not resentful. Love takes
> no pleasure in other people's sins but delights in truth; it
> is always ready to excuse, to trust, to hope, and to endure
> whatever comes.[58]

Love was not bursting with self-importance, clinging to an inflated idea of the self, but was empty, self-forgetful, and endlessly respectful of others.

The gospels, written between 70 and about 100 CE, follow Paul's line. They did not present Jesus teaching doctrines, such as the Trinity or original sin, which would later become de rigueur. Instead they showed him practicing what Mozi might have called *jian ai*, "concern for everybody." To the dismay of some of his contemporaries, Jesus regularly consorted with "sinners"—prostitutes, lepers, epileptics, and those who were shunned for collecting the Roman taxes. His behavior often recalled the outreach of the Buddha's "immeasurables," because he seemed to exclude nobody from his radius of concern. He insisted that his followers should not judge others.[59] The people who would be admitted to the kingdom would be those who practiced practical compassion, feeding the hungry and visiting people who were sick or in prison.[60] His followers should give their wealth to the poor.[61] They should not trumpet their good deeds, but live gentle, self-effacing lives.[62]

It seems that Jesus was also a man of *ahimsa*. "You have heard how it was said: *Eye for eye and tooth for tooth,*" he said to the crowd in the Sermon on the Mount, "but I say this to you: offer the wicked man no resistance. On the contrary, if anyone hits you on the right cheek, offer him the other as well."[63] When he was arrested, he would not let his followers fight on his behalf: "All who draw the sword will die by the sword."[64] And he died forgiving his executioners.[65] One of his most striking—and, scholars tell us, most probably authentic—instructions forbade all hatred:

> You have heard how it was said: You must love your neighbour and hate your enemy. But I say this to you: love your enemies and pray for those who persecute you; in this way you will be sons of your father in heaven, for he causes his sun to rise on bad men as well as good and his rain to fall on honest men alike. For if you love those who love you, how can you claim any credit? Even the tax-collectors and the pagans do as much, do they not? And if you save your greetings for your brothers, are you doing anything exceptional? You must be perfect as your heavenly father is perfect.[66]

The paradox "Love your enemies" was probably designed to shock his audience into new insight; it required kenosis, because you had to offer benevolence where there was no hope of any return.

The final flowering of the Axial Age occurred in seventh-century Arabia, when the prophet Muhammad brought the Qur'an, a divinely inspired scripture, to the people of the Hijaz. Muhammad, of course, had never heard of the Axial Age, but he would probably have understood the concept. The Qur'an did not claim to be a new revelation, but simply to restate the message that had been given to Adam, the father of humanity, who was also the first prophet. It insisted that Muhammad had not come to replace the prophets of the past but to return to the primordial faith of Abraham, who lived before the Torah and the gospel—before, that is, the religions of God had split into warring sects.[67] God had sent messengers to every people on the face of the earth, and today Muslim scholars have argued that had the Arabs known about the Buddha or Confucius, the Qur'an would have endorsed their teachings too. The basic message of the Qur'an was not a doctrine—indeed, it was skeptical of theological speculation, which it called *zannah,* "self-indulgent guesswork"—but a command to practical compassion. It was wrong to build a private fortune selfishly, at the expense of others, and good to share your wealth fairly and create a just and decent society where poor and vulnerable people were treated with respect.

Like all the great Axial sages, Muhammad lived in a violent society, when old values were breaking down. Arabia was caught up in a vicious cycle of tribal warfare, in which one vendetta led inexorably to another. It was also a time of economic and material progress. The harsh terrain and climate of the Arabian Peninsula had isolated the Arabs, but in the late sixth century CE the city of Mecca had established a thriving market economy and its merchants took their caravans into the more developed regions of Persia, Syria, and Byzantium. Muhammad was himself a successful merchant, and delivered his message to the Meccans in an atmosphere of cutthroat capitalism and high finance. The Meccans were now rich beyond their wildest dreams, but in the stampede for wealth, old tribal values, which demanded that the community take care of the weaker members of the clan, had been forgotten. There was widespread malaise, and the old pagan faith, which had served the Arabs well in their nomadic days in the desert, no longer met their altered circumstances.

When Muhammad received his first revelations, in about 610 CE, many of the Arabs had become convinced that Allah, the High God of their pantheon,★ was identical with the God of the Jews and Christians. Indeed, Christian Arabs often made the hajj pilgrimage to the Kabah, commonly regarded as Allah's shrine in Mecca, alongside the pagans. One of the first things that Muhammad asked his converts to do was to pray facing Jerusalem, the city of the Jews and Christians whose God they were now going to

★*Al-lah* simply means "God" in Arabic.

worship. No Jews or Christians were required—or even invited—
to join the new Arab religion unless they particularly wished to do
so, because they had received valid revelations of their own. In the
Qur'an, God told the Muslims that they must treat the *ahl al-kitab*,
"people of an earlier revelation," with respect and courtesy:

> Do not argue with the followers of earlier revelation
> otherwise than in the most kindly manner—unless it be
> such of them as are bent on evildoing—and say: "We
> believe in that which has been revealed to us from on
> high, as well as that which has been bestowed upon you:
> for our God and your God is one and the same, and it is
> unto him that we all surrender ourselves."[68]

This remained the policy of the Muslim empire long after
Muhammad's death. Until the middle of the eighth century CE,
conversion to Islam was not encouraged. It was assumed that
Islam was the religion of the Arabs, the descendants of Abraham's
son Ishmael, as Judaism was the religion of the children of Isaac
and Jacob, and Christianity was for the followers of the gospel.
Today some Muslims denigrate Judaism and Christianity, and
some extremists speak of the Muslim duty to conquer the entire
world for Islam, but these are innovations that break with centuries of sacred tradition.

Eventually Muhammad's religion would be called *islam* ("surrender"); "Muslims" are men and women who have made an ex-
istential surrender of their lives to God. This takes us immediately
to the heart of the Axial Age. When Muhammad asked that his
converts prostrate themselves in prayer (*salat*) several times a day,
this was hard for the Arabs, who did not approve of monarchy and
found it degrading to grovel on the ground like slaves. But the
posture of their bodies was designed to teach them at a level
deeper than the rational what *islam* required: transcendence of the
ego, which prances, preens, and postures and continually draws attention to itself.

Muslims were also required to give a regular proportion of
their income to the poor. This *zakat* ("purification") would purge

their hearts of habitual selfishness. At first, it seems, the religion of Muhammad was called *tazakkah,* an obscure word (related to *zakat*) that is difficult to translate: "refinement," "generosity," and "chivalry" have all been suggested as English equivalents, but none is entirely adequate. By *tazakkah,* Muslims were to cloak themselves in the virtues of compassion and generosity. They must use their intelligence to cultivate a caring and responsible spirit, which made them want to give graciously of what they had to all God's creatures. They must carefully observe Allah's bounteous behavior to human beings by observing the "signs" (*ayat*) of nature:

> The earth he has spread out for all living beings, with fruit hereon, and palm trees with sheathed clusters of dates, and grain growing tall on its stalks and sweet-smelling plants.[69]

By meditating on the mysteries of creation, Muslims must learn to behave with similar generosity. Because of Allah's kindness, there was order and fruitfulness instead of chaos and sterility. If Muslims followed his example, they would find that their own lives had been transfigured. Instead of being characterized by selfish barbarism, they would acquire spiritual refinement.

The new religion enraged the Meccan establishment, which did not approve of its egalitarian spirit; the most successful families persecuted the Muslims, tried to assassinate the prophet, and eventually Muhammad and seventy Muslim families were forced to flee to Medina, some 250 miles to the north. In the context of pagan Arabia, where the blood tie was the most sacred value, this amounted to blasphemy. It was unheard of to leave your kin and take up permanent residence with a tribe to whom you were not related. After their migration (*hijrah*), the Muslims faced the prospect of war with Mecca, the most powerful city of Arabia. For five years, they fought a desperate battle for survival. In pre-Islamic Arabia, warriors were merciless. If they had managed to conquer the Muslim community, the Meccans would certainly have exterminated every man, and enslaved every woman and child.

During this dark time, some of the revelations of the Qur'an instructed Muslims about conduct on the battlefield. Islam was not a religion of *ahimsa,* but the Qur'an permitted only defensive warfare. It condemned war as "an awesome evil," and forbade Muslims to initiate hostilities.[70] Aggression was strictly prohibited; there must be no preemptive strikes. But sometimes it was regrettably necessary to fight in order to preserve decent values.[71] It was permissible to defend yourself if you were attacked, and while the war lasted, Muslims must fight wholeheartedly, pursuing the enemy vigorously in order to bring things back to normal. But the second the enemy sued for peace, hostilities must cease, and Muslims must accept any terms that were offered.[72] War was not the best way of dealing with conflict. It was better to sit down and reason with the enemy, as long as arguments were conducted "in the most kindly manner." It was much better to forgive, and be forbearing, "since God is with those who are patient in adversity."[73]

The word *jihad* did not mean "holy war." Its primary meaning was "struggle." It was difficult to put God's will into practice in a cruel, dangerous world, and Muslims were commanded to make an effort on all fronts: social, economic, intellectual, and spiritual. Sometimes it might be necessary to fight, but an important and highly influential tradition puts warfare in a subordinate position. It is said that on returning from a battle, Muhammad told his followers: "We are leaving the Lesser Jihad [the war] and returning to the Greater Jihad," the infinitely more momentous and urgent challenge to reform our own societies and our own hearts. Later Muslim law elaborated on these Qur'anic directives. Muslims were forbidden to fight except in self-defense; retaliation must be strictly proportionate; it was not permitted to make war on a country where Muslims were able to practice their religion freely; civilian deaths must be avoided; no trees could be cut down; and buildings must not be burned.

During the five-year war with Mecca, atrocities were committed on both sides, as was customary in the bloodbath of pre-Islamic Arabia. Bodies were mutilated, and after one of the Jewish tribes of Medina tried to assassinate the prophet and plotted with Mecca to open the gates of the settlement during a siege, the men of the clan were executed. But as soon as the balance shifted in his favor, Muhammad cut the destructive cycle of strike and counter-strike, and pursued an astonishingly daring nonviolent policy.

In 628 CE he announced that he wanted to make the hajj pilgrimage and invited the Muslim volunteers to accompany him. This was extremely dangerous. During the hajj, Arab pilgrims could not carry arms; all violence was forbidden in the Meccan sanctuary. It was even forbidden to speak a cross word or kill an insect. In going unarmed into Mecca, Muhammad was, therefore, walking into the lion's den. Nevertheless, a thousand Muslims chose to accompany him. The Meccans sent their cavalry to kill the pilgrims, but local Bedouins guided them into the sanctuary by another route. Once they had entered the sacred territory, Muhammad made the Muslims sit down in a peaceful demonstration, knowing that he was putting the Meccans in a difficult position. If they harmed pilgrims in the holiest place of Arabia, blasphemously violating the sanctity of the Kabah, their cause would be irreparably damaged. Eventually, the Meccans sent an envoy to negotiate, and to the horror of the Muslims present, Muhammad obeyed the directives of the Qur'an and accepted conditions that seemed not only to be dishonorable but also to throw away all the advantages that the Muslims had fought and died for. Nevertheless, Muhammad signed the treaty. The Muslim pilgrims were furious, and even though mutiny was narrowly averted, they started the ride home in sullen silence.

But during the homeward journey, Muhammad received a revelation from God, who called this apparent defeat a "manifest victory."[74] While the Meccans, inspired by the violence of the old religion, had "harboured a stubborn disdain in their hearts," God had sent down the "gift of inner peace [sakinah]" upon the Muslims, so that they had been able to respond to their enemies with calm serenity.[75] They were distinguished by total surrender to God, and this separated them from the pagan Meccans and linked them with what we would call the religions of the Axial Age. The spirit of peace, said the Qur'an, was their link with the Torah and the gospel: "They are like a seed that brings forth its shoot, and then he strengthens it so that it grows stout, and in the end stands firm upon its stem, delighting the sowers."[76] The treaty that had seemed so unpromising led to a final peace. Two years later the Meccans voluntarily opened their gates to Muhammad, who took the city without bloodshed.

In every single one of the religions of the Axial Age, individuals have failed to measure up to their high ideals. In all these faiths, people have fallen prey to exclusivity, cruelty, superstition, and even atrocity. But at their core, the Axial faiths share an ideal of sympathy, respect, and universal concern. The sages were all living in violent societies like our own. What they created was a spiritual technology that utilized natural human energies to counter this aggression. The most gifted of them realized that if you wanted to outlaw brutal, tyrannical behavior, it was no good simply issuing external directives. As Zhuangzi pointed out, it was useless for Yan Hui even to attempt to reform the prince of Wei by preaching the

THE RELIGIONS OF THE AXIAL AGE TODAY.
WORLD POPULATION

Christian	1,965,993,000
Muslim	1,179,326,000
Hindu	767,424,000
Buddhist	356,875,000
Sikh	22,874,000
Daoist	20,050,000
Jewish	15,050,000
Confucian	5,067,000
Jain	4,152,000
Zoroastrian	479,000

noble principles of Confucianism, because this would not touch the subconscious bias in the ruler's heart that led to his atrocious behavior.

When warfare and terror are rife in a society, this affects everything that people do. The hatred and horror infiltrate their dreams, relationships, desires, and ambitions. The Axial sages saw this happening to their own contemporaries and devised an education rooted in the deeper, less conscious levels of the self to help them overcome this. The fact that they all came up with such profoundly similar solutions by so many different routes suggests that they had indeed discovered something important about the way human beings worked. Regardless of their theological "beliefs"—which, as we have seen, did not much concern the sages—they all concluded that if people made a disciplined effort to reeducate themselves, they would experience an enhancement of their humanity. In one way or another, their programs were designed to eradicate the egotism that is largely responsible for our violence, and promoted the empathic spirituality of the Golden Rule. This, they found, introduced people to a different dimension of human experience. It gave them *ekstasis,* a "stepping out" from their habitual, self-bound consciousness that enabled them to apprehend a reality that they called "God," *nibbana,* brahman, atman, or the Way. It was not a question of discovering your belief in "God" first and then living a compassionate life. The practice of disciplined sympathy would itself yield intimations of transcendence. Human beings are probably conditioned to self-defense. Ever since we lived in caves, we have been threatened by animal and human predators. Even within our own communities and families, other people oppose our interests and damage our self-esteem, so we are perpetually poised—verbally, mentally, and physically—for counterattack and preemptive strike. But if we methodically cultivated an entirely different mind-set, the sages discovered, we experienced an alternative state of consciousness. The consistency with which the Axial sages—quite independently—returned to the Golden Rule may tell us something important about the structure of our nature.

If, for example, every time we were tempted to say something hostile about a colleague, a sibling, or an enemy country, we considered how we would feel if such a remark were made about us—and refrained—we would, in that moment, have gone beyond ourselves. It would be a moment of transcendence. If such an attitude became habitual, people could live in a state of constant *ekstasis,* not because they were caught up in an exotic trance but because they would be living beyond the confines of egotism. The Axial programs all promoted this attitude. As Rabbi Hillel pointed out, this was the essence of religion. The Confucian rituals of "yielding" were designed to cultivate a habit of reverence for others. Before an aspirant could undertake a single yogic exercise, he had to become proficient in *ahimsa,* nonviolence, never betraying antagonism in a single word or gesture. Until this was second nature, his guru would not allow him to proceed with his meditation—but in the process of acquiring this "harmlessness" he would, the texts explained, experience "indescribable joy."

The Axial sages put the abandonment of selfishness and the spirituality of compassion at the top of their agenda. For them, religion *was* the Golden Rule. They concentrated on what people were supposed to transcend *from*—their greed, egotism, hatred, and violence. What they were going to transcend *to* was not an easily defined place or person, but a state of beatitude that was inconceivable to the unenlightened person, who was still trapped in the toils of the ego principle. If people concentrated on what they hoped to transcend *to* and became dogmatic about it, they could develop an inquisitorial stridency that was, in Buddhist terminology, "unskillful."

This is not to say that all theology should be scrapped or that the conventional beliefs about God or the ultimate are "wrong." But—quite simply—they cannot express the entire truth. A transcendent value is one that, of its very nature, cannot be *defined*—a word that in its original sense means "to set limits upon." Christianity, for example, has set great store by doctrinal orthodoxy, and many Christians could not imagine religion without their conventional beliefs. This is absolutely fine, because these dogmas often express a profound spiritual truth. The test is simple: if people's beliefs—secular or religious—make them belligerent, intolerant, and unkind about other people's faith, they are not "skill-ful." If, however, their convictions impel them to act compassion-ately and to honor the stranger, then they are good, helpful, and sound. This is the test of true religiosity in every single one of the major traditions.

Instead of jettisoning religious doctrines, we should look for their spiritual kernel. A religious teaching is never simply a state-ment of objective fact: it is a program for action. Paul quoted that early Christian hymn to the Philippians not to lay down the law about the incarnation, but to urge them to practice kenosis them-selves. If they behaved like Christ, they would discover the truth of their beliefs about him. Similarly, the doctrine of the Trinity was meant in part to remind Christians that they could not think about God as a simple personality, and that the divine essence lay beyond their grasp. Some have seen the doctrine of Trinity as an attempt to see the divine in terms of relationship or community; others have discerned a kenosis in the heart of the Trinity. But the object of the doctrine is to inspire contemplation and ethical ac-tion. In the fourteenth century CE, Greek Orthodox theologians developed a principle about theology that takes us to the heart of the Axial Age. Any statement about God, they said, should have two qualities: it must be *paradoxical,* to remind us that the divine cannot fit into our limited human categories, and *apophatic,* lead-ing us to silence.[77] A theological discussion, therefore, should not answer all our queries about the ineffable deity, but should be like a *brahmodya,* which reduced contestants to speechless awe.

Centuries of institutional, political, and intellectual develop-ment have tended to obscure the importance of compassion in re-ligion. All too often the religion that dominates the public discourse seems to express an institutional egotism: *my faith is bet-ter than yours!* As Zhuangzi noted, once people interject them-selves into their beliefs, they can become quarrelsome, officious, or even unkind. Compassion is not a popular virtue, because it de-mands the laying aside of the ego that we identify with our deep-est self; so people often prefer being right to being compassionate. Fundamentalist religion has absorbed the violence of our time and developed a polarized vision, so that, like the early Zoroastrians, fundamentalists sometimes divide humanity into two hostile camps, with the embattled faithful engaged in a deadly war against "evildoers." As we have seen to our cost, this attitude can easily segue into atrocity. It is also counterproductive. As the *Daodejing* pointed out, violence usually recoils upon the perpetrator, no matter how well intentioned he might be. You cannot force people to behave as you want; in fact, coercive measures are more likely to drive them in the opposite direction.

All the world religions have seen the eruption of this type of militant piety. As a result, some people have concluded either that religion itself is inescapably violent or that violence and intolerance are endemic to a particular tradition. But the story of the Axial Age shows that in fact the opposite is the case. Every single one of these faiths began in principled and visceral recoil from the unprecedented violence of their time. The Axial Age began in India when the ritual reformers started to extract the conflict and aggression from the sacrificial contest. Israel's Axial Age began in earnest after the destruction of Jerusalem and the enforced deportation of the exiles to Babylonia, where the priestly writers started to evolve an ideal of reconciliation and *ahimsa*. China's Axial Age developed during the Warring States period, when Confucians, Mohists, and Daoists all found ways to counteract widespread lawless, lethal aggression. In Greece, where violence was institutionalized by the polis, despite some notable contributions to the Axial ideal—especially in the realm of tragedy—there was ultimately no religious transformation.

Nevertheless, the critics of religion are right to point to a connection between violence and the sacred, because *homo religiosus* has always been preoccupied by the cruelty of life. Animal sacrifice—a universal practice of antiquity—was a spectacularly violent act designed to channel and control our inherent aggression. It may have been rooted in the guilt experienced by the hunters of the Paleolithic period when they slaughtered their fellow creatures. The scriptures often reflect the agonistic context from which they emerged. It is not difficult to find a religious justification for killing. If seen in isolation from the tradition as a whole, individual texts in, for example, the Hebrew Bible, the New Testament,

or the Qur'an can easily be used to sanction immoral violence
and cruelty. The scriptures have constantly been used in this way,
and most religious traditions have disgraceful episodes in their
past. In our own day, people all over the world are resorting to religiously inspired terrorism. They are sometimes impelled by fear,
despair, and frustration; sometimes by a hatred and rage that entirely violates the Axial ideal. As a result, religion has been impli-
cated in some of the darkest episodes of recent history.

What should be our response? The Axial sages give us two important pieces of advice. *First,* there must be self-criticism. Instead
of simply lambasting the "other side," people must examine their
own behavior. The Jewish prophets gave a particularly strong lead
here. At a time when Israel and Judah were threatened by the imperial powers, Amos, Hosea, and Jeremiah all told them to scruti-
nize their own conduct. Instead of encouraging a dangerous
righteousness, they wanted to puncture the national ego. To imagine that God is reflexively on *your* side and opposed to your enemies was not a mature religious attitude. Amos saw Yahweh, the
divine warrior, using Assyria as his instrument to punish the kingdom of Israel for its systemic injustice and social irresponsibility.
After his deportation to Babylon, when the exiles had been the
victims of massive state aggression, Ezekiel insisted that the people of Judah look into their *own* violent behavior. Jesus would later
tell his followers not to condemn the splinter in their neighbor's
eye while ignoring the beam in their own.[78] The piety of the
Axial Age demanded that people take responsibility for their own
actions. The Indian doctrine of karma insisted that all our deeds
have long-lasting consequences; blaming others without examining how our own failings might have contributed to a disastrous
situation was "unskillful," unrealistic, and irreligious. So too in our
current predicament, the Axial sages would probably tell us, reformation must start at home. Before stridently insisting that another
religion clean up its act, we should look into our own traditions,
scriptures, and history—and amend our own behavior. We cannot
hope to reform others until we have reformed ourselves. Secular-
ists, who reject religion, should also look for signs of secular fundamentalism, which is often as stridently bigoted about religion as

some forms of religion are about secularism. In its own brief history, secularism has also had its disasters: Hitler, Stalin, and Saddam Hussein show that a militant exclusion of religion from public policy can be as lethal as any pious crusade.

Second, we should follow the example of the Axial sages and take practical, effective action. When they confronted aggression in their own traditions, they did not pretend that it was not there but worked vigorously to change their religion, rewriting and reorganizing their rituals and scriptures in order to eliminate the violence that had accumulated over the years. The ritual reformers of India took the agon out of the sacrifice; Confucius tried to extract the militant egotism that had distorted the *li;* and "P" took the aggression out of the ancient creation stories, producing a cosmogony in which Yahweh blessed all his creatures—including Leviathan, whom he had slaughtered in the old tales.

Today extremists have distorted the Axial traditions by accentuating the belligerent elements that have evolved over the centuries at the expense of those that speak of compassion and respect for the sacred rights of others. In order to reclaim their faith, their coreligionists should embark on a program of disciplined and creative study, discussion, reflection, and action. Instead of sweeping uncomfortable scriptures and historical disasters under the carpet in order to preserve the "integrity" of the institution, scholars, clerics, and laity should study difficult texts, ask searching questions, and analyze past failings. At the same time, we should all strive to recover the compassionate vision and find a way of expressing it in an innovative, inspiring way—just as the Axial sages did.

This need not be a purely intellectual campaign; it should also be a spiritual process. In these perilous times, we need new vision, but, as the Axial sages tirelessly explained, religious understanding is not simply notional. Many opposed the idea of a written scripture, because they feared that it would result in slick, superficial knowledge. A self-effacing, compassionate, and nonviolent lifestyle was just as important as textual study. Even Indra had to change his belligerent way of life and live as a humble Vedic student before he could understand the deepest truths of the tradition. It also took him a long time. Because we live in a society of instant communication, we expect to grasp our religion instantly too, and can even feel that there is something wrong if we cannot appreciate it immediately. But the Axial sages tirelessly explained that true knowledge is always elusive. Socrates believed that he had a mission to make the rational Greeks aware that even when we are most rigorously logical, some aspect of the truth will always evade us. Understanding comes only after intellectual kenosis, when we realize that we know nothing and our mind is "emptied" of received ideas. The Axial sages were not timid about questioning fundamental assumptions, and as we face the problems of our time, we need to have a mind that is constantly open to new ideas.

We are living in a period of great fear and pain. The Axial Age taught us to face up to the suffering that is an inescapable fact of human life. Only by admitting our own pain can we learn to empathize with others. Today we are deluged with more images of suffering than any previous generation: war, natural disasters, famine, poverty, and disease are beamed nightly into our living rooms. Life is indeed *dukkha*. It is tempting to retreat from this ubiquitous horror, to deny that it has anything to do with us, and to cultivate a deliberately "positive" attitude that excludes anybody's pain but our own. But the Axial sages insisted that this was not an option. People who deny the suffering of life and stick their heads, ostrichlike, in the sand are "false prophets." Unless we allow the sorrow that presses in on all sides to invade our consciousness, we cannot begin our spiritual quest. In our era of international terror, it is hard for any of us to imagine that we can live in the Buddha's pleasure park. Suffering will sooner or later impinge upon all our lives, even in the protected societies of the first world.

Instead of resenting this, the Axial sages would tell us, we should treat it as a religious opportunity. Instead of allowing our pain to fester and erupt in violence, intolerance, and hatred, we should make a heroic effort to use it constructively. The trick, Jeremiah told the deportees, was not to give free rein to resentment. Vengeance was not the answer. Honor the stranger in your midst, "P" told the Jewish exiles, for you were strangers in Egypt. The memory of past distress brings us back to the Golden Rule; it should help us to see that other people's suffering is as important as our own—even (perhaps especially) the anguish of our enemies. The Greeks put human misery onstage so that the Athenian audience could learn sympathy for the Persians who had devastated their city only a few years earlier. In the tragedies, the chorus regularly instructed the audience to weep for people whose crimes would normally fill them with abhorrence. Tragedy could not be denied. It had to be brought right into the sacred heart of the city and made a force for good—as, at the end of the *Oresteia,* the vengeful Erinyes were transformed into the Eumenides, the "well-disposed ones," and given a shrine on the Acropolis. We had to learn to feel *with* people we have hated and harmed; at the end of the *Iliad,* Achilles and Priam wept together. Rage and vicious resentment can make us inhuman; it was only when Achilles shared his grief with Priam, and saw him as his mirror image, that he recovered the humanity he had lost.

We must continually remind ourselves that the Axial sages developed their compassionate ethic in horrible and terrifying circumstances. They were not meditating in ivory towers but were living in frightening, war-torn societies, where the old values were disappearing. Like us, they were conscious of the void and the abyss. The sages were not utopian dreamers but practical men; many were preoccupied with politics and government. They were convinced that empathy did not just sound edifying, but actually worked. Compassion and concern for everybody was the best policy. We should take their insights seriously, because they were the experts. They devoted a great deal of time and energy to thinking about the nature of goodness. They spent as much creative energy seeking a cure for the spiritual malaise of humanity as scientists today spend trying to find a cure for cancer. We have different preoccupations. The Axial Age was a time of spiritual genius; we live in an age of scientific and technological genius, and our spiritual education is often undeveloped.

The Axial Age needed to craft a new vision because humanity had taken a social and psychological leap forward. People had discovered that each person was unique. The old tribal ethic, which had developed a communal mentality to ensure the survival of the group, was being replaced by a new individualism. This is why so many of the Axial spiritualities were preoccupied by the discovery of the *self*. Like the merchant, the renouncer was a self-made man. The sages demanded that every single person become self-conscious, aware of what he was doing; rituals had to be appropriated by each sacrificer, and individuals must take responsibility for their actions. Today we are making another quantum leap forward. Our technology has created a global society, which is interconnected electronically, militarily, economically, and politically. We now have to develop a global consciousness, because, whether we like it or not, we live in one world. Even though our problem is different from that of the Axial sages, they can still help us. They did not jettison the insights of the old religion, but deepened and extended them. In the same way, we should develop the insights of the Axial Age.

The sages were ahead of us in recognizing that sympathy cannot be confined to our own group. We have to cultivate what the Buddhists call an "immeasurable" outlook that extends to the ends of the earth, without excluding a single creature from this radius of concern. The Golden Rule reminded the fledgling individuals of the Axial Age that I value my own self as much as you do yours. If I made my individual self an absolute value, human society would become impossible, so we must all learn to "yield" to one another. Our challenge is to develop this insight and give it a global significance. In the Holiness Code, "P" insisted that no living creature is unclean and that everybody—even a slave—has sovereign freedom. We have to "love" our neighbor as ourselves. As we have seen, "P" did not mean that we had to be filled with emotional tenderness for everybody; in his legal terminology, "love" meant being helpful, loyal, and giving practical support to our neighbor. Today everybody on the planet is our neighbor. Mozi tried to convince the princes of his day that it made good, practical sense to cultivate *jian ai,* a deliberate and impartial "concern for everybody." It would, Mozi argued, serve their own best interests. We now know this to be the case. What happens in Afghanistan or Iraq today will somehow have repercussions in

London or Washington tomorrow. In the last resort, "love" and "concern" will benefit everybody more than self-interested or shortsighted policies.

In *The Bacchae,* Euripides showed that it was dangerous to reject "the stranger." But acceptance of the alien and the foreign takes time; displacing the self from the center of our worldview demands a serious effort. Buddhists recommended meditation on the "immeasurables" to cultivate a different mentality. But people who have neither the time nor the talent for yoga could repeat the Buddha's poem "Let All Beings Be Happy"—a prayer that demands no theological or sectarian belief. The Confucians also recognized the importance of a program of self-cultivation. The rituals were designed to create a *junzi,* a mature, fully developed human being who did not treat others carelessly, perfunctorily, or selfishly. But they also transformed the person who was the object of ritual attention and brought out his or her unique holiness. A practically expressed respect for the other is probably indispensable for a peaceful global society and perhaps the only way to "reform" rogue states. But this respect must be sincere. As the *Daodejing* pointed out, people always sense the motives behind our actions. Nations will also be aware if they are being exploited or humored out of self-interest.

Suffering shatters neat, rationalistic theology. Ezekiel's terrifying, confusing vision was very different from the more streamlined ideology of the Deuteronomists. Auschwitz, Bosnia, and the destruction of the World Trade Center revealed the darkness of the human heart. Today we are living in a tragic world where, as the Greeks knew, there can be no simple answers; the genre of tragedy demands that we learn to see things from other people's point of view. If religion is to bring light to our broken world, we need, as Mencius suggested, to go in search of the lost heart, the spirit of compassion that lies at the core of all our traditions.

Notes

INTRODUCTION

1. Karl Jaspers, *The Origin and Goal of History,* trans. Michael Bullock (London, 1953), pp. 1–70.
2. Mircea Eliade, *Myths, Dreams and Mysteries: The Encounter Between Contemporary Faiths and Archaic Realities,* trans. Philip Mairet (London, 1960), pp. 172–78; Wilhelm Schmidt, *The Origin of the Idea of God* (New York, 1912).
3. Walter Burkert, *Homo Necans: The Anthropology of Ancient Greek Sacrificial Ritual and Myth,* trans. Peter Bing (Berkeley, Los Angeles, and London, 1983), pp. 16–22; Joseph Campbell with Bill Moyers, *The Power of Myth* (New York, 1988), pp. 72–74.
4. Eliade, *Myths, Dreams and Mysteries,* pp. 80–81; Mircea Eliade, *The Myth of the Eternal Return, or, Cosmos and History,* trans. Willard R. Trask (Princeton, 1959), pp. 17–20.
5. Eliade, *Myth of the Eternal Return,* pp. 1–34.
6. Huston Smith, *The World's Religions: Our Great Wisdom Traditions* (San Francisco, 1991), p. 235.
7. Eliade, *Myth of the Eternal Return,* pp. 34–35.
8. Jaspers, *Origin and Goal of History,* p. 40.

1. THE AXIAL PEOPLES

1. Mary Boyce, *Zoroastrians: Their Religious Beliefs and Practices,* 2nd ed. (London and New York), p. 2; Peter Clark, *Zoroastrians: An Introduction to an Ancient Faith* (Brighton and Portland, Ore., 1998), p. 18.
2. Mircea Eliade, *Patterns of Comparative Religion,* trans. Rosemary Sheed (London, 1958), pp. 66–68.
3. Boyce, *Zoroastrians,* pp. 9–11.
4. Ibid., p. 8.
5. Yasht 48:5.
6. Boyce, *Zoroastrians,* pp. 11–12.
7. Thomas J. Hopkins, *The Hindu Religious Tradition* (Belmont, Calif., 1971), p. 14.
8. Gavin Flood, *An Introduction to Hinduism* (Cambridge and New York, 1996), p. 44; John Keay, *India: A History* (London, 2000), p. 32.
9. Boyce, *Zoroastrians,* pp. 12–15.
10. Eliade, *Patterns of Comparative*

Religion, pp. 188–89; Norman Cohn, *Cosmos, Chaos and the World to Come: The Ancient Roots of Apocalyptic Faith* (New Haven and London, 1993), pp. 94–95; Boyce, *Zoroastrians,* pp. xiv–xv, 19.

11. Rig Veda 4.42.5, in Ralph T. H. Griffith, trans., *The Rig Veda* (New York, 1992).

12. Cohn, *Cosmos, Chaos and the World to Come,* p. 77; Boyce, *Zoroastrians,* p. xiii; Clark, *Zoroastrians,* p. 19.

13. Yasna 43.

14. Clark, *Zoroastrians,* pp. 4–6.

15. Yasna 19:16–18. Quotations from the Zoroastrian scriptures are taken from Mary Boyce, ed. and trans., *Textual Sources for the Study of Zoroastrianism* (Chicago, 1984).

16. Boyce, *Zoroastrians,* pp. 20–23; Cohn, *Cosmos, Chaos and the World to Come,* p. 81.

17. Yasna 46:2, 11; 50:1.

18. Yasna 29:1–10.

19. Yasna 30.

20. Yasna 30:6.

21. Yasna 46:4.

22. Jamsheed K. Choksy, *Purity and Pollution in Zoroastrianism: Triumph over Evil* (Austin, 1989), pp. 1–5.

23. Boyce, *Zoroastrians,* p. 32.

24. Yasna 44:15; 51:9.

25. Yasna 43:3.

26. Yasna 29, 33.

27. Yasna 33.

28. Boyce, *Zoroastrians,* pp. 23–24.

29. Ibid., p. 30; Cohn, *Cosmos, Chaos and the World to Come,* p. 78.

30. Edwin Bryant, *The Quest for the Origins of Vedic Culture: The Indo-Aryan Debate* (Oxford and New York, 2001); S. C. Kak, "On the Chronology of Ancient India," *Indian Journal of History and Science* 22, no. 3 (1987); Colin Renfrew, *Archaeology and Language: The Puzzle of Indo-European Origins* (London, 1987).

31. Keay, *India,* pp. 5–18; Hopkins, *Hindu Religious Tradition,* pp. 3–10; Flood, *Introduction to Hinduism,* pp. 24–30.

32. Shatapatha Brahmana (SB) 6.8.1.1, in J. C. Heesterman, *The Broken World of Sacrifice: An Essay in Ancient Indian Ritual* (Chicago and London, 1993), p. 123.

33. Mircea Eliade, *A History of Religious Ideas,* trans. Willard R. Trask, 3 vols. (Chicago and London, 1978, 1982, 1985), I:200–201; J. C. Heesterman, "Ritual, Revelation and the Axial Age," in S. N. Eisenstadt, ed., *The Origins and Diversity of Axial Age Civilizations* (Albany, 1986), p. 404.

34. Louis Renou, *Religions of Ancient India* (London, 1953), p. 20.

35. J. C. Heesterman, *The Inner Conflict of Tradition: Essays in Indian Ritual, Kingship and Society* (Chicago and London, 1985), pp. 85–87.

36. Jan Gonda, *The Vision of the Vedic Poets* (The Hague, 1963), pp. 14–23.

37. Renou, *Religions of Ancient India,* pp. 10, 16–18; Michael Witzel, "Vedas and Upanishads," in Gavin Flood, ed., *The Blackwell Companion to Hinduism* (Oxford,

2003), pp. 70–71; Heesterman, "Ritual, Revelation and the Axial Age," p. 398.

38. RigVeda 9.10.6, as translated in Gonda, *Vision of the Vedic Poets,* p. 17.

39. Heesterman, *Inner Conflict of Tradition,* pp. 118–24.

40. SB 7.2.1.4, in Mircea Eliade, *The Myth of the Eternal Return, or, Cosmos and History,* trans. Willard R. Trask (Princeton, 1959), p. 21.

41. Taittiriya Brahmana (TB) 1.5.9.4, ibid.

42. Heesterman, *Inner Conflict of Tradition,* p. 206; Heesterman, "Ritual, Revelation and the Axial Age," pp. 396–98; Keay, *India,* pp. 31–33; Romila Thapar, *Early India: From the Origins to AD 1300* (Berkeley and Los Angeles, 2002), pp. 126–30.

43. Jaiminiya Brahmana (JB) 2.297; Heesterman, *Broken World of Sacrifice,* p. 52.

44. Heesterman, *Broken World of Sacrifice,* pp. 2, 27, 76–79.

45. JB 2.297–99, in Heesterman, *Broken World of Sacrifice,* p. 52; Heesterman, "Ritual, Revelation and the Axial Age," p. 397.

46. RigVeda 10.33.2–3. Griffith translation.

47. Hermann Kulke, "The Historical Background of India's Axial Age," in Eisenstadt, *Origins and Diversity of Axial Age Civilizations,* p. 376; Flood, *Introduction to Hinduism,* pp. 67–68; Keay, *India,* pp. 37–40, 50–53.

48. Heesterman, *Broken World of Sacrifice,* pp. 136–37.

49. Arthashastra 6.13–15, in

Heesterman, *Inner Conflict of Tradition,* p. 149.

50. TB 1.8.4.1, in Heesterman, "Ritual, Revelation and the Axial Age," p. 403.

51. SB 5.5.2.5, ibid.

52. Mantra in Taittiriya Samhita (TS) 1.3.3, in Heesterman, *Broken World of Sacrifice,* p. 126.

53. Maitrayani Samhita 4.2.1.23:2, ibid., pp. 23–24, 134–37.

54. SB 2.2.2.8–10, ibid., p. 24.

55. Hopkins, *Hindu Religious Tradition,* pp. 17–18.

56. Kathaka Samhita (KS) 8.9.92–3; TS 4.1.2.2, in Heesterman, *Broken World of Sacrifice,* p. 113.

57. SB 7.1.1.1–4, in Eliade, *Myth of the Eternal Return,* pp. 10–11.

58. RigVeda 10.119.1, 7–8. Griffith translation.

59. Heesterman, *Broken World of Sacrifice,* pp. 171–73.

60. Louis Renou, "Sur la notion de brahman," *Journal asiatique* 237 (1949).

61. Jan Gonda, *Change and Continuity in Indian Religion* (The Hague, 1965), p. 200.

62. Heesterman, *Inner Conflict of Tradition,* pp. 70–72, 126.

63. RigVeda 10.129.

64. RigVeda 10.129:6–7. Griffith translation.

65. RigVeda 10.90.

66. *Classic of Odes* 253, in Arthur Waley, ed. and trans., *The Book of Songs* (London, 1937).

67. Jacques Gernet, *A History of Chinese Civilization,* 2nd ed., trans. J. R. Foster and Charles Hartman (Cambridge and New York, 1996), pp. 39–40.

68. Sima Qian, *Records of the Grand*

Historian 1.101; Marcel Granet, *Chinese Civilization,* trans. Kathleen Innes and Mabel Brailsford (London and New York, 1951), pp. 11–16; Henri Masparo, *China in Antiquity,* 2nd ed., trans. Frank A. Kierman Jr. (Folkestone, 1978), pp. 15–19.

69. D. Howard Smith, *Chinese Religions* (London, 1968), pp. 1–11; Gernet, *History,* pp. 41–50; Jacques Gernet, *Ancient China: From the Beginnings to the Empire,* trans. Raymond Rudorff (London, 1968), pp. 37–65; Wm. Theodore de Bary and Irene Bloom, eds., *Sources of Chinese Tradition,* vol. I, *From Earliest Times to 1600,* 2nd ed. (New York, 1999), pp. 3–23.

70. Gernet, *History of Chinese Civilization,* pp. 45–46; Gernet, *Ancient China,* pp. 50–53; Marcel Granet, *The Religion of the Chinese People,* trans. and ed. Maurice Freedman (Oxford, 1975), pp. 37–54.

71. Eliade, *Myth of the Eternal Return,* pp. 46–47.

72. Michael J. Puett, *To Become a God: Cosmology, Sacrifice, and Self-Divinization in Early China* (Cambridge, Mass., and London, 2002), pp. 32–76.

73. De Bary and Bloom, *Sources of Chinese Tradition,* pp. 10–23.

74. Oracle 38. De Bary and Bloom translation.

75. Oracle 15a–b.

76. Oracle 22a. De Bary and Bloom translation.

77. Oracle 23. De Bary and Bloom translation.

78. De Bary and Bloom, *Sources of Chinese Tradition,* p. 12.

79. Gernet, *Ancient China,* p. 62.

80. *The Book of Mozi,* 3.25, in Gernet, *Ancient China,* p. 65.

81. *Classic of Documents,* "The Shao Announcement," in de Bary and Bloom, *Sources of Chinese Tradition,* pp. 35–37. Some scholars believe that this speech was given by the duke of Shao, but de Bary and Bloom, in common with many others, assign it to Dan, duke of Zhou.

82. Ibid., p. 37.

83. Edward L. Shaughnessy, "Western Zhou Civilization," in Michael Loewe and Edward L. Shaughnessy, eds., *The Cambridge History of Ancient China* (Cambridge, U.K., 1999), pp. 313–17.

84. Ibid., p. 317.

85. Israel Finkelstein and Neil Asher Silberman, *The Bible Unearthed: Archaeology's New Vision of Ancient Israel and the Origin of Its Sacred Texts* (New York and London, 2001), pp. 89–92.

86. Ibid., pp. 103–7; William G. Dever, *What Did the Biblical Writers Know and When Did They Know It? What Archaeology Can Tell Us About the Reality of Ancient Israel* (Grand Rapids, Mich., and Cambridge, U.K., 2001), pp. 110–18.

87. Gosta W. Ahlström, *The History of Ancient Palestine* (Minneapolis, 1993), pp. 234–35, 247–48.

88. George W. Mendenhall, *The Tenth Generation: The Origins of Biblical Tradition* (Baltimore and London, 1973); N. P. Lemche,

Early Israel: Anthropological and Historical Studies on the Israelite Society Before the Monarchy (Leiden, 1985); D. C. Hopkins, *The Highlands of Canaan* (Sheffield, 1985); James D. Martin, "Israel as a Tribal Society," in R. E. Clements, ed., *The World of Ancient Israel: Sociological, Anthropological and Political Perspectives* (Cambridge, 1989), pp. 94–114; H. G. M. Williamson, "The Concept of Israel in Transition," in Clements, *World of Ancient Israel,* pp. 141–63.

89. Dever, *What Did the Biblical Writers Know,* pp. 121, 124, 267.

90. Joshua 9:15; 4:11; 1 Samuel 27:10; 30:29; Judges 1:16; 4:11; Exodus 6:15; Mark S. Smith, *The Early History of God, Yahweh and the Other Deities in Ancient Israel* (New York and London, 1990), p. 4; Frank Moore Cross, *Canaanite Myth and Hebrew Epic: Essays in the History of the Religion of Israel* (Cambridge, Mass., and London, 1973), pp. 49–50.

91. Joshua 9; Judges 8:33; 9:4, 46; Joshua 24.

92. Cross, *Canaanite Myth,* p. 69; Peter Machinist, "Distinctiveness in Ancient Israel," in Modechai Cogan and Israel Ephal, eds., *Studies in Assyrian History and Ancient Near Eastern Historiography* (Jerusalem, 1991).

93. Genesis 29:14; 2 Samuel 5:1; cf. Judges 9:1–4.

94. Frank Moore Cross, *From Epic to Canon: History and Literature in Ancient Israel* (Baltimore and London, 1998), pp. 3–6.

95. Mendenhall, *The Tenth Generation,* p. 177.

96. Cross, *From Epic to Canon,* p. 13.

97. Numbers 10:35. A very ancient text. Unless otherwise stated, all biblical quotations are taken from *The Jerusalem Bible.*

98. Cross, *Canaanite Myth,* pp. 41–84; Smith, *Early History of God,* pp. 7–12.

99. Exodus 6:3.

100. Psalms 89:10–13; 93:1–4; Isaiah 27:1; Job 7:12; 9:8; 26:12; 38:7–11; Isaiah 51:9–11.

101. Ugaritic hymn quoted in Cross, *Canaanite Myth,* pp. 148–50.

102. Ibid.

103. Ibid., pp. 162–63.

104. Judges 5:4–5.

105. Habakkuk 3:4–8.

106. David S. Sperling, *The Original Torah: The Political Intent of the Bible's Writers* (New York and London, 1998), pp. 89–90.

107. Joshua 3:1–5:15; Cross, *From Epic to Canon,* p. 44; Cross, *Canaanite Myth,* pp. 103–5, 138.

108. Joshua 3:15.

109. Joshua 5:1.

110. Joshua 4:10–12.

111. Joshua 5:13–15.

112. Joshua 6:21.

113. Cross, *Canaanite Myth,* pp. 103–24.

114. Exodus 15:1–18.

115. Exodus 15:15–16.

116. Cross, *Canaanite Myth,* pp. 133–34.

117. Ibid., pp. 112–24.

118. Exodus 15:3, 6–7.

119. Exodus 15:8.

120. Deuteronomy 32:8–9.

121. R. A. Di Vito, *Studies in Third Millennium Sumerian and Akkadian Personal Names: The Designation and Conception of the Personal God* (Rome, 1993), pp. 93–96.

122. Finkelstein and Silberman, *The Bible Unearthed,* pp. 124–42; Dever, *What Did the Biblical Writers Know,* pp. 124–64.

123. Psalm 2:7.

124. See, for example, Psalms 77 and 89.

125. Psalm 24.

126. Psalm 29:8–10.

127. Ugaritic hymn quoted in Smith, *Early History of God,* p. 46.

2. RITUAL

1. Walter Burkert, *Greek Religion,* trans. John Raffan (Cambridge, Mass., 1985), p. 47.

2. Ibid., pp. 10–16; Oswyn Murray, *Early Greece,* 2nd ed. (London, 1993), pp. 10–11; Jacob Burckhardt, *The Greeks and Greek Civilization,* trans. Sheila Stern; rev. ed. by Oswyn Murray (New York, 1998), pp. 13–16.

3. Robert Parker, *Athenian Religion: A History* (Oxford and New York, 1996), pp. 10–16.

4. Murray, *Early Greece,* pp. 69–74.

5. Burkert, *Greek Religion,* pp. 49–50.

6. Walter Burkert, *Savage Energies: Lessons of Myth and Ritual in Ancient Greece,* trans. Peter Bing (Chicago and London, 2001), p. 91; Walter Burkert, *Homo Necans: The Anthropology of Ancient Greek Sacrificial Ritual and Myth,* trans. Peter Bing (Berkeley, Los Angeles, and London, 1983), pp. 27–34; Walter Burkert, *Structure and History in Greek Mythology and Religion* (Berkeley, Los Angeles, and London, 1980), pp. 50–52.

7. Hesiod, *Theogony* 116–32, in Dorothea Wender, trans., *Hesiod and Theognis* (London and New York, 1976).

8. Ibid., 118–22. Wender translation.

9. Homer, *Odyssey,* 1:31–32.

10. Anthony Gottlieb, *The Dream of Reason: A History of Philosophy from the Greeks to the Renaissance* (London, 2000), pp. 123–25; Burkert, *Greek Religion,* pp. 134–35.

11. Gottlieb, *Dream of Reason,* pp. 138–40; Burkert, *Greek Religion,* p. 200.

12. Burkert, *Greek Religion,* pp. 237–42; Burkert, *Homo Necans,* pp. 213–35.

13. Israel Finkelstein and Neil Asher Silberman, *The Bible Unearthed: Archaeology's New Vision of Ancient Israel and the Origin of Its Sacred Texts* (New York and London, 2001), pp. 158–59.

14. 1 Kings 11:5, 7–8; Mark S. Smith, *The Early History of God: Yahweh and the Other Deities in Ancient Israel* (New York and London, 1990), pp. xxiii–xxv.

15. Smith, *The Early History of God,* pp. 44–49.

16. Mark S. Smith, *The Origins of Biblical Monotheism: Israel's Polytheistic Background and the Ugaritic Texts* (New York and London, 2001), pp. 41–79.

17. Ibid., pp. 47–48, 96, 148–51.
18. Psalm 89:5–8.
19. Smith, *Origins of Biblical Monotheism,* p. 9.
20. 1 Kings 18:3, 10, 19.
21. 1 Kings 18:20–46.
22. S. David Sperling, "Israel's Religion in the Near East," in Arthur Green, ed., *Jewish Spirituality,* 2 vols. (London and New York, 1986, 1988), I: 27–28.
23. Exodus 33:17–23; 34:6–8.
24. 1 Kings 19:11–13. This translation is suggested by Frank Moore Cross in *Canaanite Myth and Hebrew Epic Essays in the History of the Religion of Israel* (Cambridge, Mass., and London, 1973), p. 194.
25. 1 Kings 19:18.
26. Cross, *Canaanite Myth,* pp. 190–91.
27. Psalm 82.
28. 1 Kings 21:19.
29. F. Charles Fensham, "Widow, Orphan and the Poor in Ancient Near Eastern Legal and Wisdom Literature," in Frederick E. Greenspahn, ed., *Essential Papers on Israel and the Ancient Near East* (New York and London, 1991), pp. 176–82.
30. W. G. Lambert, *Babylonian Wisdom Literature* (London, 1960), pp. 134–35.
31. Anastasi II.6:5; Papyrus Harris I.
32. Norman Cohn, *Cosmos, Chaos and the World to Come: The Ancient Roots of Apocalyptic Faith* (New Haven and London, 1993), p. 120.
33. John Dominic Crossan, *The Birth of Christianity: Discovering What Happened in the Years Immediately After the Execution of Jesus* (New York, 1998), pp. 198–99.
34. 1 Kings 17:8–16; 2 Kings 4:1–7.
35. S. David Sperling, "Joshua 24 Re-examined," *Hebrew Union College Annual* 58 (1987).
36. Joshua 24:19–20, 23.
37. S. David Sperling, *The Original Torah: The Political Intent of the Bible's Writers* (New York and London, 1998), pp. 68–72; John Bowker, *The Religious Imagination and the Sense of God* (Oxford, 1978), pp. 58–68.
38. Jacques Gernet, *A History of Chinese Civilization,* trans. J. R. Foster and Charles Hartman, 2nd ed. (Cambridge, U.K., and New York, 1996), pp. 54–65.
39. Marcel Granet, *The Religion of the Chinese People,* trans. and ed. Maurice Freedman (Oxford, 1975), pp. 56–82; Henri Masparo, *China in Antiquity,* trans. Frank A. Kierman Jr. (Folkestone, 1978), pp. 134–59; D. Howard Smith, *Chinese Religions* (London, 1968), pp. 12–31.
40. *Classic of Odes* 151, in Arthur Waley, ed. and trans., *The Book of Songs* (London, 1934).
41. Michael J. Puett, *The Ambivalence of Creation: Debates Concerning Innovation and Artifice in Ancient China* (Stanford, Calif., 2001), pp. 28–36.
42. *Classic of Odes* 270. Waley translation.
43. Huston Smith, *The World's Religions: Our Great Wisdom Traditions* (San Francisco, 1991), pp. 183–85; Gernet, *History of Chinese Civilization,* pp. 31–32.

44. Smith, *Chinese Religions*, p. 24.

45. Marcel Granet, *Festivals and Songs of Ancient China,* trans. E. D. Edwards (London, 1932), p. 75.

46. Granet, *Chinese Civilization,* pp. 11–12; Granet, *The Religion of the Chinese People,* pp. 66–68.

47. Sima Qian, *Records of a Master Historian* 1.56, 79, cited in Granet, *Chinese Civilization,* p. 12.

48. Sima Qian, *Records of a Master Historian* 38, cited ibid.

49. Edward L. Shaughnessy, "Western Zhou Civilization," in Michael Loewe and Edward L. Shaughnessy, eds., *The Cambridge History of Ancient China* (Cambridge, U.K., 1999), pp. 323–34.

50. *Classic of Odes* 199. Waley translation.

51. Ibid.

52. Benjamin I. Schwartz, *The World of Thought in Ancient China* (Cambridge, Mass., and London, 1985), pp. 49–50.

53. *Classic of Odes* 235, in Wm. Theodore de Bary and Irene Bloom, eds., *Sources of Chinese Tradition,* Vol. 1: *From Earliest Times to 1600* (New York, 1999), p. 38.

54. *The Book of Xunzi* 20, "A Discussion of Music," in *Xunzi: Basic Writings,* ed. and trans. Burton Watson (New York, 2003).

55. Schwartz, *World of Thought,* p. 49.

56. *Classic of Odes* 254. Waley translation.

57. *Classic of Odes* 258, in Bernhard Karlgren, trans., *The Book of Odes* (Stockholm, 1950), p. 214.

58. Louis Renou, "Sur la notion de brahman," *Journal asiatique* 237 (1949).

59. J. C. Heesterman, "Ritual, Revelation and the Axial Age," in S. N. Eisenstadt, ed., *The Origins and Diversity of Axial Age Civilizations* (Albany, 1986), pp. 396–97.

60. Ibid., p. 403.

61. J. C. Heesterman, *The Inner Conflict of Tradition: Essays in Indian Ritual, Kingship and Society* (Chicago and London, 1985), p. 91.

62. Taittiriya Brahmana (TB) 3.7.7.14, quoted in J. C. Heesterman, *The Broken World of Sacrifice: An Essay in Ancient Indian Ritual* (Chicago and London, 1993), p. 34.

63. Taittiriya Samhita (TS) 6.4.8.1., ibid., p. 209.

64. Pancavimsha Brahmana (PB) 7.7.9–10, ibid., p. 62.

65. Jaiminiya Brahmana (JB) 1.135; TS 6.3.1.1.; Shatapatha Brahmana (SB) 36.1.27–29; ibid., p. 67.

66. SB 6.8.1.4, cited in Heesterman, "Ritual, Revelation and the Axial Age," p. 402.

67. JB 2.60–70, in Heesterman, *Broken World of Sacrifice,* p. 54.

68. SB 10.5.2.23; 10.6.5.8, ibid., p. 57.

69. SB 11.2.2.5, ibid., p. 34; cf. Brian K. Smith, *Reflections on Resemblance, Ritual and Religion* (Oxford and New York, 1989), p. 103.

70. JB 2.70, cited in Heesterman, *Broken World of Sacrifice,* pp. 54, 57.

71. R. C. Zaehner, *Hinduism* (London, New York, and Toronto,

1962), pp. 59–60; Smith, *Reflections on Resemblance,* pp. 30–34, 72–81.

72. Louis Renou, *Religions of Ancient India* (London, 1953), p. 18.

73. PB 24.11.2, cited in Smith, *Reflections on Resemblance,* p. 59.

74. PB 7.10.15; JB 3.153; SB 7.1.22, ibid., p. 61.

75. SB 10.4.2.3, ibid., p. 60.

76. SB 7.4.2.11; 6.1.2.17; PB 24.11.2; 21.2.3, ibid., pp. 64–65.

77. SB 4.2.2.16, ibid., p. 68; cf. Mircea Eliade, *Yoga, Immortality and Freedom,* trans. Willard R. Trask (London, 1958), p. 109; Mircea Eliade, *A History of Religious Ideas,* trans. Willard R. Trask, 3 vols. (Chicago and London, 1978, 1982, 1985), I:228–29; Thomas J. Hopkins, *The Hindu Religious Tradition* (Belmont, Calif., 1971), p. 33.

78. Eliade, *Yoga,* pp. 109–11; Jan Gonda, *Change and Continuity in Indian Religion* (The Hague, 1965), pp. 316–39; Hopkins, *Hindu Religious Tradition,* pp. 31–32.

79. AB 1.3, cited in Hopkins, *Hindu Religious Tradition,* pp. 31–32.

80. Smith, *Reflections on Resemblance,* pp. 104–12.

81. SB 11.2.6.13, cited ibid., p. 101.

82. Smith, *Reflections on Resemblance,* pp. 116–18.

83. TB 3.10.11.1–2, ibid., p. 117; my italics.

84. SB 11.2.3.6; 2.2.2.8, in Heesterman, *Broken World of Sacrifice,* pp. 97, 140; cf. pp. 215–18.

85. Hopkins, *Hindu Religious Tradition,* pp. 36–37.

86. SB 2.2.2.15, cited in Heesterman, *Broken World of Sacrifice,* p. 216.

87. SB 11.2.6.3, cited ibid.

88. SB 1.1.1.4; 3.3.2.2, cited in Gonda, *Change and Continuity,* pp. 338–39; Heesterman, *Broken World of Sacrifice,* p. 216.

3. KENOSIS

1. Israel Finkelstein and Neil Asher Silberman, *The Bible Unearthed: Archaeology's New Vision of Ancient Israel and the Origin of Its Sacred Texts* (New York and London, 2001), pp. 206–12.

2. G. Lenski, *Power and Privilege: A Theory of Social Stratification* (New York, 1966), pp. 161–217, 273; Andrew Mein, *Ezekiel and the Ethics of Exile* (Oxford and New York, 2001), pp. 20–38.

3. Amos 7:14–15.

4. Amos 3:8.

5. Michael Fishbane, "Biblical Prophecy as a Religious Phenomenon," in Arthur Green, ed., *Jewish Spirituality,* 2 vols. (London and New York, 1986, 1988), I:63–68.

6. Psalms 63:1–2; 84:2; C. F. Whitley, *The Prophetic Achievement* (London, 1963), pp. 16–17.

7. Amos 9:1.

8. Amos 7:17.

9. Amos 1:3–2:3; 6:14; 2:4–16.

10. Amos 5:21–24.

11. Amos 3:1–2; 9:7–8.

12. Fishbane, "Biblical Prophecy," p. 70.

13. Abraham J. Heschel, *The Prophets,* 2 vols. (New York, 1962), I:22–38.

14. Hosea 1:2; Heschel, *The Prophets*, I:52–57.

15. Hosea 3:1–5.

16. Hosea 4:2

17. Hosea 4:4–6, 12–14, 17; 5:13–14; 10:4–11; 14:4.

18. Heschel, *The Prophets*, I:57–59.

19. Hosea 6:6.

20. Hosea 11:3–4.

21. William M. Schniedewind, *How the Bible Became a Book: The Textualization of Ancient Israel* (Cambridge, U.K., 2004), pp. 24–34.

22. William G. Dever, *What Did the Biblical Writers Know and When Did They Know It? What Archaeology Can Tell Us About the Reality of Ancient Israel* (Grand Rapids, Mich., and Cambridge, U.K., 2001), p. 280.

23. Frank Moore Cross, *From Epic to Canon: History and Literature in Ancient Israel* (Baltimore and London, 1998), pp. 41–42.

24. R. E. Clements, *Abraham and David* (London, 1967).

25. Peter Machinist, "Distinctiveness in Ancient Israel," in Mordechai Cogan and Israel Ephal, eds., *Studies in Assyrian History and Ancient Near Eastern Historiography* (Jerusalem, 1991), p. 434; Michael Fishbane, *Text and Texture: Close Readings of Selected Biblical Texts* (New York, 1979), pp. 64, 124–25.

26. Exodus 24:1–2, 9–11.

27. Numbers 11:11, 14–15.

28. Exodus 21:1–27; 22:1–30; 23:1–33.

29. Exodus 24:9, 11.

30. Exodus 33:16–23; Mark S. Smith, *The Origins of Biblical Monotheism: Israel's Polytheistic Background and the Ugaritic Texts* (New York and London, 2001), p. 86.

31. Genesis 3:8–9; 6:6; 8:21; 18:1–15.

32. Exodus 3:13–15.

33. Genesis 18:1–15.

34. Genesis 18:3.

35. Genesis 22:1–10.

36. Genesis 22:1–2.

37. Mircea Eliade, *The Myth of the Eternal Return, or, Cosmos and History*, trans. Willard R. Trask (Princeton, 1959), pp. 108–10.

38. Isaiah 6:1–9.

39. Isaiah 6:11–12.

40. E. A. W. Budge and L. W. King, *Annals of the Kings of Assyria* (London, 1902), p. 31.

41. 1 Kings 16; Isaiah 7.

42. Psalm 46:5–6.

43. Isaiah 9:8; 10:12; 14:12; 16:6; 23:9.

44. Isaiah 14:30–32.

45. Isaiah 10:5–7.

46. Isaiah 2:10–13.

47. Psalm 46:9; cf. Isaiah 9:1; Psalm 76:1–3.

48. Isaiah 2:2–4.

49. Psalm 131; cf. Psalms 9:10–13; 10; Ben C. Ollenburger, *Zion, the City of the Great King: A Theological Symbol of the Jerusalem Cult* (Sheffield, 1987), pp. 58–69.

50. Finkelstein and Silberman, *Bible Unearthed*, pp. 239, 243–46.

51. 2 Kings 18:3–7.

52. 2 Kings 19:35.

53. Finkelstein and Silberman, *Bible Unearthed*, pp. 263–64.

54. Oswyn Murray, *Early Greece*, 2nd ed. (London, 1993), pp. 62–65.

55. Charles Freeman, *The Greek Achievement: The Foundation of the Western World* (New York and London, 1999), pp. 49–50, 116–21.

56. *Odyssey* 6:262.

57. Christian Meier, "The Emergence of Autonomous Intelligence Among the Greeks," in S. N. Eisenstadt, ed., *The Origins and Diversity of Axial Age Civilizations* (Albany, 1986), pp. 71–73.

58. *Iliad* 2:273; 18:105, 252; Freeman, *Greek Achievement,* p. 89.

59. Jean Pierre Vernant, *Myth and Society in Ancient Greece,* 3rd ed., trans. Janet Lloyd (New York, 1996), p. 90.

60. Ibid., pp. 29–32.

61. Walter Burkert, *Greek Religion,* trans. John Raffan (Cambridge, Mass., 1985), pp. 44–49.

62. *Iliad* 23.

63. Walter Burkert, *Homo Necans: The Anthropology of Ancient Greek Sacrificial Ritual and Myth,* trans. Peter Bing (Berkeley, Los Angeles, and London, 1983), pp. 94–103.

64. Walter Burkert, *The Orientalizing Revolution: Near Eastern Influence on Greek Culture in the Early Archaic Age,* trans. Margaret E. Pinder and Walter Burkert (Cambridge, Mass., and London, 1992), pp. 65–67; Burkert, *Greek Religion,* 199–208; Robert Parker, *Athenian Religion: A History* (Oxford and New York, 1996), pp. 34–41.

65. Pindar, *Nemean Ode* 7:44–47. In some versions of the myth, Apollo kills Pyrrhus himself.

66. Burkert, *Homo Necans,* pp. 117–30; Meier, "Emergence of the Autonomous Intellect," pp. 79–81.

67. Burkert, *Greek Religion,* p. 116; Murray, *Early Greece,* pp. 102–14; Freeman, *Greek Achievement,* pp. 65–72.

68. Burkert, *Orientalizing Revolution,* pp. 56–67.

69. Robert A. Segal, "Adonis: A Greek Eternal Child," in Dora C. Pozzi and John M. Wickersham, eds., *Myth and the Polis* (Ithaca and London, 1991); Anthony Gottlieb, *The Dream of Reason: A History of Philosophy from the Greeks to the Renaissance* (London, 2000), pp. 105–10; Pierre Vidal-Naquet, "The Black Hunter and the Origin of the Athenian Ephebia," in R. L. Gordon, ed., *Myth, Religion and Society* (Cambridge, U.K., 1981).

70. S. L. Schein, *The Mortal Hero: An Introduction to Homer's* Iliad (Berkeley, Los Angeles, and London, 1984), p. 1.

71. Burkert, *Greek Religion,* p. 121.

72. Schein, *Mortal Hero,* p. 80.

73. Ibid., p. 70; Jean Pierre Vernant, "Death with Two Faces," in Seth L. Schein, ed., *Reading the Odyssey: Selective Interpretive Essays* (Princeton, 1996), pp. 58–60.

74. *Odyssey* 11:500, in Walter Shewring, trans., *Homer: The Odyssey* (Oxford and New York, 1980).

75. *Iliad* 4:482–89, in Richard Lattimore, trans., *The Iliad of Homer* (Chicago and London, 1951).

76. Schein, *Mortal Hero,* pp. 98–128.

77. *Iliad* 9:629. Lattimore translation.

78. *Iliad* 9:629–52.

79. *Iliad* 22:345–48.

80. *Iliad* 24:39–54. Lattimore translation.

81. *Iliad* 24:479–81. Lattimore translation.

82. *Iliad* 24:507–16. Lattimore translation.

83. *Iliad* 24:629–32. Lattimore translation.

84. *Iliad* 24:634. Lattimore translation.

85. *Iliad* 22:158–66.

86. *Iliad* 5:906.

87. *Iliad* 21:385–513; 20:56–65.

88. Burkert, *Greek Religion,* pp. 114, 152; Schein, *Mortal Hero,* pp. 57–58.

89. Vernant, *Myth and Society,* pp. 102–4.

90. Ibid., p. 113; Burkert, *Greek Religion,* pp. 216–17.

91. Burkert, *Greek Religion,* pp. 219–25.

92. *Iliad* 20:48–53; 15:110–42; 21:391–433.

93. Jacques Gernet, *Ancient China: From the Beginnings to the Empire,* trans. Raymond Rudorff (London, 1968), pp. 71–75.

94. Remarks of Jacques Gernet, reported in Vernant, *Myth and Society,* pp. 80–82.

95. Ibid., p. 81.

96. Huston Smith, *The World's Religions: Our Great Wisdom Traditions* (San Francisco, 1991), pp. 161–62.

97. Marcel Granet, *Chinese Civilization,* trans. Kathleen Innes and Mabel Brailsford (London and New York, 1951), pp. 97–100.

98. Marcel Granet, *The Religion of the Chinese People,* trans. and ed. Maurice Freedman (Oxford, 1975), pp. 97–99.

99. Ibid., pp. 99–102.

100. Fung Yu-Lan, *A Short History of Chinese Philosophy,* ed. Derk Bodde (New York, 1978), pp. 32–37.

101. "The 'Canon of Yao' and the 'Canon of Shun,' " in Wm. Theodore de Bary and Irene Bloom, eds., *Sources of Chinese Tradition,* vol. I: *From Earliest Times to 1600,* 2nd ed. (New York, 1999), p. 29.

102. Ibid., p. 30.

103. Paul Dundas, *The Jains,* 2nd ed. (London and New York, 2002), p. 17; Steven Collins, *Selfless Persons: Imagery and Thought in Theravada Buddhism* (Cambridge, U.K., 1982), p. 64; L. Dumont, *Homo Hierarchicus: The Caste System and Its Implications* (Chicago and London, 1980), p. 46.

104. Gavin Flood, *An Introduction to Hinduism* (Cambridge, U.K., and New York, 1996), p. 91; Patrick Olivelle, "The Renouncer Tradition," in Gavin Flood, ed., *The Blackwell Companion to Hinduism* (Oxford, 2003), p. 271.

105. Mircea Eliade, *Yoga, Immortality and Freedom,* trans. Willard R. Trask (London, 1958), p. 186.

106. J. C. Heesterman, *The Inner Conflict of Tradition: Essays in Indian Ritual, Kingship and Society* (Chicago and London, 1985), pp. 39–40.

107. Patrick Olivelle, *Samnyasa Up-*

anisads: Hindu Scriptures on Asceticism and Renunciation (Oxford and New York, 1992).

108. Rig Veda 10:136; 1:114, in Ralph T. H. Griffith, trans., *The Rig Veda* (New York, 1992).

109. Flood, *Introduction to Hinduism,* pp. 79–80; Eliade, *Yoga,* pp. 103–4.

110. Dundas, *Jains,* p. 17.

111. Heesterman, *Broken World of Sacrifice,* pp. 164–74; Jan Gonda, *Change and Continuity in Indian Religion* (The Hague, 1965), pp. 228–35, 285–94.

112. Manara Gryha Sutra 1.1.6, cited in Heesterman, *Broken World of Sacrifice,* p. 170.

113. Shatapatha Brahmana (SB) 2.2.2.6; Taittiriya Samhita (TS) 1.7.3.1, cited in Gonda, *Change and Continuity,* p. 229.

114. SB 11.3.3:3–6; 11.5.4; 5.7.10; 11.5.6:3, ibid.

115. Gonda, *Change and Continuity,* pp. 289–90.

116. Collins, *Selfless Persons,* pp. 48–49; Flood, *Introduction to Hinduism,* pp. 87–88; Heesterman, *Inner Conflict,* pp. 42–43.

117. Gonda, *Change and Continuity,* pp. 380–84.

118. Ibid., pp. 381–82; Olivelle, "The Renouncer Tradition," pp. 281–82.

119. Collins, *Selfless Persons,* pp. 56–60; Heesterman, *Inner Conflict,* p. 42.

120. Gautama Dharma Sutra 3:26–27, in Olivelle, "The Renouncer Tradition," p. 272.

121. Aitirya Aranyaka 3.2.3; Thomas J. Hopkins, *The Hindu Religious Tradition* (Belmont, Calif., 1971),

p. 50; Mircea Eliade, *A History of Religious Ideas,* trans. Willard R. Trask, 3 vols. (Chicago and London, 1978, 1982, 1985), I:232.

122. Olivelle, *Samnyasa Upanisads,* p. 21.

4. KNOWLEDGE

1. Chandogya Upanishad (CU) 2.23.3. All quotations from the Upanishads are taken from Patrick Olivelle, ed. and trans., *Upanisads* (Oxford and New York, 1996).

2. CU 2.4.4–5.

3. Brhadaranyaka Upanishad (BU) 2.4.4–5.

4. Klaus K. Klostermaier, *A Survey of Hinduism,* 2nd ed. (Albany, 1994), p. 196.

5. BU 2.5.19.

6. CU 6.8.7.

7. BU 4.5.15.

8. Olivelle, *Upanisads,* p. xxix.

9. Ibid., p. xxxix; Michael Witzel, "Vedas and Upanisads," in Gavin Flood, ed., *The Blackwell Companion to Hinduism* (Oxford, 2003), pp. 85–86.

10. Olivelle, *Upanisads,* pp. xxxiv–xxxvi; Witzel, "Vedas and Upanisads," pp. 83–84; BU 3.5.8; 2.4.1.

11. Olivelle, *Upanisads,* p. xxxvii.

12. BU 3.4.

13. BU 3.5.1.

14. BU 4.5.13–15.

15. BU 4.1.1–7.

16. BU 4.3.

17. BU 4.3.21.

18. BU 4.4.23–35.

19. BU 4.4.5–7.

20. BU 3.2.13.

21. BU 4.5.15.

22. CU 8.15.

23. CU 6.1.2.

24. CU 6.2.

25. CU 6.8.7. My italics.

26. CU 6.13. My italics.

27. CU 6.11; 6.12.

28. CU 6.10. My italics.

29. Klostermaier, *Survey of Hinduism,* p. 522.

30. CU 6.7.

31. CU 3.7.

32. CU 6:9.

33. CU 1.12.

34. CU 8.7.1.

35. CU 8.7.2.

36. CU 8.8.3.

37. CU 8.11.1.

38. CU 8.12.4–5.

39. CU 8.11.3.

40. CU 8.12.3.

41. Charles Freeman, *The Greek Achievement: The Foundation of the Western World* (New York and London, 1999), p. 72.

42. Oswyn Murray, *Early Greece,* 2nd ed. (London, 1993), pp. 173–85; Christian Meier, *Athens: A Portrait of the City in Its Golden Age,* trans. Robert and Rita Kimber (London, 1999), p. 41.

43. Freeman, *Greek Achievement,* p. 101; Meier, *Athens,* pp. 54–56; Walter Burkert, *The Orientalizing Revolution: Near Eastern Influence on Greek Culture in the Early Archaic Age,* trans. Margaret E. Pinder and Walter Burkert (Cambridge, Mass., and London, 1992), pp. 76–77.

44. Burkert, *Orientalizing Revolution,* p. 90.

45. Murray, *Early Greece,* p. 18.

46. *Theogony* 31–35, in Dorothea Wender, trans., *Hesiod and Theognis* (London and New York, 1973).

47. *Works and Days* 248–49; 68–70. Wender translation.

48. *Works and Days* 258–67.

49. *Works and Days* 106–201. Wender translation.

50. *Works and Days* 116–18. Wender translation.

51. *Works and Days* 184. Wender translation.

52. Jean-Pierre Vernant, "At Man's Table," in Marcel Detienne and Jean-Pierre Vernant, *The Cuisine of Sacrifice Among the Greeks,* trans. Paula Wissing (Chicago and London, 1989), pp. 30–37.

53. Mircea Eliade, *Patterns in Comparative Religion,* trans. Rosemary Sheed (London, 1958), pp. 75–77; Burkert, *Orientalizing Revolution,* pp. 87–90; Walter Burkert, *Greek Religion,* trans. John Raffan (Cambridge, Mass., 1992), pp. 122–23; Jean-Pierre Vernant with Pierre Vidal-Naquet, *Myth and Tragedy in Ancient Greece,* trans. Janet Lloyd (New York, 1990), pp. 95–101.

54. *Theogony* 535–616; *Works and Days* 60–104.

55. Vernant, "At Man's Table," pp. 22–86.

56. Freeman, *Greek Achievement,* pp. 98–192; Murray, *Early Greece,* pp. 137–45.

57. Aristotle, *Politics* 5.13.10b.

58. Murray, *Early Greece,* pp. 124–37; Freeman, *Greek Achievement,* pp. 91–95; Jean-Pierre Vernant,

Myth and Society in Ancient Greece, trans. Janet Lloyd, 3rd ed. (New York, 1996), pp. 39–53.

59. Fragment 12.13–19, in Murray, *Early Greece,* p. 133.

60. Mary Douglas, *Leviticus as Literature* (Oxford and New York, 1999), pp. 26–29.

61. Murray, *Early Greece,* pp. 164–86; Vernant, *Myth and Society,* p. 47.

62. Marcel Granet, *Chinese Civilization,* trans. Kathleen Innes and Mabel Brailsford (London and New York, 1951), pp. 259–60, 308–9.

63. *Record of Rites* 1:704, in James Legge, trans., *The Li Ki* (Oxford, 1885).

64. *Record of Rites* 1:719.

65. *Record of Rites* 1.720. Legge translation.

66. Confucius, Analects 15:4, in Arthur Waley, trans., *The Analects of Confucius* (New York, 1992).

67. Granet, *Chinese Civilization,* pp. 261–79; Jacques Gernet, *Ancient China: From the Beginnings to the Empire,* trans. Raymond Rudorff (London, 1968), p. 75; Holmes Welch, *The Parting of the Way: Lao Tzu and the Taoist Movement* (London, 1958), p. 18; Huston Smith, *The World's Religions: Our Great Wisdom Traditions* (San Francisco, 1991), p. 160.

68. *Zuozhuan* ("The Commentary of Mr. Zuo") 2:29–30, in James Legge, trans., *The Ch'un Ts'ew and the Tso Chuen,* 2nd ed. (Hong Kong, 1960).

69. *Zuozhuan* 2:412.

70. *Classic of Odes* 35, 167, 185.

71. *Zuozhuan* 2:18.

72. *Zuozhuan* 2.132.

73. *Zuozhuan* 1.627. Legge translation.

74. *Zuozhuan* 1.320. Legge translation.

75. *Zuozhuan* 3.340. Legge translation.

76. *Zuozhuan* 2.234. Legge translation.

77. *Zuozhuan* 1.509. Legge translation.

78. *Zuozhuan* 1.635. Legge translation.

79. Granet, *Chinese Civilization,* pp. 287–309.

80. *Classic of Odes* 55, cited ibid., p. 288.

81. *Record of Rites* 2.263. Legge translation.

82. *Record of Rites* 1.215. Legge translation.

83. *Record of Rites* 2.359. Legge translation.

84. *Record of Rites* 2.627; Granet, *Chinese Civilization,* pp. 288–90.

85. Granet, *Chinese Civilization,* pp. 297–308.

86. Ibid., pp. 310–43; Marcel Granet, *The Religion of the Chinese People,* trans. and ed. Maurice Freedman (Oxford, 1975), pp. 82–83; Granet, *Chinese Civilization,* pp. 311–27.

87. Granet, *Chinese Civilization,* pp. 328–43.

88. Granet, *Religion of the Chinese People,* pp. 83–89.

89. Gernet, *Ancient China,* p. 75.

90. Jacques Gernet, *A History of Chinese Civilization,* trans. J. R. Foster and Charles Hartman, 2nd ed. (Cambridge, U.K., and New York, 1996), p. 60; Gernet, *Ancient China,* pp. 77–83.

91. *Zuozhuan* 2.272; text of a treaty made in 592. Legge translation.

92. *Zuozhuan* 2.453. Legge translation.

93. H. G. Creel, *Confucius: The Man and the Myth* (London, 1951), p. 19.

94. Israel Finkelstein and Neil Asher Silberman, *The Bible Unearthed: Archaeology's New Vision of Ancient Israel and the Origin of Its Sacred Texts* (New York and London, 2001), pp. 264–73.

95. 2 Kings 21:2–7; 23:11; 23:10; Ezekiel 20:25–26; 22:30; Andrew Mein, *Ezekiel and the Ethics of Exile* (Oxford and New York, 2001), p. 105.

96. Psalms 68:18; 84:12; Gosta W. Ahlström, *The History of Ancient Palestine* (Minneapolis, 1993), p. 734.

97. Finkelstein and Silberman, *Bible Unearthed,* pp. 264–73.

98. 2 Kings 21, 23.

99. 2 Kings 22:1; William M. Schniedewind, *How the Bible Became a Book: The Textualization of Ancient Israel* (Cambridge, U.K., 2004), pp. 107–8.

100. 2 Chronicles 34:1–2.

101. 2 Kings 22:8.

102. Exodus 24:3, 7. My italics.

103. Exodus 31:18.

104. Exodus 24:9–31:18; Schniedewind, *How the Bible Became a Book,* pp. 121–34.

105. Exodus 24:4–8; this is the only other place in the Bible where the phrase *sefer torah* is found. Schniedewind, *How the Bible Became a Book,* pp. 121–26.

106. 2 Kings 22:11–13.

107. Nehemiah 8:1–9.

108. 2 Kings 22:16.

109. 2 Kings 22:11.

110. 2 Kings 23:4–20.

111. Deuteronomy 6:4–6.

112. Deuteronomy 6:14.

113. Deuteronomy 7:2–6.

114. Bernard M. Levinson, *Deuteronomy and the Hermeneutics of Legal Innovation* (Oxford and New York, 1998), pp. 148–49.

115. Deuteronomy 12–26.

116. Deuteronomy 11:21; 12:5.

117. Deuteronomy 12:20–24.

118. Levinson, *Deuteronomy,* p. 50.

119. Deuteronomy 16:18–20; 17:8–13; Levinson, *Deuteronomy,* pp. 114–37.

120. Levinson, *Deuteronomy,* pp. 138–43; Schniedewind, *How the Bible Became a Book,* p. 110.

121. Deuteronomy 17:18–20.

122. 1 Kings 13:1–2; 2 Kings 23:15–18; 2 Kings 23:25.

123. Finkelstein and Silberman, *Bible Unearthed,* pp. 283–84.

124. Judges 2:7.

125. R. E. Clements, *God and Temple* (Oxford, 1965), pp. 89–95; S. David Sperling, *The Original Torah: The Political Intent of the Bible's Writers* (New York and London, 1998), pp. 146–47; Margaret Barker, *The Gate of Heaven: The History and Symbolism of the Temple in Jerusalem* (London, 1991), pp. 7–8.

126. 1 Kings 8:27.

127. Deuteronomy 15:3.

128. Deuteronomy 15:7–8, in Everett Fox, trans., *The Five Books of Moses* (New York, 1983); cf. Deuteronomy 14:29; 23:21; 24:17–18.

129. Deuteronomy 21:15–17; 24:14–15; 15:12–15.

130. Levinson, *Deuteronomy,* pp. 11–95.

131. Jeremiah 29:1–3; 36:110; 39:14; 40:6; Richard Eliott Friedman, *Who Wrote the Bible?* (New York, 1987), pp. 125–27.

132. Jeremiah 8:8–9; Schniedewind, *How the Bible Became a Book,* pp. 114–17.

133. Haym Soloveitchik, "Rupture and Reconstruction: The Transformation of Contemporary Orthodoxy," *Tradition* 28 (1994).

134. Deuteronomy 12:3.

135. Joshua 8:24–25.

136. Levinson, *Deuteronomy,* pp. 53–97.

137. 2 Kings 21:21–23.

138. 2 Kings 23:29.

5. SUFFERING

1. 2 Kings 24:16. These numbers are disputed.

2. Jeremiah 52:28–30.

3. Elias J. Bickerman, *The Jews in the Greek Age* (Cambridge, Mass., and London, 1988), pp. 46–47; Thomas L. Thompson, *The Bible in History: How Writers Create a Past* (London, 1999), pp. 217–25.

4. Ephraim Stern, *Archaeology of the Land of the Bible,* vol. 2: *The Assyrian, Babylonian and Persian Periods (732–332)* (New York, 2001), p. 303.

5. Lamentations 1:8–9.

6. Jeremiah 7:1–15; 26:1–19.

7. Jeremiah 20:7–9; 17–18.

8. Jeremiah 2:31–32; 5:7–9, 28–29.

9. Jeremiah 29:4–20.

10. Jeremiah 31:33–34.

11. Psalm 137:9.

12. Daniel L. Smith, *The Religion of the Landless: The Social Context of the Babylonian Exile* (Bloomington, 1989), pp. 39–52; Jonathan Z. Smith, *Map Is Not Territory: Studies in the History of Religions* (Chicago and London, 1978), p. 119.

13. William M. Schniedewind, *How the Bible Became a Book: The Textualization of Ancient Israel* (Cambridge, U.K., 2004), p. 152.

14. Ezekiel 3:15.

15. Ezekiel 8:1; 20:1, 3.

16. Andrew Mein, *Ezekiel and the Ethics of Exile* (Oxford and New York, 2001), pp. 66–74.

17. Isaiah 45:14; 52:2; Psalms 149; 107:14; Nahum 3:10.

18. Bickerman, *Jews in the Greek Age,* pp. 47–48.

19. Job 1:6.

20. Job 1:12.

21. Ezekiel 1:1–2:15.

22. Ezekiel 2:12–15.

23. Ezekiel 2:3.

24. Ezekiel 8–12.

25. Ezekiel 8:12.

26. Ezekiel 9:9; 11:6.

27. Ezekiel 7:23; 16:38; 18:10; 22:3.

28. Ezekiel 37:10–11.

29. Ezekiel 11:18–20.

30. Ezekiel, 40:2; 48:35; Mein, *Ezekiel,* p. 142.

31. Ezekiel 47:11–12.

32. Mein, *Ezekiel,* p. 254.

33. Mary Douglas, *Natural Symbols: Explorations in Cosmology* (London, 1970), pp. 59–64; Smith, *Religion of the Landless,* pp. 84, 145.

34. Frank Moore Cross, *Canaanite Myth and Hebrew Epic: Essays in the History of the Religion of Israel* (Cambridge, Mass., and London, 1973), pp. 321–25.

35. Leviticus 17–26.

36. Exodus 25–27; 35–38; 40.

37. Genesis 1, in Everett Fox, trans., *The Five Books of Moses* (New York, 1983).

38. Psalm 137:8–9. Jerusalem Bible translation.

39. Mark S. Smith, *The Origins of Biblical Monotheism: Israel's Polytheistic Background and the Ugaritic Texts* (New York and London, 2001), pp. 167–71.

40. Genesis 1:31. Fox translation; my italics.

41. Michael Fishbane, *Text and Texture: Close Readings of Selected Biblical Texts* (New York, 1979).

42. Exodus 35:2. Jerusalem Bible translation.

43. Exodus 39:43.

44. Ackroyd, *Exile and Restoration*, pp. 91–96.

45. Exodus 29:45–46.

46. Cross, *Canaanite Myth and Hebrew Epic*, pp. 298–300; R. E. Clements, *God and Temple* (Oxford, 1965), pp. 114–21.

47. Exodus 40:34, 36–38. Fox translation.

48. Cross, *Canaanite Myth and Hebrew Epic*, p. 321.

49. Numbers 1–4; Ackroyd, *Exile and Restoration*, p. 100.

50. Exodus 15:24; 17:3; cf. Exodus 16:2, 7–9, 12; Numbers 14:2, 27, 36.

51. Ackroyd, *Exile and Restoration*, pp. 254–55; Mein, *Ezekiel*, p. 137.

52. Leviticus 19:2.

53. Leviticus 26:27; David Damrosch, "Leviticus," in Robert Alter and Frank Kermode, eds., *The Literary Guide to the Bible* (London, 1987).

54. Leviticus 26:12; trans. Cross, *Canaanite Myth*, p. 298.

55. Leviticus 25.

56. Leviticus 19:34. Jerusalem Bible translation.

57. Mary Douglas, *In the Wilderness: The Doctrine of Defilement in the Book of Numbers* (Oxford and New York, 2001), pp. 24–25, 42–43; Mein, *Ezekiel*, pp. 148–49.

58. Numbers 19:11–22.

59. Douglas, *In the Wilderness*, pp. 25–26.

60. Leviticus 1:9, 13, 17.

61. Leviticus 1:1–3; Exodus 20:8; Mary Douglas, *Leviticus as Literature* (Oxford and New York, 1999), pp. 68–69, 135–36.

62. Leviticus 11:31–39, 43–44.

63. Numbers 11:31–33; Psalm 78:26–27.

64. Douglas, *Leviticus as Literature*, pp. 150–73.

65. Christian Meier, *Athens: A Portrait of a City in Its Golden Age*, trans. Robert and Rita Kimber (London, 1999), pp. 150–52.

66. Oswyn Murray, *Early Greece*, 2nd ed. (London, 1993), pp. 195–97.

67. Meier, *Athens*, pp. 70–71.

68. Robert Parker, *Athenian Religion: A History* (Oxford and New York, 1996), pp. 71–72.

69. Ibid., pp. 75–91; Murray, *Early Greece*, p. 270.

70. Walter Burkert, *Homo Necans: The Anthropology of Ancient Greek Sacrificial Ritual and Myth,* trans. Peter Bing (Berkeley, Los Angeles, and London, 1983), pp. 152–68; Walter Burkert, *Greek Religion,* trans. John Raffan (Cambridge, Mass., 1985), pp. 232–344; Parker, *Athenian Religion,* pp. 89–91; Louise Bruitt Zaidman and Pauline Schmitt Pantel, *Religion in the Greek City,* trans. Paul Cartledge (Cambridge, U.K., 1992), pp. 105–6.

71. Parker, *Athenian Religion,* pp. 97–100; Walter Burkert, *Ancient Mystery Cults* (Cambridge, Mass., and London, 1986), pp. 7–95; Burkert, *Homo Necans,* pp. 248–97.

72. Aristotle, Fragment 15, cited in Burkert, *Ancient Mystery Cults,* pp. 69, 89.

73. Aristotle, Fragments, cited ibid., p. 90.

74. Plutarch, Fragment 168, cited ibid., pp. 91–92.

75. Cited ibid., p. 114.

76. Burkert, *Ancient Mystery Cults,* p. 37; Joseph Campbell, *Transformations of Myth Through Time* (New York, 1990), pp. 191–93.

77. Zaidman and Pantel, *Religion in the Greek City,* pp. 198–218; Burkert, *Greek Religion,* pp. 160–66; Jean-Pierre Vernant with Pierre Vidal-Naquet, *Myth and Tragedy in Ancient Greece,* trans. Janet Lloyd (New York, 1990), pp. 384–90.

78. Zaidman and Pantel, *Religion in the Greek City,* pp. 199–200; Burkert, *Greek Religion,* pp. 290–93.

79. Marcel Detienne, "Culinary Practices and the Spirit of Sacrifice," in Marcel Detienne and Jean-Pierre Vernant, eds., *The Cuisine of Sacrifice Among the Greeks,* trans. Paula Wissing (Chicago and London, 1989), pp. 7–8; Zaidman and Pantel, *Religion in the Greek City,* pp. 158–75; Anthony Gottlieb, *The Dream of Reason: A History of Philosophy from the Greeks to the Renaissance* (London, 2000), pp. 25–26; Burkert, *Greek Religion,* pp. 296–303.

80. William K. Freist, "Orpheus: A Fugue on the Polis," in Dora C. Pozzi and John M. Wickerstein, eds., *Myth and the Polis* (Ithaca and London, 1991), pp. 32–48.

81. Gottlieb, *Dream of Reason,* pp. 4–20; Burkert, *Greek Religion,* pp. 305–11; Murray, *Early Greece,* pp. 247–51; Charles Freeman, *The Greek Achievement: The Foundation of the Western World* (New York and London, 1999), pp. 149–52; Richard Tarnas, *The Passion of the Western Mind: Understanding the Ideas That Have Shaped Our World View* (New York and London, 1991), pp. 19–25.

82. Samkhya Sutras 3:47.

83. Samkhya Sutras 3:47, in Mircea Eliade, *Yoga: Immortality and Freedom,* trans. Willard R. Trask (London, 1958), p. 12.

84. Samkhya Sutras 3:61, ibid., p. 30.

85. Samkhya Karita 59, ibid.

86. Eliade, *Yoga,* passim; Edward Conze, *Buddhist Meditation* (London, 1956).

87. Yoga Sutra 2.42, in Eliade, *Yoga,* p. 52.

88. Jacques Gernet, *Ancient China: From the Beginnings to the Empire,* trans. Raymond Rudorff (London, 1968), pp. 83–84.

89. James Legge, trans., *The Ch'un Ts'ew and the Tso Chuen,* 2nd ed. (Hong Kong, 1960), p. 109.

6. EMPATHY

1. A. C. Graham, *Disputers of the Tao: Philosophical Argument in Ancient China* (La Salle, Ill., 1989), p. 9.

2. Confucius, Analects 5:6; cf. 16:2. Quotations from the Analects are taken from Arthur Waley, trans. and ed., *The Analects of Confucius* (New York, 1992), unless otherwise stated.

3. Analects 7:8.

4. Analects 7:33.

5. Benjamin I. Schwartz, *The World of Thought in Ancient China* (Cambridge, Mass., and London, 1985), p. 62; Fung Yu-Lan, *A Short History of Chinese Philosophy,* ed. Derk Bodde (New York, 1976), p. 12.

6. Analects 12:7.

7. Analects 7:1.

8. Analects 7:19.

9. Analects 2:11.

10. Analects 5:12.

11. Analects 11:11.

12. Analects 17:19.

13. *Classic of Odes 55,* in Arthur Waley, ed. and trans., *The Book of Songs* (London, 1937); Analects 1:15.

14. Analects 12:1. Translation suggested in Schwartz, *World of Thought,* p. 77.

15. Ibid.

16. Analects 2:7.

17. Jacques Gernet, *Ancient China: From the Beginnings to the Empire,* trans. Raymond Rudorff (London, 1968), p. 116.

18. Analects 2:8.

19. Ibid.

20. Tu Wei-ming, *Confucian Thought: Selfhood as Creative Transformation* (Albany, 1985), pp. 115–16.

21. Analects 6:28, as translated ibid., p. 68.

22. Tu Wei-ming, *Confucian Thought,* pp. 57–58; Huston Smith, *The World's Religions: Our Great Wisdom Traditions* (San Francisco, 1991), pp. 180–81.

23. Analects 4:15, as translated in Graham, *Disputers of the Tao,* p. 21.

24. Analects 15:23.

25. Analects 5:11.

26. Graham, *Disputers of the Tao,* p. 19.

27. Tu Wei-ming, *Confucian Thought,* p. 84.

28. Analects 12:3.

29. Analects 12:2.

30. Analects 6:28.

31. Ibid.

32. Analects 6:20; 16:2.

33. Analects 7:29.

34. Analects 6:20; Herbert Fingarette, *Confucius: The Secular as Sacred* (New York, 1972), pp. 51–56.

35. Analects 8:7.

36. Analects 9:10.

37. Analects 11:8–9.

38. Analects 5:8.

39. Analects 9:8.

40. Analects 7:5.

41. Isaiah 44:28.

42. Isaiah 41:1–4.

43. Isaiah 51:9–10.

44. Isaiah 42:1–4; 49:1–6; 50:4–9; 52:13–53:12.

45. Isaiah 42:2–3.

46. Isaiah 50:5–6, 9.

47. Isaiah 52:13–53:5.

48. Isaiah 49:6.

49. Isaiah 41:12, 16; 51:23.

50. Isaiah 45:3.

51. Isaiah 41:17–24

52. Isaiah 44:6–20; 46:1–9.

53. Isaiah 5:7.

54. Isaiah 42:13.

55. Isaiah 42:17.

56. Isaiah 40:5; 51:3.

57. Isaiah 54:11–17.

58. Ezra 2:64.

59. Josephus, *The Antiquities of the Jews* 11:8.

60. Margaret Barker, *The Older Testament: The Survival of Themes from the Ancient Royal Cult in Sectarian Judaism and Early Christianity* (London, 1987), p. 186.

61. Haggai 1:9–11; 2:4–8.

62. Ezra 3:12–13.

63. Zechariah 8:23.

64. Zechariah 2:8.

65. Zechariah 7:1–7; 8:20.

66. Frank Moore Cross, *From Epic to Canon: History and Literature in Ancient Israel* (Baltimore and London, 1998), p. 170.

67. 2 Chronicles 30:1–14.

68. Ezra 3:13.

69. Christian Meier, *Athens: A Portrait of the City in Its Golden Age,* trans. Robert and Rita Kimber (London, 1999), pp. 157–86; Charles Freeman, *The Greek Achievement: The Foundation of the Western World* (New York and London, 1999), pp. 167–69; Oswyn Murray, *Early Greece,* 2nd ed. (London, 1993), pp. 274–81.

70. Murray, *Early Greece,* pp. 279–80.

71. Meier, *Athens,* p. 158; Jean-Pierre Vernant, *Myth and Society in Ancient Greece,* trans. Janet Lloyd, 3rd ed. (New York, 1996), pp. 92–96.

72. Heraclitus B17, in Jonathan Barnes, ed. and trans., *Early Greek Philosophy* (London and New York, 1987), p. 110.

73. Heraclitus B61, ibid., p. 104.

74. Heraclitus B125; B12; B49a; B26, ibid., pp. 117, 120, 124.

75. Heraclitus B60, ibid., p. 103.

76. Heraclitus B101, ibid., p. 113.

77. Heraclitus B119, ibid., p. 124.

78. Xenophanes B14; B12; B15, ibid., p. 95.

79. Xenophanes B23, ibid.

80. Xenophanes B26; B25, ibid., p. 97.

81. Fragment 1.22, in Anthony Gottlieb, *The Dream of Reason: A History of Western Philosophy from the Greeks to the Renaissance* (London and New York, 2000), p. 52.

82. Barnes, *Early Greek Philosophers,* pp. 129–43.

83. Gottlieb, *The Dream of Reason,* p. 52.

84. Meier, *Athens,* pp. 10–18.

85. Murray, *Early Greece,* pp. 281–83; Meier, *Athens,* pp. 219–25.

86. Murray, *Early Greece,* pp. 236–46; Meier, *Athens,* pp. 3–33.

87. Murray, *Early Greece,* pp. 281–83; Meier, *Athens,* pp. 219–25.

88. Herodotus, *Histories* 6.21, in

Jean-Pierre Vernant with Pierre Vidal-Naquet, eds., *Myth and Tragedy in Ancient Greece,* trans. Janet Lloyd (New York, 1990), p. 244.

89. Simon Goldhill, "The Great Dionysia," in J. J. Winckler and F. Zeitlin, eds., *Nothing to Do with Dionysos? Athenian Drama in Its Social Context* (Princeton, 1990).

90. Freeman, *Greek Achievement,* p. 169.

91. John Gould, "Tragedy and Collective Experience," in M. S. Silk, ed., *Tragedy and the Tragic: Greek Theatre and Beyond* (Oxford, 1996), pp. 219–24; Simon Goldhill, "Collectivity and Otherness: The Authority of the Greek Chorus," in Silk, *Tragedy,* pp. 245–60.

92. Charles Segal, "Catharsis, Audience and Closure in Greek Tragedy," in Silk, *Tragedy,* pp. 149–66.

93. Aeschylus, *The Persians* 179–84, in Philip Vellacott, trans., *Aeschylus: Prometheus Bound and Other Plays* (London and New York, 1961).

94. *The Persians* 826–29. Vellacott translation.

95. Meier, *Athens,* pp. 207–8.

96. Vernant, *Myth and Society,* pp. 133–35.

97. Aeschylus, *Agamemnon* 1592, in Robert Fagles, trans., *Aeschylus: The Oresteia* (New York and London, 1975).

98. Segal, "Catharsis," pp. 157–58; Oliver Taplin, "Comedy and the Tragic," in Silk, *Tragedy,* pp. 198–99.

99. Vernant, *Myth and Tragedy,* p. 277; Michael Trapp, "The Fragility of Moral Reasoning," in Silk, *Tragedy,* pp. 76–81.

100. *Antigone* 348–70, in E. F. Watling, trans., *Sophocles: The Theban Plays* (London and New York, 1957).

101. Thomas J. Hopkins, *The Hindu Religious Tradition* (Belmont, Calif., 1971), pp. 50–51.

102. Katha Upanishad 1.26, in Patrick Olivelle, *Upanisads* (Oxford and New York, 1996).

103. Katha Upanishad 3:2–4, 6, 8; 6:11. Olivelle translation.

104. John Keay, *India: A History* (London, 2000), pp. 47–73; Olivelle, *Upanisads,* pp. xxviii–xxix; Gavin Flood, *An Introduction to Hinduism* (Cambridge, U.K., and New York), pp. 80–81; Hermann Kulke, "The Historical Background of India's Axial Age," in S. N. Eisendstadt, ed., *The Origins and Diversity of Axial Age Civilizations* (Albany, 1986), p. 109.

105. Kulke, "Historical Background," p. 384.

106. Mircea Eliade, *Yoga: Immortality and Freedom,* trans. Willard R. Trask (London, 1958), pp. 139–40, 158.

107. Trevor Ling, *The Buddha: Buddhist Civilization in India and Ceylon* (London, 1973), pp. 78–82.

108. Eliade, *Yoga,* pp. 189–91; Hopkins, *Hindu Religious Tradition,* p. 54.

109. Paul Dundas, *The Jains,* 2nd ed. (London and New York, 2002), pp. 28–30.

110. Ibid., p. 27; Hopkins, *Hindu Religious Tradition*, pp. 54–55.

111. Dundas, *Jains*, pp. 106–7.

112. Acaranga Sutra (AS) 2.15.25.

113. AS 1.5.6.3, in Dundas, *Jains*, p. 43.

114. AS 1.4.1.1–2, ibid., pp. 41–42.

115. AS 1.2.3, ibid.

116. Dasavairtaklika 4.10, ibid., p. 160.

117. AS 1.21; 1.1.3.2.

118. Dundas, *Jains*, pp. 34–35.

119. Ibid., pp. 170–71.

120. Avashyaksutra 32, in Dundas, *Jains*, p. 171.

7. CONCERN FOR EVERYBODY

1. Margaret Barker, *The Older Testament: The Survival of Themes from the Ancient Royal Cult in Sectarian Judaism and Early Christianity* (London, 1987), pp. 201–16.

2. Isaiah 65:16–25.

3. Isaiah 56:7.

4. Nehemiah 2:14; 4:11–12.

5. Gosta W. Ahlström, *The History of Ancient Palestine* (Minneapolis, 1993), pp. 880–83; Elias J. Bickerman, *The Jews in the Greek Age* (Cambridge, Mass., 1988), pp. 29–32; W. D. Davies and Louis Finkelstein, eds., *The Cambridge History of Judaism*, 2 vols. (Cambridge, U.K., 1984), I:144–53.

6. Ezra 7:6.

7. Ezra 7:21–26; Bickerman, *Jews in the Greek Age*, p. 154.

8. Nehemiah 8.

9. Ezra 10.

10. Isaiah 63:10–19.

11. Jonah 4:11.

12. Diogenes Laertius, *Lives of the Philosophers* 9.72, in Jonathan Barnes, trans. and ed., *Early Greek Philosophy* (London and New York, 1987), p. 157.

13. Plato, *Parmenides* 127a–128d.

14. Anthony Gottlieb, *The Dream of Reason: A History of Philosophy from the Greeks to the Renaissance* (London, 2000), pp. 65–71.

15. Ibid., p. 78.

16. Plato, *Apology* 26d; Gottlieb, *Dream of Reason*, p. 84.

17. G. B. Kerferd, *The Sophistic Movement* (Cambridge, U.K., 1981); Gottlieb, *Dream of Reason*, pp. 109–28; Walter Burkert, *Greek Religion*, trans. John Raffan (Cambridge, Mass., 1985), pp. 311–17; Richard Tarnas, *The Passion of the Western Mind: Understanding the Ideas That Have Shaped Our World View* (New York and London, 1991), pp. 26–31; Christian Meier, *Athens: A Portrait of the City in Its Golden Age* (London, 1999), pp. 440–45.

18. Gorgias, Fragment 3.

19. Meier, *Athens*, pp. 405–12.

20. Antiphon, Fragment 44, in Gottlieb, *Dream of Reason*, p. 125.

21. Protagoras, Fragment 1, ibid., p. 119.

22. Protagoras, Fragment 4, in Tarnas, *Passion of the Western Mind*, p. 28.

23. Euripides, "On the Nature of the Gods." Quoted in Meier, *Athens*, p. 443.

24. *Heracles* 1307; 1341–46, in Philip Vellacott, trans., *Euripides: Medea and Other Plays* (London and New York, 1963).

25. Fragment 1018, in Burkert, *Greek Religion,* p. 319.

26. *Trojan Women* 884–88, in John Davie, trans., *Euripides: Electra and Other Plays* (London and New York, 1998).

27. *Medea* 1021–80; Bernard Seidensticker, "Peripeteia and Tragic Dialectic in Euripidean Tragedy," in M. S. Silk, ed., *Tragedy and the Tragic: Greek Theatre and Beyond* (Oxford, 1996), pp. 387–88.

28. Aristotle, *Rhetoric* 1385b.11–1386b.7, in Richard McKeon, ed., *The Basic Works of Aristotle* (New York, 2001).

29. Seidensticker, "Peripeteia and Tragic Dialectic," pp. 402–3.

30. *Heracles* 1233–38; 1398–1428. Vellacott translation.

31. Cf. *Odyssey* 11:275–76.

32. Charles Segal, "Catharsis, Audience and Closure in Greek Tragedy," in Silk, *Tragedy and the Tragic,* pp. 166–68; Claude Calame, "Vision, Blindness and Mask: The Radicalization of the Emotions," in Silk, *Tragedy and the Tragic,* pp. 19–31; Richard Buxton, "What Can You Rely on in Oedipus Rex?," in Silk, *Tragedy and the Tragic,* pp. 38–49.

33. *King Oedipus* 1297; 1312; 1299; 1321, in E. F. Watling, trans., *Sophocles: The Theban Plays* (London and New York, 1947).

34. Jean Pierre Vernant with Pierre Vidal-Naquet, *Myth and Tragedy in Ancient Greece,* trans. Janet Lloyd (New York, 1990), pp. 113–17.

35. Plato, *Symposium* 220c; 174d; 175b, in W. Hamilton, trans., *The Symposium* (Harmondsworth, 1951).

36. Plato, *Laches* 187e, in Benjamin Jowett, trans., with M. J. Knight, *The Essential Plato* (Oxford, 1871); reprinted with introduction by Alain de Boton (London, 1999).

37. Plato, *Laches,* "On Courage." Jowett translation.

38. Plato, *Apologia* 38a5–6. Jowett translation.

39. Plato, *Crito* 47e. Jowett translation.

40. Plato, *Crito* 49a.

41. Plato, *Symposium* 215de. Hamilton translation.

42. Charles Segal, *Dionysiac Poetics and Euripides' Bacchae,* 2nd ed. (Princeton, 1997); Richard Seaford, "Something to Do with Dionysus: Tragedy and the Dionysiac," in Silk, *Tragedy and the Tragic,* pp. 284–92; Oliver Taplin, "Comedy and the Tragic," in Silk, *Tragedy and the Tragic,* pp. 284–92; George Steiner, "Tragedy, Pure and Simple," in Silk, *Tragedy and the Tragic,* pp. 538–89; Vernant, *Myth and Tragedy,* pp. 381–412; Meier, *Athens,* pp. 575–78.

43. Euripides, *The Bacchae* 1168–1231, in Philip Vellacott, trans., *Euripides: The Bacchae and Other Plays* (London and New York, 1973).

44. Euripedes, *Bacchae* 1075–95.

45. Plato, *Apologia* 37e. Jowett translation.

46. Jacques Gernet, *A History of Chinese Civilization,* trans. J. R.

Foster and Charles Hartman, 2nd ed. (Cambridge, U.K., and New York, 1996), p. 62.

47. Jacques Gernet, *Ancient China: From the Beginnings to the Empire,* trans. Raymond Rudorff (London, 1968), pp. 93–94, 96–101; Gernet, *History of Chinese Civilization,* pp. 65–67.

48. *Zuozhuan* ("The Commentary of Mr. Zuo") 2:30, in James Legge, trans., *The Ch'un Ts'ew and the Tso Chuen* (Hong Kong, 1960).

49. Marcel Granet, *Chinese Civilization,* trans. Kathleen Innes and Mabel Brailsford (London and New York, 1951), pp. 32–33.

50. Sima Qian, *Records of the Grand Historian* 124, in Fung Yu-Lan, *A Short History of Chinese Philosophy,* ed. and trans. Derk Bodde (New York, 1976), p. 50.

51. Fung Yu-Lan, *Short History of Chinese Philosophy,* pp. 50–52.

52. *The Book of Huainan* 20. The *Huainanzi* is a collection of twenty-one essays compiled in the second century.

53. A. C. Graham, *Later Mohist Logic, Ethics and Science* (Hong Kong, 1978), p. 4; Gernet, *Ancient China,* pp. 116–17.

54. *The Book of Mozi* 26:4. Quotations from the *Mozi* are from Burton Watson, trans. and ed., *Mo-Tzu: Basic Writings* (New York, 1963), unless otherwise stated.

55. A. C. Graham, *Disputers of the Tao: Philosophical Argument in Ancient China* (La Salle, Ill., 1989), p. 34; Benjamin I.

Schwartz, *The World of Thought in Ancient China* (Cambridge, Mass., and London, 1985), p. 137.

56. *Mozi* 26:4.

57. *Mozi* 6:17–18.

58. Gernet, *Ancient China,* p. 116.

59. *Mozi* 3:16, trans. Fung Yu-Lan, *Short History of Chinese Philosophy,* p. 55.

60. Graham, *Disputers of the Tao,* p. 41.

61. *Mozi* 15:11–15.

62. Graham, *Disputers of the Tao,* pp. 47–48.

63. Schwartz, *World of Thought,* p. 157.

64. *Mozi* 8.

65. *Mozi* 15.

66. Graham, *Later Mohist Logic,* p. 256.

67. *Mozi* 4, in Schwartz, *World of Thought,* p. 145.

68. *Mozi* 16.

69. Ibid.

70. Majjhima Nikaya (MN) 26, 85, 100; Jataka 1.62. The Pali scriptures include four collections of the Buddha's sermons (*Majjhima Nikaya, Digha Nikaya, Anguttara Nikaya,* and *Samyutta Nikaya*) and an anthology of minor works, which include the *Udana,* a collection of the Buddha's maxims, and the *Jataka,* stories about the past lives of the Buddha and his companions. The quotations from the Pali Canon given here are my own version of the texts cited.

71. MN 26.

72. Udana 8:3.

73. MN 26, 36, 85, 100.

74. MN 12, 36, 85, 200.

75. MN 36.

76. Joseph Campbell, *Oriental Mythology: The Masks of God* (New York, 1962), p. 236.

77. MN 36.

78. Anguttara Nikaya (AN) 9:3; MN 38, 41.

79. *Vinaya:* Mahavagga 1.6. This text is part of the *Vinaya Pitaka*, the Book of Monastic Discipline, which codifies the rule of the Buddhist order.

80. Udana 3:10.

81. MN 38.

82. Hermann Oldenberg, *Buddha: His Life, His Doctrine, His Order,* trans. William Hoey (London, 1882), pp. 299–302; Edward Conze, *Buddhism: Its Essence and Development* (Oxford, 1951), p. 102.

83. AN 8.7.3.

84. Richard F. Gombrich, *How Buddhism Began: The Conditioned Genesis of the Early Teachings* (London and Atlantic Highlands, N.J., 1996), pp. 60–61.

85. Michael Carrithers, *The Buddha* (Oxford and New York, 1993), pp. 75–77.

86. AN 8.20.

87. MN 36; Samyutta Nikaya 12.65.

88. MN 36.

89. AN 10.95.

90. MN 29.

91. Karen Armstrong, *A History of God: The 4,000 Year Quest of Judaism, Christianity and Islam* (London and New York, 1993).

92. Sutta-Nipata 43:1–44. The Sutta-Nipata is an anthology of early Buddhist poetry.

93. *Vinaya:* Mahavagga 1.5.

94. Ibid.

95. *Vinaya:* Mahavagga 1.6.

96. *Vinaya:* Mahavagga 1.11.

97. *Vinaya:* Mahavagga 1.6; SN 22:59.

98. *Vinaya:* Mahavagga, 1.6.

99. MN 1.

100. MN 22.

101. Samyutta Nikaya 53:31.

102. MN 63.

103. AN 3.65.

104. Sutta-Nipata 118.

105. AN 3.65.

106. Samyutta Nikaya 3.1–8.

107. MN 89.

108. Karl Jaspers, *The Great Philosophers: The Foundations,* ed. Hannah Arendt, trans. Ralph Manheim (London, 1962), pp. 99–105.

109. AN 4.36.

8. ALL IS ONE

1. Jacques Gernet, *A History of Chinese Civilization,* trans. J. R. Foster and Charles Hartman, 2nd ed. (Cambridge, U.K., and New York, 1996), pp. 67–81; Jacques Gernet, *Ancient China: From the Beginnings to the Empire,* trans. Raymond Rudorff (London, 1968), pp. 89–114.

2. Benjamin I. Schwartz, *The World of Thought in Ancient China* (Cambridge, Mass., and London, 1985), pp. 238–39.

3. Marcel Granet, *Chinese Civilization,* trans. Kathleen Innes and Mabel Brailsford (London and New York, 1951), p. 32.

4. Analects 14:39, 41; 18:6.

5. *The Book of Zhuangzi,* 15:1, in Martin Palmer with Elizabeth

Brenilly, trans., *The Book of Chuang Tzu* (London and New York, 1996).

6. A. C. Graham, *Disputers of the Tao: Philosophical Argument in Ancient China* (La Salle, Ill., 1989), pp. 64–74.

7. *The Book of Zhuangzi* 15:5.

8. Fung Yu-Lan, *A Short History of Chinese Philosophy,* ed. and trans. Derk Bodde (New York, 1976), pp. 60–66.

9. *Annals of Spring and Autumn* 1.3.

10. *Annals of Spring and Autumn* 21.4, in Graham, *Disputers of the Tao,* p. 251.

11. *The Book of Mencius* 3B9, in D. C. Lau, trans., *Mencius* (London 1970).

12. *The Book of Mencius* 7A 26. Lau translation.

13. *The Book of Huainan,* 13.

14. *The Book of Mencius* 3B9.

15. *Inward Training* 2.100, in Graham, *Disputers of the Tao,* pp. 100–105.

16. *Inward Training* 2.102. Graham translation.

17. *The Book of Zhuangzi* 17:34. Palmer translation.

18. Graham, *Disputers of the Tao,* pp. 76–82; Schwartz, *World of Thought,* pp. 223–24; Fung Yu-Lan, *Short History of Chinese Philosophy,* pp. 83–94.

19. *The Book of Zhuangzi* 33. Palmer translation.

20. Schwartz, *World of Thought,* p. 224.

21. Fung Yu-Lan, *Short History of Chinese Philosophy,* p. 91.

22. Graham, *Disputers of the Tao,* pp. 172–203; Schwartz, *World of Thought,* pp. 215–36; Fung Yu-Lan, *Short History of Chinese Philosophy,* pp. 104–17; Mark Elvin, "Was There a Transcendental Breakthrough in China?," in S. N. Eisenstadt, ed., *The Origins and Diversity of Axial Age Civilizations* (Albany, 1986), pp. 342–46.

23. *The Book of Zhuangzi* 17.

24. *The Book of Zhuangzi* 20:61–68. Palmer translation.

25. *The Book of Zhuangzi* 18:15–19. Palmer translation.

26. *The Book of Zhuangzi* 6.53, in David Hinton, trans., *Chuang Tzu: The Inner Chapters* (Washington, D.C., 1998).

27. *The Book of Zhuangzi* 5:84.

28. *The Book of Zhuangzi* 6:29–31.

29. Elvin, "Was There a Transcendental Breakthrough in China?," p. 343.

30. *The Book of Zhuangzi* 4:26–28. Hinton translation.

31. *The Book of Zhuangzi* 2:29–31. Palmer translation.

32. *The Book of Zhuangzi* 17:3.

33. *The Book of Zhuangzi* 19:19–21; 13:70–75. Palmer translation.

34. *The Book of Zhuangzi* 2:1–3. Hinton translation.

35. *The Book of Zhuangzi* 6:93. Hinton translation.

36. *The Book of Zhuangzi* 6:19.

37. *The Book of Zhuangzi* 6:20. Palmer translation.

38. *The Book of Zhuangzi* 1:21. Palmer translation.

39. *The Book of Zhuangzi* 6:80. Palmer translation.

40. *The Book of Zhuangzi* 7:32; 13:2–6; 33:56.

41. *The Book of Zhuangzi* 6:11.

42. Graham, *Disputers of the Tao,* pp.

111–32; Elvin, "Was There a Transcendental Breakthrough in China?," pp. 340–42; Schwartz, *World of Thought,* pp. 255–90; Fung Yu-Lan, *Short History of Chinese Philosophy,* pp. 68–79; Tu Wei-ming, *Confucian Thought: Selfhood as Creative Transformation* (Albany, 1985), pp. 61–109.

43. *Mencius* 2A 1; 2B 13; quotations from *Mencius* are taken from Lau, *Mencius.*

44. *Mencius* 2A 3.

45. *Mencius* 1A 5–6.

46. *Mencius* 1A 7.

47. *Mencius* 3A 4.

48. *Mencius* 3B 9.

49. *Mencius* 2A 6.

50. *Mencius* 3A 5.

51. *Mencius* 1A 7.

52. Ibid.

53. *Mencius* 2A 6.

54. Ibid.

55. *Mencius* 6A 8.

56. Ibid.

57. *Mencius* 6A 11.

58. *Mencius* 7A 1.

59. *Mencius* 2A 2; Fung Yu-Lan, *Short History of Chinese Philosophy,* p. 78.

60. *Mencius* 7A 4.

61. *Mencius* 7A 13.

62. E. Washington Hopkins, *The Great Epic of India* (New York, 1902); Thomas J. Hopkins, *The Hindu Religious Tradition* (Belmont, Calif., 1971), pp. 87–89; Klaus K. Klostermeier, *Hinduism: A Short History* (Oxford, 2000), pp. 58–62; John Brockington, *The Sanskrit Epics* (Leiden, 1998); John Brockington, "The Sanskrit Epics," in Gavin Flood, ed., *The Blackwell Companion to Hinduism* (Oxford, 2003), pp. 116–23; R. C. Zaehner, *Hinduism* (London, New York, and Toronto, 1962), pp. 84–120; Alf Hiltebeitel, *The Ritual of Battle: Krishna in the Mahabharata* (Ithaca and London, 1976); David Shulman, "Asvatthaman and Brhannada: Brahmin and Kingly Paradigms in the Sanskrit Epics," in S. N. Eisenstadt, ed., *The Origins and Diversity of Axial Age Civilizations* (Albany, 1986), pp. 407–25.

63. *Mahabharata* 5.70.40–66.

64. *Mahabharata* 6.103.71:82–90.

65. *Mahabharata* 7.164.63, in K. M. Ganguli, trans., *Mahabharata,* 12 vols. (Calcutta, 1883–96).

66. *Mahabharata* 7.164.98–99. Ganguli translation.

67. *Mahabharata* 7.164.41–42.

68. Taittiriya Samhita 3.1.10.3; Shatapatha Brahmana 4.2.2.4.

69. *Mahabharata* 9.60.62. Ganguli translation.

70. *Mahabharata* 5.70.66. Ganguli translation.

71. *Mahabharata* 10.3.33. Ganguli translation.

72. *Mahabharata* 10.14.6–7.

73. *Mahabharata* 10.15.1–10.

74. *Mahabharata* 10.18.9cd–12, quoted in Hiltebeitel, *Ritual of Battle,* p. 334.

75. Richard Tarnas, *The Passion of the Western Mind: Understanding the Ideas That Have Shaped Our World View* (New York and London, 1991), pp. 4–54; Bernard Williams, "Plato: The Invention of Philosophy," in Frederic Raphael and Ray Monk, eds., *The Great Philoso-*

phers (London, 2000), pp. 41–75; Anthony Gottlieb, *The Dream of Reason: A History of Philosophy from the Greeks to the Renaissance* (London, 2000), pp. 169–219; Walter Burkert, *Greek Religion,* trans. John Raffan (Cambridge, Mass., and London, 1992), pp. 321–37.

76. *Seventh Letter* 326a, quoted in Gottlieb, *Dream of Reason,* p. 176.

77. Williams, "Plato," p. 47; Tarnas, *Passion of the Western Mind,* p. 13.

78. *Cratylus* 386e, trans. C. D. C. Reeve in John M. Cooper, ed., *Plato: Complete Works* (Indianapolis, 1997).

79. Mircea Eliade, *The Myth of the Eternal Return, or, Cosmos and History,* trans. Willard R. Trask (Princeton, 1959), pp. 34–35.

80. *Meno* 82 b–c.

81. Quoted in Gottlieb, *Dream of Reason,* p. 170.

82. *Meno* 81c–d, trans. G. M. A. Grube in Cooper, ed., *Plato: Complete Works.*

83. *Meno* 82b–c.

84. Gottlieb, *Dream of Reason,* p. 174.

85. Ibid., p. 207.

86. *Symposium* 210e, in W. Hamilton, trans., *The Symposium* (Harmondsworth, 1951).

87. *Symposium* 201e. Hamilton translation.

88. *Symposium* 210e. Hamilton translation.

89. *Republic* 504d–509d.

90. *Republic* 520c, trans. G. M. A. Grube and C. D. C. Reeve, in Cooper, ed., *Plato: Complete Works.*

91. *Republic* 517a. Grube and Reeve translation.

92. *Republic* 520c. Grube and Reeve translation.

93. P. E. Easterling, "The End of an Era: Tragedy in the Early Fourth Century," in A. H. Sommerstein, ed., *Tragedy, Comedy, and the Polis* (Bari, 1993).

94. P. J. Wilson, "The Use of Tragedy in the Fourth Century," in M. S. Silk, ed., *Tragedy and the Tragic: Greek Theatre and Beyond* (Oxford, 1996), pp. 314–16.

95. *Republic* 606d. Grube and Reeve translation.

96. *Republic* 603e–606b; Stephen Halliwell, "Plato's Repudiation of the Tragic," in Silk, *Tragedy and the Tragic.*

97. *Timaeus* 28c, trans. Donald J. Zeyl, in Cooper, ed., *Plato: Complete Works.*

98. *Timaeus* 39–41. Zeyl translation.

99. *Timaeus* 90a. Zeyl translation.

100. *Symposium* 202e–203a; *Laws* 834a; 729e; 941a.

101. *Laws* 771d.

102. *Laws* 653b; 654a, trans. Trevor J. Saunders, in Cooper, ed., *Plato: Complete Works.*

103. *Laws* 717b.

104. Burkert, *Greek Religion,* pp. 333–34.

105. *Laws* 716c. Saunders translation.

106. *Laws* 888b; 885b. Saunders translation.

107. *Laws* 907d; 909d.

108. *Nichomachean Ethics* 1178a, in Richard McKeon, ed., *The Basic Works of Aristotle* (New York, 2001).

109. *Nichomachean Ethics* 1177a, ibid.

110. Gottlieb, *Dream of Reason*, pp. 270–72.

111. Burkert, *Greek Religion*, p. 331.

112. *Nichomachean Ethics* 1099b11; 1179a24.

113. *Politics* 1335b.15; 1314b39; 1331a27; 1336b6; *Rhetoric* 1391b1.

114. Karen Armstrong, *A History of God: The 4,000 Year Quest of Judaism, Christianity and Islam* (London and New York, 1993), pp. 171–208.

115. Fragment 15, quoted in Walter Burkert, *Ancient Mystery Cults* (Cambridge, Mass., and London, 1987), pp. 69, 89.

116. Gottlieb, *Dream of Reason*, p. 277.

117. *Poetics* 6, 1449b28.

9. EMPIRE

1. A. C. Graham, *Disputers of the Tao: Philosophical Argument in Ancient China* (La Salle, Ill., 1989), pp. 267–76; Benjamin I. Schwartz, *The World of Thought in Ancient China* (Cambridge, Mass., and London, 1985), pp. 321–45; Fung Yu-Lan, *A Short History of Chinese Philosophy*, ed. and trans. Derk Bodde (New York, 1976), pp. 155–65.

2. Schwartz, *World of Thought*, pp. 321–23.

3. *The Book of Guanzi* 67.3.55, quoted in Graham, *Disputers of the Tao*, p. 274. The *Guanzi* was attributed to the seventh-century statesman Guan Zhong, but is actually of a much later date.

4. *Shanqiunshu* ("The Book of Lord Shang") 2:7, quoted in Fung Yu-Lan, *Short History of Chinese Philosophy*, p. 159.

5. *Shanqiunshu* 9:1.

6. *Shanqiunshu* 8:8, quoted in Schwartz, *World of Thought*, p. 328.

7. *Shanqiunshu* 20, quoted in Mark Elvin, "Was There a Transcendental Breakthrough in China?," in S. N. Eisenstadt, ed., *The Origins and Diversity of Axial Age Civilizations* (Albany, 1980), p. 352.

8. *Shanqiunshu* 20, quoted in Graham, *Disputers of the Tao*, p. 290.

9. *Shanqiunshu* 20, in Schwartz, *World of Thought*, pp. 342–43.

10. *Han Feizi* ("The Book of Han Fei") 54, in Graham, *Disputers of the Tao*, p. 290.

11. *Han Feizi* 5, ibid., p. 288.

12. Graham, *Disputers of the Tao*, pp. 235–67; Schwartz, *World of Thought*, pp. 299–320; Fung Yu-Lan, *Short History of Chinese Philosophy*, pp. 143–54; Elvin, "Was There a Transcendental Breakthrough in China?," pp. 348–51.

13. *Xunzi* ("The Book of Master Xan") 9, in Burton Watson, ed. and trans., *Xunzi: Basic Writings* (New York, 2003).

14. *Xunzi* 16.

15. *Xunzi* 16, in Schwartz, *World of Thought*, p. 305.

16. *Xunzi* 8, quoted in Graham, *Disputers of the Tao*, p. 238.

17. *Xunzi* 15:72. Watson translation.

18. *Xunzi* 17:44. Watson translation.

19. Ibid. Watson translation.

20. *Xunzi* 23:1–4. Watson translation.

21. Ibid. Watson translation.

22. Ibid.

23. *Xunzi* 21:28–30.

24. *Xunzi* 19:63. Watson translation.

25. *Xunzi* 19:17–79. Watson translation.

26. *Xunzi* 19, passim. The sentence is repeated throughout the chapter like a refrain. Watson translation.

27. *Xunzi* 21:34–39. Watson translation.

28. Ibid. Watson translation.

29. Ibid. Watson translation.

30. Graham, *Disputers of the Tao*, p. 215; Elvin, "Was There a Transcendental Breakthrough in China?," p. 352; Huston Smith, *The World's Religions: Our Great Wisdom Traditions* (San Francisco, 1991), p. 197; Max Kaltenmark, *Lao Tzu and Taoism*, trans. Roger Greaves (Stanford, Calif., 1969), p. 14.

31. Schwartz, *World of Thought*, pp. 186–215; Elvin, "Was There a Transcendental Breakthrough in China?," pp. 352–54; Kaltenmark, *Lao Tzu and Taoism;* Fung Yu-Lan, *Short History of Chinese Philosophy*, pp. 93–103; Graham, *Disputers of the Tao*, pp. 170–231; Holmes Welch, *The Parting of the Way: Lao Tzu and the Taoist Movement* (London, 1958).

32. *Daodejing* ("Classic of the Way and Its Potency") 1, in D. C. Lau, trans., *Tao Te Ching* (London and New York, 1963).

33. *Daodejing* 25. Lau translation.

34. *Daodejing* 59.

35. *Daodejing* 21; 6.

36. *Daodejing* 16. Lau translation.

37. Ibid.

38. *Daodejing* 11, in Kaltenmark, *Lao Tzu and Taoism*, p. 43.

39. Ibid.

40. *Daodejing* 16.

41. *Daodejing* 37. Lau translation.

42. Graham, *Disputers of the Tao*, pp. 223–24.

43. See *Xunzi* 17:51; *Spring and Autumn Annals* 17:7.

44. *Daodejing* 78. Lau translation.

45. *Daodejing* 43.

46. *Daodejing* 7. Lau translation.

47. *Daodejing* 31, in Kaltenmark, *Lao Tzu and Taoism*, p. 56.

48. *Daodejing* 30. Lau translation.

49. *Daodejing* 68, in Kaltenmark, *Lao Tzu and Taoism*, p. 56.

50. Ibid.

51. *Daodejing* 22, in Wm. Theodore de Bary and Irene Bloom, *Sources of Chinese Tradition from Earliest Times to 1600* (New York, 1999), p. 85.

52. *Daodejing* 49. Lau translation.

53. *Daodejing* 18; 19.

54. *Daodejing* 13, in de Bary and Bloom, *Sources of Chinese Tradition*, pp. 83–84.

55. Schwartz, *World of Thought*, p. 211.

56. Robin Lane Fox, *Alexander the Great* (London, 1973), p. 331.

57. John Keay, *India: A History* (London, 2000), p. 71.

58. Charles Freeman, *The Greek Achievement: The Foundation of the Western World* (New York and London, 1999), pp. 362–65.

59. Anthony Gottlieb, *The Dream of Reason: A History of Philosophy from the Greeks to the Renaissance* (London, 2000), pp. 283–345;

Richard Tarnas, *The Passion of the Western Mind: Understanding the Ideas That Have Shaped Our World View* (New York and London, 1991), pp. 73–85.

60. Epicurus, *Letter to Menoeceus* 125, in Gottlieb, *Dream of Reason,* p. 296.

61. Diogenes Laertius, *Lives of the Philosophers* 19.61, ibid., p. 329.

62. Sextus Empiricus, *Outlines of Pyrrhonism* 1.29, ibid., p. 335.

63. Robert Parker, *Athenian Religion: A History* (Oxford and New York, 1996), p. 280.

64. Thirteenth Major Rock Edict, quoted in Romila Thapar, *Asoka and the Decline of the Mauryas* (Oxford, 1961), p. 256.

65. *Dhamma* is the Pali form of the Sanskrit *dharma.*

66. Keay, *India,* pp. 91–94.

67. Ibid., p. 88.

68. Ibid., pp. 94–100; Romila Thapar, *Early India: From the Origins to AD 1300* (Berkeley and Los Angeles, 2002), pp. 202–4.

69. Thapar, *Ashoka,* p. 254.

70. Ibid., p. 255.

71. Thomas J. Hopkins, *The Hindu Religious Tradition* (Belmont, Calif., 1971), p. 72.

72. Shvetashvatara Upanishad 1:8, 10, in Patrick Olivelle, trans., *Upanisads* (Oxford and New York, 1996).

73. Shvetashvatara Upanishad 2:15. Olivelle translation.

74. Shvetashvatara Upanishad 3:7. Olivelle translation.

75. Shvetashvatara Upanishad 3:13. Olivelle translation.

76. Shvetashvatara Upanishad 6:23. Olivelle translation.

77. Klaus K. Klostermaier, *A Survey of Hinduism,* 2nd ed. (Albany, 1994), pp. 221–37.

78. *Bhagavad-Gita* 1:30–37. All quotations from the *Bhagavad-Gita* are taken from Barbara Stoler Miller, trans., *The Bhagavad-Gita: Krishna's Counsel in Time of War* (New York, 1986).

79. *Bhagavad-Gita* 1:47.

80. *Bhagavad-Gita* 2:9.

81. *Bhagavad-Gita* 2:47–48.

82. *Bhagavad-Gita* 4:20.

83. *Bhagavad-Gita* 4:6.

84. *Bhagavad-Gita* 4:8.

85. *Bhagavad-Gita* 9:9.

86. *Bhagavad-Gita* 11:15–16.

87. *Bhagavad-Gita* 9:18.

88. *Bhagavad-Gita* 11:32–33.

89. *Bhagavad-Gita* 11:55.

90. *Bhagavad-Gita* 18:63–66.

91. *Bhagavad-Gita* 9:32.

92. *Bhagavad-Gita* 13:7.

10. THE WAY FORWARD

1. Karl Jaspers, *The Origin and Goal of History,* trans. Michael Bullock (London, 1953), p. 51.

2. Sima Qian, *Records of the Grand Historian* 6:21, in A. C. Graham, *Disputers of the Tao: Philosophical Argument in Ancient China* (La Salle, Ill., 1989), p. 370.

3. Benjamin I. Schwartz, *The World of Thought in Ancient China* (Cambridge, Mass., and London, 1985), pp. 350–82; Fung Yu-Lan, *A Short History of Chinese Philosophy,* ed. and trans. Derk Bodde (New York, 1976), pp. 130–202; Graham, *Disputers of the Tao,* pp. 325–58.

4. A. C. Graham, *Later Mohist Logic, Ethics and Science* (Hong Kong, 1978), p. 411.

5. Sima Qian, *Records of the Grand Historian* 6:237, in Graham, *Disputers of the Tao,* p. 371.

6. Holmes Welch, *The Parting of the Way: Lao Tzu and the Taoist Movement* (London, 1958), pp. 89–98.

7. Sima Qian, *Records of the Grand Historian* 6:87, in Fung Yu-Lan, *Short History of Chinese Philosophy,* p. 204.

8. Ibid.

9. Schwartz, *World of Thought,* pp. 237–53.

10. *The Book of Zhuangzi* 33, in Martin Palmer, trans., with Elizabeth Brenilly, *The Book of Chuang Tzu* (London and New York, 1996).

11. Ibid.

12. Fung Yu-Lan, *Short History of Chinese Philosophy,* pp. 205–16; Graham, *Disputers of the Tao,* pp. 313–77; Schwartz, *World of Thought,* pp. 383–406.

13. Sima Qian, *Records of the Grand Historian* 8:1, in Fung Yu-Lan, *Short History of Chinese Philosophy,* p. 215.

14. *Hanshu* ("History of the Former Han") 130, in Graham, *Disputers of the Tao,* pp. 379–80.

15. Huston Smith, *The World's Religions: Our Great Wisdom Traditions* (San Francisco, 1991), p. 189.

16. Fung Yu-Lan, *Short History of Chinese Philosophy,* p. 215.

17. Louis Renou, *Religions of Ancient India* (London, 1953), pp. 46–47.

18. Brian K. Smith, *Reflections on Resemblance, Ritual and Religion* (Oxford and New York, 1989), pp. 195–202.

19. Baudhayana Dharma Sutra 2.6.11:2–6, in Smith, *Reflections on Resemblance,* p. 196.

20. *The Law of Manu* 3:68–69, ibid., p. 198.

21. Gavin Flood, *An Introduction to Hinduism* (Cambridge, U.K., and New York, 1996), p. 61.

22. L. Dumont, *Homo Hierarchicus: The Caste System and Its Implications* (Chicago and London, 1980), p. 54.

23. *The Law of Manu* 10.51.

24. Quoted in Klaus K. Klostermaier, *A Survey of Hinduism,* 2nd ed. (Albany, 1994), p. 222.

25. *Bhagavad-Gita* 12:8–10, in Barbara Stoler Miller, trans., *The Bhagavad-Gita: Krishna's Counsel in Time of War* (New York, 1986).

26. Bhagavata Purana (c. 800 CE), in Klostermaier, *Survey of Hinduism,* p. 229.

27. *Bhagavad-Gita* 6.32. Miller translation.

28. Freda Matchett, *Krsna: Lord or Avatara? The Relationship Between Krsna and Visnu* (Richmond, U.K., 2001), pp. 1–4.

29. Ibid., p. 5.

30. Rig Veda 1.155.4, in Ralph T. Griffith, trans., *The Rig Veda* (New York, 1992).

31. Rig Veda 7.100.2; 8.25.2.

32. Klaus K. Klostermaier, *Hinduism: A Short History* (Oxford, 2000), pp. 135–78; Klostermaier, *Survey of Hinduism,* pp. 262–69.

33. Klostermaier, *Survey of Hinduism,* pp. 307–19.

34. Astasahasrika 15:293, quoted in

Edward Conze, *Buddhism: Its Essence and Development* (Oxford, 1951), p. 125.

35. Shabbat 31a, in A. Cohen, ed., *Everyman's Talmud* (New York, 1975), p. 65. Some scholars believe that this story should be attributed to another rabbi, some two hundred years later.

36. Aboth de Rabbi Nathan 1. N, 11a, in C. G. Montefiore and H. Loewe, eds., *A Rabbinic Anthology* (New York, 1976), pp. 430–31.

37. Mekhilta de Rabbi Simon on Exodus 19:6, in J. Abelson, *The Immanence of God in Rabbinical Literature* (London, 1912), p. 230.

38. Song of Songs Rabbah 8:12, ibid., p. 231.

39. Yakult on Song of Songs 1:2.

40. Sifre on Leviticus 19:8, in Samuel Belkin, *In His Image: The Jewish Philosophy of Man as Expressed in Rabbinic Tradition* (London, 1960), p. 241.

41. Makhilta on Exodus 20:13, ibid., p. 50.

42. Sanhedrin 4:5.

43. Baba Metziah 58b.

44. Arakim 15b.

45. Midrash Rabbah, Numbers 19:6, in Gerald L. Bruns, "Midrash and Allegory," in Robert Alter and Frank Kermode, eds., *The Literary Guide to the Bible* (London, 1987), p. 632.

46. Midrash Rabbah 1.10.2, ibid., p. 627.

47. Baba Metziah 59b, Deuteronomy 30:12, in Cohen, *Everyman's Talmud,* pp. 40–41.

48. Exodus Rabbah 34:1; Hagigah 13b, in Abelson, *Immanence of God,* pp. 115–16.

49. Matthew 12:18–21.

50. Matthew 7:12; Luke 6:31.

51. Matthew 22:34–40; Mark 12:29–31; Luke 10:25–28.

52. Philippians 2:6–11.

53. Philippians 2:5.

54. Philippians 2:2–4.

55. Romans 6:1–11.

56. Romans 8:14–39.

57. Galatians 2:20.

58. 1 Corinthians 13:4–8.

59. Matthew 7:1.

60. Matthew 25:31–46.

61. Matthew 19:16–22; Mark 10:13–16; Luke 18:18–23.

62. Matthew 6:1–6.

63. Matthew 5:39–40.

64. Matthew 26:53.

65. Luke 22:34.

66. Matthew 5:43–48.

67. Qur'an 3:58–62; 2:129–32.

68. Qur'an 29:46. Quotations from the Qur'an are taken from Muhammad Asad, trans., *The Message of the Qur'an* (Gibraltar, 1980).

69. Qur'an 55:10.

70. Qur'an 2:217; 2:190.

71. Qur'an 22:39–40.

72. Qur'an 2:292.

73. Qur'an 16:125–26.

74. Qur'an 48:1.

75. Qur'an 48:26.

76. Qur'an 48:29.

77. Gregory Palamas, *Theophanes,* in J. P. Migue, ed., *Patrologia Graeca* (Paris, 1864–84), 9.932D.

78. Matthew 7:5.

Glossary

Achaean: term used to describe the Mycenaean Greeks, many of whom lived in Achaea.

Acropolis (Greek): the sacred hill outside Athens.

Agnicayana (Sanskrit): Vedic ritual; the building of a brick fire altar for Agni, god of fire.

Agon (Greek): contest; competition.

Agora (Greek): the open space in the center of a Greek city; a central meeting place.

Ahimsa (Sanskrit): "harmlessness"; nonviolence.

Ahl al-kitab (Arabic): usually translated as "the people of the Book." But as there were very few books in Arabia in the seventh century CE, when the Qur'an was revealed, the term is more accurately rendered "people of an earlier revelation."

Ahura (Avestan): "lord"; the title of the most important gods in the Aryan pantheon. The *ahuras* became the gods worshiped by the Zoroastrians.

Am ha-aretz (Hebrew): in the seventh century BCE, the rural aristocracy of Judah. After the return from exile, the term referred to the foreign people who had settled in Canaan after the Babylonian wars, and also Israelites and Judahites who had not been deported to Babylon.

Amesha (Avestan): "the Immortals." In Zoroastrian religion, the term referred to the seven gods in the retinue of Ahura Mazda, the Supreme God.

Anatta (Pali): "no self"; the Buddhist doctrine that denied the existence of a constant, stable, and discrete personality, designed to encourage Buddhists to live as though the self did not exist.

Apeiron (Greek): the "indefinite" original substance of the cosmos in the philosophy of Anaximander.

Aranya (Sanskrit): forest; jungle. The Aranyakas ("Forest Texts") give an esoteric interpretation of the Vedic rites.

Archetype (Greek derivation): the "original pattern" or paradigm. A term connected with the perennial philosophy that sees every earthly object or experience as a replica, a pale shadow of a more powerful, richer reality in the heavenly world. In ancient religion, the return to the archetypal reality was regarded as the fulfillment of a person or object. One thus attained a fuller, richer existence.

Areopagus (Greek): the rocky hillock near the agora of Athens that was the meeting place of the aristocratic Council of Elders (often known as the Areopagus Council).

Aristeia (Greek): the "victorious rampage" of the Greek warrior, who lost himself in an ecstasy of battle rage.

Arya; Aryan: literally, "honorable, noble"; the Indo-European peoples, who originated on the steppes of southern Russia and migrated later to India and Iran.

Asana: "sitting"; the correct position for yogic meditation, with straight back and crossed legs.

Asha (Avestan): the sacred order that held the universe together and made life possible.

Ashavan (Avestan): the "champions of *asha*" in Zoroastrian religion.

Asura (Sanskrit): see *ahura*. The Vedic Aryans demoted the *asuras,* who were worshiped by the Zoroastrians. They regarded them as passive and sedentary, compared with the dynamic *devas.*

Ataraxia (Greek): freedom from pain.

Atman (Sanskrit): the immortal and eternal "self" sought by renouncers and Upanishadic mystics, which was believed to be identical with the brahman.

Avatara (Sanskrit): "manifestation"; "descent"; the earthly appearance of one of the gods. Krishna, for example, is an *avatara* of the Vedic god Vishnu.

Bandhu: "connection." In Vedic ritual science, the sacrificer and priest were supposed to look for links between earthly and heavenly realities when performing a sacrifice. The *bandhu* was based on a resemblance of function or appearance, or on a mythical connection between two objects.

Basileus (Greek); plural *basileis:* "lords"; the Greek aristocrats.

Bhakti (Sanskrit): "love"; "devotion"; the name given to the Indian religion that is based on an emotional surrender to a god. A *bhakta* is a devotee of, for example, Shiva or Vishnu.

Bin (Chinese): "hosting"; the name given to the ritual banquet in honor of the ancestors, who were believed to attend. They were impersonated by younger members of the family, who were thought to be possessed by the spirit of their deceased relatives during the rite.

Brahmacarya (Sanskrit): the "holy life" of the Vedic student, during his apprenticeship under a teacher who initiated him into sacrificial lore. He had to live a humble, self-effacing life of *ahimsa* and chastity, while studying the Vedic texts. A *brahmacarin* is a Vedic student.

Brahman (Sanskrit): "the All"; the whole of reality; the essence of existence; the foundation of everything that exists; being itself. The power that holds the cosmos together and enables it to grow and develop. The supreme reality of Vedic religion.

Brahmasiris (Sanskrit): a mythical weapon of mass destruction.

Brahmin (Sanskrit): a Vedic priest; a member of the priestly class.

Brahmodya (Sanskrit): a ritual competition. The contestants each tried to find a verbal formula that expressed the mysterious and ineffable reality of the brahman. The contest always ended in silence, as the contestants were reduced to speechless awe. In the silence they felt the presence of the brahman.

Buddha (Sanskrit; Pali): an enlightened or "awakened" person.

Buddhi (Sanskrit): the "intellect"; the highest human category in the Samkhya system; the only part of the human person that was capable of reflecting the eternal *purusha*.

Cheng (Chinese): "sincerity." A person was supposed to perform the rituals of China wholeheartedly, not hypocritically or grudgingly.

Chthonian (Greek derivation): the term that refers to the Greek gods who dwelt in or beneath the earth (*chthon*), such as the Erinyes.

City Dionysia: the annual festival in honor of the god Dionysus, when the tragedies were performed in the theater on the southern slopes of the Acropolis.

Coincidentia oppositorum (Latin): the "coincidence of opposites"; the ecstatic experience of a unity that exists beyond the apparent contradictions of earthly life.

Daeva (Avestan); plural *daevas*: the "shining ones"; the gods. The Zoroastrians came to regard the *daevas* as demonic, and worshiped the *asuras*, the "lords" of the *daevas*, who were the guardians of truth and order.

Daimon (Greek): a lesser divine being. An intermediary between the higher gods and human beings.

Dao (Chinese): the Way; the correct course or path. The object of much Chinese ritual was to ensure that human affairs were aligned with the Way of Heaven. Human virtue consists of living in accordance with the *de*, the potency that expresses the *dao* on earth. In *Daoism*, the school represented in the Axial Age by Zhuangzi and Laozi, the *dao* becomes the ultimate, ineffable reality, the source from which all appearance derives, unproduced producer of all that exists, which guarantees the stability and order of the world.

Daode (Chinese): the "power of the Way," expressed particularly by the king or prince. A magical potency that brings order to the world and to the kingdom.

Demos (Greek): the people.

Deva (Sanskrit); plural *devas*: "the shining ones," the Vedic gods. Cf. *daeva*. The Zoroastrians demoted the *daevas* and regarded them as evil, violent, and demonic, but the Vedic Indians loved the dynamism of the *devas*, and worshiped them rather than the *asuras*.

Dhamma (Pali): See *dharma*. In Buddhist terminology, it generally meant the teaching of a particular school. The way of salvation.

Dharma (Sanskrit): a complicated word, with a range of different meanings. Originally it meant the natural condition of things, their essence, the fundamental law of their existence. Then it came to stand for the laws and duties of each class of Vedic society, which defined their function and way of life. Finally it referred to religious truth, the doctrines and practices that make up a particular religious system. In Pali, *dharma* became *dhamma*.

Diadochoi (Greek): the six "successors" of Alexander the Great, who fought for supremacy after his death.

Dike (Greek): justice; also the goddess of justice, one of the daughters of Zeus.

Dukkha (Sanskrit): "awry, flawed, unsatisfactory"; often translated simply as "suffering."

Dysnomia (Greek): "disorder"; an unbalanced social policy, which allowed some elements of the population to become too dominant.

Ekagrata (Sanskrit): a yogic discipline; concentration "on a single point."

Ekstasis (Greek): ecstasy; literally "stepping out," going beyond the self; transcending normal experience.

Elohim (Hebrew): term that sums up everything that the gods mean to human beings; the divine. Often also used as a formal title of Yahweh and translated as "God."

En mesoi (Greek): "in the center"; a phrase expressing the open, accessible nature of Athenian democracy.

Entheos (Greek): literally, "a god is within"; the ecstatic experience of divine possession, especially during the mysteries of Dionysus.

Erinyes (Greek): the Furies; ancient chthonian deities who avenged the unnatural murder of kinsfolk.

Eunomia (Greek): order; a balanced society in which no single element is allowed to dominate the others. This is the term for the polity established by Solon in Athens in the sixth century BCE.

Fa (Chinese): "standard, pattern, method"; often translated as "law." An important concept in the Chinese Legalist school.

Gathas (Avestan): Zoroastrian scriptures, seventeen inspired hymns attributed to Zoroaster.

Golah (Hebrew): the community of returned exiles in Judea.

Goyim (Hebrew): the foreign nations.

Grama (Sanskrit): village. Originally the term referred to a troop of trekking warriors.

Haoma (Avestan): a hallucinogenic plant used in Aryan worship. Its stalks were ceremonially gathered, crushed, and mixed with water to make a sacred, intoxicating drink. Haoma was also revered as a god. See *soma*.

Helots (Greek): the indigenous people of Messenia, who were enslaved by Sparta when their territory was conquered.

Herem (Hebrew): the "ban"; the holy war of ancient Israel.

Hesed (Hebrew): often translated as "love" or "mercy," but originally a tribal term denoting the loyalty of a kinship relationship that demanded altruistic behavior toward the family group.

Hinneni (Hebrew): "Here I am!" A cry uttered by prophets and patriarchs to express their total presence before God and their readiness to do whatever he wished. An expression of submission and devotion.

Homoioi (Greek): the "equal" or "uniform" ones; the title of the citizens of Sparta.

Hoplite: from the Greek *hopla,* "weapons." The Greek citizen-soldier who armed himself.

Hotr (Avestan; Sanskrit): the priest who was expert in the sacred chant.

Hubris (Greek): pride, selfishness; excessive behavior; the refusal to keep within due bounds; egotism.

Isonomia (Greek): "equal order"; the name given to the government devised by Cleisthenes in Athens in the early sixth century.

Jian ai (Chinese): the chief virtue of the Mohist school; often translated as "universal love," but more accurately rendered "concern for everybody," a principled impartiality.

Jina (Sanskrit): a spiritual "conqueror," who has achieved the enlightenment of *ahimsa.* The Jains were a religion of *jinas.*

Jing (Chinese): the highest form of *qi;* the sacred essence of being; existence itself; the divine quintessence of all things.

Jiva (Sanskrit): a soul; a living entity that was luminous and intelligent. The Jains believed that every single creature—humans, plants, animals, even rocks and trees—each had a *jiva* that could feel pain and distress, and which must therefore be protected and honored.

Junzi (Chinese): originally it simply meant a gentleman; a member of the Chinese nobility. The Confucians took away its class connotations and democratized it. For the Confucians a *junzi* was a mature, fully developed human being who had cultivated his innate capacities. Sometimes translated as a "profound" or "superior" person.

Karma (Sanskrit): "action." At first it referred to ritual activity, but was later extended to include all deeds, including mental acts such as fear, attachment, desire, or hatred.

Karma-yoga (Sanskrit): the phrase coined by Krishna in the *Bhagavad-Gita* to describe the yoga of the warrior, who learned to dissociate himself from his actions, so that he was no longer interested in gaining any benefit from them.

Katharsis (Greek): "cleansing, purification." It referred originally to the purification of sacrifice and ritual; in tragedy, the audience cleansed their emotions of hatred and terror.

Kenosis (Greek): "emptying." In spirituality, the word is used to describe the emptying of self, the dismantling of egotism.

Kshatriya (Sanskrit): "the empowered ones"; the Indian warrior class, who were responsible for the government and the defence of the community.

Li (Chinese): rite; ceremony; the range of ritual lore that regulated the entire life of a *junzi*.

Logos (Greek): "dialogue speech"; reasoned, logical, and scientific thought. In some philosophies, such as Stoicism, it refers to the rational, ruling principle of nature.

Mandala (Sanskrit): a symbolic, pictorial representation of the universe, which is always circular in shape to indicate an all-inclusive pervasion; an icon of contemplation.

Mantra (Sanskrit): a short prose formula, chanted during a ritual. Sound was sacred in Vedic religion, so a mantra was divine, a *deva*. Mantras could encapsulate the divine in the human form of speech.

Messiach (Hebrew): "anointed one." Originally the term referred to the king of Israel and Judah, who was anointed during his coronation ceremony and achieved a special, cultic closeness to Yahweh. He became the "son of God," and had a particular divine task. By extension, Second Isaiah applied the term to Cyrus, king of Persia, who was Yahweh's king and doing Yahweh's work.

Miasma (Greek): a contagious, polluting power inherent in a violent atrocity against a family member or neighbor. It had an independent life of its own; it could contaminate perfectly innocent human beings who were related to the perpetrator or simply happened to be in the vicinity. Not dissimilar to radioactivity. Once the evil deed had been committed, its *miasma* could be eliminated only by the punishment—usually the violent, sacrificial death—of the perpetrator. The Erinyes were responsible for the elimination of *miasma* and hounded the guilty.

Mitzvah (Hebrew); plural *mitzvoth*: the "commandments" of Yahweh's Torah.

Moksha (Sanskrit): "liberation" from rebirth and the ceaseless round of samsara; the consequent awakening to one's true self.

Monolatry (Greek derivation): refers to the worship of a single god. Monolatry is not the same as monotheism, the belief that only one god exists; a person who practices monolatry may believe in the existence of many deities, but has made the decision to worship only one of them. The prophets of Israel probably believed that other gods existed, but wanted the people to worship only Yahweh and take no part in the cults of other gods.

Muni (Sanskrit): a "silent sage"; a renouncer.

Mystai (Greek): people who undergo the initiation into a Greek mystery religion that gives them a personal and intense experience of the divine.

Mythos (Greek): "myth." A reality that in one sense happened once, but that also happened all the time. The mythical discourse that deals with elusive, timeless truth and the search for ultimate meaning, which is complemented by *logos*.

Nibbana (Pali): "extinction"; "blowing out"; the extinction of the self, which brings enlightenment and liberation from pain and suffering. In Sanskrit, this becomes *nirvana*.

Niyama (Sanskrit): the preparatory "disciplines" of the yogin, including the study of the guru's teaching, habitual serenity, and kindness to all.

Nous (Greek): "mind."

Panathenaea (Greek): the new year's festival of Athens, which celebrated the birth of the city. It consisted of a procession through the streets of Athens up to the Acropolis, where a new robe was presented to Athena for her cult statue.

Pesach (Hebrew): "crossing"; the name of the spring Passover festival, which eventually celebrated the liberation of the Israelites from Egypt, when the angel of death passed over the houses of the Israelites but slew the first-born sons of the Egyptians.

Physikoi (Greek): the "physicists," the natural scientists of Miletus and Elea in southern Italy.

Purusha (Sanskrit): "person." The term first applies to the primordial human Person who voluntarily allowed the gods to sacrifice him in order to bring the world into being. This archetypal sacrifice was celebrated in the Purusha Hymn of the Rig Veda. Later the Purusha was merged with the figure of the creator god Prajapati, and thus became crucial to the ritual reform that began India's Axial Age. In Samkhya philosophy, the *purusha* referred to the eternal, sacred self of every single individual, which had to be liberated from nature.

Polis (Greek); plural *poleis:* the Greek city-state.

Pranayama (Sanskrit): the breathing exercises of yoga, which induce a state of trance and well-being.

Prophet (Greek derivation): a person who "speaks for" or on behalf of God.

Qaddosh (Hebrew): "separate, other," and, by extension, "holy."

Qi (Chinese): the raw material of life; its basic energy and its primal spirit; it animates all beings. Endlessly active, it conglomerates in different combinations, under the guidance of the *dao,* to form individual creatures; after a time, the *qi* disperses, the creatures die or disintegrate, but *qi* lives on, combining in new ways to bring quite different beings into existence. *Qi* gives everything its distinctive shape and form. To allow the *qi* to flow freely through the human person became the chief aim of Chinese mysticism: it was the base of the personality, the ground of being, and therefore in perfect harmony with the *dao.*

Raja (Sanskrit): "chief, king."

Rajasuya (Sanskrit): the ceremony of royal consecration.

Rang (Chinese): "yielding"; the attitude inculcated by the Chinese rituals of reverence and respect.

Ren (Chinese): originally, "human being." Confucius gave the word new significance, but refused to describe it because it transcended any of the intellectual categories of his time. It was a transcendent value, the highest good. *Ren* would always be associated with the concept of humanity and has been translated as "human-heartedness." Later Confucians equated it with benevolence or compassion. It is the chief Confucian virtue.

Rig Veda (Sanskrit): "Knowledge in Verse"; the most sacred part of the Vedic scriptures, consisting of over a thousand inspired hymns.

Rishi (Sanskrit): "seer." The term applied to the inspired poets of the RigVeda. Also a visionary; a mystic or sage.

Rita (Sanskrit): the sacred order. See *asha*.

Ru (Chinese): the ritual experts of China.

Sabaoth (Hebrew): "of armies"; the chief epithet of Yahweh.

Samkhya (Sanskrit): "discrimination." A philosophy, akin to yoga, that analyzed the cosmos into twenty-four different categories and devised a cosmology that was intended as an object of meditation to induce *moksha*.

Samsara (Sanskrit): "keeping going"; the cycle of death and rebirth, which propelled people from one life to the next. It often referred to the restlessness and transience of the human condition.

Sangha (Sanskrit): originally the tribal assembly of the Aryan clans. By extension, it referred to the religious orders of renouncers.

Satrap (Persian): governor.

Sefer torah (Hebrew): the scroll of the Law discovered in the Jerusalem temple in 622 BCE.

Shen (Chinese): the divine, numinous quality that made each person unique. It was the *shen* that enabled a person to survive as an individual in Heaven and become a sacred ancestor in the cult. In Chinese mysticism, the *shen* referred to a person's deepest, divine self, which is one with the *jing* of existence.

Shi (Chinese): the lower aristocracy of China, the ordinary gentlemen. Often they did the less prestigious jobs in the administration, serving as men-at-arms, specialists in the various branches of knowledge, guardians of the written traditions, and scribes. The sages of the Chinese Axial Age usually came from this class.

Shruti (Sanskrit): "that which is heard"; revelation.

Shu (Chinese): "likening to oneself." The Confucian virtue of consideration, linked with the Golden Rule: never do to others what you would not like them to do to you.

Shudra (Sanskrit): the non-Aryan population of India, the lowest class of Vedic society, whose function was to supply labor.

Soma (Sanskrit): see *haoma*. A hallucinogenic plant used in Aryan ritual; in India, Soma was also a divine priest, who protected the people from famine and looked after their cattle.

Sympatheia (Greek): "feeling with"; a profound affinity with the ritual, and later, by extension, with other suffering human beings.

Tapas (Sanskrit): "heat"; an ascetical exercise, in which people sat by the sacred fire, sweated, and felt a surge of warmth rise up within that was experienced as a divine and creative force. By extension, the word often means "asceticism."

Techne (Greek): technology.

Theoria (Greek): contemplation.

Thetes (Greek): the lowest classes of Greek society.

Torah (Hebrew): the "teaching"; the divine Law of Israel, said to have been transmitted to Moses by God on Mount Sinai.

Upanishads (Sanskrit): "to sit down near to"; esoteric mystical scriptures, revered as the culmination of the Veda. Thirteen classical Upanishads were composed between the seventh and second centuries BCE.

Vaishya (Sanskrit): clansman. The third class of Vedic society, whose function was to create the wealth of the community; first by stock breeding and agriculture, and later by trade and commerce.

Veda (Sanskrit): "knowledge." The term used to denote the huge corpus of sacred literature of the Aryan Indians.

Wu wei (Chinese): "doing nothing."

Xian (Chinese): the Mohist "men of worth"; practical men of action.

Xie (Chinese): bands of peripatetic military specialists.

Yamas (Sanskrit): the five "prohibitions" of the preliminary training of the yogin, who had to master them before he began to meditate; also called the five "vows." They forbade violence, stealing, lying, sex, and intoxicating substances that clouded the mind and hindered concentration.

Yoga (Sanskrit): "yoking." Initially the term referred to the yoking of draft animals to war chariots at the beginning of a raid. Later it referred to the "yoking" of the powers of the mind to achieve enlightenment. The meditative discipline designed to eliminate the egotism that holds us back from *moksha* and *nibbana*.

Yogin: a practitioner of yoga.

Yu wei (Chinese): disciplined, purposeful action.

Yuga (Sanskrit): an age, era; a cycle of history.

Bibliography

Abelson, J. *The Immanence of God in Rabbinical Literature.* London, 1912.

Ackroyd, Peter R. *Exile and Restoration: A Study of Hebrew Thought in the Sixth Century BC.* London, 1968.

Ahlström, Gosta W. *The History of Ancient Palestine.* Minneapolis, 1993.

Alt, A. *Essays in Old Testament History and Religion.* Trans. R. A. Wilson. Oxford, 1966.

Alter, Robert, and Frank Kermode, eds. *The Literary Guide to the Bible.* London, 1987.

Bareau, A. *Recherches sur la biographie du Buddha.* Paris, 1963.

Barker, Margaret. *The Gate of Heaven: The History and Symbolism of the Temple in Jerusalem.* London, 1991.

————. *The Older Testament: The Survival of Themes from the Ancient Royal Cult in Sectarian Judaism and Early Christianity.* London, 1987.

Batto, B. *Slaying the Dragon.* Philadelphia, 1992.

Bechert, Heinz. "The Date of the Buddha Reconsidered." *Indologia Taurinensia* 10, n.d.

Becking, B., and M. C. A. Korpel, eds. *The Crisis of Israelite Religion: Transformations and Religious Tradition in Exilic and Post-Exilic Times.* Leiden, 1999.

Belkin, Samuel. *In His Image: The Jewish Philosophy of Man as Expressed in Rabbinic Tradition.* London, 1960.

Ben-Tor, Amnon, ed. *The Archaeology of Ancient Israel.* New Haven, 1992.

Bespaloff, R. *On the Iliad.* Trans. M. McCarthy. 2nd ed. New York, 1962.

Biardeau, Madeline. "Etudes de mythologie hindoue." *Bulletin de l'Ecole Francaise d' Extreme-Orient* 63 (1976).

Biardeau, Madeline, and Charles Malamoud. *La sacrifice dans l'Inde ancienne.* Paris, 1976.

Bickerman, Elias J. *From Ezra to the Last of the Maccabees.* New York, 1962.

————. *The Jews in the Greek Age.* Cambridge, Mass., and London, 1988.

Birrell, Anne. *Chinese Mythology: An Introduction.* Baltimore and London, 1993.

Boccaccini, Gabriele. *Roots of Rabbinic Judaism: An Intellectual History from Ezekiel to Daniel.* Grand Rapids, Mich., and Cambridge, U.K., 2002.

Boedeker, Deborah, and Kurt A. Raaflaub, eds. *Democracy, Empire and the Arts in Fifth-Century Athens.* Cambridge, Mass., and London, 1998.

Boodberg, Peter. "The Semasiology of Some Primary Confucian Concepts." *Philosophy East and West* 2, no. 4 (October 1953).

Booth, Wayne C. *Modern Dogma and the Rhetoric of Assent.* Chicago, 1974.

Bottero, Jean. *The Birth of God: The Bible and the Historian.* Trans. Kees W. Bolle. University Park, Pa., 2000.

Bowman, J. *Samaritan Documents Relating to Their History, Religion and Life.* Pittsburgh, 1977.

Boyce, Mary. *A History of Zoroastrianism.* 2 vols. Leiden, 1975, 1982.

————. *Zoroastrians: Their Religious Beliefs and Practices.* 2nd ed. London and New York, 2001.

————, ed. and trans. *Textual Sources for the Study of Zoroastrianism.* Chicago and London, 1984.

Brickhouse, Thomas C., and Nicholas D. Smith. *Plato's Socrates.* London and New York, 1994.

Brockington, John. *The Sanskrit Epics.* Leiden, 1998.

————. "The Sanskrit Epics." In Gavin Flood, ed., *The Blackwell Companion to Hinduism.* Oxford, 2003.

Bronkhorst, Johannes. "Dharma and Abhidharma." *Bulletin of the School of Oriental and African Studies* 48, no. 2 (1985).

Bruns, Gerald L., "Midrash and Allegory." In Robert Alter and Frank Kermode, eds., *The Literary Guide to the Bible.* London, 1987.

Burckhardt, Jacob. *The Greeks and Greek Civilization.* Ed. Oswyn Murray. Trans. Sheila Stern. New York, 1999.

Burkert, Walter. *Ancient Mystery Cults.* Cambridge, Mass., and London, 1986.

————. *Greek Religion.* Trans. John Raffan. Cambridge, Mass., 1985.

————. *Homo Necans: The Anthropology of Ancient Greek Sacrificial Ritual and Myth.* Trans. Peter Bing. Berkeley, Los Angeles, and London, 1983.

————. *The Orientalizing Revolution: Near Eastern Influence on Greek Culture in the Early Archaic Age.* Trans. Margaret E. Pinder and Walter Burkert. Cambridge, Mass., and London, 1992.

————. *Savage Energies: Lessons of Myth and Ritual in Ancient Greece.* Trans. Peter Bing. Chicago and London, 2001.

————. *Structure and History in Greek Mythology and Ritual.* Berkeley, Los Angeles, and London, 1980.

Buxton, Richard. *Imaginary Greece: The Contexts of Mythology.* Cambridge, U.K., 1994.

————, ed. *Oxford Readings in Greek Religion.* Oxford, 2000.

Campbell, Joseph. *The Hero with a Thousand Faces.* Princeton, 1949.

————. *Oriental Mythology: The Masks of God.* New York, 1962.

————. *Primitive Mythology: The Masks of God.* New York, 1959.

————. *Transformations of Myth Through Time.* New York, 1990.

Campbell, Joseph, with Bill Moyers. *The Power of Myth.* New York, 1988.

Carrithers, Michael. *The Buddha.* Oxford and New York, 1983.

Carroll, Robert. "Psalm LXXVIII: Vestiges of a Tribal Polemic." *Vetus Testamentum* 21, no. 2 (1971).

Cartledge, Paul. *The Spartans: An Epic History.* London, 2002.

Chakravarti, Sures Chandra. *The Philosophy of the Upanishads.* Calcutta, 1935.

Chang, K. C. *Art, Myth and Ritual: The Path to Political Authority in Ancient China.* Cambridge, Mass., 1983.

————. *Early Chinese Civilization: Anthropological Perspectives.* Cambridge, Mass., 1976.

Chaudhuri, Nirad C. *Hinduism: A Religion to Live By.* New Delhi, 1979.

Ching, Julia. *Mysticism and Kingship in China: The Heart of Chinese Wisdom.* Cambridge, U.K., 1997.

Choksky, Jamsheed K. *Purity and Pollution in Zoroastrianism: Triumph over Evil.* Austin, 1989.

Chottopadhyana, D. *Indian Atheism.* London, 1969.

Clark, Peter. *Zoroastrianism: An Introduction to an Ancient Faith.* Brighton, U.K., and Portland, Ore., 1998.

Clements, R. E. *Abraham and David.* London, 1967.

————. *God and Temple.* Oxford, 1965.

————, ed. *The World of Ancient Israel: Sociological, Anthropological and Political Perspectives.* Cambridge, U.K., 1989.

Clifford, Richard J. *The Cosmic Mountain in Canaan and the Old Testament.* Cambridge, Mass., 1972.

Cogan, Mordechai, and Israel Ephal, eds. *Studies in Assyrian History and Ancient Near Eastern Historiography.* Jerusalem, 1991.

Cohen, A. *Everyman's Talmud.* New York, 1975.

Cohn, Norman. *Cosmos, Chaos and the World to Come: The Ancient Roots of Apocalyptic Faith.* New Haven and London, 1993.

Cohn, Robert, and Laurence Silberstein. *The Other in Jewish Thought and History: Constructions of Jewish Culture and Identity.* New York, 1994.

Colaiaco, James A. *Socrates Against Athens: Philosophy on Trial.* New York and London, 2001.

Collins, Steven. *Selfless Persons: Imagery and Thought in Theravada Buddhism.* Cambridge, U.K., 1982.

Conze, Edward. *Buddhism: Its Essence and Development.* Oxford, 1951.

————. *Buddhist Meditation.* London, 1956.

————. *A Short History of Buddhism.* Oxford, 1980.

Cooper, John M., ed. *Plato: Complete Works.* Indianapolis, 1997.

Cornford, F. M. *From Religion to Philosophy: A Study in the Origins of Western Speculation.* New York, 1957.

Creel, H. G. *Confucius: The Man and the Myth.* London, 1951.

————. *The Origins of Statecraft in China.* Chicago, 1970.

Cross, Frank Moore. *Canaanite Myth and Hebrew Epic: Essays in the History of the Religion of Israel.* Cambridge, Mass., and London, 1973.

————. *From Epic to Canon: History and Literature in Ancient Israel.* Baltimore and London, 1998.

Crossan, John Dominic. *The Birth of Christianity: Discovering What Happened in the Years Immediately After the Execution of Jesus.* New York, 1998.

Csikszentmihalyi, Mark, and Philip J. Ivanhoe, eds., *Religious and Philosophical Aspects of the Laozi.* Albany, 1999.

Damrosch, David. "Leviticus." In Robert Alter and Frank Kermode, eds., *The Literary Guide to the Bible.* London, 1987.

————. *The Narrative Covenant: Transformations of Genre in the Growth of Biblical Literature.* San Francisco, 1987.

Davids, T. W. Rhys. *Dialogues of the Buddha.* 3 vols. London, 1899, 1910, 1921.

Davie, John, trans. *Euripides: Electra and Other Plays.* London and New York, 1998.

Davies, W. D. *The Territorial Dimension of Judaism.* Berkeley and Los Angeles, 1982.

Davies, W. D., with Louis Finkelstein. *The Cambridge History of Judaism.* 2 vols. Cambridge, U.K., 1984.

Dawson, Raymond. *Confucius.* Oxford, Toronto, and Melbourne, 1981.

De Bary, Wm. Theodore, and Irene Bloom, eds. *Sources of Chinese Tradition.* Vol. I, *From Earliest Times to 1600.* 2nd ed. New York, 1999.

Detienne, Marcel. *Masters of Truth in Archaic Greece.* Trans. Janet Lloyd. London, 1996.

Detienne, Marcel, with Jean-Pierre Vernant. *The Cuisine of Sacrifice Among the Greeks.* Trans. Paula Wissing. Chicago and London, 1989.

Dever, William G. *What Did the Biblical Writers Know and When Did They Know It? What Archaeology Can Tell Us About the Reality of Ancient Israel.* Grand Rapids, Mich., and Cambridge, U.K., 2001.

Di Cosmo, Nicola. *Ancient China and Its Enemies: The Rise of Nomadic Power in East Asian History.* Cambridge, U.K., and New York, 1992.

Di Vito, R. A. *Studies in Third Millennium Sumerian and Akkadian Personal Names: The Designation and Conception of the Personal God.* Rome, 1993.

Dubs, H. H., ed. and trans. *The Works of Hsuntze.* London, 1928.

Dull, Jack. "Anti-Qin Rebels: No Peasant Leaders Here." *Modern China* 9, no. 3 (July 1983).

Douglas, Mary. *Implicit Meanings: Essays in Anthropology.* London, 1975.

————. *In the Wilderness: The Doctrine of Defilement in the Book of Numbers.* Oxford and New York, 2001.

————. *Leviticus as Literature.* Oxford and New York, 1999.

————. *Natural Symbols: Explorations in Cosmology.* London, 1970.

————. *Purity and Danger.* London, 1966.

Dumezil, Georges. "Métiers et classes fonctionelles chez divers peuples indo-européens." *Annales (Economies, Societies, Civilisations 13e Année)* 4 (October–December 1958).

Dumont, L. *Homo Hierarchicus: The Caste System and Its Implications.* Chicago and London, 1980.

Dundas, Paul. *The Jains.* 2nd ed. London and New York, 2002.

Durham, J. I., and J. R. Porter, eds. *Proclamation and Presence: Essays in Honour of G. Henton Davies.* London, 1970.

Durkheim, Emile. *The Division of Labour in Society.* 2 vols. Trans. George Simpson. London, 1969.

Dutt, Sukumar. *Buddha and Five After-Centuries.* London, 1957.

———. *Early Buddhist Monarchism, 600 BC to 100 BC.* London, 1924.

Duyvendark, J. J. L., trans and ed. *The Book of Lord Shang.* London, 1928.

Eck, Diana L. *Banaras, City of Light.* New York, 1999.

———. *Darsan: Seeing the Divine Image in India.* New York, 1996.

Edwardes, Michael. *In the Blowing Out of a Flame: The World of the Buddha and the World of Man.* London, 1976.

Eisenstadt, S. N., ed. *The Origins and Diversity of Axial Age Civilizations.* Albany, 1986.

Eliade, Mircea. *A History of Religious Ideas.* 3 vols. Trans. Willard R. Trask. Chicago and London, 1978, 1982, 1985.

———. *The Myth of the Eternal Return, or, Cosmos and History.* Trans. Willard R. Trask. New York, 1959.

———. *Myths, Dreams and Mysteries: The Encounter Between Contemporary Faiths and Archaic Realities.* Trans. Philip Mairet. London, 1960.

———. *Patterns in Comparative Religion.* Trans. Rosemary Sheed. London, 1958.

———. *The Sacred and the Profane.* Trans. Willard R. Trask. New York, 1959.

———. *Yoga, Immortality and Freedom.* Trans. Willard R. Trask. London, 1958.

Elvin, Mark. "Was There a Transcendental Breakthrough in China?" In S. N. Eisenstadt, ed., *The Origins and Diversity of Axial Age Civilizations.* Albany, 1986.

Epsztein, Leon. *Social Justice in the Ancient Near East and the People of the Bible.* London, 1986.

Erdosy, G. *Urbanization in Early Historic India.* Oxford, 1988.

Fagles, Robert, trans. *Aeschylus: The Oresteia.* London and New York, 1966.

Faraone, C., and T. H. Carpenter, eds. *Masks of Dionysus.* Ithaca, 1993.

Fensham, F. Charles. "Widow, Orphan and the Poor in Ancient Near Eastern Legal and Wisdom Literature." In Frederick E. Greenspahn, ed., *Essential Papers on Israel and the Ancient Near East.* New York and London, 1991.

Fingarette, Herbert. *Confucius: The Secular as Sacred.* New York, 1972.

Finkelstein, Israel, and Neil Asher Silberman. *The Bible Unearthed: Archaeology's New Vision of Ancient Israel and the Origin of Its Sacred Texts.* New York and London, 2001.

Finkelstein, Israel, and Nadar Na'aman, eds. *From Nomadism to Monarchy: Archaeological and Historical Aspects of Early Israel.* Washington, D.C., 1994.

Fishbane, Michael. *The Exegetical Imagination: On Jewish Thought and Theology.* Cambridge, Mass., and London, 1998.

————. *Text and Texture: Close Readings of Selected Biblical Texts.* New York, 1979.

Flood, Gavin. *An Introduction to Hinduism.* Cambridge, U.K., and New York, 1996.

————, ed. *The Blackwell Companion to Hinduism.* Oxford, 2003.

Fox, Everett, trans. *The Five Books of Moses.* New York, 1983.

Frankfort, H., and H. A. Frankfort, eds. *The Intellectual Adventure of Ancient Man: An Essay on Speculative Thought in the Ancient Near East.* Chicago, 1946.

Frauwallner, E. *The Earliest Vinaya and the Beginnings of Buddhist Literature.* Rome, 1956.

Frawley, David. *Gods, Sages and Kings: Vedic Secrets of Ancient Civilization.* Salt Lake City, 1991.

Freedman, David N., ed. *The Anchor Bible Dictionary.* 6 vols. New York, 1992.

Freeman, Charles. *The Greek Achievement: The Foundation of the Western World.* New York and London, 1999.

Freist, William K. "Orpheus: A Fugue on the Polis." In Dora C. Pozzi and John M. Wickersham, eds., *Myth and the Polis.* Ithaca and London, 1991.

Freud, Sigmund. *New Introductory Lectures on Psychoanalysis.* Trans. and ed. James Strachey. New York, 1965.

Friedman, Richard Eliott. *Who Wrote the Bible?* New York, 1987.

Fung Yu-Lan. *A Short History of Chinese Philosophy.* Ed. and trans. Derk Bodde. New York, 1976.

Ganguli, K. M., trans. *Mahabharata,* 12 vols. Calcutta, 1883–96.

Gernet, Jacques. *Ancient China: From the Beginnings to the Empire.* Trans. Raymond Rudorff. London, 1968.

————. *A History of Chinese Civilization.* 2nd ed. Trans. J. R. Foster and Charles Hartman. Cambridge, U.K., and New York, 1996.

Ghosh, A. *The City in Early Historical India.* Simla, 1973.

Girard, René. *Violence and the Sacred.* Trans. Patrick Gregory. Baltimore, 1977.

Girardot, N. J. *Myth and Meaning in Early Taoism.* Berkeley, 1983.

Gokhale, B. G. "The Early Buddhist Elite." *Journal of Indian History* 42, part II, n.d.

Gombrich, Richard F. *Buddhist Precept and Practice: Traditional Buddhism in the Rural Highlands of Ceylon.* London and New York, 1995.

————. *How Buddhism Began: The Conditioned Genesis of the Early Teachings.* London and Atlantic Highlands, N.J., 1996.

————. *Theravada Buddhism: A Social History from Ancient Benares to Modern Columbo.* London and New York, 1988.

Gonda, Jan. *Change and Continuity in Indian Religion.* The Hague, 1965.

————. *Notes on Brahman.* Utrecht, 1950.

————. *Vedic Literature.* Wiesbaden, 1975.

————. *The Vision of the Vedic Poets.* The Hague, 1963.

Goody, Jack, and Ian Watt. *Literacy in Traditional Societies.* Cambridge, U.K., 1968.

Gordon, R. L. *Myth, Religion and Society.* Cambridge, U.K., 1981.

Gottlieb, Anthony. *The Dream of Reason: A History of Philosophy from the Greeks to the Renaissance.* London, 2000.

————. "Socrates." In Frederick Raphael and Ray Monk, eds., *The Great Philosophers.* London, 2000.

Graham, A. C. *Disputers of the Tao: Philosophical Argument in Ancient China.* La Salle, Ill., 1989.

————. *Later Mohist Logic, Ethics and Science.* Hong Kong, 1978.

Granet, Marcel. *Chinese Civilization.* Trans. Kathleen Innes and Mabel Brailsford. London and New York, 1951.

————. *Festivals and Songs of Ancient China.* Trans. E. D. Edwards. London, 1932.

————. *The Religion of the Chinese People.* Trans. and ed. Maurice Freedman. Oxford, 1975.

Green, Arthur. *Jewish Spirituality.* 2 vols. London and New York, 1986, 1988.

Greenspahn, Frederic E., ed. *Essential Papers on Israel and the Ancient Near East.* New York and London, 1991.

Griffith, Ralph T. H., trans. *The Rig Veda.* Reprinted New York, 1992.

Hamilton, G., trans. *The Symposium.* Harmondsworth, 1951.

Haran, Menahem. *Temples and Temple-Service in Ancient Israel: An Inquiry into the Character of Cult Phenomena and the Historic Setting of the Priestly School.* Oxford, 1987.

Hatto, A. T., ed. *Traditions of Heroic and Epic Poetry.* London, 1980.

Havelock, Eric A. *Preface to Plato.* Cambridge, Mass., and London, 1963.

Heesterman, J. C. *The Ancient Indian Royal Consecration.* The Hague, 1957.

————. *The Broken World of Sacrifice: An Essay in Ancient Indian Ritual.* Chicago and London, 1993.

————. *The Inner Conflict of Tradition: Essays in Indian Ritual, Kingship and Society.* Chicago and London, 1985.

————. "Ritual, Revelation and Axial Age." In S. N. Eisenstadt, ed., *The Origins and Diversity of Axial Age Civilizations.* Albany, 1986.

Heschel, Abraham J. *The Prophets.* 2 vols. New York, 1962.

Hilliers, Delbert. *Covenant: The History of a Biblical Idea.* Baltimore, 1969.

Hiltebeitel, Alf. *The Ritual of Battle: Krishna in the Mahabharata.* Ithaca and London, 1976.

Hinton, David, trans. *Chuang Tzu: The Inner Chapters.* Washington, D.C., 1998.

————, trans. *Mencius.* Washington, D.C., 1998.

Holloway, Richard, ed. *Revelations: Personal Responses to the Books of the Bible.* Edinburgh, 2005.

Hopkins, D. C. *The Highlands of Canaan.* Sheffield, 1985.

Hopkins, E. Washington. *The Great Epic of India.* New York, 1902.

Hopkins, Thomas J. *The Hindu Religious Tradition.* Belmont, Calif., 1971.

Hubert, H., and M. Mauss. *Sacrifice: Its Nature and Functions.* Trans. W. D. Halls. Chicago, 1981.

Ivanhoe, Philip J. *Confucian Moral Self-Cultivation.* 2nd ed. Indianapolis, 2000.

———. *Ethics in the Confucian Tradition.* 2nd ed. Indianapolis, 2002.

Jacobi, H., ed. and trans. *Jaina Sutras.* 2 vols. Oxford, 1882–85.

Jaspers, Karl. *The Great Philosophers: The Foundations.* Ed. Hannah Arendt. Trans. Ralph Manheim. London, 1962.

———. *The Origin and Goal of History.* Trans. Michael Bullock. London, 1953.

James, E. O. *The Ancient Gods: The History and Diffusion of Religion in the Ancient Near East and the Eastern Mediterranean.* London, 1960.

Jowett, Benjamin, trans., with M. J. Knight. *The Essential Plato.* Oxford, 1871. Reprinted with introduction by Alain de Botton. London, 1999.

Kak, S. C. "On the Chronology of Ancient India." *Indian Journal of History and Science* 22, no. 3 (1987).

———. "The Structure of the Rgveda." *Indian Journal of History and Science* 28, no. 2 (1993).

Kaltenmark, Max. *Lao Tzu and Taoism.* Trans. Roger Greaves. Stanford, Calif., 1969.

Karlgren, Bernhard, trans. *The Book of Odes.* Stockholm, 1950.

Keay, John. *India: A History.* London, 2000.

Keightley, David N. "The Making of the Ancestors: Late Shang Religion and Its Legacy." *Cahiers d'Extreme-Asie,* n.d.

———. "The Religious Commitment: Shang Theology and the Genesis of Chinese Political Culture." *History of Religions* 17, nos. 3–4 (1978).

———. "Shamanism, Death and the Ancestors: Religious Mediation in Neolithic and Shang China ca. 5000–1000 BCE." *Asiatische Studien* 52, no. 3 (1998).

———, ed. *The Origins of Chinese Civilization.* Berkeley, 1983.

Keith, Arthur Berridale. *The Religion and Philosophy of the Veda and Upanishads.* Cambridge, Mass., and London, 1925.

Kennedy, K. A. R., and G. L. Possehl, eds. *Studies in the Archaeology and Palaeoanthropology of South Asia.* New Delhi, 1983.

Kerferd, G. B. *The Sophistic Movement.* Cambridge, U.K., 1981.

King, Ursula. *Women in the World's Religions, Past and Present.* New York, 1987.

King, Winston L. *Buddhism and Christianity.* Philadelphia, 1962.

Kirk, G. S., and J. E. Raven. *The Pre-Socratic Philosophers.* Cambridge, U.K., 1960.

Klawans, Jonathan. *Impurity and Sin in Ancient Judaism.* Oxford, 2000.

Kline, T. C., III, and Philip J. Ivanhoe. *Virtue, Nature and Moral Agency in the Xunzi.* Indianapolis, 2000.

Klostermaier, Klaus K. *Hinduism: A Short History*. Oxford, 2000.

———. *A Survey of Hinduism*. 2nd ed. Albany, 1994.

Kosambi, D. D. *The Culture and Civilization of Ancient India, in Historical Outline*. London, 1965.

Kramer, Samuel N. *Sumerian Mythology: A Study of the Spiritual and Literary Achievement of the Third Millennium BC*. Philadelphia, 1944.

Kramrisch, Stella. *The Presence of Siva*. Princeton, n.d.

Kulke, Hermann. "The Historical Background of India's Axial Age." In S. N. Eisenstadt, ed., *The Origins and Diversity of Axial Age Civilizations*. Albany, 1986.

Lambert, W. G. *Babylonian Wisdom Literature*. London, 1960.

Lane Fox, Robin. *Alexander the Great*. London, 1973.

Langdon, Stephen. *Babylonian Wisdom*. London, 1923.

Lattimore, Richmond, trans. *The Iliad of Homer*. Chicago and London, 1951.

Lau, D. C., trans. *Lao-tzu: Tao Te Ching*. London, 1963.

———, trans. *Mencius*. London, 1970.

Legge, J., trans. *The Ch'un Ts'ew and the Tso Chuen*. 2nd ed. Hong Kong, 1960.

———, trans. *Classic of Filial Piety (Hsiao Ching)*. Oxford, 1879.

———, trans. *The Li Ki*. Oxford, 1885.

Leick, Gwendolyn. *Mesopotamia: The Invention of the City*. London, 2001.

Lemche, N. P. *Early Israel: Anthropological and Historical Studies on the Israelite Society Before the Monarchy*. Leiden, 1985.

Lenski, G. *Power and Privilege: A Theory of Social Stratification*. New York, 1966.

Lenski, G., and J. Lenski. *Human Societies: An Introduction to Macrosociology*. 2nd ed. New York, 1974.

Lesky, A. "Decision and Responsibility in the Tragedy of Aeschylus." *Journal of Hellenic Studies* (1966).

Levinson, Bernard M. *Deuteronomy and the Hermeneutics of Legal Innovation*. Oxford and New York, 1998.

Lévi-Strauss, Claude. *The Savage Mind*. Chicago, 1966.

———. *Structural Anthropology*. New York, 1969.

Liao, W. K., trans. and ed. *Han Fei Tzu*. 2 vols. London, 1938, 1959.

Lieb, Michael. *The Visionary Mode: Biblical Prophecy, Hermeneutics and Cultural Change*. Ithaca and London, 1991.

Ling, Trevor. *The Buddha: Buddhist Civilization in India and Ceylon*. London, 1973.

Lloyd, G. E. R. *Adversaries and Authorities: Investigations into Ancient Greek and Chinese Science*. Cambridge, U.K., 1996.

Loewe, Michael, and Edward L. Shaughnessy, eds. *The Cambridge History of Ancient China*. Cambridge, U.K., 1999.

Lopez, Donald S. *Buddhism*. London and New York, 2001.

Machinist, Peter. "Distinctiveness in Ancient Israel." In Mordechai Cogan and Israel Ephal, eds., *Studies in Assyrian History and Ancient Near Eastern Historiography*. Jerusalem, 1991.

———. "Outsiders or Insiders: The Biblical View of Emergent Israel in Its Contexts." In Robert Cohn and Laurence Silberstein, *The Other in Jewish Thought and History: Constructions of Jewish Culture and Identity*. New York, 1994.

Mann, Th. W. *Divine Presence and Guidance in Israelite Traditions: The Typology of Exaltation*. Baltimore, 1977.

Masparo, Henri. *China in Antiquity*. 2nd ed. Trans. Frank A. Kierman Jr. Folkestone, 1978.

Matchett, Freda. *Krsna: Lord or Avatara? The Relationship Between Krsna and Visnu*. Richmond, U.K., 2001.

McCrindle, J. W. *Ancient India as Described by Megasthanes and Arrian*. Calcutta, 1877.

McKeon, Richard, ed. *The Basic Works of Aristotle*. New York, 2001.

Mei, Y. P., ed. and trans. *The Ethical and Political Works of Mot-tse (Chapters 1–39; 46–50)*. London, 1929.

Meier, Christian. *Athens: A Portrait of the City in Its Golden Age*. Trans. Robert and Rita Kimber. London, 1999.

———. "The Emergence of Autonomous Intelligence Among the Greeks." In S. N. Eisenstadt, ed., *The Origins and Diversity of Axial Age Civilizations*. Albany, 1986.

Mein, Andrew. *Ezekiel and the Ethics of Exile*. Oxford and New York, 2001.

Mendenhall, George W. *The Tenth Generation: The Origins of Biblical Tradition*. Baltimore, 1973.

Miller, Barbara Stoler, trans. *The Bhagavad-Gita: Krishna's Counsel in Time of War*. New York, Toronto, and London, 1986.

Montefiore, C. G., and H. Loewe, eds. *A Rabbinic Anthology*. New York, 1974.

Mote, Frederick F. *Intellectual Foundations of China*. New York, 1971.

Moulinier, L. *Le pur et l'impur dans la pensée et la sensibilité des Grecs jusqu'à la fin de IV siècle avant J-C*. Paris, 1952.

Muffs, Yochanan. *Love and Joy: Law, Language and Religion in Ancient Israel*. Cambridge, Mass., 1992.

Mujamdar, B. P. *Socio-Economic History of Northern India*. London, 1960.

Muller, Max. *The Six Systems of Indian Philosophy*. London, 1899.

Murray, Oswyn. *Early Greece*. 2nd ed. London, 1993.

Nanamoli, Bhikku, trans. and ed. *The Life of the Buddha, According to the Pali Canon*. Kandy, Sri Lanka, 1972.

Narain, A. K. ed. *Studies in the History of Buddhism*. Delhi, 1980.

Needham, Joseph. *Science and Civilization in China*. Cambridge, U.K., 1956.

Neusner, J. *The Idea of Purity in Ancient Israel*. Leiden, 1973.

Nicholson, Ernest. *The Pentateuch in the Twentieth Century: The Legacy of Julius Wellhausen*. Oxford, 1998.

Niditch, Susan. *Oral World and Written Word: Ancient Israelite Literature*. Louisville, 1996.

Noth, Martin. *Exodus*. London, 1960.

―――. *A History of Per*

Oldenberg, Hermann. *B*[RAPHY]

Hoey. London, 1882.

Olivelle, Patrick. "The Ren[heffield, 1981.]

well Companion to Hindu[trine, His Order. Trans. William]

―――. *Samnyasa Upanisads.* [531]

Oxford and New York, 19

―――, ed. and trans. *Upanisa*[in Flood, ed., *The Black-*]

Ollenburger, Ben C. *Zion, the C*

the Jerusalem Cult. Sheffield, [*and Renunciation.*]

Otto, Rudolf. *The Idea of the Holy*

Idea of the Divine and Its Relatio

Oxford, 1923.

Owen, E. T. *The Story of the Iliad.* 2n[*Symbol of*]

Palmer, Martin, with Elizabeth Breui

don and New York, 1996.

Pankenier, David W. "The Cosmo-Poli[*in the*]

date." *Early China* 20 (1995).

Parker, Robert. *Athenian Religion: A Histo*

Patai, Ralph. *Man and Temple.* London, 199

Poliakov, L. *The Aryan Myth.* New York, 19

Polley, Max E. *Amos and the Davidic Empire:*

York and Oxford, 1989.

Pozzi, Dora C., and John M. Wickersham, eds

London, 1991.

Puett, Michael J. *The Ambivalence of Creation: D*

Artifice in Early China. Stanford, Calif., 2001.

―――. *To Become a God: Cosmology, Sacrifice, and*

China. Cambridge, Mass., and London, 2002.

Rahula, Walpola. *What the Buddha Taught.* 2nd ed. C

Raphael, Frederic, and Ray Monk, eds. *The Great Ph*

Redfield, J. M. *Nature and Culture in the Iliad: The Trag*

and London, 1975.

Redford, D. B. *Egypt, Canaan and Israel in Ancient Times.*

Renfrew, Colin. *Archaeology and Language: The Puzzle of*

London, 1987.

Renou, Louis. *Religions of Ancient India.* London, 1953.

―――. "Sur la notion de *brahman*." *Journal Asiatique* 237 (

Rickett, W. Allyn, ed. and trans. *Guanzi (35 Chapters).* Prince

―――, ed. and trans. *Kuan-tzu (10 Chapters).* Hong Kong, 1

Roth, Harold D. *Original Tao: Inward Training and the Foundatio*

Mysticism. New York, 1999.

Rowley, Harold H. *Worship in Ancient Israel: Its Form and Meanin*

1967.

532

Sandars, N. K., trans. and ed. *Poems of Heaven* ...*cient Mesopotamia. Harmondsworth, 1971. ...d. Berkeley, Los

Schein, Seth L. *The Mortal Hero: An Intro*...inceton, 1996.
Angeles, and London, 1984. ...*t. Textualization of*

———, ed. *Reading the Odyssey: Selec*... . Cambridge,

Schniedewind, William M. *How the* ...*nscripts.* New
Ancient Israel. Cambridge, U.K ...

Schwartz, Benjamin I. *The World* ...*ies." Critical Quar-*
Mass., and London, 1985. ...

Scott, James. *Domination and t*... r, Tragedy and the
Haven, 1990. ...*of Dionysus.* Ithaca,

Seaford, Richard. "Dionys... ...d ed. Princeton,
terly 31 (1981).

———. "Dionysus as ... re des Religions* 42
Polis." In C. Fara...
1993.

Segal, Charles. D...*rchaeological Real-*
1997. ...*dies in the Archaeology*

Senart, Emile. ...*ncient India.* Delhi,
(1900).

Shaffer, J. G... ...d New York, 1980.
ity." I... ...hin and Kingly Para-
and ... d., *The Origins and*

Sharm...

...*l Beyond.* Oxford, 1996.
Sh...ingham, U.K., 1994.
S...1951.
New York and London,

...*Religion.* Oxford and

...*ocial Context of the Babylon-*

...*isdom Traditions.* San Fran-

...A. T. Hatto, ed., *Traditions of*

Self-Divin...

...Oxford and Bosto...
...ilosophers. London, 2...
...dy of Hector. Chicago...
Princeton, 1992.
...Indo-European Origins.

...1949).
...ton, 1985.
...965.
...s of Taoist
...g. London,

Smith, Jonathan Z. *Imagining Religion: From Babylon to Jonestown.* Chicago, 1982.

———. *Map Is Not Territory: Studies in the History of Religions.* Chicago and London, 1978.

Smith, Mark S. *The Early History of God: Yahweh and the Other Deities in Ancient Israel.* New York and London, 1990.

———. *The Origins of Biblical Monotheism: Israel's Polytheistic Background and the Ugaritic Texts.* New York and London, 2001.

Smith, Wilfred Cantwell. *Faith and Belief.* Princeton, 1979.

———. *Towards a World Theology.* London, 1981.

Snodgrass, A. N. *The Dark Age of Greece: Archaeological Survey from the Eleventh to the Eighth Centuries BC.* Edinburgh, 1971.

Soggin, J. Alberto. *A History of Israel from the Beginnings to the Bar Kochba Revolt, AD 135.* Trans. John Bowden. London, 1984.

Soloveitchik, Haym. "Rapture and Reconstruction: The Transformation of Contemporary Orthodoxy." *Tradition* 28 (1994).

Sommerstein, A. H., ed. *Tragedy, Comedy and the Polis.* Bari, 1993.

Sperling, S. David. "Israel's Religion in the Near East." In Arthur Green, ed., *Jewish Spirituality,* vol. 1. London and New York, 1986.

———. "Joshua 24 Re-examined." *Hebrew Union College Annual* 58 (1987).

———. *The Original Torah: The Political Intent of the Bible's Writers.* New York and London, 1998.

Staal, Fritz. *Rules Without Meaning: Ritual, Mantras and the Human Sciences.* New York, 1989.

Stern, Ephraim. *Archaeology of the Land of the Bible,* vol. 2, *The Assyrian, Babylonian and Persian Periods (732–332 BCE).* New York, 2001.

Stevenson, Margaret Sinclair. *The Heart of Jainism.* London and New York, 1915.

Sukhtankar, V. S. *On the Meaning of the Mahabharata.* Bombay, 1957.

Tarnas, Richard. *The Passion of the Western Mind: Understanding the Ideas That Have Shaped Our World View.* New York and London, 1991.

Thapar, Romila. *Asoka and the Decline of the Mauryas.* Oxford, 1961.

———. *Early India: From the Origins to AD 1300.* Berkeley and Los Angeles, 2002.

Thomas, Edward J. *The Life of Buddha as Legend and History.* London, 1969.

Thompson, P. M. *The Shen-tzu Fragments.* Oxford, 1979.

Thompson, Thomas L. *The Bible in History: How Writers Create a Past.* London, 1999.

Torwesten, Hans. *Vedanta: Heart of Hinduism.* Trans. John Phillips. Ed. Loly Rosset. New York, 1985.

Trautmann, T. R. *Kautilya and the Arthasastra.* Leiden, 1971.

Tu Wei-ming. *Confucian Thought: Selfhood as Creative Transformation.* Albany, 1985.

Van Buitenen, J. A. B., ed. and trans. *The Mahabharata.* 3 vols. Chicago and London, 1973, 1975, 1978.

Van Buitenen, J. A. B., with Mary Evelyn Tucker. *Confucian Spirituality*. New York, 2003.

Van der Toorm, K. *Sin and Sanction in Israel and Mesopotamia: A Comparative Study*. Assen, Netherlands, 1985.

Van Nooten, Barend A. *The Mahabharata*. New York, 1971.

Van Seters, J. "The Religion of the Patriarchs in Genesis." *Biblica* 61 (1980).

————. "The Yahwist as Theologian? A Response." *Journal for the Study of the Old Testament* 3 (1977).

Vandermeersch, Léon. *La formation de légisme*. Paris, 1965.

Vellacott, Philip, trans. *Aeschylus: Prometheus Bound and Other Plays*. London and New York, 1961.

————, trans. *Euripedes: The Bacchae and Other Plays*. Rev. ed. London and New York, 1973.

————, trans. *Euripides: Medea and Other Plays*. London and New York, 1963.

Vernant, Jean Pierre. "Death with Two Faces." In Seth L. Schein, ed., *Reading the Odyssey: Selected Interpretive Essays*. Princeton, 1996.

————. *Myth and Society in Ancient Greece*. 3rd ed. Trans. Janet Lloyd. New York, 1996.

————. *Myth and Thought Among the Greeks*. Trans. Janet Lloyd. Boston, 1983.

Vernant, Jean Pierre, with Pierre Vidal-Naquet. *Myth and Tragedy in Ancient Greece*. Trans. Janet Lloyd. New York, 1990.

Vetter, Tilmann. *The Ideas and Meditative Practices of Early Buddhism*. Leiden, New York, Copenhagen, and Cologne, 1988.

Vidal-Naquet, Pierre. "The Black Hunter and the Origin of the Athenian Ephebia." In R. L. Gordon, *Myth, Religion and Society*. Cambridge, U.K., 1981.

Wagle, N. K. *Society at the Time of the Buddha*. London, 1966.

Waley, Arthur, ed. and trans. *The Analects of Confucius*. New York, 1992.

————, ed. and trans. *The Book of Songs*. London, 1937.

————, ed. and trans. *The Way and Its Power*. London, 1943.

Warren, Henry Clarke. *Buddhism in Translations*. Cambridge, Mass., 1900.

Watling, E. F., trans. *Sophocles: The Theban Plays*. London and New York, 1947.

Watson, B., ed. and trans. *Chuang Tzu*. New York, 1968.

————, ed. and trans. *Han Fei Tzu: Basic Writings*. New York, 1964.

————, ed. and trans. *Hsun-Tzu: Basic Writings*. New York, 1963.

————, ed. and trans. *Mo-Tzu: Basic Writings*. New York, 1963.

————, ed. and trans. *Records of the Grand Historian of China*. New York, 1961.

————, ed. and trans. *Xunzi: Basic Writings*. New York, 2003.

Weinfeld, Moshe. *Deuteronomy and the Deuteronomic School*. Oxford, 1972.

————. *Social Justice in Ancient Israel and in the Ancient Near East*. Jerusalem and Minneapolis, 1995.

Welch, Holmes. *The Parting of the Way: Lao Tzu and the Taoist Movement*. London, 1958.

Wender, Dorothea, trans. *Hesiod and Theognis*. London and New York, 1976.

Wheatley, Paul. *The Pivot of the Four Quarters: A Preliminary Enquiry into the Origins and Character of the Ancient Chinese City.* Chicago, 1971.

Whitley, C. G. *The Prophetic Achievement.* London, 1963.

Whitman, C. H. *Homer and the Heroic Tradition.* Cambridge, Mass., 1958.

Widengren, G. "What Do We Know About Moses?" In J. I. Durham and J. R. Porter, eds., *Proclamation and Presence: Essays in Honour of G. Henton Davies.* London, 1970.

Wijayaratna, Mohan. *Le moine bouddhique selon les texts du Theravada.* Paris, 1983.

Williams, Bernard. "Plato." In Frederick Raphael and Ray Monk, eds., *The Great Philosophers.* London, 2000.

Winckler, J. J., and F. Zeitlin, eds. *Nothing to Do with Dionysos? Athenian Drama in Its Social Context.* Princeton, 1990.

Winnington-Ingram, R. P., ed. *Classical Drama and Its Influence: Essays Presented to H. D. F. Kitto.* London, 1965.

Witzel, Michael. "Vedas and Upanisads." In Gavin Flood, ed., *The Blackwell Companion to Hinduism.* Oxford, 2003.

Yandell, Keith E., ed. *Faith and Narrative.* Oxford, 2001.

Yerushalmi, Y. H. *Zakhor: Jewish History and Jewish Memory.* Seattle, 1982.

Zaehner, R. C. *Hinduism.* London, New York, and Toronto, 1962.

Zaidman, Louise Bruitt, and Pauline Schmitt Pantel. *Religion in the Greek City.* Trans. Paul Cartledge. Cambridge, U.K., 1992.

Index

Page numbers in *italics* refer to illustrations.

*Grateful acknowledgment is made to the following for permission
to reprint previously published material:*

The Arthur Waley Estate: Excerpts from *The Analects of Confucius* translated
by Arthur Waley (Allen & Unwin, 1938). Copyright © by The Arthur Waley
Estate. Reprinted by permission of The Arthur Waley Estate.

Bantam Books: Excerpts from *Bhagavad-Gita* by Barbara Stoler Miller.
Reprinted courtesy of Bantam Books, a division of Random House, Inc.

Columbia University Press: Excerpts from *Xunzi: Basic Writings* translated
by Burton Watson. Reprinted by permission of Columbia University Press.

Doubleday: Excerpts from *The Jerusalem Bible* by Alexander Jones. Reprinted
courtesy of Doubleday, a division of Random House, Inc.

Oxford University Press: Excerpts from *Upanisads* edited and translated by
Patrick Olivelle (Oxford University Press, 1996). Reprinted by permission of
Oxford University Press.

Penguin Group (UK): Excerpts from *Mencius* translated with an introduction by D. C. Lau (Penguin Classics, 1970). Copyright © 1970 by D. C. Lau.
Reprinted by permission of Penguin Group (UK).

The University of Chicago Press: Excerpts from *The Iliad of Homer* translated by R. Lattimore. Reprinted by permission of The University of Chicago
Press.